Turn Away Thy Son

TURN AWAY THY SON

LITTLE ROCK, THE CRISIS THAT SHOCKED THE NATION

Elizabeth Jacoway

The University of Arkansas Press

Fayetteville

2008

Originally published by

FREE PRESS
A Division of Simon & Schuster, Inc.
1230 Avenue of the Americas
New York, NY 10020

Designed by Kyoko Watanabe

Manufactured in the United States of America

12   11   10   09   08   5   4   3   2   1

Library of Congress Cataloging-in-Publication Data Control Number: 2006041334

ISBN-13: 978-0-7432-9719-6
ISBN-10: 0-7432-9719-9

In memory of my father

BRONSON COOPER JACOWAY

Who always encouraged me to see the other fellow's point of view

When the LORD thy God shall bring thee into the land whither thou goest to possess it, and hath cast out many nations before thee, . . . And when the LORD thy God shall deliver them before thee; thou shalt smite them, and utterly destroy them; thou shalt make no covenant with them, nor shew mercy unto them. Neither shalt thou make marriages with them; thy daughter thou shalt not give unto his son, nor his daughter shalt thou take unto thy son. For they will turn away thy son from following me, that they may serve other gods. . . .

—DEUTERONOMY 7:1-4

Do not weep. Do not gnash your teeth. Understand.

—SPINOZA

CONTENTS

CHAPTER 9

CHAPTER 10

CHAPTER 11

CHAPTER 12

CHAPTER 13

CHAPTER 14

CHAPTER 15

CHAPTER 16

CHAPTER 17

CONCLUSION

AFTERWORD

PREFACE

As a child of thirteen growing up in Little Rock, I lived through the 1957 desegregation crisis with my eyes closed. My "Uncle Virgil" Blossom was superintendent of schools, but I was more interested in the fact that my cousin was a cheerleader and "popular" than that her father was instituting a dramatic social revolution in my city. I knew of course that Orval Faubus was governor of my state, but I was more impressed by the fact that my older brother made fun of Farrell Faubus's socially unacceptable, "country" white socks and blue jeans than that the governor was resisting integration. "Brooks" was my father's old family friend Representative Brooks Hays, whom my congressman-grandfather had mentored in Washington, but no mention was ever made around our dinner table that Dad's friend was somehow involved in resolving one of the great crises of our time. "Amis" was one of several men to whom my father delivered presents on Christmas afternoon while the Jacoway kids rode in the backseat, at least until Amis Guthridge became the attorney for the Capital Citizens' Council, an ardent segregationist group. I never noticed that the Christmas deliveries had ceased. "Uncle Dick" was Richard C. Butler, the lawyer who argued the key Little Rock case before the United States Supreme Court, and who had served as best man in my parents' wedding, but no one mentioned his role in the crisis in my presence.

It did not occur to me that I was being shielded purposely from affairs beyond my limited little world, although my father did explain often that girls should not think about "unhappy things." The carefully cultivated product of a patriarchal culture, I floated blithely through those days believing that if anything ever went wrong in my world, the men would fix it. A rigorously and self-consciously "good" little girl, I had always worked hard to fulfill my parents' expectations of me, which included being proper, pretty, and popular, in that order. It did not occur to me until many years later that I had been sealed in an airtight box because female questioning could somehow threaten the established order in worlds beyond my own.

Little Rock's high schools were closed in 1958–59, the year I was in ninth grade, and in tenth grade I attended a private, Catholic girls school, just in case the public schools failed to reopen. No one talked about the complicated, confusing legal and social problems that swirled around far above our heads. By the time I made it to Hall High School, the men had, indeed, "fixed" the problem in Little Rock, assigning three lonely black girls to attend school with the children of the city's elite. In a form of unintended cruelty that to this day hurts me to recall, my friends and I ignored those frightened young pioneers.

I started my undergraduate education at a lovely women's college in Virginia, which was academically rigorous when it came to art history and classical Greece, but where I also encountered my first hard-edged racism in dormitory ditties and "funny" stories. The song I remember most vividly changed "We Shall Overcome" to "We Shall All Be Beige." Transferring to the University of Arkansas after two years, I majored in sorority life and earned a teaching certificate.

In one of his greatest gifts to me, my Harvard Law–trained father insisted that I go to graduate school, although he envisioned for me a career in secondary teaching if I somehow failed to make a good match in the marriage market. I stumbled into a southern history seminar at the University of North Carolina, taught by a great historian, George Tindall, as a result of a last-minute opening in his class. For the first three weeks I perused the group skeptically, evaluating each class member on the basis of whether she or he would have been invited into one of the elite sororities or fraternities I had so cherished as an undergraduate. But as it began to dawn on me that these strange people were talking about things that *mattered,* and that they cared deeply about things I knew nothing about, I had a Damascus Road experience.

My intellectual awakening began with the realization that I had mindlessly participated in and benefited from a racist culture. From that point on, the earning of my Ph.D.—and the writing of this book—became a personal quest, aimed not so much toward a career in teaching as toward achieving an explanation of what had happened in Little Rock and why I had missed it. The deaths of some close family friends and relatives freed me to write this story without having to protect individuals whom I loved but who I came to realize had failed Little Rock and its children. Maturity at length emboldened me to say the things that need to be said despite the certainty of a hostile reception in some quarters.

The story of the Little Rock crisis has most often been told as a conflict between state and federal authority, a standoff in which an opportunistic governor defied federal attempts to impose a dreaded cultural change on his unwilling constituents. While power and politics—and high drama—are certainly parts of the story, my years of digging in ever-widening circles revealed that the foundations of the governor's behavior were enormously complex, and that the subtext of the whole experience was the most important layer. That bedrock was a white fear of miscegenation, or more specifically, allowing black men to have access to white women. In the mannerly, distinctly southern environment of Little Rock, such sexual concerns rarely rise to the level of verbal discourse, and almost never in the company of women, then or now. But with the blinders of traditional racial and gender expectations removed, I began to see patterns in the Little Rock crisis that at last brought home to me some crucial, neglected dimensions of that experience. I offer these now as tools for reassessing the meaning and significance of that landmark episode in American history.

The white fear of what the segregationists called "race-mixing" neither started nor ended in Little Rock. A burgeoning historical literature has noted the operation of this fear in every era and in every section of the country, demonstrating that it is a fundamental animator of American racism, and suggesting, therefore, why it has been impervious to change. Cold War imperatives may have necessitated modifications of American law, putting an end to the formal practice of segregation, but even the heroic sacrifices of civil rights activists and such belated federal initiatives as the Civil Rights and Voting Rights acts failed to change the hearts and minds of white Americans who feared the defilement of their culture. That fear drove legions of whites into the suburbs. Worse, after fifty years of attempting integration, America has resegregated. This countrywide, across-the-board reality reflects much deeper and more pernicious problems than manipulation by greedy or class-conscious elites.

Elizabeth Eckford, the young black warrior whose troubling photograph at Central High School flashed around the globe and became an icon of the Civil Rights Movement, commented at a conference recently that "we cannot have any real healing in this country until we face the truth about our past." That truth involves not only our actions but also our attitudes; until we name the disease we cannot hope to find a cure. Only a candid examination of our past can open the way toward reconciliation and a new beginning. In that spirit I offer this work, which is sure to be painful to all who read it. My hope is that out of that pain may be born a new clarity about where we have been and where at last we can begin, together, to go.

TURN AWAY
THY SON

MISCEGENATION AND THE BEAST

F IFTEEN-YEAR-OLD ELIZABETH ECKFORD WANTED TO BE A LAWYER. Thurgood Marshall was her hero, and although she had never dared to hope she might one day meet the man who had argued and won *Brown v. Board of Education* before the United States Supreme Court, the African-American youngster dreamed of doing the same kinds of daring things for her people. When, however, her principal at all-black Horace Mann High School asked in the spring of 1957 who wanted to help pioneer desegregation at Little Rock Central High School in the fall, shy, serious Elizabeth did not raise her hand. Explaining her hesitation several years later, she recalled that she had thought she could not reach such an important decision without a lot of careful deliberation.[1]

As a consequence, Elizabeth was not included among the sixteen students Superintendent Virgil Blossom had selected to initiate desegregation in September. She knew she wanted to go to college, however, and she knew that Central High School offered courses she would not be able to take if she stayed at Horace Mann. After thinking about it all summer, Elizabeth finally told her mother in August she wanted to go to Central High. Birdie Eckford hoped her quiet, studious daughter would change her mind.[2]

In her own childhood Birdie Eckford had witnessed in her hometown the death of a black man at the hands of a white mob that was similar to a gruesome 1927 lynching on the streets of Little Rock. She had felt the same wave of panic wash over the black community, much as it had in Little Rock when a black man captured after the rape and murder of a young white girl had been hanged, riddled with over two hundred bullets, dragged by the head for blocks behind an automobile, and then thrown on the trolley tracks at the intersection of Ninth and Broadway in the heart of the black business district and set ablaze.[3]

Along with other members of Little Rock's African American community,

Birdie Eckford had absorbed from such experiences the lessons of growing up black in the South, and she feared the white beast that could rise up at any moment and strike her people. Her husband, Oscar, had learned in his Little Rock childhood that any time a white woman came toward him on the street he should cross to the other side, just to remove all possibility of her sensing anything untoward in his glance or manner. For their own survival, southern blacks had to understand and explain to their children, especially their sons, the chemistry that could unharness the beast.[4]

Elizabeth Eckford had learned from her parents, and from the grandfather who doted on her, the demands and the function of hard work. Her father later told a visiting reporter that he was the only man in Little Rock who worked nine days a week: seven nights at the Little Rock railroad station, and two days cleaning the home of a white Arkansas National Guard colonel. Birdie taught laundry skills at the Arkansas School for the Blind and Deaf Negro, where she had a son enrolled, and she also took correspondence courses in psychology and English literature. Grandfather Oscar owned a grocery store and worked long hours; he catered to an integrated clientele, and Elizabeth had noted he was as forthright and dignified with his white patrons as with his black ones. Of all his grandchildren Oscar Eckford Sr. had a special bond with tiny Elizabeth, apparently seeing in her some of the spunk he valued in himself. As Elizabeth's father explained, "Maybe Papa felt that he and I didn't do nothing, so maybe Elizabeth would."[5]

Elizabeth persevered in badgering her reluctant mother, and finally Birdie agreed to take her second daughter for an interview with Superintendent Virgil Blossom. Elizabeth had all A's and B's and her school record was a model of citizenship. After keeping Elizabeth and her mother waiting for a very long time, Dr. Blossom tried to discourage the youngster, as he had all the other applicants, by explaining she would not be allowed to participate in any extracurricular activities. The determined fifteen-year-old quietly held her own against the imposing former football coach, however, and Blossom added Elizabeth Eckford to the list of students already slated to enter Central High School the next week. As a consequence of her late decision, Elizabeth missed the preparation some of the other students had been receiving at the home of Daisy Bates, state president of the National Association for the Advancement of Colored People.[6]

ELIZABETH HAD PAID attention throughout the summer as an increasingly vocal group of white people, the Capital Citizens' Council, had mounted a propaganda campaign against the planned desegregation of Central High School.

She had been confident, however, that school authorities and the local police would maintain order at the high school, and she felt nervously excited rather than fearful as the opening of the fall term approached. In preparation for that day, in her small, crowded household, she laid out on the living room floor the fabric and pattern for a new dress, a beautiful white shirtwaist with a deep gingham hem, to wear on the first day of school. Her sewing occupied her thoughts in the last few days. Even as Governor Orval Faubus surrounded her new high school with armed National Guardsmen on the night of September 2, Elizabeth fretted over her new white buck loafers and bobby socks, making sure that everything was ready for this exciting new chapter in her life.

Birdie Eckford was terrified by the Arkansas governor's actions. She thought she heard him say on television that if the black children insisted on pressing their right to attend Central High School at that time, "blood will run in the streets" of Little Rock. The next day the black children stayed home while the Little Rock School Board went into federal court to ask for a temporary delay of its integration plan. Federal Judge Ronald Davies, visiting from North Dakota to clear up a backlog of cases, noted the governor had said his Guardsmen would function neither as integrationists nor segregationists but only to preserve the peace. He ordered the School Board to proceed immediately with its federally mandated plan. The children and their parents had met that same afternoon with Superintendent Blossom, and when they got home Birdie Eckford insisted the family pray together. After dinner Birdie instructed Elizabeth to read Psalms 27 and 4.[7]

Filled with excitement and a growing apprehension, Elizabeth tossed and turned all night, finally rising early on the morning of September 4 to iron her new dress one last time. When her little brother turned on the television and the announcer blared that a crowd was already forming in front of Central High School, Birdie shouted from the kitchen "Turn that TV off!" Oscar Eckford paced back and forth through the house chewing on his pipe and carrying a cigar, both unlit, and Elizabeth would have laughed if she had not been so nervous. After reading Psalm 27 one last time, the plucky teen told her parents not to worry and boarded the city bus, alone, for the short ride to Central High School.[8]

Elizabeth did not know that late the night before, Daisy Bates had arranged for the black children to assemble at her home in order to drive them as a group to meet with city policemen two blocks from the school. From that point, a group of black and white ministers planned to escort the children to the school grounds and to offer themselves as a moral shield of protection in the event a hostile crowd assembled outside the school. Working into the early morning hours to call all of the parents, an exhausted Bates realized at length the Eck-fords did not have a telephone. She fell into bed making a mental note to find Elizabeth in the morning. The next morning, Bates forgot about Elizabeth in the crush of activity at her home. Meanwhile, Governor Faubus was changing his orders to the National Guard, instructing them not simply to "keep the peace" as he had the day before, but to bar the black children from the campus of Central High School.[9]

WHEN THE BUS deposited her at the corner of Twelfth and Park Streets Eliza-beth could see the large crowd that had formed in front of the massive buff brick school. As she approached the corner of Fourteenth and Park, she felt comforted by the presence of the National Guardsmen ringing the school, and she headed for the sidewalk behind the line of soldiers so they would be between her and the noisy protesters. Elizabeth neared the soldiers and was relieved to see a white girl pass between them. One of the Guardsmen, however, motioned for her to cross to the other side of the street, suggesting she should approach the decid-edly unfriendly throng of about two hundred whites.[10]

Obedient as always, Elizabeth did as she was told, and the whites initially drew back to let her pass. When, however, she heard one man say "Here she comes, now get ready!" she felt the first real fear surge through her. She moved to the middle of the street, walking with the soldiers on her right and the large band of increasingly hostile whites on her left.[11]

Elizabeth saw some white students pass through the line of soldiers about halfway down the two-block campus, and she headed for that spot. Whites were crowding close behind her saying such things as "Go back where you came from! Go home before you get hurt, nigger. Why don't you go back to the god-damn jungle!" As she told a local white minister several days later, she began to grow fearful, but the proud and dignified young girl also worried she would "bust out crying and I didn't want to in front of all that crowd."[12]

When the frightened child finally arrived at the midpoint of the campus and tried to pass between two soldiers, they raised their guns and barred her entry. Her knees now shaking, Elizabeth turned to face the mob, hoping to find a friendly or compassionate soul. One grey-haired woman seemed to have a kindly manner, but when the black girl looked at her beseechingly, the woman spat in her face.[13]

With dignity and composure, Elizabeth turned and walked briskly toward the Sixteenth Street bus stop. As she traveled that nightmarishly long block, an aroused mob trailed closely behind her hurling threats and epithets. "Lynch her!"

was the one she remembered. At some point during the seemingly endless journey, a young photographer for the *Arkansas Democrat* snapped a haunting picture that soon traveled around the globe, later becoming an icon of the Civil
Rights Movement. That picture of a stoic Elizabeth Eckford absorbing an out-
pouring of white rage suggested the depth of black courage, endurance, and
hope.[14]

Elizabeth made her way to the bus stop at Sixteenth and Park and considered sitting on the bench. With the mob at her heels, however, she decided to
cross over to Ponder's Drug Store and use their telephone to call a taxi. As the
terrified child approached the store, someone inside locked the door. Elizabeth
went back to the bench and sat down, while people around her shouted "Lynch
her!" and "Nigger bitch!" A black man she had never met materialized beside
her—it was L. C. Bates. He pulled back his coat to show he had a gun in his belt
and invited her to leave the scene with him. Elizabeth knew her strict mother
would never approve her leaving with a strange man, and she declined.[15]

Handsome Terrence Roberts sat down beside her, another one of the black
students Virgil Blossom had selected who had also been turned away, and he
suggested they walk home together. Elizabeth knew he lived closer to the school
than she did, and she feared what any whites who chose to trail along behind
them might do to her once Terrence went into his own home. She decided to
wait for a bus.[16]

As Elizabeth began to cry, *New York Times* education editor Benjamin Fine
sat beside her on the bench and laid down his notepad, abandoning his role as
a journalist. Putting an arm around her he lifted her chin and said, "Don't let
them see you cry." It helped the frightened child regain her composure. Now the
mob descended on the Jewish New Yorker, shifting easily from racism to anti-
Semitism, and threatened the small, appalled newsman that if he did not stop
interfering they would castrate him. Elizabeth sat frozen, raging in her mind
against Virgil Blossom, Daisy Bates, and the other white newsmen and photographers who were doing nothing to help her. When word went through the
crowd that more black children were trying to enter the school, most of the
newsmen abandoned Elizabeth to her tormentors and dashed the length of the
campus to cover the new action.[17]

While the minutes ticked away, Elizabeth's pulse began to return to normal
as the milling crowd lost interest in her and shifted its attention to events at the
other end of the long block. Suddenly a white woman appeared and began to
berate the crowd for its mistreatment of Elizabeth. "She's scared," Grace Lorch
challenged the mob. "She's just a little girl. . . . Six months from now you'll be

ashamed at what you're doing." Cries of "Nigger-lover!" flew up on all sides.
Mrs. Lorch, the wife of a mathematics professor at the local black college, Philander Smith College, was also a member of the Communist Party. Elizabeth
did not know this, of course, but she thought in terror that the woman was trying to incite a riot. Finally a city bus arrived and Elizabeth rose to board it, as
did Mrs. Lorch.[18]

A few young toughs stood in front of the bus and said to the older woman,
"You nigger lover, you are not going to get on this bus." Mrs. Lorch raised her
hands and said, "I am just aching to punch someone in the nose. This is what I
have been wanting to do, just waiting for. You stand there and you will get your
nose punched in." The bullies backed down and faded away. Glad as she was to
escape the situation, Elizabeth believed Mrs. Lorch demonstrated a lack of sincere concern for her when the older woman got off the bus a few blocks later
without seeing the frightened teenager safely to her destination.[19]

Elizabeth rode the bus to her mother's school. When she arrived at the laundry area where Birdie worked she found her mother standing by the window
with head bowed, terrified after hearing accounts on the radio of her daughter's
ordeal. Elizabeth collapsed into her mother's arms and wept. As Mrs. Eckford
recalled, "I went with her to the rest room, and she braced up and came on
home alone." The two women then did what their survival under segregated
oppression had taught them to do: they squared their shoulders, and they raised
their chins.[20]

NATIONAL COUNCIL OF Churches representative Will Campbell, who was in
town as an observer, had volunteered to join Ministerial Alliance President
Dunbar Ogden in escorting the black children to Central High when Ogden
was unable to secure such a commitment from any other white minister in Little Rock. Forty years later Campbell looked at the pictures of that day and said,
"'Where,' the photographs cry out, 'are the white Christians in this scene?'" In
the same volume of images Hazel Bryan, the young white girl who shouted
"Nigger!" at Elizabeth Eckford in Will Counts's haunting picture, described herself as having been "very religious" at the point in her life when she hurled such
slurs. Hazel Bryan's story complicates the standard narrative seemingly depicted
in Counts's iconic photograph.[21]

Hazel had grown up in the country close to Pine Bluff, one of the centers of
black population and white racism in Arkansas. She had had affectionate relationships with several older black women in her poor, rural community. As a
child she was never encouraged explicitly to hate blacks, but as she recalled years

later, ". . . you just somehow knew from the expression or the tone of 'nigger.'" According to Hazel, both of her parents were "very racially prejudiced," as were literally all of the whites of their acquaintance. A member of the Church of Christ, which was among the most rigid practitioners of Christian fundamentalism, she never heard directly from the pulpit that the races should be kept separate, but in thinking back to those days, she remembered ". . . you always got the idea that you weren't supposed to marry, intermarry. . . ."[22]

Hazel's family had moved to Little Rock when she was nine so her mother could take a job at the Westinghouse lightbulb factory. Her father was a disabled veteran who stayed at home and drove the children to school. Hazel had spent the summer of 1957 dancing to rock 'n' roll music in the numerous lakeside pavilions around Little Rock, and especially on the popular afternoon television program *Steve's Show*, where she had gotten to be friends with the other white girl in Will Counts's picture, Sammie Dean Parker. Parker later became one of the ringleaders of the segregationist students inside Central High School, while Hazel's parents withdrew her from Central and sent her to one of the county high schools, mainly for what they perceived to be her "protection." Hazel's addiction to rock 'n' roll and her swooning over the highly sexualized, black-influenced sounds and gyrations of Elvis Presley caused her parents to fear, as did so many other white parents across the nation, that traditional cultural norms were giving way to something base and sinister.[23]

Hazel's father took her to school on September 4, as did Sammie Dean's father, and they met in the carnival atmosphere of the crowd outside the school. Boys waved Confederate flags, a man played "Dixie" on his coronet, and a minister with a bullhorn bellowed at the crowd, "They don't want in your school, they want in your bedroom!"[24]

Suddenly Elizabeth Eckford appeared in Hazel and Sammie Dean's line of vision, coming toward them with a crowd at her heels. As she passed, they fell in behind her followed by Sammie Dean's father, the menacing-looking man in Counts's photograph. The two girls, both show-offs with an unexpected audience of photographers, and getting swept up into the spirit of the moment, joined the heckling. Hazel had no awareness of the issues involved, and as a typical 1950s teenage girl, she had no interest in the larger world of politics and social concerns. She recalled years later that Mr. Parker was angry with his daughter for placing herself in such a dangerous situation. Instead of heckling Elizabeth Eckford, as countless viewers of the photograph have assumed over the years, he was ordering Sammie Dean off the street.[25]

Hazel knew immediately she had made a mistake, and as the Civil Rights

Movement unfolded and she understood increasingly the depth of her error, she called Elizabeth and apologized in 1962. She kept quiet about her role in the affair for the next thirty-five years, until the fortieth anniversary of the Little Rock crisis in 1997, when she attempted to do penance for her behavior by confessing it publicly and apologizing again to Elizabeth. By that time she had experienced dramatic growth in her religious and racial views. She had left the church and worked for a number of social betterment causes in Little Rock, especially in programs to help black children learn to read. Hazel's story reveals unexamined dimensions of the struggle for desegregation in Little Rock, and elsewhere. Her experience adds depth and texture to Will Campbell's oversimplified question concerning the apparent contradiction between Christianity's central command to "love thy neighbor" and the segregationists' hate-filled treatment of the black people in their midst.[26]

The sources of white hatred and rage toward African-Americans were as old as relationships between the two races on the American continent. White racism stemmed primarily from the fear in white minds of pollution, of race-mixing, of miscegenation, of "mongrelization." It stemmed from a fear of the loss of racial purity, the loss of control of white women, the loss of potency, both social and physical. It stemmed from a fear of black sexual exuberance and capacity. That fear was at the heart of white America's perception of black character and personality. Once aroused, it often became the operant element in unleashing primitive, irrational behavior. Elizabeth Eckford did not know, when she alighted from her bus at Twelfth and Park, that she was walking into the jaws of the beast.[27]

CHAPTER ONE

DEFINING THE DEBATE

Harry Ashmore

The "City of Roses" was beginning to bloom. June in Arkansas has always been delightful, and in the early summer of 1957 it was especially so. Temperatures in Little Rock hovered around 75 degrees through clear and balmy days, children played in backyards and collected lightning bugs in mason jars at dusk, and the gifted young editor of the *Arkansas Gazette* spent long, pleasant afternoons in his downtown office crafting the final phrases of the book about southern life he had been preparing himself for twenty years to write.

Harry Ashmore had come to Little Rock ten years before at the age of thirty-one to direct the editorial page of Arkansas's leading newspaper. In that postwar decade he had seen the city take on new business vigor under the blandishments of returned World War II veterans such as himself. He had also participated in the realignment of Arkansas politics under the liberal leadership of another young veteran, his friend and ally in numerous causes, former Governor Sid McMath.

By the summer of 1957 the city fathers of Little Rock had reason to believe they were on the threshold of a promising new era in Arkansas's history and development. Following the leadership of a group of young veterans who had broadened their vision in their sojourns out into the world beyond the South, the Little Rock Chamber of Commerce had overseen the development of an industrial district and had participated in attracting an Air Force base to the metropolitan area. In the summer of 1955 the Little Rock School Board had announced its plans for voluntary desegregation of the city's public schools. The following year the city's business leadership had succeeded in changing their community from a mayoral to a city manager form of government, a "reform" that aimed to make the city more responsive to the needs and desires of the business community.[1]

In the winter 1957 session of the state legislature, the reform-minded young governor, Orval Faubus, had pushed through a dramatic increase in the state's sales tax that promised to make possible some desperately needed improvements in education and other state services in Arkansas. By all accounts Little Rock enjoyed an earned reputation as one of the most progressive cities in the South with regard to race relations, and visitors from other regions and countries frequently responded with genuine surprise to its beauty, graciousness, and sophistication. In short, all of the elements seemed to be in place for Little Rock's long-delayed entry into the mainstream of American life.[2]

IN THIS UPBEAT environment, Harry Ashmore thought he could see the coming together of several themes, or "great impersonal forces," he had first detected at work in the South Carolina of his youth. He believed he was witnessing the end of an era in the South, and as the pleasant days of an Arkansas June began to wilt into the steam and sweat of midsummer, the celebrated young editor put the finishing touches on an elegant and hopeful study that he titled *An Epitaph for Dixie*.[3]

In this slim volume Ashmore prophesied a new order for the South, one he believed was the inevitable result of the passing of the Old South's "peculiar institutions" of the agrarian economy, one-party politics, and legal segregation, all three of which were tied to the white man's determination to control the position of the Negro in southern society. In the face of the dramatic population shifts of black Americans from the southern countryside to the cities, especially the northern cities, and as a result of the *Brown* decisions outlawing segregation in the public schools, Ashmore argued that white southerners would follow their own economic self-interest into a new ordering of race relations. In particular, the New South's businessmen, "the bustling gentlemen at the local Chambers of Commerce or the state Industrial Development Commissions," would lead the way into a more democratic and rational future, and they would bring their communities and their region along with them. At last, thought Ashmore, the white people of the South could affirm of their own accord the reality of the accommodation the nation had reached at Appomattox almost a hundred years before. However haltingly such an effort might proceed, the young writer predicted the people of his native region would head in that direction, and the road they would take "leads inevitably to reunion."[4]

Harry Scott Ashmore had spent his formative years in the South Carolina piedmont, or the "upcountry." A member of an extended kin network of respectable farmers, merchants, and politicians, he found abundant opportu-

nities from an early age to develop his twin passions of reading and studying
politics. In the stratified society of white South Carolina he developed a fasci-
nation with the concept of aristocracy, and perhaps a sense of injustice that his
family could not lay claim to the grand traditions of elegance and preference
that accrued to their low-country neighbors. An able student, he was
undoubtedly chagrined by his father's bankruptcy during his high school years,
a circumstance that sent him into his first journalistic employment as a newspaper boy. He attended Clemson because as a state-supported institution it had
no tuition fees, and he joined the Reserve Officer Training Corps because it paid
a small stipend to "a chronically broke student."[5]

Upon completing college in 1937, Ashmore returned home to work as a cub
reporter for the *Greenville Piedmont,* eventually transferring to the *Greenville
News* and assuming the courthouse beat in the state capital of Columbia. Here
he cut his journalistic teeth on the Byzantine intricacies of southern life and
politics that compelled and fascinated him until he thought he had captured
them in his second book, *An Epitaph for Dixie.*[6]

In 1941 the young reporter applied for and was awarded a Nieman Fellowship to study for a year at Harvard. After a semester of reveling in the study of
history (and especially southern history) under a variety of challenging professors, the former R.O.T.C. student found himself called to active duty in the
Army as a result of the bombing of Pearl Harbor. Ashmore served with distinction on the front lines in France as an officer with the 95th Infantry, and after
the victory in Europe he assumed a post at the Pentagon until the war's end.
Always a voracious reader, he devoured Gunnar Myrdal's newly-released *An
American Dilemma* while still in the Army, and when he returned to the South
in 1945 his eyes had been opened by all these experiences to the tragedies of the
southern past and the possibilities for its future. He came home with a determination to be a part of shaping that future.[7]

Ashmore knew he would have greater opportunities to be heard and understood as a journalist outside the South, but he had already decided to pursue his
career within the region. In response to an offer to assume Wilbur J. Cash's old
position as editorial page editor of the *Charlotte News,* Ashmore had written
from Europe in 1944, "I've come to believe that the important things, the essen-
tial freedoms, the democratic processes, are luxuries, not inalienable rights, and
the price we must pay for them is high. Sometimes we fight to preserve them with
guns, sometimes with typewriters, but always we must stand ready to fight."[8]

Ashmore understood that the nature of the postwar fight in the South
would be a struggle for the long-denied civil rights of the region's black popu-

lation, but he was not yet committed to the goal of social equality. Like other southerners of his place and time he had grown up wearing blinders to the plight and condition of the blacks among whom he lived. In his youth, he wrote some years later, he believed "Negroes handled menial chores and performed personal services and were to be treated with tolerance and even affection, but were not exactly people. Negroes, I understood, were inextricably bound up in the Southern Way, but in that simple time they had not even risen to the status of a Problem."[9]

By the time he returned from the war against Hitler's armies, Ashmore saw things differently. Although he was still willing to take a gradualist approach to the solution of the South's racial problems, the young editor was now clear-sighted about the need to prepare for the demands of the future. His next move took him into the very heart of the struggle to shape that world.[10]

MOVING TO LITTLE ROCK in 1947 to accept the position as editorial page editor and later executive editor of the *Arkansas Gazette*, Harry Ashmore found an ally and a lifelong friend in another recent addition to the top tier of the *Gazette* hierarchy, Hugh B. Patterson. Patterson had married owner and editor J. N. Heiskell's daughter, Louise, in 1943, and had joined the newspaper's staff on the business side after completing his military service in 1946. Although he was the boss's son-in-law, from the beginning of his tenure Patterson insisted on playing an integral role in the life of his paper, and he proved to be much more than a figurehead when he assumed the business direction of the *Gazette*. Possessed of a merry disposition and an ability to tell a good story, Patterson complemented Ashmore's forceful personality and mordant wit, and the two became constant companions. Significantly for the future of the paper, Patterson also functioned as a loyal advocate with Mr. Heiskell—one longtime staffer remembered that "Hugh ran interference for Harry"—in behalf of the advanced positions of the celebrated newcomer who now graced the editorial page of the *Arkansas Gazette*.[11]

One of Ashmore's early challenges came in his first discussion with Heiskell of a specifically racial matter, when he addressed the *Gazette*'s customary practice of refusing to use courtesy titles such as *Mr., Mrs.,* and *Miss* when referring to blacks. "It simply had not occurred to him," Ashmore wrote years later, "that the conventional address he had used all his life was offensive, and no one had ever called the matter to his attention." Ashmore suggested dropping *Mr.* for whites as well as blacks, and to use *Miss* and *Mrs.* for all women, largely to clarify their marital status in news stories. Heiskell listened carefully and then agreed, but not, thought Ashmore, "as a matter of correcting an injustice, but because he was a meticulous grammarian who could see that the style forced clumsy convolutions in the use of his beloved English language." But the *Gazette* continued to separate its obituaries for whites and blacks, it did not carry pictures of black brides, and it identified Negroes as such in many news stories, including police news. Although Harry Ashmore was not yet an advocate of complete social equality, he must have chafed under these constraints.[12]

JUST A FEW WEEKS after Ashmore joined the *Gazette* in the fall of 1947, he found himself embroiled in "political combat, Arkansas style." In an effort to secure the Democratic Party's 1948 presidential nomination, Harry Truman had adopted the political strategy of wooing northern and black voters, and he had in 1946 appointed a special commission to study and make recommendations regarding minority civil rights. When the commission released its report in October 1947, titled *To Secure These Rights,* a firestorm of protest erupted across the southern states. The following spring Arkansas Governor Ben T. Laney, believing that the presidential commission's recommendations represented a major threat to the South's racial mores, assumed the chairmanship of a region-wide faction—soon to be called Dixiecrats—committed to opposing Truman's nomination.[13]

As editor of Arkansas's leading newspaper, Harry Ashmore soon charged into battle with the governor of his adopted state. In a radio debate with Governor Laney in May of 1948, Ashmore hammered away at his insistence on party loyalty, while Laney emphasized his opposition to the president's endorsement of anti-lynching, anti–poll tax, anti-segregation, and Fair Employment Practices Commission legislation, calling all of it unconstitutional and even communistic. Ashmore was convinced that nefarious economic and political considerations lay behind the Dixiecrats' use of the race issue, as they had in many other instances in the southern past.[14]

In the question-and-answer period after the radio debate with Laney, Ashmore deflected a question along the lines of "Would you want your sister to marry a Negro?" attempting to prevent the dialogue from descending into a discussion of the horrors of miscegenation. This line of argument seemed to him to be so irrational that he dismissed it as one of the "absurdities" he railed against all his life. He also thought it was an emotional smoke screen that southern whites used to cover their opposition to any alteration of the racial power relationships from which they had always benefited.[15]

Harry Ashmore believed the region's rejection of the Dixiecrats indicated the South might be willing to accept a softened version of the Truman civil rights package. Senator J. William Fulbright and Congressman Brooks Hays were working feverishly on just such a proposal, soon to be known as "The Arkansas Plan." Ashmore endorsed the Hays-Fulbright effort in an editorial titled "The Area of Compromise," arguing that there was a difference between segregation and discrimination, and that southerners would accept proposals to modify some practices, such as the poll tax, that discriminated against blacks.[16]

But Ashmore also argued there were limits beyond which the South could not be expected to go, and that the region "for many years to come will continue to reject anti-segregation and fair employment laws." Unfortunately, Senator Fulbright proved unwilling to press for the changes Ashmore was advocating. As one biographer noted, "Fulbright did not have the political courage to put his public stamp of approval on even as modest a plan as this [the Arkansas Plan]."[17]

As a result, mild-mannered and conciliatory Brooks Hays stood boldly alone in presenting his compromise package in a speech to the Congress on February 2, 1949. Exactly one year to the day after Harry Truman had proposed legislation drawn from *To Secure These Rights,* Hays pointed out that Congress had not approved any of the president's major recommendations, and his compromise proposals eliminated all of the Truman recommendations that did not provide for voluntary, state-controlled mechanisms of enforcement. This toothless approach met with derision on the floor of the House of Representatives, and so Harry Ashmore and his allies went back to square one in their effort to avoid a southern split and keep the South in the embrace of the Democrats.[18]

THE NEXT SPRING, at Governor Sid McMath's invitation, Harry Ashmore stepped up to the microphone at the Southern Governors' Conference to deliver what he hoped would be the fatal blow to the third-party threat. The Dixiecrat movement had been born at the 1948 Southern Governors' Conference, and President Truman had gotten wind of the fact that many of the still-disaffected southern leaders intended to use the occasion of the 1951 conference to plot their strategy for the next election, hoping to prevent Truman's renomination and eliminate civil rights from the 1952 Democratic platform. In a move to control the tone of the conference, Sid McMath invited Harry Ashmore and House Speaker Sam Rayburn, another Truman loyalist, to give the two key addresses.[19]

Rayburn's speech emphasized party loyalty and raised a few Dixiecrat hackles. Ashmore's speech addressed southern race relations directly, and it was met with stony silence. "We went through a tragic and divisive internal politi-

cal struggle in 1948," he reminded his audience, most of whom had been participants in that struggle. "The makings of another great political rebellion are here
in this room, and again it is the peculiar institution of the one-party South—
with its roots in the basic problem of race relations—that is its cause." Finding
his stride, he continued: "The practical problem before the South is to preserve
social segregation while at the same time meeting the conditions of a Constitution and a national tradition which demand that full civil liberties and full
equality of opportunity be extended to all citizens without discrimination...."[20]

Ashmore argued that in all activities supported by tax funds, "the Negro must
either be treated without official prejudice or in absolute, incontrovertible fact
be provided with separate but equal facilities." When the South had done these
things, the young editor suggested, "we may then insist that matters involving
the private relationship between the two races are, and should be, beyond the
reach of the law." Attempting to allay his listeners' fears about miscegenation,
Ashmore added, "I happen to be one who believes that segregation in the relationships that are essentially private in character can endure in the South without violation of any of the real civil rights of members of either race."[21]

Despite his attempts at diplomacy, Ashmore recalled years later that two of
the southern governors, Jimmy Byrnes of South Carolina and Herman Talmadge
of Georgia, walked out in the middle of his speech, and when he concluded his
remarks only Theodore McKeldin, Republican governor of Maryland,
applauded. In reaction to a question from the *New York Times'* John Popham,
Governor Byrnes could only sputter "Why, I believe I know that boy's family!"
The press contingent in the back of the room, however, who had turned out in
full force expecting fireworks from the meeting, were elated. As John Popham
wrote six days later, "I can't begin to tell you . . . just how enthusiastic all the newspaper boys were in expressing in their little groups for several days the high regard
they had for you and your speech. . . . You were one hell of a hit with the gang,
Harry, and that's as much bouquet as I'm going to give you from now on."[22]

Emboldened by the reactions of Popham and others, Ashmore actively
sought a wider audience for his views. Less than a week after his speech he sent
a copy to his friend Charles Morton, editor of the *Atlantic Monthly.* Ashmore
responded enthusiastically to Harold Fleming's invitation to publish the speech
in the Southern Regional Council's *New South,* and to Louis Lyons's request to
include it in Harvard's *Nieman Reports.* Harry Ashmore had now tasted the
heady wine of influencing national policy and had found it addictive. He would
never retreat from the impulse to be involved in the shaping of national public
affairs.[23]

One secret to Ashmore's remarkable productivity seems to be his ability to write quickly. Louise Patterson was accustomed to watching her father "give birth" to his editorials, but she remembered that "Words just poured from Harry like liquid." Journalist Roy Reed, who was a young *Gazette* reporter at the time, described Ashmore's abilities with awe. "We used to see him come into the newsroom and just hang around, talking, gossiping, telling jokes," Reed recalled, "and suddenly an editorial would come upon him . . . and he would commandeer some reporter's typewriter and just sit down and bat it out right there. And of course, it would read just perfectly the next morning."[24]

Some of this ability to write quickly came from the fact, as Reed described it years later, that Ashmore had "perfect pitch with the language." Probably the greater part of Ashmore's facility with writing stemmed from his great assurance, when he sat down to give voice to an idea, that he was right. Unburdened by self-doubt, and possessed of immense powers of persuasion, Ashmore was unaccustomed to finding himself challenged effectively.[25]

This gift carried with it an equal and troublesome sting: as charming and as forceful as he was universally acclaimed to be when speaking from the podium, in personal exchanges Ashmore was widely perceived in Arkansas to be intellectually arrogant and disdainful of points of view that differed from his own. A description he wrote of one of his reporters probably applied with equal force to himself: "he . . . has little tolerance for fools and he considers himself outnumbered." This disdain was not reserved exclusively for Dixiecrat politicians or people he dismissed as "rednecks." He was especially impatient with the country club set, whom he called the "establishment," perhaps because he believed he should be able to expect more enlightened views from them, perhaps because he felt himself to be a natural aristocrat and he mocked their pretensions, perhaps because he sensed that they looked down on him.[26]

Although his office correspondence shows a high level of professionalism in dealing with people who challenged his editorials, in his personal interactions with people who disagreed with him Ashmore's haughtiness and dismissive tone prevented his having an effective voice within the social circles where community decisions were made. This was a real failing by his own standards, for as he wrote in the Introduction to his first book, one of his "cherished theories" was that "journalism should serve as a two-way bridge between the world of ideas and the world of men."[27]

Harry Ashmore felt a passionate commitment to the Democratic Party, but he was always more of an elitist than a populist. As he told his friend and fellow journalist John Egerton toward the end of his life, "the only justification for democracy" is that it "puts a constraint on the elitists who are going to run the damn government anyway. But, as far as effecting a policy change, it won't do that. It will probably go the other way. The best you can hope for is when they are quiescent, when they let a little progress happen, which is what happened in the South."[28]

WITHIN HIS PROFESSION Ashmore had legions of admirers, and a stature and reputation that Little Rock citizens did not realize. His elegant and accessible writing style, his persuasiveness with pen or microphone, and his forthright stands on a variety of tough issues caused his journalistic peers to regard him as a leader. His gifted storytelling, unfailing mirth, and prodigious capacity for alcohol made him a valued companion, whether entertaining visiting journalists and singing hillbilly songs on his patio in Little Rock, or sitting around smoky hotel bars and swapping tales from the front at journalism conventions. His lifelong friend Bill Emerson described him this way: "Ashmore was a warrior. He would join in battle against the enemy with fierce glee. He laughed when he fought like the Celt that he was . . . If you search for Ashmore in the bosky dell—that is in the grove of academe—he might appear in the distance to be half scholar, half Dionysus, but on an editorial mission that would take no prisoners."[29]

Ashmore prided himself on having helped turn the tide at the Southern Governors' Conference at Hot Springs in 1951. At the Democratic National Convention in Chicago the next summer the southern states stayed within the fold of the Democratic Party, and even the inclusion of a strengthened civil rights plank in the platform did not occasion a fight on the convention floor. By this time Ashmore had become enamored of the sophisticated Adlai Stevenson, who was destined to become the Democratic nominee, and he worked behind the scenes to secure the vice presidential nomination for his friend Bill Fulbright, whom President Truman had recently branded "an overeducated S.O.B." Disappointed in this effort, he returned to Arkansas with a renewed commitment to the Democratic faith and ready to train the heavy artillery of the *Arkansas Gazette*'s editorial page on the Republican Party and its nominee, Dwight Eisenhower.[30]

THE 1952 PRIMARY season in Arkansas also brought with it the defeat of Ashmore's friend Sid McMath, who was swept from the governorship by a combination of popular outrage over questionable dealings in his highway department, opposition from the mighty Arkansas Power & Light Company, and a revulsion against Truman. As an article in the *Arkansas Democrat-Gazette* explained years later, "Toward the end of McMath's second term in office, the Highway Audit Commission concluded that there was an 'apparent practice' of requiring businessmen to contribute to a political fund under [Henry] Woods' control to get state contracts." An associate justice of the Arkansas Supreme Court wrote to Francis Cherry, the new governor, "One of the most tragic phases of the McMath fiasco was that he followed, blindly and eplicitly [*sic*], the Harry-Harry (Truman-Ashmore) philosophy of socialism. . . . I predict that your worst headache will not be with the Legislature, as Mr. Ashmore assumes, but rather with the Gazette and its policy of higher taxes and more socialism." The justice's comments reflected a skepticism that was spreading throughout Arkansas about the reformist ideas of the liberal Mr. Ashmore.[31]

Early in 1952, the Ford Foundation–sponsored Fund for the Advancement of Education invited Ashmore to chair a project assessing the state of Negro education in the South, in preparation for the expected Supreme Court decision concerning segregation in public education. When the Ford Foundation's director approached Ashmore about overseeing this effort, the young editor wondered why someone with academic credentials was not being given the job. As he soon learned, "no university administration was prepared to face the political heat an impartial appraisal of the disparities in the dual school system was bound to engender." Although intrigued, his first concern was the risk to the *Gazette* his involvement in such a project would incur. In a meeting with Heiskell and Patterson in which he laid out the possibilities, his boss "said dryly that this was a financial matter and he would leave it to the publisher." Hugh Patterson, who had become the second in command at the newspaper, replied immediately, "Of course it is. It would be an act of fiscal imprudence if we didn't insist that Ashmore accept. When that Supreme Court decision comes down every newspaper in the South is going to have to deal with the consequences, and we'll have the best-informed editor available—at Ford Foundation expense."[32]

In theory the Ford Foundation project, which quickly came to be called the Ashmore Project, was to be strictly a fact-finding mission conducted by a team of forty sociologists, economists, educational experts, and legal scholars, with Ashmore compiling the results into an objective appraisal of the needs and deficiencies of black education. In fact, as Ashmore soon wrote to a confidant, the goal of the project was to find out "what happens in the South and everywhere else in the country for that matter if the Supreme Court knocks out segregation in the schools. Part of it is pure research; we hope to find out by examining existing sources what the problems really would be. . . ." The other part, however, "is necessarily a quiet public relations job intended to line up some of the big wheels in the South to step forward [if] the blow falls and urge everybody to count up to ten before they start talking about blood in the streets."[33]

Ashmore may have realized he had taken on far more than an editing assignment, but he also found that he enjoyed the work immensely and that he was able to bring to bear on a real-world problem all the thinking, studying, and caring he had invested in the southern region over the last twenty years of his life. Upon surveying the findings of his team of researchers, the logical Ashmore felt confident that anyone who "considered the implications of the changing demographic patterns revealed by the pages of tables and graphs, could not doubt that time was running out on the rigidly segregated society hammered into place eighty years before."[34]

The conclusion to his study reflected his optimism, as well as his lifelong desire to be seen as a prophet. "In the long sweep of history," he wrote, "the public school cases before the Supreme Court may be written down as the point at which the South cleared the last turning in the road to reunion—the point at which finally, and under protest, the region gave up its peculiar institutions and accepted the prevailing standards of the nation at large as the legal basis for its relationship with its minority race." Even more hopefully he wrote, "This would not in itself bring about any great shift in Southern attitudes, nor even any far-reaching immediate changes in the pattern of bi-racial education. But it would re-define the goal the Southern people, white and Negro, are committed to seek in the way of democracy."[35]

Ashmore finished *The Negro and the Schools* and sent it off to the University of North Carolina Press in January of 1954. Imposing an extraordinarily streamlined publishing schedule, the press worked feverishly to publish the volume before the announcement of the Supreme Court's decision on segregation. With remarkable timing the press actually released the book on Sunday, May 16, 1954, the day before the United States Supreme Court handed down its decision in *Brown v. the Board of Education of Topeka, Kansas.*

Ashmore clearly believed that one of his responsibilities in conjunction with the Ford Foundation project was to prepare a wide range of southern leaders for the effects of the upcoming Supreme Court decision. As he wrote to George Mitchell of the racially progressive Southern Regional Council, "There is going to be much work to do in the wake of the Court decision. . . . I like the term Jonathan Daniels used . . . to the effect that the white and Negro people in the South now have important business together."[36]

Ashmore was making quiet contacts in Arkansas as well. His membership on both the statewide Citizens' Steering Committee for Public Schools and the Arkansas Department of Education's Special Committee on Negro Education put him in touch with a wide range of community leaders, and in these and other forums he had access to the kind of "big wheels" who he hoped would step forth to speak for calm and reason in their communities. He also met frequently with the Little Rock School Board's new superintendent, Virgil Blossom, to whom he became "very close." As he recalled years later, "I was taking the position that this was not going to create any fast, rapid, social change. That it was the beginning of a process . . . that we were at the end of a historical epoch and we were just going to begin come what may. . . ."[37]

ON THE FOURTH Monday in May the Supreme Court handed down its historic *Brown* decision, mandating an end to segregation in the nation's public schools. Governor Cherry announced almost immediately that Arkansas would comply with the Supreme Court mandate, as did the Little Rock School Board. At this point Hugh and Louise Patterson had to take J. N. Heiskell "by the hand" and drag him into the new order in the South. Years later Louise recalled that her father's devotion to the rule of law caused him to bend before this new dispensation. "You've got to realize that he was born in 1872," Louise Heiskell recalled, and "in [the] post–Civil War [era], the bitterness was very strong. He grew up with that attitude. . . . I don't think he changed his mind; I just think he knew he had to accept it." The reluctance and dismay of the old editor reflected the majority sentiment in the white South, and as Harry Ashmore eventually realized, the "road to reunion" stretched far beyond the horizon.[38]

Ashmore was momentarily euphoric. His book received glowing reviews in newspapers across the nation, and he found himself "rushing around the country" to promote it. He also found himself being praised and criticized at the same time, and he took obvious pleasure in writing to his old friend Tom Waring of the *Charleston News and Courier* that the reviewer for the *Saturday Evening Post* detected "a current of bias against the South's pattern of school segregation" and yet the reviewer for the *San Francisco Chronicle* "charged that despite my best efforts at objectivity there flowed through the work a definite bias against integration."[39]

As Hugh Patterson had predicted, Harry Ashmore was now the recognized authority on the new demands facing the South's schools and communities. Ashmore also put the finishing touches on a new agency he had helped the Fund for the Advancement of Education to design and staff, the Southern Education Reporting Service (SERS). Overseen by a blue-ribbon, interracial board

of editors and educators, SERS was touted as an objective, nonpartisan reporting agency that would monitor the progress of desegregation and disseminate
that information through the publication of a new weekly, *Southern School
News.* From the first SERS attempted "to meet the needs of the communications media," and as Ashmore later explained, it became the primary means by
which the press was "able to make any sense at all out of this dark and tangled
tale. . . ."[40]

Ashmore's old Little Rock nemesis, John Wells, editor and publisher of the
conservative weekly the *Arkansas Recorder,* took immediate exception to *The
Negro and the Schools,* and to SERS. The Wells-Ashmore feud dated back to the
Dixiecrat crusade and continued through Wells's brutal and effective assault on
the McMath administration. Wells's initial reaction to the *Brown* decision had
been to cry, "If freedom is to be preserved, or rather reinstated, as the first consideration of our government, a new party must rise to carry the burden of
disciplined self-government that both Democrats and Republicans have cast off
in bidding for votes of organized minorities. It's time the majority organized."
Charging that SERS was designed to be "a Southwide propaganda mill," the
unhappy Wells thought the Supreme Court would simply "wait for the propaganda to take hold before it renders its final decrees in the segregation cases."
Far from being an isolated crackpot, Wells's views mirrored those of many concerned citizens across the South.[41]

ORVAL FAUBUS HAD considered running for governor in 1954, but when he
went to Little Rock to explore the possibilities, the political kingmaker who was
backing Governor Cherry, Witt Stephens, told him "You wait two years and we'll
be for you, . . . You run this time and we'll beat your ass." Stephens also informed
Faubus that if he ran, "they" would find an opponent for his friend and mentor, Congressman Jim Trimble. Taking Stephens's advice to heart, Faubus went
home to the Ozarks and bided his time until the day before the filing deadline,
then he slipped into Little Rock and filed his candidacy just minutes before the
office closed, thereby preventing a challenge to Trimble. This kind of wily
maneuvering offered a taste of how the next twelve years of Arkansas politics
would be flavored.[42]

Sid McMath had brought Orval Eugene Faubus into Arkansas politics.
Another returning GI, Faubus had delivered his home county to the victorious
McMath gubernatorial campaign in 1948, and McMath had rewarded him by
making the mountaineer a member of the powerful Highway Commission (and
later its chairman), and then his administrative assistant. In these capacities

Faubus had worked closely with Sid McMath and especially with his executive secretary, Henry Woods. In the process he had learned a great deal about the people of Arkansas and the functioning of their politics, and he had come to the conclusion in 1953 that Governor Francis Cherry was beatable.[43]

Henry Woods had opposed Faubus's entering the gubernatorial race. Woods knew that in the same campaign season McMath would be attempting a political comeback by challenging Senator John McClellan, and he believed a Faubus candidacy would draw energies and funds away from the McMath network he had so carefully constructed. Faubus persisted despite Woods's opposition, and in the first primary he surprisingly made it into a runoff, while McMath met defeat.[44]

A flustered and increasingly desperate Governor Cherry made a strategic error when he bowed to the lead of some of his advisers, primarily John Wells, and launched a McCarthy-like attack on Orval Faubus. Waving papers before television cameras that purported to show Faubus had once been a student at the "communist" Commonwealth College in Mena, Arkansas, Cherry brought the red menace home to a people who had heretofore felt insulated and safe.[45]

Henry Woods was incensed by this smear campaign and distressed by Faubus's apparent inability to deal with it effectively. Woods told Faubus he had run into Harry Ashmore and Harry was disgusted by the whole incident, so disgusted in fact that Woods thought he could get Ashmore to write a speech for Faubus to deliver. Henry Woods and Harry Ashmore and their liberal compatriot Edwin Dunaway spent the whole afternoon preparing the Faubus defense. First they wrote a double-page newspaper ad, and then while Dunaway solicited donations for television time, Woods supplied the facts and Ashmore wrote the candidate's speech. As Henry Woods remembered it, "we handed him the damn speech, and . . . he read it in the damn car from the damn airport going to the damn station. . . . the truth of the matter is that Ashmore and I elected the son of a bitch."[46]

Harry Ashmore wrote a brilliant speech that made Orval Faubus the governor of Arkansas. In it he sounded all the themes the populist candidate had employed in his campaign against a stuffy establishment lawyer. He explained that in his callow youth as a poor mountain boy he had found his way to the left-leaning college, but that he had been offended immediately by some of the things he heard there and he had not stayed. One of Ashmore's phrases stuck in the candidate's mind for the rest of his life: "When I went out from the green valley of my youth. . . ." Midway through it, as Faubus' biographer told the tale, "Faubus glanced up from his text and saw the spectators moving closer. They made no sound, but he saw women wiping away tears." He knew then that his campaign had turned the corner. From that day forward, Orval Faubus knew he owed Harry Ashmore a great debt, a debt that he acknowledged many times through the rest of his life. He even told Ashmore he owed the editor "a blank check" that could be redeemed at any time. Ashmore never collected.[47]

FOR HARRY ASHMORE, the real excitement of the busy summer of 1954 was his own emergence on the national scene as a commentator, expert, and guide. To his great pleasure he was now called upon with increasing frequency to share his insights with a world that felt a new urgency about understanding the South. As he realized, the "accidents of birth and occupation" had "thrust upon me a singular concern" with understanding the intricacies and implications of American racism, "the issue that holds the undisputed American course record for public and private ambivalence."[48]

The time now seemed to be right for Ashmore to write a book of his own, one that would elucidate his understanding of America's racial dilemma and the prospects for escaping the grip of that ancient curse. Writing to Howard W. Odum, the venerable Chapel Hill scholar whose work had first introduced him to the academic study of the southern region while he was an undergraduate at Clemson, Ashmore responded to the older man's praise for *The Negro and the Schools* by saying, ". . . having been now well bitten by the bug, I am toying with the notion of a book developing the theme of an epitaph for Dixie. This one, heaven preserve us, would be a personalized volume in which I would present all sorts of splendid generalizations totally unbuttressed by scientific research."[49]

Within a matter of months Ashmore had secured a contract from W. W. Norton & Company for just such a book, and now his busy days took on an even more urgent, if pleasantly rewarding, feel. In the meantime, *The Negro and the Schools* went on the bedside table of Chief Justice Earl Warren, and undoubtedly those of many southern school officials and editors who carried the major responsibility for the coming changes.[50]

About this time Ashmore took another step he hoped would contribute to smoothing the transition in Little Rock: he went on the founding board of the new Arkansas Council on Human Relations (ACHR), an interracial offshoot of the Southern Regional Council, in which capacity he developed a good working relationship with the young president of Arkansas' National Association for the Advancement of Colored People, Mrs. Daisy Bates. As a board member of the Southern Regional Council in 1953, Ashmore had helped secure a large grant for that organization from the Ford Foundation's Fund for the Republic.

Ashmore believed that without help from outside the region, funding for organizations such as the Southern Regional Council would dry up in the South,
especially as ultraconservatives began to draw an equation between communism and the threat to segregation.[51]

Ashmore's decision to join the ACHR board simply confirmed the suspicions of many in Little Rock that he was an "integrationist," as did his decision
to join the national board of the aggressive and well-endowed Fund for the
Republic. As Ashmore described the loosely formulated goals of the Fund for
the Republic, it aspired to "guarantee freedom of thought." With characteristic
irreverence, Ashmore wrote an inquirer: "What the Ford people did was give the
Fund $15,000,000 and run for the high ground." The Fund became an ardent
supporter of civil rights, especially in the South, and in affiliating himself with
this effort Ashmore placed himself directly in the line of fire of people such as
John Wells, who felt certain that Ashmore was the agent of a vast communist
conspiracy to undermine southern institutions, especially segregation.[52]

ON MAY 31, 1955, the United States Supreme Court handed down its implementation guidelines for desegregation, known widely as *Brown II*. Harry Ashmore wrote what he called "a fan letter" to Chief Justice Earl Warren. "It is my
considered opinion," the young editor suggested, "that the Court's handling of
the complex and explosive school segregation cases may very well rank as the
greatest act of judicial statesmanship in the nation's history. . . ." Writing with
unbridled enthusiasm Ashmore continued, "The unequivocal initial ruling, the
year's cooling off period, and the moderate procedures outlined in today's
orders remanding the cases have enabled the South to see the issue in perspective. It will take time, of course, to end segregation in the schools. But we are on
our way, and thanks to you and your colleagues, we are proceeding in reasonably good order."[53]

The Little Rock School Board had announced its plan for desegregation a
week before *Brown II* appeared. Called the Blossom Plan for its creator, Superintendent Virgil T. Blossom, it was a limited, phased program that intended to
start at the high school level and proceed downward through the grades over
the succeeding six years. Ashmore and Blossom envisioned it as a "pilot project"
that could show the South how easily desegregation could be accomplished.
Ashmore did have doubts about the burly, high-strung superintendent whom
he described as "a natural-born Rotarian" (not intended as a compliment), but
he kept his reservations to himself and hoped for the best.[54]

Ashmore was pleased with the immediate response of Governor Orval

Faubus, who, as the editor wrote years later, "greeted *Brown II* with as moderate a statement as any made by a major Southern officeholder." As the Arkansas governor suggested, "Our reliance now must be upon the good will that exists between the two races—the good will that has long made Arkansas a model for the other southern states in all matters affecting the relationship between the races." The progressive young governor's stance boded well for the future of the desegregation effort in Arkansas, and for this reason Ashmore did not think it necessary to lobby Governor Faubus and secure his support for compliance with the two *Brown* decisions, as he was doing with other decision-makers in the state.[55]

ANOTHER PRESIDENTIAL election was shaping up. An invitation arrived to join the campaign of Adlai Stevenson to secure the Democratic Party's nomination, and Ashmore could not resist. He announced his intention to take a year's leave of absence, signed on as Stevenson's press secretary (and as it turned out, his speechwriter and adviser on civil rights), and moved his family to Chicago. The next year was a whirlwind of purposeful activity and a refreshing change from the pace of life in a newspaper office. As Ashmore described his role in the campaign, "I was . . . expected to provide a conspicuously non–Ivy League persona in Stevenson's immediate entourage, and establish an informal relationship with the media. The term had not yet been coined, but as the correspondents began to arrive at our downtown headquarters I soon realized that I had become a spin doctor."[56]

Stevenson's main challenge in the 1956 campaign was to figure out how to reconcile the country's divergent views on race, or in other words how to be a "moderate," in a year in which race had become "an absolutely critical issue." Stevenson supported the *Brown* decisions, and one of Ashmore's key assignments was to make that support palatable to southern audiences. The young editor hoped to fashion a stance for Stevenson allowing him to be a statesman in a situation that necessitated embracing widely conflicting loyalties and commitments. At one point he even suggested Stevenson consider Arkansas's progressive young governor, Orval Faubus, as his running mate.[57]

In March of 1956 the Stevenson candidacy suffered a crippling blow when ninety-seven southern Democratic congressmen, and three Republicans, signed a Declaration of Constitutional Principles questioning the legitimacy of the *Brown* decision. Popularly known as the "Southern Manifesto," this document proclaimed: "We regard the decision of the Supreme Court in the school cases as a clear abuse of judicial power. It climaxes a trend in the Federal Judiciary undertaking to legislate, in derogation of the authority of Congress, and to encroach upon the reserved rights of the States and the people. . . ." Ringing on the coveted southern theme of states' rights, it went even more directly to the heart of southern fears of Yankee force when it concluded, "We pledge ourselves to use all lawful means to bring about a reversal of this decision which is contrary to the Constitution and to prevent the use of force in its implementation."[58]

With this action the candidacy of Adlai Stevenson had been, in Ashmore's words, "very nearly submerged." The Arkansas editor remained convinced ever after that the Republican victory in November was a result of "the default of the Southern political leadership," and that Stevenson's statesmanship in trying to fashion a moderate course "had been rewarded by an act of Southern sabotage." Ashmore was chastened by this experience, and also by his failure to deliver his own state's delegation at the Democratic National Convention. Orval Faubus had received word that Averell Harriman was considering him as a possible running mate, and he refused to go for Stevenson on the first ballot. Ashmore returned to Arkansas with an abiding sense of grievance against the young governor who owed him so much.[59]

J. N. Heiskell had major surgery in the summer of 1956, and Hugh Patterson summoned Ashmore home. And so after the Democratic Convention and the successful nomination of his candidate, Harry Ashmore returned to Little Rock and resumed editorial direction of the *Arkansas Gazette*. In the year of his absence he had missed the buildup of a spirit of massive resistance to desegregation in his city, especially the birth of the Capital Citizens' Council. He had missed the 1956 political season in Arkansas, and as a consequence he had not paid close attention to the charged racial currents that swirled around his state, particularly in the race for governor between the progressive incumbent, Faubus, and the fiery states' rights advocate, Jim Johnson. His inattention to the tone of that campaign hobbled him in his attempts to understand what happened in his city the next year.[60]

But for the present he had his hands full reestablishing his routine as an editor, dealing with his disappointment about Stevenson's anemic candidacy and eventual defeat, and writing a book. By early 1957 he was ready to capture on paper his analysis of the forces that were shaping a new South, insights that had led him to believe the time had come, at last, to begin the preparation of an epitaph for Dixie.[61]

After spending the winter and spring of 1957 deeply engaged in his book project, Ashmore and his family left Little Rock for a month of vacation and rest in July. He returned in August to discover that his city editor had been out for weeks caring for his fatally stricken wife. Ashmore at this point assumed control not only of the editorial but also of the news-gathering functions of his paper, and in the crush of work resulting from the addition of this commitment to the backlog of work accumulated during his vacation, he failed to take notice of the escalating tensions in Little Rock. And so, imperfectly informed about affairs in his city, the self-styled "prophet" was completely taken by surprise when a racial confrontation of national and international proportions erupted under his very nose.[62]

With characteristic haste and assurance, Harry Ashmore immediately suspected Faubus of using race, "the old black magic," cynically to further his political career. Within days he was writing about "The Crisis Mr. Faubus Made," and soon he charged that the governor was seeking nothing nobler than a third term in the statehouse. With his immense powers of persuasion, his carefully nurtured prestige within his profession, his strategic placement as an expert at the heart of the action, and his preconceived theories about the sources of resistance to desegregation, Harry Ashmore fashioned over the next months an interpretation of events in the unfolding "Little Rock Crisis" that traveled around the globe, and that stood, practically untouched, for the next fifty years.[63]

CHAPTER TWO

MASSIVE RESISTANCE
Jim Johnson

L IKE SUMMER THUNDER, JIM JOHNSON ARRIVED ON THE ARKANSAS political scene seemingly out of nowhere, challenging the progressive, modernizing forces at work in his state, dragging into the political arena the oppressive attitudes and values of an older, vanishing South. In the summer of 1957 he was preparing himself for a second run for governor. Darkly handsome, slim and courtly, at thirty-three he was one of the youngest talents on the Arkansas political horizon, and yet in his command of a rhetoric that expressed the fears and anxieties of a largely rural electorate he was one of the most accomplished. Johnson had run for governor in 1956 and had pushed the incumbent Orval Faubus far to the right. Only once in Arkansas history had a governor been elected to a third successive term in office, and Jim Johnson fully expected Orval Faubus to aspire to a higher office in the summer of 1958.[1]

Johnson was a master of the rhetoric of "massive resistance" to desegregation. A protege of former Arkansas governor Ben Laney, who had spearheaded the Dixiecrat effort in 1948, Johnson had in the ensuing years established close working relationships with many of the regionwide leaders of the southern resistance movement. In part at their urging, but more directly in response to both his political ambition and his genuine fear of the impending destruction of white supremacy, Johnson employed every weapon in his arsenal to cause Orval Faubus to hold the line against desegregation in Little Rock.

Throughout the late spring and summer of 1957, Johnson used his influence and contacts to augment the program of intimidation Little Rock's Capital Citizens' Council (CCC) had undertaken. Targeting Governor Faubus and School Superintendent Virgil Blossom, the CCC initiated a barrage of anonymous telephone calls threatening violence if Little Rock Central High School were to be integrated in September as planned. These calls became increasingly ominous to both the governor and the superintendent, who began to meet with escalating frequency to discuss plans and contingencies for the integration process. They were so concerning to Blossom, in fact, that he persuaded the Little Rock School Board to send its attorney to Washington to seek assistance and direction from the Justice Department, and he also made arrangements for his daughter to attend school in another town.[2]

Jim Johnson's most important contribution to the campaign to intimidate Orval Faubus was his invitation to his friend Governor Marvin Griffin of Georgia, to come to Little Rock and address a huge Citizens' Council gathering in a last-ditch effort to forestall integration before the schools opened in September. Griffin brought his friend Roy Harris, firebrand director of the States' Rights Council of Georgia. They came in August, and their visit had the desired effect, demonstrating to Arkansas' first poll-watching governor that "the people" would not support integration at Little Rock Central High School. The day after the Georgians' speeches to the Capital Citizens' Council, Jim Johnson had breakfast at the Governor's Mansion with Faubus, Griffin, and Harris, and he observed with great pleasure the dilemma he had created for his old foe.[3]

JAMES DOUGLAS JOHNSON came into this world in 1924 in the Arkansas delta town of Crossett, just eight miles north of the Louisiana line and less than seventy miles west of the Mississippi River. His was a rowdy sawmill town, a company town that was "owned" by the bosses of the Crossett Lumber Company. His father despised the system that made his neighbors the virtual slaves of the company. They were paid in scrip, which they could then redeem only at the company store. Jim Johnson's father operated an independent grocery on the edge of town, often forcing prices down at the company store. Johnson later remembered his father's store as "a little pocket of freedom in a sea of control." And as he commented more than half a century after that boyhood, "I just detest control."[4]

Jim's mother, whose maiden name was Long and who thought herself to be related to the legendary Huey, one of his political heroes, complained bitterly about the pennies in sales tax "the government" forced her to assess and then record. His father preached daily about the virtues of being free to work for a fair wage and then to spend one's wages in a free and open market. These early lessons hit their mark with the boy who, as captain of the football team and president of the student body, had the gift of leadership, and they were themes that later emerged time and again in a political career spent fighting the intractable forces of an expanding federal government. In these early years of living "beyond the pale" in a company town, Johnson also forged a conception of himself as an outsider, a self-image he carried into politics, and one that served him well with a constituency that increasingly felt itself to be outside the main currents of American thought.[5]

In 1948 Jim Johnson was twenty-three, a veteran of World War II and a newly minted attorney. On the advice of a trusted older lawyer whom he admired and emulated he had skipped college, a decision he always regretted, and gone straight to Cumberland University Law School in Tennessee after serving in the Marines. He returned to his hometown of Crossett to establish a law practice. At the invitation of former Governor Ben Laney of nearby Camden, another of his and his mother's political heroes, he jumped into Arkansas politics as a district manager of Strom Thurmond's presidential campaign on the Dixiecrat ticket. In that heady experience, Johnson cut his teeth on the conservative issues that had been the hallmarks of the southern political tradition: small government, states' rights, and white supremacy. Laney put into his hands a copy of President Truman's Commission on Civil Rights report titled *To Secure These Rights,* and Johnson studied it religiously, finding it to be an alarming assault on traditional patterns of both Democratic Party politics and southern race relations.[6]

The young Johnson also studied and absorbed uncritically an address Thurmond had made to a Democratic Party rally in May of 1948, recalling later that this speech "was literally scripture to me." In this speech, Thurmond excoriated the "party bosses and ward heelers who have kidnapped the Democratic Party and deserted its principles," laying out the course the Dixiecrats eventually followed in an effort to convince the Democratic leadership "that the South's electoral votes are no longer in the bag for the Democratic Nominee." In the process of working for Thurmond and the Dixiecrats, Johnson learned the language of resistance and the stance of using high-toned rhetoric to mask his darker obsession with the threat of black defilement.[7]

A major theme of the Thurmond speech, and of Johnson's subsequent career, was its conspiratorial, paranoid line of argument. Holding that powerful forces in the North had long worked to keep the South in economic subjugation, Thurmond suggested that freight rate differentials and tariffs were instruments of economic exploitation that had been imposed when the South was in a weakened state after the Civil War, and that any time the old Confederacy began to improve economically, northerners pulled out the race issue and used the threat of civil rights or "Force" legislation to whip the South back into line. By 1948, for example, it was the South's successful industrialization that caused Congress to debate civil rights legislation that was "calculated to throw us into confusion and distract our attention from our industrial program, in which our efforts have been succeeding so markedly in recent years."[8]

Similarly, Johnson made frequent allusion to the threat of communist subversion. He echoed Mississippi's Senator James O. Eastland, another of Johnson's mentors, who as chairman of the Senate Internal Security Subcommittee developed an obsession with the communist menace as a source of the movement for desegregation. With these twin engines of paranoia, Johnson began to envision for himself a political future as a deliverer of his people and his region from the evils abroad in the land. A self-styled defender of traditional conceptions of constitutional government, Jim Johnson embarked on what proved to be a lifelong career as a champion of the past.[9]

TWO YEARS AFTER his colorful introduction to the exhilaration and the narcotic power of the political process, Johnson ran for the Arkansas state legislature at the age of twenty-five, securing a seat in 1950 as the youngest state senator in Arkansas history. He began immediately to distinguish himself as an activist legislator, sponsoring eighty-five bills in his first term, all of which he and his wife, Virginia, wrote themselves. Finding himself unopposed at the end of his first term in the Senate, in 1952 Johnson and his wife went to work as "Cherry Pickers" in the gubernatorial campaign of Judge Francis Cherry against Sid McMath. Cherry declined to return the favor two years later when Johnson ran for attorney general and lost, but the young senator had made an outstanding record. Senate President Ellis Fagan stated that Johnson "had introduced and sponsored more constructive and progressive legislation than any senator in his memory," and Johnson clearly had a bright future in Arkansas politics.[10]

Two months before Johnson's race for attorney general in the summer of 1954, the United States Supreme Court handed down its decision in *Brown v. Board of Education of Topeka, Kansas.* While he made minimal use of the race issue in that campaign, Johnson was profoundly disturbed by what he perceived to be the Court's assault on the constitution and the nine justices' willingness to use judicial means to accomplish legislative ends. He agreed fervently with Senator Eastland's assessment of the *Brown* decision as an act of judicial tyranny, and in time he realized he had found his issue.[11]

ALTHOUGH ARKANSAS is not a Deep South state, portions of its Mississippi River delta area, the Arkansas black belt, can be considered Deep South in outlook as well as in geography. Jim Johnson's home in Crossett was south of Atlanta, south of Birmingham, south of the Sunflower County of his neighbor and friend, Senator Eastland of Mississippi. Johnson's outlook was much more closely aligned with the Old South sympathies of Jackson, Mobile, or Charleston than with the bustling, progressive hopefulness of Little Rock. Something about his ideas and presentation of himself appealed to a colorful character with a shady past named Curt Copeland, who observed Johnson in his 1954 race for attorney general and was impressed. Copeland found his way to Crossett after the election and persuaded the young state senator that the newly elected governor, Orval Faubus, could be beaten in 1956, and before long Jim Johnson had set his sights on a new goal. He soon found himself in the vanguard of another crusade to save the southern way of life, at least as many whites defined it.[12]

Contemporary observers often wrote of the apparent quiet and calm that descended on the South after the *Brown* ruling. In truth, the lull presaged a storm. In the black belt areas of the Deep South, a counterrevolution was in the making; a cauldron was being readied that would boil over with heated fervor after the Court spelled out its implementation decree in May of 1955, with *Brown II.*[13]

In the summer of 1955, resistance groups began to spring up all across the southern region; foremost among them was the Citizens' Council movement, which came into being in Senator Eastland's Sunflower County, in Indianola, Mississippi, just across the river from Jim Johnson's home in Arkansas. A grassroots movement of respectable small-town citizens, the Citizens' Councils eschewed the methods and the violence of the Ku Klux Klan, seeking instead to arouse white public opinion to the threat of desegregation and to dissuade southern blacks from seeking to exercise their newly articulated rights.[14]

By the end of the summer of 1955, Jim Johnson and Curt Copeland had organized the White Citizens' Council of Arkansas, a thinly veiled vehicle for Johnson's campaign in the upcoming race for governor. They were also preparing to launch a new publishing effort for former editor Copeland; to be titled *Arkansas Faith,* ostensibly a Citizens' Council publication, it was actually the rallying cry of the Johnson gubernatorial campaign.[15]

A small group of white men in heavily black Pine Bluff beat Johnson to the punch in establishing a segregationist resistance organization in Arkansas. Calling their group White America Inc., they proclaimed that the *Brown* decision "was not, in our opinion, a democratic process, but was handed down in a dictatorial manner. . . ." They organized White America to "perpetuate the white race and endeavor to have this and future generations remain free of contamination of Negro blood." Integration of the schools would mean that "in a few years we wouldn't be able to identify ourselves as either white or black."

White America soon established chapters in communities throughout the delta region of Arkansas, as well as in Little Rock, where the Capital City Chapter became a forceful advocate for maintaining segregation in that city. Foremost among the leaders in the Little Rock chapter of White America was lawyer and furniture dealer Amis Guthridge, perennially unsuccessful candidate for public office in Arkansas. By the end of the year Jim Johnson and Amis Guthridge joined forces.[16]

Jim Johnson launched his career as a public speaker in September 1955, in the Arkansas black belt town of DeWitt, a region in which blacks often outnumbered whites two to one. Handbills posted around the county summoned citizens to a mass meeting on the courthouse square on September 12 for "a frank discussion" about segregation. When the crowd gathered on the courthouse lawn, and also in later meetings at Lake Village, Walnut Ridge, Dermott, England, Sheridan, Forrest City, and Hamburg, they heard a recording of what was supposedly a speech by "Professor Roosevelt Williams of Howard University" at a "secret NAACP meeting in Mississippi in December of 1954."[17]

Professor Williams said, among other things, ". . . the whole world knows that the white man strongly prefers the Negro women with [their] strong, rich ancestors and warm, full-blooded passions than recline in the spiritless women of his own race. . . ." Furthermore, according to Williams, Negro men ". . . have long known that the white woman is violently dissatisfied with the white man . . ." In response to this dissatisfaction, he continued, "we demand the right for any Negro man or woman to marry a member of the white race if he [or she] can find one fit to marry. . . ."[18]

Citizens' Council chapters played "Professor Williams'" speech across the South through the fall of 1955 and the spring of 1956, until a small Georgia newspaper reported there was no Professor Roosevelt Williams on the faculty of Howard University, and there never had been. When contacted for comment on this situation, its originator replied, "We never claimed it [the speech] to be authentic." Jim Johnson, nonetheless, maintained as late as 2002 that he never was convinced the recording was a fraud.[19]

Enthusiastic letters of support began to pour in to Johnson's law office in Crossett. Johnson and Copeland made an effective team on the stump, starting with a little gospel singing by the Jeffress Quartet from Crossett, then with Copeland warming up the crowd with racist invective that Johnson later admitted made him "cringe." At length Johnson rose to the microphone, taking the high ground and thundering against the mounting threats to constitutional government and the southern way of life.[20]

Johnson always claimed in these speeches that he did not hate black people. African-American reporter Carl Rowan heard him speak in Montgomery, Alabama, in January of 1956, and reported Johnson's message. "'You know,' he said as he built up his case against race-mixing, 'it's not within my make-up to hate, but I'll tell you one thing: I love some people a helluva lot more than I do others.'" Johnson then launched into a full-blown attack on miscegenation, asking ". . . do you think that children who attend integrated schools with integrated faculties will think it is wrong to intermarry?" He also played on the white southerner's darkest fears about desegregation when he suggested restricting integrated swimming pools to boys one day and girls the next. "Then you won't find 'em [Negroes] going to your swimming pools if they don't think they're going in swimming with your white daughters."[21]

Johnson had a winning smile and an easy manner in one-on-one encounters, but from the courthouse steps or the back of a flatbed truck he took on the persona of an Old Testament Jeremiah, railing against the sins of the federal government, the communists, and the NAACP. One observer described him as "altogether the most effective wielder of the language that Arkansas had seen in many years."[22]

Jim Johnson delivered one of the most significant speeches of his career at Walnut Ridge in September of 1955. The school board of neighboring Hoxie had voted to stop busing its few black children twenty-five miles away to Jonesboro and instead to integrate them into Hoxie's formerly all-white schools. The summer term had opened in July with twenty-five black children attending, and despite some grumbling, things had gone smoothly for three weeks. Yet after an article appeared in *Life* magazine entitled "A 'Morally Right' Decision," white supremacist literature began to pour into the little farming community, and soon outraged local citizens formed a protest organization and selected local farmer and auctioneer Herbert Brewer to lead them. At their first meeting this group decided to defeat desegregation by boycotting the school, which they did beginning on August 4. Brewer claimed a 50 percent absentee rate the first day. Within days, the Brewer group petitioned the school board to restore segregation in the Hoxie schools. The board refused.[23]

On August 13, Amis Guthridge, the newly appointed executive secretary of White America Inc., went to Hoxie to speak at a segregationist rally and declared "integration will lead to intermarriage; they want in the white bedroom." Herbert Brewer reported he had been to Mississippi to meet with Senator Eastland, who had promised to come to Hoxie in September, and a Missionary Baptist preacher remarked in his invocation he thought God would condone violence in Hoxie if it were necessary to preserve the purity of the white race. By the end of the week, Guthridge presented the Hoxie School Board with a petition signed by almost 1,100 citizens requesting the resignation of the board. Instead, the board suspended the summer term two weeks earlier than planned, ostensibly to let tempers cool.[24]

The board's attorney, Bill Penix, soon sought assistance from the United States Department of Justice, where his friend and fellow Arkansan Arthur Caldwell was head of the Civil Rights Section. His father, Roy Penix, also wrote to U.S. Attorney General Herbert Brownell that a "well organized and well financed" movement based in Mississippi was trying to force the board to abandon integration, and that anyone who stood up for law and order had been subjected to "all forms of intimidation." Roy Penix reported, "The matter has gone so far that many thinking people in the community are afraid to speak up for the School Board and officials, resulting in the situation that the board and Superintendent stand virtually alone and undefended."[25]

One of Brownell's lieutenants, Warren Olney III, wrote a memo to his boss suggesting "it would have a beneficial effect if the Bureau were requested to send immediately a group of agents into the Hoxie area and interrogate as large a number of people as possible concerning the activities of White Americans [*sic*] Inc., the White Citizens Councils, and any other organizations attempting to interfere with the rights of colored children to attend non-segregated schools." Brownell approved, and by early September the Civil Rights Section replied to Roy and Bill Penix that it had authorized a full FBI investigation.[26]

Johnson and Copeland arrived in Hoxie in September and located Brewer's home after dark. It was surrounded by cars. Brewer greeted them at the door with a look of alarm, put his finger to his lips as if to suggest they not say a word, and then led his intrigued visitors into the yard.

Brewer had circulated a petition, and within days a gaggle of FBI agents had descended on Hoxie. Armed with photocopies of the petitions, agents went from home to home, flashing their FBI credentials to the alarmed housewives and farmers. The agents told these simple country folk that inasmuch as they had signed a petition opposing the supreme law of the land, the agents had come to take a statement, which could be used against them in a court of law. As Jim Johnson recalled, the citizens of Hoxie were not only in awe, they were literally "scared to death that they had committed some grave wrong." Herbert Brewer was persuaded his home had been bugged. The sight of such intimidation among American people, in Johnson's words, "shook every fiber of my being."[27]

In Jim Johnson's recollection of that episode, he was absolutely thunder-

struck. All his paranoid tendencies came to the fore, and he felt a deep, smoldering anger forming in his gut. He spent a sleepless night in a cheap motel, and
well before dawn he was up and girding himself for battle. As soon as the sun
was up Johnson and Copeland set out, with a loudspeaker atop their car, and
Herbert Brewer showing the way. "I covered every highway, street, road, and pig
trail in the school district begging the people to meet with me on the Lawrence
County courthouse square at 2 o'clock that afternoon. Without taking time to
eat or wash our face we promoted the meeting right up to the starting time."[28]

When the crowd began to form, and Johnson was setting up his micro-
phones and loudspeaker equipment, various citizens pointed out to him FBI
agents in the crowd, saying, "There's the one who came to my house . . . and
there's one . . . and there. . . ." Johnson was simply furious, and by the time he
began to speak, he was shaking. He told his listeners they were citizens of the
United States of America, they had the right to petition their government for
redress of grievances, they had done nothing wrong, and if the FBI came to their
homes again, these simple rural folk should tell the United States government
to "go straight to Hell!"

The crowd erupted. Johnson felt that a boil had been lanced, and that these
people's citizenship rights had been returned to them. The United States government did not see it that way. Within weeks they had branded Johnson an
"outside agitator" and enjoined him from interfering further with the attempts
of the Hoxie School Board to integrate.[29]

JIM JOHNSON HAD reason to be paranoid about the role of the United States
government at Hoxie. Arkansas native Arthur Caldwell was chief of the Civil
Rights Section of the Eisenhower Justice Department at that time, and despite
the president's reluctance to get involved in the civil rights struggle, Caldwell
had hoped to make moderate Arkansas an early example to the rest of the South
of the federal government's determination to implement and enforce the spirit
of the *Brown* decision. As Warren Olney wrote to the U.S. solicitor general,
"Because of the importance of this one case to the success of the integration
program in the entire South, Mr. Caldwell and members of his staff have
endeavored to assist Mr. Penix, unofficially, as much as possible." Although
President Dwight D. Eisenhower was not committed to the required changes in
civil rights, and his failures of leadership in that arena contributed to southern
recalcitrance to the acceptance of desegregation, Arthur Caldwell maneuvered
without Attorney General Herbert Brownell's approval to allow the Justice
Department to participate in the Hoxie case.[30]

In time the case of *Brewer v. Hoxie School Board* was resolved in a manner favorable to the school board's efforts to desegregate, and Arthur Caldwell could report that the United States government had played a role in supporting this voluntary effort by a group of "small town merchants and farmers" when they "stood up and fought for what they believed was right, and won their battle without any help from the NAACP." What Caldwell did not report was that he had called the NAACP's Thurgood Marshall and asked him to stay out of the Hoxie case. The wheels of justice turn very slowly, however, and by the time the final decision was handed down two years later the forces of massive resistance had hobbled the federal government's will to act decisively and its ability to do so. More immediately, the episode fueled Jim Johnson's determination to combat what he perceived to be an escalating federal juggernaut, and it persuaded Senator Eastland that a regionwide organization was needed to coordinate the counterrevolution.[31]

IN THE LATE FALL of 1955 Jim Johnson set out in his aging Chevrolet for Virginia, to consult with James Jackson Kilpatrick of the *Richmond News Leader,* and then South Carolina, to visit Tom Waring of the *Charleston News and Courier.* This trip introduced Johnson to the emerging doctrines of massive resistance. When the fiery fighter arrived back in Arkansas, he proposed an amendment to the Arkansas Constitution:

> From and after the Adoption of this Amendment, the General Assembly of the State of Arkansas shall take appropriate action and pass laws opposing in every Constitutional manner the Un-Constitutional desegregation decisions of May 17, 1954 and May 31, 1955 of the United States Supreme Court, including interposing the sovereignty of the State of Arkansas to the end of nullification of these and all deliberate, palpable and dangerous invasions of or encroachments upon rights and powers not delegated to the United States nor prohibited to the States by the Constitution of the United States and Amendments thereto, and those rights and powers reserved to the States and to the People thereof by any department, commission, officer, or employee of such department or commission of the Government of the United States, or of any government of any Nation or Federation of Nations acting upon the apparent authority granted them by or assumed by them from the Government of the United States. Said opposition shall continue steadfast until such time as such Un-Constitutional invasions or encroachments shall have abated or shall

have been rectified, or the same shall be transformed into an Amendment to the Constitution of the United States and adopted by action of three-fourths of the States as provided therein.[32]

In later years Johnson described his amendment as "damned near a declaration of war against the United States. It'd kill corn knee high. It was strong." It came to be known as the Interposition Amendment, or the Johnson Amendment. In the spring of 1956 the still-undeclared candidate sold his idea all over Arkansas, explaining to enthralled audiences that if massive resistance worked properly, "there wouldn't be enough jails" to hold all the state and local officials who were willing to show the federal government what they could do with their "unconstitutional" Supreme Court decision.[33]

Before putting his amendment in final form, Johnson drove over to Ruleville, Mississippi, and shared it with Senator Eastland, thinking he had hit on a solution that would work for the whole South. Eastland was at that moment working on a project that had captured his interest for almost a year, and he invited young Jim Johnson to join him in that work. Early in 1955 Eastland had begun to formulate plans for an effort to be called the Federation for Constitutional Government, and in December of that year he had formally inaugurated this enterprise at a large meeting in Memphis. Boasting a distinguished roster of one hundred senior political figures from most of the southern states, the Federation aimed to serve as a clearinghouse for the ideas of the emerging massive resistance movement. In many ways a continuation of the Dixiecrat crusade in personnel as well as ideology, the Federation appealed to some of its members as a potential third-party force in American politics, and from the outset it aimed to extend its message to conservative groups beyond the southern region.[34]

The Federation for Constitutional Government played a major role in Jim Johnson's career, placing him on a first-name basis with such southern luminaries as Senators Eastland and Thurmond, Governor Marvin Griffin and Roy Harris of Georgia, Leander Perez and Willie Rainach of Louisiana, Judge Tom Brady and Congressman John Bell Williams of Mississippi. Many of these men came to his aid in his gubernatorial bid, and all of them were significant sounding boards for his ideas about a constitutional amendment. Among the most important of the many contacts Johnson made through his participation in Federation activities was Dean Clarence Manion of the Notre Dame Law School. A leading conservative thinker, Manion endorsed the idea of the Johnson Amendment and even attended a rally in El Dorado, Arkansas, to watch Johnson make his pitch to voters.[35]

Unfortunately the young crusader made a fatal error in calculating the means by which to get his amendment onto the ballot. Lacking funds, a tested political base, and anything resembling a machine to assist him, Johnson used little more than race-baiting. As he has explained in numerous interviews over the years, always with an apology and a candid acknowledgment of his responsibility and guilt, he believed that the necessary thousands of names on hundreds of petitions could only be inspired by rank emotion. In his words, "I meant to stir everything up that I possibly could to make these people react in a way that would be positive toward this petition. . . . Now there are things you can do with money and there are things you can do without money, and we had to do it without money; and the way you did it without money was emotional." Johnson succeeded in securing the necessary thirty thousand names, and the Johnson Amendment went on the Arkansas ballot in 1956.[36]

Johnson's campaign publication, a series of six issues entitled *Arkansas Faith,* left an even more damaging legacy. Distributed initially free of charge to ten thousand Arkansas homes in November of 1955, it was blatantly racist and tasteless in tone. The same themes reappeared throughout the series: the illegalities of the *Brown* decision; the threat of communism; the dangers presented by the left-wing *Arkansas Gazette* and especially the "pinko," foundation-funded Harry Ashmore; the horrors of miscegenation, demonstrated by photographs of black men dating and kissing white women; the inadequacies of Orval Faubus (Awful Fabalouse) and his Yankee, Urban League–supporting friend, Winthrop Rockefeller; the glories of interposition; and the ultimate salvation of the Johnson Amendment. Orval Faubus branded *Arkansas Faith* "the vilest, most dissolute, neo-pornographic publication it has ever been my disgust to see."[37]

Every issue of *Arkansas Faith* included quotations from leaders of the southern resistance. The inaugural issue contained the classic protest from James Jackson Kilpatrick of the *Richmond News Leader.* "In May of 1954, that inept fraternity of politicians and professors known as the United States Supreme Court," Kilpatrick wrote with feeling, "chose to throw away the established law. These nine men repudiated the Constitution, spit upon the tenth amendment, and rewrote the fundamental law of this land to suit their own gauzy concepts of sociology. If it be said now that the South is flouting the law, let it be said to the high court, *You taught us how.*"[38]

The March 1956 issue of *Arkansas Faith* included the complete text of the "Declaration of Constitutional Principles," or the Southern Manifesto. This was the high-water mark of the massive resistance effort in the South, the moment at which success in defying the federal government seemed to be within reach.

Jim Johnson was jubilant that the region's political leaders had so forcefully endorsed the position he had been advocating with fervor for months. *Arkansas Faith* immediately editorialized, "the Congressmen and Senators from the South have taken the pro-segregation movement to a new sphere. . . . With this action by the Southern lawmakers comes the strong probability that the South will win a reversal of the Court's political decisions."[39]

IN THIS ATMOSPHERE of euphoria Jim Johnson decided the time had come to make his candidacy for governor official, but not until he had established that his friend and mentor, former Governor Ben Laney, had no interest in trying to reclaim the post. In what one journalist has described as "a triumph of theatricality," Johnson staged a "draft" of himself to run for governor. He arranged a "states' rights constitutional rally" with Governor Marvin Griffin of Georgia as the featured speaker and Ben Laney as master of ceremonies. Before an emotional audience of two thousand Arkansans, the thirty-two-year-old Johnson "agreed" to run after Herbert Brewer came to the stage at the end of the program and "suggested" it. As the *Arkansas Gazette* reported the story the next day, "The suggestion touched off a demonstration that lasted more than 20 minutes. People streamed down the aisles to toss money into the orchestra pit to make up Johnson's $1,500.00 filing fee. They crowded onto the stage and milled around Johnson shaking his hand and wishing him luck." Years later Johnson recalled that Robert B. Patterson, executive secretary of the Mississippi Citizens' Councils, was so impressed by the performance he told the young campaigner he should go to Hollywood.[40]

JOHNSON HAD THOUGHT Orval Faubus to be vulnerable ever since the new governor had failed to mention segregation in his January 1955 inaugural address, and especially after he failed to get involved in the Hoxie situation the following summer. Although Faubus had toyed with playing the race card in the 1954 gubernatorial election, he backed off that strategy when the *Arkansas Gazette* scolded him for an early pronouncement that segregation would be the most important issue in the campaign. After that Faubus tried to operate on the theory that the less said about desegregation the better.[41]

Jim Johnson would not let him get away with lying low. *Arkansas Faith* had made Faubus furious, but as a careful political observer he knew that it resonated with a significant element of his own constituency and that the concerns it voiced could not be ignored, especially in light of Johnson's campaign slogan, "Think Right . . . Vote White" and his campaign song, "Dixie." After employing a private pollster, Eugene Newsom, to conduct a poll regarding Arkansans' attitudes toward desegregation, the formerly moderate Faubus announced on January 27, 1956, that 85 percent of the people of Arkansas opposed integration, and that consequently "I cannot be a party to any attempt to force acceptance of a change to which the people are so overwhelmingly opposed."[42]

Soon Faubus appointed a blue-ribbon committee of east Arkansas political leaders to go to Virginia and study that state's plan for resisting implementation of the *Brown* decision. They returned with two proposals: a pupil placement plan that assigned students to schools without mentioning the criterion of race, and a watered-down version of the Johnson Amendment. Jim Johnson had begun to shape the 1956 gubernatorial campaign before he even declared himself a candidate.

Orval Faubus lobbied hard and successfully to persuade both Brooks Hays and his old mentor Congressman Jim Trimble to sign the Southern Manifesto, ostensibly in an effort to dampen the power of the Citizens' Councils, but probably also in an effort to shift the momentum and responsibility for the integration debate from the state to the national level. In the spring 1956 atmosphere of escalating support for massive resistance, Faubus, always the shrewd political analyst, noted with alarm the rising power of the Johnson effort. As he wrote years later, "To sit still and become known as a do-nothing governor in the face of this tide of public sentiment, especially after the issuance of the Southern Manifesto, would be inviting disaster. If Jim Johnson with his zeal, eloquence and diligence, should attract some able and respected assistants, he could well be the full recipient of this strong tide of sentiment." And so however reluctantly, Orval Faubus found himself being pushed to the right on the very issue he had hoped to avoid.[43]

After Jim Johnson formally declared his candidacy, Faubus claimed lamely that he did not think segregation would be "too much of an issue" in the campaign. "So long as I can keep the faith and confidence of the ordinary people," the governor stated wishfully, "I will not be too concerned with the political maneuvering of others." This was for public consumption, of course. In private, Faubus was terrified by his personal attorney's assessment that if he did not secure enough signatures on the petitions to get his pupil placement and interposition initiatives on the ballot, the Johnson campaign would sink him.[44]

Faubus was trying to steer a perilous course between the unyielding dogmatism of Jim Johnson on the right and the pragmatic, gradualist stance of Harry Ashmore and Faubus's black supporters on the left. Personally devoid of the racist mentality that infected many white residents of the black belts, and consequently lacking the passion to maintain segregation, he did not genuinely care about or understand the southern determination to defeat the *Brown* decision. What he did care about was poor people, black and white, and he apparently hoped he could wiggle through the narrow passages of the desegregation debate so he could survive to improve the educational opportunities and the public services of a desperately impoverished state. Jim Johnson shut off Faubus's wiggle room.[45]

At the traditional Fourth of July picnic and political rally at Portia, a command performance for all Arkansas politicians, Johnson vowed that if elected he would close down the schools at Hoxie, Charleston, and Fayetteville, the three Arkansas school districts that had integrated voluntarily, "forcing the children to apply for readmission under a student assignment plan." He also accused Faubus of "pussy-footing" on the integration question, charging the governor with "waiting for sentiment to develop before taking a stand on the issue." Faubus responded by questioning Johnson's own commitment, countering that Johnson "didn't mention the [integration] issue when he ran for attorney general two years ago" and suggesting that Johnson was trying to make money out of the campaign.[46]

Two weeks later, after a punishing schedule of campaign appearances, Faubus took off the gloves and charged that Johnson had "made a living for the last year as a purveyor of hate." Warming to his subject, he continued, "Not until he was sure that there was a marginal market for hate did he find anything of consequence in such a vital matter. . . ." Faubus, by contrast, promised "I shall strive with every personal resource, and with every resource vested by law and tradition in the office of governor of Arkansas to maintain segregation in a calm, orderly, thoughtful and completely legal manner." And then the governor found himself making a promise that he could not have imagined just a few months before. "There will be no forced integration of our public schools and institutions as long as I am governor." He continued with words that later came back to haunt him: "Nor will races be pitted against each other for political advantage."[47]

ORVAL FAUBUS WON the election overwhelmingly, carrying sixty-seven counties to Jim Johnson's seven. As one Faubus biographer wrote, Faubus had "successfully co-opted the segregationist doctrine and superimposed it on his own moderate image." Although Johnson took comfort in later years from the realization that his vote total was the highest amassed by any Faubus opponent in Faubus's last five primary campaigns, he also found himself deeply in debt, and he reluctantly suspended publication of *Arkansas Faith*. Nonetheless, his amendment was on the November ballot, so he could not step all the way to the sidelines, though he thought it was "almost unseemly for the person who has been defeated to still be hanging around."[48]

Harry Ashmore was now back in Arkansas after his service to the Stevenson campaign, and he editorialized frequently against the Johnson Amendment, even on the front page. This opposition inspired Johnson to stay active in the campaign, and it may even have contributed to the ultimate success of the amendment, especially among the many people who believed Ashmore and the *Gazette* were agents of the "leftwing conspiracy" to integrate Arkansas schools. In the November election the people of Arkansas approved the Johnson Amendment by a significant margin: 185,374 for and 146,064 against. Arkansas voters also approved Faubus's two proposals to maintain segregation, convincing Jim Johnson that this election was a turning point in Orval Faubus's thinking, that it was "one poll he didn't have to pay for." Johnson believed ever after that the politically astute Faubus saw what the people of Arkansas wanted at that point, and then he simply waited for an opportunity to get out in front and lead the parade. Johnson always believed that opportunity arose at Little Rock Central High School.[49]

Jim Johnson knew his amendment would be meaningless if the governor in power refused to implement its provisions. Consequently, the defeated candidate went to work immediately to keep the pressure on Faubus to maintain segregation. Before the Arkansas General Assembly came into session in the winter of 1957, Johnson and other segregationist leaders drafted four bills to maintain segregation, all of which passed the legislature. The House passed them with only two dissenting votes.[50]

In the Senate the segregation bills ran into a stumbling block, apparently in part because Faubus waffled in his support and acceded to demands that they be given a public hearing. In a forum staged before nine hundred spectators, numerous religious leaders spoke against one bill to create a State Sovereignty Commission, designed to "resist the usurpation of the rights and powers reserved to this State or our sister states by the Federal Government. . . ." Opponents of the bill seconded Winthrop Rockefeller's concern that it would create "an Arkansas gestapo."[51]

Daisy Bates, Arkansas president of the National Association for the Advancement of Colored People, had spoken earlier against another bill that required "certain organizations" to register their membership lists with the Sovereignty

Commission. Bates remarked that the legislation "obviously is aimed at destroying the NAACP in Arkansas. I frankly don't know what the outcome will be because I still can hardly believe that the sovereignty commission bill says what it does." The other two bills provided legal assistance for any school board that wanted to resist desegregation and waived the compulsory attendance law for any child in an integrated school.[52]

All four bills ultimately received Governor Faubus's endorsement. Commentators at the time and since have speculated that Faubus traded his support of the bills for east Arkansas (black belt) legislators' votes for his $22 million dollar tax increase. Faubus biographer Roy Reed concluded that no such deal was necessary, however, because the east Arkansas legislators remembered with gratitude the governor's efforts of the previous fall "to try to stall integration." William J. Smith, the architect of the legislative package and Faubus's personal attorney, also denied in a candid interview many years later that any deal had been struck.[53]

The Senate amended two of the bills, and Faubus signed them into law within a week. Faubus later recalled that he was merely trying to avoid "the detriment of being classified as an extreme liberal in order to survive in Arkansas politics." The specter of Jim Johnson still lurked in the shadows.[54]

THROUGH THE SPRING of 1957, Johnson tried to keep a low profile, although he kept in constant telephone contact with friends and allies. The immediate concern of all Arkansas segregationists was the upcoming fall integration of Little Rock Central High School. Johnson knew agitation in Little Rock was in the capable hands of the newly formed Capital Citizens' Council, and since he had had a political falling out with the CCC's Amis Guthridge, he watched from the wings while that group initiated an escalating assault on both school Superintendent Virgil Blossom and Governor Faubus.[55]

After stumbling in the March school board elections and seeing both of its candidates lose to men who had pledged to uphold the district's desegregation plan, the CCC found an effective tool in an open letter to Governor Faubus, published as an ad in a local newspaper in April. It argued that Faubus had the ability to prevent integration through the employment of his police powers. The CCC republished this letter and others like it throughout the summer, always with the suggestion that citizens should write to the governor and ask him to exercise his police powers to prevent integration.[56]

The height of Citizens' Council agitation came when Jim Johnson persuaded Governor Marvin Griffin of Georgia to come to Little Rock for a CCC rally. Before an audience of 350 "handsomely dressed Arkansas segregationists" at a ten-dollar-a-plate dinner, Griffin declared that the public schools of Georgia would not be integrated as long as he was governor. Griffin's friend Roy Harris took up the refrain, bellowing that the "second Reconstruction" was already under way, and that it had as its object "the mixing of races." At speeches' end, as inspired Citizens' Council members made their way out of the Hotel Marion ballroom, a smiling Jim Johnson greeted them at the exit, trying to shake hands with everyone who passed through the door. Someone asked Johnson's aide and friend Phil Stratton if Johnson was "running again." "'He hasn't stopped running.' Stratton said. 'He knows how to win now.'"[57]

CHAPTER THREE

PATERNALISTIC GENTLEMEN

Archie House and the Establishment

I N THE LATE SUMMER OF 1957, HARRY ASHMORE GLANCED OUT HIS office window and spied Archie House loping south on Louisiana Street, undoubtedly headed to lunch around the corner at the Little Rock Club. It was a steamy summer day, and Archie had on his signature seersucker suit and flat straw hat—both from Brooks Brothers and both decades out of style. Archie House was an institution in Little Rock, a central figure in the downtown establishment, a welcome and sought-after guest in the city's leading social circles, a somewhat eccentric, lovable old bachelor with one of the best law practices in town. Local lore had it that as a young man in the 1920s, when he was president of the Boat House down on the Arkansas River where the Peabody Hotel later stood, he had done a back-flip off the top of the Main Street Bridge, landing safely in the water below to the applause and delight of an admiring throng. In 1957, as attorney for both the Little Rock School Board and the *Arkansas Gazette*, Archie House found himself vaulted into a different kind of gymnastics.[1]

Born in 1892 and bred in elegance and privilege in Little Rock, Archie House at sixty-five embodied the values and ideals of a vanishing age. The senior partner in the city's premier law firm, the venerable old Rose firm, House was universally admired for his integrity and was described in later years by one of his partners as "the soul of honor." This same partner characterized him as "always honest, open and fair with everyone in business and personal relationships," but also a man who "did not hide his disapproval of those who were dishonest, devious, mean, lazy or greedy." And as would be expected of such a southern gentleman, "He treated women with great courtesy and respect, and abhorred off-color language in their presence."[2]

Despite the youthful leap from the Main Street Bridge, Archie House's mature behavior always expressed a strong sense of propriety. In his one hundredth year, he continued to dress in coat and tie even in the nursing home. At about that same time he also confided to an interviewer his shock at Lyndon Johnson's behavior and language as portrayed in Robert Caro's *Means of Ascent*. Fundamental to his notion of propriety was his conviction that the control of civic affairs should reside in the hands of the elite, those who were best suited by breeding, education, and character to decide which courses of action were most expressive of "the public good." As he explained to a student in 1972, describing the role of the extreme segregationists in "igniting" Little Rock in 1957, the masses needed to be "suppressed" by keeping the right people in control.[3]

House's paternalism was certainly benign. As his old friend Harry Ashmore commented at the time of House's retirement from the practice of law in 1970, "Among his peers Judge House has a deserved reputation as an uncompromising adversary of public and private wrongdoers, and a witty and merciless deflator of the self-important." And yet at the same time, "to the humble, maimed victims of society he has accorded a boundless compassion. In court and in the private places of power he stood up for the poor and the black and the scorned, and I suspect a true reckoning would show that he had given away more legal services than he ever billed." Compassionate as he was, however, House's sympathy for the ignorant and the downtrodden did not include the notion that they should govern themselves.[4]

Instead House espoused an approach to public affairs that one student has called the "civics" mentality of the Little Rock elite. The customary approach was for a small group of civic leaders to identify a preferred course of action and then use the existing machinery of government, quietly, toward the accomplishment of that end. So in the case of the School Board elections, which the business and professional leaders deemed vital to the economic well-being and growth of the community, the proper authorities complied in holding elections at times when turnout promised to be light, and the "right" people could be counted on to go to the polls and ratify the candidates the businessmen had selected and endorsed. In this way the civic elite controlled the affairs in their community, as Archie House believed they should.[5]

As an upper-class gentleman, Archie House shunned publicity, never even writing a letter to the editor. But although he confined his maneuvering to the shadows, he played a major role in the drama that unfolded in his city in the fall of 1957. He had grown fond of Harry Ashmore, and he found himself agreeing with Ashmore's assessment of the "inevitability" of desegregation in a changing South. Over long lunches at the Little Rock Club or in the Men's Grill at the Country Club of Little Rock, or during elegant dinner parties in lovely, sophisticated homes, Archie House used his wit and intellect to persuade the city's leadership to accept the coming changes in southern racial patterns. As attorney for the Little Rock School Board, House was a key player in the deliberations that led to his city's stepping forth voluntarily with one of the earliest desegregation plans in the South.[6]

By all accounts the majority of Little Rock's citizens had resigned themselves to accept in the fall of 1957 the School Board's plan for desegregation. Former Governor Sid McMath reflected years later that Little Rock "was the last place in the South where [a crisis] should have happened, because we were making so much progress, and the people had been accepting this thing in a proper frame of mind." Arkansas Education Association Executive Secretary Forrest Rozzell recalled that even though most Little Rock people opposed the *Brown* decision in principle, they were willing to go along. Most educators, Rozzell noted, worried about the impact of desegregation on educational standards, but most also believed that the transition could be effected with a minimum of disruption.[7]

The front person selling the School Board's plan, the person who worked the hardest to create it, stood to benefit the most from implementing it, and for whom the plan was named, was Little Rock School District Superintendent Virgil T. Blossom, whom Archie House described as "a wonderful man." Harry Ashmore claimed that Archie House was the source of Virgil Blossom's strong stand for compliance.[8]

Virgil Blossom moved to Little Rock in January of 1953 from Fayetteville, Arkansas, where he had enjoyed great success in his eleven years as superintendent of schools. In Fayetteville Blossom had undertaken a massive building program, persuaded the citizenry to double the school budget, and annexed seventeen adjoining school districts to the Fayetteville district. He wrote proudly of his time in northwest Arkansas: "Fayetteville became a kind of showplace that was studied by many educators from other parts of the country as an example of what could be done to improve the school program and school facilities 'in the backwoods.'"[9]

Blossom arrived in Little Rock filled with expectation, and he immediately sought to consolidate all three school districts in Pulaski County (including North Little Rock). He planned a major new building campaign, and he worked toward the merger of Little Rock Junior College with the University of Arkansas. By 1955 the *Arkansas Democrat* had named him Little Rock "Man of the Year," and his office mail routinely contained congratulatory, supportive letters from a broad spectrum of Little Rock's citizens. Everyone agreed that Virgil Blossom was very capable, and for a time he was very popular.[10]

The *Brown* decision did not catch Blossom by surprise. A professional educator, he had monitored the court cases calling for the equalization of black and white teachers' salaries, and especially of those providing greater opportunities for blacks in public education. Within twenty-four hours of *Brown,* Blossom had assembled his six-member School Board to discuss its implications, and within three days he had convinced his somewhat reluctant board to issue a statement announcing they would comply with the new "Federal Constitutional Requirements." As Archie House recalled later, Virgil Blossom "thought that he could talk all of his Board members into acceptance and the right philosophic attitude, and move forward with the new ideas and everything would be wonderful. And he convinced me that he could."[11]

Harry Ashmore had to have been pleased with Blossom's success in persuading his board to step out front with a positive response to the *Brown* decision. Ashmore's close friend and publisher Hugh Patterson recalled years later that Blossom was in and out of the *Gazette* office very frequently, and that Ashmore, Patterson, and Blossom were plotting the strategy to implement desegregation. Archie House was one of the strategists, and his perception was that he and Blossom were "the real supporters of compliance with the law." Orval Faubus, however, wrote of Blossom's reaction to the *Brown* decision in terms that reflected a more widespread sentiment in Little Rock. "Soon after the original U.S. Supreme Court decision of May 17, 1954," Faubus recalled in his memoir, "the Little Rock School Board and Supt. Virgil Blossom announced they would integrate the Little Rock schools. It was as if they welcomed the opportunity to try the new social experiment."[12]

Virgil Blossom threw himself into devising a plan of integration for his city with characteristic vigor. His initial inquiries around town had persuaded him that the white citizens of Little Rock would accept only a bare minimum of integration, and that he would have to proceed slowly. His primary concern, and that of his board, was to maintain educational "quality" (presumably for white students, since the low quality of the black schools had activated the Court). As one of the School Board members recalled, "We didn't set out to integrate the schools, we set out to continue education during the integration process, and we were much more interested in the education process than we were in integration."[13]

Blossom spent the remainder of 1954 researching the problems of integration, attending a wide variety of community meetings to discuss the issue, and taking informal polls. He eventually concluded that while some in the black community believed integration should begin immediately, and some in the white community believed it should not begin at all, most Little Rock citizens, black as well as white, understood the necessity of going slowly. One of Blossom's major concerns was his fear that if integration proceeded too rapidly and encountered too much opposition in Little Rock, the state legislature would abolish the public schools. As he explained in his memoir, "Our purpose was to comply with the law in a manner that would be accepted locally, not to wreck the school system."[14]

In time Blossom came to believe he had devised a workable solution to the South's desegregation problem, and he grew increasingly excited over the prospect of his city's becoming another "showplace." As one observer put it, Virgil Blossom envisioned Little Rock's desegregation as "the prototype for the rest of the South." Being in the spotlight was a position Blossom had always enjoyed.[15]

VIRGIL BLOSSOM WROTE in his memoir, *It HAS Happened Here,* that he had originally believed desegregation should begin at the elementary school level. "It seemed to me," he recalled, "that six-year-old children would be the least concerned about the color of the skin of classmates." Although this plan looked good on paper, Blossom's meetings with PTA groups quickly convinced him that the parents of small children opposed integration more strongly than the parents of older youngsters. His surveys of the school district also demonstrated to him that in the eastern section of the city, black children in some elementary schools would outnumber whites by as much as fifty to one. Based on widespread reports of educational difficulties in the nation's capital, he was convinced that integration had failed in Washington, D.C., because many classrooms had a majority of black students, and he was determined to keep Little Rock from repeating that mistake.[16]

The determining factor, however, in Blossom's decision to start integration at the high school level, an issue Blossom and his board discussed at great length, was the widespread fear of miscegenation. School Board president William G. Cooper explained decades later, "We went back and forth on that forever. We thought that people would be more liable to accept their daughters, females, being put with black men at the time when they were competent adults. That was what swung us to do it. As far as practical results are concerned . . . I think it would have worked better . . . if they had started out when they didn't know any better. We were pretty solid on our decision at the time."[17]

The official explanation the School Board gave for the decision to start integration at the senior high level was that there were fewer buildings and fewer students at that level, and presumably there would also be fewer problems. The real explanation, of course, was that Blossom was responding to white parents' desires that their children develop "appropriate" racial attitudes before they were thrown into daily contact with black children. As the line in the popular Broadway play *South Pacific* made clear at about that time, children have to be "carefully taught" to love and hate.[18]

In September of 1954, the executive board of the Little Rock NAACP met with Virgil Blossom and the School Board. Blossom outlined the plans the board was contemplating. He explained that the school district was in the process of building two new high schools and that upon their completion, probably in September of 1956, integration would begin at all four of Little Rock's high schools. He also suggested that integration would be complete, based on attendance zones. He said junior high school integration would commence the year after that, and somewhat later, integration would proceed at the elementary level.

Reaction from the NAACP board was mixed. The more militant members opposed the plan "on the grounds that it was vague, indefinite, slow-moving, and indicative of an intent to stall further on public-school integration." The majority, however, argued the School Board "should be given adequate time to demonstrate their good faith in effectuating the plans drawn up by Mr. Blossom." The dominant moderate faction on the NAACP board hoped "Little Rock might show the rest of the South that peaceful and voluntary compliance with the Supreme Court decision could be realized."[19] Virgil Blossom hoped the same thing.

Between September of 1954 and May of 1955, the Little Rock superintendent changed his mind about key elements of what came to be called "The Blossom Plan," undoubtedly in part as a result of the reaction to the first *Brown* decision in Washington. President Eisenhower refused to draw on his enormous popularity or moral authority to endorse the mandated changes in public education, and Congress also failed to offer vigorous and principled support for the position the Supreme Court had espoused. When Blossom encountered vocal opposition in the local white community, he backed away significantly from the position he had outlined to the NAACP executive board the previous fall. Among the concerns of many white citizens, apart from deep-seated racism, were fears that desegregation would lower academic standards in the schools, impede the progress of white children, decrease community support for public education, cause a shift to private schools, displace Negro teachers, and curtail social activities as well as create social problems in the schools. Whatever the explanation for the change, the School Board unveiled a very different plan in May of 1955 from the one it had contemplated in the fall of 1954.[20]

Although the School Board plan announced on May 24, 1955, did not say so, it apparently started from a premise articulated in a later draft, which stated: "The reorganization of a school system that has been racially segregated from its beginning presents major problems of creating 'teachable groups' of children for instructional purposes in an integrated system of Public Education, if it is done too quickly." Therefore, the district proposed a "phase program" of school integration, with the process to begin in grades ten through twelve, probably in the fall of 1957. Upon completion of a successful program of integration at the senior high school level, grades seven through nine would become involved; upon successful completion of the program at the junior high level, the program would begin in the elementary schools. The later draft of the plan specified that even though the entire process might take as many as six years, "To move faster than the *'deliberate time schedule'* outlined could easily result in placing our system of Free Public Education in danger."[21]

The element that caused the most consternation among critics was the introduction of a system of transfers, by which children did not have to attend the school in their designated zone if such attendance placed them in a racial minority in that school. As critics quickly noted, only Central High School faced significant integration. The faculty at the new Horace Mann High School, in a predominantly black zone, remained all black; the faculty at Central High, Technical High, and the new Hall High remained all white. Most alarming of all, from the perspective of the NAACP, Horace Mann, slated to open in February 1956, was described as a segregated black institution, without even the pretense of voluntary integrated attendance.[22]

On May 31, 1955, nine days after Virgil Blossom announced the "Little Rock Board of Education Plan of School Integration," the United States Supreme Court handed down *Brown II*. In highly ambiguous terms, the justices called for changes "with all deliberate speed" and for a "prompt and reasonable start" toward integration. The justices set no deadlines for the initiation of integration, and they offered no guidelines for compliance. They placed responsibility for administering the changes in the hands of southern federal judges, who had no enforcement machinery, and local school boards, who were directed to craft their plans based on local needs.[23]

Many members of the Little Rock chapter of the NAACP understood that Blossom and his board "now intended to integrate the public schools only on a token basis, if at all." The Blossom Plan was a flawed attempt to achieve white acceptance by retaining as much segregation as possible. NAACP state president Daisy Bates expressed the dominant view when she wrote, "Superintendent Blossom was more interested in appeasing the segregationists by advocating that only a limited number of Negroes be admitted than in complying with the Supreme Court decision."[24]

IN JULY, THE BOARD of directors of the newly formed Arkansas Council on Human Relations, a biracial group, requested an audience with Virgil Blossom. Daisy Bates, Harry and Barbara Ashmore, Fred Darragh, and Reverend J. C. Crenchaw all pressed the superintendent to tell them why the schools could not be integrated immediately. Rumblings began to spread through the Little Rock chapter of the NAACP that the group should bring a lawsuit to enjoin the School Board from opening Horace Mann as a segregated school. Many members concluded that "without a court order the Board would never integrate a single school."[25]

The NAACP's regional field office in Dallas advised against pursuing a lawsuit, thinking it would bring adverse publicity, and the Little Rock leadership renewed its attempts to meet again with the School Board in an effort to resolve their differences. The School Board refused all overtures to meet. In the white community, the NAACP was seen as an "extremist" organization. Therefore in December of 1955, with Horace Mann High School scheduled to open the following month, the local branch of the NAACP voted to file suit against the Little Rock School Board if three conditions could be met: if students could be found whose parents would allow them to attempt to register at Central High School, if sufficient funds could be raised to pay a lawyer, and if a lawyer could be secured for the fee the branch could afford. To the surprise of the local branch, it was able to meet all three conditions with relative ease.[26]

Pine Bluff attorney Wiley Branton, one of the first black graduates of the University of Arkansas Law School and chairman of the Arkansas NAACP's Legal Redress Committee, agreed to represent the Little Rock chapter when its usual attorneys declined to participate. Georg C. Iggers, the white chairman of the Education Committee, raised considerable money through an appeal to family and friends in other parts of the country, and he also secured donations from a tiny cadre of supporters in Little Rock's white community. Finally, Iggers, L. C. and Daisy Bates, and other representatives of the NAACP visited black homes throughout the district, seeking parents willing to attempt to register their children at white schools.[27]

On the day that Horace Mann opened, January 23, 1956, twenty-seven black children and their parents appeared at four white elementary, junior high, and high schools seeking to register. When they were rebuffed, Daisy Bates took a group of the children to Virgil Blossom's office, where he formally denied her request for immediate integration. In a statement to the press after the meeting, Bates told reporters, "I think the next step is obvious. We've tried everything short of a court suit. How soon we can file a suit depends on how busy our attorneys are. It could be a week and it could be a month." Two weeks later, on behalf of thirty-three black children, Wiley Branton filed suit against the Little Rock School District, its officers, and its superintendent in the United States District Court for the Eastern District of Arkansas. The case became known as *Aaron v. Cooper*.[28]

Virgil Blossom immediately put together team of lawyers he called a "brain trust" to meet the NAACP's challenge. Hoping to demonstrate the practicality of the Blossom Plan and foster public support for it, he selected a cross-section of the city's best legal talent, four lawyers from leading firms, to work under the supervision of Archie House: Leon Catlett was widely regarded as the best trial lawyer in the state; Richard C. Butler, a member of U.S. Senator Joe T. Robinson's old firm, was a recent president of the Little Rock Chamber of Commerce and one of the leading lights in the movement to attract industry to Arkansas; Henry Spitzberg was a highly regarded attorney and a leader in the Jewish community; Frank Chowning was a socially prominent, socially conservative proponent of continued segregation who reluctantly recognized the need to obey "the law of the land" as expressed in *Brown*. House initiated a series of meetings and communicated with his team regularly through formal memoranda.[29]

ARCHIE HOUSE, like Blossom, reflected the limitations of Little Rock's "Establishment." He accepted the fact that integration had to occur, yet he tried to appease opponents by moving slowly, and he relied entirely on procedural maneuvering. House noted in his early memoranda that no local black attorney had signed the complaint initiating the suit, and he believed if he could demonstrate that dissension existed within the local chapter he could weaken the NAACP's case. He worked to show that local conditions had been subordinated to the aggressiveness of the NAACP's national leaders and that therefore "reasonableness" resided on the side of the Little Rock School District. In keeping with *Brown II*'s demand for a "prompt and reasonable start," Archie House argued that the only question in the case was whether the Blossom Plan was "reasonable" in light of local conditions.[30]

Federal Judge John Elvis Miller, a former Arkansas U.S. senator and congressman, and a longtime close friend of Senator Joe T. Robinson, heard the case. In one of his first elective offices, while serving as prosecuting attorney of St. Francis County in 1919, Miller had suppressed evidence of a white massacre of dozens and perhaps hundreds of blacks, allowing that episode to enter the historical record as the Elaine "race riots." A salty, aging jurist much given to colorful language who made it a point to hunt or fish one day a week, Miller disagreed with the *Brown* decision. But while he thought the Court had no right "to impose its sociological beliefs on others," he had stated publicly he could take no other attitude than to "enforce the law as it was declared by the high court."[31]

At the trial, Archie House hammered home the theme that the Little Rock School District had voluntarily made "a prompt start" toward desegregation, and that the Blossom Plan had been crafted to meet local needs. Wiley Branton, on the other hand, yielded control of his case, reluctantly, to the NAACP regional attorney, U. Simpson Tate. Tate flew in from Dallas, neglected to consult with the local representatives, and argued to their consternation that the proposed Blossom Plan was unconstitutional and that it should be thrown out altogether. This argument was more in line with the thinking of the national NAACP office than the gradual integration Wiley Branton had been willing to accept based on his recognition that the Blossom Plan was probably constitutional. Predictably, Judge Miller ruled in favor of the Little Rock School District, and the case of *Aaron v. Cooper* became an early indication of the federal judiciary's willingness to support southern school boards in their efforts to slow the full implementation of *Brown*.[32]

Judge Miller held that the Little Rock plan "which has been adopted after thorough and conscientious consideration of the many questions involved is a plan that will lead to an effective and gradual adjustment of the problem and ultimately bring about a school system not based on color distinctions." Miller also incorporated into his opinion Archie House's post-trial suggestion that the federal court should retain jurisdiction in the case.[33]

House wisely looked toward the next stage of the litigation process, the appeal to the Eighth Circuit Court, noting the "weak spot" in the School Board's plan: its failure to specify dates for integration at the junior high and elementary school levels. The School Board's lead attorney consequently advised his team of lawyers that in order to deflect attack, "it seems to me it would be wise to suggest to Judge Miller that he approve the Plan in its present form, but subject to later modification if it is shown to him that there is any evidence of bad faith in advancing into phases 2 and 3. . . . In following this suggested plan we have nothing to lose and much to gain in the way of winning appellate court approval." The NAACP did appeal Judge Miller's decision, and the wisdom of House's strategy became apparent when the Appeals Court also endorsed the Blossom Plan.[34]

Virgil Blossom immediately hailed Judge Miller's decision as "a complete endorsement" of the School Board's program. "This gives us an opportunity to integrate the schools and at the same time maintain our educational standards. We will move along in good faith." Daisy Bates told the *Arkansas Gazette* she thought the School Board was using "delaying tactics" instead of acting in good faith on the integration problem. "I think a definite starting date should have been named," she said. "Their plan has too much 'probability' and 'maybe' in it."[35]

The *Arkansas Gazette* editorialized that despite some "extremist" criticism, the School Board's program "has the support of a considerable majority of the citizens of Little Rock of both races, who accept it as a practical solution to a difficult problem." The newspaper also suggested the Blossom Plan "might well set a pattern for the Upper South and point a way out of the dilemma that now faces many Southern communities." While Harry Ashmore's editorial may have boosted Virgil Blossom's spirits and ego, events soon made clear that the *Gazette*'s endorsement did not reflect the sentiments of most Arkansas citizens. In fact, the approval of the Little Rock newspaper may have hurt Virgil Blossom's efforts to sell his plan to the people whose children would actually be involved in the desegregation process.[36]

THE BLOSSOM PLAN had a major flaw. The community's elite, who tended to live in the newer area to the west called "the Heights," did not expect to have their children participate in the integration process under the revised plan that the federal judge approved. Hall High School, the new western campus that was slated to open in 1957, had only six black children in its carefully gerrymandered district. By 1957 this number had dropped to two, neither of whom requested entry into Hall High. Hoping to sell his plan to the community's elite, the group he viewed as his primary constituency, Virgil Blossom had given them a free pass. He also intended to use Hall High School as a haven for citizens who wished to avoid integration, and he reportedly advised numerous people, such as attorney William H. Bowen, that if they wanted to keep their children in segregated schools they should move to the Heights. Respected Little Rock attorney and Faubus adviser William J. Smith recalled many years later that Blossom "advised many close friends to move to the western part of Little Rock if they didn't want their children attending integrated schools. He talked with me several times about it. . . . I do know younger people whom he told they should buy their residences . . . in the area where Hall High was later built." Blossom reportedly told Frances Sue Wood, principal of Forest Park School in one of the elite neighborhoods, that there would "never" be any black children in the schools in the Heights.[37]

Keeping his focus on the community's power structure had worked for Blossom in the majority-white, university town of Fayetteville. In Little Rock, however, the new superintendent exacerbated class conflict and ultimately doomed his carefully crafted plans for integration. Trying to sell his plan in over 225 speeches around the community, Virgil Blossom spoke most frequently to middle-class organizations such as the Rotary Club and the Kiwanis Club. He did not consider the views of the blue-collar workers who lived around Central High School, people who felt great concerns about their property values, the threat of miscegenation, and the inherent unfairness of a fundamental adjustment of their cultural patterns that was not being demanded of their wealthier neighbors to the west. The removal of elite children from the equation virtually guaranteed that the people who were most likely to provide a moderating hand in any community dispute were not involved.[38]

IN HIS SPEECHES Blossom stressed the minimum nature of the School Board's plan. Referring to integration in the South as "the sixty-four-thousand dollar question," the superintendent insisted that he and his board personally opposed integration, but since they had to obey the law of the land they had devised a program that would provide the least amount of integration over the longest period of time the courts would permit.[39]

Foremost among Blossom's critics was Disciples of Christ minister Colbert Cartwright, chairman of the board of the Arkansas Council on Human Relations. In an article titled "Failure in Little Rock," Cartwright charged that "white persons hearing a presentation of the school plan by Dr. Blossom left well-assured that every effort was being made to keep the number of Negroes entering white schools to a minimum," and that Blossom placed the school problem "in the context of maximum avoidance of racial mixing. . . ."[40]

Blossom's approach was a flawed attempt to gain community acceptance, and it reflected the School Board's fundamental strategy of attempting to maintain educational quality through a gradual process of minimal change. Whereas Blossom viewed his own stance as moderate in comparison to the "extremes" of the NAACP and the White Citizens' Councils, one critic has argued impatiently that "in fact, minimum compliance was merely a diluted form of resistance, providing a subtle and insidious way of frustrating the process of school desegregation."[41]

Virgil Blossom saw it differently. As he wrote in the *Saturday Evening Post,* "I have no doubt many persons will regard such a plan as an evasion or an unworthy compromise. I can only say that such persons fail to understand the circumstances. . . . Our purpose was minimum compliance with the law in a manner acceptable to the courts and the community—not to wreck the school system by arousing resentment."[42]

Other critics of Blossom's handling of the desegregation process charged that he was autocratic in his approach. A researcher for the Anti-Defamation League, who conducted interviews with Little Rock leaders in the spring of 1958, heard repeatedly that "development of policy was kept the exclusive prerogative of the school superintendent and the board." One respondent declared "No one had anything to do with it but the board. . . . Virgil Blossom decided the plan and they went along. The Board would not listen to anyone who disagreed, black or white." Another interviewee suggested, "Blossom saw himself as a great leader who would handle the thing alone. It was a personal offense with Blossom if questioned on the school plan." This man did feel, however, that Blossom "led the board further than they would have gone alone. [But] the Board would possibly have encouraged more participation on the part of the community without Blossom."[43]

Directing its sharpest criticism at Blossom himself, a preliminary report on the ADL study declared, "Even his supporters like Harry Ashmore indicate that he is an authoritarian, does not delegate responsibility, is stubborn and dogmatic." When the Interdenominational Ministerial Alliance of Greater Little Rock, a black group, suggested a biracial committee to help prepare the community, Blossom rejected the proposal. When the Little Rock Ministerial Alliance, a white group, offered to endorse the Blossom plan publicly and officially, Blossom asked them not to do it. Several civic leaders discussed the idea of bringing in a law enforcement expert to help the School Board and the city plan for any disturbance that might mar the opening of school; Blossom replied that he had the situation under control and needed no outside help. When a group of professional educators suggested to Blossom in the fall of 1955 that informal meetings should be held to air feelings and discuss problems the group would face the next year, Blossom thought the idea unwise.[44]

Within Central High School many individuals suggested ways to prepare both students and teachers for the changes they would soon undergo. Principal Jess Matthews alerted both the Guidance Committee and the Community

Cooperation Committee during the summer of 1955 that "both would have much to do in preparing the public for the integration which was to occur in the fall of 1957 . . . ," and that the committees "should begin formulating plans." When the committees began meeting in the fall of 1955, however, Matthews directed them to hold off for the time being, explaining that Blossom wanted to handle these matters himself. The committees never functioned. Teachers also heard that Blossom would eventually give the word to initiate a transition program of preparations; the word never came.

Arkansas Democrat reporter George Douthit charged years later that Blossom had refused all interviews with the press, trying to keep the lid on the community's reaction to his plan until he was ready to release the information. A memo in the files of the Southern Regional Council complained, "The plan of desegregation supported by the Superintendent of Schools did not provide for preparation of students, faculty, and parents for the advent of integration. The Superintendent took the viewpoint that the least said the better. Thus the Arkansas Council [on Human Relations] was thwarted in its efforts to help the school system prepare in advance." The paternalistic, autocratic approach of Virgil Blossom, the School Board, and Little Rock's community leaders had the tragic consequence of leaving the community "without resources, common denominators, and networks of interested individuals who could come together to help them turn the tide of an impending crisis."[45]

IN NOVEMBER OF 1956 Arkansas voters adopted the Johnson Amendment. In February of 1957 the Arkansas General Assembly passed four laws designed to protect the right of school districts to maintain segregation. In March of 1957, by contrast, Little Rock voters overwhelmingly elected two new members to the School Board who had campaigned on a platform of obeying the law of the land. Little Rock was out of step with the majority sentiment in the rest of the state, and soon the forces of massive resistance would launch an all-out assault on the desegregation efforts planned for the capital city. Little Rock was unprepared for the assault that ensued. But for the moment, Virgil Blossom and his School Board felt vindicated by the March elections, and the civic elite felt secure in their ability to control the affairs of their city.[46]

The process leading to the School Board elections was instructive. Wayne Upton had been working in his law office one morning in February of 1957 when James Penick, president of Worthen Bank, called to say that he and R. A. "Brick" Lile, a School Board member and business leader, wanted to come over for a visit. "So they came in and . . . sat down, and they sat there, and there was no conversation going on to amount to anything, and finally Brick Lile said: 'This is not a subject we can build up to gradually. . . . We want you to run for the School Board, . . . and now you understand there is no hurry. . . . We don't need your answer until two o'clock this afternoon.'" Upton's visitors told him it would not cost him anything to run, "and I didn't spend a penny, not even the dollar necessary to get my name on the ticket. I don't know who circulated the petition, it took only twenty-five names. . . . I know I didn't pay the dollar, I never saw the petition, I don't know who signed it." Henry Rath received a similar visit from Jim Penick and some other businessmen. Rath and his wife were active in their children's PTAs and they had become close friends of Virgil Blossom. Rath had "expressed the feeling that he wanted to see this integration thing work," and he later believed "that was why I was backed by this group." Wayne Upton recalled that "Henry and I were running as a team" against two strong segrega-tionists, Robert Ewing Brown and George P. Branscum, and "this was the first School Board race in which [desegregation] was an issue." Two of Little Rock's top business leaders, John Riggs and Harvey Couch, handled all of the fund-raising and advertising; as Upton later recalled, "I never saw any money and I never had the slightest idea who contributed. . . ."[47]

Wayne Upton was a young lawyer with one of Little Rock's respected law firms. During World War II he had worked for Naval Intelligence, and in that capacity he had helped investigate Commonwealth College, the leftist school that Orval Faubus attended briefly. By 1957 he described himself as being "just on the periphery" of affairs in Little Rock, someone who had never been inter-ested in running for public office. He also considered himself fairly oblivious to the issue of desegregation. Still, he approved of the approach the School Board had taken, because he knew "deep down" that segregation in public schools could not be defended "on the basis of sound Christian principles. . . . I had never really thought about it . . . but to me it just didn't make sense that [blacks] should be denied the same opportunity for an education as anybody else."[48]

Henry Rath had grown up in Hawaii, the son of social workers, and as he explained "in the islands we are somewhat more liberal. . . ." He had moved to Little Rock to be close to his wife's family, who were a part of the city's social elite but were also known to be more liberal in their thinking than most of their peers. Originally trained in accounting, Rath was the comptroller for Meyer's Bakery. Other members of the School Board later described him as "a Yankee." Upton and Rath won their races by two-to-one margins, with the majority of their votes coming from the fifth ward (the Heights) and the black ward, a long-standing coalition in Little Rock politics.[49]

The real Yankee on the School Board was William G. Cooper, by 1957 the longest-serving member of the board and its president. Educated at Exeter, Harvard, and Yale, he was a widely respected surgeon whose interest in public affairs paralleled that of his father, who had also been president for many years of the local school board in his New York community, Ogdensburg. Virgil Blossom described Cooper as having "the highest IQ in Little Rock," and Cooper was equally complimentary of Blossom's character and efforts. He was very close to Archie House, and House described him as a strong supporter of the movement toward integration. Cooper recalled years later that he worried about diluting educational standards when the *Brown* decision was first handed down, but "I thought about it, and thought about it, . . . and I came to the conclusion that things were not separate but equal and it was just not correct."[50]

The other long-serving member of the School Board was R. A. Lile, who had attended his first board meeting in January of 1953, at the same time that Virgil Blossom attended his. Archie House described Lile as "a damned segregationist," but Wayne Upton thought he was the dominant member of the board, saying "he had ideas of his own and we respected them. . . ." Upton admitted Lile was a segregationist but described him as "a very practical man." Willie Cooper also thought of Lile as "a real brain, real good person." Lile was the son of professional educators (his father had been president of Ouachita Baptist University in Arkadelphia, Arkansas), and he was a successful businessman who had been involved with many projects to develop the community. He was a close personal friend of Virgil Blossom, and each had a great deal of respect for the other's views and capabilities.[51]

The other segregationist on the School Board was Dr. Dale Alford, a respected ophthalmologist. Alford won his seat on the board in 1955, before the Blossom Plan was announced, in a rare successful effort against the chosen candidate of the downtown business elite. Archie House described Alford as a "fanatic" on the segregation issue. Despite his strong racial views, however, Alford was certainly accepted in social circles in the Heights, and he considered himself a good friend of School Board president Cooper.[52]

Sometime before the fall of 1957, Alford "openly admitted" to the rest of the School Board that he represented the segregationist point of view and segment of the community. He also became a liaison with Orval Faubus, providing the governor with inside information about the thinking of the School Board. Increasingly the other board members chose to meet without Alford when they wanted to discuss particularly sensitive issues and information.[53]

The final member of Little Rock's six-man School Board was also elected in

1955, just weeks before the Blossom Plan was announced. Harold Engstrom was an engineer at Arkansas Foundry, an old homegrown industry. He was naive when he went on the board, later confessing "I didn't even know about . . . integration as a problem when I agreed to run for the School Board." As was typical, several prominent businessmen approached him about running. They did not make him promise to support or oppose anything, and they offered financial assistance. In this way the civic elite had for many years maintained control of the Little Rock School Board.[54]

IT WAS ONLY WEEKS after the election that the Appeals Court upheld the Blossom Plan. Four days later, however, on April 30, the Capital Citizens' Council launched a blast against the Blossom Plan that shattered every hope for a peaceful, uncontested desegregation process. In an open letter to Governor Faubus, the Citizens' Council quoted Senator Eastland of Mississippi to the effect that the only way to protect segregation was to use the power of the states. "If we contest at the local level," the letter suggested, "by individual school district, or by a county, or on a community basis, we are sitting ducks and will be picked off one by one. The state can take action which the individual district cannot."[55]

Reminding the governor that the people of Arkansas had expressed their overwhelming desire for segregation in the November 1956 election, the CCC letter launched into a personal attack on Virgil Blossom. "The Little Rock School Board, dominated by its superintendent, who was born, reared, and educated just below the Iowa state line in Northwest Missouri, announced a school race-mixing policy one week after the federal Supreme Court's May 17, 1954, opinion." Furthermore, "The school board and the superintendent played along with the N.A.A.C.P. and wound up in federal court on the question of should we mix completely now, or just start with the high schools."[56]

The heart of the letter developed an argument that Governor Faubus found compelling. "Under the sovereignty of the State of Arkansas," the Citizens' Council stated, "you can, under our police powers, in order to preserve domestic tranquility, order the two races to attend their own schools. As the sovereign head of a state, you are immune to federal court orders." Citing the examples of Mansfield, Texas, and Clinton, Tennessee, where the governor intervened and the federal government backed down in integration disputes, the letter placed responsibility for preserving segregation squarely in the governor's lap, concluding "Governor, as executive head of this state, please act forthrightly, because the problem will not go away unless you solve it. An ounce of prevention is still worth a pound of cure. You, Governor, and you alone, can act on this most serious matter—will you?"[57]

Signed by Robert Ewing Brown, president of the Capital Citizens' Council, this letter soon blanketed the city of Little Rock in pamphlet form. With one masterful stroke of the pamphleteer's pen, Faubus found himself on the spot. For the remainder of the spring and summer, Virgil Blossom and Orval Faubus engaged in an elaborate dance, one whose steps and rhythms responded to the governor's urgent need to find political cover.[58]

HOUSE AND BLOSSOM initially reacted as Establishmentarians: they asked Judge Miller to respond to the letter. But the judge refused, and in fact he could have done little apart from issuing a statement. Miller did make one suggestion that Archie House took to heart and soon pursued: he recommended that the School Board attorney go to Washington to seek guidance and assistance from the Justice Department. On May 28, 1957, House called Arkansas native and longtime friend Arthur Brann Caldwell, who had served since 1952 as head of the Justice Department's Civil Rights Section, requesting an appointment. House indicated he "represented some clients who were greatly concerned about the integration problem in Little Rock," but he refused to be more specific on the telephone.[59]

When House arrived in Washington on June 5, he gave Caldwell a copy of the Capital Citizens' Council pamphlet, and he informed the Justice Department lawyer that Virgil Blossom and the Little Rock School Board were "greatly concerned about the possibility of violence when school opens in September." He had come to Washington "to alert the Department to the potential trouble and to seek whatever assistance the Department might render to the Little Rock officials."[60]

Caldwell decided to travel to Little Rock to investigate the situation himself. In his new position as assistant to the assistant attorney general, he had just been given "more power as a troubleshooter on the civil rights front," and he undoubtedly hoped to enhance his position in the department by forestalling difficulties in Little Rock. Apparently he was also hoping to secure the position of director of the Civil Rights Division, a branch of the bureaucracy that had been prepared for Congress as part of Eisenhower's civil rights bill.[61]

Actually, as Archie House had no way of knowing, Arthur Caldwell was headed for a crippling collision with U.S. Attorney General Herbert Brownell. According to Justice Department insiders, Caldwell had been "the principal author of the administration's original civil rights bill," particularly the highly contested Section III. In March, Brownell had arranged for Caldwell to make a presentation at a Cabinet meeting, offering a detailed explanation of the proposed bill. President Eisenhower left midway through the presentation and did not hear the information about Section III, which vastly increased the powers of the attorney general. Indeed, in the Senate debate later in the summer, Richard Russell of Georgia charged that the intent of the bill was to "bring to bear the whole might of the Federal Government, including the Armed Forces if necessary, to force a commingling of white and Negro children in . . . the South." Russell claimed further that Section III gave "an unlimited grant of powers . . . to govern by injunction and federal bayonet."[62]

When disgruntled southern leaders complained to Eisenhower about "the drastic nature of Section III," the president had to admit he had not known the specifics of the bill. Eisenhower then reacted by "sharply chiding Brownell for not keeping him fully informed . . . ," and Brownell reacted by removing Caldwell from the Civil Rights Section over the protest of Caldwell's immediate superior, Assistant Attorney General Warren Olney III. After the passage of the truncated civil rights bill, minus the objectionable Section III, when Olney recommended Caldwell to head the newly created Civil Rights Division, Brownell replied with a flat "No."[63]

ARTHUR CALDWELL ARRIVED in Little Rock in late June of 1957, still hoping for a promotion. At House's suggestion he conferred at length with Virgil Blossom, who left him cold; Harry Ashmore, whom he had long admired; Osro Cobb, the United States attorney; Marvin Potts, the chief of police; and Al Bryant, the local agent-in-charge of the FBI. As School Board member Harold Engstrom described Caldwell's visit, the Justice Department "had sent a special man here who tried to stay in the background. . . . He was Brownell's man who was in charge of the integration problem for Brownell, . . . but we didn't have any open above-board discussions with him. . . ."[64]

Caldwell's assessment of Blossom and his board was scathing. As he later wrote Archie House, "it was fairly clear to me from the beginning that, in view of the frightened and reluctant attitude of Virgil Blossom and the School Board the plan never had much chance of success. . . . A plan which is 'designed to give the least amount of integration over the longest period' (to use Virgil's description) is a plan of evasion, not sincere compliance." Arthur Caldwell was not inspired to offer the assistance of his department to a School Board he felt was evading the spirit of the *Brown* decision.[65]

On June 27, Archie House and Arthur Caldwell drove to Fort Smith to see

Judge Miller. The judge suggested that the School Board petition him to grant "a motion for declaratory judgment concerning the constitutionality of certain new Arkansas laws recently enacted by the State legislature." He hinted that he would hold those state laws unconstitutional. This suggestion apparently made only a slight impression on Caldwell and House, but in a few weeks Miller made the same suggestion to Orval Faubus, and it fell on fertile ground.[66]

Meanwhile, in his report to his Justice Department superiors concerning the June visit to Little Rock, Caldwell concluded that "unless and until some party does file a petition for a restraining order directed at the Capital City [*sic*] Council no action can be taken by the court." In his recommendations for "Possible Action by the Department" he considered the idea of using the FBI to investigate possible conspiracies, since it was apparent to him that "members of the Capital Citizens Council are endeavoring to bring pressure on the Governor to take some action that would stop integration this fall." Yet, incredibly, Caldwell concluded that "at the present time it would be wiser to wait until receipt of more evidence of affirmative action by the Capital Citizens Council before instituting any investigation." Despite the School Board's frightened and frustrated plea for help, and despite the federal judge's unwillingness or inability to provide any relief, Arthur Caldwell recommended that the Justice Department do nothing to help a school board that was voluntarily complying, in however flawed a manner, with federal guidelines in the face of mounting opposition from the local citizenry.[67]

During the summer of 1957, Archie House recalled years later, segregationist opposition to the Blossom Plan grew with mounting ferocity. House's paternalistic mind-set, and that of the School Board, when combined with the federal government's failure to function as a deterrent, left the city's traditional leaders unable to respond effectively to the unexpected challenge from the lower classes. The flood of carefully crafted segregationist propaganda that poured into Little Rock that summer swept away vast portions of the popular willingness to bow to the "inevitability" of integration. That flood also left a school superintendent and a governor struggling frantically to stay afloat.[68]

CHAPTER FOUR

BLUE-COLLAR OPPOSITION

Amis Guthridge

AMIS GUTHRIDGE LIVED SEVERAL MILES TO THE WEST OF LITTLE ROCK on Highway 10. A part-time lawyer and an aspiring politician (he also refinished antique furniture and sold it in his wife's small store), he faced a long drive each time he headed downtown. In July, as he passed the rolling farms in the pleasant valley on the edge of town or the lovely homes amid landscaped yards along the highway, the beauty of the view clashed with the crushing, wilting heat. In 1957, however, his mind was on other things, more important things, things that promised to bring him the recognition and status he lacked, and craved, all his life.[1]

Amis Guthridge was the kind of man who would say to an interviewer years later, "obviously why you're talking to me is because I was a leader, there's no question about that, in this situation here. . . . I was well known from Bobby Kennedy, Herbert Brownell, all of them up and down the track." Guthridge led Little Rock's segregationist forces, thanks both to his ability to articulate the inchoate fears and concerns of the middle to lower classes of the city's white citizens and to his willingness to engage and challenge the arrogant, paternalistic attitudes of the civic elite.[2]

Guthridge had been bitten by the political bug when he was elected president of the student body at Fort Smith High School, and he had been dabbling in politics ever since. He had worked hard for the Dixiecrats in 1948, championing the maintenance of states' rights and the South's old racial patterns. In 1952 he had run for Congress against Brooks Hays and had been soundly defeated. But in the years since the *Brown* decision he had found the issue he believed would carry him to victory in his next attempt.[3]

Amis Guthridge may have been the prototype for what Harry Ashmore called disdainfully the "thin-lipped men," the small-minded, mean-spirited men the Arkansas editor warned against and feared. Guthridge could have been ordered up from Central Casting to play the part of a Citizens' Council member. His smooth, rounded face bore no distinctive features except a prominent nose and a mildly cleft chin. With pale blue eyes, oiled back sandy-blond hair, shiny suits and dusty shoes, he may have appealed to an occasional Arkansas jury, but he failed completely to win the regard of the respectable men of affairs who were working to put Little Rock on a competitive footing with Dallas, or Memphis, or St. Louis. Archie House called him a "loud mouth creature." Harry Ashmore claimed that "nobody ever listened to Amis Guthridge, he was a blithering idiot. . . ." However, to the letter carriers, gas station attendants, beauticians, factory workers, and especially the men from the railroad yards and the small sect churches of Little Rock, Amis Guthridge offered hope that their children could be spared from the "black plague of race-mixing," and that their tenuous hold on self-respect through racial superiority could be preserved.[4]

By June of 1955 Guthridge had joined the legal staff of White America Inc. One of the early press reports describing White America quoted its president, L. D. Poynter, as saying his organization wanted the problem of integration settled "on a peaceable basis—through legal action. If that fails, then the people are going to take matters into their own hands. . . ." Two weeks after the United States Supreme Court handed down *Brown II,* Amis Guthridge informed a cheering White America audience that the Supreme Court decision on desegregation "did not apply directly to Arkansas, since none of the five cases on which the decision was made involved Arkansas school districts." He also promised that White America chapters would be organized in every Arkansas school district and would fight "any attempts by Negroes to enter white schools." He himself helped to form one of the first new chapters in Little Rock.[5]

L. D. Poynter informed the June meeting of the Capital City Chapter of White America that his organization opposed gradualism in integration just as vigorously as it opposed a sudden change, because both would have the same effect on "racial integrity." "Our organization does not advocate the abolition of the public school system . . . ," he offered, but "personally, I would rather see public schools abolished than to see my grandchildren sit in classes with Negroes."[6]

At the August 1955 meeting of the Little Rock chapter, Guthridge flexed his political muscle and took aim at Governor Orval Faubus. "Pretty soon we're going to tell Faubus he's either for the white folks or for the NAACP," Guthridge barked, "and we don't want any smart remarks." Ten days later Guthridge represented White America at a meeting in Hoxie of seven hundred citizens who were protesting integration in their tiny northeast Arkansas hamlet. Guthridge bellowed there was "not one man holding state office or a congressional seat" who had "guts enough to take a stand against integration." Then he warned that in the 1956 elections politicians would have to make their positions clear.[7]

Within a week the newly-formed, segregationist Hoxie Citizens Committee had hired Amis Guthridge to represent them in a potential suit against the school board. Guthridge announced to his Hoxie supporters that while he was not running for governor, "someone is getting ready to who will say the same things I do." Guthridge and Jim Johnson then worked together closely until they split in the spring of 1956.[8]

IN MID-OCTOBER, Amis Guthridge and Jim Johnson announced a set of tactical maneuvers they had devised to circumvent the *Brown* decisions, the most noteworthy of which was their proposal to promote abolition of the public schools "if necessary," by electing school boards who would "reduce the millage rates to nothing." Accusing the NAACP of seeking federal control of the public schools, Guthridge charged, "They couldn't get it done through Congress, so they are trying to do it through the Supreme Court. . . . Now the Supreme Court sets itself up as an all-powerful government, is trying to take over the executive department, and wants to administer the law through the federal district courts."[9]

By March of 1956 Guthridge and Johnson had parted company, probably because Guthridge was talking openly about swinging the support of White America behind the reelection campaign of Faubus. Faubus had announced his version of an interposition resolution and a pupil assignment plan, and Guthridge commended him for finally declaring himself "for the principles which White America stands for." After Jim Johnson's defeat in the summer elections, however, White America and the White Citizens' Council merged under the title of the Associated Citizens' Councils of Arkansas, with the aging L. D. Poynter as president. Into the leadership vacuum stepped Guthridge, commanding the forces of the newly configured Capital Citizens' Council, which had become "the largest and most vocal segregation group in the upper South."[10]

In other southern cities the leadership of the Citizens' Council movement emerged from the traditional civic elite. In Little Rock, by contrast, the CCC leaders, as well as their followers, were decidedly lower-middle-class. People who traditionally had functioned on the fringes of politics and the economy, these council members found themselves "feeling threatened and yet powerless to influence the finer machinations of the political process. . . ." *Arkansas Gazette* publisher Hugh Patterson expressed the disdain his class felt for the Citizens' Council's members, while at the same time explaining some of the source of their influence. "It's interesting—they're tolerated by people who have found them to be disreputable and sort of unclean before, but somehow they're tolerated by people who don't themselves want to expose a profile for attack."[11]

Virgil Blossom shared the elitist assumptions of his friends Hugh Patterson and Harry Ashmore, and he had failed completely to court the Citizens' Council types in his campaign to "sell" the Blossom Plan. When, however, the CCC distributed 100,000 copies in Little Rock of a pamphlet containing its April 30 appeal to Governor Faubus to stop the integration of Central High School, Blossom saw the error of his ways and began to court Amis Guthridge. Guthridge recalled later that he had liked Virgil Blossom, and that Blossom had taken him out to dinner and tried to win him over. But by then it was too late. As Arkansas Education Association Executive Director Forrest Rozzell explained, the segregationists were the only group in the community that had organized. The educators, the businessmen, the religious leaders—all were foundering while the CCC perfected its organization and strategy. Amis Guthridge and his followers were beginning to discover new avenues to power.[12]

THE NEW HALL HIGH SCHOOL in west Little Rock was scheduled to open in the fall of 1957 with seven hundred whites and no blacks. In the neighborhoods surrounding Central High School, however, most of the families belonged to the lower and middle classes, and many of these parents believed Virgil Blossom had made a "deal" with the city's upper-class groups whereby the wealthier residents of the western neighborhoods would support the Blossom Plan in return for the promise of a new, segregated school in the Heights. As Harvard sociologists Thomas Pettigrew and Ernest Q. Campbell explained, after conducting extensive interviews in Little Rock, working-class parents believed that the city's leaders did not want their own children to attend integrated schools, "but nonetheless desire Little Rock to have a reputation as a progressive and enlightened city, thereby attracting northern industry." That all six School Board members *and* Superintendent Blossom lived in the Heights strengthened the public perception of preference. As Amis Guthridge expressed his assessment of the plan to, in effect, integrate only Central High School, the rich and well-to-do were going to see to it that the "only race mixing that is going to be done is in the districts where the so-called rednecks live."[13]

Virgil Blossom's heavy-handed maneuvers only made matters worse. Blossom had refused to grant transfers out of the Central High district to white parents who wanted to keep their children in segregated schools, and yet he offered transfers to Hall High for the children of the vocal Reverend Wesley Pruden and Chief of Police Marvin Potts. Pruden refused indignantly, although Chief Potts accepted the transfer for his daughter until the Capital Citizens' Council circulated a petition calling for his removal from office.[14]

Blossom's attempts at appeasement were also inept. Calling the principals of the black junior and senior high schools into his office, he instructed them to "screen" the students who were eligible to attend Central High in the fall to make sure that only the most suitable would be accepted. Only eighty black children had indicated an interest in enrolling at Central High, and as Blossom wrote in his memoir, "following conferences among teachers, parents, and Negro leaders, this number was reduced to seventeen who were regarded as qualified and who actually applied and were approved by me." Arthur Caldwell explained to his superior in the Justice Department the procedure that Blossom used. "His argument to the colored principals," Caldwell wrote, "was that in the interest of successful integration the colored principals should see to it that only the very best qualified colored students should be transferred to the white high schools, and any colored student who was low scholastically or likely to be a disciplinary problem should not be approved for transfer."[15]

The result, in Caldwell's words, was "integration reduced to the barest minimum. . . ." NAACP attorney Wiley Branton later wrote that by the summer of 1957, "having further reduced the number of black children who might possibly attend Central High School that year, the board gave tentative approval for approximately . . . ten percent of the number they had told the court would be attending."[16]

Not surprisingly, Blossom's actions all but destroyed his credibility in the black community. Nat Griswold traced a lingering result. "Virgil Blossom's acts of bad faith" the former ACHR executive secretary told an interviewer, "have created a continuing sense of distrust by the Black community in the acts and words of white leaders. At first Blacks believed what Blossom said, but they were completely disillusioned." NAACP activist Ozell Sutton said it more simply: "Virgil Blossom was an instrument of chicanery and trickery . . . [T]hat was all of our view of Virgil Blossom through that time."[17]

AMIS GUTHRIDGE HAD a field day with Blossom's missteps. His primary strategy was to sow distrust concerning the intentions of authority figures such as Blossom and Harry Ashmore. He talked frequently of the people who were "imported" to set Little Rock up as "the first old Confederate state to comply with the United States Supreme Court decision." Presumably he meant Blossom and Ashmore, as well as, perhaps, NAACP lawyers such as Thurgood Marshall and Robert Carter.[18]

Guthridge and Pruden also insisted that the movement toward integration was a part of the international communist conspiracy. Pruden took out an ad in the *Arkansas Democrat,* paid for with his own (or his church's) money, that proclaimed: "Race-mixing in our schools is a Communist Doctrine. . . . Racial mixing of children in schools will lead to undue familiarity and encourage intermarriage. This would corrupt both races and create a mongrel people. Segregation has Christian sanction, integration is Communistic." Guthridge often said in his speeches that "the Communists actually took over the operation of the government of the United States from the inside when Franklin Delano Roosevelt was made President in 1933. And they have been determining our policies, in my opinion, ever since."[19]

Their arguments were often deeply flawed, yet these segregationist leaders had influence. When Pruden argued "since there was nothing in the Constitution that gave the federal government power over the schools or over the states, . . . the federal government's action was completely illegal," he spoke with authority to an uneducated, uncritical audience predisposed to accept his pronouncements with enthusiasm. This understanding of constitutional law had become, by 1957, an article of faith among Little Rock's segregationists. In its primary, stated functions of education and propaganda, the Capital Citizens' Council had been wildly successful, and it continued for two years to have an impact far beyond its membership.[20]

IN LATE JUNE OF 1957 Amis Guthridge and CCC president Robert Ewing Brown traveled to Tulsa to speak to the Tulsa Citizens' Council; they and Wesley Pruden would do the same elsewhere. Borrowing a phrase from Fort Smith, Arkansas' legendary territorial judge, "Hanging Judge Parker," Guthridge said there would be "Hell on the border" in Little Rock in September if the schools integrated. As the *Arkansas Democrat* described his speech, Guthridge "loosened all his guns from the minute he took the speaker's stand until he sat down." Blasting Orval Faubus as "a do-nothing governor on the segregation issue," Guthridge fired verbal salvos at everyone from Chief Justice Earl Warren to Arkansas' liberal Republican Winthrop Rockefeller. He undoubtedly said, as he later claimed to have included in all his speeches, that "the first Negro child that crosses the threshold of a public school would sound the death knell to the public school system." The "fired-up Arkansas attorney" ended his remarks by predicting "a resounding victory" not only for the Capital Citizens' Council but for all of the South's Citizens' Councils, and he left his audience with the firm conviction that there was a way to avoid desegregation.[21]

The following Thursday, Guthridge and Pruden appeared before the Little Rock School Board and formally requested that, in accordance with Act 84 of the Arkansas legislature that had created a State Sovereignty Commission, the School Board provide segregated schools for those white students who opposed integration. Quoting the opinion of Federal Judge John J. Parker of the Circuit Court of Appeals in Charlotte, North Carolina, that the *Brown* decision "does not require integration. It merely forbids discrimination," he reminded the School Board that Judge Miller had included this thinking in his August 1956 decision, and that the Eighth Circuit Court of Appeals had upheld Miller's decision in April 1957. Guthridge argued that the Supreme Court therefore had not mandated "compulsory integration."[22]

After citing the four laws the Arkansas legislature had passed in February 1957 to preserve segregation, the attorney concluded, "I am asking you not to attempt any compulsory integration in this district and to provide schools where white children will not have to attend with children of another race. . . ." He added that there had been much discussion about the rights of Negro children, but that he represented "some white children who have rights, too, you know." He brought to the meeting one of his clients, Mrs. Eva Wilbern, whose daughter was slated to be a student at Central High School in the fall. He asked for a transfer to Hall High School for Mrs. Wilbern's daughter, Kay.[23]

Wesley Pruden also addressed the School Board, informing the members that his people were disturbed about how integration would work in the social functions sponsored by the schools like the senior dances. "If Negro children go to integrated schools, . . . will they be permitted to attend school sponsored dances and would the Negro boys be allowed to solicit the white girls for dances?" Pruden assured the board that, based on a verbal opinion he had secured that week from an assistant state attorney general, if a Negro were enrolled in high school "there would not be any legal way to keep him from coming to any school sponsored function." Superintendent Blossom asked Guthridge and Pruden to submit their questions to the board in writing, and president William G. Cooper assured the two CCC representatives they would have an answer by the time of the next School Board meeting in July. Cooper was persuaded, however, that Guthridge's motives were "just political," and he confided to an interviewer years later that Guthridge was "not an impressive person."[24]

Next, the Capital Citizens' Council opened a full-scale assault on Governor

Faubus. They began by publishing Robert Ewing Brown's April 30 letter to Faubus in a three-quarter-page advertisement in the *Arkansas Democrat,* just in case anyone had missed seeing one of the one hundred thousand pamphlets they had distributed in Little Rock in May. Blaring in large block letters that "Race-Mixing! . . . Can Be Stopped By the Governor," they limned out the mantra they would chant for the next year:

> Since a sovereign state is immune to federal court orders . . .
> Since the governor as head of the sovereign state is also immune to
> federal court orders . . .
> Since the Governor, himself, placed on the ballot in last November's
> general election a resolution of interposition calling for the use of
> these sovereign powers to protect our people . . .
> Since the people of Arkansas by a tremendous, overwhelming majority
> approved the Governor's resolution for this purpose . . .
> Since the legislature backed up the people by voting overwhelmingly
> and passing four segregationist laws . . .
> **The Governor Should Exercise This Sovereignty to Protect the People**
> **of Arkansas. He Was Elected on This Basis.**

The Citizens' Council ad encouraged Arkansans to "write, wire or phone the Governor" and "urge him to use these powers now." In small print the ad went on to charge that white and Negro "revolutionaries" supported by wealthy tax-exempt foundations were trying to "FORCE RACE MIXING" on the unwilling people of Arkansas. Claiming that the aim of all Citizens' Councils throughout Arkansas was to use every legal resource available to them to stop such "vile schemes," the CCC ad promised that "race mixing" could be stopped by perfectly legal means.[25]

Faubus did nothing. A week later he called for the addition of more blacks to the Arkansas Democratic Party's Central Committee, which "strengthened the long-held opinion of many that their governor was an outright integrationist." In June he had minor surgery to correct an ulcer and then treated himself to a family reunion in California. He and his wife, Alta, had planned to extend their vacation with a leisurely train trip into Mexico, but his health problems worsened and he returned to Little Rock and checked himself back into the hospital. Meanwhile, the Capital Citizens' Council struck with their second ad.[26]

Quoting Faubus's own words in the Resolution of Interposition he had sponsored in the 1956 election, the ad reminded the people of Arkansas that their governor had promised to operate the public schools "on a racially sepa-rate but substantially equal basis," and that by ratifying the Fourteenth Amend-ment the people of Arkansas had not delegated to the federal government the power to control the domestic institutions of Arkansas, "any and all decisions of the federal courts or any other department of the federal government to the contrary notwithstanding." Faubus found himself caught in a web of his own making. Hammering home the point that Faubus had assumed responsibility for maintaining segregation, the ad reminded Arkansas citizens that in the 1956 campaign Faubus had promised that no school district in Arkansas would be forced to "race-mix" against its will. In block letters the ad asked pointedly "WHEN WILL THE GOVERNOR SPEAK?"[27]

Barely out of the hospital and testy, Faubus snapped to a reporter that he had not read the Citizens' Council ads. For the moment the pressure shifted away from him and back to the School Board when Wesley Pruden released to the press the questions he submitted to the School Board on July 8. Reverend Pruden asked about some of the "serious problems that are sure to arise if we abandon our segregated school system"—such as integrated social events, inte-grated restroom facilities and showers, integrated drama classes (with the pos-sibility of love scenes), and more.[28]

The next day Amis Guthridge found the superintendent and delivered his formal, written request for separate schools. Repeating the arguments he had made verbally at the School Board meeting on June 27, Guthridge added a con-cern that would bedevil the School Board. "Under Mr. Blossom's plan of inter-mingling the races," Guthridge wrote pointedly, "the negro [sic] pupils may choose to go to their negro [sic] school or to the white Central High School. But the white children are 'trapped' under the plan, and would be forced to attend Central High with negroes [sic], regardless of their desires." Guthridge quoted Act 84 of the 1957 Arkansas General Assembly, one of the four segregation bills, which specified that no child should be required to attend any school wherein both white and Negro children were enrolled; he also referred to the section of the Arkansas Constitution that provided for free public schools for all children between the ages of six and twenty-one.[29]

The superintendent barely had time to catch his breath before the CCC published its third ad in as many weeks, titled "Virgil Blossom and Little Rock School Board: SPEAK UP SO WE CAN HEAR YOU!" Printing in full the questions Wesley Pruden had submitted to the School Board, the ad asked Blossom and his board, "Come out in the open and let us know in plain words what you are planning to do with our children! When you start your race-mixing . . . where are you going to stop?" For example, the CCC asked, "Because of the high vene-real disease rate among negroes [*sic*], the public is wondering if the white chil-dren will be forced to use the same rest rooms and toilet facilities with negroes [*sic*]. Or will discrimination be permitted here?"[30]

Of course the third ad included the now-customary charges about "a small clique" of revolutionaries and the spread of "the black plague of race-mixing." Some historians have dismissed these charges as crude racism and lurid propa-ganda, but such characterizations trivialize and obscure the depths of the seg-regationists' concerns about miscegenation. These advertisements articulated the deep-seated fears and heartfelt beliefs of many Little Rock citizens, animat-ing them to take a stand in defense of the things they held dear. Virgil Blossom later wrote that they were very damaging to the cause of peaceful integration.[31]

AFTER THE THIRD Citizens' Council ad, Amis Guthridge got a call from his old friend Jimmy Karam, one of Little Rock's more colorful characters. Karam had had many incarnations, and he would have many more. He had been a strike-breaker, a football coach, a clothier, a leader in the biracial Urban League, and an active member of the Arkansas Council for Human Relations.[32] He had been elected "Mr. Little Rock" for his success in taking the Little Rock Junior College football team to a championship. Above all, Karam had been a hard-living, hard-drinking *bon vivant* with a desperate desire for acceptance. Born in Lake Village to Lebanese Catholic parents, which he described as "worse than being black where I'm from in south Arkansas," Jimmy Karam had grown up with a chip on his shoulder. He learned to fight early—"I was going to force people to look up to me"—and he fought a losing battle to "make people respect my parents."[33]

Jimmy Karam had appeared out of nowhere in Orval Faubus's first cam-paign for governor. Faubus remembered him materializing on a windy baseball field to hold the pages while the candidate delivered an important speech. From there Karam ingratiated himself with the new governor by teaching Faubus's chubby son Farrell, a sophomore at Central High School and an easy target for some of the young toughs, how to play football. In the summer of 1957 Jimmy Karam saw that "his" governor had the opportunity to be elected to a third term and perhaps more if he would align himself with the Citizens' Council, and so despite his liberal credentials he set himself the task of turning Orval Faubus into a segregationist. As he recalled years later, "I wanted Faubus to be re-elected, and I knew that if he didn't make the stand against [integration], that he could pack up and go back to Huntsville" [his home]. Out of the blue Jimmy Karam called a surprised Amis Guthridge and said, "Amis, would you all support Orval Faubus for a third term if he would stop integration of Central High School?" Guthridge stammered out an affirmative reply and Karam said, "All right, he wants to meet with you."[34]

At a clandestine night meeting on the mezzanine of Jimmy Karam's store, Governor Faubus sat down with the inner circle of the Capital Citizens' Council: Amis Guthridge, Wesley Pruden, Robert Ewing Brown, and Will J. Smith (not to be confused with Faubus's attorney, Bill Smith). As Guthridge remembered it, "We were there to meet with the Governor, and Jimmy Karam and the Governor came up the alley. . . . we met for a long time that evening . . . [and] he indicated to us very strongly that he was going to stop it, the integration of Central High School." He did not actually say he would intervene, but he left his co-conspirators with that impression. Guthridge came away from the meeting with the impression that Faubus was going to stop integration by using the Arkansas State Police; Brown later recalled the governor had said he was not going to let the national Republican Party dictate to him.[35]

Karam had mentioned the third term, and the CCC leaders were predisposed to believe that was the purpose of the meeting, but no evidence exists to suggest that Faubus understood what Jimmy Karam had wrought. In fact, as one of the governor's closest confidants and aides described Faubus, he was a listener. He smiled, and nodded, and made all supplicants believe he agreed with them, but he rarely committed himself. Reporters at the time noted the same thing: the governor "wouldn't comment. He'd sit back and smile. Well, hell, you could interpret his smile anyway you wanted to, couldn't you?" The wily governor always played his hand close to the vest, and through the years many people thought they had secured his commitment when actually he had only smiled and nodded.[36]

Jimmy Karam said years later that Orval Faubus never did understand racism. Faubus later claimed he had tried to convince Guthridge and Pruden that blacks deserved better treatment, and he said that the segregationists were never really happy with him. Guthridge and the CCC leadership believed Faubus was "a political opportunist," and that despite his leftist credentials they could manipulate him. The governor's actions demonstrated that the segregationists' assessment was correct, but Orval Faubus did not become an enthusiastic segregationist until he felt he had been thoroughly betrayed. In the meantime, Jimmy Karam stayed by his side. Speaking of the last weeks of the summer Karam later told an interviewer, "I slept and ate with him and I answered all the phones, and I wouldn't let anybody get to Faubus unless they believed the way that I believed, that the whites ought to be in that school alone.... I guess if we had of let nobody but Ashmore and his group talk to him, he'd have gone on and integrated."[37]

Despite his secret meeting with the CCC, Faubus soon told a press conference that "everyone knows no state law supersedes a federal law. If anyone expects me to try to use them to supersede federal laws they are wrong." That same day, a fiery segregationist preacher and radio broadcaster from Dallas, Reverend J. A. Lovell, told a cheering CCC rally of 250 people in Little Rock, "If the integration of the races continues while the Supreme Court and other public officials keep their weak-kneed attitude, there are people left yet in the South who love God and their nation enough to shed blood if necessary to stop this work of Satan." He added that race-mixing was "a Device by Satan to destroy the fertility of the white man's brain."[38]

Robert Ewing Brown presided at the rally and urged his audience to join the "50-million Club." Its aim, he explained, was to send postcards to commercial sponsors of radio and television shows that featured whites and blacks appearing together, informing the sponsors that "we bid farewell to your products." This was the first public mention in Arkansas of using economic boycotts as a tool of persuasion, though Little Rock would hear much of this standard Citizens' Council tactic in the months to come. The CCC now started hosting meetings two or three times a week, and the audiences were no longer just a handful.[39]

On July 20, a Sunday, the Little Rock School Board released a four-page statement explaining its desegregation policy. The School Board's limp statement was negative, reactive, and almost whiny in tone. Denying the segregationists' central contention that the Johnson Amendment and the four segregation laws made it unnecessary for the School Board to comply with the *Brown* decision, the board invited the segregationists to sue them if they wanted to obtain a definite judicial answer. The School Board statement admitted that the individual members disapproved of the *Brown* decision, but suggested that because they felt "a duty to obey," they had prepared their plan of integration. Quoting the supremacy clause of the United States Constitution, the statement also said that state laws must yield to federal laws. It was hardly a ringing endorsement of *Brown*.[40]

IN LATE JULY, Amis Guthridge insisted on having an audience for his July meeting with the School Board, and he got his way. Virgil Blossom complained of the large, noisy crowd, including reporters and photographers, and he wrote later that one of his segregationist School Board members (probably Brick Lile) muttered in disgust as they left the meeting together, "When I have to go

through meetings like this one . . . it almost makes me an integrationist."
Guthridge suggested before an admiring audience that the School Board provide a school for white and black students who wanted to be integrated, and
that it leave all existing schools segregated. He averred that only a small building would be needed, because few students would want it, and "if they have any
trouble getting a building the Capital Citizens' Council will provide one and
pay the rent to get it started. . . ."[41]

Responding to reporters' questions about whether or not he intended to file
suit, Guthridge replied, "They know I can't do that until I have exhausted all
administrative remedies available through the Board. . . . They also know that
school is starting soon and time is of the essence. That is why I want an answer
at this meeting." The board refused to reply to Guthridge at the meeting, and
they also refused to respond to the appeal he had made to them in June, saying
he would receive their answer in a few days in the mail. The board thereby
missed an opportunity to capitalize on the available media coverage.[42]

Two days later the board sent Amis Guthridge and the local newspapers the
opinions of its five lawyers, and once again their dry legalistic document paled
beside the rhetoric of the Citizens' Council. In response to the suggestion that the
School Board establish separate schools for white and Negro children, the lawyers
wrote, "The establishment of a segregated school plainly violates the rule of the
Brown case. . . ." In response to the charge that white children were "trapped" in
the Central High School attendance area, they wrote, "It is evident that he is confusing the Brown case with this gradual plan of integration." Most damaging of
all, the letter contained the admission, "The plan was developed to give as little
integration as possible over as long a period of time as it is legally possible to
have." It was not only uninspiring, it was a formula for defeat.[43]

SCHOOL BOARD PRESIDENT William G. Cooper later admitted, "I don't think
we appreciated the [segregationist] feeling, but it was certainly there. I personally thought it was unreasonable and I didn't give it much credence." School
Board member Harold Engstrom agreed, recalling that the board misjudged
"emotions" among "that segment of the community" with which they did not
have much contact. The School Board's failure to realize the strength and extent
of opposition to their plan stemmed from elitist disdain for points of view different from their own. They simply were not accustomed to taking into consideration the feelings or concerns of people outside their own privileged, limited
group. While there was very little, if anything, they could have said to mollify
those who cried "Never!" a respectful bow in the direction of at least hearing

their critics' concerns would have defused some of the class tensions that under-lay the worsening situation in Arkansas's capital city.[44]

Orval Faubus suffered a similar fate at the hands of the Little Rock power structure. One of the most galling, embarrassing moments of his life came shortly after his first gubernatorial election in the fall of 1954. Asked to crown the Jaycees' Miss Hospitality at a Razorback football game in Little Rock, he walked out on the field at halftime to a thundering chorus of boos. His wife was mortified, and he became newly, painfully aware of his outsider status in the capital city of the state he had been elected to govern. His son Farrell received the same kind of treatment at Central High School, as he himself did when he went along to help Farrell register for classes.[45]

Faubus's old friend and compatriot from the McMath administration, Henry Woods, told the story years later about how Little Rock people had thought Orval and Alta were "so country," and how the mountaineers simply had not fit in with the upwardly mobile smart set in Little Rock. Because of these experiences, and more importantly because of a deeply ingrained sense of social conscience and populism, Faubus felt an affinity for the rank and file of the lower to middle classes in Little Rock. By the summer of 1957 he was willing to agree that the lower classes should not have to bear the burden of integration if the "nabobs" did not have to do so as well. Above all, the besieged governor wanted to remain uninvolved, because he could see only danger from any position in the battle.[46]

Virgil Blossom was determined to get Orval Faubus involved. Since at least May of 1954 Blossom had envisioned himself as a heroic figure in the southern effort to desegregate the schools, and now he needed the governor's help to ensure the success of his plan. Blossom had also begun to envision a future for himself in politics, and he had even let it be known around Little Rock that he might like to be governor some day. Harold Engstrom spelled it out most clearly: "I don't know whether I should put it in a public document or not, but Virgil's private ambition was to be governor. . . . That's one of the reasons he worked eighteen and twenty hours a day."[47]

Blossom relied on Engstrom as one of his confidants—he had many—and he would arrive at Engstrom's home at all hours of the night, wake Engstrom up, and they would either drink coffee in the living room or ride around in Blossom's car. As Engstrom recalled years later, "In one of those unloadings, when he was very frank and open about all of his feelings and problems, he admitted that that [being governor] was really what he would like to do, and was trying to achieve some day." In retrospect Engstrom believed that Blossom's private ambition contributed significantly to his inability to deal successfully with Orval Faubus in the summer of 1957. "Blossom was a big man in the community at that time," Engstrom recalled. "And he felt that on this issue he would make a considerable personal advance—or it might be his downfall. I think that put a little more pressure on the man than some men can normally stand. . . ."[48]

The Citizens' Council media blitz put additional pressure on Blossom, as did the telephone campaign of anonymous threats and intimidation that he and all the School Board members began to experience after July. The increasingly agitated superintendent considered sending his high school–age daughter to Jonesboro to live with his brother-in-law, and he began to haunt the homes and offices of the School Board members whose advice he valued most—Brick Lile, Wayne Upton, and Harold Engstrom. After unknown assailants fired a shot through his car and another through his kitchen, the aggressive, overbearing Blossom was well on his way to becoming what Harry Ashmore would eventually call him, a "towering mass of jello."[49]

Orval Faubus was having stress problems of his own. All through the summer of 1957 his ulcer bothered him, and he could not eat solid food. Aside from the pressure of the Little Rock situation, he was grieving over the prospect of having to assume responsibility for the execution of a young murderer and rapist, Emmett Earl Leggett. As much as he liked Virgil Blossom, whom he had known when they were both living in northwest Arkansas and who had worked with him to get his tax package through the legislature in the winter of 1957, he felt that Blossom's approach drew attention to Little Rock, and that made him nervous. Perhaps a touch of ego or competition lay behind Faubus's irritation when he said, "Virgil Blossom became imbued with the idea that he was going to become a national hero." He believed that if Blossom had not pursued such widespread publicity for his plan, it would not have come to the attention of either the NAACP, or the South-wide Citizens' Councils, or even the federal government.[50]

Politically, Faubus needed local school districts to maintain a low profile when they decided to integrate. He had established the pattern of not interfering where the local school patrons initiated desegregation, and in time one of his mantras would be that "integration had occurred in more public schools in Arkansas than in eleven other states that had a comparable problem." When Blossom's School Board directed him to secure a statement of support from the governor, the superintendent at first felt confident he could handle the job. But as the days and weeks passed with no commitment, the light began to dawn on Blossom that all he was getting from the governor was smiles and nods. In the summer of 1957, his unease began to turn to panic.[51]

The board also wanted statements from Chief of Police Potts and Judge

Miller. A reluctant Chief Potts told Blossom, "I'll carry out my oath. . . . The police will protect life and property and preserve the peace. . . . But let me be clear that I do not regard it as my job to integrate the schools." When Blossom asked Judge Miller "to issue a public statement that he would tolerate no interference with peaceful implementation of the gradual integration plan which his court had approved," however, the ever-cautious federal judge declined.[52]

Virgil Blossom was an old football coach who was accustomed to winning, and as Harold Engstrom reflected later, "his technique was that if he were having difficulty achieving some objective, just to try harder. And in his effort to convince Faubus, he was over-zealous, and he over-extended himself, I believe, and he pushed Faubus harder than a person like Faubus should have been pushed." Faubus said later that Blossom began to "haunt" him, calling him six times a day, and appearing at the Governor's Mansion so often he became a "nuisance."[53]

As his anxiety rose, Blossom began to increase the decibels of his appeal, providing frightening tidbits such as the conversation he had had with Amis Guthridge earlier in the summer, when Guthridge had told him about a group of segregationists who would not join the White Citizens' Council "because the Council acted legally and constitutionally, but this group said they would, at the proper time, 'take over' with guns and pistols." And as his anxiety turned into panic, Blossom pressed Faubus over and over to tell him if he and the School Board could count on the National Guard if they needed it to supervise carrying out the Blossom Plan. Faubus said later that Blossom "gave me more information than anyone else on impending violence and disorder," and it was the superintendent who convinced the governor that the threat of violence at Central High School was very real.[54]

Faubus needed political cover. He knew the Arkansas segregation laws would not stand up to a court test, but until they were actually eliminated he felt bound to abide by them. He also knew he could not directly defy a federal court order without placing himself in contempt of court, and even if he had wanted to, he had promised his most important political adviser, Bill Smith, that he would never violate a court order. He knew Texas Governor Allan Shivers had succeeded in defying the federal government in 1956 when he called out the Texas Rangers to stop integration at Mansfield, and President Eisenhower had backed down. Faubus also knew, however, that 1956 had been the year of a national election and that Texas commanded a large number of electoral votes. Furthermore, Shivers had been a major player in the "Democrats for Ike" movement in Texas in 1952 that had been a key element in Eisenhower's victory. Tiny Arkansas commanded only eight electoral votes, and the astute Faubus understood that the federal government would not back down from a direct confrontation with his state.[55]

Finally, after many conversations, Virgil Blossom asked Faubus point-blank, "Governor, just what *are* you going to do in regard to the Little Rock integration plan?" After a long pause the governor replied, "When you tell me what the federals are going to do . . . then I will tell you what I am going to do." Faubus always insisted the federal government should enforce its own court orders, that it was not fair to expect state governments to do the political "dirty work" the federal government did not want to touch. The image he used was a telling one: "never did a federal agent say to a sheriff, 'There's a still out there, you go out and capture it, he's violating the federal law.'" Virgil Blossom reported to his School Board, "We know where we stand with the city police and Judge Miller. But the Governor is unpredictable. I don't know what he will do." Neither did Faubus.[56]

On August 20, 1957, the Mothers' League of Central High School was born. Amis Guthridge later said that the Mothers' League worked "hand in glove" with the Capital Citizens' Council, although the CCC initially denied any association between the two organizations. At the organizational meeting at the home of Mary Thomason, the conversation inevitably turned to the effects of integration "such as inter-racial marriages and resulting diseases that might arise." A Canadian broadcaster soon reported of one League member, "She was genuinely convinced that allowing Negroes into white schools would promote widespread miscegenation . . . and she was convinced that if the federal government persisted in forcing the integration of the schools, it would lead to bloodshed." Championing nonviolence as well as states' rights and segregation, the League became a powerful if symbolic voice in the community, investing the segregationist cause "with the unassailable twin mantles of Christianity and the sacred authority of southern mothers."[57]

The acme of the CCC's summer crusade came on August 22, when Governor Marvin Griffin of Georgia and his aide Roy Harris spoke in Little Rock at a Citizens' Council rally. Three hundred fifty people paid ten dollars a plate to hear Griffin and Harris blast Orval Faubus for succumbing to the federal court's scheme to destroy the southern way of life. The Capital Citizens' Council taped the Griffin speech and played it repeatedly on KARK radio.[58]

The Mothers' League staged a rally at the Hotel Lafayette on August 27, where an audience of 250 heard a minister from Dallas explain that "communism is behind every effort of the National Association for the Advancement of Colored People" and heard Wesley Pruden urge that integration be opposed "in a Christian way." To the consternation of Amis Guthridge, as well as the Mothers' League leadership, an unidentified man in the audience asked "how many persons would be at Central when classes begin next Tuesday to 'push back' any Negroes who seek entry," and then followed his remarks with the comment "I imagine there are a few shotguns in Little Rock, too." His remarks were met by silence and a few groans, and League president Mrs. O. R. Aaron took the microphone to tell the man that the mothers were "trying to keep down violence."[59]

When reporters asked Amis Guthridge if there had been any indication that segregationist troublemaker John Kasper might be thinking of coming to Arkansas, Guthridge replied, "We have not heard any report that he might do so. We do not want him in Arkansas. He will not be welcome in Arkansas; we will not have anything to do with him." Asked if his group had any plans to help keep down the possibility of violence, Guthridge replied, "We will fight through the greatest court of all, the court of public opinion."[60]

The Mothers' League adopted a petition urging Governor Faubus to prevent "forcible integration of the Little Rock schools." When they presented it to him by hand the next day at the Governor's Mansion, Faubus told the group he believed that the majority of Little Rock people opposed integration. Nonetheless, he refused to commit himself to any course of action, saying he must exercise his own best judgment if "pending litigation" failed.[61]

The pending litigation to which Faubus referred included a suit the Mothers' League's recording secretary, Mary Thomason, had filed in Pulaski County Chancery Court asking for a temporary injunction against integration. While the Mothers' League wanted to stop integration altogether, Faubus hoped that the Thomason suit, if it was successful and the injunction were granted, would delay integration only until the other cases then pending in state and federal courts could determine the unconstitutionality of the state's segregation laws. Faubus would then be off the hook, he would have the political cover he needed, and he could say to the people of Arkansas that, however distasteful it might be to him, he had to abide by the laws of the land. Although many hands had been involved in crafting this lawsuit in an attempt to delay integration—including those of Orval Faubus, Virgil Blossom, and Judge Miller—it would prove unable to withstand the forces pressing for accommodation to the *Brown* decision in Little Rock.[62]

CHAPTER FIVE

A TIME OF PANIC

Virgil Blossom

"HAIL TO THE OLD GOLD, HAIL TO THE BLACK!" STRAINS OF THE Central High School *alma mater* wafted across the field from where the band was practicing in the late summer of 1957. The boys on Central High's formidable football team, the Tigers, fantasized about the days just ahead, when Quigley Stadium would be filled with roaring, adoring crowds, and star players Bruce Fullerton, Billy Moore, Bill May, and Ralph Brodie would dazzle the home folks. But first, the boys had to sweat and groan through double-session practices in the oppressive heat and suffocating humidity of the August mornings and the scorching, relentless, stifling blaze of the Arkansas afternoons. Wilson Matthews was their tough coach and his boys produced. As an old football player and coach himself, Virgil Blossom usually felt his pulse quicken in August when the "two-a-days" started, but this year Blossom was much too busy to think about football.[1]

Little Rock's burly superintendent had grown up the hard way, and he understood demanding, unrelenting work. Because his father was paralyzed, the big, athletic boy had gone to work at the age of thirteen, helping after school to put food on the table for his family. He had earned an athletic scholarship to Missouri Valley College, and his determination was so great that when the school offered a prize of one hundred dollars to whoever made the first touchdown in the new stadium, the competitive defensive tackle managed to grab the ball and win the cash. After college he worked as a coach in a string of little towns, eventually landing in Fayetteville, Arkansas, where he became superintendent. There, he married the mayor's daughter, cute, perky Clarrene Tribble, in a Depression-era triple wedding with her two sisters. Soon the new couple had two daughters.[2]

In 1957 Virgil Blossom was forty-eight years old. Tall, barrel-chested, at least fifty pounds overweight, Blossom filled a room with his size and his intensity. Gifted as an athlete and an administrator, he did not have a light touch. He was earnest, businesslike, and serious, and he tended to dramatize or magnify the things that concerned him. As his good friend Wayne Upton described him years later, "Mr. Blossom was a very intense man. He was . . . a very determined person, . . . who was a driver, just always on the go, . . . [and] if he had to run over some people to get the things done which he thought needed to be done, he didn't mind doing it."[3] Blossom's horn-rimmed glasses added to the impression of severity, sometimes giving him an owlish quality. In the late summer and fall of 1957 they contributed to the deer-in-the-headlights look that marked many photographers' images of Little Rock's superintendent of schools.

Arkansas Council on Human Relations Executive Director Nat Griswold recalled that Blossom had "a tremendous ego" and "a certain feeling of insecurity in that ego." Griswold also noted that "everything indicated a desire for recognition." School Board member Harold Engstrom thought Blossom's ambition showed "in how he handled himself when hell broke loose" in Little Rock. In later years Engstrom came to believe that because Blossom wanted to be governor, "perhaps he might not have been the person to handle Faubus that summer. . . . I just can imagine . . . it had some effect on the way he . . . reacted to Faubus's reluctance to agree to what he wanted to do."[4]

The evidence suggests that the superintendent and the governor developed a bond of understanding and even of affection during the summer of 1957, during many late-evening conversations at the Governor's Mansion. In later years, each wrote sympathetically and admiringly of the other. They were sharing information and even strategizing together, both searching for political cover and trying to avoid a crisis in their state. Blossom was also sharing with the Little Rock School Board his growing understanding of the nature of Orval Faubus's dilemma. Some members of that board soon demonstrated a willingness to accommodate the governor's political needs.[5]

ON AUGUST 13, Little Rock School Board member Wayne Upton, an attorney, went to Fort Smith for a pretrial conference with Judge John Miller on a case unrelated to the Little Rock school matter. At the conclusion of the conference, Upton told the judge that he wanted to discuss a personal matter with him, "at which point Judge Miller stated that he probably knew" what it was. Upton told Miller there was a possibility a lawsuit might be filed in state court "to enjoin the School Board from integration." Apparently he was testing the water to see whether the judge would welcome it. To Upton's delight, Judge Miller told him "he would hate to see a suit filed by the wrong type of people, but if such a suit were filed and an injunction granted, the School Board should come to him and he would consider ordering a stay of the original integration order until the legality of the State action" could be determined. This was the "political cover" both Orval Faubus and Virgil Blossom needed. If they could seem to comply with Arkansas's new segregation laws until those laws were declared unconstitutional, they could then say in all candor they had no choice but to abide by the law of the land.[6]

Wayne Upton could hardly wait to get back to Little Rock and tell Virgil Blossom of this promising development. As Blossom's across-the-street neighbor, Upton felt himself to be at that time the superintendent's "chief sounding board," and they were very close. Upton recalled years later that he and Blossom would take drives in the superintendent's automobile, and Blossom leaned "more heavily on me for a short time there than on most anybody else because I was so handy."[7]

Blossom already had a date scheduled for August 15 for one of his frequent breakfast meetings with Faubus, and after learning of Judge Miller's proposal he called to ask the governor if he could bring a School Board member out to the Mansion to join their visit. Faubus invited Blossom and Upton for the next morning. Over breakfast, Upton explained Miller's suggestion. The governor agreed it was a good idea and confided to his visitors "he did not think that the State Statutes relating to integration were legal." Faubus recalled saying to the duo, "It's up to you people to figure out something to do. If you think this isn't going to work . . . then you have other alternatives. . . . Since this is more or less voluntary on the part of the School Board and Superintendent . . . you can do something to give this situation and tension that's building an opportunity to dissipate, or to come up with something that might be more acceptable." Blossom recalled in his memoir that Faubus suggested the School Board should arrange for a court suit testing the validity of the four new laws the legislature had enacted in February. Blossom and Upton offered to consider this suggestion and they felt that "if we arranged for a test suit the Governor would cooperate with us and, if necessary, issue the statement we wanted" [stating that the governor would not tolerate violence at Central High School].[8]

That night Blossom and Upton returned to the Mansion, arriving during a reception for the High School All-Star coaches. They told the governor they had brought him a lawsuit the School Board attorneys had drawn up. The School Board had five attorneys, and it is not clear which ones, if any, of them had been involved in this effort, or if Upton had drawn the suit himself. The suit they brought to the Mansion asked for an injunction against the School Board.[9]

Governor Faubus took his two visitors upstairs to meet with two of his key advisors, R. B. McCulloch and J. L. "Bex" Shaver. McCulloch, a graduate of Harvard Law School, the son of a former chief justice of the Arkansas Supreme Court, and a highly respected east Arkansas attorney, had authored Arkansas's *amicus curiae* brief in the *Brown II* case as well as helping to craft the four seg-regation laws the Arkansas legislature had passed in February. Shaver, also from the black belt of east Arkansas, was a member of the State Sovereignty Commission he had helped to create, and he had chaired the five-man committee (which included McCulloch) that went to Virginia in 1956 to study the Gray Commission's plan to institute "freedom of choice" in Virginia's schools.[10]

Shaver recalled later that in the summer of 1957 he had been in and out of the Governor's Mansion repeatedly, trying to find a solution that would quell the growing segregationist clamor. McCulloch and Shaver met with Blossom and Upton and discussed the proposed plans for a lawsuit, and after the two school men left the lawyers advised the governor they could see nothing that needed to be changed, and they thought such a suit might help. Faubus asked McCulloch and Shaver to handle the business of finding an attorney and a plaintiff; soon McCulloch's cousin, Little Rock attorney Griffin Smith, was involved in a suit in state court seeking an injunction against the School Board.[11]

All through that day Blossom and Upton had been trying to get in touch with Bill Smith, the governor's personal attorney and his most important adviser. Smith was a close friend of School Board member Brick Lile, with whom he had organized and created Riverdale Country Club, and also of School Board member Harold Engstrom and School Board attorney Leon Catlett. Smith had played golf several times with Engstrom in recent months, and he had heard enough to be alarmed about the School Board's concerns that violence would erupt when school opened in September. Engstrom had told him in absolute confidence about threats Virgil Blossom was receiving and about the board members' escalating concerns that blood would be shed when school opened, which led Smith to conclude that Little Rock was going to have a "blood bath."[12]

On the night of August 15, Virgil Blossom located Bill Smith by telephone at Riverdale Country Club, and Smith later described Blossom as "having a fit." Blossom begged Smith to come by his house after he had finished dinner, and finally "he begged me so to come to his home that I did go," arriving at Blossom's house about 9:00 or 9:30; he found Blossom "scared to death." Smith said later that Blossom "was like a wild man" because of the violence he feared was going to flare up at Central High School when the schools opened in a couple of weeks. According to Smith, Blossom opened a desk drawer and took out a number of knives and said, "This is just a few. Last year we took all kinds of knives and brass knuckles and everything else away from our boys in Central High that they claimed were being prepared for this year, and had them in their lockers, and we conducted locker searches and everything."[13]

At this point Blossom and Upton, who had joined the group after Smith's arrival, "begged" him to bring a suit for a private citizen in state court, "to enjoin the School Board from implementing the integration plan that had been approved." Smith responded "Well, Virgil, this is your plan. You've been going all over town making speeches to civic clubs and women's clubs and everybody else." To which Blossom responded, "There's going to be bloodshed if this thing's not stopped." The two school men told Smith the purpose of the suit was "to delay integration in the Little Rock Public Schools until the legality of the State Statutes regarding integration could be determined."[14]

Bill Smith told Upton and Blossom he was leaving for New York the next day to be gone on state business for a week or perhaps two. He offered to check with his law partners before he left town to see what they thought about getting involved in the School Board's scheme, and he promised to call them and let them know what his partners thought. Smith recalled later that as they were leaving Blossom's house, and standing on the front lawn, Blossom grabbed Smith by the lapels of his suit and implored him, saying, "Bill, you've got to save me. You've got to save me."[15]

According to Smith, Blossom continued, "there's going to be bloodshed if this thing's not stopped. . . . If you've answered the phone at your house and heard people threaten your daughter's life and your wife's life and threaten to throw bombs in your home, you'd know what I was talking about." Smith felt Blossom at that point was "on the verge of hysterics." He jerked loose from Blossom's grasp and said, "Virgil, I've got problems enough of my own." Apart from the fact that Blossom was a very large, intimidating man, some of Smith's irritation stemmed from the fact that he believed Blossom felt he needed to be "saved" because he wanted to run for governor. As Smith told an interviewer years later, Blossom thought "if he could pull off the integration of the schools peacefully . . . and he laid the groundwork for it and everything, that it would elect him governor."[16]

Bill Smith talked to his law partners "at great length" the next morning before he left town for New York, and they all agreed "We don't want any part of it. . . ." Smith could not get through to Blossom to convey this information, so he left a message with the superintendent's secretary. Even though his own firm did not want to get involved in the School Board scheme, something about Blossom's urgency had touched Smith, and somehow he managed to find time before he left town to locate a lawyer who said he *would* be willing to represent the School Board's plaintiff.[17]

Arthur Frankel was a longtime Little Rock lawyer, a respected member of the legal establishment. He told the FBI "another lawyer" had asked him to get involved in what became the Thomason suit, but he refused to answer more of the Bureau's questions because he believed the investigation was politically motivated in an effort to discredit Orval Faubus. Wayne Upton told Virgil Blossom that Bill Smith had secured Frankel, and Upton later informed the FBI that "Mr. Frankel told him, in confidence, that the suit had been prepared at the request of Mr. William F. Smith, personal legal advisor for Governor Faubus." Archie House reported to the FBI, incorrectly, that Smith's law firm prepared the Frankel suit. Because of Smith's involvement in locating Frankel, the federal government concluded, incorrectly, that Orval Faubus had conceived the resulting suit.[18]

Upon reaching New York, Smith called Faubus to discuss his bizarre encounter with Blossom and Upton at Blossom's house. This information, and especially the stories about the drawer of knives and the threats Blossom had received, intensified the governor's growing sense of alarm about the potential for violence at Little Rock Central High School. As Faubus later wrote about his communications with Blossom, "As the time for school opening drew near his concern grew to alarm and even fear. He told me of growing opposition and then of reports of organized resistance to the court-approved plan of the school board. He was so concerned, he said that he was making arrangements to send his children to another school." Blossom's brother-in-law, state Senator Marvin Melton, told Faubus "Virgil's awfully worried. He's already made arrangements to send his children to stay with me and attend school at Jonesboro." Blossom had by this point descended into what Nat Griswold termed a "paralyzing panic."[19]

After leaving the Governor's Mansion on the morning of the 15th, Blossom had gone by the office of William F. Rector, a socially prominent, highly regarded businessman who handled the insurance for the Little Rock School District, and to whom Blossom had talked earlier about the possibility of filing a suit either for an injunction against the School Board or for a declaratory judgment regarding the four segregation laws. Blossom asked Rector to proceed and Rector agreed, mainly because the vice president of the Capital Citizens' Council, T. A. Dillaha, had aroused his ire by seeming to threaten him with a loss of business if he did not join the CCC.[20]

Rector however, refused to go the whole way and file suit for an injunction barring the School Board from proceeding with its plan for desegregation. Instead, on August 16 his attorney, Bernal Seamster, filed suit in Pulaski County Chancery Court seeking a declaratory judgment on the four segregation laws. Although Wayne Upton later told the FBI he was the only School Board member who knew the origins of this suit, other evidence suggests that most, if not all, members of the board were in on this maneuvering. As School Board attorney and former Chamber of Commerce President Richard C. Butler told the Eisenhower Administration Project's interviewer in 1971, "*We* were just trying to explore every possible way of trying to avoid what appeared to be the inevitable confrontation of people who were being carried too fast in accepting something, figuratively at gunpoint, that some of us felt might have a chance of working in a somewhat cooler climate."[21]

On Sunday afternoon, August 17, Wayne Upton, Virgil Blossom, and Harold Engstrom made the four-hour drive to Fort Smith to have a private meeting with Judge John Miller. Engstrom recalled later that the meeting "seemed to me to be kind of unethical, but [Judge Miller] welcomed us to do it." Engstrom was initially doubtful that Upton had heard Judge Miller correctly, and that Miller had actually volunteered to delay the Blossom Plan based on a state court's action. As Engstrom recalled, "So we discussed it. And I think one of the reasons I went [was that] I couldn't believe that a federal judge would . . . talk like that. And Upton insisted he had it right. And so because I was a little hard to convince that was the reason I went."[22]

The trio met with the judge on the mezzanine of the historic old Ward Hotel at six o'clock. As Upton explained to the FBI almost three weeks later, they discussed the Rector suit, but "Judge Miller said that he did not think that any action on this suit would give a reasonable legal basis for him to take any action. Judge Miller said that the only possible action, as he saw it, would be through an injunction." Virgil Blossom later reported to the FBI that at the conclusion of this meeting, Harold Engstrom asked the judge if he would be willing to "express his preference relative to possible delay in order to have state segregation legislation cleared up prior to integration." According to Blossom, Judge Miller then told Engstrom he felt "some delay might be desirable."[23]

Harold Engstrom was appalled by the behavior of the federal judge. As a young engineer, he had held judges and the legal system in the highest esteem— he said later he was in "awe of the federal court"—and he was stunned that the judge would "more or less make a deal with us." Engstrom had a lot of reservations about being involved in any backroom deals, and he was amazed that the judge "allowed us to appear before him and tell him what we were trying to do, and he'd tell us what the alternatives were that he could do."[24]

Harold Engstrom's distress was the least of Wayne Upton's worries. Having learned that the Rector suit was inadequate to his purposes, he had to persuade the School Board to let itself be sued for a delay of the start of integration. As he probably anticipated, Archie House would have none of it. When informed thirty years later of the School Board trio's meeting with Judge Miller, House replied, predictably, that he just could not believe the three had done anything "unbecoming of gentlemen."[25]

Harold Engstrom recalled that the School Board discussed for days whether to participate, if only secretly, in a suit for a delay. Both Upton and Blossom advocated postponing integration, but eventually the board members instructed Blossom to call Judge Miller and tell him they intended to proceed. Upton and Blossom, undaunted, proceeded privately with their maneuvering. Blossom continued to meet with Faubus to seek some common ground and later passed on to the FBI some information Faubus had given him during this period. "The Governor said he tried to postpone the appointment of the Sovereignty Commission as set up by the legislature," Blossom reported to the FBI, "but he was mandamused by East Arkansas citizens to appoint the said Commission." Blossom also called United States Attorney Osro Cobb repeatedly, seeking assistance, finally coming to Cobb's office and saying, "Osro, we have got to find some way to defer the program, or all hell could break loose." Cobb told him that "the only chance of relief was by petition to the federal court . . . ," but Blossom was not willing to pursue that option.[26]

Meanwhile Orval Faubus was casting about on his own. On August 20 he telephoned Washington "to find out what the Department of Justice could and would do in the event of an outbreak of violence in Little Rock." Faubus claimed in his memoir, *Down From the Hills,* that he had called twice before with no response, and he was beginning to grow angry over what he perceived to be the federal government's "cowardice" in refusing to help resolve a problem Washington had created. As Faubus wrote, "Since the plan to integrate Central High School was now in response to and by the direction of a federal court, I was sure the federal authorities had devised some procedures and formulated some plan of action to be followed in view of the difficulties, disorder and violence which had already occurred in various places . . ." such as Clinton, Tennessee, and Louisville, Kentucky. "I wanted to discuss the Little Rock situation with some knowledgeable person in the Department, to be informed on their plans and preparations, and be assured that violence and disorder would not result in destruction of school buildings, and the injury or death of students, school personnel or others." Deputy U.S. Attorney General William P. Rogers informed Faubus the Justice Department could do "very little," but Rogers did offer to send a department representative to Arkansas to talk to the beleaguered governor. Incredibly, that representative, Arthur Caldwell, waited a week before he traveled to Arkansas to meet with Faubus.[27]

Always a man to help himself, Faubus went fishing over the weekend with Judge Miller. No record remains of their conversation, though Faubus biographer Roy Reed contended that Faubus told him he never made a "deal" with the judge. Upon his return to Little Rock, Faubus visited with Virgil Blossom and suggested the School Board should file a suit to delay integration. Blossom shared this idea immediately with Archie House, who exploded in anger and declared Faubus's proposition "absurd."[28]

On the following day, Monday, August 26, Faubus invited the Little Rock School Board to join him for lunch at the Albert Pike Hotel, and at that meeting he tried to sell his idea to the whole group. Citing information he said he could not give them, which had been provided in large part by Blossom, Faubus claimed there was a significant danger that violence would erupt at Central High School if the School Board chose to proceed with its plan of desegregation. He apparently thought he was pursuing a course the board would endorse when he then told them he had made arrangements to have a suit filed in Chancery Court asking for a temporary delay of the Blossom Plan, that he "had a judge that would fix it up and take the heat off the school district" by granting a temporary injunction, and that the School Board would then be "protected." He said at that point the School Board could petition the federal court for a postponement of desegregation. Sounding curiously like Judge Miller, Faubus suggested this suit would be filed "by a reputable attorney who was representing a reputable citizen and not by Amis Guthridge or any of his group."[29]

Rising up to his full and considerable height, Archie House informed the governor that what he was suggesting was "conspiracy to violate federal law." House barked at Faubus that the School Board "had worked long and hard with this plan and had reduced it to the barest minimum of integration and, in addition, had secured its approval by both the Federal District Court and the Eighth Circuit Court of Appeals, and this being true they would not now back down or refuse to go through with the plan." House reflected years later that the members of the School Board may have been segregationists, but they would not have engaged in such an underhanded scheme.[30]

Blossom and Upton had given it their best shot, but they had been unable to persuade the School Board to buy into any arrangement that would offer the increasingly wobbly superintendent a reprieve. The next day, in Pulaski County Chancery Court, Arthur Frankel filed *Mrs. Clyde Thomason v. Dr. William G. Cooper, et al.,* seeking an injunction to prohibit desegregation, temporarily, at Central High School. In Washington, the Civil Rights Bill of 1957, a toothless tiger that contained no provisions for allowing the Justice Department to initiate action against recalcitrant school districts, cleared the final hurdle and became the law of the land.[31]

ON WEDNESDAY, AUGUST 28, Arthur Caldwell finally came face to face with Orval Faubus. An Arkansas native, a graduate of George Washington University Law School, and a veteran of extended service both to the powerful Senator Joe T. Robinson and to the United States Department of Justice, Caldwell felt great disdain for the self-taught mountaineer who now occupied the Arkansas governor's office. Caldwell's immediate superior, Warren Olney III, ostensibly sent Caldwell to Arkansas in response to Faubus's pleas for help, but the Justice Department representative's actual mission was to "check on warnings from local sources about Faubus' plans."[32]

Attorney General Herbert Brownell was already furious with Caldwell for not apprising him fully of the nature and import of Section III of the proposed Civil Rights Bill, and so Olney decided to keep the Caldwell mission to Arkansas a secret. When Caldwell got to Arkansas he requested to meet "secretly and on a confidential basis" with the Arkansas governor. Brownell's learning of the trip seems to have been the final straw that cost Caldwell his job as assistant to the assistant attorney general, and it also dashed Caldwell's hopes of being appointed to head the new Civil Rights Division of the Justice Department.[33]

In a detailed report to Olney, Caldwell described his hour-and-a-half meeting with Governor Faubus. At the outset, Faubus asked what action the Department of Justice might take in the event violence erupted at Central High School the following Tuesday, September 3, when the semester began. Caldwell hastened to explain that because Section III of the Civil Rights Bill had failed to pass the Senate "the new Civil Rights legislation would have no effect whatever on any school situation."[34]

Caldwell then outlined the provisions of the United States Code that might allow for the application of criminal statutes to potential school integration difficulties, and he explained how the precedent of the Hoxie case could allow the federal government to enter some suits as *amicus curiae*. Finally, he reviewed the Clinton, Tennessee, situation of the previous year as an example of how the Justice Department might join a contempt proceeding. In the Clinton experience, he explained, the school board had requested an injunction against certain named persons from interfering with the school board's plans, but the Little Rock School Board was unwilling to seek such an injunction. Of necessity, Caldwell had to conclude "the development of a disturbance at the school would not of itself provide any basis for action by federal authorities."[35]

Faubus wrote in his memoir he was "amazed" to learn of the federal government's attitude in relation to "its own court orders." According to the governor,
"It was with utter astonishment and some consternation that I learned that the
federal authorities would do nothing about any disorder and mob violence that
might be created solely by reason of its own actions . . . ," and he was equally
amazed when Caldwell said to him, "Governor, we can't do a thing until we find
a body." Faubus began to explain to Caldwell his dilemma. He said that he was
"gravely concerned" about violence when school opened on Tuesday. Just one
month before, he continued, "the community of Little Rock was . . . resigned to
integration and would have accepted it without protest or violence at that time."
But as a result of the activities of the Capital Citizens' Council, and in particular the Marvin Griffin speech, the situation was now completely changed.[36]

In a surprising move from a man not known for candor, Faubus then
revealed his hand. He may have been lulled into this lack of vigilance by the fact
that he felt he had "no stronger supporter" than Caldwell's father, who was the
librarian for the Arkansas Supreme Court. Faubus told Caldwell he was so concerned about violence "he had arranged to have a law suit filed" in Pulaski
County Chancery Court asking for a temporary injunction to prevent the Little Rock School Board from carrying out its plans for integration. The governor informed the Justice Department representative he hoped the chancellor (a
Faubus appointee) would issue the injunction restraining the School Board,
"thus placing them in such a position the School Board would be forced to go
back to Federal Judge John Miller for permission to postpone integration of
Little Rock schools this Fall, or at least a postponement until the constitutionality of the Arkansas Statutes could be determined."[37]

Faubus stressed he was taking this action through the Chancery Court because
he thought it was "the only way to avoid bloodshed." When Caldwell asked him if
he had any evidence or information he would turn over to the FBI or the local
police, Faubus claimed his information was "much too vague and indefinite" to
be of any value to the law enforcement agencies. The governor ended the conference by pointing with pride, as he always did, to the substantial progress Arkansas
had made during his administration in integrating almost all of its colleges and
universities, as well as Little Rock's public transportation system.[38]

Caldwell was not impressed. He told Faubus in response that he could
under no circumstances approve the action the governor was proposing. He
also shared with Faubus the results of his own investigations with the chief of
police and the FBI, all of which pointed to the conclusion that there would be
no violence at Central High on Tuesday.[39]

When Arthur Caldwell left the governor's office, he decided to remain in Little Rock to attend the Chancery Court hearing the next morning. Undoubtedly, Caldwell reported the results of his conference to his old friends Harry Ashmore and Archie House. It would not strain credulity to suggest that Caldwell also called Judge Miller to alert him of the scheme and probably to offer unrestrained criticism of what he perceived to be an unworthy attempt to sidestep federal directives.

THE SCHOOL BOARD had formally disavowed any connection with the Thomason suit. House had said they would fight it; Blossom had told the judge to count them out. But Leon Catlett, one of the School Board lawyers, asked attorney Griffin Smith to take over the trial portion of the case because "they" didn't like the way Arthur Frankel planned to argue it. Frankel had planned to present his evidence in writing but call no witnesses, and according to Griffin Smith, the unspecified "they" thought this was no way to win a lawsuit. Frankel's client, Mary Thomason, who asked to speak to "her attorney, Arthur Frankel" when the FBI interviewed her a week later, went into Chancery Court seeking an injunction and represented by Griffin Smith. Mary Thomason was recording secretary for the Mothers' League of Central High School, and the common perception was that this organization was behind the suit. In fact it was not.[40]

According to Orval Faubus, Virgil Blossom visited the Governor's Mansion one or two evenings before the Chancery Court hearing near hysteria, "fearful for his life, fearing violence," begging the governor to testify in the Thomason suit. Mrs. Thomason's attorney had subpoenaed Faubus to appear as a witness for the plaintiff, but according to the law at that time, a governor did not have to obey such a subpoena. Faubus agreed to appear.[41]

The morning of Thursday, August 29, 1957, just five days before the start of the fall school term, the Pulaski County Courthouse hummed with activity as the two-hour Thomason hearing attracted an assemblage that was unaccustomed to viewing such a legal display. Noting that the courtroom was filled to capacity with members of the Central High Mothers' League, Archie House later recalled that he and Virgil Blossom felt themselves to be lonely sentinels at the witness table on behalf of a most unpopular position. None of the other School Board lawyers participated in this suit.[42]

In the brief he filed for Mary Thomason, Arthur Frankel had argued, "Due to the uncertainty of the law, the conflicting court decisions and general state of confusion and unrest, there is possible danger of civil commotion if the defendants proceed with their announced plan." Archie House brushed aside this concern in his opening argument, telling the court "an allegation that bloodshed will occur doesn't make it so." Griffin Smith, a close friend of Blossom, represented the plaintiff, Mary Thomason, and called her as his first witness. Mrs. Thomason expressed strong class concerns about the Blossom Plan, feeling that Central High School "was being singled out and thus was being discriminated against," since Hall High School did not have any black students.[43]

According to Arthur Caldwell's careful description, Mary Thomason testified she was afraid that both black and white children "might be injured if the integration plan proceeded." She could offer very little evidence to substantiate these fears, except that she had heard "rumors from a filling station operator whose name she would not divulge, that there was a possibility of shotguns and shooting in Central High School if the colored children entered." She also reported she had heard rumors of "gangs of white children and gangs of colored children being formed with a view to some sort of violence." In short, Mrs. Thomason said that the mothers were "terrified" at the situation, and they were "afraid to send their children to school." A loving mother concerned for the well-being of her offspring, Mary Thomason made a strong witness.[44]

Archie House then called Virgil Blossom to the stand. Most of Blossom's testimony dealt with the specifics of the Blossom Plan, and he stressed his belief that while most Little Rock citizens did not favor integration, they had accepted the School Board's plan as "the best solution to a difficult problem." He also testified that Police Chief Marvin Potts had assured him there would be no violence, but under questioning he admitted he did not know what specific plans had been made to prevent such a possibility.[45]

Governor Faubus arrived at the hearing late, quietly seating himself to one side of the courtroom as Blossom testified. "Almost immediately," he wrote later, Faubus noted and was puzzled by Blossom's "extremely evasive attitude in response to questions about possible difficulties." When Archie House asked if he feared violence, Blossom responded, according to Faubus, with "considerable hesitation accompanied by nervous body movements and erratic nodding of the head, '. . . I've never given it a thought.'"[46]

Orval Faubus was stunned—"dumbfounded . . . amazed"—by Virgil Blossom's performance. Violence was all the superintendent had been talking about to him all summer, and as Faubus sat listening to Blossom testify the thought came to him repeatedly that this was simply a change of strategy of which he had not been informed. Faubus had "done a lot of checking and information-gathering" on his own about the possibility of violence at Central High, and he had concluded that "Trouble was brewing and appeared to be serious." As he later recalled, "I confidently expected my testimony to back up Blossom's stronger evidence and the extensive information he had obtained as to impending opposition that could lead to disorder. I expected my testimony to bolster his genuine concern and fear for the safety of the Negro students, as well as his concern for the welfare of himself, his family and others."[47]

Griffin Smith then called Orval Faubus to the stand. The governor testified he feared there would be "rioting and bloodshed if the city program was put into effect," and he informed the court he had learned "the federal government would not intervene." He testified that revolvers had been found on white and black students, that the Marvin Griffin speech had crystallized sentiment against integration, and that the present time was one of "the worst times possible" to impose desegregation on Little Rock because of the heightened tensions of the summer. The governor said he had noted recent statements of segregationist leaders deploring violence, but he added "a crowd can assemble with the best intentions and become a mob just because of two or three hot-headed people." Faubus urged the court to enjoin the School Board from proceeding with its plans. When he finished, the courtroom "broke into applause and the Governor bowed."[48]

School Board member Harold Engstrom recalled years later that the board members felt they had a responsibility to the community to downplay the threat of violence. They always discussed the dangers of the charged emotional situation in Little Rock; the School Board concluded consistently, however, they "had to be careful and not take the position . . . that this was a very dangerous thing because that in itself would encourage . . . violence." Time and again they came to the conclusion that "to go to the federal marshals and ask for their protection, we would have to argue that we needed it. And at the time we were not of the opinion that that was the prudent thing to say to the community or to the press." Perhaps that explains Blossom's testimony.[49]

In a typically cautious portion of his statement to the FBI, Blossom later claimed, "I did not have any knowledge of impending violence at Central High School prior to the opening of school September 3, 1957." He suggested that his first inkling of violence came from Faubus. "I heard, in chancery court," Blossom argued, "Governor Faubus' statement of his knowledge of the existence of conditions that would produce violence." Downplaying his own involvement, he continued: "During the past summer, I talked with Governor Faubus about isolated incidents involving guns on Negro children in the previous school year, expressing to him the feeling that there was some restlessness caused by the general tension over integration in the South." What later proved to be a successful attempt to place all the blame on Orval Faubus for the disaster in Little Rock had begun.[50]

Predictably, Chancellor Murray Reed ruled in favor of the plaintiff on August 29, saying "in view of the testimony and the show of the threat of violence, riots and bloodshed, and particularly in the opinion of Governor Faubus, I feel that I can only rule to grant the injunction." Judge Reed declared that his temporary restraining order was "designed solely to preserve order at a time when forces beyond the control of individuals involved here have created a situation which is perilous to the community and its citizens." Archie House, however, had come to the Reed hearing prepared for such an eventuality, and he had already secured a commitment from Arthur Frankel and Griffin Smith that "if the court did grant an injunction that the usual notice of ten days would be waived and the matter could be presented in federal court immediately."[51]

House's petition to the Federal District Court asked for an injunction restraining Mrs. Thomason from using Judge Reed's injunction "in any way that would interfere with the Little Rock School Board and its integration of Little Rock high schools." When House went to the federal courthouse to file his petition, however, he discovered that Judge John Miller was no longer on the case. Another agent of the federal government had failed Orval Faubus, and he would not be the last.[52]

UPON LEARNING THE results of the hearing in Judge Murray Reed's court, federal Judge John Miller immediately called Chief Judge Archibald Gardner of the Eighth Circuit Court of Appeals and asked to be relieved of any further responsibility for the Little Rock school case. Gardner complied, and within the hour he notified Judge Ronald N. Davies, of Fargo, North Dakota, who had arrived in Little Rock only days before to fill the vacancy in the Eastern District of Arkansas, that henceforth Davies would handle all further proceedings in the case. Virgil Blossom, Wayne Upton, and Orval Faubus must have been stunned by this development. Blossom and Faubus had both thought Miller would save them; both thought they had an informal commitment from the judge that if they followed his suggestions he would sustain Judge Reed's temporary injunction, thereby providing time for litigation to proceed to determine the constitutionality of the state's four segregation statutes. But now Judge Miller had bailed out. No record has come to light of John Miller's thinking or motivation in this instance, but several possibilities suggest themselves.[53]

Herbert Brownell indicated to President Eisenhower that Judge Miller felt burdened by a backlog of cases, and that as soon as Ronald Davies arrived on the scene, Miller was anxious to be relieved of some of them. Warren Olney argued that Little Rock lawyers had complained of the inconvenience of having to travel to Fort Smith to do business with Judge Miller, and that as soon as Davies arrived in Little Rock Miller was happy to accommodate them by asking to be relieved of the Little Rock school case. Harold Engstrom suggested years later that "all the rest of us were trying to figure out how we could back out of it, too. He probably grabbed at the chance when Davies showed up." None of these possible explanations seems adequate to warrant Judge Miller's walking away from his implied commitment to Faubus and Blossom just days away from school opening with no viable plan in place. The day after Miller recused himself, the United States Senate approved unanimously a bill that Arkansas Senator John L. McClellan had proposed that would add an additional judge to the Eighth Circuit Court of Appeals. As the *Arkansas Gazette* reported the next day, "Reliable sources say it would go to federal District Judge John E. Miller of Fort Smith. . . ." Miller's long-held dream was within his grasp, and he did not need to jeopardize his chances by involving himself in a no-win situation in Little Rock.[54]

That afternoon Blossom's teenage daughter Gail picked up the telephone to hear a man's voice spewing the frightening message, "You girls will not be alive this time tomorrow. . . ." Blossom told the FBI this was one of a number of calls received by his family containing threats, not only on the night of August 29, but on subsequent nights. Blossom immediately called Chief of Police Marvin Potts and requested police protection for his home, "knowing that it would be somewhere from eleven to Midnight before I would be there." Not only did Blossom have a School Board meeting to attend, he also had an important visit to make before he could let this exhausting day come to an end.[55]

In Orval Faubus's telling of the tale, Virgil Blossom appeared at the front door of the Governor's Mansion that night, and as Faubus let him in, the superintendent entered with his hand outstretched and said with great earnestness, "Oh, I want to thank you! I'll never forget you! I'll do anything for you! Just let me know when you need me! I'm forever in your debt!" Faubus realized "he was thanking me for not exposing him in my testimony earlier in the day." In an instant Orval Faubus realized that Blossom's behavior in the courtroom had not been the result of a change in strategy. To the contrary, instead of "bringing out in court the evidence and information of growing opposition to their integration plan, they had denied the facts by deliberately obscuring and suppressing the evidence." Faubus asked Blossom why he had not testified to all the information he had given the governor over the preceding weeks. Blossom replied, "Governor, all I can say . . . I just couldn't." When Faubus pressed him to know why he couldn't, he was evasive, finally responding, "You know who I'm with." Faubus later observed that Blossom's stay that night was briefer than usual, and it was "the last of our many private, friendly discussions."[56]

Upon reflection, Faubus realized that Blossom could not be forthcoming in the courtroom because "then I think perhaps the school board members would have known something which he may not have let them know. . . . and he was caught. Virgil was caught [between] two of the greatest conflicting forces that I've ever seen. And . . . actually I kind of sympathized with him." But as he thought it through, Faubus came to the conclusion that "I had 'been had.' I had been double crossed and betrayed by those I had dealt with in good faith." Despite his anger and disillusionment, Faubus claimed that he could never bring himself to believe "that Virgil Blossom was guilty of such perfidy of his own free will and accord. Someone or some group, I am convinced, took mental and verbal control of Virgil Blossom, assumed complete domination of his actions, gave him a 180-degree turn and set him on the course which became apparent in his testimony. He was never permitted to deviate from that course during his remaining months in Little Rock."[57]

In one day, themes had been etched into Orval Faubus's mind that shaped his thinking and actions for the rest of his life. Added to his long-standing grievance that the federal government should have assumed responsibility for implementing and enforcing its own court orders was the strong belief that he had been double-crossed and betrayed by people he had thought he was helping, as well as the unshakable conviction that those people were seeking national glory at his expense. Old Sam Faubus, the governor's father, said in later years that something had happened to change his son, to harden him and to turn him away from the idealism of his youth. While Sam Faubus could never identify the experience that had had such a profound impact on his son, Virgil Blossom's betrayal of Orval Faubus seems a likely candidate.[58]

WHEN FEDERAL JUDGE John Miller removed himself from involvement in the Little Rock school case, his action initiated a frenzy of activity in Little Rock. The ensuing frantic week was just the beginning of a siege that ultimately sank Virgil Blossom's plan for integration, his hopes for a political future, and his career in Arkansas. His lack of candor and fairness with Orval Faubus pushed the governor into an untenable position, and it proved to be the final straw. Faubus felt himself to be victimized by Attorney General Brownell, betrayed by Judge Miller, under siege by segregationists from across the southern region, and now made to look like a fool by the Little Rock School Board. Sincerely concerned about violence, though with his eye, as always, on his own political viability, Orval Faubus charted the only course he thought he could manage.

INTERREGNUM

THE CHOSEN FEW

T HE ENTIRE DRAMA CENTERED ON ONLY NINE STUDENTS. THAT THERE were not more is a tragedy, and one of the key stories of the crisis.

Two hundred black children had initially been eligible to attend Central High School under the Blossom Plan, because they lived in that attendance zone. Of these, only 70 to 80 expressed interest in transferring to the formerly all-white school. In the spring of 1957, Virgil Blossom instructed the black junior and senior high principals of those children's current schools to begin "screening" them.

One close observer became convinced that the purpose of this process was to talk the black children out of transferring to Central High. He understood that Blossom and the School Board were attempting "to desegregate legally without having any appreciable mixing of the races," that they wanted to do "the legal minimum."

Of the thirty-seven students who remained after the initial screening, Blossom required that they and their parents meet with him for interviews. Daisy Bates believed these interviews were designed to be intimidating and demeaning. She requested her own meeting between some representatives of the NAACP and the superintendent.[1]

The feisty Bates had made it her business to nettle Virgil Blossom over the past two years, and it gave her pleasure to do so. She had followed him around from one location to another as he made speeches all over Little Rock promoting his plan of gradualism and tokenism; she routinely asked vexing questions from the floor, pointing out that he was saying one thing to black audiences and another to white. Bates had long since decided she did not trust the burly superintendent, and the hard-driving former coach undoubtedly responded in kind.

At a June 2, 1957, meeting with Bates and several other African-Americans, Blossom explained that the "screening" he and the principals of the black junior high and high schools was conducting sought to ensure that the first year of integration would be a success. As the superintendent explained in his memoir, they

101

simply wanted to discourage students with weak academic standing, poor self-discipline, or emotional instability from attempting the transition, in an effort to assure that only those black children who would be "a credit to their race" would pioneer this historic effort.[2]

Bates saw a more ominous reality. Not only was the superintendent eliminating all students who wished to participate in such extracurricular activities as athletics, clubs, or the band, he had even discouraged one girl because she was "too pretty," saying all of the white boys would be attracted to her. Bates believed the real goal of the screening was to find the most timid students so they would drop out, or at the very least, not fight back. Whether this was true cannot be established at this late date; what is demonstrable is that not one of the thirty-three children involved in the NAACP's initial suit in January 1956 was selected to attend Central High School in the fall of 1957. NAACP attorney Wiley Branton believed the School Board intended to get "good Negroes and none of those radicals who sued us. They were [only] going to let a few good Negroes in."[3]

Daisy Bates also believed the School Board intended to select only "light Negroes" for the first Central High students. She claimed to have told Blossom, "We've got 215 kids. You can take the cream of the crop, or you can take all of them." He finally retorted in defense of the screening process, "I know it is undemocratic and I know it is wrong, but I am doing it." He also threatened to use the recently adopted Pupil Placement Act to effect a reduction of black participants if his critics did not go along with his interviews and dissuasion.[4]

The early June meeting with the Bates group came shortly after the Capital Citizens' Council published Robert Ewing Brown's open letter to the governor asking why Little Rock had to comply with the *Brown* decision when the Arkansas legislature had recently enacted laws protecting the state from such unwanted federal intrusion. Virgil Blossom and the board reacted to it with panic, unaccustomed as they were to criticism from the erstwhile silent, powerless masses. It made the screening process more urgent.

Daisy Bates used the youth arm of the NAACP, the Little Rock Youth Council, to find out what kinds of questions Blossom was asking in order to prepare as many children and parents as possible for their encounters with the superintendent. She worked in parallel with the Arkansas Council on Human Relations' summer program, which prepared black and white church youth groups for integration. She spent the summer encouraging black students, and their parents, to summon the courage to attend Central High School.[5]

Virgil Blossom eventually approved a grand total of only seventeen black children to attend Central High. Eight of them withdrew their applications the first day of the fall term, leaving the others to march into history as the Little Rock Nine. All of them were from stable, middle-class homes. All of them had parents who valued education and supported their decision to be pioneers for their race. All of them wanted to better themselves and thought the opportunities at Central High School offered the way up.

Elizabeth Eckford was the second of six children born to parents who both worked. Her mother taught blind black children laundry skills; her father worked for the railroad. Her grandfather, who doted on her, was an institution in the black community, an independent grocer who dealt fearlessly with all people, white as well as black. Shy to a fault, Elizabeth had babysat for a white doctor in the Heights, where she had seen a higher standard of living. Elizabeth wanted to be a lawyer, and she thought an education at Central High School would help her get there.[6]

Gloria Ray was the indulged youngest child of a retired, relatively affluent agricultural extension agent and a Welfare Department field worker. She had signed up to go to Central without her parents' permission; her father's first knowledge of it would be when he heard her name on the radio on September 4. Impish and cute, she wanted to be an atomic scientist. Her father had studied under George Washington Carver at the famed Tuskegee Institute.[7]

Jefferson Thomas had been president of the student body at Dunbar Junior High the year before, and he expected to succeed at Central before going on to study electronics in college. Although he was an athlete and had a good sense of humor, he was tentative and only fifteen, and he was destined to become a favorite target of segregationist abuse inside Central High.[8]

Carlotta Walls was the youngest of the group at fourteen, but she was tall, athletic, and good-humored, and she had grown up playing with white children in an integrated neighborhood. Her father was a brick mason who worked with integrated crews; he had fought in World War II and he said often that his tax dollars were not segregated. Her mother had completed three years of college. Carlotta was fearless and self-reliant, and she received relatively little abuse inside the walls of the formerly segregated school.[9]

Thelma Mothershed had been president of the National Honor Society at Dunbar Junior High, where she had made straight A's. Her father was a psychiatric nurse in the employ of the federal government; her mother was a housewife. Because of Thelma's heart problems her mother had refused when she asked permission to transfer to Central, but since the two older Mothershed girls were desegregation pioneers, Thelma persisted and eventually prevailed.[10]

Terrence Roberts was the best student in the group of nine, and perhaps for that reason he was to become one of the main targets of the segregationists. His father was a Navy veteran and a dietitian; his mother was a cateress. The large Roberts family were Seventh-Day Adventists and very religious. Terrence's father had attended meetings all summer discussing integration but remained ambivalent about his son's attending Central, until the governor's actions made it a matter of principle. When newsmen asked Terrence if the NAACP had pressured him to attend Central, the idealistic fifteen-year-old responded, "Nobody urged me to go. The school board asked if I wanted to go. I thought if I got in, some of the other children would be able to go . . . and have more opportunities."[11]

Pretty Melba Patillo wanted to be an entertainer. Vivacious and determined, she had copyrighted two songs, "Teen Age Dreams" and "Let's Make Up or Break Up." She spoke with perfect diction that persuaded her tormentors she had been imported from the North, a persistent rumor about the Nine that the NAACP eventually tried to dispel with a press release. Melba and her little brother and her mother, a teacher, lived with her grandmother, who was a shaping presence in the young teenager's life.[12]

Minnijean Brown, vivacious and outgoing, was the daughter of a stonemason and a practical nurse. Her father was determined that Minnie go to Central; her mother had to struggle with fears about her daughter's safety. Minnijean wanted to make friends and like most adolescents needed recognition. Even though she had studied nonviolence and worked hard not to respond to segregationist taunting, she was high-spirited and outspoken, and she became the primary target of the segregationists.[13]

Ernest Green was the only senior and the natural leader. His father had died when he was thirteen, and he had had to take a leadership role in the family. An Eagle Scout, a sports enthusiast, a church usher, he played the tenor sax, and he had had many jobs since he was eleven. The summer before going to Central he worked at Little Rock's Jewish Country Club, where he made friends with some of the white kids he would know at Central. The son and nephew of respected teachers, Ernest expected the transition to be smooth, and for him it was relatively so. Even if it had not been, he was willing to pay the price of being a pioneer; as he told one interviewer "it's cheap—because of what's involved." Almost fifty years later, Ernest Green reflected on his decision to attend Central High School. He had taken a "Negro history" course at Horace Mann; he had read about the Montgomery Bus Boycott and the Emmett Till murder; he had followed Jackie Robinson's career; he had watched his mother earn a Master's degree from the University of Arkansas by correspondence and then be barred from marching in the graduation procession. He had come to the conclusion that "if things were going to change, it wasn't going to be handed to you. And I always thought after the '54 decision that there might be a window in which I'd have an opportunity to play some sort of role, and I always said to myself that if that opportunity came I wanted to be there."[14]

As the Arkansas governor headed into the weekend that would change his life, and the nation's, these nine children and their parents prepared for what they hoped would be a bright new beginning in American education. The Little Rock Nine knew they were about to attempt something historic, but they had no idea how historic, or how challenging, it would be.

CHAPTER SIX

THE CRISIS BREAKS
Orval Faubus

BEADS OF SWEAT TRICKLED DOWN THE GOVERNOR'S NECK AND BACK, causing his shirt to stick to his skin in uncomfortable patches that shifted as he moved. A mountaineer, he had never grown accustomed to the suffocating summer humidity on the flatlands of central Arkansas, and he doubted he ever would. Even in his shirtsleeves, with his tie loose and askew, Orval Faubus could not escape the relentless, paralyzing heat that rose in dizzying waves from the scorching pavement and the parched earth. But late summer was also the season for campaigning in Arkansas, a time for barbeques, fish fries, water carnivals, and speeches. Most important, it was a time for meeting the people, *his* people, the little people he felt he understood and wanted to serve. Despite the heat, the gifted politician loved an Arkansas August.[1]

Orval Faubus had been born in a log cabin. A frail and quiet child, he had grown into a man of slight build and undistinguished features—except for the crooked nose, which became the centerpiece of many a political cartoon. Sensitive from childhood, he carried about himself an aura of sadness and a great dignity. He had clawed his way out of the mountain barrenness of his youth and had achieved distinction in both his nation's Army and his state's government. He had come through heavy fighting in World War II unscathed, although a majority of his unit had been killed, and he believed "Providence had spared him for some great purpose."[2]

Faubus had come to the governor's office filled with a passion to improve the lives of people who needed better schools, better health care, and better highways, and with extraordinary political courage and skill he had conceived and sponsored a legislative package that made these improvements possible. His political advisers had told him that the property reassessment at the heart of his 3 percent tax hike would alienate every tax assessor in the state, and that the taxpayers would abandon him in droves when they began to feel the pinch in their pocketbooks. Faubus had persisted and prevailed, and after his success in the legislative session in February of 1957, the executive secretary of the Arkansas Education Association, Forrest Rozzell, had come to the governor and asked him to consider running for a third term in the statehouse.[3]

Faubus had his eye on bigger game. He had been touted as a possible vice presidential candidate in 1956, with both Adlai Stevenson and Averell Harriman floating the suggestion they might consider him. The United States congressman in his district had been in poor health, but until Jim Trimble decided to step aside, Faubus's strong sense of loyalty prevented him from running against his former political mentor. He seems to have had his heart set on the Senate seat held by J. William Fulbright, but that seat would not come available again until 1962. In the murky interim until the governor's political prospects clarified, Orval Faubus's first concern in the spring of 1957 was to remain politically viable, whether or not he ran for a third term. He thought initially he might be able to accomplish this by naming his successor and retaining control of certain patronage appointments. But as the year unfolded and the segregationist resistance intensified, Faubus, the savvy navigator and strategist, could see only danger in the troubled waters ahead.[4]

ON FRIDAY MORNING, August 30, 1957, the day after his "betrayal" by both Superintendent Blossom and Judge Miller, Governor Faubus convened a meeting of his department heads and commissioners. Apprising his "official family" of the reports he had received, from unnamed sources, of an increase in the sales of guns and knives in Pulaski County, and of a flurry of telephone calls "from persons who feared violence and trouble if integration should take place," Faubus remarked that it had never been his policy to interfere with integration. He told his Cabinet he had repeatedly advised his callers "he was not for or against integration in this matter, but only in preserving peace and order." He also told them there were towns already integrated and some about to be integrated "in which he took no part and which he intended to take no part if these towns should desire to peacefully integrate their schools."[5]

The governor then invited discussion regarding the question of "whether to take a precautionary step or wait until some violence actually occurred over the integration issue before doing anything about it." The majority of his Cabinet responded that if he thought trouble was brewing "he should certainly act in preventing violence." Herman Lindsey, director of the Arkansas State Police, endorsed the governor's assessment of the situation. At the governor's direction, Lindsey had used the state police to conduct his own investigation of the threat of violence, and he was alarmed by his findings.[6]

Arkansas State Comptroller Kelly Cornett informed Federal Bureau of Investigation interviewers a week later that someone at this meeting had suggested the possible use of the National Guard and the political consequences that would arise from such an action, and that Governor Faubus had "declared that he was not concerned with the political aspects of such action, and that his only concern was . . . the prevention of any violence." Cornett also recalled that Faubus made the statement that he would consider calling out the National Guard "only as the last resort to maintain the peace and order." Of course as members of the governor's Cabinet, these men were Faubus loyalists, and they would have been inclined to put the most favorable slant on the governor's actions in their interviews with the FBI.[7]

Faubus inquired what the law "would allow him to do in regard to calling out the National Guard," but no one knew the answer and the meeting seemed to be at a stalemate. At length Insurance Commissioner Harvey Combs suggested that no decision be made until after that day's rehearing of the Thomason suit in federal court; if the visiting federal judge upheld Murray Reed's injunction preventing the Little Rock School Board from proceeding with its plans for integration, which Faubus thought was highly unlikely, then the questions the governor's advisers were discussing would become moot. About 12:15 P.M. the Cabinet meeting adjourned. Faubus directed Sherman Clinger, adjutant general of the Arkansas National Guard, to place the Guard on alert status.[8]

VIRGIL BLOSSOM WROTE in his memoir that Judge Murray Reed's injunction against starting integration "left the School Board dangling between conflicting federal and state court orders" and that the board thereupon instructed Archie House to go immediately to the federal district court "to ask for relief." With Judge Miller recused, that put a recently appointed jurist, Judge Ronald N. Davies, in the spotlight. He had been in Little Rock for only three days when he received the call from Chief Judge Archibald Gardner assigning him to the Little Rock school case. Davies invited Archie House and National Association for the Advancement of Colored People attorney Wiley Branton into his chambers for a private conference. Following the meeting, House formally filed a petition in United States District Court requesting that Mrs. Clyde Thomason "and the class she represents be enjoined from using in any manner the Order of the Pulaski County Chancery Court . . . , and that they be enjoined from taking any steps in said Pulaski Chancery Court which might cause [the school officials] to be punished for contempt in treating the order of that court as void and in proceeding to integrate on September 3, 1957, ..."[9]

In an amendment to his petition, House also requested that if the court allowed a postponement of the Blossom Plan, the judge should also "define specifically the responsibilities and duties of [the school officials]." NAACP attorney Wiley Branton noted years later he was "strongly of the view that most of the school officials were really hoping that the court would find a need to delay the implementation of the integration plan and that they preferred this relief rather than any injunction against Mrs. Thomason."[10]

Judge Davies granted the School Board's petition for an injunction, concluding that the Pulaski County Chancery Court lacked jurisdiction to interfere with the operations of the Little Rock School Board's federal court-approved plan of integration. He then proceeded to order "that Mrs. Clyde Thomason, and the Class she represents, *and all others*" be enjoined from using the state court order to prevent or interfere with the opening of the integrated high schools in Little Rock. Years later Wiley Branton described Davies's demeanor as a "no-nonsense judge," and the new jurist certainly acted with dispatch in demanding that the Blossom Plan be allowed to proceed.[11]

The School Board had begun to get wind of Faubus's potential use of the National Guard. One member heard from a neighbor, whose daughter was dating a Guardsman, that at his unit's last drill the young soldier was instructed to bring his firing pin in his rifle rather than leave it at home. The School Board quickly concluded that Orval Faubus had decided to use their dilemma at Central High for his own political gain. Virgil Blossom shared this suspicion with Harry Ashmore and Hugh Patterson, and Orval Faubus's opportunism became an article of faith in Harry Ashmore's thinking from that day forward.[12]

On Friday night the School Board members invited Faubus to an evening meeting at their favorite haunt, the lovely old Albert Pike Hotel downtown. Three of the board's attorneys were present, Archie House, Richard Butler, and Frank Chowning, as was Superintendent Blossom. Faubus did not think to take a lawyer or an aide with him and he immediately felt overmatched; as he recalled years later, "They were all together. I was alone."[13]

Faubus waited "coolly" to learn the purpose of the meeting, and after some preliminary pleasantries one of the School Board members held up a copy of that afternoon's *Arkansas Democrat*, which carried the story that North Carolina Governor Luther Hodges had announced he would tolerate no disorder in his state when school opened the following week. Brick Lile, who was seated next to Faubus, said, "Now, Governor, we're not expecting you to be for integration. What we're expecting you to do and asking you to do is to make the same sort of announcement . . . that you're going to see that there's no violence, that you're going to maintain law and order."[14] This was the statement of assurance that Virgil Blossom had been trying to secure from the governor all summer.

Lile's recollection was that Faubus responded he "couldn't do that, it wouldn't be good politics." At length Virgil Blossom blurted out that the School Board simply had to know what the governor was planning to do. Blossom's blunt manner, added to his performance in Judge Reed's court the day before, offended the governor and left him thinking, "They must have thought they were dealing with a country bumpkin, a coward, or a vacillating weakling. . . . The group's attitude was more one of disdain than hospitality although I was a guest at the members' request." Faubus's social insecurities colored his judgment; in addition his deepest fear, of being made to look like a fool, now had him in its grasp.[15]

In Harold Engstrom's description, Faubus at this point "turned as pale as a sheet and asked to be excused. And he got up and went to the . . . restroom. And somehow or other we got the impression that he vomited. And he came back in the room and just had a hard time talking and wouldn't commit himself to what he was going to do." Engstrom recalled Faubus eventually offered "a politician's answer to the question in which he talked about it a lot but he didn't say anything conclusively. . . . He was very convincing, that he was interested in the problem and trying to do what he thought was best. But we were not reassured very much that he was going to do what we thought he should do." Many years later Harold Engstrom reflected, "I believe the man was in more turmoil than Virgil Blossom was in, . . . and more turmoil than we were in."[16]

Orval Faubus's perception of the meeting with the School Board differed significantly from the reports of his adversaries. In his recollections, he looked around that private dining room on the second floor of the Albert Pike Hotel and his gaze moved from Dr. William G. Cooper, "the immigrant Northerner," who "bore an attitude of superiority"; to Brick Lile, who, as "a business associate and satellite of Winthrop Rockefeller" could be expected to be an integrationist; to Wayne Upton, who "appeared nervous, his eyes shifting about in his pallid features"; to Virgil Blossom, who was "nervous and hesitant"; to Archie House, who had "deliberately sought to avoid disclosure of evidence in Judge Reed's court." Clearly, Faubus was in the presence of people he did not feel he could trust. As he told an interviewer over a decade later, he had been "double-crossed by the School Board . . . and then they wanted him to bail them out."[17]

In Faubus's telling of the tale he informed the School Board that if they were correct in their predictions that there would be no trouble at Central High, as they had reported in both state and federal courts in the last few days, "then I will do nothing, for there will be nothing for me to do." He reminded the board that he had no authority in their school district. "This is your problem and your responsibility." His problem was the maintenance of law and order. He did not want any "disorder or rioting in this city with damage to property and injury to people as have occurred for the past two years in other sections of the nation, and which are occurring now as all of you know."[18]

Faubus reported that his information, which he had "carefully and diligently gathered" over the past several days, was at variance with the School Board's pronouncements that the Blossom Plan could "become a model for all of Arkansas and for the South." To the contrary, based on Faubus's information, there was "a good possibility of trouble." He concluded that if there were "disorder or the dire threat of disorder and violence, then I will use my best judgment based on the best information I can obtain, and act accordingly. I can't tell you what I'm going to do, because I have no way of knowing myself. My actions will be determined by developments, whatever those developments may be, and my evaluation of the situation."[19]

The next day, the Saturday before school opening on Tuesday, the Little Rock School Board issued a public statement signed by all six members saying that because of Judge Davies's order they were "compelled to proceed" with the first phase of desegregation of the schools. With characteristic lack of force they concluded, "We earnestly solicit and confidently expect the understanding and cooperation of all students and adults in the peaceful solution of this difficult problem, in order that the best interests of all may continue to be served."[20]

A FEW MONTHS EARLIER, in late spring of 1957, probably after the Capital Citizens' Council published its open letter calling on the governor to use his police powers to block integration, Faubus had discussed with at least one of his allies the possibility of blocking integration at Central High School. Wayne Glenn was executive secretary of the Arkansas AFL-CIO, and as an ally of Sid McMath and Henry Woods he had worked in both of Faubus's gubernatorial campaigns. When he began to hear rumors that the governor was considering interfering with the federal court order, he called Faubus and scheduled a Sunday afternoon visit. The two men talked in the governor's capitol office for four hours, with Faubus saying repeatedly, "I'm not going to enforce the Court's orders. In fact, I'm going to see to it that the Feds have to enforce it." For weeks, if not months, then, Faubus had been pondering his options.[21]

On Saturday, August 31, Faubus received a telephone call from his favorite reporter at the *Arkansas Democrat*, George Douthit. Douthit informed him he had just read a dispatch from the Washington bureau of the *New York Times* revealing that Arthur Caldwell had met in Little Rock with Faubus. Caldwell had asked the Arkansas governor to keep their meeting confidential and Faubus had complied with that request. Certain that he had been betrayed again, the governor was livid, replying to Douthit, "They told me to keep this confidential. That just shows how much faith you can put in the national administration." Faubus continued heatedly that the government was "cramming integration down our throats, but they are going to make us handle the enforcement of their own orders."[22]

U.S. Attorney Osro Cobb's office staff sprang into action after they received word that Governor Faubus would be quoted in the afternoon paper to the effect that the federal government had no means of enforcing its own orders. Warning that the "full resources" of the United States Justice Department stood ready to enforce Judge Davies's orders prohibiting interference with the School Board's integration program, these federal officials based in Little Rock issued a statement explaining that Judge Davies could direct the FBI to investigate any alleged violations of his injunction. "This announcement," they continued, "is in accordance with the statement of President Eisenhower made several months ago that the Justice Department stands ready to step into integration cases at any time the local district court requests it."[23] The Justice Department was implementing damage control in response to Arthur Caldwell's clumsy handling of the Arkansas governor.

At some point during that long Saturday, Sid McMath and Henry Woods called their former protégé to tell him, as McMath later recalled, "that if he mobilized the Guard and opposed the admission of these children to the high school, that he would have a confrontation with the United States government, and that it would not only cast a cloud on our state, but it would do irreparable damage to the United States in the eyes of the world, particularly among the uncommitted countries." At the same time, McMath also suggested, "I couldn't tell him that it wouldn't help him. I told him that I thought maybe it would elect him. . . ." Though Orval Faubus claimed steadfastly until his death almost forty years later that he had not yet decided to seek a third term, nobody believed him.[24]

Henry Woods recalled that many other people telephoned Governor Faubus over the weekend, trying to discourage him from defying the federal courts.

Harry Ashmore, Hugh Patterson, and Sid McMath spent "endless hours" that weekend in Virgil Blossom's room at the Sam Peck Hotel "trying to figure out how Faubus could be persuaded not to follow this reckless course. . . ." Ashmore remembered the "blank check" the governor had offered him in 1954 and wondered aloud if he should try to cash that blank check now, but Patterson discouraged him. "I remember asking Hugh if he thought that I should go out and try to talk to Orval," Ashmore recalled years later, "and Hugh said no, let's don't touch the son of a bitch, . . . we don't want to get compromised with whatever he's going to do." If Ashmore and Patterson had not been so convinced that Faubus was operating strictly from political motives, the Little Rock situation might have ended very differently.[25]

Arkansas Gazette reporter Tom Davis told an audience thirty years later that he found Virgil Blossom in a hotel room that weekend, and that Blossom "had turned to jelly." Harry Ashmore wrote of Blossom, "Virgil was near hysteria, and tended to gibber under the best of circumstances. . . ." Completely distraught, the big man could see the Blossom Plan, and his own political viability, going up in smoke. Despite his courtroom protestations that he expected no violence at Central High School, Blossom met on Saturday morning with Assistant U.S. Attorney James F. Gallman, Police Chief Marvin Potts, and Archie House in an effort to gain "assurance as to what could be done to enforce the Court's order should there be any violations of it."[26]

LATE SATURDAY NIGHT Virgil Blossom and Brick Lile drove the sixty-five miles out of Little Rock to Petit Jean Mountain to see Winthrop Rockefeller at his fabulous Santa Gertrudis cattle operation, Winrock Farms. Lile was Rockefeller's accountant and friend; Rockefeller was Lile's major client. Rockefeller had worked closely with the governor as director of the Arkansas Industrial Development Commission, one of Faubus's premier initiatives, and Blossom and Lile were hoping to persuade him to use his influence with the state's chief executive to forestall any planned use of the National Guard at Central High School.[27]

Harry Ashmore in the meantime wrote an editorial for use in Sunday morning's newspaper. Titled "A Time of Testing" and placed conspicuously at the top right of Page One, Ashmore's editorial praised Judge Davies's "clear and forthright ruling in the Little Rock school case," claiming that the judge had "swept away the legal confusion generated by the apparent conflict between state and federal laws." The Little Rock editor argued that although "there are those who have suggested" violence would occur when fifteen Negro children enrolled at Central High School along with more than two thousand whites, those doomsayers had "too little faith in the respect of our people for law and order." Offering up words of support for the School Board by writing that it was "simply carrying out its clear duty," Ashmore concluded, "We are confident that the citizens of Little Rock will demonstrate on Tuesday for the world to see that we are a law-abiding people."[28]

Orval Faubus had a firmer grasp than the celebrated editor of the elements controlling popular thought in Arkansas. As he wrote in his memoir, "The editorial referred to 'changes in the law,' and the people asked, 'What change in what law?' Congress made federal laws, not the Supreme Court. Judge Davies could make no law." Faubus knew that in the eyes of most Arkansas people, a call for law and order was a "hypocritical way of calling for integration." In short, Faubus argued, Ashmore's editorials "had no influence in cooling the anger of the people or in clearing the air of confusion."[29]

FAUBUS HEARD A great deal on Sunday from what he called his "little people," waiters, hairdressers, bartenders, etc., who were in a position to overhear discussions and pass on information from their unsuspecting clients, and who recognized Orval Faubus as one of their own. Repeatedly he heard that the Central High Mothers' League had organized a telephone campaign for the next day. He also heard reports of a more alarming kind, such as Arkansas State Police Director Herman Lindsey's announcement that he had disarmed one old fellow who had threatened to gun down any Negro children who attempted to integrate Central High School on Tuesday.[30]

Probably of equal significance, the governor received a telegram from his old foe Jim Johnson congratulating him, in a message Johnson had also released to the Associated Press, for his recent published comments in support of state sovereignty. Johnson's wire said no court could interfere with the governor in preserving domestic tranquility, and it suggested that Governor Allan Shivers of Texas, in the Mansfield case the year before, "gave you ample precedent to follow in the face of a federal court order." Johnson had been using his network of political connections to sustain a swarm of telephone calls to the governor, and his pressure on Faubus to move in support of protecting "the southern way of life" was ultimately so effective that it robbed the fiery segregationist of his own political base. Members of the Capital Citizens' Council, especially Wesley Pruden, Malcolm Taylor, and Robert Ewing Brown, also orchestrated a stream of calls to the governor all through the weekend.[31]

The phone calls hit their mark. Governor Faubus moved a step closer

toward intervening in the Little Rock situation when Bill Smith and his law partner Pat Mehaffy came to the Mansion and Faubus asked Smith to write a proclamation for potential use in mobilizing the National Guard. Smith was alarmed
by the idea. As many of Faubus's other advisers had already suggested, Smith
counseled a course of prudence, saying, "Governor, there'll always be those
who'll say that there was no real and apparent danger of a breach of the peace,
and you're the preservator of the peace, I know that, under the constitution. But
the safest thing for you to do is to wait for trouble to erupt and then you can call
the Guard." Orval Faubus responded to this advice in words that his attorney
never forgot, conveying a message that Bill Smith said later was "a pretty hard
thing for a man to say to another." According to Smith's recollection, Faubus
said, "Bill, I've been elected to keep the peace, that's my responsibility . . . and
you're asking me to follow the course of a moral weakling. You're asking me to
let somebody's blood be shed to protect my political position."[32]

As Smith recalled with clarity almost fifteen years later, Faubus then said,
"Now, I know in the long run I can't win, as an office holder. If I call out the
Guard and there's no trouble, people will always say, particularly those people
who hate me and I've got my share of those and going to get some new ones out
of this, that there never would have been any trouble." (And in fact, this is precisely what Harry Ashmore would say for the rest of his life.) "On the other
hand, if I don't call out the Guard, people will say that I knew there was going
to be a race riot and I didn't have courage enough to stop it before it occurred."
Smith encouraged his client to delay making a definite decision about using the
state militia. Faubus agreed to do so, and Smith left after the long Sunday meeting thinking the governor would not make up his mind about using the
National Guard until after school opened Tuesday morning.[33]

While Faubus and his attorney were meeting at the state capitol, Virgil Blossom held a meeting several blocks away with the black students who had survived the screening process and still wanted to attend Central High School. He
employed several means of persuasion to encourage them to return to Horace
Mann. This was the first time the full group had assembled and they, along with
their parents and the uninvited Daisy Bates, met in Superintendent Blossom's
office, ostensibly to get instructions regarding the first day of school.[34]

The lone senior, Ernest Green, looked around the room in surprise that so
few students were there.[35] The son and nephew of respected teachers, Green had
wanted to transfer to Central because he knew it was a more rigorous school
than Horace Mann, and he hoped by doing so he would strengthen his chances
of earning a college scholarship.[36] Shy Elizabeth Eckford had imbibed the mes-

sage of her black teachers that she had an obligation to her race to improve herself and help lift her race by going to college. She knew that an education at Central High School would offer her many more advantages than Horace Mann.[37] Tiny Thelma Mothershed wanted to go to Central simply because her two best friends, Minnijean Brown and Melba Patillo, had said "Let's do it!" and she was thrilled as she entered the room to see that the two of them had also passed Blossom's rigorous inspection.[38]

Focusing on more substantive issues, the parents were dismayed by Blossom's requirement that they not accompany their children to school on the first day. Imogene Brooks Brown, Minnijean's mother, asked repeatedly if her child would be safe.[39] The superintendent suggested that in the event of conflict it would be easier to protect the children if black adults were not in the picture.[40] After a summer of escalating segregationist rhetoric in the newspapers and in numerous public meetings, the prospect of placing their children in harm's way required extraordinary courage and resolve from these seemingly ordinary parents.[41]

Blossom attempted to dissuade some of the children and parents who were wavering by promising them that if they would go to Horace Mann for the first few days, they could transfer to Central High after the semester had started. Eight of the seventeen eventually took him up on his offer, undoubtedly responding as well to the frightening rumors and threats that were swirling around Little Rock. Blossom, however, reneged on his promise. As Bates recalled, "When the nine went into Central, these children appealed to the school board again for admittance. They were told then to wait until things quieted down." Things never quieted down.[42]

A FEW HOURS AFTER Faubus and Smith finished their conference in the governor's office, Faubus drove downtown to meet Winthrop Rockefeller at the Albert Pike Hotel. Rockefeller had made an urgent call that morning requesting a meeting with the governor. Faubus always regretted that he went alone. Rockefeller brought with him one of his assistants at the Arkansas Industrial Development Commission, Bill Ewald.[43]

From the moment he arrived, Rockefeller worked to persuade Faubus to use the power of the state to implement the federal court order. The Arkansas governor suspected that the Republican Rockefeller had been sent to confer with him at the request of the White House, and with some heat he replied, "How can I assist the federal authorities when they are unprepared to do anything and whose official policy is to do nothing?"[44]

When the governor revealed he had alerted the Arkansas State Police and the Arkansas National Guard, Rockefeller suggested that the use of the National Guard in defiance of a federal court order "would be a serious blow to the state and the Arkansas Industrial Development Commission." Faubus commented that "violence would be even worse." Undaunted, Rockefeller pressed ahead, suggesting that Governor Faubus do as Luther Hodges had done in North Carolina by making a public pronouncement that he would not tolerate violence when school opened on Tuesday in Little Rock. Faubus pointed out that Texas Governor Shivers had used the National Guard at Mansfield the previous year and integration there had been halted and bloodshed averted. With some consternation, Rockefeller confessed to Brick Lile and Virgil Blossom after the meeting that he "doubted that he had influenced the Governor's position."[45]

In his interview with the FBI a week later, Rockefeller also reported that Faubus "appeared to be more concerned about political obligations and the future than he was with the integration of Little Rock schools." He said Faubus told him that his 1956 platform of "moderate segregation" had saved the state from the racial extremists, and if he did not hold the support of eastern Arkansas, then Jim Johnson, Amis Guthridge, and Bruce Bennett, the ambitious, segregationist attorney general, would take over the political life of the state in the next election. Many years later, Faubus recalled he had told Rockefeller, "if I should do some of the things you are suggesting that I do, you'd be dealing with Jim Johnson in the next term, because it would give them the ammunition which they need and the issues there, not handled properly, could be fatal." Despite their differences, Faubus and Rockefeller parted amicably, and according to uncorroborated information reported by the flamboyant and mercurial Jimmy Karam they went to another room in the Albert Pike, where they joined Harry Ashmore, Hugh Patterson, Virgil Blossom, and Rockefeller's attorney, Edwin Dunaway, in a party that was already under way.[46]

Jimmy Karam claimed he had moved into the Governor's Mansion about a week before in order to screen Faubus's phone calls to assure that only staunch segregationists got through to talk to the governor. He also contended that he went everywhere with Faubus, and press reports from that time did make frequent mention of his being in the governor's company. Karam reported that on this particular night the Ashmore group told Faubus they were going to make him "the biggest man in the world, biggest man in America." Despite Karam's efforts to align Faubus with the segregationists, he had the feeling that the governor was about to yield to Ashmore's charm and persuasive powers—he was "just on the verge of it," it was "nip and tuck."[47]

Faubus and Ashmore had been friends and occasional social companions up to this point, and Faubus reported years later that he missed the jovial editor after the Little Rock crisis caused them to part company. Apparently Karam had good reason to be "scared to death" that Ashmore could influence Faubus, and from that night forward he "did not let a man get on that phone or a woman that thought their way. Nobody." From then on, Karam claimed, he did not let anybody get information to Faubus "except what we wanted him to have. We wouldn't let him go to conferences, wouldn't let him get on the phone—all the people he thought was calling him was everybody that thought just one way. . . . 'There's going to be blood in the streets.' Oh yes. That's all he heard."[48]

Orval Faubus got back to the Governor's Mansion about ten o'clock that evening, picked up the telephone, and invited Virgil Blossom to come for a late-night visit after this very long day. Blossom soon arrived and the two men conferred for about three hours. The superintendent later wrote in his memoir that he did most of the talking, "and at times the Governor seemed to be sunk in serious meditation." At several points Blossom thought Faubus was going to agree to issue the statement the School Board had requested, and he could sense that the governor was deeply conflicted. Blossom pleaded, "Governor, we have worked almost three years to get past this problem peacefully. We will now succeed if only you will issue a statement that you will not tolerate defiance of the law." Faubus shook his head. "I'll call you when I decide," he said, "but I don't think I'm going to let you do it." Faubus told Blossom he would know at nine-thirty the next morning what, if any, public statement would be made. The next morning, Labor Day, gubernatorial aide Claude Carpenter called the superintendent to say there would be no statement.[49]

THE MOTIVES BEHIND Orval Faubus's decision to station the Arkansas National Guard at Little Rock Central High School were discussed and dissected in a frenzy of analysis by journalists at the time and by numerous historians in the years afterward. With few exceptions commentators followed Harry Ashmore's lead and argued that Faubus simply used the emotional issue of race to win a third term in the Arkansas statehouse. Rarely in the years since has Orval Faubus been given a forum to explain his actions on his own terms. An extraordinary interview that Faubus gave to the Eisenhower Administration Project was an exception to this pattern.[50]

In 1971 Columbia University Oral History Program interviewer John Luter asked Governor Faubus if he had decided to run for a third term when he called out the National Guard. Faubus answered, "No. But I had always had the idea that I might, and I still fully believe . . . that I could have been elected to a third term had this never occurred. . . . Of course, my enemies promoted the idea, you know, that I did it for political gain, because your enemies seldom attribute anything to you except ulterior motives. This is the law and the nature of politics. . . ." But despite his detractors' analysis of his opportunism, Faubus thought he could have survived without the Little Rock crisis because "we had done something that, if the Little Rock situation hadn't occurred, was as dramatic as anything that had occurred in Arkansas in years and years." That was the program of tax increases he had put through the legislature in early 1957 that had enabled "every school in Arkansas for the first time in all its history to have a full nine month term, teachers' salaries being increased over 100 percent, welfare grants more than 100 percent. . . ." So many good things had been created for the people of Arkansas that "everyone was happy, and when people are happy and doing well, they'll usually support the incumbent."[51]

Faubus felt Virgil Blossom was a large part of his problem with the school crisis. "Virgil was ambitious," Faubus told Luter. "He'd had a successful career in Fayetteville just 30 miles from where I lived, and then he'd moved to Little Rock, and somehow or other he got imbued with all these delusions of glory, and then when he'd get in a crisis he'd vacillate. I don't blame him for being concerned. It was one hell of a situation for a man to be in." Luter asked if Blossom's ambitions were political or if they were confined to educational circles, and Faubus answered, ". . . he was already talking about running for governor. Some of his friends were talking about running him, and you see, after he got into the thing, well, it's kind of like Napoleon at Waterloo, you know. He could see all the glory or all the degradation, one way or the other." Faubus always maintained that had it not been for the widespread publicity Blossom and his allies sought and obtained for their efforts, Little Rock could have integrated peacefully.[52]

His decision made, Faubus called in his top aides, administrative assistants Claude Carpenter and Kay Matthews, and Executive Secretary Arnold Sikes, and informed them of the course he had charted. About noon he issued the order to Adjutant General Sherman T. Clinger to station the National Guard around Central High School that night at 9:00. When an aide called the local television station to reserve air time for the governor to make an evening address to the people of Arkansas, that was the first public indication the governor had arrived at a decision.[53]

Faubus then summoned Bill Smith. As they sat facing each other across the governor's big desk, Bill Smith listened while Orval Faubus explained what he had decided to do, saying, "Bill, we're going to have bloodshed. We're going to have a race riot. I've got the evidence, without question. I've had my troopers out, private investigators, checking, and we've got the evidence. I'm going to call out the guard. I'm going to stop it before it occurs." The governor continued: "I want you to tell me what my legal rights are and legal responsibilities. . . ." Smith read him the pertinent portions of the state constitution, the necessary provisions, and the implementing statutes. The two men discussed them at some length, and then Faubus concluded, "I want you to write me a proclamation, to activate the Guard."[54]

Years later Orval Faubus remembered saying to his friend and counselor when Smith protested, "All right, Bill, I'm placing myself in the same place as a parent out there who has a child going to school." Striking to the heart of the matter, Faubus continued: "Suppose a mother, black or white, comes into this office and sits across the desk from me where you are sitting now and inquires of me, 'Governor, you testified in court that you had heard of possible violence at the high school. Did you believe there was going to be trouble?'" Faubus knew that if his reply was "yes," as he now thought it would have to be, that mother could ask in all fairness "Then why didn't you do something to stop it? If you had acted my child would still be alive today." He told his attorney that while he appreciated his concern for the governor, he did not call Smith to his office to discuss the matter. "My decision is already made. I will use the Guard if I judge it to be necessary. I called you here to write the proclamation for me. If I get into trouble, you will bear no part of the blame for you have had no part in the decision." Smith wrote the order.[55]

About two-thirty P.M., while Faubus was talking to Bill Smith about the course he had decided to pursue, the phone rang. Virgil Blossom was on the other end of the line, very excited. At this point the story diverges, depending on who is telling the tale. Faubus in his memoir wrote that Blossom was "more excited and agitated than I had ever heard him . . . ," expressing alarm over reports he was receiving of caravans that were converging on Little Rock from Texarkana, El Dorado, Crossett, and Monticello, and concluding, "One group has already arrived from northeast Arkansas and a number of them are now at the Marion Hotel." Faubus recalled he asked Blossom, "Virgil, . . . do you think you need protection?" And Blossom replied emphatically "Yes, I do!" Remembering the "double-dealing" he felt he had experienced at Blossom's hands in Judge Reed's courtroom, Faubus replied cautiously, "All right, Virgil, . . . you write out a brief statement to that effect. It need not be long. Just state that in view of the reports you have received of opposition to integration which may lead to disorder, and which may jeopardize your safety and the safety of your home, that you feel you need protection." Faubus then offered to send a state police officer to pick up the note, and upon his receipt of the note, "I will provide you with all the police protection that you need." Blossom hesitated, and then said, "I'll call you back." He never called.[56]

Faubus referred to this call in his televised address that night, necessitating an explanation from Virgil Blossom. In his own memoir, Blossom stated he had called Faubus to request information about whom Police Chief Potts should call in case of an emergency. While he was trying to get the governor on the line, his secretary came into his office, "pale and shaken," to tell him that an anonymous telephone call had just been received saying that "several extremist segregation leaders from other parts of the state had arrived or would soon arrive in Little Rock with more than 150 others who were 'out to get Blossom.'" Blossom instructed his secretary to call the police, and by the time he got Faubus on the telephone, a police lieutenant was sitting beside his desk. Blossom claimed that he asked the governor for the information the police chief needed, and then he "also mentioned the anonymous warning I had received, and asked him where I could get in touch with the director of State Police in an emergency." According to Blossom the governor asked, "Do you need protection?" and the superintendent responded, "Do you think I need protection?" In Blossom's version Faubus then suggested, "I wish you would write me a letter asking for it," to which Blossom replied, "You know I won't do that," and hung up the telephone. Blossom recalled that he turned to Lieutenant Carl Jackson and said, "I think Governor Faubus himself is behind this program of intimidation."[57]

Several blocks away from both the Governor's Mansion and the School Board office, Harry Ashmore and Hugh Patterson launched a campaign against Orval Faubus, an effort that eventually cost the *Arkansas Gazette* a million dollars in lost subscriptions and advertising. Feeling keenly their responsibility to be fair with Mr. Heiskell, who owned the paper and would sustain the losses, Ashmore and Patterson met with the old gentleman in his office at the *Gazette* building that Labor Day afternoon. They gave "Mr. J. N." their assessment of Faubus's intentions and motivations, and of the probable effect on Heiskell's beloved community. In Ashmore's words, J. N. Heiskell sat for a long moment looking out his office window at the town he had lived in and loved all his adult life, and then he said, "I'm an old man and I've lived too long to let people like that take over my city." With the old editor's blessing, and not dreaming that their actions would be so costly for the newspaper, Ashmore and Patterson inaugurated a lonely offensive against what they perceived to be the forces of both misguided ambition and a discredited past.[58]

Late in the afternoon all of the School Board members except Dale Alford gathered at the Albert Pike for a hastily convened meeting to discuss the new developments. Wayne Upton reported to the group that Governor Faubus was going to tell the people "that Negroes would not be allowed in Central High School" on Tuesday, "and that the militia would be called out for the purpose of establishing peace and order." Blossom reported in his memoir that he got a call from "a newspaperman" during the meeting asking, "Did you hear Faubus is calling out the Guard?" Not long after that, about 9:00, Harry Ashmore called Virgil Blossom to tell him that Central High School was surrounded by soldiers and that the governor would speak at 10:15. "My God!" said Blossom, and the meeting broke up, to hear Faubus on TV. Harold Engstrom reported that the School Board watched "with astonishment and dismay" as Orval Faubus in a twenty-five minute speech wrecked their plans for an orderly process of integration at Central High.[59]

The governor began by describing in elaborate detail the recent accomplishments Arkansas had made in improving the lot of its black citizens. "These facts are given as irrefutable proof," Faubus suggested, "that the citizens of Arkansas have not been unmindful of their problems as they relate to the good relations of the races and that the citizenship as a whole have met their responsibilities. . . ." However, he said, since the federal District Court at Little Rock had ruled the past Friday that integration must proceed, "the evidence of discord, anger and resentment has come to me from so many sources as to become a deluge." The governor listed seven areas of concern: 1) Virgil Blossom had appealed to him for protection; 2) a telephone campaign "of massive proportions" was under way calling on the mothers of white children to assemble at Central High Tuesday morning; 3) caravans were descending on Little Rock from many parts of the state and were planning to converge on the high school as well; 4) numerous telephone calls had come into the governor's office and home expressing fear of disorder and violence; 5) according to police reports, unusually large numbers of weapons had been sold in the Little Rock area, "mostly to Negro youths" but many to whites; 6) several revolvers had been taken from high school students, both black and white; 7) litigation "seeking to determine the validity of recently enacted state segregation laws" had not been concluded. Referring to this last point the governor said, "I feel strongly that time should be given to litigate these measures to final conclusion in order that we may see clearly and unmistakably what is the law of the land—either state or federal. . . ."[60]

Because of all these concerns, Faubus announced he had come "prayerfully" to the decision to place units of the National Guard and the state police at Central High School "with the mission to maintain or restore the peace and good order of this community." Faubus insisted that the state militia would not act "as segregationists or integrationists," but would "protect the lives and property of citizens." He ended his speech, however, by saying that since it would not be possible for the soldiers to accomplish their mission "if forcible integration is carried out tomorrow in the schools of this community . . . ," the "inevitable conclusion" must be that the schools in Pulaski County "must be operated on the same basis as they have been operated in the past." The governor was in effect calling for, and enabling, the maintenance of segregation.[61]

This was the point at which Orval Faubus seemed to cross the line and embrace massive resistance, although he had not yet bought fully into that philosophy. While he used the language of the resisters in his speech when he railed against "forcible integration," the governor did not, in his written orders, specify that the black children should be turned away from Central High School. Those orders proclaimed only that a state of emergency existed in Pulaski County and that as a consequence the governor was calling into active duty certain units of the state militia "to accomplish the mission of maintaining or restoring law and order and to preserve the peace, health, safety and security of the citizens of Pulaski County, Arkansas."[62]

All across the city people looked at one another and asked, "What did he say?" The *Arkansas Gazette* reported that within an hour after the governor finished his speech, the newspaper's switchboard received more than a dozen calls from people asking, "Is there going to be integration tomorrow? Should I send my child to school tomorrow? What did he say?" Assistant U.S. Attorney James F. Gallman believed and reported to his superiors that Faubus had been vague on purpose, in order to avoid stating openly that he was interfering with the process of integration and thereby placing himself in danger of being found in contempt of court. Faubus maintained in the days and years ahead that he was not trying to "interpose" himself between the people of Arkansas and the federal court system, he was simply attempting to preserve the peace.[63]

Virgil Blossom, like many, found himself swirling in a sea of confusion. At Archie House's insistence, the School Board voted to keep the ten remaining black children who wanted to attend Central High School out of school "until conferences could be held with the Federal Judge." (Seven black children had withdrawn their applications that afternoon.) Wayne Upton later explained to the FBI: "this was not done to interfere in any way with the integration order but rather to save students embarrassment or possible harm."[64]

At 11:00 P.M., just fifteen minutes after Faubus finished his speech, the School Board released to the press a statement announcing, "Although the Federal Court has ordered integration to proceed, Governor Faubus has said that schools should continue as they have in the past and has stationed troops at Central High School to maintain order. In view of this situation, we ask that no negro [sic] students attempt to attend Central or any white high school until this dilemma is legally resolved." Virgil Blossom then went into a meeting at the School Board offices with the principals of the black junior and senior high schools and advised them "to notify students to remain home on September 3, 1957." He spent the remainder of the night dealing with the logistics of informing all black staff personnel to stay away from Central High and figuring out how to serve lunch to two thousand children without a staff in the cafeteria. At dawn the next morning, when he saw 270 soldiers surrounding the school, he felt "only a deep sadness."[65]

Two other members of the local establishment who were sleep-deprived on September 3 were Orval Faubus and Harry Ashmore. Ashmore reportedly stayed up late into the night trying to persuade the governor not to pursue the course on which he had embarked. Failing in that effort, he oversaw the production of the next morning's edition of the *Arkansas Gazette,* which was a classic example of the practice for which that newspaper was often criticized, blurring the distinction between news and opinion. The lead article referred to the governor's "extreme action" and his "apparent direct defiance of a specific federal court order," declaring, "In effect he personally interposed the office of governor between the local School District and the United States Supreme Court."[66]

Orval Faubus received his friend, Reverend Dale Cowling, at the Governor's Mansion on the morning of September 3 with tears in his eyes, saying, "You just can't imagine the pressure. . . ." Cowling said, "Orval, you have got to explain this to me. I know you are not a segregationist. Why have you made this decision?" According to Cowling's recollection almost fifty years later, Faubus replied, "Dale, you'll never understand unless you are in politics, but I promised the farmers of east Arkansas that I would take care of them on the segregation issue if it ever came to that. . . ."[67]

After weighing the various factors that were pressing down on him from all sides, Orval Faubus had taken a flying leap in the direction of maintaining the peace and, perhaps more important, maintaining his own political viability.

Thinking he was courting disaster no matter which way he leapt, he would not know until three weeks had passed how wildly popular his actions had made him in locales far beyond the borders of Arkansas.

BY 8:00 A.M. ON THE first day of school, September 3, 1957, an estimated four to five hundred people had gathered across Park Street from Central High School. Composed primarily of Citizens' Council and Mothers' League members, as well as an assortment of disgruntled parents and students, the crowd remained peaceful, if rowdy. Mary Thomason sang "Dixie" as she waved a Confederate flag, and Margaret Jackson distributed petitions calling for the removal of Superintendent Blossom. One student wore a Rebel cap and unfurled the South's battle flag, but police quickly told the youth to put the banner away and he complied. Most in the crowd apparently intended only "to make a peaceful point of . . . opposition," and when no blacks showed up to attend school, the crowd dispersed.[68]

Jim Johnson later admitted to Faubus biographer Roy Reed that he was the driving force behind the threats of the caravans that never materialized. "There wasn't any caravan. But we made Orval believe it. We said, 'They're lining up. They're coming in droves.' . . . The only weapon we had was to leave the impression that the sky was going to fall."[69]

Jim Johnson may have thought he was bluffing, but the threat of caravans of armed men was very real. Faubus biographer Roy Reed discovered, through some persistent detective work, that one group of men from south Arkansas had stopped at the home of Joe Foster in England, on the edge of the delta, and Foster had persuaded them to leave their guns stacked on his back porch. Orval Faubus claimed many times in later years that these men, and others, would have stopped integration violently if he had not called out the National Guard.[70]

AT ABOUT THE SAME time that Mary Thomason sang "Dixie" across the street from Central High, President Dwight Eisenhower held a press conference in Washington, D.C. When asked his thoughts about Governor Faubus's use of the National Guard, the president commented first that Attorney General Herbert Brownell was "taking a look" at the Little Rock situation, and that Brownell would "discuss it with the federal judge." He then went on to reflect "you cannot change people's hearts merely by laws." Fumbling for words, the president continued, "Now it is for this reason because I know this is a slow process the Supreme Court in its decision of '54 pointed out the emotional difficulties that would be encountered by a Negro even if given . . . equal but separate schools. . . .

But there are very strong emotions on the other side. People that see a picture of mongrelization of the race, they call it."[71]

Eisenhower had been listening when FBI Director J. Edgar Hoover briefed the president's Cabinet on the southern opposition to desegregation in March of 1956, introducing the term "mongrelization" in attempting to explain the heart of the southern resistance. Despite Attorney General Brownell's racial liberalism and activism, President Eisenhower had never been a supporter of using federal force to change southern racial mores. The worsening situation in Little Rock eventually forced him into a posture that he assumed only reluctantly.[72]

Shortly after the president finished speaking, Faubus convened his own press conference in his office at the state capitol building. A local press report described him as "looking fresh and relaxed though a squawky radio made him jump." Dressed in coat and tie despite the heat and the absence of air-conditioning, Faubus answered questions and posed for thirty local and national newsmen and photographers who were more appropriately clad in shirtsleeves and open collars. This briefing focused heavily on Faubus's reasons for mobilizing the National Guard, and the governor eluded his questioners' attempts to lead him into saying that his action was intended to defy federal authority. When asked "Have you instructed the National Guard to prevent . . . Negro students from enrolling today," the governor answered, "I have instructed the Guard to maintain peace and order and that they may use their discretion . . . as it affects the situation as relates to the peace and stability of the community."[73]

The press conference rambled widely over a variety of topics, but ended with the following exchange with James W. Erwin of Movietone News: "Governor, your action possibly is going to be interpreted as an invitation to test out the police powers of the state as compared to the powers of the federal government. Was your action in calling out the Guard prompted in any way as perhaps an invitation to such a legal principle?" Governor Faubus answered, "No, Jim. . . . It might be interpreted that way in some quarters. I think that any prudent and judicious official with the responsibilities that I have would certainly make the decision to prevent disorder and violence rather than having it occur and then step in even though he did so at the risk of being misunderstood and I realize that that is a possibility." If the prevention of violence was, in fact, one of the governor's primary motivations, he was right to fear that he would be misunderstood.[74]

THAT AFTERNOON, September 3, Archie House filed a pleading in Judge Davies's court asking for further instructions and explaining the Little Rock School Board was "helpless, caught between the District Court order and the governor's troops." That board's lead attorney also requested exemption for his clients from any charge of contempt of court for failing to integrate. At seven-thirty that evening, Judge Davies convened a five-minute hearing in his courtroom. After House explained that the School Board statement of the previous evening "did not in the least suggest that there was any deviation planned [from the Blossom Plan], and there is not a word in it that shows any retreat as to the plan itself . . . ," Davies replied with astonishment, "That is the sum and substance of the position of the Little Rock School Board?" When House replied in the affirmative, Davies quoted Faubus's statement that the state militia "will not act as segregationists or integrationists[,]" and then concluded "I am taking the statements of the Governor of Arkansas at their full face value" and ordered the School Board to "put into effect forthwith" its plan of integration.[75]

Sometime after midnight on September 4, Faubus changed the orders of the National Guard, instructing the soldiers explicitly to prohibit the black children from entering Central High School. He said in an interview years later that all through the day his "undercover people" who were circulating through the crowd at Central High had reported that there was going to be "disorder whenever the black children came. . . ." Although he understood the course he was pursuing could be interpreted as defiance of Judge Davies's order, he wanted to believe that because of his progressive record and his support for integration where it had occurred in other Arkansas towns, his argument that he was merely preserving the peace would be accepted.[76]

Faubus always held that his primary concerns had been to maintain order, see to it that no one was injured or killed, and prevent property damage. In his words, "We'd just had a tax increase, fighting for money to increase teachers' salaries, and I dreaded the thought to see a bunch of buildings destroyed and then have to use that money to have to replace them . . . when it should go to the teachers." Faubus suggested in later years he was also trying to protect his Guardsmen, since he realized they were at risk of losing their commissions and pensions if they refused to implement the judge's order.[77]

It is more likely that Faubus initially hoped to provoke the Eisenhower administration into an action that would take him off the hook, one that would provide protection against violence while at the same time allowing him to claim he had tried to hold out but had been overwhelmed by the superior might of the federal government. Legal historian John Thomas Elliff concluded, after a close examination of the behavior of the Justice Department in this controversy, that the department "could have taken limited independent legal actions that would

have given Governor Faubus an excuse to bow to federal executive authority."
Apparently the federal government had no interest in helping Orval Faubus.[78]

Neither did Harry Ashmore. In a front-page editorial in the September 4
Arkansas Gazette, Ashmore laid out an interpretation of Faubus's actions that
has remained the dominant view of the governor's behavior from that day to
this. Titled "The Crisis Mr. Faubus Made," the Ashmore editorial argued that in
the face of Judge Davies's most recent directive, the Arkansas governor now had
to decide "whether he intends to pose what could be the most serious constitutional question to face the national government since the Civil War." Claiming
that Faubus had taken a local problem and turned it into a state problem when
he testified in state court to the threat of violence, Ashmore argued that Faubus
had then made it a national problem by calling out the National Guard. The
clear message of this editorial and its headline was that Orval Faubus had will-
fully chosen to employ the massive resistance strategy of interposition in direct
defiance of federal authority.[79]

Harry Ashmore knew otherwise. He knew about Blossom's "deal" with Judge
Miller and he had worked assiduously to bring Blossom back onto the course
he wanted the superintendent to pursue. His placing of all the blame on Orval
Faubus was disingenuous and less than fair. Years later, Bill Smith told a story to
an Eisenhower Administration Project interviewer that was very revealing. Finding himself seated with Ashmore in a group of eight or ten men in the bar at the
Riverdale Country Club, Smith remarked, "Harry, . . . I'd just like for you to tell
me how it feels to win the Pulitzer Prize for accurate reporting, when you know
in your own conscience that you were sending out fictitious stories, and the public was not being told the truth?" According to Smith, Ashmore replied, perhaps
half in jest, "Bill, I'm prepared to defend what I did on the grounds that it would
not have been in the best interests of the public to know the truth."[80]

SID MCMATH GAVE dozens of interviews in the fifty years after the Little Rock
crisis in which he elaborated on the Ashmore thesis. Orval Faubus, he would
say, was "not racially prejudiced," but in order to overcome the Arkansas tradition against a third term "he needed a highly volatile issue, and he appropriated
the racial issue for political purposes." Frightened by his 1956 race against Jim
Johnson, McMath argued, Faubus recognized "the tremendous emotional value
to him politically of this race issue" and "staged the Little Rock High School
incident." According to McMath, Faubus encouraged the opposition to desegregation "and then called out the Guard in order to put down the mob which
he had organized." An old political foe with an axe to grind, McMath enhanced

his liberal credentials and burnished his tarnished reputation with his ever-quotable, increasingly fashionable assessments.[81]

Forrest Rozzell had a clearer vantage point from which to appraise Faubus's actions and motives. As executive secretary of the Arkansas Education Association, Rozzell had worked closely with Faubus in frequent meetings through the spring and summer of 1957, and the gentle, liberal educator recalled in an interview fifteen years later that when Faubus called out the National Guard, his own reaction was one of total surprise. According to Rozzell, Blossom and the School Board had thrown a curveball at the governor, and Faubus had simply reacted without calculation. Recalling that Faubus had never been a segregationist, Rozzell suggested that the governor had always had a deep respect for his fellow man regardless of color. Asked if he thought Faubus had manufactured a crisis in Little Rock for political purposes, Rozzell replied that he did not think so. He acknowledged that for a few years Faubus did use the integration issue for political purposes, but he thought that in 1957 the governor probably felt that he was facing political danger no matter which way he moved.[82]

Forrest Rozzell got it about right. Although Faubus-bashing became a minor industry in the national press after 1957, the liberal mountaineer who charged into battle seeming to carry the banner of massive resistance, to the complete surprise of the massive resisters, went to his grave maintaining that he had acted to prevent violence in Little Rock. He never revealed his evidence, as he had promised to do, and his detractors cited this as proof that the evidence did not exist. Faubus had evidence, and the FBI uncovered some of it, but upon sober reflection the crafty mountaineer must have realized he had been led astray.[83]

During sleepless nights at the Governor's Mansion, or during quiet hours fishing the lakes or walking the woods he loved, the man who feared most of all being made to look foolish must have realized he had been used for others' purposes and benefit. Virgil Blossom, Jimmy Karam, Jim Johnson, all had their agendas, and all accomplished their objectives at the expense of the ideals and convictions of the man they used. Animated by a complex mix of idealism and calculation, Orval Faubus backed into the arms of the segregationists; in order to avoid looking like a fool, he stayed there.

CHAPTER SEVEN

THE MINEFIELD IN THE MIDDLE
Brooks Hays

SEPTEMBER IN ARKANSAS BRINGS THE FIRST RELIEF FROM LONG WEEKS of blazing sun, and words like "partly cloudy" and "mild" begin, mercifully, to creep into the weather forecast. In September of 1957, the front page of the *Arkansas Gazette* predicted "partly cloudy" conditions or "considerable cloudiness" every day but one. Those predictions proved to be an apt description of Congressman Brooks Hays's attempts to provide leadership for his beleaguered city.

They described many of the issues facing Little Rock, as well: the proper relationship between the powers of the states and those of the federal government; the powers, and especially the intentions, of Governor Orval Faubus; the authority and designs of Federal Judge Ronald Davies, and the assistance he received from the United States Department of Justice and the Federal Bureau of Investigation; the repeated staging of complicated legal maneuvers; the daily appearance of conflicting press accounts and disturbing images; Harry Ashmore's behind-the-scenes efforts both to control Little Rock's mayor and to influence the Eisenhower administration; and, not least, the motives and purposes of Congressman Hays himself. A sweet, gentle, Christian soul, the mild-mannered public servant embarked on his mission with a lack of clarity that ultimately damaged Governor Faubus and the state of Arkansas, President Eisenhower and the United States government, and the Little Rock Nine and the cause of civil rights.

Lawrence Brooks Hays grew up surrounded by politics. His father at one time had been the chief clerk of the Arkansas House of Representatives and had made an unsuccessful run for the congressional seat his son eventually held. Young Brooks decided early upon a political career and made all the right stops along the way, including the University of Arkansas, where he joined the Sigma Chi fraternity, also the university home of Senator Fulbright, and George Washington Law School in Washington, D.C. An idealistic, youthful reformer, Hays early attempted three unsuccessful political races (two for the governorship and one for Congress), before concluding in 1933, in the words of one biographer, that "the Democratic establishment of Arkansas was so fed up with his crusading that it was determined to use any means, legal or otherwise, to keep him from elective office." Disappointed and bitter, Hays retired temporarily from the political arena to a law office in Little Rock, eventually accepting a series of appointments with the Roosevelt administration and moving to Washington. After a decade of federal service, Hays felt emboldened to stand for office once again, this time securing the former congressional seat of his political mentor, Henderson M. Jacoway, whose district included Little Rock.[1]

Hays developed what he called "a passionate concern for justice," especially racial justice, during his childhood in Arkansas. The poverty of his neighbors and the inequities suffered by black Arkansans weighed heavily on his heart.[2] While working for the Roosevelt administration he became an expert on farm tenancy, eventually helping to write the Bankhead-Jones Act which created the Farm Security Administration, and he became an active member of the racially progressive Commission for Interracial Cooperation, a forerunner of the Southern Regional Council.[3]

In 1949 Hays introduced into Congress what he called his Arkansas Plan, which provided for federal action only in the event that the states did not act, and which was an attempt to keep the Dixiecrats within the Democratic Party in the face of President Harry S. Truman's assault on traditional southern racial practices. Increasingly, Hays found himself traversing the nebulous, conflicted ground of "the southern moderate." Understanding fully the dilemma of the Christian democrat in a segregated society, Hays argued that "no man ought ever to be excoriated for speaking softly when he carries grave responsibilities, and has to consider the attitude of the segments within the political community."[4]

The *Brown* decision caught Brooks Hays by surprise. Years later he recalled, "I just couldn't conceive of the court over-ruling [*Plessy v. Ferguson*] particularly considering the possibility of violence...." Realizing that his home constituency would oppose both *Brown* and anyone who championed this fundamental alteration of southern culture and mores, Hays knew his moderate middle ground was a minefield. Trying, he said later, to defuse "the extremists" in both North and South, and swept along by the enthusiasm of the rest of the Arkansas congressional delegation, in March of 1956 Hays signed the Southern Manifesto, declaring an intent to resist integration. He regretted it immediately. In later years, Hays said of his signing of the Manifesto, "It has embarrassed me ever since. . . . It wasn't worthy of me."[5]

As one who was known for his "long-standing and widely publicized support of civil rights for southern blacks," Hays increasingly found himself "on the fringe of political insecurity." Fifty-nine years old in the fall of 1957, Brooks Hays had just been elected president of the nationwide Southern Baptist Convention, and he longed to be relieved of the necessity of continuously tap-dancing around the uneven stage of civil rights. Gradually he began to hope that the judiciary might offer him a route out of his dilemma, and he let his old friend Sherman Adams, Eisenhower's chief of staff, know that he would be delighted to be appointed a federal judge. As unlikely as it was to think a Democrat might receive such a plum in a Republication administration, in the late summer of 1957 Adams advised the Arkansas congressman that he was under consideration. Hays had done Adams and Eisenhower favors in the past, and soon both the *Washington Post* and the *Arkansas Gazette* discussed his candidacy. The crisis in his city seemed to offer Brooks Hays an opportunity to bring together his intellectual commitment to federalism, his moral passion for racial justice, and his ambition.[6]

ORVAL FAUBUS HAD staggered into a constitutional crisis, seeming to defy a federal court order, and seeming to employ the massive resisters' strategy of interposition. On both counts, Faubus wanted to argue that his actions remained within the constitutional bounds of the governor's role as he struggled to maintain peace and order within his state's borders. Numerous factors had impaired his judgment: sleep deprivation; panic; severe intestinal discomfort caused by ulcers; his conviction that Virgil Blossom and Judge John Miller had betrayed him; his anger that the federal government offered him no assistance in implementing what he saw to be "their" court order; his alarm concerning the reports of impending violence he was hearing from people like Jimmy Karam; his belief that Hugh Patterson, Virgil Blossom, Harry Ashmore, Sid McMath, and Henry Woods sought to become national heroes at his expense; his fear that the extremists in the Arkansas legislature would impeach him if he did not uphold the new Arkansas laws requiring segregation; his chagrin at feeling disdained by the Little Rock School Board and the Little Rock elite.

For the first few days after he called out the National Guard, the governor simply allowed his tactics to evolve day by day. But no matter how he turned it over in his mind, Orval Faubus did not see how he could survive politically. In his words, ". . . I didn't think I could win no matter what I did. I had very definite feelings that the action I was taking would in likelihood finish my political career." Bill Smith advised him that it was not his responsibility to enforce the federal government's new mandate in the *Brown* decision, saying after the governor had called out the National Guard, ". . . when the government accepts its responsibility of enforcing its own court orders, then you just withdraw." As Smith recalled years later, "And Governor Faubus made this statement publicly, time and again, that he would never as Governor assume the responsibility of enforcing a federal court order. Now the Governor of Tennessee had fallen into that trap previously. And we didn't propose for the Governor of Arkansas to fall into that trap, and he didn't."[7]

After several days, Brooks Hays came to Governor Faubus and offered to arrange a meeting with President Eisenhower where the two men could discuss their differences. Faubus needed help, and he responded to Hays's generous offer to run interference between the state and federal governments. Hays was noted for his ability to effect compromises, and he had amassed an impressive record in Congress of reconciling the differences between his northern and southern colleagues on racial issues. But when the hapless governor put himself in the hands of gentle, foggy Brooks Hays, his cause was sunk.[8]

Brooks Hays arrived in Little Rock by train on the night of September 4, exhausted after the long congressional struggle over the civil rights bill. Thursday morning, September 5, he opened the *Arkansas Gazette* and saw on the front page the sickening picture that had been flashed around the globe showing dignified, fifteen-year-old Elizabeth Eckford walking resolutely past unyielding National Guard soldiers with a howling, hate-filled mob at her heels. Hays's heart sank. He had thought Little Rock was doing so well, and that significant progress was being made on the civil rights front.[9]

Reactions to Faubus's use of the National Guard were intense. Little Rock Mayor Woodrow Mann resented what he regarded as the governor's usurpation of his authority. On the same page of the morning paper that featured Elizabeth Eckford's distressing picture, the city's readers discovered that the mayor had termed Governor Faubus's claims of the threat of violence at Central High "a hoax," contending that "the governor has chosen to use this city as a pawn in what clearly is a political design of his own." With this blast, Woodrow Mann inaugurated a brief period of service as Harry Ashmore's puppet. It was a choice that soon cost Mann his business and led to his departure from Little Rock. But for a few heady weeks, the mayor who had lost his job amid charges of corruption found himself the darling of the liberal press and the confidant of officials at the highest levels of the national government.[10]

Ashmore was furious at Faubus. He had just developed the thesis in his forthcoming book that the South suffered from a "default of leadership," and he was certain that Faubus's actions stemmed from no other purpose than a craven desire for a third term. The next day, when he read an interview in the *Arkansas Democrat* in which Faubus suggested that the Little Rock situation "possibly could develop into a Southwide test" of federal authority over state laws, Ashmore concluded that Faubus had fallen under the spell of a cabal of southern fire-eaters, probably led by Marvin Griffin of Georgia. As he soon wrote, ". . . there is every evidence that the Arkansas governor's gesture was the signal of a revolt of Southern governors. . . ." Ashmore at this point flew into high gear in defense of his city, his moral principles, and his thesis. As one of his journalistic colleagues, David Halberstam, wrote several years later, "This was the moment, he was sure, when he would be judged with a finality." By the end of the month, Harry Ashmore received notification of his formal nomination for a Pulitzer Prize.[11]

ALTHOUGH PEOPLE ON the ground in Little Rock did not know it, on September 3 Attorney General Herbert Brownell had initiated an intensive study of federal authority both to review the legitimacy of Faubus's actions and to enjoin him from continued use of the National Guard at Central High School. Brownell wrote in his memoir that the Eisenhower administration had expected a conflict such as the one they believed they were seeing in Little Rock. As he recalled, ". . . we had increasingly realized that a clash of historic importance was inevitable between the president, who was required by the Constitution to enforce the law of the land, and political leaders in the South, who had announced their plan to resist the enforcement of the *Brown* decisions." A report prepared later for Brownell, which showed the Justice Department's thinking in early September, read in part, "As the Governor's action *appeared on its face* to be a mere device to obstruct the court order for integration, active consideration was given to the possible counter-moves." Convinced that Faubus was acting primarily to block integration, the attorney general's assistants dismissed out of hand the governor's claims that he was using the Guard to preserve peace and order in Little Rock.[12]

The Justice Department was struggling through what the United States attorney in Little Rock, Osro Cobb, called "a legal thicket." Unclear themselves about whether the recently passed Arkansas laws could withstand a court test, Justice Department attorneys attempted to secure a delay for the government by pressuring the Little Rock NAACP's attorney to withdraw the nine black children from Central High School. As Wiley Branton recalled, Osro Cobb argued "we should allow a year for attitudes to change and tempers to cool before making any further attempts to integrate the schools."[13]

Cobb repeatedly pressured Branton not to bring Thurgood Marshall into the Little Rock situation, flattering him that he could handle the situation alone. As Branton recalled, Cobb "told me what a fine lawyer he and his colleague thought me to be and suggested that I was really the chief counsel and certainly did not need Thurgood Marshall to tell me how to handle the Little Rock school case." Other "well-placed individuals in Little Rock" suggested that Branton's future in Arkansas would be far more promising "if I would support a one-year delay."[14]

Branton refused to dispense with the assistance of the noted civil rights attorney, who was also his role model and friend, and Marshall quickly muddied the waters for the federal government. As Branton recalled, "Marshall had a verbal clash with the Justice Department official [undoubtedly Cobb] who insisted that his immediate superior in Washington had directed him to suggest the delay. Marshall countered by stating that he had just spoken that morning with the Attorney General himself and that the suggested delay was not what had been agreed to." The black attorneys refused to withdraw the nine children from Central High School.[15]

The Justice Department considered three alternative courses of action. The first was a contempt citation against the governor and the Guard commander for violating Judge Davies's August 30 order that Mrs. Clyde Thomason "and all others" should desist from interfering with integration at Central High School. Brownell's advisers recommended against pursuing this course because they realized Judge Davies's order had been too broad. The second alternative, federalization of the National Guard, they deemed premature, because the governor's action "might conceivably be supported judicially." Even the Justice Department attorneys conceded the possibility that Faubus may not have exceeded his authority. Department officials also understood President Eisenhower's opposition to the "use of force in carrying out the Supreme Court's school integration decision." The third alternative, which they eventually chose, aimed at "obtaining judicial determination of the legality of the Governor's action through an injunction proceeding . . . ," but Justice Department advisers specified that this action would have to await "the Court's request for assistance. . . ." Since U.S. Attorney Cobb had an office next door to Judge Davies and their staffs frequently had meals and coffee breaks together, it seems likely that staffers shared the Justice Department's thinking with the federal judge. Whatever the source, Judge Davies soon asked the department for assistance.[16]

After National Guard soldiers turned away the black teenagers who tried to integrate Central High School on September 4, Judge Davies asked the Justice Department "to conduct an investigation and report to the court respecting obstruction of its orders." Davies directed his request to Cobb, "who had been in constant touch with the Department from the beginning." Reflecting the assumptions that underlay its approach, the ensuing Federal Bureau of Investigation report bore the title "Integration in Public Schools, Little Rock, Arkansas—Civil Rights; Contempt of Court; Obstruction of Justice."[17]

Orval Faubus maintained steadfastly throughout the month, and for almost forty years afterward, that he had called out the National Guard to prevent violence and preserve the peace in Little Rock, and that under the constitution of the state of Arkansas he had the authority to do so. From the standpoint of the governor, he had the executive discretion to determine when such a threat existed and when he should act. From the standpoint of the federal government, and much of the press, Faubus's credibility rested squarely on whether he could produce evidence that the threat of violence had in fact existed. The public—national as well as local—was confused by the situation, and media analysts proclaimed vociferously on both sides of the issue. Increasingly, however, the new medium of television reduced the struggle in Little Rock to a morality play between the black children and the segregationists, and the underlying issue of the conflict between state and federal authority got lost in the shuffle. And Orval Faubus's options narrowed.[18]

MANY LITTLE ROCK citizens had been reading the newspapers with mounting concern. They read of an exchange of telegrams between the governor and the president, with Faubus charging that federal agents had tapped his telephone and that he felt in danger of being taken into federal custody. They read that Faubus had, as a consequence, surrounded the Governor's Mansion with National Guard troops, that he was cloistered inside with his closest advisers, and that he would not leave the grounds even for a televised interview. They read that a flood of telegrams and letters had begun to arrive at the Mansion, most of them supporting the governor's stand; that large, ugly crowds were gathering daily outside Central High School; and that spokesmen for the Justice Department were predicting a conflict "that could reach historic proportions." They also read that President Eisenhower had flown to Newport, Rhode Island, for a golfing vacation, and that he and wife Mamie expected to have "the time of our lives. . . ."[19]

When he got in touch with close friends in Little Rock, Brooks Hays found them all shocked and dismayed by Faubus's actions. Little Rock's business leadership saw the Chamber of Commerce's carefully mounted industrial campaign in serious jeopardy. Arkansas's educational leaders were numb with disbelief that Faubus would bring such unfavorable publicity to a defensive little state that was already suffering from major image problems. And of course Harry Ashmore was seething. Hays's most troubling conversations were with his friend Virgil Blossom, from whom he learned that the School Board had decided to go back to Judge Davies and ask for permission to delay their integration plan as a result of the ongoing disruptions to the educational environment. The judge announced he would not rule on the School Board's request for two days, possibly in the hope that the FBI investigation would yield some guiding information by that time.[20]

Hays also learned from Blossom about the FBI's interviews. The early phases of the investigation focused on whether or not Governor Faubus had any credible evidence of impending violence when he called out the troops at Central High. School Board members met repeatedly in preparation for their FBI interviews and apparently decided upon a common strategy of denial: every member of the School Board reported to FBI investigators they had no warning of potential violence prior to September 3, even though they had been discussing the danger and threat of violence all summer long. Virgil Blossom even went so far as to tell the FBI that Governor Faubus's behavior was "motivated entirely by political expediency." Mayor Mann told FBI investigators he had had no foreknowledge of plans to incite violence, and he announced in one of his many prepared statements, which the *Arkansas Gazette* dutifully printed, that he and Little Rock Police Chief Marvin Potts had made extensive preparations to handle the few "cranks" they expected to cause trouble, but they had anticipated no real difficulty.[21]

On September 6, in a telegram to President Eisenhower, Faubus offered to show the FBI "certain evidence upon which I acted to preserve the public peace" by suggesting they interview both his personal attorney, Bill Smith, and his state police director, Herman Lindsey. Before the day was out, the FBI had interviewed Smith, and they quickly dismissed most of his account. Smith told Bureau investigators about the meeting with Upton and Blossom where the two had implored him to file a suit to delay integration, about the threats of violence Virgil Blossom had been passing along to Faubus all summer, and about reports he had heard of Blossom and Upton's meetings with Judge Miller. Virgil Blossom (in a second interview) denied all of Smith's claims, as did Wayne Upton. The Bureau's summary of the Smith interview treated the rest of his information as frivolous.[22]

On September 7, the *Arkansas Gazette* reported that Justice Department "sources" had informed the Little Rock newspaper that "the Arkansas chief executive's action in ordering out the National Guard must not be allowed to become a precedent for defying desegregation orders. Unless the federal government successfully asserted its constitutional authority, they said, the situation at Little Rock Central High School almost certainly would be repeated elsewhere." Reflecting this thinking, Federal Judge Ronald Davies on that day rejected the School Board's request for a delay and ordered that integration proceed immediately.[23]

As Brooks Hays commented later, Davies "made it hard to sell judicial judgment to the people." He seemed cocky and abrupt, and his disdainful dismissal of the School Board's arguments was a psychological and public relations blow to the six citizens who had assumed the increasingly unpopular position of complying, however gradually, with the courts' mandates. As one observer described the courtroom scene on that Saturday, September 7: "Judge Davies issued his order after allowing less than 20 minutes of arguments on the petition filed by the School Board Thursday. He cut attorneys off abruptly at two different points, walked out of the courtroom and was back some 40 minutes later with his order."[24]

Davies informed the packed courtroom, reading from a prepared statement, "The testimony and arguments this morning were, in my judgment, as anemic as the petition itself; and the position taken by the school directors does violence to my concept of the duty of the petitioners to adhere with resolution to its own approved plan of gradual integration in the Little Rock public schools." After citing the public statements of Mayor Mann, who had not testified, that "there has been no indication from sources available to him that there would be violence in regard to this situation . . . ," Davies ended with what he intended to be a flourish but instead was a gaffe, saying, "In an organized society there can be nothing but ultimate confusion and chaos if court decrees are flaunted [he meant 'flouted'], whatever the pretext."[25]

Jim Johnson was among the 150 spectators in Judge Davies's court, and after leaving the courtroom he handed out a typewritten statement in which he charged "apparent collusion" between Davies and the Justice Department, suggesting Davies had arrived at his decision "prior to the presentation of evidence in open Court." Johnson also charged, "It is contrary to any concept of American jurisprudence for a federal judge to permit the Justice Department to instruct him on what to do. . . ." When confronted with Johnson's statements, Davies replied heatedly, "I have never talked to Mr. Brownell and

I never intend to." The *Arkansas Gazette* had reported the day before that Brownell's man in Little Rock, U.S. Attorney Cobb, "was making interim reports daily to Judge Davies" on the status of the FBI investigation. The *New York Post* had also reported that the Justice Department and Judge Davies had mapped out a plan to "nibble at" Governor Faubus. The line of demarcation between the executive and judicial branches of government was getting blurred.[26]

Orval Faubus issued a statement refusing to "abdicate my office and let a Federal Judge substitute his judgment for mine on this issue. . . ." The governor concluded, "As duly elected Governor of this State by will of the people, I have not become its chief executive in order to surrender its sovereign powers." Faubus left the National Guard at Central High. That night, a cross was burned on the front yard of Mayor Mann.[27]

EISENHOWER AND HIS advisers did not have to be reminded of their dilemma. Although they were apparently stalling until they had concrete results from the FBI investigation, Sherman Adams and Herbert Brownell were already working around the clock to try to resolve the impasse. On the Saturday of Judge Davies's hearing in Little Rock, the president flew to Washington, D.C., to strategize with key members of his staff.

From the federal government's perspective, more was at stake than defining the proper relationship between state and federal powers. In a world of Cold War tensions and realities, the situation in Little Rock was becoming a greater embarrassment and liability every day, as world attention focused increasingly on the United States' apparent failure to guarantee the blessings of liberty to all its citizens. Deeply concerned about the image of the U.S. abroad, the men around Eisenhower felt extraordinary pressure to bring the unruly governor under control.[28]

The forty-five-minute conference among Eisenhower and his advisers centered on the same three options the department had been discussing since September 3: a contempt citation, federalization of the Guard, or issuance of an injunction. In the end, nothing was decided. Presidential press secretary James Hagerty announced at the end of the meeting that the president had decided against any federal intervention until Judge Davies had had an opportunity to study the results of the FBI investigation, which was still under way. This undoubtedly explains why Davies at this point denied the Little Rock School Board's request that he direct the United States marshal to provide them much-needed assistance. Yet Attorney General Brownell was determined to have his

Justice Department involved, and he needed only a request from the federal court to intervene. That could be arranged.[29]

IN HIS MEMOIR, *Hearts and Minds*, Harry Ashmore wrote of his astonishment upon reading a September 7 United Press account that "Attorney General Herbert Brownell, Jr., was without any immediate strategy or policy to pursue. . . ." The UP article continued, "There has been a feeling around town [Washington, D.C.] that Brownell was stalling for time or a policy inspiration." Ashmore had already concluded that Faubus had stumbled into calling out the Guard with no real plan in mind; now he concluded that the Eisenhower administration "seemed to have no more idea what to do next than Faubus did." Since Eisenhower and Brownell had just sponsored and fought for the civil rights bill, Ashmore thought the administration "ought to have realized that somewhere down the line it would have to make its stand—and been prepared accordingly."[30]

The Arkansas editor now took the lead in pursuing contacts in Washington, starting with *Washington Post* publisher Phil Graham. Graham saw immediately that the situation in Little Rock could only hurt his candidate for president, Lyndon B. Johnson. Johnson had just fought mightily to shepherd the Civil Rights Bill through the Senate in a manner that would remove civil rights issues from the forefront of public consciousness and allow the gaping wounds within the Democratic Party to heal. Graham launched into a frenzied quest to call everyone he could think of who might be able to influence the situation— to resolve it and remove it from the front pages—from friends in the White House to acquaintances in Little Rock to national black leaders. With each phone call, to Brownell, Vice President Nixon, Deputy Attorney General William Rogers, presidential advisers Sherman Adams and Maxwell Rabb, Graham passed on Ashmore's assurances that Orval Faubus was motivated by nothing more substantive than his opportunistic desire for a third term in the Arkansas statehouse. Among the people he called was his old friend, Congressman Brooks Hays.[31]

Phil Graham thought the best person to redirect the Arkansas governor's thinking would be Faubus's old hero, former President Harry S. Truman. At Graham's request, Brooks Hays telephoned Truman and asked him to call Faubus, but Truman declined, pleading ignorance of the local situation. Truman's "close friends . . . in Arkansas," obviously Sid McMath and Henry Woods, approached the former president as well, assuring Truman that he alone could get through the "vehement segregationists" who were screening the calls at the Governor's Mansion and explain to Faubus that "his armed defiance of a federal court's school integration order is damaging the country, the South and the Democratic Party—and in the long run, it cannot succeed."[32]

About this time Faubus wired the president, informing him that he would be glad to have his attorney, Bill Smith, meet with representatives of the Justice Department to try to work out a solution. Eisenhower wired back his acceptance. Smith telephoned Osro Cobb and told him they would meet in Smith's office, but at the appointed hour FBI representatives appeared and announced that "the Justice Department had determined that the United States district attorney should not come because he may be involved in litigation. . . ." As Smith recalled years later, "I'll tell you one thing, that the national administration didn't do one thing that it agreed to do, throughout the entire controversy. . . ."[33]

Bill Smith met with an unnamed member of the Justice Department on September 8 and 9, trying to hammer out a compromise. First Smith suggested the court delay the order for integration until "the legality of the Governor's action" had been ruled on. By this he undoubtedly meant, as Faubus said consistently throughout this period, he wanted the courts to rule on the constitutionality of the Arkansas segregation laws. The Justice Department rejected this option immediately. The department's representative then suggested, amazingly enough, "closing the schools until the court made its decision." Smith and Faubus rejected this option in turn. Finally, Smith suggested "voluntary abstention by the Negro students" provided Faubus agreed to abide by the court's decision. Apparently officials at Justice were willing to entertain this notion until they realized that Faubus meant "he would agree to abide only by a final court order after all appeals had been exhausted and . . . he wanted Negroes excluded until that time." Department representatives found this option "wholly unsatisfactory" and broke off further discussion.[34]

Brooks Hays made one last-ditch attempt to mediate between the White House and the governor. The congressman did not understand the position Orval Faubus had assumed, and he operated from the outset on the assumption that he, or Eisenhower, could convince the governor to capitulate. As he admitted years later, "My sympathies were on the side of the federal government, though I was not forced to show my hand."[35] Hays had the inspiration to try to set up a meeting between Eisenhower and Faubus, and he presented his ideas to the governor in person. The governor agreed.

As Hays was leaving the Governor's Mansion that September afternoon, Faubus told him "he was convinced that the overwhelming sentiment of the state and of Little Rock was in opposition to the admission of the nine Negroes to Central High School. . . ." What Faubus did not tell Hays was that his private pollster, Eugene Newsom, had recently discovered that the people of Arkansas by large margins supported his stance in Little Rock. Always alert to popular sentiment, Faubus began in earnest to educate himself about the arguments behind massive resistance. Undoubtedly aided by new supporters such as Richard Russell and James J. Kilpatrick, Faubus became convinced within a matter of days that the *Brown* decision had been improperly decided and that he was truly dealing with a constitutional as well as a racial issue. By the time he met with Eisenhower the next week, he had accepted the questionable theory that the *Brown* decision was the "law of the case" and not the "law of the land." This line of thinking held that only Congress could make laws that were binding on all the people, and therefore the Supreme Court did not have the power to effect such sweeping change as was now being required of him as governor of Arkansas. It was a position he never abandoned.[36]

OFFICIALS IN THE Justice Department continued to digest FBI efforts to prove contempt of court or obstruction of justice, the twin goals of the investigation, on the part of Governor Faubus. By September 8, Bureau agents had conducted only about half of their projected interviews, but none had provided the factual evidence they needed. Whereas Justice Department officials had expected to find no evidence of the threat of violence—since Harry Ashmore, Mayor Mann, and others had assured them that the threat was "manufactured"—they found instead troublesome statements from cabinet members, Central High Mothers' League members, and School Board members that Orval Faubus was genuinely alarmed and apparently had reason to be. They also found disturbing evidence of a federal judge's impropriety, a school superintendent's double dealings, and significant indicators of the potential for violence in Little Rock before September 3.

Osro Cobb passed the FBI's incomplete findings to Judge Davies on Sunday afternoon, September 8. Davies studied the eleven pages of summary and 437 pages of text for about two hours and then appeared next door in Cobb's office, his face betraying "the mounting tension, apprehension, and . . . determination to ride out the judicial storm that he had inherited by being assigned to Little Rock." Apparently Davies had realized that this was far from an open-and-shut case, and that the subtleties and complexities in the materials he had been studying outstripped his expertise. He informed Cobb he would need "the active help of the United States in the case" and suggested Cobb should begin preparations to get involved. Cobb immediately called Deputy Attorney General William Rogers to advise him of Davies's anticipated action.[37]

On Monday afternoon, Davies issued an order directing the United States attorney general and the U.S. attorney in Little Rock to enter the case of *Aaron v. Cooper* as *amicus curiae,* or "friend of the court," a legal maneuver designed to give the Justice Department the authority "to intervene in the case and advise the Court." The judge's order specifically authorized the named parties "to submit to the Court pleadings, evidence, arguments and briefs, and . . . to initiate such further proceedings as may be appropriate." Less than a week later Orval Faubus would contend that this provision gave Herbert Brownell the authority to advise the court in favor of a delay of integration in Little Rock, and it was a major factor in shaping the governor's strategy regarding his approach to President Eisenhower.[38]

Davies's order directed Brownell and Cobb "to file immediately a petition" against Governor Faubus and the two National Guard commanders "seeking such injunctive and other relief as may be appropriate to prevent the existing interference with and obstruction to the carrying out of the orders heretofore entered by this Court in this case." William Rogers told United Press reporters that he planned to work through the night to prepare the requested materials, and the next day Brownell and Cobb dutifully filed their petition. The next-to-last paragraph of the document spelled out the whole point of the exercise, saying, "In order to protect and preserve the integrity of the judicial process of the courts of the United States and to maintain the due and proper administration of justice, it is necessary that Governor Faubus, General Clinger, and Lt. Col. Johnson be made additional parties defendant and enjoined from obstructing or interfering with the carrying out and effectuation of said orders of this Court."[39]

In the absence of clear evidence of contempt of court or obstruction of justice, which the FBI investigation had failed to provide, troubling legal questions surrounded the matter of whether or not the federal courts had the authority to move against Governor Faubus until he was named an actual defendant in the case. As Assistant U.S. Attorney Walter Riddick explained years later, the Justice Department had to secure "judicial control." In Herbert Brownell's mind, the Little Rock case had implications far beyond Little Rock, and he felt it was imperative to establish precedents that could be used if other southern governors chose to attempt the interposition and even nullification he thought he was seeing in Little Rock.[40]

NOW THAT THE DECISION had been made to intervene, Justice Department sources made much of the fact that the department was trying to give Governor Faubus his "day in court" and to foreclose any possible suggestion of "precipitate or unfair" action by federal authorities. The department knew it was taking a highly unusual and perhaps even unprecedented action by entering into the case under these conditions, but part of the difficulty of justifying its *amicus* role vanished when "attorneys for the Negro students filed a supplemental pleading also asking for an injunction against Governor Faubus." Despite the Justice Department's desire for a speedy hearing in the matter, Judge Davies set a trial date for September 20, giving himself time to attend the wedding of his youngest daughter in Fargo, North Dakota. The ten-day delay of the hearing also gave ample time for sentiment to harden on all sides.[41]

The federal government had finally awakened, and not just the judicial branch. That same day saw the quiet launching of "Operation Arkansas," an effort on the part of the U.S. Army to prepare for the contingency of using federal troops to implement desegregation in Little Rock. Actual preparation of "preliminary draft plans for calling the Arkansas National Guard into federal service" had begun on September 5, when General Maxwell D. Taylor became concerned about the situation in Little Rock. On September 10 these plans underwent significant modification at the Pentagon. General Edwin Walker assumed command of the projected operation in Little Rock. One battle group of the 101st Airborne Division initiated riot training, and the order came down that if the National Guard were federalized most of the Arkansas boys would "remain at home station," thereby removing them "from local participation." Orval Faubus had set in motion forces far beyond what he had anticipated or imagined.[42]

As Brooks Hays continued to try to negotiate between Faubus and Washington, the governor agreed to send a telegram requesting a meeting with Eisenhower. Hays was working through his old friend Sherman Adams, who insisted that Faubus initiate the request for a conference and that he include a statement of his intent to abide by court orders. Faubus agreed, but the crucial sentence in his telegram hedged in important ways, saying, "All good citizens must of course obey all proper orders of our Courts and it is certainly my desire to comply with the order that has been issued by the District court in this case, consistent with my responsibility under the constitution of the United States and that of Arkansas." Was the *Brown* decision a "proper" order? Was a "desire" to comply a commitment to comply? Was Faubus's responsibility to the Constitution of the United States or to "that of Arkansas"? Generous, trusting Brooks Hays missed the implications of the telegram's wording, and he blithely reported to Adams "that Faubus was prepared to go along fully. . . ."[43]

Faubus had convinced Hays that he wanted a "truce," or a compromise, and that if the start of integration could be delayed until January, he would support it. Faubus was undoubtedly thinking that a delay would allow the cases then

pending in state and federal courts to be litigated, thereby ascertaining the constitutionality of the four state laws mandating segregation. Despite the opposition of Herbert Brownell and others, Eisenhower agreed to meet.[44]

Justice Department officials generated a truly astonishing document on the
day before the meeting. Although signed by Warren Olney III, one of several
assistant attorneys general and director of the Justice Department's Criminal
Division, the document may in fact have been written by Olney's assistant,
Arthur Caldwell, who was probably the most alarmed of anyone by the president's decision to meet with Faubus. Addressed to the attorney general, the
four-page memorandum was entitled "Summary of FBI Report in Little Rock,
Arkansas integration difficulty."[45]

Likely designed for release to the press, this document did find its way into
the hands of key officials and favored reporters. Filled with half-truths and outright misstatements of fact, it directly contradicted another document titled
"Director's Brief," which Bureau operatives prepared for J. Edgar Hoover when
the investigation was actually complete. Most astonishing is a claim at the end
of the first paragraph; referring to the 450 interviews FBI agents had conducted,
the memo asserted, "Not a single individual had any knowledge of any act of
violence or actual threats of violence prior to the time the Governor called the
Guards on September 2, 1957." The Director's Brief noted that "Sixty-nine persons stated they heard rumors of violence. . . ."[46]

The Olney report dismissed Dallas P. Raney's FBI interview in which he
stated he had visited Virgil Blossom's office on the morning of September 2 to
share with the superintendent an alarming piece of information. A black man
whom he knew well but did not wish to identify had told him that morning
"that his brother would not permit his daughter to go to Central High School,
she being one of the approved Negro girls selected to attend, as her father had
information certain Negroes and white persons had bought a large number of
knives from one hardware store, identity unknown." Perhaps unaware that Blossom had approved seventeen students and not just nine, the FBI interviewed
only the fathers of the girls among the nine who actually attended Central High
School; when they could not corroborate Raney's story they dismissed it as
false, but of course the parents of the eight students who chose not to attend
Central may have returned their children to Horace Mann in response to
rumors or threats of violence. Numerous other interviews included evidence of
threatened violence that the FBI chose to ignore.[47]

The Olney "Summary" presented Virgil Blossom's claims as if they were facts,
and then concluded, "The result of the entire investigation shows that the Gov-

ernor did not at any time have any real evidence of impending violence or even serious threats of violence in order to justify mobilization of the Arkansas National Guard." Furthermore, "The investigation reveals that the Mayor of Little Rock was correct when he described the Governor's action as a hoax perpetrated for political reasons, that it could be explained 'only as a political move.'"[48]

This was the document Herbert Brownell carried with him when he flew to Newport, Rhode Island, for his meeting with Eisenhower and Faubus the next day. There can be little doubt he shared it with the president before Faubus had the chance to make his pitch. Soon the press leaks began. *New York Times* education editor Benjamin Fine, who was in Little Rock to cover the crisis, wrote, "Those aware of the contents of the [FBI Report] . . . said that it was 'devastating' in its analysis of the Governor's position." Similarly, *Gazette* stringer Liz Carpenter wrote from Washington, "The report is considered fatal to the governor's claim that the threat of violence justified his calling out the Guard." The FBI investigation of the "integration difficulty" in Little Rock was never made public, yet the falsity of the Olney report came back to haunt its authors. Olney resigned five days later, and Brownell soon followed him.[49]

The FBI report the Department of Justice prepared was a travesty of justice. It reflected a culture of arrogance and secrecy within the national government that alienated civil rights and antiwar activists in the next decade, and that contributed materially to the disintegration of the fabric of national unity created by World War II. A backwoods governor and a small, poor state served as convenient targets of northern, liberal wrath, tools rather than objects of sincere study. As symbols of southern wrongdoing they merited no mercy, and in the long term they offered psychic release and satisfaction to a broad spectrum of the American population who wanted to rail against America's racial failings without having to confront the evidence of similar behavior in their own backyard.

In the short term, bereft of allies in high places, Orval Faubus walked into the lion's den armed only with his native charm and intelligence. Even so, he almost prevailed.

CHAPTER EIGHT

IN SEARCH OF COMPROMISE

Faubus, Hays, and Eisenhower

T HANKS TO BROOKS HAYS'S ARRANGEMENTS, FRIDAY THE 13TH WAS the day that Orval Faubus flew to Rhode Island, to meet President Eisenhower at Newport. Hays took note of the governor's unaccustomed silence and wondered if he had lost Faubus's confidence. By contrast, Hays was excited, he later recalled, "by the feeling that this could become a great turning point in the civil rights relationship of state and federal government and that we could find a milestone conversation at Newport, that we might reach a conclusion that would be historic." Hays also felt "it would be a supreme moment in my own life to see something like this take place. No one needed to throw any laurels or put any laurels on my brow. The inner satisfaction I would get would be sufficient compensation." At the same time, as he admitted, "I certainly can't deny that I was giving some thought to that as every man in public life does if he is a rational person, that this is a great moment in my life and some of the things that I have fought for are now coming to the surface."[1]

National papers had reported the day before that Faubus seemed ready to "throw in the sponge" in his visit with the president. These reports troubled the Arkansas governor, although Orval Faubus said years later he went to Newport willing to compromise. Faubus did not take an attorney because he did not know Brownell was going to be there, and he thought the best approach to the president would be a personal one. He felt certain that if Eisenhower understood the situation, he would be willing to agree to a delay, and Judge Davies's *amicus* order had given him hope that the court order for immediate integration could be modified. He was to be disappointed on all counts.[2]

Hays and Faubus, the governor's Executive Secretary Arnold Sikes, and two commercial pilots spent Friday night in Providence. On Saturday morning government helicopters transported the three officials to the naval base at Newport, where Eisenhower had his "summer White House." Sherman Adams met the three at the airport and escorted them through "a maze of pushing and shoving reporters," until finally they arrived at the building where Eisenhower had his office. Sikes and presidential press secretary James Hagerty remained outside, Hays and Adams visited in a connecting waiting room, and Eisenhower took Faubus into his private office. Faubus believed this encounter had been designed to intimidate him as "originally a country boy, governor of a small state," but he claimed years later, "It didn't happen that way. I wasn't any more in awe of the President than I was anybody you'd meet on the street. He's another individual, he had virtues and he had defects, just like anyone else. . . ." Faubus may have been engaging in a bit of bravado and exaggeration, but it is true that he possessed enormous dignity and self-confidence.[3]

According to Faubus's recollections of the meeting, from which most of the following description is drawn, the president made a brief presentation, "and he seemed to be trying to follow a script from memory. . . ." At first he assumed the attitude "of a general lecturing a lieutenant about something embarrassing . . . , not something to be court martialed for, but to be reprimanded and sort of straightened out." The Arkansas governor had the strong feeling that someone had coached the president and advised him to take this approach; Faubus had the sense that Eisenhower expected him to cave in. The visiting governor repeatedly reassured the president that he was a loyal citizen and that he recognized the supremacy of federal law and courts. Eisenhower admonished him to go home and change the orders of the National Guard, continuing to preserve order but allowing the black children to enter Central High School. If he took this action promptly, the president suggested, the Justice Department could go to Judge Davies and ask for a suspension of the court proceedings planned for September 20. Stressing that it would not be to either party's advantage to have "a trial of strength between the President and a governor . . . ," Eisenhower concluded with the assurance, "I don't want to see any governor humiliated."[4]

Eisenhower reported in his memoir that the governor seemed "very appreciative" of his point of view, and the president "definitely got the understanding that, upon returning to Arkansas, he would within a matter of hours revoke his orders to the Guard to prevent re-entry of the Negro children into the School." Faubus later claimed consistently that he never gave Eisenhower these assurances, and neither Hays nor Adams reported these assurances in his memoirs. It is likely that the man who had cultivated a pattern of smiling and nodding and seeming to agree without specifically committing himself, caused a man who was accustomed to having his orders obeyed to conclude that he had carried the day.[5]

Faubus listened politely and then said, "Mr. President, I'd like to tell you something about the situation in Arkansas." He then told Eisenhower that Arkansas had more public schools integrated "than eleven other states combined with a comparable problem." He told the president that all of the state's institutions of higher learning had experienced integration under his administrations. So had all the transportation systems, both intrastate and interstate, and there had been "no great difficulties." Many businesses had been integrated. Faubus's administration was integrated; his staff meetings were integrated. Faubus had put blacks on the Arkansas Democratic Party's Central Committee, making Arkansas the first southern state to do so since Reconstruction. As Faubus recalled, "The president didn't know any of this. It was a complete surprise to him." The Arkansas governor thought back to his own wartime experience and realized that if General Eisenhower had had a staff officer "who had failed to inform him on a military situation as badly" as the president had been briefed about the situation in Arkansas, "someone would have been cashiered."

Faubus had planned carefully his presentation about Arkansas's progress in integration because he wanted to build up to his central argument by reflecting on *Brown II* and the concept of "all deliberate speed." "Mr. President," he said, "if any state . . . has attained or approached deliberate speed then Arkansas has, and I personally feel . . . that we should be entitled to some credit for this and not be pushed in such an extreme measure as we are being pushed in Little Rock at the present time." Then the governor presented what he hoped would be his most compelling argument, using a military analogy to suggest that Little Rock had been made "a focal point in the contest."

Governor Faubus explained there had been a great deal of publicity of the Little Rock School Board's plan of integration, and many newspapers were beginning to editorialize that Little Rock would be the model "for all of Arkansas and all of the South." The other school districts in Arkansas that had integrated had done so quietly, except Hoxie, and always they had succeeded and had avoided creating widespread consternation because they had not tried to set themselves up as an example. But in Little Rock Ashmore's editorials had aroused people in other districts and caused them to say, "Well, if Little Rock is going to be a model for us we better interest ourselves in it."

Having caught Eisenhower's interest, Faubus concluded with a concept he knew the old general could readily grasp, saying "you know in wartime you'll commit a platoon for some minor skirmish to clean out one pill box and the other side will commit a company, so then you commit a company and they commit a battalion, and you commit a regiment, and what started out to be a little minor skirmish develops into a major battle. That's how Little Rock developed." Faubus added a line he would later repeat, saying, "Now if Blossom and those who promoted integration of our schools had stated publicly over and over, 'This is our problem alone in Little Rock, it doesn't concern you other people,' it wouldn't have become the focal point in the contest which it became."[6]

At this point Faubus had already made the sale, but he added one other element to his argument. He explained to the president that constitutional lawyers had tried to persuade the public that the *Brown* decision was "the law of the land," when in fact it was only "the law of the case." In the words of the Arkansas governor, "The law of the land is made by congress, the law of the state is made by the legislature. The courts then interpret whether or not the law is in conformity with the state constitution or the federal constitution." In the case of the *Brown* decision, "the court changed the law of the land and the court has no authority to do that under the constitution of the United States. It has to go through the Congress. . . ."[7]

Sensing that the president was in agreement with most of what he was saying, Faubus went in for the kill and asked for a delay. Admitting that he did not know whether his approach would work or not, Faubus suggested "if we had a cooling off period of ten days, thirty days, three months, something like that, some of these people might lose . . . the determination which is apparent now . . . and they might be able then to admit the blacks without difficulty." The governor ended his presentation with a resounding plea, saying, "I won't tell you this will solve the problem, but I *am* telling you this is the only chance for it at the present time under the present conditions—with everyone in Arkansas, and the South as well, now interested in Little Rock because of its having become the focal point in the contest."

Eisenhower bolted from his office, wanting to verify with Brooks Hays that the things Orval Faubus had been telling him were true. Hays confirmed everything the governor had told him, adding "yes, Mr. President we very badly need a cooling off period." The four men had a rambling discussion for an hour or so, and Faubus happened to mention that he thought integration would have a better chance of working if it were started at the first grade, when little children had not formed racial prejudices. Eisenhower was not so sure, replying, "Yes, but Governor, I've talked to a lot of my Southern friends, and they don't think you can just dismiss this matter of the difference between the sexes . . ."[8]

According to Brooks Hays's recollection, the president continued, "I've got a lot of friends down in Georgia who have discussed this with me, and they say that you're not going to make these little white children even as early as the first grader unaware of the attractiveness of this cute little colored girl sitting next to him." The president smiled and said to Faubus, "You're not getting rid [of], if that's the thing that you're worried about, intermarriage ultimately and the new relationships." The long-standing southern fear of miscegenation had made its way into the consciousness, and the policy formation, of the president of the United States.[9]

Faubus indicated the compromises he was willing to make, including letting the black children into the school after a "cooling off period," and he made it clear that he intended to obtain a decision from the courts on the constitutionality of the Arkansas segregation laws during this period of delay. Eisenhower told him emphatically that he believed the states were responsible for maintaining law and order and that the governor's primary responsibility in this regard should be respected. "I do not criticize you for calling out the Guard," he assured Faubus, "our only difference is that I would have given them different instructions."[10]

Eisenhower then summoned his attorney general, Brownell, and asked, "Can't you go down to Little Rock and ask the court to delay the implementation of this order for a brief time, decide on whether it would be days or weeks, give the people a chance to cool off, and then we can go from there?" Faubus recalled that Brownell looked "sickly," and at first he hesitated about answering, but then he said, "We can't do that." Eisenhower just kept looking at Brownell and said he did not accept that as an answer, so Brownell replied, "We can't do it legally." Faubus's immediate thought, unexpressed, was that what Brownell was telling the president was "a barefaced lie, because the order of the federal judge inviting the Justice Department into the case was to provide any information or recommendations which it saw fit," but Faubus did not have a copy of the court order with him. He believed Brownell could legally have requested a delay, but he was not a lawyer, and he did not think he was in any position to argue with the attorney general of the United States.[11]

Faubus looked to Hays, who was a lawyer, but "Hays was sitting with his head down because then he was hoping he might get an appointment as federal judge and Brownell was the one who made the selections." Faubus then looked to the president, who seemed disappointed, but Eisenhower "just dropped his head and he kind of shook it for a moment," seeming to accept what his attorney general was telling him. At that, Faubus knew his case was lost. He got up from where he was sitting and moved across the room to a divan closer to Eisenhower and said ". . . well, perhaps there is another solution. Mr. President, I can let you crucify me. . . ." Faubus recalled Eisenhower's reaction almost forty years later, saying, "I never saw such a startled look on a man's face."

The conference was over. Faubus had made the president no promises; the president had offered no assurances. Brooks Hays was dismayed the conference had come to such an abrupt end; he had assumed that the group would reassemble after lunch to try to hammer out a compromise. The attorney general was "absolutely amazed [that] Faubus was capitulating . . . because I knew from my sources that politically he couldn't afford to let the black children into the high school. It would defeat him for re-election." Brownell nonetheless congratulated his boss, Hays and Faubus, thinking incredulously, "It was . . . one of the biggest constitutional crises in the history of the nation and it evidently had been solved at one conference." Brownell flew away from Newport smug in the assurance that something was amiss. As the Arkansas men headed for their helicopter, Faubus later claimed, he noticed Eisenhower was "already heading for the golf course."[12]

THE NOISE IN THE helicopter precluded any talking, but as soon as Hays and Faubus got back to their hotel the governor said, "Brooks, Brownell is wrong," and then he explained to the congressman about the court order inviting the Justice Department into the case. Hays was not "all that familiar with it," but at length he said, "Now Governor, I believe you're right," and he agreed that as soon as Faubus got back to Little Rock the governor should air mail a copy of the court order to Hays's office in Washington, and Hays would try to get it into the hands of the president. Faubus dared to hope Eisenhower would then see "that the Justice Department could intercede and that it could agree to some modification or at least a postponement of the implementation date until tempers and attitudes could cool off and the intense interest would decline. . . . [T]hat was my hope, that was the only hope that I had then."

Brownell's attitude left the governor no alternative except "abject surrender." As he wrote in his memoir, by the time he went to Newport he had also come to believe that such surrender "would not involve just me and the Little Rock situation, but the constitutional rights of all the states, all state officials and all the people of the United States." Faubus had taken several giant steps toward the leading edge of massive resistance.[13]

While the content of the Newport discussion was not to be made public, since, as Sherman Adams said, it was "subject to the customary restrictions on executive communications," Adams and Hays had decided that the waiting press deserved some information and they agreed to issue joint statements later that afternoon. As the appointed time drew near and Hays realized Faubus was making no move toward preparing a statement, the congressman suggested he would be willing to write out some thoughts. The governor replied, "Oh, I wish you would." Hays had hoped Faubus would recognize that Arkansas "was in a highly strategic position to make a demonstration of the reconciling of these two forces of federal power and state power, . . . and that some of the goals that I had visualized could actually be reached." Brooks Hays liked to tell himself he was working for Orval Faubus's benefit, but clearly he was pursuing his own agenda without much consideration of the governor's stated position.[14]

Hays undertook the assignment of preparing a statement for the governor to endorse. He went into another room and called Sherman Adams to inquire what the governor's statement should say. Adams told the congressman he and Brownell "wanted Faubus to say that he would comply with the law and withdraw the National Guard troops from the high school." Hays wrestled with both the wording and the governor and then called Adams again; Adams later reported that after he had "a long and baffling conversation" with Hays, the congressman persuaded Faubus to offer a statement that was "far short" of what Adams and Brownell had wanted. The Eisenhower team wondered if anything at all had been accomplished at Newport.[15]

Hays later explained that while he was writing the governor's statement, he was keenly aware that he, himself, would be up for reelection the following summer, and while he was willing to assume a certain amount of risk, he was not willing to take on "unnecessary ones." He only managed to get the governor to say the people of Little Rock expected to obey "valid court orders," along with the comment "I expect to accept the decisions of the court. . . ." Finally, after considerable pressure, Hays even persuaded Faubus to include the assertion that the *Brown* decision "is the law of the land and must be obeyed."[16]

Hays persuaded himself that this careful declaration was a commitment of some sort, and as he recalled later he thought this "was exciting from my point of view because I thought Governor Faubus and I, I'll put myself in a little secondary position, had pulled it out of the fire. We had rescued Little Rock. Naturally, I was elated." Hays commented years later, ". . . if Faubus had stayed by the commitment of the statement that I wrote for him at his request we wouldn't have had the trouble we had in 1957."[17]

Eisenhower released his own statement: "The governor stated his intention to respect the decisions of the United States District court and to give his full cooperation in carrying out his responsibilities in respect to these decisions." The Eisenhower statement implied that the conferees had reached an agreement, but of course they had not. In reflecting on the Newport meeting years later, Faubus charged, "My biggest complaint of Congressman Hays' role in the affair is that he did not warn me of the devious strategy of the White House and the efforts of entrapment."[18]

In explaining his actions at Newport, Orval Faubus eventually fell into an error of speech that followed him to the grave. Appearing on the national telecast *Face the Nation* a year later, Faubus suggested the *Brown* decision was not binding on him because it was "the law of the case" and not "the law of the land." A reporter asked him, "Here you said in this statement you recognized the Supreme Court decision as the law of the land and now you say it isn't the law of the land?" Faubus explained the pressures on him to make the statement at Newport and then concluded, "Anyhow, because I said it then doesn't make it so." He meant that his saying it was the law of the land did not make it the law of the land, but critics immediately interpreted the governor's comment to mean, "You can't depend on anything I say." The phrase "Because I said it doesn't make it so" haunted him for the rest of his life.[19]

THE DAY AFTER his return from Newport, Orval Faubus subjected himself, over his advisers' objections, to a televised interview by a young, feisty Mike Wallace. Faubus managed Wallace deftly, responding to all his barbed, loaded questions with courteous, reasoned answers. As Osro Cobb wrote of the exchange, "From this and other performances, ... it became apparent [Faubus] had no ghost writers but was providing his own ammunition from day to day." Equally important, Wallace's aggressive treatment of the governor infuriated many viewers; Faubus claimed in his memoir that Wallace called him a "hillbilly from Greasy Creek" and blew smoke in his face. The governor's courteous, smiling responses earned him legions of new supporters, and from that point on "telegrams came in by the bale."[20]

Brooks Hays called from Texas to check on the governor and Faubus pleaded with him to come to Little Rock, saying, "This thing isn't smoothing out like I hoped it would." Hays returned to Little Rock "with forebodings." The congressman and the governor spent hours secluded together at the Governor's Mansion, and Hays became very fond of the man who began to call him "my bishop." But no amount of good feeling could mask the fact that the weary congressman was urging a course of surrender.[21]

After almost continuous meetings all day Tuesday, on Wednesday morning, the 18th, Hays finally persuaded Faubus to let the National Guard be federalized, thereby removing responsibility for them from the governor. Yet Sherman Adams refused to go along, and the Justice Department refused to allow federal marshals to be used. On Thursday Faubus told him "Brooks, I can't do this.... It would be political suicide."[22]

Hays's influence and role were rapidly waning. His meetings with the governor were supposed to be confidential, and yet time and again Faubus heard from his sources that Hays went directly to Harry Ashmore and reported the substance of their discussions. Faubus later told the Eisenhower Administration Project he quickly realized Hays "wasn't playing as straight with me as I'd thought. . . . [W]hen he came in with his ingratiating and friendly way, naturally I gave him heed, gave him an audience. I would have anyone. But before it was over with, I found out that the things he and I talked about in confidence, I'd get them back from downtown fifteen minutes after he left."[23]

Harry Ashmore and Sid McMath were the two people in Little Rock that Faubus had publicly identified as his "enemies." He felt certain the two men, along with Hugh Patterson and Henry Woods, were working purposefully to discredit him with the visiting press in daily sessions at the Little Rock Press Club across the street from the *Gazette*. (Most of the out-of-town newsmen used the *Arkansas Gazette* as their headquarters.) As Faubus wrote years later, "There with the whiskey and conversation flowing freely, [McMath] visited with the out-of-state and foreign press representatives, becoming quite a hero to them as he helped Harry Ashmore and the *Gazette* editors indoctrinate the strangers against me."[24]

Faubus claimed before he left for Newport that McMath had turned on him at the outset of the Little Rock crisis "when he got mad because I wouldn't turn everything over to him." He later elaborated, saying, "McMath and Woods were pretty condemnatory of me at the time, and they tried to portray me as a country hick who didn't know my way about, and then of course they had to find some way to discredit me. So they . . . began to use the theory that I did it all for politics." This view of Faubus found its way into a *Time* magazine article about Little Rock that even staffers at the *Gazette* agreed was over the top. For Faubus, there were fewer and fewer intermediaries whom he could trust.[25]

PRESIDENT EISENHOWER had expected Faubus to go home from the Newport conference and either remove the National Guard or change its orders. Now, he felt betrayed. He called Herbert Brownell and said "you were right . . . Faubus has gone back on his word." The attorney general wrote of the president in his memoir, saying, "I could tell he was furious. His voice was tense. He was acting as a military commander-in-chief, dealing with Faubus as a subordinate who had let him down in the midst of battle." Brownell knew the president did not want to use military force to effect desegregation in Little Rock, for he feared the Arkansas governor would simply shut down the schools and Faubus's pattern of noncompliance would be adopted all over the South. Nonetheless, the

Justice Department began contingency planning to employ federal troops if Faubus refused to submit to the injunction that Judge Davies was poised to issue on September 20.[26]

Faubus's legal advisers had been maneuvering since September 10 to prepare for their appearance before Judge Davies, continuing to strategize through the Newport conference and the week after. In consultation with Senator Richard Russell, Faubus's lawyers assured the governor repeatedly he was on firm legal ground, he was not in defiance of Judge Davies's orders, and as they eventually decided, he was not even subject to the jurisdiction of Judge Davies's court, because "the action was against a sovereign state and jurisdiction could only be vested in the Supreme Court." When they submitted a brief to Judge Davies arguing the last point, Brooks Hays realized his efforts at compromise had failed, and his frustration deepened when Harry Ashmore called him to say he thought it was time for Hays to pull out of the negotiations.[27]

Meanwhile, Bill Smith received word that the federal government planned to file suit against Governor Faubus. Thinking the governor would hide behind the National Guardsmen stationed at the Governor's Mansion, federal officials reportedly thought they could blast Faubus through the press as "a process-dodger." When he learned of this scheme Smith called the U.S. attorney and said, "Osro, I understand you're getting ready to file an action against Governor Faubus. When you do, if you will send Beal Kidd, the United States Marshal, to the Mansion, if you'll let me know what time you'll be here, Governor Faubus and I will walk down to the front gate and he'll accept service." Smith recalled years later that this action "staggered" Cobb, and when the governor put out a press release announcing his plans, Cobb was "staggered" again. Smith and Faubus actually did walk down to the gate to accept service, where they were photographed by numerous national press services. As Smith explained years later, "I had one understanding with Governor Faubus, that he would never violate a court order, and if he did, why, I'd withdraw. He said he had no intention of violating a court order, but he had stated his position, and if it was changed it had to be changed by court order."[28]

Judge Davies's courtroom on Friday, September 20, was a spectacle. The hallway outside "looked like something out of a Hollywood premiere. . . . The cameras whirred and flashbulbs flashed when the principals of the drama went out of the courtroom and into the floodlights." Judge Davies had reserved the jury box for the press, since this was a nonjury trial, and Bill Smith estimated that Davies also reserved half of the spectators' seats in the courtroom for newsmen. As Smith recalled, "I have seen some despicable actions by judges in my day, but I've never seen anything like Davies. . . . It wasn't a trial, it was a star chambers proceedings. . . ." The point at issue in the case was whether Governor Faubus's use of the National Guard violated Davies's orders that integration proceed. Bill Smith had advised Faubus "it was not the duty of the Governor to enforce any federal court order, and that to do so could become a great financial burden to the state of Arkansas. . . ." The eyes of the world now focused on the packed courtroom in Little Rock to see if the judge agreed.[29]

JUDGE DAVIES BEGAN by dismissing two motions which claimed that he should recuse himself and that he did not have jurisdiction in the case. At that point, Faubus's lead attorney asked the judge for permission to be excused, and the governor's lawyers—Tom Harper, Kay Matthews, and Walter Pope— stunned everyone by walking out of the courtroom. At the Governor's Mansion, when a young reporter had told the governor that he was just hanging around to get his reaction "in case they started crucifying him in the courtroom downtown," Faubus and his aides had laughed. Now, the governor sat down and wrote a statement that opened with the words: "Now begins the crucifixion."[30]

Faubus explained to the young reporter, Bob McCord, that just the day before, he had secured a copy of a mimeographed letter Osro Cobb had sent to many of the two hundred people he had subpoenaed to appear as government witnesses, informing them their presence in the courtroom was no longer necessary. The governor believed Cobb had mailed this letter to "all of those persons who made statements upholding the stand I have taken in this matter," making it clear to Faubus that the hearing was going to be "a very one-sided affair" and that "the Justice Department is not in this thing as an impartial friend of the court." Faubus told McCord that with a group of "carefully-selected witnesses," no cross-examination, and no evidence presented to support his allegations of the threat of violence, "[t]he results are a foregone conclusion."[31]

The trial proceeded through four hours of testimony, with Osro Cobb eliciting information from only ten witnesses: Superintendent Virgil Blossom, Mayor Woodrow Mann, Chief of Police Marvin Potts, National Guard General Sherman Clinger, Central High Principal Jess Matthews, School Board President William G. Cooper, and students Ernest Green and Elizabeth Eckford. At length Judge Davies issued a 250-word ruling in which he said, "It is very clear" Little Rock's plan for gradual integration "has been thwarted" by Governor Faubus's use of the National Guard at Central High School. Dismissing the governor's concerns about the potential for violence in Little Rock, Davies argued, "It is equally demonstrable from the testimony here today that there would have been no violence in carrying out the plan of integration, and that there has been no violence. . . ." Based on that judgment, Judge Davies granted Herbert Brownell's petition for a preliminary injunction against Faubus and the National Guard officers and ordered that integration at Central High School "should proceed forthwith."[32]

Judge Davies never mentioned the FBI report that was lying on his bench throughout the hearing. Most likely the judge did not base his ruling on that report because he would then have had to share it with Faubus's lawyers on appeal, and Justice Department staffers had already realized the report contained ample, damning evidence of the potential for violence in Little Rock. The report was never made public, and its findings died the quiet death J. Edgar Hoover and Herbert Brownell hoped they would.[33]

THAT AFTERNOON GOVERNOR Faubus obeyed the judge's injunction and ordered the National Guard removed from Little Rock Central High School. The governor and his advisers thought the judge had ordered him to withdraw the Guard completely, and he soon found himself subject to new criticism for leaving the city unprotected. In a televised speech that night, Faubus announced that the litigation in Judge Davies's court had proceeded "as expected," and that the judge had, among other things, overruled the governor's motion to dismiss for lack of jurisdiction "even though the Justice Department attorneys were unable to, and did not attempt to answer most of the points of law presented by the motion. In doing so," Faubus claimed, the judge "ignored the law and permitted the Justice Department to assume to itself authority expressly denied to it by action of the most recent Congress."[34]

Faubus made much of the fact that the government had subpoenaed two hundred witnesses and then dismissed most of them. The governor claimed these were witnesses "who had knowledge of and would have testified as to the true facts of the situation." Faubus also claimed their dismissal was "another indication of the number of witnesses which the Justice Department did not want the Court to hear."[35]

Faubus denounced Sid McMath and Henry Woods as the source of "the slanted and falsified reports" in *Time* and *Newsweek,* Harry Ashmore and Hugh Patterson as "ardent integrationists" who had tried to indoctrinate the visiting press "with a biased and prejudiced viewpoint" toward the governor, and Woodrow Mann as "the discredited and repudiated politician" who said that no disorder or violence was imminent, yet currently had two Little Rock policemen assigned "to the protection of his home and person." Faubus worried aloud that "disorder and violence, which has so far been prevented," would now occur, and he implored the NAACP to withhold the black students from Central High "until a cooling-off period" had elapsed.[36]

The governor concluded with a disturbing thought: "With the curtailment by the order of Judge Davies of my authority to preserve the peace and good order of the community and protect all citizens, I now can only say that I will use all other means at my command to preserve the peace, and sincerely hope that all citizens will cooperate in this endeavor." With that he flew away to Sea Island, Georgia, for the Southern Governors' Conference and a new career as a southern folk hero.[37]

NINE OF THE ORIGINAL seventeen black children approved for enrollment at Central High School had maintained their resolve to attend. The nine had been at loose ends for three weeks and were falling far behind their peers, although Daisy Bates had struggled to provide them with tutors and some kind of structure. Now, despite Governor Faubus's urgent pleas that they remain out of school through a cooling-off period, they began to prepare for what promised to be a frightening situation on Monday morning.[38]

Mayor Mann spent much of Saturday, September 21, scrambling about Little Rock trying to put in place the forces he would need in order to preserve the peace on Monday. Police Chief Marvin Potts promised the mayor his men would do their best to keep order, but he refused to use police officers to escort the black children into the school. Fire Chief Gann Nalley refused to allow his hoses to be used for crowd control even though, as Mann later noted, "police officials had made it clear that success in mob control depended largely on the supplementary use of water." Mann made a brave statement to the press urging Little Rock residents to accept integration peacefully at the school and warning that "local law enforcement officers" would deal with anyone who attempted to create disorder.[39]

At Sherman Adams's request, Brooks Hays returned to Little Rock Saturday afternoon, albeit without enthusiasm and with considerable apprehension for his future. Sunday morning he was dismayed to read on the front page of the *Arkansas Gazette* an article by Liz Carpenter speculating on his prospects for securing the appointment as federal judge. Carpenter reported the Washington scuttlebutt that some Republican leaders thought Eisenhower's reliance on the Democratic Hays had damaged the GOP's chances of success in the 1960 elections, because they thought (incorrectly) that Hays had played a role in Eisenhower's "failure to act" when Faubus called out the National Guard. Carpenter concluded with the thought that any judicial appointment would have to have the approval of Arkansas's senior senator, John McClellan, who had publicly supported Faubus, and that "he, too, may be re-evaluating the contenders in light of their action in the Arkansas crisis." Hays soon wrote to Sherman Adams apologizing for the article and removing his name from consideration if it became politically necessary for Adams to make such an announcement.[40]

About the time Hays finished digesting the newspaper, his telephone started ringing. First Mayor Mann, despite weeks of claiming otherwise, "now expressed concern to me over the danger that the disorder might be too great to be controlled by his small police force," and he asked for Hays's assistance. Then Virgil Blossom appeared at Hays's hotel, imploring the congressman to call Washington and line up some federal marshals to help keep the situation in Little Rock under control. Hays called Sherman Adams, who said he would talk to Deputy Attorney General Bill Rogers. Within an hour, Adams called back to inform Hays that Rogers had agreed to call Osro Cobb and tell him "to work with us on this and to get in touch with Blossom and to do what he was suggesting." Hays called Cobb himself and said, "They're waiting to hear from you. Call them and get some clear instructions now and work with them." Cobb later told Hays, "They didn't give me any such instructions. They gave me anything but that." The naive Hays later pondered this "fault" in the lines of communication between Little Rock and Washington.[41]

Soon Hays's phone rang again, and this time it was Henry Woods, Sid McMath's law partner and Woodrow Mann's attorney, reporting that the mayor had heard rumors of a mob being formed to descend on Central High School on Monday. Woods invited the congressman to his home for a strategy session. Hays was not sure he should go, for he feared he might be drawn into "the orbit of political opposition to Governor Faubus, and I was trying hard to escape involvement in the feud which had developed between McMath and the Governor." Blossom persuaded Hays they should both go see the mayor, for all hope for preserving the peace now rested upon the local police "and such other help as the Mayor could muster."[42]

When Hays and Blossom arrived at Woods's home they were greeted by Woods, McMath, Mann, Edwin Dunaway, and Harry Ashmore, a veritable Who's Who of Faubus opponents. Woods had called Dunaway because of his close friendship with Daisy Bates, and because he felt the group needed to know what the black children were going to do on Monday. He had called Ashmore, he said later, because he thought "the paper needs to know about this and Ashmore needs to know." He had also called Osro Cobb, but Cobb made no appearance at the little house in the Heights. Woods later told a colleague that he and the others worked that day to keep Virgil Blossom "from having a breakdown. . . ."[43]

The group stayed at Woods's house all day, considering a variety of options. Hays called Sherman Adams to talk about marshals. Dunaway called Assistant Police Chief Gene Smith, an old friend, to ascertain if the largely segregationist police force could be counted on to maintain order at Central High; Smith was doubtful, so the group got Chief Potts to assign Smith to the high school, thereby getting Potts "off the spot." Woods called Lieutenant Governor Nathan Gordon, a friend from law school who was now officially in charge of the state police and the National Guard while Faubus was out of the state; Woods recalled years later that Gordon "didn't want to get into the picture. It was a hot political issue." Blossom called Judge Davies to ask for federal marshals. Judge Davies directed the superintendent to call Osro Cobb. The tiny band of planners realized immediately, with alarm, they were back to square one.[44]

Mayor Mann had already tried to persuade Fire Chief Nalley to be prepared to use his hoses against the crowd. Nalley had refused and threatened to resign if he were ordered to do so. Mann was increasingly concerned that some black children might be killed the next day "and that it would precipitate one hell of a race riot over there in that part of town." The man who had said publicly for three weeks there was no danger of violence in Little Rock now saw things in a different light.[45]

Every person at Henry Woods's house had participated in the process of pushing Orval Faubus into a narrowing corridor. Whether out of ideological commitment, lack of clarity, or self-interest, all had made choices that limited those of the governor, pointing him increasingly in the direction of his own political advancement down a path that he did not, from his background and inclination, want to take. Faced with repeated betrayals from old friends and former allies, as well as from the government agencies he might have expected to oppose him, Orval Faubus finally hardened, and succumbed to opportunism.

IN THE FINAL ANALYSIS, two questions beg for answers: How threatening was the situation? Can Faubus's behavior fairly be labeled defiance? Bulky and disorganized as it is, the FBI Report (finally secured through use of the Freedom of Information Act) yields impressive evidence of the threat of violence in Little Rock, as the Justice Department ultimately conceded in its own internal memorandum. In addition, the behavior of key players is instructive. Daisy Bates, of course, had many instances of violence directed against her home, which she detailed in her memoir, *The Long Shadow of Little Rock.* Virgil Blossom also chronicled in his memoir, *It HAS Happened Here,* many threats directed at him. Perhaps more revealing are the admissions of fearfulness elicited in private interviews: School Board members Harold Engstrom and William G. Cooper took special precautions to protect their families; Henry Rath and Wayne Upton had Little Rock police officers stationed at their homes for several days in September; Arkansas state troopers guarded Osro Cobb, Bill Smith, and Orval Faubus. The state police gave Alta Faubus a little gun to carry for her own protection; federal marshal Beal Kidd guarded Brooks Hays for a week; and Wiley Branton, Woodrow Mann, and Judge Ronald Davies had police protection around the clock. With regard to the second question, despite Faubus's reputation, he was never in direct defiance of the court. He was never cited or arrested for contempt. As he said to researchers Jack Bass and Walter DeVries in 1974, "I never did defy a court order. When they issued a court order directly to me I evaded each time. I never was in defiance of a court order."[46]

Liberal columnist Walter Lippmann posed the question in terms that came to define the textbook narrative of Little Rock. "The issue, in short," he wrote on the day of Judge Davies's final hearing, "is whether a Governor may use the National Guard to enforce segregation." In the end, Lippmann suggested, Faubus "must recognize his responsibility to enforce the law, not to nullify it." Conservative columnist David Lawrence disagreed, however, arguing that the Justice Department's injunction against Faubus had created a situation in which "the representative or republican system of government would be suspended by the order of a federal judge. Never before in American history has the Constitution been so flagrantly defied and disregarded by the executive." Political rhetoric aside, this exchange frames the constitutional debate at issue in the Little Rock crisis, underscoring the conflict between the view on the one hand that Faubus had a responsibility to uphold federal law, and the view on the other hand that a governor should be allowed to determine when a threat to domestic tranquility existed in his state. The bottom line, of course, is that Faubus attempted to preserve the peace by using the National Guard to keep the black children out of Central High School. If he had used the Guard to preserve the peace while letting them *in* there would have been no constitutional crisis— although there may well have been bloodshed. In the end Orval Faubus succumbed to frustration, vanity, and ambition, and his turn toward opportunism removed him from the forward march of history in 1957.[47]

CHAPTER NINE

CENTRAL HIGH SCHOOL, ACT ONE

Daisy Bates

Aᴼᵀᴱᴿ ᴀ ᴡᴇᴇᴋᴇɴᴅ ᴏғ ᴛʜᴜɴᴅᴇʀsᴛᴏʀᴍs, Mᴏɴᴅᴀʏ, Sᴇᴘᴛᴇᴍʙᴇʀ 23 dawned clear and cool at Little Rock Central High School. Birds chirped in the many trees that dotted the huge campus while squirrels scampered about the grounds, oblivious to the drama that was about to be played out in the surrounding streets. Often called "the most beautiful high school in America" since its completion thirty years before, the massive buff-brick structure fronted along two city blocks. Its five stories rose majestically out of a typical southern working-class neighborhood of modest white and black homes, the grandeur of its facade conveying the hope that Little Rock nurtured for its youth and its future.[1]

Driving up to the intersection of Park and Fourteenth (now named Daisy L. Gatson Bates Avenue), the first-time visitor to Central High School feels surprise, awe, and intimidation in the presence of the overpowering fortresslike structure that rises improbably from its humble surroundings. Set well back from the street, the immense building is almost medieval in effect. The lush, well-tended grounds render it serene, even ethereal, and one almost expects knights on white steeds and magical unicorns to appear from the wings. Passing a reflecting pool and colonnade on the ground level, the visitor approaches the elevated front entry by climbing winding sets of stairs, arriving eventually at a central exterior piazza. Three oversized wood and glass double doors open beneath equally large glass-paned arches; rising above the entrance on four concrete pillars, massive neo-gothic statues depict "Ambition," "Opportunity," "Personality," and "Preparation." Ranking for years among the top high schools in the country in academic performance and college preparation, by 1957 this yellow brick school had opened avenues of opportunity for three decades of Little Rock's youth—provided they were white.

Several blocks away stands a smaller redbrick replica of Central High School, for many years a beacon of pride and hope for Little Rock's African-American community. Until it was supplanted by the new Horace Mann High School in 1956, Paul Lawrence Dunbar High School, built about the same time and on a similar floor plan as Central High, although one-third the size of its white sister, had a strong faculty and an impressive impact on the community it served. Principal L. M. Christophe had the only earned doctorate in the Little Rock school system. All of his high school teachers held bachelor's degrees, and almost half of his faculty held or were working toward master's degrees.[2]

At the forefront of the social elite in the black community, Dunbar's teachers set a standard of achievement in their classrooms and rectitude in their personal lives that had served as a palpable example of "the way up" for two generations among Little Rock's people of color. In time the school became such a source of pride and inspiration that it developed a vibrant and loyal alumnae group of thousands of members. For many years, promising African-American children from communities all over Arkansas, for whom educational opportunity ceased after the eighth grade, made their way to Little Rock to live with relatives and attend Dunbar High School. Scores of Dunbar's graduates went on to fruitful professional and business careers. With the construction of Horace Mann, the white officials of the Little Rock School Board sacrificed the Dunbar tradition, joining the frantic southern effort to stave off integration by providing, at the last minute, "separate but equal" schools for all children.[3]

Like many Dunbar students, the beautiful, fiery young president of Arkansas's statewide NAACP, Daisy Bates, had finished eighth grade in a tiny south Arkansas sawmill town. Yet when Daisy Lee Gatson moved to Little Rock, it was not for schooling. Her formal education had ended in her hometown of Huttig. Bates believed that three white men had raped and murdered her mother when she was an infant, and she carried into adulthood a smoldering anger and hatred of all white people. Both the date of her birth and the date of her marriage to the older Lucious Christopher Bates remain shrouded in mystery, but by 1941 she and L.C. had moved to Little Rock where he had founded a crusading newspaper, the *Arkansas State Press*. Partners in the operation of their newspaper and in the fight to improve the lives of Little Rock's black citizens, Daisy and L.C. Bates were also partners in the struggle to achieve integration in the Little Rock public schools.[4]

Daisy Bates's moving autobiography, *The Long Shadow of Little Rock*, reveals her to have been bright and aggressive from childhood, eager to compete and win, even against the big boys. Shaped both by her hatred of whites and her love of her gentle, funny, irreverent adoptive father, Daisy grew into a strikingly beautiful, vivacious, forceful woman who yearned for distinction and recog-

nition and who seized eagerly the opportunity to join her husband in his crusade against discrimination and injustice. L.C. reminded Daisy of her father,
and he seemed to take the same kind of pleasure her father had experienced in
watching her flex her ego and dazzle the crowds. Fine-boned and petite, with a
mop of loosely curled hair and a penchant for heavy makeup, Bates cut a fine
figure in the social circles she entered in Little Rock, although she and L.C. were
never fully accepted by the black social elite. That elite—many of them Dunbar
graduates—valued education, and Daisy was painfully aware of her lack of
schooling. Nonetheless, her high energy and exuberance made her a force to be
reckoned with among people who might otherwise have been inclined to dismiss her because of her country background and her grammatical lapses.[5]

Daisy Bates felt immense impatience with the black elite's accommodation-
ist approach to the indignities of segregation. Her protege, Ozell Sutton, suggested that the Bateses were "as condemning of complacent black leadership as
they were of what they considered to be reactionary white leadership." Bates
took an increasingly active role within the Arkansas conference of the National
Association for the Advancement of Colored People, becoming president in
1952; her official title was President of the State Conference of Branches. Bates
also served on the board of the Arkansas Council on Human Relations, an affiliate of the Southern Regional Council, where she had more opportunities than
the vast majority of Little Rock's African-Americans to interact with whites as
social equals. On the ACHR board she developed cordial working relationships
with three white men, Harry Ashmore, Edwin Dunaway and Fred Darragh, that
served her well in the subsequent civil rights battles in her city. Understanding
the class tensions that ran through the Little Rock crisis, Bates commented to
Ashmore, "You may deserve Orval Faubus, but by God I don't!"[6]

BATES BELIEVED SHE understood "the timeworn lust of the white man for the
Negro woman," but nothing in her writing or her behavior suggested she understood a related element of that compulsion, the white fear of miscegenation. An
unsigned, undated memorandum in the Daisy Bates Papers reflects the efforts
of the NAACP national office to bring Bates up to speed on the subject. Providing several examples of the "bedroom theme" Citizens' Council speakers often
developed, the memo quotes White Citizens' Council founder Robert B. Patterson of Indianola, Mississippi, saying, "All of us feel that integration is impossible here because we are realists enough to know that it would eventually lead to
intermarriage, mongrelization and the destruction of the white race in the
south. Racial intermarriage and a preference for light skinned women by many

so called negro leaders has shown their belief that the racial problem can best be solved in the bedroom."[7]

Bates may have shared some of her Little Rock friends' understanding of the white fear of black male potency and power. As black activist and longtime Bates friend Annie Abrams expressed it years after Daisy Bates's death, the "one-drop" rule of the segregationist's racial calculus seemed to imply superiority of the black seed. If interracial sexual liaisons resulted in the erosion of white racial characteristics and the introduction of black traits, did that not suggest a genetic black supremacy? Many in the black community believed this was the source of white fear of the black male. As a woman, many believed, Daisy Bates was far more effective in dealing with whites than her "handsome, erect black husband" would have been, or than any black male could have been.[8]

Under Daisy Bates's leadership the Arkansas NAACP had been pushing for immediate integration ever since the *Brown* decision. The group waited patiently, though not meekly or silently, for over a year for the Little Rock School Board to formalize its plans before filing its lawsuit in February 1956. Its loss had given judicial sanction to Virgil Blossom's plan for gradual integration. The NAACP had appealed, then lost again. In consultation with the national office, however, the Little Rock chapter of the NAACP had decided not to appeal the Circuit Court's decision because of the risk that with Supreme Court approval the Blossom Plan could become the standard for integration everywhere. Meanwhile, members of the local chapter grew increasingly dismayed that the Little Rock School Board continually whittled down its plan.[9]

Some of the black students selected to go to Central High had never met Daisy Bates before Sunday, September 1, when she arrived at Virgil Blossom's office as he met with the seventeen selected for Central High. With characteristic boldness the NAACP president was determined to propel her organization into the forefront of the integration process in Little Rock. Some of the chosen few had worked with her in the Little Rock Youth Council, and she claimed later that they invited her to function as their mentor as they initiated the transition into the formerly all-white school. Whatever the origin of her involvement, she quickly assumed a leadership position as the coordinator of the group and the liaison between school officials and the black children.[10]

Bates had taken it upon herself to organize a biracial group of ministers to accompany the children the first day. This group, in turn, secured a statement from the National Guardsmen that they were barring the children on orders of the governor. She had enlisted tutors for the children during the three weeks they were out of school from September 4 to September 23, and she had also run interference between the children and the scores of reporters who wanted to interview them at all hours of the night and day. Through all of the activities of that harried and much-publicized period, the names of the NAACP, and especially of Daisy Bates, were inescapably linked to the activities of the group that soon earned the sobriquet "The Little Rock Nine."[11]

Daisy Bates had long known she and her husband were visible targets as a result of their war on segregation. They had been jailed for libel for criticizing a white judge; the Arkansas Supreme Court later overturned their convictions. They had lost white advertising after their outraged reporting of the killing of an African-American soldier by white policemen in 1942, and that loss had led to a strategic decision to depend on subscriptions from the black community rather than the beneficence of the white community. They had been harassed by telephone invective and drive-by taunting on many occasions. They had had two crosses burned on their lawn after the race-baiting governor's race in 1956. But the most harrowing assault on Daisy Bates came on August 22, 1957, after Marvin Griffin's speech to the Capital Citizens' Council. Sitting quietly in her living room in the home that she and L.C. had built two years before with the earnings from their successful newspaper, Bates was stunned when a large rock came hurtling through the plate-glass window that faced the street. Collecting herself from the floor where she had instinctively thrown herself, the young civil rights leader retrieved the rock from the shards of glass that littered the carpet, untied the attached note and read the almost illegible scrawl, "Stone this time, dynamite next."[12]

Daisy Bates did not sleep much that night, but by the next morning she was ready to commit herself to the fight of her life, and that is exactly what it proved to be. In the ensuing weeks segregationists burned more crosses on the lawn; vandals broke the picture window numerous times until the Bates installed a steel screen over it; an insurance agency cancelled the family's household policy; and armed guards began to protect the house, and its residents, around the clock. NAACP regional director Clarence Laws arrived from New Orleans to provide tactical and moral support, and the national office of the NAACP began to provide daily guidance and counsel. (Unlike Rosa Parks, Bates had had no advance training or preparation for the role she would play in Little Rock.) Bates took this opportunity to appeal to Gloster Current, NAACP director of branches, and then to Roy Wilkins, NAACP executive director, for financial support for the now-troubled *Arkansas State Press*, which had begun to founder as a result of the recent, massive loss of white advertising. Daisy Bates became a fighting machine, running on adrenaline, and she relished her dramatic role at the white-hot center of what she envisioned as a titanic struggle between the forces of darkness and light.[13]

BEFORE ORVAL FAUBUS removed the National Guard from Central High School on Friday, September 20, he thought Daisy Bates had agreed not to try to integrate the school in his absence. In his televised speech he had implored the black parents of those selected for desegregation to keep their children at home for a few days in order to allow passions to cool. One of Daisy Bates's young NAACP workers, Ozell Sutton, heard the broadcast and rushed immediately to the Bates home to urge her not to heed the governor's importuning. A committed proponent of integration, Sutton was convinced that if the black children did not press their advantage now, they would lose momentum and their parents would lose heart.[14]

On Saturday the *Arkansas Democrat* had printed Virgil Blossom's announcement that no nonstaff adults would be allowed inside Central High School on Monday, although the superintendent admitted he had had no indication of whether the nine Negro students planned to attend school Monday "or when they will come." Sunday morning the *Arkansas Gazette* reported, "Spokesmen for the Negro students indicated [they] would return soon—though they wouldn't say exactly when. . . ." Clarence Laws had returned to New Orleans and reported later he did not know the nine were planning to attend Central High on Monday until he heard on the radio they had gone in. All of these bits of evidence support the conclusion that Daisy Bates had not originally intended to send the black children into Central High School on Monday morning—but something changed her mind. Perhaps it was Ozell Sutton's pleadings. Or perhaps it was the arguments of the little band of conspirators at Henry Woods's house in the Heights, partisan workers who wanted to prove that Orval Faubus had manufactured a crisis and that nothing untoward would happen in the absence of his interference.[15]

Daisy Bates reported to Gloster Current at the national NAACP headquarters that she spent all day Sunday, September 22, working with Harry Ashmore, Edwin Dunaway, and Woodrow Mann, who were at Henry Woods's house, to try to get the federal government to provide some kind of protection for the black children to enter Central High School. The Justice Department, of course, refused. Police Chief Marvin Potts refused to order his men to "escort" the Negro children into the school. Acting Governor Nathan Gordon had 150 National Guardsmen ready for use at Central High School, but he said he would not call out the Guard to restore order at the school without a request from school or city officials. He said any request from Mayor Mann would have to be in writing because he wouldn't take "Mann's word for anything." Similarly, when the mayor called Governor Faubus at Sea Island to request the use of Arkansas state policemen, and Faubus consented, state police director Herman Lindsey, undoubtedly remembering Virgil Blossom's denial of having asked Orval Faubus verbally for protection, demanded a written request for aid before he agreed to authorize the use of fifty state troopers at Central High.[16]

Late Sunday night Virgil Blossom called Daisy Bates and told her to have the children at her house first thing Monday morning and then await instructions on how to proceed. Monday morning's *Arkansas Gazette* carried a statement by Mrs. Margaret Jackson, vice president of the Mothers' League of Central High School, saying "we hope to have a big demonstration [on Park Street in front of the school] to show that the people of Little Rock are still against integration. I hope they [Negroes] won't get in." At Daisy Bates's house, where eight of the children, several parents, and a handful of reporters had gathered to prepare for the children's second attempt to enter Central High, radio reports informed the anxious little band that an unruly crowd had heeded Mrs. Jackson's wishes and had formed once again in front of the school. Radio commentators broadcast sidewalk interviews, and the group assembled at Bates's home heard one man say, "Just let those niggers show up! Just let 'em try!" Another man fumed "We won't stand for our schools being integrated. If we let 'em in, next thing they'll be marrying our daughters." Minnijean Brown's mother sat with her hands folded in her lap, her lips moving in prayer; Elizabeth Eckford's father bowed his head. The irreverent Daisy Bates found that she, too, was praying.[17]

Finally the telephone call came from Gene Smith, assistant police chief, saying that plans were in place to allow the children to enter the school through one of the out-of-the-way doors on the south side. The white reporters at Bates's home left immediately; four black reporters stayed behind, hoping to get more details so they could have exclusive coverage of the historic moment. Rushing to leave, Bates told them if they arrived at the school on the Sixteenth Street side, they could see the children enter. As he drove four of the children and Daisy Bates in his car toward Central High School, Chris Mercer, a young black lawyer and former associate director of the Arkansas Council on Human Relations, thought that there would be no real violence that day in Little Rock. These children were not warriors, he thought, they were just kids who had never had any real leadership roles or training, and surely in this day and age they would not be placed in harm's way.[18]

Recalling her terrifying first attempt to enter Central High, Elizabeth Eckford wondered nervously if she and her friends would have protection this time. With characteristic teenage invincibility, Ernest Green never dreamed he might be hurt. Sensitive and studious Terrence Roberts felt scared but determined, and he believed that once he got into the school, "the kids will accept me and not cause any trouble." Only Daisy Bates had the sickening fear that something might go terribly wrong, but she was prepared to sacrifice lives—her own or the children's—in that cause.[19]

As the children pulled up to the Sixteenth Street entrance and alighted from their cars, the mob of over a thousand people that was assembled on Park Street in front of Central High seemed to be surging away from the building and down the street. Little Rock police officers in bright blue shirts lined the street. Everyone's attention seemed to be focused on something beyond the vision of the children as they made their way quickly into the school. The unintended decoy proved to be the four black reporters, whose arrival just ahead of the children had triggered a savage outburst of violence. It could have proved murderous if someone had not noticed the nine children entering the building and shrieked "Oh god! The niggers are in the school!"[20]

Margaret Jackson was in the crowd she had encouraged to form on that pretty September day. Her two daughters were students at Central, and she feared for their moral well-being; she believed that "allowing Negroes into White schools would promote wide scale miscegenation," and she was convinced that if the federal government persisted in forcing the integration of the schools, "it would lead to bloodshed." Another Mothers' League member in the crowd that morning, Mary Thomason, tried to break through the police lines when she saw the black children going into the school. Failing to get through, she screamed at the men around her, "Where's your manhood? . . . Why don't you do something to get these people?" then collapsed into sobs as she wailed, "My daughter's in there with those niggers. Oh, my god! Oh, God!"[21]

From the front entrance where he had been stationed to ward off any unwanted intruders, football coach Wilson Matthews thought he saw a group of black men being killed. When he reported this in the office, vice principal for girls Elizabeth Huckaby, thinking the children were being attacked, felt physically ill. Mrs. Huckaby was soon relieved to see student leader Craig Raines walking toward her office with the black children, whom she immediately took into Principal Jess Matthews's office. Thelma Mothershed, the girl with a heart problem, promptly sank to the floor with an erratic pulse, and Mrs. Huckaby called the school nurse. As if this were not enough excitement, the student body then let out a collective roar from each of the home rooms to cheer the football team toward victory in Friday night's game; the press and the mob interpreted the outburst as violence inside the school, and the rumor mills cranked into high gear.[22]

White students began to slip out of the building, supposedly in protest of the black children's entry. Some of them provided the eagerly waiting reporters with lurid, and false, details of the supposed violence taking place inside the school. One account that went out on the radio and landed in the *Arkansas Democrat* that night horrified citizens and frightened parents. "Several fights broke out among Negro and white students in the corridors of Central High School after the Negroes entered, a student who left the school building said today. The youth said he saw three Negroes with blood on their clothing. He said Negro students were chased through the hallways inside the building, and that 'several fights had broken out.'" After each report, Daisy Bates received an assurance from Gene Smith that it was false, but Oscar Eckford spoke for the assembled parents when he screamed at Bates, "Well, if it's not true, why would they say such things on the air?"[23]

White parents also found the radio reports frightening, and they began to arrive at the school demanding their children be allowed to leave. All such requests were honored, though one big high school boy may have spoken for his peers when he responded with embarrassment to his frantic mother's demand that he leave his class by stammering, "Aw, Mom!"[24]

The view from inside the school was far different from the reports being issued on the outside. Ernest Green recalled later that he could not hear the noise coming from the street, and that many of the white students were friendly to him because the avid segregationists were boycotting the school. Terrence Roberts and Thelma Mothershed reported in that night's *Arkansas Democrat* that "nothing much happened" inside Central High School during their first day of classes. Melba Patillo encountered a white mother in the halls who spit on her and shrieked that "next thing, you'll want to marry one of our children!" Melba had classes on the Park Street side of the school, and she described the sound of the mob as having an "animal quality." The school library was also on the Park Street side, and librarian Lola Dunnavant described the sound as being like an earthquake or storm, "a steady, deep roar all the time." Frightened Miss Dunnavant feared for the black children's safety, and in her memoir she described a poignant encounter with a terrified black maid who apparently was hiding in the restroom.[25]

Stymied in their attempt to prevent the black children from entering Central High, members of the increasingly frustrated and steadily growing mob cast about for other targets for their abuse. *Arkansas Gazette* reporters received much verbal taunting, but they had grown accustomed to being called "nigger lovers" and "communists." More serious were the assaults on the out-of-town reporters. After the four African-American newsmen—Alex Wilson of the *Tri-State Defender* in Memphis, James Hicks of the *Amsterdam News* in New York City, Moses Newsome of the Baltimore *Afro-American,* and Earl Davy, photographer for the Bates's *Arkansas State Press*—had been beaten and run off, a crew from *Life* magazine received such a severe beating that police arrested them for their own protection. L. C. Bates wandered ill-advisedly through the crowd but was not attacked; as his biographer noted, he had a gun in his pocket "and he had his hand on it all the time."[26]

Most observers reported that a large percentage of the mob at Central High came from places other than Little Rock, although one observer told two Harvard-based researchers he counted twenty-two local segregationist ministers in the crowd that day. Daisy Bates informed the national NAACP office that her people knew the Little Rock segregationists, and with the exception of the ministers Wesley Pruden and M. L Moser, the crowd at Central High was made up of "real red necks," mostly from the delta area east of Little Rock. Virgil Blossom's memoir noted that local reporters checked the car license plates and found that most of them were from other counties and states. Elizabeth Huckaby, Henry Woods, and Roy Reed all concurred that the crowd at Central High did not represent their city, but the people of Little Rock bore the stigma forever after for the disgraceful occurrences of September 23, 1957.[27]

The *Arkansas Gazette* reported that the scene at the school "was one of almost unrestrained hysteria throughout the morning. But the police held." Assistant Police Chief Gene Smith told Harry Ashmore from a pay phone outside the school that his feet hurt. When Ashmore asked why, Smith responded, "' . . . hell, I've walked a thousand miles today.'" Ashmore said, "walked a thousand miles where?" Smith responded "inside the police line, from one end to the other." He added, "I've told those sons of bitches if any of them step back I'd shoot them in the back of the head." *New York Times* reporter Claude Sitton later wrote, "It is said in Little Rock, and only half in jest, that what kept police lines from breaking during the rioting that day was that 'those policemen were more afraid of big Gene Smith than they were of the mob.'"[28]

THE OFFICIALS RESPONSIBLE for the situation felt unnerved by the potential for violence, especially since Superintendent Blossom, Mayor Mann, and Principal Matthews all had children inside the building. Shortly after the black students went into the school, when the violence outside hit its ugliest, Virgil Blossom telephoned Brooks Hays and asked if federal troops were coming, apparently in reference to tentative plans made the day before at Henry Woods's house. Mayor Mann then called Hays and admitted that while his public pronouncements had attempted to maintain a brave facade, Chief Potts had just informed him that fighting had broken out and that he needed "about 150 soldiers as soon as possible." Hays promptly telephoned Sherman Adams to inquire about the status of federal troops. Adams replied cryptically, "That's all the information I need," and promised to call back. Assistant Attorney General William Rogers called Harry Ashmore, who from his command post at the *Arkansas Gazette* was hearing from myriad local and visiting reporters blow-by-blow accounts of the excitement at Central High. When asked to describe the situation Ashmore responded, "I'll give it to you in one sentence. The police have been routed, the mob is in the streets and we're close to a reign of terror."[29]

Almost two hours after his call to Adams, Hays had heard nothing from the White House when Virgil Blossom called him "in an almost hysterical attitude" and asked, "Are the troops coming or aren't they? . . . The safety of the children depends on it." Hays called Washington and talked to Maxwell Rabb, Eisenhower's special assistant for minority affairs, and said, ". . . for goodness sakes, . . . send help, send troops." Rabb replied, "They'll be on their way." About this time Mayor Mann received an urgent phone call from his son Woody, a senior at Central High. Fearing for Woody's safety, Mann had Gene Smith bring his son to the police chief's office downtown, where the boy told his father rumors were flying around the school that "the Negro students will be taken care of at noon time." Alarmed, Mann talked the situation over with his attorney Henry Woods, who was at the *Gazette* office with Harry Ashmore, and then called Virgil Blossom telling him to "have the Negro students removed." Blossom agreed, though he said difficulties with the telephone lines, undoubtedly the influx of calls from worried parents, had made it impossible for him to reach Principal Matthews. Mann then radioed Gene Smith and told him to remove the children from the school for their own safety. As Mann reported later, "Chief Smith said . . . he also felt that it was necessary for the safety of all students in the school building."[30]

The black children left the school with considerable consternation, spirited out of the back of the building in two police cars. They headed for Daisy Bates's home. Bates announced emphatically to reporters that afternoon, after talking to Harry Ashmore, "The children will not return to Central High School until they have the assurance of the President of the United States that they will have protection against the mob." Orval Faubus commented from Sea Island that the violence in Little Rock was what he had tried to avoid by calling out the National Guard on September 2. Central High School vice principal for girls Elizabeth Huckaby recalled in her memoir she was dismayed at "our scandalous and humiliating failure." Arkansas Congressman Brooks Hays "shared the feelings of horror" of most of the residents of Little Rock.[31]

DESPITE PRESIDENT Eisenhower's July 17 statement that he could not imagine any set of circumstances "that would ever induce me to send federal troops into . . . any area to enforce the orders of a federal court . . . ," he now began to set in motion the process of sending armed paratroopers into Little Rock. Clearly the old military man felt he could not allow his authority to be flouted. At a 4:48 P.M. news conference his press secretary, Jim Hagerty, issued a "Statement by the President" declaring Eisenhower would "use the full power of the United States including whatever force may be necessary" to carry out the orders of the federal court. As a preliminary step, laws required the issuance of a "cease and desist" order, and at 6:23 P.M. Eisenhower signed one, calling upon the citizens of Little Rock to refrain from their "wilful obstruction of justice," and disperse.[32]

The president's order outlined the three sections of the United States Code under which Eisenhower claimed the power to use federal authority. However, from Sea Island Orval Faubus declared, ". . . it is clearly defined under the constitution and the law that the forces of the federal government cannot be employed except on request of the governor of a sovereign state," and "I do not intend to make any such request." From Washington, D.C., Arkansas Senator John McClellan also challenged the president's authority to use federal troops. He said contempt proceedings were the only enforcement powers available under the *Brown* decision, and "if this approach by the administration is right, that means we have a military government." McClellan also said the recently passed Civil Rights Bill repealed the president's power to use troops. In fact, McClellan was largely correct. Eisenhower's authority to use the army on American soil was shaky, at best.[33]

WHILE THE EISENHOWER team grappled with the legalities of sending the Army into Little Rock, Mayor Mann and his advisers, Harry Ashmore, Hugh Patterson, and Henry Woods, crafted a telegram to send Eisenhower placing blame for Monday's "disgraceful occurrences" squarely on the shoulders of Orval Faubus. "The mob that gathered was no spontaneous assembly," the telegram informed the president, "it was agitated, aroused, and assembled by a concerted plan of action." Naming Jimmy Karam as "one of the principal agitators" in the crowd and identifying him as "a political and social intimate" of the governor, Mann drew the "inevitable conclusion" that "Governor Faubus at least was cognizant of what was going to take place."[34]

Herbert Brownell immediately ordered a new FBI investigation, this time of the violence at Central High and particularly Jimmy Karam's role in it. After an extensive investigation, one that a reporter on the scene called the most massive FBI investigation on record, researchers concluded in their report to bureau Director J. Edgar Hoover that they had found "no evidence" of "any organized campaign of violence to prevent integration" at Little Rock Central High School. As was the case with the earlier investigation into the circumstances surrounding Faubus's use of the National Guard, the FBI report exonerating Jimmy Karam, and by extension Orval Faubus, was never made public, thereby leaving the impression in many people's minds that Jimmy Karam had directed the mob and that Orval Faubus had authorized him to do it. Jimmy Karam's iniquity became another component of Harry Ashmore's growing mythology about the Little Rock crisis.[35]

Jimmy Karam *was* at Central High School all morning on September 23. He told all who asked him that he had two children in the building and he was there to check on their welfare. Arkansas Council on Human Relations Executive Director Nat Griswold was not convinced Karam had planned the violence, or that he was acting at Faubus's direction. As he recalled years later, "Frequently at news conferences at the Mansion, Jimmy Karam was right in with him. But how much this was a conspiracy on the part of Mr. Faubus with Jimmy, I don't know. Jimmy did so many things on his own that were fantastic, it's just unbelievable."[36]

The next day's *Nashville Banner* charged, "The governor's political enemies were making veiled accusations that the violence was 'carefully planned' for the express purpose of vindicating Faubus. . . ." Apparently this reporter had heard the scuttlebutt coming out of Harry Ashmore's office that led to the sending of Woodrow Mann's telegram, which was not released to the press. The FBI pushed Mann hard about supplying evidence to support his charges; Mann eventually waffled and told investigators Henry Woods had all the information. Woods finally admitted his conclusions had been based on "hearsay and logical deductions," since he had been in the *Gazette* office the morning of September 23 and heard many reporters talk about Jimmy Karam's activities at Central High School. Woods "assumed" Faubus told Karam to direct the mob, and he "deduced" Faubus wanted to run for a third term as governor. The FBI was not impressed.[37]

THE NIGHT OF September 23, while President Eisenhower watched *Song of the South* at the vacation White House in Rhode Island, Little Rock police stopped a caravan loaded with guns and dynamite one block from Daisy Bates's home. Neighbors guarded her house with guns, and the harried NAACP leader got two hours of sleep.[38]

The next morning, Bates announced that the nine black children were not going to Central High. She told her superiors at the national NAACP office she was "afraid the children may be killed. . . ." She responded to the president's proclamation by remarking it was "gratifying and a step forward" but that "a little more assurance" would be necessary before the students returned to school. "I want to be absolutely sure that they will be protected and how," she said, "before they will be advised to return."[39]

Tuesday's crowd at Central High School exceeded no more than four hundred people as classes began, and it dwindled to 150 by 8:45 and to twenty-five by 10:30. Little Rock police had arrested forty-five people through the evening of the 23rd, and they seemed to have communicated to the city's rougher element that they meant business. It is also possible that if Jimmy Karam did have paid goons at the school on Monday, he only paid them for one day. Whatever the explanation, the crowd that assembled in front of Central High was quiet and orderly.[40] Mayor Mann reported otherwise to the President of the United States.

Mann and his handlers sent a hysterical telegram to President Eisenhower at 9:16 on the morning of September 24, claiming:

> The immediate need for federal troops is urgent. The mob is much larger in numbers at 8AM than at any time yesterday People are converging on the scene from all directions Mob is armed and engaging in fisticuffs and other acts of violence. Situation is out of control and police cannot disperse the mob I am pleading to you as President of the United States in the interest of humanity law and order and because of democracy world wide to provide the necessary federal troops within several hours. Action by you will restore peace and order and compliance with your proclamation.

In a classic case of understatement, the Army's account of the situation read: "The reports that reached the President from Mayor Woodrow Wilson Mann portrayed a far more dangerous situation than the Army reports indicated."[41]

The reason the Mann telegram differed so significantly from the Army's on-the-scene observations was that the Justice Department worded the telegram. Henry Woods, Sid McMath, Harry Ashmore, Virgil Blossom, Brooks Hays, Edwin Dunaway, and Woodrow Mann had reassembled at Woods's house Monday afternoon and decided "the only way you were going to restore order was to get troops in here." In a telephone interview with his mentor at Harvard the next day, Ashmore admitted his sense of desperation about the inability of the Little Rock police to control the mob, concluding, "Apparently it can only be handled by Federal troops."[42]

Working from the thesis he had so recently articulated in *An Epitaph for Dixie,* Ashmore was predisposed to believe that if the federal government took a strong stand, the segregationist resistance across the South would crumble. As he said on a nationally televised program on October 6, 1957, the South was laboring under a "false hope" that "somehow there was a way to head off integration." The self-assured young editor suggested if a "mild president" such as Eisenhower could be persuaded to use federal troops, then the South's "false hope" would be shown to be groundless.[43]

The Ashmore group decided not to ask for the National Guard. They also talked to Daisy Bates and urged her not to send the children to school until Eisenhower had sent in federal troops to protect them. In time the little band of Faubus adversaries found themselves talking to the U.S. attorney general's office, and according to Henry Woods "they told us in Washington exactly how that telegram ought to be phrased."[44]

Herbert Brownell felt he had ample moral justification for whatever measures might be necessary to crush what he saw as the forces of massive resistance in the South. As he wrote in his final report to President Eisenhower upon his resignation as attorney general, "When an unruly mob arrogates to itself the power to nullify" a valid court order, "it may reasonably be assumed that the danger of a fast-moving, destructive volcanic force is immediately present. Success of the unlawful assemblage in Little Rock inevitably would have led to mob rule, and probably a breakdown of law and order in an ever-increasing area." With schoolyard braggadocio, Brownell concluded, "When a local and State government is unable or unwilling to meet such a threat, the Federal Government is not impotent." And indeed it was not.[45]

According to Eisenhower biographer Stephen Ambrose, the president now "found himself in precisely the situation he had most wanted to avoid. His options had run out. Mayor Mann's telegram gave him no choice but to use force." Believing, incorrectly, that the situation was out of control in Little Rock and that significant elements of the population were defying his authority, President Eisenhower reverted to a military mentality. Justice Department officials had long since completed preparations for using military force if necessary, and now those officials persuaded a reluctant Eisenhower that military intervention was the only remaining option.[46]

THE JUSTICE DEPARTMENT's use of the Army required considerable jimmying of the law. Chapter 15, Title 10, Section 331 of the U.S. Code specified that a request by a governor or a state legislature was a prerequisite of presidential use of military force. Another federal statute prohibited the president from employing the U.S. Army as a "*posse comitatus . . .* for the purpose of executing the laws." Justice Department officials therefore decided to rely on Chapter 15, Title 10, Sections 332 and 333 of the U.S. Code, which gave the president the discretion to remove obstructions "against the authority of the United States," or to put down violence which hindered the execution of the "law of the United States." As Herbert Brownell recalled, somewhat disingenuously, "We felt that it was necessary for local officials to appeal to Washington for assistance before the federal government would send in troops. The mayor of Little Rock did appeal to Washington on the ground that the rioting and the threatened rioting there meant that local law enforcement authorities could not handle the situation. That gave the legal authority which, under the Supreme Court cases, we thought was necessary to have."[47]

On September 24, 1957, at 11:22 A.M. Little Rock time, President Dwight Eisenhower affixed his signature to Executive Order 10730, authorizing the Army to subdue a mob—one that local authorities had already brought under control. The real purpose of the order, of course, was to put down a perceived rebellion generated by the governor, and to serve notice on any other southern governors who might be considering similar tactics. The president dispatched units of the famed 101st Airborne Division to Little Rock from Fort Campbell, Kentucky, and his orders also federalized the Arkansas National Guard, thereby taking it out of Faubus's hands. Communicating these orders by telephone to the 101st Airborne commander, General Maxwell Taylor concluded the conversation by saying, "The President of the United States is watching your move personally. Make it expeditious and a good airborne move." The move was in fact expeditious, taking military precision to new heights by accomplishing the operation ahead of schedule.[48]

By late afternoon 856 soldiers had landed at the Little Rock Air Base just north of the city, and by nightfall 319 of these men, all white, had taken up stations around Central High School under the command of General Edwin Walker. Another ninety-nine men arrived by land the next day, and an additional five hundred soldiers remained in readiness in Kentucky if needed. The troops brought with them an irritant gas dispenser, tear gas, and vomiting gas, which occasioned much local and press comment.[49]

When informed of these developments, Orval Faubus said smilingly for the press that he felt "like MacArthur" since he had been "relieved of my command." Privately he felt a great sense of relief, and he admitted years later, "This is what I had been wishing for, some kind of action which would show that a federal court order was going to be enforced by the federal authorities which authored it." Faubus believed Brownell had wanted to use troops all along, to recoup the political losses incurred during the struggle over the Civil Rights Bill.

Faubus may have been right. Brownell admitted at a 1990 conference that Justice Department officials believed the use of troops was the only way to enforce the law, and that "Eisenhower's decisive action at Little Rock crushed the forces behind the southern manifesto."[50] As Brownell told interviewers for the *Eyes on the Prize* documentary series, "We felt that this was the test case that had to [be] made in order to dramatize to everyone that when it came to a showdown the federal government was supreme in this area. The situation was as close as you could get to an irreconcilable difference between the North and the South. There'd been nothing like it since the Civil War."[51]

Eisenhower biographer Stephen Ambrose concluded that the troop use convinced most white southerners "they could not use force to prevent integration." It also convinced many of them they could not trust their own government, and that the dreaded specter of "Yankee force" was abroad in the land. While Eisenhower's use of the Army may have persuaded many southerners the tactics they had been employing were flawed, in time it also hardened a spirit of alienation in many quarters and signaled the need for more subtle means of resistance.[52]

More immediately, the use of federal troops enraged large numbers of southerners and made many in Little Rock feel they had been "invaded," or as Orval Faubus described it, "occupied." One typical reaction came from a former president of the Little Rock Chamber of Commerce, Harvard-educated A. Howard Stebbins III, who reflected years later, "Once you laid down the gauntlet, which the government did, I think many of us felt like we should rally around the only leader we've got right now and that's Faubus. . . . Now you can criticize that attitude, looking back on it, but at the time, why we hadn't had federal troops since '67! That was so shocking that we didn't know whether we should support the government or not."[53]

As Sid McMath had feared would happen, ". . . even people who were opposed to Orval Faubus and opposed to his position supported him when the 101st Airborne came in." Sharing the reaction of most Little Rock citizens, Governor Faubus's top adviser Bill Smith simply felt disbelief when the federal troops arrived, "disbelief that the federal government would go that far without exhausting the less radical procedures." One Arkansan who responded with a different kind of disbelief was NAACP lawyer Wiley Branton, who heard the announcement on his car radio that Eisenhower was sending in the Army and said to himself "Wow, what have I started?"[54]

AT 7:00 P.M. Little Rock time, President Eisenhower gave a televised address to the nation, explaining his actions in Little Rock and stressing that he had not sent the troops to effect integration but instead to enforce a court order. This became the basic theme of all his comments about Little Rock in succeeding days and weeks, but as his biographer noted, few southerners grasped "the difference between using troops to enforce integration on one hand, or to uphold the law on the other. The result, after all, was the same."[55]

The central theme of Eisenhower's message stressed that the situation in Little Rock transcended legal questions to encompass Cold War considerations. "At a time when we face grave situations abroad because of the hatred that Communism bears toward a system of government based on human rights," he argued, "it would be difficult to exaggerate the harm that is being done to the prestige and influence, and indeed to the safety of our nation and the world." Claiming the nation's enemies were "gloating over this incident" the president called upon the citizens of Little Rock to put an end to defiance and obstruction of the law.[56]

Even as President Eisenhower spoke, the Capital Citizens' Council held a large meeting in downtown Little Rock, attended by over one thousand people who had responded to Sunday's newspaper invitation to "all . . . who are against race-mixing in our schools. . . ." Deploring violence, Amis Guthridge and Wesley Pruden harangued the outraged citizens and announced, incorrectly, that Central's teachers were planning to walk out en masse. They also blamed the NAACP for the disturbances then taking place in Little Rock, and they led the meeting to adopt a resolution calling for a special session of the legislature to abolish the public school system.[57]

DAISY BATES REPORTED to her superiors in the national office that Harry Ashmore and Edwin Dunaway, based on a mysterious source of authority, had decided the black children would attempt to enter the school again at noon on Wednesday. Virgil Blossom had wanted Wednesday to be a day for passions to cool in Little Rock, and when he had not called Bates with plans by 10:00 P.M. Tuesday she called all the parents and told them the children would not be going to school the next day. Shortly after midnight Blossom called Bates and informed her the children were to go into the school first thing the next morning. Bates protested that she would not be able to reach the parents because they had an agreement to take their telephones off the hook at midnight in order to avoid harassing calls. Blossom would not be dissuaded, saying that Major General Edwin Walker insisted that the children be delivered to Mrs. Bates' house at 8:30 A.M. The indefatigable Daisy Bates, joined by black principals L. M. Christophe and Edwin Hawkins, set out at about 1:00 A.M. and visited each child's home, awakening frightened families to deliver the news. Gloria Ray's elderly father answered the door with a shotgun in his hand, furious. Hearing Blossom's instructions, Mr. Ray exploded, "I don't care if the President of the United States gave you those instructions! . . . I won't let Gloria go. She's faced two mobs and that's enough."[58]

Daisy Bates fell into bed that night after 3:00 A.M., not knowing how many of the black children would appear at her house the next day. She was sure of only three. To her relief and delight, all nine appeared, including Gloria Ray. A subdued Mr. Ray delivered his daughter and said, looking down at his daughter with pride, "Here, Daisy, she's yours. She's determined to go." That fighting spirit would stand the Little Rock Nine in good stead through the long, lonely months that lay ahead of them.[59]

When the Army station wagons arrived at the Bates home to pick up the nine children and deliver them to Central High, the normally exuberant Minnijean Brown said solemnly, "For the first time in my life, I feel like an American citizen." Tears of pride and relief rolled down the faces of the parents and friends assembled in Daisy Bates's living room. The children rode the few short blocks to Central High School, disembarked into a cordon of helmeted soldiers carrying rifles with bayonets affixed, and marched triumphantly into the massive school in what was surely one of the most photographed events in modern history. Ernest Green recalled, "Walking up the steps that day was probably one of the biggest feelings I've ever had." Melba Patillo remembered years later, "I went in not through the side doors, but up the front stairs, and there was a feeling of pride and hope that yes, this is the United States; yes, there is a reason I salute the flag; and it's going to be okay."[60]

The impressive military presence made short work of the slight resistance that erupted from the spectators across the street when the nine went into the school. The soldiers reestablished their perimeter an additional block from the school building, and the Army's analysis of the first day was that the initial show of force was "an unqualified success."[61]

Militarily, perhaps, it was a success; politically it was a disaster, as Eisenhower realized almost immediately. The president started the very next day trying to reduce the number of soldiers and withdraw from Little Rock. He had met his match in Orval Faubus, however. He would have to stay all year.

CHAPTER TEN

INTO THE CAULDRON

The Little Rock Nine

I N ONE OF WHAT HAD RECENTLY BECOME DAILY TELEPHONE CONVER-
sations with Daisy Bates, Gloster Current, director of NAACP branches,
remarked on September 26, "We are winning many friends because so many
people are conscience stricken because of what is happening to the children. . . ."
By this time, everyone in the New York office had realized that the Little Rock
crisis was a public relations windfall for the NAACP. A September 19 press
release out of the national office had announced that contributions had
increased because of Little Rock, and that Elizabeth Eckford had become a symbol for many people of what was at stake in the emerging civil rights movement. One powerful letter to Elizabeth quoted in this release read "you have
made the people of America take sides." Another letter a week later read, "The
picture in the newspapers of that poor girl holding her head high and brave
while being followed and spat upon and called ugly names by supposed Americans reminded me of Nathan Hale. And I cried." A third read, "I don't know
the specifications used by the Carnegie Committee in making their annual
heroism awards, but I would like to nominate for consideration these First Children of the Land."[1]

The national NAACP understood the potential for building their organization with the Little Rock Nine.[2] By late September they were pressing Bates to
schedule appearances for the Nine on such television programs as Dave
Garroway's *Today* show and Chet Huntley's *Outlook*. They also began to schedule speaking engagements and fund-raising tours all over the country for Bates.
Her calendar filled quickly though she worried aloud about the wisdom of
spending so much time away from Little Rock and the children. As John Morsell
in the New York office explained the concept to Clarence Laws in Little Rock,
"The basic problem is to make a big splash with this thing; to make it apparent
that there is a group which could serve as a rallying point for the average citi-

zens who would like to see an end to all this regardless of their views on integration and who want to see the law observed in peace."[3]

Bates worked tirelessly to court the press, always with an eye to stressing the
role of the NAACP. Many black reporters stayed in her home, and most seem
to have used it as a social and professional headquarters. Late on the afternoon
of September 24, Bates complained to Gloster Current in New York, "I don't see
how I have stood it. I have all the radio people here—NBC, ABC, and all the
reporters have been out here to my house." Understanding fully the need to use
the situation to build the NAACP, she reported to Current, speaking of black
reporter James Hicks, "I told him that when he printed his story to make sure
to print what the NAACP had been doing. That we are making history and the
NAACP is doing it. We have to get our story told in a manner it should be told."
Soon the national association recognized Bates's efforts and her value to the
organization by electing her to their board of directors.[4]

In daily telephone conversations, the NAACP national office guided Bates's
efforts to brief the children on such things as what to say to the press, how to
understand their proper role in the civil rights struggle, and how to avoid developing a martyr complex. In daily after-school debriefings and makeshift ther-
apy sessions at her house, Bates helped the children deal with the stresses of
their situation, blow off steam, and support one another. She minced no words,
pushing and prodding each day to shape them into warriors. As she recalled
one episode, "So I told them that one of us might die in this fight. And I said to
them, 'If they kill me, you would have to go on. If I die, don't you stop. If Jeff
died. . . .' He said: 'I ain't going to die' (laughs)."[5]

ON SEPTEMBER 25 the Army created a public relations disaster for itself and
for Eisenhower by ordering the creation of four 1000-man task forces to prepare plans, "as a precautionary measure in event troops are required in situations similar to that now current in Little Rock . . . ," and also to make a survey
of the availability of riot control materials at supply depots in the United States.
The gist of the order leaked to the press and to Congress almost immediately,
with predictable results. Secretary of the Army Wilber Brucker rescinded it the
next day. As the Army's analysis of the situation concluded, however, "the damage had already been done, for some members of Congress interpreted the version of the message which they had heard to mean that the Army was planning
to use troops to enforce integration throughout the South." Eisenhower's political predicament deepened.[6]

On September 26, the day after the Army's arrival, General Walker reduced the hall guards inside Central from thirty-eight to twenty; he also reduced the soldiers outside the building from 319 to 270. Attendance at the school went up from 50 percent on the 25th to 67 percent on the 26th. The Little Rock police withdrew protection from the homes of the nine black children and from the Bates home, and the city attempted to return to some semblance of normality.[7]

On that day Brooks Hays spoke to his own Little Rock Lions Club chapter and lectured his listeners on the morality of the federal government's use of soldiers to enforce integration. He was very troubled by his cold reception. On the same day, Hays wrote to Sherman Adams expressing his appreciation for Eisenhower's actions in sending federal troops, and he withdrew his own name from consideration as a federal judge.[8]

Also on September 26, Senator Richard Russell of Georgia, the chairman of the Senate Armed Services Committee and a noted student of the Constitution, sent a telegram to the president describing Eisenhower's actions in Arkansas as "highhanded and illegal methods . . . which must have been copied from . . . Hitler's storm troopers. . . ." At about the same time, Governor LeRoy Collins of Florida, chairman of the Southern Governors' Conference, requested a meeting between the president and a delegation of southern governors to discuss getting the troops out of Little Rock. Eager for help from any quarter, Eisenhower scheduled the meeting for October 1.[9]

That night, an impassioned Orval Faubus went on national television with the plaintive plea, "What is happening in America?" Displaying disturbing, and misleading, pictures of coeds with bayonets at their backs, and of a railroad worker who had been hit in the face with a rifle butt while standing on private property, Faubus charged the FBI had held teenage girls incommunicado for hours without the knowledge of their worried parents. Articulating a theme he stressed through the rest of his life, Faubus castigated "the cleverly conceived plans of the Justice Department, under Herbert Brownell, for the military occupation of Arkansas. . . ."[10]

The Army scored a few points in football-crazed Arkansas by allowing Friday night's game to proceed against Istrouma High of Baton Rouge, and by sending the troop commander and a handful of soldiers to cheer the Central High Tigers to their thirty-third straight gridiron victory. At his headquarters office in downtown Little Rock, however, General Edwin Walker found his situation to be anything but improved, spending the weekend dealing with a tangled mess of difficulties resulting from the hasty deployment of troops and the unusual addition of National Guard soldiers into the force under his control. General Walker and Sherman T. Clinger, adjutant general of the Arkansas

National Guard, clashed over lines of command. Walker clearly did not trust the Arkansas soldier who had just the week before overseen the effort to keep the black children *out* of Central High.[11]

Camp Robinson, where the Army was housed, proved to be run-down and inadequate, and the generals came belatedly to the realization that Orval Faubus had the power to evict their troops from the camp by vetoing their request to use it. The Secretary of the Army eventually decided to overlook the regulation requiring a request, and General Walker never asked Faubus for permission.[12]

With the situation seemingly quieting in Little Rock, and with Eisenhower pressing to get out, Army officials made the decision to scale back their military presence. On Monday, September 30, students arrived to find the outside troops reduced considerably, and the hall guard cut to fifteen. As the soldiers started to be withdrawn, Melba Patillo recalled in her memoir, "I had never before felt such fear." Senator McClellan telegrammed the president, asking respectfully that all the soldiers be withdrawn, and Eisenhower responded with his mantra: the troops had not gone to Arkansas to solve the problem of integration, but to "assure that the law should not be flouted." Even Clarence Laws suggested to his superiors in New York it would be a good public relations move to have the black children request the Army be withdrawn; Henry Moon responded on the other end of the line, "Let's not push the matter about having the troops out too soon." Hopes ran high in Washington and elsewhere that the meeting between the president and a committee from the Southern Governors' Conference, planned for Tuesday, would be able to get the soldiers out of Little Rock.[13]

Tuesday morning, October 1, the National Guard took over both inside and out at Central High School. The nine black children suffered harassment all day from about two hundred white students, in the form of "name-calling, thrown objects, trippings, shovings, kickings." The segregationists had started returning to school, and they were testing the resolve of the National Guard to hold the line as forcefully as the regular Army had done. Daisy Bates reported that one of her girls went to a Guardsman stationed inside the building and asked him to whom she should report instances of badgering. "The guard didn't answer, but just turned away," Mrs. Bates reported.[14]

Clarence Laws informed the national NAACP office that "one girl who went in to take a shower after her gym class, found that her books and clothing were scattered all over the floor. One girl was shown a knife by one of the students and was told that unless she moved her locker from so near his, that tomorrow he would use the knife on her." Elizabeth Eckford finally went to Mrs. Huckaby's office in tears, saying she wanted to go home. The vice principal for girls would not allow it. "It would not do for one of the Nine to leave," Huckaby wrote in her memoir. "It would make it harder for them to return; it would prolong the necessity for armed guards; it would put pressure on everyone involved, from the president on down." Mrs. Huckaby appealed to Elizabeth's pride and courage and ultimately convinced the tormented girl to stay. At the end of the day she found Elizabeth and asked if she were not glad she had stayed at school. "No, I'm not," Elizabeth replied forlornly, undoubtedly reflecting the sentiments of all nine of the children.[15]

THE MEETING BETWEEN the president and the southern governors did not go well. All of the five governors, except Theodore McKeldin of Maryland, the lone Republican in the group, knew they were treading in dangerous political waters by agreeing to meet with Eisenhower. Marvin Griffin of Georgia dropped out of the group when Eisenhower suggested he intended to discuss the whole issue of integration. The other three Democrats, all of them thought to be racial moderates (LeRoy Collins of Florida, Frank Clement of Tennessee, and Luther Hodges of North Carolina), had received numerous telegrams urging them not to meet with the president, but they had persuaded themselves they could craft a workable compromise between Faubus and Eisenhower. Clement had assembled a group of his state's leading lawyers and constitutional scholars and had spent several days studying the issues before he went to Washington. Through numerous telephone calls among themselves and with Faubus, the governors had fashioned a statement they thought would be acceptable to both sides, and they had sent Frank Bane, executive secretary of the Council of State Governments, to Arkansas to clear their ideas with Faubus. Faubus had given Bane a handwritten proposed statement, in which he pledged to the president and the five governors that he would use the facilities at his command to keep order at Central High School, and Bane had carried the Faubus statement to Washington for the governors' meeting with Eisenhower.[16]

Sitting down with the governors and Sherman Adams, but not Herbert Brownell, the president insisted the Arkansas governor must promise two things before he withdrew the Army: not to obstruct the orders of the federal courts demanding immediate integration, and to maintain law and order in Little Rock. Upon receipt of such a declaration, Eisenhower agreed to return the command of the Arkansas National Guard to Faubus and withdraw all federal troops.[17]

Since Faubus had already agreed to these conditions in prior discussions with the governors' committee, the mood was one of nervous optimism in

Washington. Indeed, when Faubus read his statement to reporters assembled at the Governor's Mansion, he said, in part, ". . . it has never been my intention to obstruct the orders of the federal courts, . . . the orders of the federal courts will not be obstructed by me, and . . . I am prepared, as I have always been, to assume full responsibility for maintaining law and order in Little Rock. This has been consistently my stand and viewpoint throughout the controversy." Further- more, Faubus declared, ". . . upon withdrawal of federal troops, I will again assume full responsibility, in co-operation with local authorities, for the main- tenance of law and order, and . . . the orders of the federal courts will not be obstructed by me."[18]

Yet Herbert Brownell inspected this statement carefully and rejected it as inadequate. President Eisenhower then issued a press release that read, "The statement issued this evening by the Governor of Arkansas does not constitute in my opinion the assurance that he intends to use his full powers as Governor to prevent the obstruction of the orders of the United States District Court." (As the *Christian Science Monitor* pointed out the next day, the original joint state- ment that Eisenhower and the governors' committee issued "had made no spe- cific mention of Governor Faubus' using his full powers.") The Eisenhower press release continued, "Under the circumstances, . . . the President of the United States has no recourse at the present time except to maintain Federal surveillance of the situation."[19]

What had gone wrong? At his news conference the next morning, Eisen- hower's press secretary, Jim Hagerty, suggested the two words "by me" were a part of the problem, since they seemed to imply Faubus would not guarantee he would prevent other people from obstructing implementation of the court's orders. Notes Eisenhower's staff prepared for his October 3 press conference prompted the president to say, "Faubus has not said that he would do other than use the National Guard, if returned to his [control], for the same purpose he originally did—i.e., to prevent the Negro children from going to school."[20]

Facing two hundred newsmen in the Arkansas capitol building Wednesday morning, an uncharacteristically nervous and irritable Orval Faubus described himself as "amazed and disappointed" the president had refused to accept his statement. Amid charges in the national press that he had "double-crossed" the southern governors and the president, Faubus claimed he had told the gover- nors by telephone he intended to use the phrase "by me," and that apparently Eisenhower wanted assurances Faubus would "take my troops and put bayonets in the backs of students of my state, and bludgeon and bayonet my own peo- ple. . . ." In later years, Faubus claimed the southern governors apparently wanted him to be "a complete puppet" of the Eisenhower administration and to assume the Justice Department's responsibility for enforcing its own orders. More ominously, and giving credence to Brownell's skepticism, Faubus also told the assembled newsmen "keeping Negro pupils out of Central High School, as he had ordered his National Guard to do for three weeks, was still the best way to keep peace in Little Rock."[21]

An explanation for the failure of the negotiations between the southern governors and the president rests quietly in the archival materials of the NAACP. In one of her daily conversations with the national office, on October 2 Daisy Bates reported that after the terrible harassment of the children the day before, the day of the president's meeting with the southern governors, vice principal for boys J.O. Powell had come to her home to get her assessment of the situation. She had informed him of "the position of the kids," which apparently was that they felt they needed the Army's presence for protection. Bates reported that Powell and others with whom he was working felt they "had to get it to Washington as quickly as possible to work on the President to reject Faubus' statement." Bates reported she "got in touch with Ashmore and he got in touch with General Walker and Blossom. Harry called Rogers up and Harry called me back and said he had talked with Rogers and they were waiting for the Governor's statement."[22]

In the meantime, Thurgood Marshall telegrammed President Eisenhower and reported, "Today, after withdrawal of federal troops from Central High School in Little Rock, Arkansas, Negro children were harassed by groups of other children inside of the school. Their complaints to the National Guard were ignored and laughed at. This is typical of what can be expected if federal troops are withdrawn." In a conclusion that went straight to the heart of Herbert Brownell's concerns, Marshall predicted, "Any weakening of the federal government's position in Little Rock will encourage others to risk presence of federal troops if they are only to be there for a week." Apparently Brownell, Rogers, et al. felt it was safer to blame the president's rejection of Faubus's statement on the duplicity of the damaged Arkansas governor than to admit that the need for continued protection of the children was the real reason for deciding to leave the Army at Central High.[23]

In his press conference on October 3, Eisenhower stressed that the troops were in Little Rock to support the courts, not to implement desegregation. Revealing his own inner anguish about the situation, the president lamented, "No one can deplore more than I do the sending of Federal troops anywhere. It is not good for the troops; it is not good for the locality; it is not really American, except as it becomes absolutely necessary for the support of the institutions that are vital to our form of government."[24]

ON OCTOBER 2, Daisy Bates gave the nine black children money for the pay phones if they needed to call for help, and with great trepidation she sent them off with their Army escort. Shortly after an Army station wagon and two jeeps left her house, the worried young civil rights leader drove by Central High School with her husband and Clarence Laws, stopping just long enough to ask one of the patrolling National Guardsmen if the children had made it into the school without incident. In fact, when the black children had alighted from the Army station wagon and headed for the front entrance, they found their way blocked by a large group of hostile students. Veering off toward the south entrance, they heard one of the white boys yell "Get those coons!" A pack of students swarmed down the steps from their viewing area above. As the white boys yelled "Chicken!" the black children made a dash for the south door and went straight to their lockers, young "hoods" trailing after them.[25]

According to Terrence Roberts, he and Jefferson Thomas were at their lockers when a group of boys started roughing them up, pushing and shoving, and trying to knock the books out of their arms. The young toughs followed Terrence and Jeff down the hall. "Every once in awhile one would stop and push you and knock one of our books down," Terrence reported. "They kept on doing it until they knocked all my books out of my arms." As Principal Jess Matthews's report described the situation, "The National Guard group accompanying these Negro pupils made little if any effort to prevent, intercede, or assist in clearing the halls and dispersing the large groups of students in the halls." Elizabeth Huckaby happened upon this scene and immediately grabbed two of the white boys by their arms and marched them into the principal's office. As she wondered to herself where the National Guardsmen were, she saw a group of them "looking on from the door of the conference room" next to her office. "None of them had made a move toward the scramble" she had interrupted. The two white boys told Jess Matthews, "We wanted to make the niggers so miserable they would leave Central." Matthews suspended the boys for two days.[26]

In the school assembly that morning, a group of white boys pushed Melba Patillo into a darkened corner under the balcony, and while one of them pressed his forearm against her throat another hissed, "We're gonna make your life hell, nigger. You'all are gonna go screaming out of here, taking those nigger-loving soldiers with you."[27]

About ten o'clock, Melba and Minnijean asked Mrs. Huckaby for change for a quarter, planning to call Daisy Bates. Huckaby implored them to report their concerns to Jess Matthews before they called Mrs. Bates, and they agreed reluctantly to do so. Melba, very upset, said she felt in danger in the remote areas of the school, where white students threw pencils at her and jeered and insulted her. Melba claimed there had been "a big change in the atmosphere yesterday and today, and that it is worse today." She felt that more guards, "or different guards" were needed. Minnijean reported she had walked up to a guard who seemed to be "in command" and asked for more protection, but he replied "he had to follow orders." Melba added that many white students had been friendly, "but that they were as afraid of the 'tough' students" as the black children were. Elizabeth Eckford later reported many of her white neighbors recognized her inside the school, ". . . but when I saw them I saw fear in their eyes [that said] 'don't let them know you know me.'"[28]

After they made their report to the principals, the two girls called Mrs. Bates, who told them they would have to go home if they were not to be better protected. Jess Matthews called General Sherman Clinger to come to his office, and General Walker came as well; together they worked out a plan to assign two guards to each black student. The military men also strengthened the order concerning the handling of incidents in the school, specifying, "Should military personnel on duty in the school observe an incident which takes place or should an incident be reported to military personnel on duty, the soldiers concerned will immediately intervene, quell the incident, and escort the offender(s) to the principal's office." The children called Bates to tell her what was being done to assure their safety, and she agreed to let them stay.[29]

Under constant attack inside the enormous school, the black children began to realize the emotional as well as the physical price they would have to pay to stay there. Increasingly isolated and lonely, Melba Patillo described their plight. "I was treated as though I were an outside observer," she wrote years later, "sitting and looking into a glass room that held all the white students, separate and apart from me. I was never really included in what they were doing. With that realization, a new pain seeped into my heart. . . . I was treated as if I didn't exist. Would it be this way all year long?"[30]

AT THIS POINT the withdrawal of the Nine from Central High School became a very real possibility. General Walker had assured Daisy Bates that "he was going to have plenty of people in that building" on Wednesday, and they would "watch the students as well as the National Guard." But Clarence Laws talked to two of General Walker's aides, informing them that the parents of the black children were extremely concerned, and that he wanted to meet with the general "and ascertain exactly what his plans are to protect the persons of these children."[31]

Laws was equally concerned about the cavalier attitude of Principal Jess Matthews, who told him the harassment of the black children was "more psychological than anything else." Not only was Matthews apparently unmoved by the plight of the black pupils, but Laws reported to his superiors in New York that "the Principal said this morning that he would not presume to tell General Walker how to run his business. . . . The school authorities take the position that it is the Army's position to maintain order." Jess Matthews did enlist the aid of the football team to try to discourage incidents inside the school, but they apparently worked primarily to provide protection for white students such as Blossom's daughter Gail who might have been subject to attack by segregationists.[32]

VIRGIL BLOSSOM WAS monitoring the situation inside the school, and in his characteristic frantic manner he called the Episcopal Bishop of Arkansas, Robert R. Brown, whose former parishioner had become an assistant secretary of state, and asked that Brown use his influence to put him in touch with President Eisenhower. Word got to Secretary of the Army Brucker that the superintendent was trying to complain to the president. At 12:30 P.M. Secretary Brucker called General Walker and talked for thirty minutes, making it clear that "more positive steps would have to be taken the next day to insure the safety and well-being of the Negro students inside the school."[33]

At 3:35 P.M. a representative of Secretary Brucker's office called Walker again, saying Brucker was "quite concerned about the situation at Little Rock," and requesting he be informed immediately of any significant change. Eisenhower had realized the nine black children were seriously contemplating withdrawal from Central High School, and as the Army's historian analyzed the situation, "Withdrawal would have defeated the whole purpose of the operation the President had ordered." The political blood Ike had spilled would have been in vain.[34]

General Walker responded to the pressure from Washington by reversing his earlier initiative to withdraw the Army as quickly as possible, now reassigning the 101st to duty both inside and outside the school building. Walker also changed the wording of the orders to the troops inside the school, commanding them to "prevent disorder" instead of simply maintaining order, as the earlier directive had charged. As the Army's analysis read: "It was a show of force again, not this time to quell a mob but to assure protection for the Negro children against a more subtle form of pressure inside the school." The persecution of the black children ceased temporarily, but now General Walker had to start over in his efforts to withdraw from Little Rock.[35]

AT THE HEIGHT of the disturbances Wednesday morning, October 2, vice principal for boys Jay Powell telephoned Daisy Bates and urged her not to take the children out of Central High School. "He begged me not to pull them out," she reported to the New York office; "he told me I had worked too hard to get them in." Bates claimed Virgil Blossom called her as well and pleaded with her not to let the children withdraw. The *New York Times* reported that the parents of the nine black students, "worried by radio reports of violence, were thinking of keeping their children home tomorrow." The *Times* noted editorially such action would support Faubus's contention that removing the black children from Central High was the only way to restore law and order. Ernest Green said years later that Daisy Bates kept the group together, she kept the parents informed, and she was an inspiration. Apparently she worked her magic the evening of October 2, because the next day the black children went back to Central High School, reportedly "in high spirits," and all of the parents agreed they should go.[36]

Ernest Green had realized the nine children could not quit, because the fight was too important. An unusually strong bond was forming among these nine young warriors, and each felt a growing determination to continue the struggle for the sake of the others. Elizabeth Eckford believed she had to continue the fight, because she could not let the others down. As she recalled years later, nobody on the outside knew what torments the black children were enduring, and she felt that she could not just walk away from the others. Jefferson Thomas spoke in Thelma Mothershed's church forty-five years later and said sometimes he had wanted to quit, but then he thought of little ninety-pound Thelma who had a heart problem but was not quitting, and he kept going back. Minnijean Brown carried a burden of guilt for forty years that her eventual retaliation against her white tormenters, which led to her expulsion from Central High School, left the other eight to carry on without her. Terrence Roberts recalled years later that at one point early in October he thought of quitting, saying to himself "' . . . okay, I've done my bit; I've had enough.' But then as I thought about that, other voices from the past would pop into my head. Voices of people who had given their lives in this struggle. Voices of freedom fighters. . . . And I could almost see the panorama of people over the years who had died in this struggle and that was the thing that turned it around for me." So they supported each other, and the black community supported them.[37]

Occasionally, expressions of support materialized from the white community that had a powerful impact on the group's resolve. October 4 was Elizabeth Eckford's birthday, and on that morning a white man, a stranger, appeared at her front door with a watch for Elizabeth. He said his wife was dying of cancer and she wanted Elizabeth to have that watch. Elizabeth was shocked that anyone knew her birthday, and that a stranger would care, and she wondered about that dying woman for a long time. But she was also accustomed to having people in Little Rock reach out to each other regardless of color. Her home backed up to a white neighborhood, and so she knew that there were kind white people, and also that there were mean-spirited people in her own neighborhood.[38]

A CONTEMPORARY STUDY of black Little Rock conducted by two African-American sociologists reported the unusual cohesion in the black community that had emerged from the crisis. Not only was there a growing unity over the need for desegregation, and the feeling that this was a "kind of second emancipation," but "Everyone felt the morale of the children had to be protected." The nationally acclaimed psychologist Dr. Kenneth Clark came to the same conclusion, writing of Little Rock's black community that they were "fearless, determined, and stolid. There is an almost oriental quality in the relentless refusal to move backwards."[39]

Without question, the key to black unity and success in Little Rock was Daisy Bates. The national NAACP office realized that "one person and one person alone" had carried the ball in Little Rock, and increasingly they realized she was a potent symbol of relentless struggle for African-Americans everywhere. Through seemingly tireless efforts to support the children, encourage the parents, keep pressure on the military, hold accountable the school administration, court the press, strategize, and plan, she was a one-woman show that kept the Little Rock effort on course. As she recalled years later, "We were determined that they were not going to chase us out of town. This was the big thing they wanted to do. Had they chased us out of town, the movement would have died." Through sheer determination and unflagging courage, Daisy Bates and the Little Rock Nine kept that movement alive.[40]

CHAPTER ELEVEN

A CRISIS OF LEADERSHIP
Robert R. Brown and the Civic Elite

T HE NEW EPISCOPAL BISHOP OF ARKANSAS, ROBERT R. BROWN, HAD been in the state just two years when the Little Rock crisis threw his city into upheaval. Dark-haired and handsome, with an athlete's vital, compact build, the forty-seven-year-old cleric was noted for his powerful preaching and his commanding presence. A Texan by birth and education, he had attended seminary in Alexandria, Virginia, where he had met and married his aristocratic wife, Warwick, the daughter of a politician who was a staunch segregationist and member of the Byrd machine. Bishop Brown shared by instinct and background the South's traditional paternalistic views toward his social "inferiors," though his seminary training had caused him to question the contradictions between the brotherhood of man and a segregated social order.[1]

Brown's initial reaction to the crisis in Little Rock was to attempt to work behind the scenes, since, as a relative newcomer, he was wary of resentment among his flock. Other Little Rock ministers struggled with the same conflict between their obligation to speak out against social injustice and their responsibility to keep parishioners in the pews. Three members of the Little Rock School Board, Dale Alford, William G. Cooper, and Wayne Upton, were Episcopalians, and Brown hoped initially to be able to work through them. He learned through one of his staunch church members, a Faubus appointee, that the governor was anxious for help in mediating the crisis, and he sent numerous proposals and counterproposals for the governor to consider. He spent long hours debating strategy with respected citizens and members of the vestry at Trinity Episcopal Cathedral. He struggled to inspire the Greater Little Rock Ministerial Alliance to work together to alleviate the crisis, though the group was reluctant. Only when violence flared on September 23 did Bishop Brown decide it was time for swift and purposeful action.[2]

By 11:00 A.M. that Monday, after two hours of rioting in the streets around Central High School, the bishop had convened a meeting of the Ministerial Alliance and galvanized it into action. Finally able to see the desegregation problem in theological terms, Brown argued that in light of the violence, "to remain silent was to condone the sin, and to appear neutral was to commit a real Christian heresy." Meeting next with the city's Episcopal clergy, the bishop concluded that duty compelled him to write a pastoral letter to all Arkansas Episcopalians outlining the proper response of the Christian in the present crisis, which he did that afternoon. Brown threw himself into his letter with a passion and an abandon that he later came to regret. Endorsing the position of his national church "that we consistently oppose and combat discrimination based on color or race . . .", he directed his flock "to refrain from every word or deed which is not consistent with the teachings of Jesus Christ concerning the brotherhood of man." In a phrase that revealed much about his mind-set, he also admonished Arkansas Episcopalians "to make a firm resistance against every pressure of an unthinking society."[3]

Brown believed the actions of the segregationists stemmed from unthinking emotion. Convinced that mindless prejudice lay behind concerns about such things as "race-mixing" and "mongrelization," Brown was baffled by his inability to lead his parishioners into a more enlightened approach to race relations. He lamented the "vast distance . . . between altar, pulpit, and pew," and he was astounded by the "unawareness of the people" and their failure to follow their "more spiritually experienced pastors." Brown believed that if church members would be "obedient" to the Gospel as he now understood it, they would raise up a cry against the continued resistance to desegregation.[4]

While acknowledging that those among the segregationists he labeled "extremists" held views "bordering on religious fanaticism," Bishop Brown could not bring himself to take those views seriously. Even though he later wrote, "Little Rock has become the symbol of a national attack upon a sacred southern tradition . . . ," he could not seem to fathom that most Little Rock people responded to racial issues with more deeply rooted beliefs than his newfound understanding of the demands of the "brotherhood of man." Certain of his own intellectual and spiritual superiority, Bishop Brown was just as paternalistic as Little Rock's other civic leaders. One of the casualties of the Little Rock crisis would be the easy assumption among the civic elite of the right to lead, since the heretofore docile majority increasingly asserted the right to follow leaders of their own choosing.[5]

THE MONTH OF SEPTEMBER had brought a succession of shocks to Little Rock's civic leadership: when Orval Faubus surrounded Central High with the National Guard, when unruly mobs formed in front of the high school, when disturbing images of a stoic Elizabeth Eckford circled the globe, when Eisenhower and Faubus failed to reach a compromise at Newport, when rioting occurred on September 23, when federal soldiers marched into an American city, *their* city. As one of Little Rock's business leaders expressed it, "... we were resentful of the whole incident. It was making something of our town which we were ashamed of. We were, we *knew* that we were more progressive in the beginnings of racial integration than most of the South, and most *all* of the North, so our feelings were: 'Why us?'" Little Rock's business and professional men began to meet in offices, in coffee shops, and on street corners, expressing the sentiment over and over, "Somebody should do something!" The realization eventually began to dawn that "we were somebody."[6]

Within hours of the arrival of federal troops in Little Rock, the city's traditional leadership began to rally. At the urging of Brooks Hays's close friend and adviser, Clyde Lowry, the twenty-five former presidents of the Little Rock Chamber of Commerce (and Hays) began to meet daily at the Chamber office, seeking a means toward withdrawing the federal troops and getting their city off the front pages of the world's newspapers. Yet many of them were shocked by the range of sentiment within the group, and especially the heat with which others were willing to defend Faubus in the face of the federal government's show of naked force.[7]

Thursday, September 26, the day after federal troops escorted the Little Rock Nine into Central High School, three self-described segregationist candidates filed for positions on the soon-to-be elected City Council. Many of Little Rock's civic leaders read this news in the morning paper with alarm, because in the fall of 1956 they had participated in a successful "good government" campaign to replace the supposedly corrupt and inefficient mayor-alderman form of government, based on representation from each ward, with a more "scientific" city manager–council arrangement based on citywide voting and therefore more easily controlled. The chairman of the Good Government Campaign was Clyde Lowry. Little Rock's civic leaders had worked for a year to nurture the new plan, hoping to make local government more responsive to what they perceived to be the city's best interests. Now just a month away from the November election, these leaders did not want to see their efforts jeopardized by the injection of the integration controversy into the campaign. With the entry of three vocal and decidedly nonelite candidates into the race, Little Rock's civic leadership faced the uncomfortable realization that they had a fight on their hands for control of local affairs.[8]

Two days after federal troops surrounded Central High, the Capital Citizens' Council ran an ad in the *Arkansas Democrat* naming fifteen white ministers who had publicly opposed Faubus's use of the National Guard and challenging those clerics to act on their stated convictions: ". . . we recommend and urge all ministers who believe that our children should have racially mixed schools forced upon them to immediately take steps to integrate their churches by publicly inviting the colored people to their services. . . . Under this arrangement, the children would not be asked to accept a situation which the adults are unwilling to tolerate." After a summer of relentless harassment of Governor Faubus and the School Board, the Citizens' Council had its publicity mechanisms securely in place; and after the boon of having federal troops sent into Little Rock, the organization's coffers began to overflow. In November Amis Guthridge told a South Carolina audience, "We weren't solidified in Arkansas before that happened [sending in the troops]. But we are now. We've had to hire a fulltime secretary to handle the business of our Capital Citizens' Council. I once might have been from that state in the Southwest but tonight the majority of people in Arkansas are from the Deep, Deep South." Flush with its windfall of unexpected funds, the Citizens' Council stepped up its advertising campaign.[9]

Friday, September 27, the same day the Citizens' Council ran its ad, Mrs. Margaret Jackson released a statement for the Central High School Mothers' League pleading with Governor Faubus to close the school because the mothers felt the lives of their children "were being endangered by the federal troops." Faubus told reporters he was also under pressure to call a special session of the state legislature. As the next day's *Arkansas Gazette* noted the situation, "Some legislators reportedly advocated shutting off state funds to integrated schools. Faubus has said, however, that he does not favor such drastic action."[10]

On Saturday the 28th Faubus met at the Governor's Mansion with a delegation of 136 members of the Mothers' League, led by Margaret Jackson, who fervently requested both the school closing and the special session of the legislature. In an impromptu press conference on the Mansion steps after the meeting, Faubus told reporters such a special session could pass laws that would take Central High School out of the control of federal troops. Reflecting the thinking of some of his advisers, and perhaps testing the waters, Faubus suggested that abolition of the public school system, the creation of private schools, or the withholding of state aid from public school districts that had integrated schools were among the options under consideration. But with characteristic caution he added, "I haven't said that I favor any of those—I'm just listing the possibilities." The governor emphasized he did not want to close the schools and "jeopardize the progress of the state." Faubus also told the reporters assembled on his front lawn, jokingly, "If we are occupied much longer . . . we will deal with the United Nations and seek some Marshall Plan aid."[11]

Faubus now found himself subject to pressures from every conceivable direction. On the right were the segregationists, his erstwhile foes, who did not trust him and thought him too liberal. On the left, among his erstwhile friends, Faubus found only condemnation and disdain. Sid McMath, just three years removed from his last political race and hoping to offer himself as a liberal alternative, seized every opportunity to portray the beleaguered governor as a "Dixiecrat" and a potential third-party threat to the anxious Democratic faithful. Similarly, Harry Ashmore suggested on *Face the Nation* that Faubus had invited a split in the Democratic Party that would leave the South "in far worse shape in trying to deal with its problems."[12]

More astute in managing Governor Faubus than either of the strident groups on his right or his left, Little Rock's businessmen launched a "courteous campaign" that refrained from attacking the governor and thereby forcing him into positions they did not want him to take. Typical of the group was Josh Shepherd, gentlemanly insurance executive, former president of the Chamber of Commerce, and a committed member of the Governor's Advisory Commission on Education. Shepherd had spent September vacationing in Canada, and he returned home to the surreal spectacle of federal troops in his city's streets. Reading that Faubus was contemplating calling a special session of the General Assembly, he knew "if those legislators had come to Little Rock and had seen federal troops marching in front of the high school[,] passions might have risen so high that the results might have been extremely injurious to our public education system." Shepherd went out to the Mansion to see the governor and pleaded for time and patience.[13]

Little Rock's leaders realized that Mann and McMath had both been ineffectual because they had attacked Faubus mercilessly. Schooled throughout their lives in the niceties of southern manners, the city's leading businessmen approached the governor in a manner that was "polite but purposeful." Organizing very quietly and working through the weekend, the civic leaders strove to surround Faubus with evidence that segregationist sentiment would ultimately win less favor with the voters than "devotion to law and order, preservation of the public school system, and restoration of the state's good name in the nation." Running up their long-distance telephone bills, leaders such as Josh

Shepherd, Chamber President William Shepherd (no relation), financier Raymond Rebsamen, and legislator Jack East Jr. called Faubus's friends and close political associates and persuaded them to the businessmen's point of view. Suddenly, as the *Wall Street Journal* described it, the governor "found himself surrounded by mobilized moderates."[14]

State legislators began to make statements to the press suggesting they opposed a special legislative session. Sunday's *Arkansas Democrat* reported Representative C. E. Yingling of Searcy had said, "This would be the worst possible time to call such a session. . . . this is a time to sit down, cool off, and act like human beings." The twenty-five past presidents of the Little Rock Chamber of Commerce issued a mild statement Monday morning that they thought it would be "unwise" to convene the legislature "while emotions are aroused and the situation is yet tense." By Monday afternoon, Faubus had backed off the idea of calling a special session.[15]

When the southern governors and the president failed to reach a compromise, Eisenhower himself began to harbor the unrealistic hope that local church and business leaders could "create a climate that would permit the Little Rock integration program to proceed peacefully, regardless of the Governor's stand, without either Federal or state intervention." Undoubtedly this strategy grew in part from Brooks Hays's misplaced assurances that Little Rock's clerical and business leaders were now rallying and that they could regain control of their city. Hays informed reporters that "informal discussions" were under way "in an effort to develop some specific plan that would bring about the withdrawal of the troops."[16]

President Eisenhower initially placed his hope for resolution of the Little Rock crisis on two initiatives of local leaders. One was an abortive public relations campaign that the past presidents of the Chamber of Commerce attempted to orchestrate. The other was a timid and ineffectual citywide prayer service. On October 2 the twenty-five past Chamber presidents (joined again by Brooks Hays) released a vague "Statement of Objectives and Rededication to Principles" specifying only that the people of their city supported law and order, condemned violence, had faith in democratic legal processes, and needed "a period of continual calm consideration of all the facts and circumstances." The last item in the list sounded very much like a request for the "cooling-off period" or the "breathing space" that Orval Faubus had been seeking for weeks.[17]

The businessmen's statement also called upon the people of Little Rock to resolve that they would "a. Uphold those who enforce laws without reservation. b. Condemn violence and the threat of violence or the encouragement of violence. c. Join unitedly in daily prayer for guidance and counsel for all who lead our people." The *Arkansas Gazette* story that accompanied this statement claimed that it called for "peaceful compliance to court-ordered school integration," but it did nothing of the sort. As Bishop Brown explained in his memoir, severe disagreements within the group precluded the businessmen's efforts to craft a strong statement in support of compliance. "Many admitted publicly," the bishop wrote, "that they did not mind saying they were for law and order, but that they were still going to stop integration in Little Rock if they could."[18]

The efforts of the religious leaders were no more promising. Under Bishop Brown's prodding, an ecumenical group of prominent clerics—Protestant, Catholic, and Jewish—and the ubiquitous Brooks Hays had met at Brown's home and crafted a plan to hold citywide prayer services on Columbus Day. The day after the meeting, Bishop Brown went out to the Governor's Mansion to see Orval Faubus. He thought he secured a commitment from the governor to let him serve as a mediator in the crisis, which would have been very pleasing to Brooks Hays and President Eisenhower. Apparently this was another example of a forceful personality deceiving himself that he had persuaded the governor to his own point of view, when actually Faubus had only smiled and nodded.[19]

On October 3 about forty ministers, all white, met at Trinity Episcopal Cathedral to plan the day of prayer, or the "Ministry of Reconciliation" as Brown preferred to call it. The bishop read letters of support from President Eisenhower, Governor Faubus, and the Little Rock School Board, and then the group decided that the October 12 services would include prayers for the community, state and nation; for the students at Little Rock Central High School; for support of law and order; for "understanding and compassion" to replace "rancor and prejudice"; for the people to resist "unthinking agitators"; and, from the Episcopal Book of Common Prayer, a confession "that we have done those things which we ought not to have done and not done those things which we ought to have done." Church leaders stressed in their public statements that these services were not to address the question of integration or segregation, but instead they should stand apart from what one leader called "the ministry of judgment."[20]

The vague and nonjudgmental language elicited a strong response from one of the uninvited ministers Bishop Brown labeled an "extremist," Reverend L. D. Foreman, pastor of Antioch Missionary Baptist Church and one of the prominent participants in the mob at Central High School throughout September. Foreman told the *Arkansas Democrat* "they're covering the subject (integration) with a veneer of prayer . . . making prayer the outer shell. It's an act of cowardice of the men participating. Instead of committing themselves on integration, they're saying let's get together and pray." Brother Foreman spoke in harsher, more direct tones than the city's clerical leadership was accustomed to using, but his critique of the projected day of prayer was widely shared. President Eisenhower's hopes for a change in public opinion soon disappeared under a flood of newspaper advertising that echoed Reverend Foreman's point of view.[21]

Harvard sociologists Thomas Pettigrew and Ernest Campbell traveled to Little Rock in the fall of 1957 and conducted an investigation of white attitudes toward desegregation. Based on that research they constructed a "Creed of Segregation" that they argued was significantly at odds with the "American Creed" Swedish sociologist Gunnar Myrdal had postulated as the basis for his seminal 1944 study of American race relations, *An American Dilemma*. Among the eight tenets Pettigrew and Campbell found at the heart of segregationist thought were these four:

- Forced, as contrasted to voluntary, racial desegregation is un-Constitutional since it violates traditional American freedoms of self-determination and local autonomy.
- Were segregation un-Constitutional, then the Supreme Court, under any reasonable assumption of competency, could not have delayed the discovery until 1954.
- Were segregation un-Christian, then all of the major Christian bodies would not have established segregated churches.
- Equality is in some ways desirable, but it is unattainable. If equality does not exist within racial groups, by what justice is it foisted between groups?

After extensive study of this intricate and elaborate system of thought, Pettigrew and Campbell concluded, "Of this much we are sure: Whatever its dynamics or its origins, it is a staunch bulwark. It will not quickly dissipate."[22]

Many critics of the segregationist line mistakenly believed it was of lower- to lower-middle-class origins. As Central High School vice principal for girls Elizabeth Huckaby wrote in her memoir years later, "Our worst error in judgment had been in underestimating the opposition to integration. The local leaders of that cause were, in general, not people one would call the backbone of the community." But although the Amis Guthridges, Wesley Prudens, and L. D. Foremans carried the banner for the segregationist cause, most observers in 1957 Little Rock agreed that the vast majority of the population espoused the segregationists' arguments and favored their goals if not their methods.

Pulitzer Prize–winning journalist Relman Morin, who was in Little Rock from September 10 to October 1, wrote that the majority of Little Rock's citizens ". . . overwhelmingly oppose integration and want no part of it. But they also believe in obeying the law. And there is the dilemma. It is not easy to obey a command that [roils] your deepest sensibilities, nor readily comply with an order that you feel, in blood and fibre, is wrong. . . ."[23]

On October 8, Reverend M. L. Moser of Central Baptist Church announced a prayer service to be held in his small sanctuary the Friday night before the Columbus Day observances. The stated purpose of the Moser event was to pray for "the transfer of the Negro students back to Horace Mann High School." Moser stressed he had no connection with the planned Saturday morning prayer service. "We have nothing in common with those ministers," he stressed, "many of whom are modernists and liberals while we are conservatives and fundamentalists. . . ." Two days later Moser ran another ad, this time listing the three things for which his service would now pray: "1. For our National leaders. That they be guided by Constitutional Law rather than politics. 2. For our State leaders. That they be given the wisdom and the courage to fulfill their responsibilities to the citizens of the State of Arkansas. 3. For all citizens. That under these trying circumstances, no overt acts be performed for which we would later be sorry." Stated with clarity and force, this announcement was a far cry from the fuzzy "things we have left undone" for which the mainstream ministers had proposed to pray.[24]

SATURDAY MORNING SAW more than five thousand Little Rock residents praying in their churches, over half of them Catholics, whose children did not attend public schools. Of the two hundred Little Rock churches to whom invitations had been sent, only eighty-five held some kind of service, and twenty of these were black. A few churches held full, hourlong services; most provided prayers only; and some simply opened their doors for their parishioners to enter and pray. Little Rock Ministerial Alliance president Dunbar Ogden, pastor at Central Presbyterian, told the *Arkansas Democrat* that the spirit of the services indicated "a strong concern in the minds and hearts of the people to know what is the right thing to do." Bishop Brown claimed, somewhat disingenuously, that the morning's attendance was "beyond what I had anticipated" and that this indicated a desire for "God's guidance in matters of law and order. . . ." He also claimed, curiously, that "these men and women gave their own silent witness against violence." He did not claim that the morning's attendance suggested support for integration, or even for law and order.[25]

That evening's *Arkansas Democrat* carried a large advertisement entitled "Can A Christian Be A Segregationist?" Quoting at length a (purportedly) communist publication outlining the party's intention to stir discontent among blacks and guilt among whites and also to aid blacks to advance materially and socially, Reverend Wesley Pruden included one of the author's claims: "With this prestige, the Negro will be able to inter-marry with the whites and begin a process which will deliver America to our cause." Pruden editorialized, "Could anything be plainer than the fact that race-mixing in our schools is a Communist Doctrine." Pruden continued, "Racial mixing of children in schools will lead to undue familiarity and encourage inter-marriage. This would corrupt both races and create a mongrel people." The Baptist preacher concluded with his real message, "Our Lord was born into the most segrated [*sic*] race the world has ever known. Under this system He lived and died. Never did He lift His voice against segregation. Segregation has Christian sanction, integration is Communistic."[26]

Extreme as Pruden's reflections may seem, Pettigrew and Campbell stressed that it would be a mistake to "minimize the dissident ministerial elements by saying that they are poorly educated, fanatical pastors whose small flocks lack community influence." The fact was that "the Reverend Pruden and his confederates encouraged partially latent but very powerful sentiments present in every congregation in the city. Indeed, they found themselves in the happy circumstance of expressing not only the nearly unanimous views of their own congregations but also feelings of a large part of the entire community."[27]

After the Columbus Day services, most mainstream ministers declined further involvement in the integration dispute. A similar phenomenon seems to have occurred in the business community. The segregationists were making such strong and noisy arguments that moderate men and women of goodwill could not hold the line. As the Harvard sociologists argued, in this kind of community conflict, the middle ground becomes untenable. In their words, "As a movement grows and the issues are hotly debated, attitudes begin to polarize toward two extremes—either for or against; the middle ground becomes almost impossible to maintain."[28]

Socially questionable groups such as the Capital Citizens' Council and the Mothers' League, and the marginal people Pettigrew and Campbell called the "sect ministers," were hardly the only sources of arguments against integration and in support of Orval Faubus, although they were clearly the most vocal and blatant. As early as October 7 the *Arkansas Democrat* had started referring to "the forced integration" of Central High School; columnist Karr Shannon wrote frequently under such arresting headings as "Who Knows What 'The Law of the

Land' Is," "Is the 14th Amendment Valid," and "The Troops are There to Enforce What Law?" Every day, Faubus's favorite reporter, George Douthit, presented the governor's positions sympathetically, arguing frequently that the federal government had put Faubus in an untenable position, making unreasonable demands.[29]

The *Arkansas Democrat*'s owner and publisher, K. August Engel, was one of the most respected men in the community, long involved in a host of initiatives to promote community betterment, and voted by his peers in 1958 as one of the twelve men in the city "most important in the formation of public policy." Harry Ashmore later charged that the *Democrat*'s positions reflected a cynical decision to capitalize on the *Gazette*'s growing unpopularity and that it was a decision driven by greed. What Ashmore failed to admit was that the *Arkansas Democrat* reflected and reinforced the dominant sentiment in the community, at all levels of the social hierarchy.[30]

By mid-October, Little Rock's leadership was in disarray. The mayor and the City Council had been repudiated at the polls the previous year and the new municipal leadership would not take over until November. Brooks Hays spoke everywhere, ineffectually, about the need for "moderation" and "Christian love." Senator Fulbright had fled to Europe. Harry Ashmore was increasingly suspect. *Arkansas Gazette* owner J. N. Heiskell was silent, primarily because his daughter and son-in-law had had to lead him by the hand into an acceptance of his own paper's position. Worthen Bank President Jim Penick was silent; a man who characteristically worked behind the scenes, he would not have been inclined to step out front, especially not when east Arkansas depositors were threatening to close their accounts and move their substantial funds to Memphis. The gates were open wide for hotheads to take the field, and in marched Amis Guthridge, Wesley Pruden, and Margaret Jackson.[31]

For the first time, Little Rock's white citizens had to confront unexamined assumptions and unspoken expectations that touched every aspect of their lives. Until the glare of national and world attention beamed relentlessly on their public and private arrangements, most Little Rock whites had not brought into clear focus the contradictions inherent in accepting segregation in a democratic nation. Now many people began the process of sorting out what they believed and what they valued, and the costs of holding on or of letting go. It was a painful process, one that would remain unfinished many, many years in the future.

During the two weeks that President Eisenhower waited for public sentiment to crystallize in favor of yielding to integration in Little Rock, he had many occasions to question the wisdom of his decision to send federal troops into Arkansas. He grew increasingly insistent that means must be found to get the Army out of Little Rock, if not by persuading Faubus to assume responsibility for the children's safety then by working through Little Rock's community leaders. The presence of the troops was creating negative political fallout for all of the southern Republican congressmen, as well as for the president, and Faubus repeatedly found ways to exploit the situation and suggest through the press that soldiers were behaving inappropriately in the presence of American schoolchildren. The hasty call-up of troops and the incorporation of the Arkansas National Guard had invited multiple bureaucratic nightmares for the Army, with in-processing and out-processing of soldiers overlapping for weeks. In addition, the monetary costs of the operation were staggering. Military analysts reported that the National Guard alone was costing $79,000 per day, and the *Arkansas Democrat* reported that if the National Guard remained mobilized for the full school year, the cost to American taxpayers of keeping the nine black children in Central High School would reach $23 million. Eisenhower needed an escape hatch.[32]

Faubus was adamant he would not agree to any resolution of the crisis that called upon him to "give up my discretionary powers as governor of the state." After Eisenhower rejected his written offer the day of the meeting with the southern governors, Faubus made it clear that he thought all of the proposed settlements had asked him to relinquish powers to which he believed himself constitutionally entitled as governor of a state. Primary among these was the power to preserve peace and order within his own borders. Another point that Faubus began to treat as nonnegotiable was his demand for a "cooling-off period." On October 6 the *Arkansas Democrat* announced that Faubus would make a new effort to seek a "breathing spell," which the newspaper correctly pointed out the governor had "long sought unsuccessfully."[33]

Over the summer Faubus had suggested to Virgil Blossom that a delay would give him political cover by allowing time to litigate the many cases then resting on court dockets questioning the constitutionality of the new Arkansas segregation laws. Faubus had made the same argument to the Little Rock School Board over lunch in late August, and a day later to Arthur Caldwell of the Justice Department. He had presented the identical case to President Eisenhower at Newport and to Brooks Hays in Little Rock. Back in the summer it had been a reasonable request, and if the Little Rock School Board and the Justice Department had been inclined to work together toward that end, a way might have been found to effect such a compromise. By October of 1957 the granting of a delay was a much more difficult prospect for the federal government to entertain, but it became a central element in Orval Faubus's negotiating position.[34]

At his next scheduled press conference, which he attended despite his having fallen victim to the influenza epidemic that had swept Little Rock, Faubus announced the necessity of a "cooling off period" in order to resolve the crisis. The *New York Times* reported the governor as saying the city needed time "to allay tensions, time for litigation of the half-dozen lawsuits in Federal and state courts, and . . . time for people to accept peacefully what now is being crammed down their throats at bayonet point." Faubus commented that a temporary withdrawal of the nine Negro students was "a necessary prerequisite under the present circumstances. . . ."[35]

On Monday, October 14, Faubus held a press conference and announced plans to meet on Tuesday with a "businessmen's committee," which turned out to be a six-man subgroup of the Chamber of Commerce twenty-five. Routinely called "the Guy Committee" after its chairman Walter C. Guy, it more accurately could have been called "the Hays Committee" because of Brooks Hays's active involvement through one of its members, his friend and patron Clyde Lowry. In their two-hour meeting, Faubus gave his visitors an illuminating history of the events, conditions, and personalities leading to the crisis, which the committee members found persuasive. The substance of the meeting remained a closely kept secret.[36]

In its written report, which was never delivered to the larger Chamber of Commerce group, the Guy Committee expressed its belief that "the settlement of our Central High School situation must be brought about without embarrassment at both the State and National level." The mechanism the subcommittee suggested for enabling the governor and the president to save face specified that the Little Rock School Board should go back to the federal judge and ask for a "Stay of Compliance" of its desegregation program. Echoing Governor Faubus's oft-repeated arguments, the report argued that the greatest need at the present was for a "cooling-off period" during which the state's new segregation laws could be tested in the courts and their constitutionality determined. The Little Rock School Board eventually did seek from a federal judge the delay the Guy Committee and Governor Faubus had recommended, but not while Judge Davies was still on the bench in Little Rock. The subcommittee's report concluded with the hope that during the "cooling-off period," Congress might rectify the "lack of congressional laws" demanding an end to segregation and "we may find spelled out for us and the Nation more definite rules and regulations governing the integration process."[37]

On the same day as the meeting between Faubus and the businessmen, the federal government reduced dramatically the number of troops stationed in Little Rock, perhaps in an effort to show that it was willing to soften its position. Despite the cut in numbers, however, the power arrangement remained unaltered, and Faubus commented [this] "doesn't change a thing; we're still occupied." As the governor noted, "There are just as many troops on active duty at Central High School as there were before. And the number of troops on duty exceeds the number of students in school by some 400." Faubus knew he was in a position to benefit from Eisenhower's political quagmire, and even if he had been inclined to negotiate at this point, he felt he had ample reason to distrust the good intentions of either the White House or the Justice Department.[38]

Unfortunately for all concerned, Governor Faubus made an ill-advised comment at his Wednesday press conference, and the *Arkansas Democrat* reported it in that night's paper. Asked if he thought Arkansas National Guardsmen would resign from the Guard once they were released from their federal service Faubus suggested they would probably not resign for that reason, but "if I gave an order to the Guard to enforce integration in certain schools, hundreds of them would resign rather than be a party to forced integration in this state." Not stopping there, the article went on to say, "Previously the governor had said that a basis offered for settlement of the Central High School crisis was that he would have to agree to obey court orders, which he interpreted to mean he would be asked to use the Guard to enforce integration wherever it is ordered by the federal courts. He has indicated that he would not agree to such action." The Chamber of Commerce group withdrew from further negotiations between Faubus and Eisenhower.[39]

IN THE TWO WEEKS while the governor and the president waltzed back and forth, making bows to their respective admirers and trying not to step on toes, the black children at Central High School strengthened their resolve to stay the course. Some of them had moments of doubt, and the *Arkansas Democrat* reported on every absence, apparently hopeful that the nine youngsters would lose heart and return to Horace Mann High School. On October 17 the *Democrat* reported, obviously skeptical, ". . . only six of the nine Negro students attended CHS classes today. Elizabeth Eckford was reported absent due to illness. Melba Patillo and Terrence Roberts have been absent several days, with illness said to be the cause." Terrence Roberts told the United Press that white students had made him so miserable that for a time he was ready to abandon the desegregation effort. As the *Arkansas Gazette* quoted Roberts, "They . . . had been giving me a bad time, throwing erasers and saying things in the halls. But I'm going back, some time this week, I hope." Melba Patillo told Homer Bigart of the *New York Times* she "hadn't even considered quitting. The only way I'll quit is for them to kick me out," she said. "Whether the troops are there or not I'm going to school. There is too much at stake." Daisy Bates had done her job well inspiring the students to rise to the obstacles being thrown in their paths.[40]

SHORTLY AFTER THE Little Rock businessmen failed in their attempt to secure a compromise between Faubus and Eisenhower, George Douthit captured the essence of Orval Faubus's dilemma. "Arkansas' Governor Faubus has become a nationwide symbol of resistance to integration," Douthit wrote, "but few people understand that he does not control either the resistance or the removal of it." Douthit observed that thousands of Arkansans' racial attitudes were deeply ingrained and there was very little the governor could do to change that reality. "So long as he moves in the direction they want him to move, he is their accepted leader and they will cheer him. Anytime he reverses himself and starts enforcing integration, they will desert him."[41]

In a piece reprinted in the *Arkansas Democrat,* an editorial writer from outside the state, trying to make sense of Faubus's behavior in light of his liberal roots, suggested, "He has apparently split with them altogether but an experienced politician would not have risked such a split with his early backers unless he knew that he had the support of other substantial elements in the population. . . . he is obviously an astute politician who has managed to sense public opinion in his state and to congeal it in his favor." An inveterate poll taker, Faubus did indeed keep himself abreast of public opinion in his state, but rather than "congeal it in his favor" he began to mold himself to fit its contours.[42]

In the words of his biographer, Roy Reed, Orval Faubus saw politics as "the great game." Not having grown up surrounded by racism, and not comprehending either the sources or the moral dangers of the disease, Faubus viewed race as just one more pawn to be moved about the board to gain advantage. By mid-October of 1957, with every attempt at compromise frustrated and all sources of trust depleted, a weary Faubus stopped listening to the better angels of his nature and yielded to the lure of the segregationists.[43]

When he picked up his local newspapers on October 15, Faubus read that the city councils in both Little Rock and North Little Rock had adopted the new "Bennett Ordinance," named for Arkansas Attorney General Bruce Bennett, who had his sights trained on the gubernatorial nomination in the summer of 1958. Designed to cripple the NAACP, the ordinance imposed a penalty against any organization that refused to furnish information regarding membership, officers, and sources of income. The city councils of both municipalities, and others across the state, jumped on the Bennett bandwagon to silence the organization they thought was at the root of their integration woes. Faubus took note.[44]

More compellingly, Jim Johnson bought airtime to broadcast two speeches to the people of Arkansas, ostensibly to firm up their resistance to the integration menace, but actually to communicate to Orval Faubus what stance would be most politically beneficial to assume. Johnson and his massive-resistance confederates had been unable to make contact with Faubus, who was closeted in the Mansion behind legions of handlers, and they wanted desperately to influence his course of action. Knowing that Faubus's paid pollster, Eugene Newsom, kept the governor apprised of every blip on his public opinion radar, Johnson had the inspiration of speaking directly to the people and thereby influencing the governor's understanding of popular sentiment. His speech was a bombshell of massive resistance rhetoric.[45]

Demanding that the governor call a special session of the legislature, Johnson thundered, "I expect the people of Arkansas who agree with me to echo this demand." Johnson left no doubt that the purpose of the special session would be to get the State Sovereignty Commission to function in protecting Arkansas against Eisenhower and the NAACP. He also suggested that if Faubus did not perform as the segregationists wished, they would implement provisions of the Johnson Amendment enabling them to evict him from office.[46]

A combination of factors led Orval Faubus to see the wisdom of throwing in with the segregationists. Foremost was the near-universal conclusion, reached by Faubus pollster Newsom, Harvard researchers Pettigrew and Campbell, and a host of journalists on the scene, that the vast majority of the people of Arkansas opposed integration. His stance against the federal government, crafted day by day with no master plan other than maintaining his own political viability, had proved to be wildly popular in Arkansas and beyond. As one perceptive journalist assessed Faubus's prospects in mid-October, "The moderates in Arkansas are outspokenly critical of him. And the people who don't want integration but do want law and order and prestige for the state are against him. On balance, however, his position looks very strong today." By October 26 he was saying publicly that he had no intention of using the National Guard to enforce integration under his command.[47]

Within a matter of weeks Orval Faubus and Bill Smith summoned Jim Johnson to the Governor's Mansion, where they told him the governor had decided to run for a third term, suggesting obliquely that if Johnson ran for the Supreme Court they would help him. This was a courtesy of course, but it was also good politics. Johnson had demonstrated his ability to create problems for the governor, and they wanted to bring him under control. For his part, Johnson knew that Orval Faubus had "pulled every tooth in his head," and had taken his army. More to the point, as a true believer in the morality and constitutionality of segregation, Johnson was grateful to Faubus for holding the line against the federal government.[48]

This was the point at which Faubus began to think seriously about a third term. This was his moment of decision. Through the events of September and October of 1957 he had abandoned the notion of challenging Senator McClellan in 1960, and Senator Fulbright's seat, which he coveted, would not be open to contest until 1962. The missteps of the president and the Justice Department, the ham-handed assaults of McMath and Ashmore, the unanticipated allure of the segregationists, all combined to make Orval Faubus see the unmistakable direction in which his own best interests lay. From that point forward he abandoned his liberal heritage and descended into demagoguery. Although it earned him four more terms in the statehouse, it was a choice he came to regret in the quiet reflection of old age.[49]

ON OCTOBER 28, the *Arkansas Democrat* carried a Capital Citizens' Council advertisement addressed to all twenty-one candidates in the upcoming election for city directors. "Are you for race-mixing?," the ad began. "If so . . . Let the Public know now, Before We Vote! The seven who are elected . . . on November 5, will come face-to-face with this problem in making rules for our Parks, Playgrounds, Swimming Pools, Golf Courses, Buses and other city facilities. We await your public answer before we vote!"[50]

The next day's paper carried a CCC ad for a "States Rights Rally!" to be held on October 30 and inviting "All Who Believe in States Rights and Racial Integrity" (the Citizens' Councils always linked the two). Amis Guthridge took the stage before a crowd of eight hundred people and informed the audience that the Good Government Committee, which had handpicked and endorsed seven candidates for the city director positions, was "a clique of civic hypocrites" and that their candidates would permit not only integration of schools but also use by Negroes of public swimming pools and golf courses. Guthridge also said he "had word" that Little Rock Negroes were planning to "bloc vote" for the Good Government Committee's candidates. Lead speaker William M. Rainach of Louisiana, president of the Association of Citizens' Councils of America, then told his receptive audience that the real goal of the Good Government effort was "not to help the Negroes but to get the Negroes' votes."[51]

The *Arkansas Gazette* described the Good Government Committee as a "Committee of leading residents . . . ," and in fact the *Gazette,* along with the *Democrat,* had been among the originators and sponsors of the effort to adopt a new pattern of municipal government. The segregation issue had been injected in the campaign late in the game, and to the GGC leaders this seemed an unfair twist in their carefully laid plans. Indeed, after the election was over, one of the winners commented that "none of the 21 candidates differed substantially on segregation. . . ."[52]

School Board attorney and former Chamber president Richard Butler spoke in a televised advertisement promoting the Good Government candidates. Saying that they had been "unjustly accused of being integrationists," Butler urged the voters to "put the demagogues and falsifiers in the[ir] proper place" by voting for the people the Good Government Committee had endorsed. On election day Little Rock's voters did accept six of the seven GGC candidates, but by very slim margins. Significantly, an analysis of the voting revealed that the Good Government candidates won as a result of an alliance between blacks and voters in the "silk stocking" wards in the Heights. L. C. Bates wrote in the *State Press* that "a heavy Negro vote saved the city of Little Rock from losing its face to a biased group." Predictably, Amis Guthridge soon charged that the City Council elections had been "rigged from the beginning."[53]

The civic elite had been preparing for the November 5 election for a year, and under normal circumstances they could have expected the voters to follow their lead quietly as they had usually done in the past. This election delivered a loud message to the traditional civic leadership that something fundamental had changed in Little Rock. Recovering from this shock, the old leaders realized only gradually that the gentlemanly, paternalistic pattern of civic affairs had slipped into the past, and a new kind of politics had arrived to take its place. For the first time, nonelite activists had discovered they could hurl the charge of "integrationist" against anyone who opposed their agenda and be heard. Although the segregationists failed to carry this election, they had discovered a potent weapon they could use indiscriminately to slash and maim anyone who disagreed with them. As the traditional leadership retreated into shock and confusion, they lost control of their city.[54]

FOR THE NEXT YEAR and a half Little Rock would be a divided city, while Bishop Brown, Richard Butler, and other members of the civic elite struggled with not only their shock at the intemperate attitudes and behavior of people they had thought they knew, but also their outrage over the damage to their community's "image," their resentment against the federal government, and often, their own deeply ingrained attitudes and assumptions. As leading businessman Frank Lyon explained, "There was a lot of confusion. A lot of businesses were going to suffer repercussions. . . . There's never been anything here in my lifetime where there was as much polarization. . . . There was absolutely no middle ground, and so that would naturally divide a community rather sharply."[55]

As Lyon explained the business leaders' dilemma, "They were not only struggling with their own feelings. Their institutions or their industry or their business could be almost immediately boycotted, not by a few folks but by the majority. Now you may say 'That's a poor excuse! That's putting money before principle!' . . . But you must take into consideration not only the people that worked there but the people who owned . . . stock, sometimes hundreds of owners." In Lyon's estimation the business owner, banker, or industrialist had more at stake than just his own point of view, and even though he may have opposed the segregationists on strong moral grounds, he felt he had "no right to assume that risk and jeopardize all those people's jobs. . . ."[56]

Sociologists Pettigrew and Campbell observed that in the fall of 1957, "In Little Rock's white community any position that was not blatantly pro-segregation was regarded as dangerously pro-integration."[57] The "moderates" had been marginalized. The Capital Citizens' Council had taken the field. Enjoying both a significant head start as a result of their summer-long propaganda campaign and a dramatic infusion of outside capital after Eisenhower played into their hands and sent in federal troops, the segregationists used every means possible to drive home the point that their position was not just preferable, it was close to sacred. They touched every chord: motherhood, democracy, states' rights, and most important, protection of white blood lines. They argued that Harry Ashmore's mantra of "law and order" meant only one thing, integration, and they were right. Successfully challenging traditional means of control, they used polarization and fear to push Little Rock's white leaders down a steep and perilous slope. The community had to descend even farther into darkness before the old leadership found the path, and the courage, to start the long climb back toward sanity.

CHAPTER TWELVE

TORMENTS BEHIND CLOSED DOORS

Minnijean Brown

P EOPLE AROUND THE WORLD KNEW OF THE LITTLE ROCK NINE AND
drew mental images of them from the many photographs taken outside
Central High at the start of the school year. What happened to them later, inside
the building, is much less well known, and almost unrelentingly painful. By
mid-October, the nine black students had settled in for a long season of torment. Federal, state, and local governments—and school officials—abandoned
the young pioneers to the fiendish efforts of a small band of student segregationists, misfits who were committed to forcing the black children's withdrawal
from Central High.

Bright, vivacious, emotionally unguarded, and thoroughly adolescent in her
need for recognition and acceptance, Minnijean Brown had thought that going
to Central High School with her two best friends, Melba Patillo and Thelma
Mothershed, would be a lark. She had always been fascinated by the castlelike
high school for whites, and she thought it was "true proof that more money
was being spent [on whites] so it must have had something in it that was of use
to me because otherwise it wouldn't be so big. . . ." A voracious reader and a
strong student, Minnijean had no doubt she could compete academically, and
her musical gifts made her feel certain that the white kids would like her as soon
as they heard her sing. An adventurous girl who had already begun to test the
rules of segregation by refusing to ride in the back of the city buses and getting
kicked off as a result, Minnie had no way of knowing that her high spirits, her
need for peer acceptance, and her unwillingness to identify herself as a social
subordinate would lead to the Central High School officials' labeling her a troublemaker, and the segregationists' focusing on her as a target.[1]

Elizabeth Huckaby wrote in her memoir that at the beginning of the year
Minnijean had been "too effervescent" as well as a "show-off and braggart."

When Richard Boehler tripped Minnie in French class early in the fall, she called him "white trash" and summoned her guard into the classroom, alienating the already-overwhelmed first-year teacher. She challenged her American history teacher about the slim treatment of slavery in the class's textbook. She called a segregationist girl who was verbally persecuting her "a midget." She earned a seat in early-morning detention hall for being tardy to class five times.[2]

The other black students were more guarded in their interactions with whites and their respect for the rules, but they too suffered relentless harassment from a small group of vicious white "hoods," the black-jacketed, blue jeans wearing, James Dean and Elvis wannabes that haunted the nightmares of school officials all over the country. Beginning with what Virgil Blossom dismissed as a "campaign of petty harassment"—shoving, name-calling, throwing sharpened pencils and spitballs—in the absence of any significant administrative response these young delinquents graduated to more dangerous, threatening behavior.[3]

The school staff counseled the nine black children repeatedly not to respond to this harassment, as Blossom said, "in the hope it would die out." But it only escalated. On October 28, after a month of unremitting daily attacks, such as kicks to the shins and ankles, assaults with a closed fist, or treacherous shoves down the numerous stairwells, the Nine and their parents met with school officials in Superintendent Blossom's downtown office. Worried about the rapidly diminishing numbers of soldiers inside the school and expecting to hear some plans for the protection of their children, the parents were astonished to hear Blossom counsel the Nine once again not to respond to their attackers. The superintendent also explained that a teacher had to witness and report any instances of abuse, because if the staff started suspending students simply on the word of other students, in no time at all the segregationists could have the black children out of the school. Impatient with this approach, the customarily circumspect Lois Patillo stood up and confronted Blossom, asking what plans school officials had made to provide protection for her daughter. "That's none of your business!" the burly superintendent growled. Mrs. Patillo thought her child's welfare was very much her business, and she and the other parents left the meeting with a renewed sense of unease.[4]

After the meeting, Minnijean Brown ran up to Mrs. Huckaby in the parking lot and asked if she could be in the Glee Club's Christmas program, exclaiming that she needed to know soon so she would be able to buy a white dress. Girls' Chorus was Minnijean's favorite class. It was the one place she felt relaxed and accepted, the one class where the teacher treated her well. But Mrs. Huck-aby thought that Minnijean's participation in the Christmas program would stir "the deep fears and prejudice of the whites."[5]

In her memoir Mrs. Huckaby also related that one of the white girls in the National Honor Society had started eating lunch each day with Ernest Green. When Principal Jess Matthews heard that this "looked like a love affair," he asked Ernest to "insulate" this girl from criticism by making sure that a black girl sat with him every day. Apparently the members of the Capital Citizens' Council and the Mothers' League were not the only ones who feared that integration would lead to "race-mixing."[6]

On November 12, with all of the 101st paratroopers removed from the scene and only six National Guardsmen remaining inside the school, Jefferson Thomas stood facing his opened hall locker when Hugh Williams dashed behind him, hit him on the side of the head with some kind of hard object, and knocked him unconscious. Williams later confessed to the incident and was suspended for three days, the customary slap on the wrist for segregationist infractions. Clarence Laws took Jeff to see a doctor, who ascertained that no real damage had been done, and the indomitable Jeff insisted on going back to school the next day. Daisy Bates took Jeff shopping for running shoes, so he could run away from his attackers in the halls. The resourceful boy also reported to Bates that he had started buttoning the top button of his shirts so no one could drop cigarettes down his back. School authorities called the attack on Jefferson Thomas "noth-ing to get excited about," and Virgil Blossom later described the incident as "a scuffle."[7]

The afternoon of the attack on Jefferson Thomas, Daisy Bates went to Cen-tral High to complain about the escalating harassment of the black students, but she got little satisfaction. The Associated Press quoted her that evening as say-ing the children "are being bullied and harassed to try to force them to leave. But they're not going to give in." An irritated Army captain called Bates want-ing to know "who gave the information to the newspaper about the incident at the school today?" Bates replied with characteristic bite, asking if he was more interested in publicity than in the welfare of the children.[8]

NAACP Field Secretary Clarence Laws reported to his superiors in New York that there seemed to be a lackadaisical attitude on the part of Army per-sonnel in Little Rock. He gave as an example the fact that Minnijean Brown had turned over three threatening notes to a National Guardsman, and yet when Laws asked J. O. Powell about it that night at Mrs. Bates's house, Powell knew nothing about them. When the vice principal inquired at the school, he learned that the National Guardsman had placed the notes in an intelligence file down-town at Army headquarters.[9]

On the morning after the attack on Jefferson Thomas, Daisy Bates and Clarence Laws went to see Virgil Blossom. They asked him "what he intended to do about the continued brutal attacks on the children by the organized gang—attacks that had been reported many times." When Blossom said he was not aware of a large number of offenses, Bates handed him the list she had been keeping based on the children's reports to her. Bates wrote in her memoir, "As he looked at the long list of names and the repeated brutalities against the nine children, his expression lost some of its hardness, and his face seemed to soften." Yet she miscalculated when she admonished him, "If you are really interested in clearing up this trouble, you should expel some of these repeated trouble-makers." Blossom bristled at the suggestion and retorted, "You can't tell me how to run my school." Bates dug in, saying "No, I can't . . . but it's up to you—not the Army—to maintain discipline inside the school. By not doing so, you are subjecting the children to physical torture that you will have to live with the rest of your life." The feisty Bates knew when she left the superintendent's office that she had lost a potential ally, and she was correct.[10]

On November 14 Clarence Laws telephoned a formal statement to the NAACP's New York office protesting the continuing reduction of troops at Central High in the face of escalating attacks on the black children. He also proposed to school officials a means of resolving "the present school problem"; he requested that Superintendent Blossom and Principal Matthews issue a firm statement "making it crystal clear that full cooperation with the integration plan is expected of each and every teacher" at Central High. He also suggested that Matthews release a separate directive announcing that continued harassment of the black students "will not be tolerated." Finally, he requested the creation of an interracial student committee to help resolve problems within the school. School officials ignored all of Laws's suggestions. The torment of the nine children escalated.[11]

On November 18 three of the black girls received telephone calls at their homes telling them there was going to be a lynching in Little Rock. "Do you know Emmett Till?" one malicious caller asked. "The same thing is going to happen to you." About the same time, segregationist pastors instructed their high school–aged members to encourage the black children to withdraw by ignoring them. The Nine would have been happy if being "ignored" was the worst of the cruelty practiced upon them.[12]

ASTONISHINGLY, PRINCIPAL Jess Matthews explained to Minnijean Brown that she could not participate in the Glee Club Christmas program because the status of the Nine was not yet settled. "When it is definitely decided that Negroes will go to school here with the whites," he told her, "and the troops are removed, then you will be able to participate in all activities." Jess Matthews had been a popular principal of Little Rock Central High School for many years, and he took great pride in his school's outstanding academic and athletic records. Described by several former students as a "gentle giant," Matthews was the kind of principal who wanted everyone to be happy, and who wanted everyone to like him. He was unwilling to stir the wrath of the segregationists.[13]

Vice principal J. O. Powell, a Little Rock native and a Central High graduate, could hardly contain his dismay over Jess Matthews's unwillingness to intervene aggressively and stop the persecution of the nine black children in his school. Powell frequently went to Daisy Bates's home, providing the civil rights leader with much valuable information about conditions and policies her nine young charges struggled so heroically to accept and endure. In an unpublished memoir, Powell credited the principal's "gelatinous attitude of permissive negligence" for the breakdown of discipline and authority inside Central High School. Powell also claimed that since the principal was resentful of the Army's presence and yet wanted the assistance of the soldiers, Matthews created an "artificially induced smokescreen" behind which he could avoid his responsibility to protect the black children. According to Powell, Matthews was a politician first, then a school administrator.[14]

As Powell described Matthews's early counseling sessions with the school's segregationist tormentors, the avuncular principal often counseled the segregationist tormenters by saying, "You're not going to solve this thing by punching niggers. This thing is bigger than you and me and Congress and the Governor and everybody else, and it's not going to be solved any time soon. We don't like it any more than you do. But it's here. . . . You start thinking about your education and quit worrying about integration and niggers."[15]

Although Superintendent Blossom told him explicitly to weed out the troublemakers, and Powell claimed there were only fifty or so "hard core" offenders, Matthews refused to do it. His explanation was that any time he disciplined a segregationist, that child's parents either asked for a hearing before the School Board or threatened to file a lawsuit, and as Powell wrote, ". . . the principal was not accustomed to defending his judgment or having his professional posture publicly or privately scrutinized." The predictable effects were that the troublemakers became "more overt and more arrogant" and the teachers became less vigilant, inclined increasingly to believe that reporting infractions was "a waste of time." J.O. Powell had no way of knowing, of course, that a part of Jess Matthews's difficulty sprang from the Little Rock School Board's ambivalence about discipline.[16]

ELIZABETH HUCKABY WROTE that in mid-November Jess Matthews was deeply hurt by a Capital Citizens' Council petition calling for his dismissal for supposedly "selling out to the Virgil Blossom crowd." Blossom was actually the segregationists' primary target. As Blossom wrote, the segregationists described all the school officials, and especially the superintendent, as race-mixers and advocates of communism, and they kept harping "without much imagination" on the theme of miscegenation. A native of Missouri who had little familiarity with the sources and content of southern racism, Blossom failed completely to understand that fears about race-mixing formed the very heart of his community's rejection of his plan and efforts. This was not empty rhetoric designed to mask an intent to exploit blacks economically; this was the vital center of the southern resistance to desegregation.[17]

Virgil Blossom and his family endured merciless telephone harassment and numerous threats. Bitter and condemnatory letters poured into his home and office. Scurrilous ads and "Letters to the Editor" appeared frequently in the *Arkansas Democrat*. Leaflets and circulars blanketed the city. The segregationists said on numerous occasions they intended to make an "example" of Blossom, so that no other superintendent would dare propose a plan of integration. The relentless campaign caused attitudes to harden in Little Rock, and by the time of the November 5 city board elections, Blossom was aware of "much stronger anti-integration sentiment than existed before the school term opened."[18]

By mid-November, Blossom and the Little Rock School Board had become completely marginalized, largely abandoned by the erstwhile moderates who were now either struggling with their own values and emotions or working behind the scenes to effect some kind of compromise. A part of the problem was of Blossom's own creation, for the autocratic administrator continued to rebuff people who made overtures of support. In a September 30 interview, one reporter suggested to him that the business and civic leaders of Little Rock were letting school officials carry the load alone. Responding that this was not the case, Blossom said "he had received offers of supporting statements from Little Rock organizations but suggested they be withheld." Blossom wanted to be the man in charge, and he was especially resistant to the continuing efforts of the Chamber of Commerce's Guy Committee to tinker with the configuration of his plan.[19]

ORVAL FAUBUS HAD said on October 9 that the only solution to the Little Rock crisis was for the black children to withdraw from Central High School. On November 17, in a long, relaxed interview with journalist Relman Morin, Faubus reiterated this view, commenting, "I have always believed, and still do, that you have to create a climate of community acceptance before integration can be successful." It was almost an invitation to the hoods to step up the harassment.[20]

Daisy Bates heard an alarming rumor that someone had offered a ten thousand dollar reward to anyone who succeeded in getting the Nine out of Central High School. Soon Thelma Mothershed's mother came to Bates's home to tell her that black politician I. S. McClinton, who had close ties to Governor Faubus, had visited her and attempted to persuade her to remove Thelma from Central High. A local black preacher went with McClinton to see Mrs. Mothershed and told her that the Nine and their parents were "tearing up the town." Bates wrote a front-page article in the *Arkansas State Press* threatening to print the names of those resorting to such methods, and soon efforts from within the black community to get the black children to withdraw from Central High School ceased.[21]

In mid-November Brooks Hays told the Arkansas State Chamber of Commerce that he intended to introduce a bill at the next session of Congress calling for a reexamination of the *Brown* decision, basically supporting Orval Faubus's position that the city of Little Rock and the whole southern region needed a "breather," to allow time to test the constitutionality of state segregation laws. Having argued recently that *Brown* was a "mistaken law," Hays now said he would call on Congress to correct the Supreme Court's error.[22]

On November 19 the Army announced it planned to withdraw the 101st Airborne Division from Little Rock after Thanksgiving, leaving control of affairs at Central High School to the Arkansas National Guard. Governor Faubus said he would not protect the black children if control of the National Guard were turned over to him, and he commented that it was unfair to expect the Arkansas Guardsmen to perform the "distasteful" task of enforcing integration because they did not enlist to do that but instead "to defend their country in time of need."[23]

Elizabeth Huckaby wrote in her memoir that she felt fearful when she heard the Army was leaving, for she knew the situation inside Central High School to be very dangerous. Daisy Bates was also fearful, asking, "We wonder if the intelligence upon which the withdrawal of the 101st Airborne Division was based included recent reports from the Negro parents and children directly involved in the Little Rock school integration problem." The Army simply wanted out, as they had wanted ever since the day after their arrival. They had waited until after the city elections, hoping the moderates would assume control of their city, but their optimism had been misplaced.[24]

Secretary of the Army Wilber Brucker had wanted to force local authorities to take responsibility for the situation in Little Rock, but he had never been able to figure out how to make that happen. Since early October his paramount concern had been, "No situation could be allowed to develop in which the Negro students would be forced to withdraw by physical violence." Now he apparently deceived himself into believing that the situation had achieved a level of stability that would allow decreased vigilance inside Central High.[25]

ON OCTOBER 31, the U.S. attorney general convened a meeting to consider the possibility of extending Judge Davies's injunction to include "organizations which had been opposing integration in Little Rock." Such a move by the federal government to curb the activities of the Capital Citizens' Council, the Mothers' League, and others would have provided material support to Virgil Blossom and the Little Rock School Board, but FBI Director J. Edgar Hoover indicated that any expansion of the injunction would be "undesirable." Hoover opposed using injunctions once his staff's investigation revealed that only a few housewives and ministers had been found to be prosecutable, and he did not want to make "martyrs" of such sympathetic types because he believed such action would "solidify a large segment of the public."[26]

Throughout October and November interested parties on all sides waited expectantly to see what role the Justice Department would play in prosecuting the troublemakers who had been arrested during the rioting at Central High School in September. Virgil Blossom, Harry Ashmore, Daisy Bates, J. William Fulbright, and many others had expressed their certainty that when the federal government showed its resolve to deal harshly with those who had resorted to violence to oppose integration, then the vocal minority who were willing to defy law and order would be intimidated and silenced. To the shock and dismay of those who were struggling in Little Rock to uphold the law as it had been newly interpreted in the *Brown* decision, on November 20 Justice Department spokesmen announced they had decided not to prosecute the troublemakers at Central High. "U.S. Officials Drop Plans to Prosecute Agitators at School" blared the headline on page one of the *Arkansas Gazette*. News articles suggested that unnamed Little Rock people had given Justice Department officials "assurances" that in the absence of further difficulties, they could handle the situation in their city.[27]

The report of local assurances was Justice Department double-talk. New city director and mayor Werner Knoop soon made clear that he had no intention of assuming responsibility at Central High, and prospective city manager Dean Dauley told the *Arkansas Gazette* that the City Board had told him "the city shouldn't try to enforce the Supreme Court order alone, without any aid" from the federal government. On the same day the Justice Department announced its decision not to pursue prosecutions in Little Rock, Municipal Judge Harry Robinson also dismissed charges against six of those who had been arrested on September 24. In ensuing days, Robinson dropped or reduced charges against the remaining mob members who had been arrested on the streets outside Central High School.[28]

The entire responsibility for implementing the Blossom Plan now rested on the Little Rock School Board, Virgil Blossom, and Central High School officials. The School Board immediately threw in the towel, yielding to the Guy Committee's encouragement to abandon its unpopular plan, and the members began to craft an approach to the federal court seeking a delay of desegregation in Little Rock. They also undertook a prolonged effort to persuade a reluctant Virgil Blossom to accept defeat. School Board attorney Richard C. Butler, a member of the Chamber of Commerce's Guy Committee and a close friend of Blossom, proved instrumental in persuading the superintendent to his point of view.[29]

WHILE THE JUSTICE Department backed away from Little Rock, and U.S. Attorney General William P. Rogers pressured General Edwin Walker to reduce the numbers of troops stationed at Central High, the state attorney general, Bruce Bennett, extended his campaign to destroy the NAACP in Arkansas. Twelve Arkansas communities had adopted "Bennett Ordinances," which provided that the NAACP and other organizations had to disclose their membership and their sources of income. These ordinances had embroiled NAACP officers in expensive and time-consuming litigation through much of the fall, and they had frightened members into failing to send in their dues and renew their support for the organization. By December 17, Daisy Bates was writing to Roy Wilkins that the Little Rock chapter was broke because of the harassment.[30]

One of the Little Rock Nine, Melba Patillo, wrote in her memoir, "The adults we counted on were showing ever more stress." The Bateses' newspaper was being strangled; the Bennett Ordinances were crippling the NAACP. As Melba wrote in her diary at the time, "If they're busy defending themselves, who will see after us?"[31]

Another organization that came under relentless segregationist attack was the *Arkansas Gazette*. On December 13 Harry Ashmore printed a front-page editorial quoting in full a letter that had been sent to all local merchants and businessmen who advertised in the pages of the *Gazette;* the letter had threatened to launch a "crusade" not only against the newspaper but also against the offending businesses. Harry Ashmore feebly responded in an editorial that accompanied the reproduced letter, saying, "The Gazette has never advocated integration. The Gazette has never called for the breaking down of our segregation laws. On the contrary, the Gazette has consistently supported every legal effort to maintain the social patterns of segregation, and will continue to do so." Explaining that the *Gazette* supported the Blossom Plan because it called for "maintaining separate schools for whites and Negroes, with only a minimum of mixed classes . . .", Ashmore warned against the descent into anarchy that would result from the community's abandonment of a commitment to maintain law and order. In time the *Arkansas Gazette* lost a million dollars in subscriptions and advertising as a result of the segregationist boycott, but the Jewish owners of the large downtown department stores never wavered in their support of the beleaguered newspaper.[32]

The *Gazette* headline on December 3 read "9 Negroes Begin 12th Week at CHS with No Incidents." Melba Patillo Beals wondered how the editors had come to that conclusion "since they didn't have anyone inside the school to see us being kicked or inked or spat upon or scalded in the showers." Beals thought the editors were like so many of the adults who surrounded the Nine, willing to deceive themselves that all was well. But the children had painful, daily reasons to know better. "Our day-to-day experience showed us that the situation was worsening." Actually the Army's Counter Intelligence Corps, stationed inside the building at Central High, was reporting incidents daily and in some detail to General Walker, Attorney General Rogers, and Secretary of the Army Brucker. One of these transmissions was that a National Guard soldier had reported "some of the students at the school had ropes in their lockers with which they were going to do something to Minnie. . . ." In response to this information, Attorney General Rogers commented, "we ought to give the Little Rock matter a chance to rest for a while." He said he did not think it desirable from the standpoint of public interest to make statements about the Little Rock controversy.[33]

MINNIJEAN'S EXCLUSION FROM the Christmas program was not her first. She had also been left out of the student talent show, and she was bitterly disappointed over not being able to sing "Tammy" in front of the student body.

Melba Patillo Beals wrote years later that Minnijean "was beginning to be deeply affected by what was being done to her at Central High," and that Minnie's "sadness over being left out was clouding her view." Mrs. Huckaby reported a poignant episode in the fall when Minnijean wore Central High's school colors, gold and black, on her sweater before a football game and a segregationist girl challenged her right to wear them. Minnijean tore off the colors and stepped on them; about this same time she went sobbing to Mrs. Huckaby that she just wanted to quit.[34]

Melba Patillo was also chafing from the isolation imposed on her, as would any normal teenager. As she wrote in her memoir, "a deep yearning for human contact was growing inside me.... I longed for someone to acknowledge that I was alive by saying something pleasant to me, and allowing me to say something back." The white students treated her as if she were invisible. "Sometimes when a classmate said something funny, I would smile and even laugh out loud, forgetful for just one instant of my predicament. 'We weren't talking to you, nigger,' they would say. Jolted back to reality by their cruelty, I would catch myself, neutralize my expression to hide my feelings, and stare straight ahead." Thelma Mothershed confessed years later her loneliness at Central High. "I didn't want to go to Central some mornings" she recalled. "Being a junior in high school and you know that you will be ignored all day.... It was lonely, so some mornings I got a lump in my throat because I didn't want to go, but I went on ahead and went." Elizabeth Eckford's loneliness was compounded by her determination to protect her parents from knowing of her torment. "I could not share the daily abuse with anyone or seek justice." As one sympathetic observer of her predicament reported, "That isolation, day after day, proved to be her worst trial."[35]

Isolated inside Central High, the black children also lost their friends from Horace Mann. Melba Patillo's old friends were afraid to come to her home and resentful of the dislocations in their own lives caused by Melba's and the others' collective decision to integrate Central High. Thelma Mothershed remembered years later that a few of the Nine, probably her best friends Melba and Minnijean, went to a sock hop at Horace Mann in the fall of 1957 and their old friends asked, "Why are you coming over here? You belong over there with those white kids." The girls knew then they were not welcome anywhere: "white kids didn't want us, and black kids didn't want us." Thelma thought perhaps some of her old friends were jealous of the attention she was receiving as a member of "The Little Rock Nine." Nat Griswold heard similar reports ten years later when he was collecting information for a book on the Little Rock crisis. In his words, "Some of the Negro students who early entered Central High reported they received strong social disapproval from some teachers and some students of Horace Mann High, from which they transferred. 'Do you think you are better than we are?' was the question posed and imposed by their critics."[36]

Deeply distressed by her daughter's unhappiness, Mrs. Brown requested a conference with Jess Matthews to discuss his decision about the Christmas program. She requested that Elizabeth Huckaby and J. O. Powell be present. At the appointed hour on December 9, Matthews was dismayed to find Mrs. Brown had invited Daisy Bates to come along as well. Jess Matthews told Mrs. Brown that Minnijean could not sing in the Glee Club Christmas program, explaining only that it would be "unwise under present circumstances." What he did not say was that the adult crowd he was expecting would be beyond the school administration's control, and that he had heard from some white boys what would happen to Minnie if she appeared on the program.[37]

Daisy Bates took the occasion of the conference to challenge the school officials about their lax discipline of the children's segregationist tormentors. Mrs. Huckaby found her to be an impressive adversary and believed they had a good exchange that cleared the air a bit. All were surprised when an article appeared in the *Arkansas Democrat* on December 12, quoting Mothers' League sources and charging that Daisy Bates had been involved in "grilling" students at Central High School. Soon Jess Matthews received a letter from Margaret Jackson, also released to the press, claiming that this was a "disgraceful betrayal" of the trust white parents had placed in Matthews. Jackson concluded her letter with a jab at the "negro dominated school administration."[38]

BLOSSOM'S SCHOOL BOARD struggled to prepare a petition to the federal court asking for a delay of integration. On December 3 J. Edgar Hoover received information from a source "close to the Little Rock School Board" that at the next hearing in federal court, the board would ask for a delay based on two points: 1) Melba Patillo, Jefferson Thomas, and Minnijean Brown were "unadjusted," and 2) the community was not ready for integration. According to reports turned in to Army analysts, Melba, Jeff, and Minnijean were responsible for the attacks on themselves because they were "antagonistic."[39]

Because of her persistence in wanting to participate in school affairs, and also because of her mother's much-publicized conference with Matthews and Bates, Minnijean now became the primary target of segregationist torment. Many white students teased her mercilessly about being left out of the Christmas program. One boy reported her for supposedly "shooting the bird," or giving him the finger. Numerous students provoked Minnijean to respond to them verbally. She thought they were trying to "break" her by getting her to cry, and she struggled to maintain her composure—but they were content to get a rise out of her. Melba Patillo recalled that all of the Nine were suffering from "extreme fatigue," and that the taunting whites worked especially hard to get Minnijean to "blow her fuse."[40]

With just one day left before the much-needed rest of Christmas vacation, the segregationists scored a victory. Minnijean went into the cafeteria about 1:30 P.M., during the second lunch period. As she carried her tray toward the table where Melba, Ernie, and the others sat waiting for her, four boys pushed their chairs into the aisle, blocking her passage. She waited a moment, and the boys withdrew the chairs. As soon as she started to move again, the boys pushed the chairs back into her path, then removed them once again. This time, as Minnijean tried to proceed sideways between the tables, Rob Pittard started to get up from his seat, pushing his chair directly in front of her. Minnijean had been provoked previously in the same location and had warned the boys "they might get something on them." Melba could tell that an incident was building, but she knew she could not help without starting a riot; as she wrote, "they outnumbered us two hundred to one."[41]

Melba described the scene in her memoir. "As more and more people realized something was brewing," she wrote, "the chatter in the cafeteria quieted down. I could tell Minnijean was trapped and desperate, and very fast running out of patience. She was talking back to the boys in a loud voice, and there was jostling all around her.... It was as though she were in a trance, fighting within herself." Minnijean stood with her tray poised above the head of Dent Gitchel. Suddenly she just let it fall, covering Pittard and Gitchel with an abundance of chili, milk, fork, and straw. After a moment of complete silence in the cavernous hall, the black cafeteria workers burst into applause. Almost as quickly, the segregationist students became jubilant, realizing they had finally provoked one of the Nine into a response that would get her suspended from school.[42]

Two National Guard soldiers collared Minnijean and the two boys, taking them directly to the principal's office. There Dent Gitchel, still dripping, rushed to Minnijean's defense, saying he "knew she'd been through a lot of strain recently and could be expected to pop off." Gitchel, who had not been involved in previous racial incidents, suggested to Jess Matthews "that maybe this evened things up somewhat and that the matter be dropped." Matthews had other ideas. After interviewing Minnijean and ascertaining that the incident was not entirely accidental, Matthews suspended her from school for an indefinite period. Mrs. Huckaby wrote in her daily report, "Thanks to ... sharp observation on the part of two national guard sergeants in federal service, a possibly riotous incident was prevented. Poor Minnie."[43]

Where were the "good" white students while all of this harassment was going on? Student Body President Ralph Brodie recalled years later that he never saw any incidents, which can probably be explained by his student leader status, his athletic prowess, and his height at 6'5"; few "hoods" would have chosen to ply their trade in his presence. The larger explanation seems to be that those white students making overtures of friendship or assistance to the black children soon found themselves harassed and often threatened by segregationist callers. Their resultant silence mirrored the growing silence of moderate elements in the larger community. Enough of these students reported to Bishop Brown their concerns about the absence of discipline at Central High that he wrote in his memoir, "The other students were resentful of the ability of 'these hoods to get away with it.' However, the opinion became widespread that the matter had reached the point where the school officials themselves should take over the discipline within the school."[44]

SEVERAL DAYS AFTER Christmas, the *Arkansas Gazette* reported that the federal Appeals Court in New Orleans had granted the school board of Dallas, Texas, a delay in proceeding with the integration it had been under court order to begin in January. Almost immediately Orval Faubus suggested that Little Rock should go back to the federal courts seeking a delay, and Amis Guthridge threatened to sue the School Board if it did not "take advantage" of the Dallas ruling. The Little Rock School Board had already instructed Archie House to study the Dallas ruling "to determine whether it offers any prospects of temporary or permanent change" in the federal court order governing Little Rock's situation. Now only the NAACP stood as an open advocate of desegregation in Arkansas.[45]

The first day back at school after Christmas vacation set the pattern for a deteriorating situation inside Central High School, presaging what ACHR Executive Director Nat Griswold described as a "reign of terror." An anonymous caller telephoned the school office with the threat of a bomb inside the school; many such threats had come across the wires in the preceding months, and each one necessitated an extensive and costly search of the building. As had all the others, this threat proved to be false.[46]

In the face of what J. O. Powell called a "near total collapse of administrative discipline," the nine black children were alarmed to arrive back at school amid rumors that the Capital Citizens' Council was offering a reward to any-one who could incite them to misbehave and get expelled. Throughout the hol-idays, the segregationists had been busy scheming, hoping in effect to nullify the federal court order by forcing the removal of the black children.[47]

The lengthening chronicle of harassment of the Nine led *New York Times* reporter Gertrude Samuels to suggest, "The mob has moved inside the school." Darlene Holloway pushed Elizabeth Eckford down the stairs and was sus-pended for three days. Another student tripped Carlotta Walls as she left her biology class and then followed her briefly to step on her heels. Yet another threatened to kill her while he sharpened his pencil standing close to her desk. Sammie Dean Parker (a female) and Wanda Cole shoved Melba Patillo as she bent over to pick up her books and sent her sprawling spread-eagle on the floor. Sammie Dean Parker and David Sontag squirted ink on Melba Patillo's new pink felt skirt in the cafeteria, as had been done to Thelma and Minnijean in the days immediately preceding.[48]

Herbert Blount, who had been suspended in October for kicking Terrence Roberts and knocking his books out of his arms, claimed that Terrence had called him a son-of-a-bitch and challenged him to a fight; when Terrence did not respond and simply kept his hands in his pockets, Blount told J. O. Powell, "That nigger's got more nerve than anybody I ever saw. . . ." In gym class, where the abuse was the worst, Terrence suffered through many basketball games; as journalist Ted Poston described Terrence's plight, "Some of the boys are trying to harm him and they are doing a good job of it."[49]

Minnijean Brown had been admitted back into the school after a conference in Superintendent Blossom's office that included her parents and Mrs. Huck-aby, and after she had promised not to retaliate in any future incidents. She returned on January 13 and almost immediately found herself squirted with ink. On the 16th, David Sontag dropped a bowl of soup on her in the cafeteria, claiming that she had always called him "white trash." With David at the time were Sammie Dean Parker, Wanda Cole, and Darlene Holloway. Minnijean did not respond, other than to turn to Elizabeth Eckford, who was sitting at the table beside her, and say "Oh, well, they got even with me."[50]

At its regularly scheduled January board meeting, the Little Rock School Board finally enunciated a discipline policy, including the timid assertion: "Because of integration, there has been more tension in our school system than usual; therefore, our staff has moved slowly and with restrained mildness in handling all children." On January 20, officials found dynamite at Central High School, and Virgil Blossom told a press conference that a few persons were try-

ing to force the closing of the school. In response to this remark, Citizens' Council President Wesley Pruden called for the resignations of Blossom and all the
Central High officials, saying that Blossom and the Little Rock School Board
created the problem by volunteering to integrate in the first place. By January
24, Central High School had suffered through bomb scares every school day
since the Citizens' Council had held a rally on the 14th.[51]

Nat Griswold's quarterly report to the Southern Regional Council included
this assessment: "The school officials and Board neglected rather obvious remedies at hand—recognized methods of discipline of students and a request to
the Court for an injunction against interference with school operations. . . .
There were reliable reports of ignoring of many incidents of abuse of the Negro
students." Griswold echoed one of J. O. Powell's concerns when he wrote, "By
and large the public had little knowledge of the serious breakdown of school
discipline . . . ." Powell claimed in his memoir that Jess Matthews and Virgil
Blossom routinely censored public reports, and that Matthews crusaded for his
staff to "keep quiet" about the internal affairs at Central High School.[52]

On January 20 school authorities found dynamite in the basement at Central High. On January 23 they found a firecracker bomb in a locker. The director of school plant services, O. W. Romine, who had a child in the building,
reported constant damage to the school and made arrangements to guard the
furnace room around the clock, seven days a week. J.O. Powell wrote, "Over a
thousand dollars monthly was paid to civilian security guards to patrol the
building and grounds on a twenty-four-hour schedule." Powell also wrote about
uncurbed vandalism and locker damage from hoax bomb scares and dynamite
threats. Every bomb threat, and there were forty-three during the year, necessitated a check of every student locker in the building, and when officials could
not open the combination locks with the codes students had provided, they had
to cut off the locks and replace them at school expense. In addition to the locker
damage, Powell added that "juvenile racists dug, stained, painted, gouged, and
burned unprintable anti-Negro propaganda and segregationist slogans into
window-glass, furniture, walls, and any other surface at hand." Vandals started
many nuisance fires throughout the winter, and in one particularly creative
form of protest they urinated on the steam radiators in the bathrooms, sending fumes throughout the building.[53]

The absence of discipline began to turn into something more dangerous on
January 27, when a male student dared a National Guardsman to lay a hand on
him. Passing Minnijean Brown in the hall, the boy called her a "nigger-looking
bitch." The National Guardsman directly behind him told him to go to the prin-

cipal's office and he replied, "No, I'm not going, and you can't make me," then
threw his books on the floor, squared off with his fists doubled up at his sides,
and told the Guardsman he had better not touch him. At length Mrs. Huckaby
intervened and persuaded the boy to go to Jess Matthews's office. Matthews
called his father, a painter, who came immediately and promised that his son
would not get into "any more trouble with niggers." The boy was given a tardy
slip and went to his next class.[54]

General Walker was alarmed by this incident and soon asked for a judgment
from the Army's judge advocate general regarding what action to take if a similar situation arose again. Walker also suggested the Justice Department should
seek an injunction against unruly students inside Central High School. Nothing ever came of this suggestion, although by January 31 Clarence Laws was
telling the New York office of the NAACP that he and Mrs. Bates had learned
through "a most reliable source" that the National Guardsmen had been given
new instructions with regard to handling incidents. "In the future no guard is
to place a hand upon any student. If the student has committed an act, the
guard may attempt to block him if he should try to leave the school, but no
other action is to be taken." Bates and Laws asked what would happen if a
Guardsman came upon a student or students assaulting another who would
not stop upon his orders. "The reply was we do not have the answer now."[55]

ON JANUARY 29, Richard Boehler was suspended from school for academic
reasons. Before he left the campus, a student heard him threaten to "get" Minnijean Brown. At 3:30 in the afternoon he returned to the campus to pick up his
carpool, left his car, approached a group of five students including Brown, and
kicked Minnijean repeatedly from behind. Minnijean did not strike back. An
Army observer described the scene: "He had a pocket knife in his hand which
was not open. A teacher, Mrs. Brandon, had observed . . . [his] actions and
grabbed the boy before he could open his knife (which he attempted to do).
Mr. Powell, principal for boys, also grabbed the boy and took the knife
away . . . [the boy] had kicked the girl . . . several times during the fracas." Taken
to the principal's office, Boehler gave a deposition of the incident in which he
said, "I kicked her because she stomped on my leg in French class one afternoon." Minnijean had dropped French in October.[56]

Minnijean's mother was driving carpool that day and witnessed the assault,
to her horror. Although Minnie tried to stop her, Mrs. Brown dashed into the
school to report the incident. Minnie kept saying, "Don't go in there because
they are not going to listen to you," and she did not want her mother to be hurt

"by going in and trying to present this and having them treat her like they treated us." Minnijean's recollection years later was that school officials responded to her reports of mistreatment by saying things such as, "You're just so excitable, now are you sure that happened? And do you know his name? Did a teacher see it? Uh, well, I don't think there is anything we can do if no one saw it."[57]

Mrs. Brown did not stop with the evasions of the school officials. The next morning she went to Prosecuting Attorney Frank Holt's office and attempted to file formal charges against Richard Boehler. Although the Army observer wrote that "there seemed to be grounds for criminal prosecution," Frank Holt refused to issue a warrant for Boehler's arrest. The *Arkansas Gazette* quoted Boehler as saying that Minnijean had come up to him in French class and said "move your feet, white boy." Forty-five years later when her daughter asked her about this comment, Minnijean replied, "Think about it. In your wildest imaginings of me being stark raving nuts, is that the kind of thing I would do? . . . I'm in a situation of 2,000 to 9 and I'm going to be that volatile? and I'm going to be talking back? . . . To me it's the ultimate, ultimate put-down because it says 'she's so stupid that she's going to be acting like a crazy person with these odds in all this danger.'"[58]

Melba Patillo Beals wrote that Minnijean was getting weary. It was obvious to the black children that school officials were increasingly nervous and even that Mrs. Huckaby was afraid. Melba wrote in her diary, "I don't know if I can make it now. . . . I wish I were dead."[59]

On January 31, Elizabeth Eckford left school saying she could not stand it anymore. In a meeting the next day with Virgil Blossom, Mrs. Huckaby, and her grandfather, Elizabeth claimed that the white girls in her gym class were singing songs to humiliate her. Blossom suggested she ignore the songs, and sweet, gentle Elizabeth "agreed this would be the best remedy." When Mr. Eckford asked why school officials could not control the segregationist troublemakers, Mrs. Huckaby explained to him they could not discipline the students without community backing.[60] On February 4, Terrence Roberts reported that a classmate had kicked him. No one had witnessed the incident, but the accused boy's school file revealed seven previous instances of disciplinary action. J. O. Powell recommended permanent expulsion for the white boy, but no action was taken.

February 6 was the most hectic day the school had experienced, with two bomb scares, the terrorizing of Terrence Roberts's mother, and the suspension of Minnijean Brown. A teacher had reported to Mrs. Huckaby on the 5th that two white girls were following Minnijean murmuring "nigger, nigger, nigger" all the way down the hall. Mrs. Huckaby had intended to be in that hall before school started on the 6th but she was compelled to stay in her office to deal with a truant. Soon a Guardsman brought Minnijean and Frankie Gregg, one of the white girls from the day before, into Mrs. Huckaby's office.[61]

Brown reported that Gregg had been following her all week calling her a "nigger." On this morning when Frankie turned to say something to a friend, Minnijean stopped dead in her tracks and Gregg ran into her. The white girl then said, "If you stop again, I'll kick you like that boy did," adding a vulgar gesture, and continued to call her names all the way down the hall. The official description of the ensuing incident read: "After provocation of girl student, she [Minnijean] called the girl 'white trash,' after which the girl threw her purse at Minniejean [sic]." Brown claimed years later that the situation happened in reverse, that after a group of students called her names and pushed her against the wall, Frankie Gregg threw a purse full of combination locks and hit her in the back of the head; Minnie then picked up the purse, considered what to do with it, and finally threw it on the floor at Frankie's feet and said "Leave me alone, white trash."[62]

Jess Matthews told both girls to stay away from each other. Minnijean agreed and Matthews sent her on to class. Frankie responded, "I don't know," so the principals called her parents to come get her. Frankie's father arrived and withdrew her from Central High School, commenting that some child, white or black, was going to get hurt in that environment. Shortly before noon, Terrence Roberts's mother arrived at the school, distraught because someone had called to say her son had been injured in an altercation. Mrs. Huckaby took her to look through the glass pane in the door of Terrence's classroom, and when she ascertained that her son was all right she left the school, much relieved.[63]

When Mrs. Huckaby returned to her office she found Minnijean in the hall, trembling and crying. Some of the students in Girls' Chorus had stood behind her blaming her for Frankie Gregg's withdrawal from Central High and threatening to tell Sammie Dean Parker, who supposedly reported such things to Governor Faubus. The vice principal calmed the shaken girl and sent her on to lunch, but in the cafeteria a student, who had half a dozen racial incidents on his school record, spilled soup down her back. Minnijean burst into tears, but did not respond. Nonetheless, when Jess Matthews got back to campus after his weekly lunch with the Rotary Club, he announced he had decided to suspend Minnijean for calling Frankie Gregg "white trash," since her reinstatement on January 13 had been based on "the agreement that she would not retaliate verbally or physically, to any harassment but would leave the matter to school authorities to handle."[64]

Minnijean admitted to an Associated Press reporter "I just can't take everything they throw at me without fighting back." Relating a story of harassment by whites "that you just wouldn't believe," Minnijean said, "I don't think people realize what goes on at Central. . . . They throw rocks, they spill ink on your clothes, they call you 'nigger,' they just keep bothering you every five minutes." She said school officials had ordered her and the other eight black children to "be humble" to the white students. She also said she had not realized how deeply the epithet "white trash" hurt white people. A product of a strictly segregated culture, Minnijean Brown had no way of knowing how rigidly stratified Little Rock's white world was, or how deeply alienated many children of blue-collar families felt as a result of their exclusion from the seemingly glamorous activities of children from "the Heights." All Minnijean knew was that she had tried hard to live by the rules school officials had established for her, and she felt profoundly guilty because she had failed. That guilt would haunt her throughout her life.[65]

On February 4 the Little Rock School Board members decided to seek a delay in their program of integration, although they did not announce their decision publicly for another two weeks.[66] In Washington, D.C., the new director of the Justice Department's Civil Rights Division, W. Wilson White, sent a February 10 memo to the FBI requesting extensive investigation into the "harassment incidents" at Central High School. The written chronology of FBI involvement in the Little Rock crisis included the following item: "In view of the highly controversial nature of the investigation requested with probably adverse criticism to Bureau and Department the Director instructed the request be discussed with W. Wilson White." White withdrew his request the next day.[67]

For some time the parents of the Nine had requested a meeting with school officials to protest the absence of discipline and protection for their children. Finally on Sunday, February 9, they met for over two hours with Virgil Blossom, J. O. Powell, and Elizabeth Huckaby. Jefferson Thomas's father, serving as spokesman for the black parents, urged officials to call a student assembly and "lay down the law" concerning mistreatment of the black children. The school officials vetoed that suggestion. As Elizabeth Huckaby explained in her memoir, "most of our students didn't need scolding, and the others probably would have caused a demonstration." Mr. Thomas read a list of the names of boys and girls who were persecuting the black children. He said he had called and talked to some of these students' parents and had gotten cooperation from some of them. It appears that no school official ever did the same.[68]

On February 12, Virgil Blossom met with Minnijean Brown and her mother, telling them he had decided to recommend to the Little Rock School Board that Minnijean be expelled for the duration of the year, not only from Central High but from all Little Rock schools. Mrs. Brown protested vigorously, but to no avail. As Elizabeth Huckaby wrote in her memoir, school officials had come to the conclusion that "we could no longer run the school if Minnijean was there. There were plenty of marginal youngsters who would be glad to be put out of school to gain the approval of their group by souping Minnijean week after week—or even day after day. Their target had been selected." Clarence Laws immediately prepared a harsh statement for the press, apparently never released, in which he charged, "Whether by design or otherwise, Minnie Jean's [sic] expulsion was almost inescapable." Referring to the requirement that Minnijean not respond to her tormentors, no matter what the provocation, Laws wrote, "Yet those who contrived this agreement did nothing to deter her tormentors who increased day by day. No normal youth could eternally endure this inequity. No fair minded persons would impose it."[69]

In a lengthy telephone conversation on February 13, Clarence Laws and Daisy Bates spelled out for the New York office of the NAACP their suspicions regarding the absence of discipline inside Central High School. Referring to what he called "a well-laid conspiracy," Laws maintained: "It is stated that there are some important people in business here who are behind this and their plans are for getting the kids out and saying that the community is not ready for integration." Southern Regional Council Assistant Director Fred Routh wrote to Thurgood Marshall on February 12, saying "the school administration may use the disciplinary question to oust the Negro children from the school and ask the court for a delay in compliance. This would play directly into the hands of the segregationist element in the State Legislature. They would then take legislative steps to delay further desegregation in Little Rock." This prediction came to fruition within a matter of months.[70]

J. O. Powell believed Blossom and the School Board were allowing the disruptions to continue inside Central High in order to demonstrate to the federal judge that they needed a delay. In fact, Powell may have been correct. In its final report to the Chamber of Commerce committee of past presidents, dated February 17, 1958, the Guy Committee noted that when they had recommended that the School Board seek a delay back in October, the board's attorneys had "considered the request for a review as being weak and not founded on actual conditions existing in Central High School. Therefore, they felt they had no case." After six months of disruptions inside the school, however, they apparently felt that they did have a case, and in fact they built their case around those very disruptions. Only at that point did they enunciate a firm disciplinary policy.[71]

Virgil Blossom had long resisted the Guy Committee's efforts to get him to admit defeat and yield to their desire to seek a delay from the federal judge. Committed as he was to the plan that bore his name and in which he had invested four years of his life (and fond hopes for political advancement), he wanted to believe that in time the resistance movement in both the school and the community would subside. He apparently had persuaded himself that if he and his school officials charted a steady course and downplayed the disruptions inside Central High School, the segregationists would tire of the struggle and simply fade away.[72]

Yet as Daisy Bates had feared, assaults on the remaining black children inside Central High School escalated. Jeff, Gloria, Terrence, and Elizabeth all reported their lockers had been broken into and smashed, and their books stolen. Jess Matthews warned several of the worst troublemakers "against any further misbehavior against Negro students"; and yet within two days, one of these boys spit on Terrence and Jeff in the cafeteria but no action was taken, even though a teacher witnessed and reported the incident. J. O. Powell called in the boy's parents and they seemed to appreciate the opportunity to be involved, promising that in the future their son would behave. The next day the boy appeared in televised news reports throwing snow-covered rocks at the Negro children.[73]

The violent rock-throwing incident was the only time that year that Thelma Mothershed was reduced to tears. As National Guardsmen and policemen stood by with their arms folded, a pack of boys attacked several of the girls as they waited for their rides home after school. Melba Patillo Beals recalled of the Guardsmen, "Even when we pleaded for their assistance, they did nothing." Mr. Eckford bolted from the car he was driving to try to rescue the children, but he, too, was bombarded with snow-covered rocks. As Thelma described the incident years later, "When my mother came they kept on throwing rocks, even at the car. I think that was the only time I really cried, throwing rocks at the car. . . . The job [the Guardsmen] were supposed to do was to protect us; they didn't say one word to those boys. They were grinning and throwing these things. We were trying to jump out of the way. . . ." A young teacher who observed the incident, Susie West, reported it to the office, in tears herself. J. O. Powell dashed outside and identified nine of the boys as they made their escape. "It was the worst damn thing I ever saw," Mrs. Huckaby reported him as saying. "The police were there, but they did nothing." Powell recommended suspension of the nine boys. No action was taken.[74]

The *Arkansas Gazette* rarely reported the incidents of harassment the black children endured. Years later Harry Ashmore attempted to justify this editorial decision by writing of the "almost insuperable problem for responsible journalists trying to treat inherently sensational developments so as to minimize any further increase in racial tensions." As a result of the *Gazette*'s abandonment of the field to the openly segregationist *Arkansas Democrat,* most adults in the community had no idea of the extent of the harassment inflicted on the black children inside Central High School.[75]

As Ashmore explained in a speech at Harvard, many citizens were also deeply conflicted about the presence of the black students inside Central High. "Caught between the committed and dedicated partisans," Ashmore suggested, "was a substantial and silent mass of plain citizens—confused and deeply disturbed. They were people who deplored desegregation and also deplored violence. They felt, many of them, a deep compassion for the nine Negro children exposed to the anger and contempt of a white mob. But they also felt that the Negro children should not be attending the white school in the first place."[76]

ON FEBRUARY 16 the Little Rock School Board issued a "Statement of Policy" warning that the board would take all actions necessary to protect education, including expulsion of any student whose conduct was unsatisfactory. Signed by all six members in a paid advertisement in the *Arkansas Gazette,* the statement led to sharp criticism. As a Capital Citizens' Council circular soon brayed, "The School Board threatens stern measures. They strongly intimate that wholesale and permanent dismissal will be visited on all those children who do not cease to resist enforced race-mixing." Calling integration an "outrage" that was being forced on Little Rock's children by "booted soldiers," this circular claimed that the School Board's program was making Central High School's white students participate in "a way of life foreign to their training, contrary to their convictions, and nauseating to their esthetic being." As the circular concluded, ominously, "The ultimatum has been served. The crackdown on our children has started. The School Board gives us only one choice—*Submit.* And that's a terrible word for a red-blooded American."[77]

The day after the School Board announced its new get-tough policy, National Guard Sergeant Roy Blackwood caught Sammie Dean Parker passing out cards that read "One Down . . . Eight To Go." Little cards like this one had popped up all year at Central High, sometimes bearing Virgil Blossom, Daisy

Bates, and Harry Ashmore's home addresses and telephone numbers, sometimes carrying such doggerel verse as:

> *That white trash Matthews named Jess,*
> *sure got Central High in a mess;*
> *the kids—if they're white,*
> *he deprives of their rights—*
> *he's a Kansas nigger-lover, I guess.*

Or:

> *Little nigger at Central High—*
> *has got mighty free with his eye.*
> *Winks at white girls.*
> *Grabs their blond curls;*
> *little nigger sure is anxious to die.*[78]

Sammie Dean Parker was a good student and a natural leader. She had
barely missed national notoriety on September 4 when she turned her head to
speak to her father just as photographer Wilmer Counts snapped the infamous
picture of Hazel Bryan spewing hateful epithets at Elizabeth Eckford. Parker
had been involved in numerous harassing incidents—Mrs. Huckaby said the
list of her infractions filled three typewritten pages—and officials from Virgil
Blossom to Secretary of War Brucker knew that she reported regularly to
Arkansas State Police Captain Alan Templeton, who was conducting an investigation of Central High School integration difficulties for the Arkansas Legislative Council, the research arm of the Arkansas General Assembly.[79]

On February 17, when Sergeant Blackwood caught her distributing cards
that Matthews and Huckaby believed expressed "an overt threat to the school
and some of its students" as well as being "subversive of school policy and of
federal court orders . . . ," Sammie was astonished to find herself suspended for
several days. As Mrs. Huckaby described the scene: "She cried. She sobbed. And
then she shouted and bawled. She left the office. In a very few minutes her father
came in. He was fully as angry and almost as noisy as his daughter." But
Matthews and Huckaby stayed the course.[80]

Similarly, Howard Cooper earned a three-day suspension for wearing on
his shirt one of the "One Down . . . Eight To Go" cards. School authorities had
previously found Cooper in possession of anti-integration literature, but in a

conference with his father and school officials, he had agreed not to engage in any further harassing activities. Now Matthews suspended him. A history teacher, Dorothy Lenggenhager, watched in horror as another student pushed Gloria Ray down the stairs. She took the boy to the office, where J. O. Powell described him as "congenial and happy over his accomplishment." He told Matthews he pushed Gloria because "she's a nigger." Matthews suspended him for three days.[81]

On the same day of the three white suspensions, Virgil Blossom formally announced the School Board's decision to expel Minnijean Brown. Blossom claimed he had made the decision to expel her, since she had not "adjusted."[82] As Elizabeth Huckaby confessed, Minnijean's expulsion "was an admission of defeat on our part. . . . It was not volatile, natural Minnijean that was our difficulty. It was just that she and our impossible situation would not mix."[83]

Daisy Bates and her friend Kenneth Clark secured a scholarship for Minnijean to attend the experimental, interracial New Lincoln School in New York City, where she lived with the Clarks. Asked if she was happy that her child had been granted a scholarship, Mrs. Brown commented, "While I am gratified I am not happy. I am not happy that our daughter must go away at this time to attend school. I am not happy that our own hometown is permitting this to happen to us. I am not happy that children of both races are being hurt by selfish and hateful men."[84]

When Minnijean arrived in New York she described her new school as "lovely." With sophistication and diplomacy beyond her years, hard-earned in Little Rock, Minnijean faced the press and said she bore no animosity toward the segregationist students. "They felt as right as I did," Minnijean suggested. "I don't hate them. They felt they were right and I felt I was right." She did, however, predict that the segregationists would "get" another student. "There was a campaign to get everybody out and I was first," the plucky teenager declared, as she turned her back on the torment she had endured and prepared to start a new life.[85]

On February 19, Walter C. Guy released to the press a letter to the Little Rock School Board that twenty-four of the past presidents of the Chamber of Commerce had approved. The group advised the School Board to go back into federal court and seek a delay. The School Board was already engaged in the lengthy process of preparing such a request, and the next day's *Gazette* headline read "Board Asks Court to Delay Integration."[86]

Declaring themselves to be "personally opposed to integration" but compelled by their oaths to comply with the law, the School Board members argued their petition was not an act of defiance. They did, however, invite segregationists to join them in their quest for relief. "Individuals and groups who proclaim the supremacy of State laws are invited to intervene" in *Aaron v. Cooper,* they declared, and "there by legal means assist the District in obtaining the relief sought" or in developing alternative theories to render null and void the federal court order.[87]

The Little Rock School Board had a more immediate problem on its hands in dealing with the case of Sammie Dean Parker. On the same Friday it filed its petition for delay, the board met to hear Parker's father plead for her reinstatement. Amis Guthridge was now representing Parker and Howard Cooper, demanding their immediate reinstatement and threatening to charge the board with "malfeasance, misfeasance or nonfeasance" if his demands were not met. Thumbing their noses at Guthridge, the Little Rock School Board extended the suspensions of Parker and Cooper from three days to two weeks.[88]

Elizabeth Huckaby wrote that the atmosphere at Central High School improved dramatically in Sammie Dean Parker's absence. That improvement stemmed in part from the expulsion for truancy of Sammie's boyfriend, David Sontag, who, before leaving the building, spit on one teacher's floor, called Mrs. Huckaby a "bitch," and announced that if Negroes could go to the school and he could not then he would "blow it up." On Wednesday morning Virgil Blossom's secretary ended the peaceful interlude by requesting Huckaby's presence at a meeting with Parker and her parents that night, supposedly to discuss the girl's willingness to change her attitude in order to be reinstated in school. Buffeted by a soft rain as they entered the superintendent's office, Huckaby, Blossom, Jess Matthews, and the Parkers were the only people in the building.[89]

Sammie immediately took charge of the meeting, expressing "extreme hatred" of Mrs. Huckaby and Mr. Matthews because of their "persecution" of her. Blossom dismissed Matthews and Huckaby and attempted to deal with the girl and her parents on his own. As Mrs. Huckaby stood in the lobby putting on her raincoat, Sammie and her mother ran up behind her. Thinking they had had a change of heart, Huckaby turned smilingly toward them; to her shock, Sammie seized the vice principal's umbrella while her mother grabbed the glasses off her face, saying, "I'm going to hit you for what you have done to my daughter." Jess Matthews pushed between the women, saying, "Here, you can't hit a lady," while Sammie screamed, "Don't you dare touch my mother," waving the umbrella at the group. Huckaby hurried down the corridor to tell Virgil Blossom to call the police, and as she retreated she heard Mrs. Parker call out, "Two hundred women have called me and said they would pay my fine if I'd hit her!"[90]

The School Board expelled Sammie Dean Parker for the rest of the year. Mr. Parker told an *Arkansas Democrat* reporter that his daughter "has been crucified by three people who are determined to beat into submission all opposition" to integration, and he soon had Amis Guthridge file a lawsuit against the School Board contending they had expelled his daughter "without any just or legal cause or reason" and "arbitrarily abused their discretion." Naming as defendants Virgil Blossom, Jess Matthews, Elizabeth Huckaby, and the Little Rock School Board, Guthridge's petition asked that the case be heard on its merits within seven days.[91]

Now enjoying a state police escort, Sammie continued to dance every afternoon on the locally televised *Steve's Show,* and she augmented her schedule of speaking engagements at segregationist meetings. Earlier in the school year she had claimed that one of the black boys was being "familiar" with her and "winking" at her. Sammie reported to her segregationist allies that she was receiving humiliating phone calls from black men. She charged that Ernest Green had telephoned to invite her for a date. Sammie then spread the word that *Ebony* magazine had called and asked her to pose for them nude. She was doing her best to stir "red-blooded American" males to defend the alabaster blond.[92]

The Little Rock School Board waffled. Fearful of letting Sammie's case go to court, lest it be lost, Virgil Blossom persuaded his board to compromise with Parker and let her back in school if she promised to refrain from all segregationist activity during school hours. One board member told the *New York Post* the School Board did not want to give the segregationists a "martyr." They asked the girl to sign a statement that contained no acknowledgment of error on her part and no mention of her attack on Mrs. Huckaby. J. O. Powell wrote that the reinstatement of Sammie Dean Parker devastated staff morale at Central High. Nat Griswold wrote that the widely publicized expulsions of Minnijean Brown and Sammie Dean Parker caused many people to ponder the state of discipline inside the school, and "for the first time a few influential persons, clergymen and other citizens, became skeptical of the good faith or the adequacy of the school administrators."[93]

After Minnijean's expulsion, the segregationists inside Central High School went wild, their cruelty unrestrained. As Melba Patillo Beals wrote in her diary, "I think only the warrior exists in me now. Melba went away to hide. She was too frightened to stay here." She struggled not to be jealous of Minnijean's "escape" and began to feel "kind of numb, as though nothing mattered anymore." Yet she felt pain "stinging my heart every time someone called me a nigger."[94]

Writing to Secretary of the Army Wilber Brucker, Roy Wilkins commented poignantly, ". . . we are confronted with the incredible spectacle of the government of the United States placing the burden of enforcing the orders of its Courts upon the slender shoulders and the young hearts of eight teen-age Negro students." An editorial in the *New York Post* argued that firm disciplinary measures could easily stop the persecutions inside Central High. "Instead the picture that emerges is of a band of courageous Negro children fighting a long battle while the community waits for them to surrender. Will the soldiers 'intervene' in the Washington sense only when the fight becomes a lynching bee? The role played by the U. S. Army in the Battle of Little Rock shames the nation. For gallantry in action, the Negro kids take all the medals."[95]

CHAPTER THIRTEEN

THE BATTLE IN THE COURTS
Richard C. Butler

DICK BUTLER UNDERSTOOD MORE CLEARLY THAN MOST THE IMPLI-cations of the dreary saga in his city. A member of the team of lawyers the Little Rock School Board had employed in 1956 to defend the Blossom Plan in federal court, Butler was also a past president of the Little Rock Chamber of Commerce. In his work for the Chamber, he had come to understand the importance of industrialization for the future growth and prosperity of his city, and he had become one of the key promoters and developers of the Little Rock Air Force Base and the Little Rock Industrial District.[1]

A partner in the law firm founded by Senator Joe T. Robinson and Hamilton Moses (later president of Arkansas Power & Light Company), Butler was sensitive to the thinking and desires of the large utilities and other major corporations in Arkansas. One of many impressive graduates of the Little Rock schools, Butler understood the value and necessity of a strong public education system. A Republican by virtue of having married into one of Arkansas's most prominent families of that persuasion, and an aspirant to the currently vacant position as federal judge for the Eastern District of Arkansas, Richard Butler saw clearly the dangers and the opportunities the crisis in his city offered for his own, as well as his community's, welfare.[2]

Tall, lean, and handsome, endowed with a resonant voice and a rich laugh that bubbled up at the slightest provocation, deeply thoughtful and yet personable and engaging, Dick Butler was a natural leader of men. A Little Rock native, he had lost his father in his early teens and had had to sustain his mother and two sisters by learning to manage his father's real estate holdings, especially by collecting the rent. Many of his renters were in the black community, and he had learned to deal fairly with all kinds of people and to have compassion for those whose financial plight was even more desperate than his own. These were powerful, shaping experiences for a young boy, and Butler carried throughout his life an understanding of the importance of planning for the future, looking ahead with vision rather than just plodding along, and cultivating the people who could help a man implement his plans and achieve his dreams.[3]

Graduating from Little Rock High School in one of its first classes, Dick Butler put himself through Little Rock Junior College and then the University of Arkansas at Fayetteville. Like many other young people of that era, he had to drop out of the university's law school after two years when the money ran out in 1933. He "begged" Archie House's brother Joe to let him study at a table in his law firm, where he eventually moved up to working on a case-by-case basis and being paid by the case. Joe House introduced him to gardening, especially the breeding of irises, jonquils, and day lilies, and in later years Butler became a master gardener and a regional vice president of the American Iris Society. By the time he married Gertrude Remmel in 1935, he was making fifty dollars a month, and the two young people felt secure enough at last to start a family.[4]

After a stint in the Army Air Corps during World War II, Butler was made a partner by his old firm of House, Moses, and Holmes, who obviously realized his potential for contributing to their enterprise as well as to the community. Butler was one of the many young southern men whose experiences in World War II changed forever their perceptions of what was possible for their cities and their region, broadening their horizons and fostering dissatisfaction with the older, lower levels of expectation. By 1951 he was serving as president of the Little Rock Chamber of Commerce, promoting industrialization. In the same year he received a much-coveted invitation to join XV, the exclusive gentlemen's club of fifteen men that represented the summit of elite status and recognition in Little Rock.[5]

A great admirer and friend of Virgil Blossom, Butler responded to the superintendent's urgent request that he join the "brain trust" of lawyers Blossom put together in 1956 to argue the case of *Aaron v. Cooper* before the federal district court. From that point on, he worked closely with Blossom in attempting to fashion a response to the growing segregationist opposition to integration in Little Rock. In the summer of 1957, as he listened to the superintendent's descriptions of his conversations with the governor, he had felt considerable sympathy for Orval Faubus's argument that the federal courts had issued an order to desegregate and that consequently the federal government should enforce its own order. He was also aware of Blossom's attempts at that time to find a private citizen to institute a suit to delay integration.[6]

A member of the six-man Guy Committee, which had concluded as early as October 17 that the School Board should petition the federal court for a delay, Butler had understood Blossom's reluctance to abandon his plan and he affirmed the superintendent's desire to stay the course as long as the unsympathetic Judge Davies was still on the bench in Little Rock. In short, Dick Butler understood as clearly as anyone in Little Rock the situation his city faced and the options that now lay open for the School Board he represented. In the months ahead he labored mightily to fashion a solution to the crisis that loomed over his city's future and that threatened to damage or destroy all that he had worked for as one of Little Rock's most esteemed civic leaders.[7]

By February of 1958 the Little Rock School Board had lost its resolve in the face of relentless community opposition and harassment, and especially in the absence of any show of support from the Justice Department. Declaring publicly for the first time its opposition to integration, the Little Rock School Board filed a petition in federal court on February 20, 1958, asking for a delay until desegregation could be accomplished "without an impairment of educational standards." Throughout the subsequent months of litigation, as their case journeyed up through the federal court system, the School Board and its attorneys maintained this focus on the preservation of educational quality.[8]

The heart of the School Board petition argued that the district found itself in "a most difficult position in providing satisfactory education for its pupils." While on the one hand it was under court order to implement the Blossom Plan, on the other hand "it has no power to enforce the provisions of the plan." The School Board argued that successful implementation of desegregation depended on community acceptance of the federal court's decisions and orders, and that in the absence of that community sentiment, it was powerless to force the issue. The attorneys concluded plaintively that the Little Rock School Board, which had complied voluntarily with the *Brown* decision out of respect for the law of the land, was left "standing alone, the victim of extraordinary opposition on the part of the State government and apathy on the part of the Federal Government."[9]

Although it did not specify a time frame, the School Board wanted the federal courts to suspend integration for several years while the public became "educated" and the courts and Congress acted. Whatever the board's long-range expectations, its immediate goals were local and political: to achieve relief from the twin pressures of the segregationists, who demanded increasingly a solid front against any acquiescence to federal demands, and of the businessmen, who wanted to get Little Rock off the front pages of national and international newspapers. Another political goal, not widely understood at the time, was Virgil Blossom's desire to position himself to run for governor.[10]

Even Harry Ashmore endorsed the School Board's petition for a delay, writing that the board had made an "unassailable case of having attempted in all good faith to comply with the mandate of the courts . . ." and that its petition "might move the courts to look anew at the whole subject of integration. . . ." Ashmore was now in the process of reexamining his own commitment to the "full speed ahead" position of the National Association for the Advancement of Colored People and the Arkansas Council for Human Relations. He still had not changed his mind, however, about the long-range effects of industrialization on the South. As he wrote to an admiring friend shortly after *An Epitaph for Dixie* was released on January 11, "Actually, Little Rock changed none of the conclusions I had reached in the original version. . . . Hence it seems to me that an epitaph for Dixie is more than ever in order." Ashmore would have reason to reconsider this conclusion as summer approached.[11]

A WEEK AFTER THE School Board filed its petition asking for a delay, the NAACP's Legal Defense Fund (LDF) responded by filing a motion in federal court in Little Rock. Attorneys Wiley Branton of Pine Bluff and Thurgood Marshall of New York City argued that the School Board's petition was "insufficient in the law," because it spelled out no claims for relief that could be granted under the Federal Rules of Civil Procedure. In their brief filed a week later, Branton and Marshall concluded that those rules were not "intended to afford machinery to relieve aggrieved, unsuccessful litigants who merely seek to express their dissatisfaction." In the first phase of litigation, in federal district court, the LDF based its entire case on this line of argument, and it went to trial in June objecting to the School Board's request for a delay as "inappropriate and irrelevant." A battle was joined, one that would become a landmark—if underrecognized—Supreme Court case.[12]

On March 5, Orval Faubus announced his decision to run for a third term, to the surprise of no one. Jim Johnson had realized in September that Faubus had taken his nickel and "hit the jackpot," and consequently he had announced in January that he would not be a candidate for governor. But in order to keep up the pressure on Faubus, Johnson also announced in January that he was sponsoring a new "omnibus" amendment to the Arkansas Constitution, one that contained many provisions gleaned from his segregationist allies across the South. Among the schemes Johnson included were provisions for the closure and sale of integrated public schools, the recall of offending school board members, the elevation of the State Sovereignty Commission to become a constitutional body above the courts, the disbarment of any lawyers convicted of barratry (solicitation of clients—this section was clearly aimed at the NAACP), voting regulations designed to disfranchise Negroes, and many others.[13]

Harry Ashmore perceived correctly that Johnson's deepest concern was the prevention of miscegenation, and he hastened to write, "We do not, of course, believe that any such police-state procedure is necessary for the preservation of the prevailing social patterns in Arkansas." Black leader C. H. Jones also proclaimed in response to Johnson's proposals that even though he was announcing the creation of a new organization, the State Voters Association, there was no reason for persons opposed to Negro voting to "be afraid of us" because blacks did not desire intermarriage with whites.[14]

In mid-March Jim Johnson spoke to the Central High Mothers' League, promoting his amendment and seeking some of the 40,000 signatures he needed to place it on the November ballot. The signers of these and earlier petitions had become his "troops," the hard-core, true believers he called on throughout his political career. The centerpiece of his speech to the Mothers' League was the charge that "communists" lurked at the heart of the integration difficulties in Little Rock. Johnson's charge heralded the inauguration of a new strategy among the practitioners of massive resistance in the South. Having learned from the Little Rock crisis that the old strategy of interposition would not work in preserving segregation, the architects of southern resistance now turned to the threat of communism to accomplish their purposes. Through the next decade, across the entire southern region, they tried to demonstrate that proponents of black civil rights were a part of the "communist apparatus." In Little Rock as elsewhere, the twin evils of communism and miscegenation became entwined in the public mind with the drive toward integration.[15]

On March 30 the *Arkansas Gazette* announced that the State Board of Education would meet in a special session on April 7 to consider a "new plan to restore racial harmony in Arkansas," naming Little Rock businessman Herbert Thomas as the sponsor. The Thomas Plan, as it came to be known, called specifically for abandonment of the Blossom Plan at the end of the current school year. In its place Thomas proposed to create an interracial commission to meet with individual school boards around the state in an effort to let each local board decide on the meaning of "all deliberate speed" within its own district. Those districts that chose to integrate could go ahead and do so; those that did not feel themselves ready to integrate would be encouraged to make their facilities for Negro students truly equal, even though separate.[16]

A cardinal element of the Thomas Plan provided that the black children currently enrolled at Central High School would go back to a segregated Horace

Mann High School the next year. A further element called for an end to all lit-igation promoting integration. Thomas said the interracial commission would operate without legal authority of enforcement, "but because of its very nature it would operate with tremendous moral persuasion toward improved race relationships." Completely ignoring the fact that the Little Rock School Board was under federal court order to implement its current plan for integration, Thomas urged the state board to recommend instead the adoption of his "State Plan of Voluntary Progress."[17]

Brooks Hays's fingerprints were all over the Thomas Plan, and the very mixed reaction the proposal received was typical of the responses to some of his other ideas. The State Board of Education (appointed by Governor Faubus) went into executive session to consider Thomas's proposal, but it quickly announced it would have to defer judgment. The Guy Committee endorsed the business leader's plan, of course, and even Wayne Upton, president of the Little Rock School Board, commended Thomas for his efforts. Governor Faubus declined to comment on the merits of the plan, but he did note that one point Thomas had stated clearly was that "the present plan won't work." This was an idea Orval Faubus had been trying to sell since September.[18]

Herbert Thomas was increasingly frustrated by the silence of the "moder-ates" who had encouraged him in private. He had little luck persuading them to come out publicly in support of his plan. The May 2 meeting of the State Board of Education could not summon a quorum, ostensibly because of rain and flooding, and as a result the board's chairman postponed action on the Thomas proposal until the June meeting, too late to affect the federal court hearing on the School Board petition. The Thomas Plan died a quiet death without Orval Faubus ever having to show his hand.[19]

ON APRIL 21 THE *Arkansas Democrat* announced that Chief Judge Archibald Gardner of the Eighth Circuit Court of Appeals had appointed Judge Harry J. Lemley to handle all litigation in the Little Rock school integration suit until September 1. Many felt encouraged by the news, first because Judge Davies would not be hearing the case, and second because Judge Lemley was known to be a painstaking jurist with roots deep in the South. Lemley had even been heard to say the South "is almost a religion with me." Franklin Roosevelt had appointed the judge to the federal bench in 1939, and since that time he had acquired a reputation as "a meticulous and fair jurist." An amateur archaeologist and a stu-dent of the Confederacy with wide-ranging interests, Lemley occasionally aston-ished expert witnesses with his knowledge of their fields. Although Archie House later described him as a segregationist, in two prior education equalization cases Judge Lemley had ruled in favor of the black plaintiffs. Still, a palpable wave of relief swept over Arkansas at the news of his appointment.[20]

Judge Lemley held a hearing on April 28, one week after his appointment. Saying he did not understand the School Board's request for a "realistic reconsideration" of its plan in the light of "existing conditions," Lemley directed the board to clarify its position specifying the facts that entitled it to relief and stating precisely how long a delay it was requesting. Judge Lemley said in conclusion that the burden of proof would be on the School Board, but that if the board made a case for relief "under the law and the evidence, then appropriate relief will be granted." The School Board was now on notice that it could not simply complain about being left "standing alone." It had to present convincing evidence that the educational standards inside Central High School had been lowered, and that things were unlikely to improve if integration continued.[21]

Early in May the Pulitzer committee awarded prizes to the *Arkansas Gazette* for "demonstrating the highest qualities of civic leadership, journalistic responsibility and moral courage in the face of mounting public tension during the school integration crisis of 1957," and to Harry Ashmore for the "forcefulness, dispassionate analysis and clarity of his editorials on the school integration conflict in Little Rock." Locally, Ashmore and the *Gazette* had become so unpopular that the *Arkansas Democrat* did not even report the honor, and there was little open rejoicing beyond the halls of the morning newspaper. Shortly thereafter, President Eisenhower announced he was ordering the troops out of Central High School on May 29. Governor Faubus received no official word of this decision, but when reporters informed him of it he replied, "It is hoped that never again will any national administration embark upon such an unwise and illegal invasion of powers of state and local governments."[22]

For Central High School the month of May was traditionally a time of celebration. Ernest Green, however, was excluded from the fun. He stayed home from the senior prom, the senior play, and Class Day at War Memorial Park. As early as March a reporter for the *New York Times* had written that it was an "open secret" in Little Rock that plans were afoot to keep Green from graduating with his class. Mrs. Huckaby noted that after Minnijean's expulsion, Ernest had become the next target of the segregationists. When Sammie Dean Parker's father charged publicly that Ernest was winking at his daughter, the unflappable boy only redoubled his efforts to be circumspect at all times. Ernest's mother tried to prepare her son for the possibility of his not being able to walk in the graduation procession with his class. "I keep telling Ernest that pioneers have to go against the odds," she explained to a reporter. "Here at home we're trying to condition him that if he doesn't get to march with the class, well, it's the diploma that counts and he will have that. I tell him, 'You can always remember that you paved the way for others.'"[23]

The School Board and city officials were fully aware of the dangers of the situation. So was Secretary of the Army Brucker, who directed that "no hair on the head of one Ernest Green be harmed." General Walker was reluctant for his troops to play a major role, feeling that "any considerable show of force would provide ammunition for the segregationists who could claim that the troops were necessary to enforce integration at CHS from beginning to end of the school year." Walker relented, however, when Daisy Bates insisted that Green needed protection, and especially when Police Chief Gene Smith requested assistance, telling the general he and city officials feared disturbances. Walker planned to hold soldiers in reserve in case they were needed, and he also authorized the placement of four hundred security officers throughout the stadium where graduation was to be held.[24]

On Sunday, May 25, the *Arkansas Democrat* announced the School Board's decision that admission to graduation and Sunday night's Baccalaureate would be by ticket only. That night, after the traditional blessing of the seniors, the first hint of trouble flared when senior Curtis Stover spit in the face of one of the girls who was walking with Ernest Green's family. Police Chief Gene Smith had positioned himself directly behind Green and observed the incident, and he immediately arrested Stover and put him in a police car. Curtis's mother became overwrought and grabbed a "no parking" sign on a wooden stake and swung it at a *Democrat* photographer who was taking her picture. At the police station Mrs. Stover shrieked and fainted when her son was booked. When her son's case came before segregationist traffic judge Robert W. Laster, however, the judge cleared the boy of all charges, declaring "There's no insult worse than spitting in someone's face but if anyone is to be blamed it should be Dwight D. Eisenhower."[25]

On May 27, 1958, Ernest Green graduated with his class, without incident. Martin Luther King sat with Green's family in the stadium, as did Presbyterian minister Dunbar Ogden, one of the few courageous whites who had consistently supported the families of the Nine and their quest throughout the year. (Ogden soon lost his pulpit and moved away from Little Rock.) Listening to the ceremony on the radio at home, Melba Patillo's grandmother India stood and applauded when Green received his diploma. Inside the stadium there was only silence. The next day Ernest went back to school to clean out his locker and pick up his grades, and one of his classmates waved to him and yelled across the courtyard, "Wish you luck, Green!" Ernest smiled and waved back. The long year was over.[26]

On May 29 the Army pulled out of Little Rock. The orders relieving the National Guard included a statement from President Eisenhower that read: "The law of this land and the lawful orders of its courts must be honored or our nation will lose its vital heritage of freedom under law." Many in Little Rock and across the South agreed, though they pointed to the federal courts as the lawbreaker. But what would the courts do next?[27]

On May 8, Richard Butler had filed an amended petition with Judge Lemley, removing his clients' earlier request for a delay until the term "all deliberate speed" could be clarified and asking instead for a delay of two and one-half years. On May 24, Butler filed a pretrial brief in federal court delineating the basic outlines of his argument. Citing the numerous bomb threats, incidents inside Central High School, and the distribution of literature to students by "outside forces" designed to create agitation, the School Board's brief contended that the board members recognized the "binding force" of the *Brown* decision and yet they had "become pessimistic as to their ability adequately to serve the needs of education and have grown weary of the abuse they have received in trying to do their duty without the assistance of this court and in the face of the determined opposition of the forces of state government." Going to the heart of the matter, the School Board attorney suggested that the thrust of the *Brown* decision was unrealistic, for "any court which assumes that a judicial fiat will change . . . mores is simply mistaken." He asked for a delay because the provisions of *Brown II* calling for integration with "all deliberate speed" acknowledged that local conditions would vary and could be considered in designing and implementing desegregation programs.[28]

The LDF contended in its brief that Judge Lemley had no right to grant such a delay. Filed by Wiley Branton and Thurgood Marshall, the document argued that the School Board had a constitutional obligation to follow through on the court-approved Blossom Plan, with or without opposition. Branton and Marshall suggested that while *Brown II* had enumerated the ways local communities might vary, it had not considered the possibility of a delay once a plan was in the process of being implemented. Branton and Marshall also argued that under the terms of *Brown II*, the existence of disorder did not constitute a valid reason to postpone integration.[29]

ON JUNE 3, 1958, before a packed courtroom in the federal building in Little Rock, Judge Lemley began a three-day hearing in which witnesses for the School Board testified to all the difficulties of the past year. Richard Butler and Archie House made a strong case that the situation inside Central High School had disintegrated into "chaos, bedlam and turmoil," thereby making it impossible for "teachers to teach and students to learn." Wiley Branton and Thurgood Marshall introduced only two witnesses, who suggested that school administrators were at fault for the breakdown in educational standards because they had failed to impose discipline inside Central High School.[30]

The two vice principals, Elizabeth Huckaby and J. O. Powell, made strong impressions. Huckaby was not in sympathy with the abandonment of integration, but she realized that if school authorities had to bear the complete burden of implementation without the cooperation and active assistance of the federal courts and the Justice Department, "we could not run the school with safety for children of either race." She said she had devoted 75 to 90 percent of her time to disciplinary problems, because the Negro children "were under constant threat." Powell claimed he did not normally have as much as one uninterrupted hour on school business on any day during the school year. He suggested that 90 percent of his time during the year had been "channeled into problems relating to integration." Teachers and other staff members offered similar testimony.[31]

The NAACP attorneys did not even attempt to call any local witness to the contrary. Yet when School Board president Wayne Upton testified that the general feeling among the many people he had talked to in Little Rock—that an order of the Supreme Court was not the "law of the land" since it had not been passed by a legislative body—he provided an opening for the black lawyers. Under cross-examination Wiley Branton made mincemeat of Wayne Upton's arguments. Branton asked: "Now, is it the Board's position that this Court ought to give relief to the Board because of the fact there is a defiance on the part of a small group of students in Central High School?" Upton fumbled for words. In the midst of a proceeding that seemed to be going against his arguments, Wiley Branton managed to get into the court record an interpretation of the issues that became dominant on appeal. The School Board argument about maintaining educational quality began to be pushed aside by the LDF lawyers' aggressive focus on the constitutional rights of the black children.[32]

Struggling to correct Wayne Upton's damaging testimony, Richard Butler called the imposing Virgil Blossom to the stand, who testified that the dominant community attitude in Little Rock was that the federal court order "was a nullity." Blossom told the court, "The fact that these local laws have not been

repealed creates a tremendous problem, honestly, in the minds of many people"
and there will be "many, many months ahead before there will be any decision
on them, to where there is a clear-cut situation between state and federal law on
this problem, and that, in itself, creates this dilemma." With the conclusion of
Blossom's testimony, the School Board lawyers rested their case.[33]

After the hearing, Judge Lemley told U.S. Attorney Osro Cobb he had been
shocked by the teachers' testimony, for he had had no idea of the level of disruption within the school. Cobb passed this information on to his superior in the
Justice Department, Wilson White, now head of the Civil Rights Division, along
with his speculation that Lemley would grant the School Board's request for
relief. Judge Lemley's shock is significant. An intelligent, informed, concerned
citizen with a definite interest in the case, Lemley had not gleaned from news
accounts an understanding of the turmoil inside Central High School. This is a
clear indication of the care with which Virgil Blossom and school officials had
censored the news and controlled the flow of information from inside the school
out into the community.[34]

ON THE FIRST NIGHT of the Lemley hearing, after a long day of testifying and
listening to her colleagues tell their stories, Elizabeth Huckaby put on her best bib
and tucker and went to a dinner honoring Harry Ashmore and the *Arkansas
Gazette.* Little Rock's grand old lady, Mrs. Adolphine Fletcher Terry, had decided
that despite the widespread hostility to Ashmore and the *Gazette,* something
needed to be done to celebrate the newspaper's Pulitzer Prizes. Fearful initially
that no one would show up, Mrs. Terry was relieved and gratified when the ballroom of Hotel Marion filled to capacity with over nine hundred Little Rock citizens. For some of them, it was their first halting steps toward challenging the
closed-mindedness, anger, and fear that had descended upon their city. As Huckaby recalled, finding a huge crowd in the ballroom, "For the first time all year, I
did not feel isolated." Elsewhere that week, the NAACP announced that it would
award its Spingarn Medal, given annually to an African-American for distinguished achievement, to the Little Rock Nine and Daisy Bates for "their
courageous self-restraint in the face of extreme provocation and peril" and for
"their exemplary conduct in upholding the American ideal of liberty and justice."[35]

At the end of the week, Judge Lemley announced his decision to grant the
School Board a thirty-month delay. The judge's thirty-five page, carefully constructed opinion argued, "When the interests involved here are balanced, . . . the
personal and immediate interests of the Negro students affected must yield tem-

porarily to the larger interests of both races." Holding that "a tactical delay is not the same as a surrender," Judge Lemley noted that if anti-integration legislation were ruled invalid during the period of the delay, "the people of Little Rock might be much more willing to acquiesce in integration as contemplated by the plan."[36]

Judge Lemley concluded that while the *Brown* decisions had provided that "the Negro students in the Little Rock district have a constitutional right not to be excluded from any of the public schools on account of race . . . the board has convincingly shown that the time for the enjoyment of that right has not yet come." All across the South, political leaders voiced their approval of the Lemley decision, and in Little Rock Amis Guthridge and Wesley Pruden were especially pleased. Legal scholar J. W. Peltason wrote it was "a major victory for the segregationists."[37]

Wiley Branton immediately announced an appeal and filed a request for a stay until it could be heard. Judge Lemley denied the stay, primarily for the reason that from a practical standpoint "to stay the enforcement of our judgment would to a large extent nullify our order in the case since it will in all probability take months to carry the case through the court of appeals and the United States Supreme Court." Since the Eighth Circuit judges planned to start their summer recess in two weeks, Branton feared Central High School would be resegregated in the fall of 1958.[38]

On June 26, after a frantic scramble by a team of LDF attorneys to strategize and prepare complicated paperwork, Wiley Branton and Thurgood Marshall went directly to the United States Supreme Court and asked it to hold a special session and overturn the Lemley decision. The Court denied their request.[39] Nonetheless, under pressure of school reopening and the threatened loss of the hard-won gains of the city's young black warriors, the judges of the Eighth Circuit and the justices of the Supreme Court rushed to fashion a response to the perceived rebellion in Little Rock that would send an unmistakable message to those in other parts of the South who might be contemplating a resort to massive resistance. Richard Butler and Archie House now found themselves carrying the entire burden, practically alone, of interpreting southern white concerns for the benefit of the federal judiciary. The resulting clash between white and black attorneys led to nothing less than a revised and expanded conception of American justice.

On June 29, Orval Faubus formally opened his campaign for reelection by attacking his "real" opponents who "reach from the editorial office of the *Arkansas Gazette* and the home of Daisy Bates in Little Rock into every section of this broad land." In a thirty-minute telecast, Faubus said of Ashmore and Bates, "Their methods are unscrupulous. Fairness to them is a sign of weakness. They listen not to an appeal to reason; they heed not the voice of compromise. Once victorious they would be deaf to any plea for tolerance and understanding." Directing most of his criticisms at the campaign proposals of his registered opponents, Chris Finkbeiner, a meatpacker, and Lee Ward, a chancery judge, Faubus outlined the accomplishments of his administration and then reiterated his opposition, in the words of one observer, to "integration by force, and at bayonet point, declaring his belief in the preservation of southern traditions and democratic processes."[40]

On July 2 Faubus campaigned in his native hills of northwest Arkansas. At Harrison he said the basic choice in the campaign was not between him and the other two candidates, but between "me and Harry Ashmore and the other outsiders who are assisting him." He said Ashmore had made fun of him in a recent editorial "for protecting the state from the pink bollworm, fire ants, and the invasion of a federal Army." Faubus suggested that Ashmore had failed to realize the seriousness of these problems "because he has never brushed elbows with people such as us." Faubus said if Ashmore was not in his air-conditioned office "he's in his private club or maybe on the golf course. You couldn't get in his club unless I took you and that's only because I'm governor."[41]

On election day Orval Faubus won a stunning endorsement from the people of Arkansas: he garnered 68 percent of the vote, he carried all seventy-five Arkansas counties, and he won more votes than any other gubernatorial candidate in Arkansas history. The jubilation at Faubus headquarters was electric. Roy Reed of the *Arkansas Gazette* described it as being "like Mardi Gras on Markham Street." As the returns rolled in, a hand-lettered crayon sign appeared on one wall saying "Epitaph for Dixie Mr. Ashmore? Man You All Are So Wrong! Thru Governor Faubus and God the South Will Live Again!" As Faubus was leaving his campaign headquarters at one point during the celebration, one of his supporters said jokingly, "Don't leave now Governor, Ike is on the phone." The vindicated governor replied, to the delight of all, "Tell him to call back later." The next day, Harry Ashmore editorialized, "The moderate position formerly espoused by many Southern political leaders, and by this newspaper as a matter of principle, has been rejected by the mass of voters in this Upper Southern state and is now clearly untenable for any man in public life anywhere in the region."[42]

Among other significant results in the Democratic primary were Jim Johnson's election to the Arkansas Supreme Court over well-respected, moderately segregationist incumbent Minor Millwee, Brooks Hays's defeat of Amis Guthridge in a race for Hays's House seat, and Griffin Smith's failure to unseat long-serving Justice Ed McFaddin. Johnson's election surprised most observers, but later analysts concluded that he had won with Faubus's support. The Faubus organization had also promised initially to assist Griffin Smith, the attorney who had argued the Thomason suit in 1957, but they withdrew their support late in the game, apparently in an effort to save face when they concluded he could not win. Guthridge had little chance of unseating incumbent Hays, but the gentle congressman's easy victory gave him a false sense of security going into the fall election that proved to be a factor in his eventual defeat.[43]

IN AUGUST, THE LDF changed its strategy, this time arguing in the Eighth Circuit Court of Appeals in St. Louis that community opposition provided no legal basis for overturning a court-approved plan for integration. The Little Rock School Board's brief contended that the *Brown* decision did not exclude suspensions of integration plans that were already under way, and it called attention to the violence and the unusually heavy opposition to integration in Little Rock. On August 4 all seven judges of the Eighth Circuit Court of Appeals sat *en banc* in St. Louis to hear one hour of argument from each of the parties to the case. All of the judges were midwesterners.[44]

Tall, self-assured Thurgood Marshall argued that the School Board had been lax in its discipline inside Central High School. Archie House defended the Little Rock School Board, arguing that the Supreme Court's phrase "all deliberate speed" should be translated into existing conditions. The aging barrister in the rumpled suit said that any southern school board attempting to implement the *Brown* decision faced two great problems: the mores of the community, and the federal government's lack of power to enforce integration. Richard Butler suggested that the School Board had only two choices: "Either they could be a party to the destruction of what they had built up [quality education] or take legal action." Butler said there were state laws on the books in Arkansas that prohibited integration, and while "some find these to be unconstitutional, . . . who is to know until they reach the courts? The Board had to take them into consideration as well." Referring to the previous week's landslide victory of Governor Faubus, Butler argued, "The mandate of the people of Arkansas shows they are opposed to desegregation of schools."[45]

Two weeks later, on August 18, in a six-to-one decision, the Court of Appeals overruled Judge Lemley, agreeing with his findings of fact, but disagreeing with his conclusions. Accepting the LDF's arguments that the Lemley decision would amount to an "open invitation" to violence and that the real issue was whether public resistance should be allowed to nullify the order to proceed with desegregation, Judge Marion C. Matthes wrote for the majority, "*We say that the time has not yet come in these United States when an order of a federal court must be whittled away, watered down or shamefully withdrawn in the face of violent and unlawful acts of individual citizens. . . .*" The judges also suggested that "if more rigid and strict disciplinary methods had been adopted and pursued" against the ringleaders inside Central High School, much of the turmoil could have been eliminated. The Appeals Court opinion acknowledged that conditions inside Central High adversely affected educational quality but concluded "such incidents are insufficient to constitute a legal basis for suspension of the plan to integrate the public schools in Little Rock."[46]

It was a stunning reversal, yet there was one more possibility of appeal by the School Board. Richard Butler told reporters that until the court's mandate, or official order, arrived in Little Rock, the School Board would not have specific instructions on how it must proceed, and this could take as long as twenty days, which would run a week beyond school opening. In the meantime, however, Butler assured reporters that he would file an appeal with the United States Supreme Court. Butler also suggested he might seek a stay of the Appeals Court ruling. In later years Dick Butler acknowledged that all these legal maneuvers caused "utter confusion" in Little Rock.[47]

Individual Arkansas legislators responded to reporters' questions that night by saying they were ready for a special session of the General Assembly on a moment's notice. State Senator Charles F. (Rip) Smith of West Memphis, a member of the Sovereignty Commission, said the state should act quickly, and he favored "anything short of violence" to prevent integration. "The time has come for the state to use all of its resources, legislative, judicial and executive, to protect our way of life." A possible remedy was a law to close schools integrated by court order, an idea Governor Faubus (and Jim Johnson before him) had floated in the past. According to the *Arkansas Gazette,* the temper of some of the legislators was such that they were "prepared to adopt any new segregation law now and worry later about fighting it through the courts."[48]

JUDGE LEMLEY WAS personally distressed by the reversal of his decision. Richard Butler later said it "hastened his trip to the grave." Lemley soon announced plans to retire from the bench, ostensibly for matters of health, but also probably because he did not want to preside over implementation of a plan he personally opposed. Letters of condolence poured into the judge's home, as did offerings such as the one from a Mrs. Livingston. "Only God knows what is to become of our precious teen-age girls," the distressed woman wrote, "among colored school boys and older ones who have no respect for women of any color or age. . . . the whole thing is not a question of education but of physical safety. . . . Pardon length of this letter—I am troubled."[49]

On the ropes by this point, the School Board members hastened to meet with their lawyers. Whereas their situation had been "intolerable" the year before, now they faced the prospect of having to reopen the schools integrated in less than two weeks, having made no preparations to do so, and knowing that the Arkansas people had given their governor a "mandate" to oppose such a move. They knew as well from bitter experience that the Justice Department was unlikely to offer meaningful support, and they feared the return of federal troops. Having subordinated the School Board's concerns about maintaining educational quality to the necessity of implementing desegregation, the court had also placed all responsibility for enforcement of Judge Davies's court order on these private citizens' shoulders. After three hours of deliberation over dinner at the Albert Pike Hotel, Virgil Blossom announced to the press that the School Board had decided to seek a stay from the Appeals Court and a writ of certiorari (a request that the Appeals Court materials be forwarded for review) from the Supreme Court. It had also decided to seek a meeting with Governor Faubus to discuss suggestions he had recently released to the press.[50]

On August 21, at his weekly press conference, President Eisenhower delivered a prepared statement regarding the Appeals Court's reversal of the Lemley decision. Declaring that each state must uphold the decisions of the federal courts, Eisenhower told reporters that defiance of this duty would present serious problems. "[T]here can be no equivocation as to the responsibility of the federal government in such an event," the president suggested, then added, "My feelings are exactly as they were a year ago."[51]

Governor Faubus announced he would meet with the Little Rock School Board that night, at their request. The School Board requested all the deliberations be kept off the record, and Faubus honored that request, revealing to the press no details of the content of their conversations. Yet the presence at the meeting of the state's legislative leadership led one close observer to conclude, "The hopelessness of school officials under the pressures created by the new court decision, piled on the unresolved impasse of conflicting influences inside Central High School, seemed to have pushed them to accept the Governor's proposed solution (to close the high schools) as the only practical relief." The next day, Governor Faubus alerted the members of the General Assembly to stand by for a special session, tentatively scheduled for the following Monday, August 26.[52]

On August 21 the Eighth Circuit Court of Appeals unexpectedly announced a decision to grant the Little Rock School Board a stay of its order until the Supreme Court ruled on the case. Now, either the schools would be segregated when they opened on September 2, or the Supreme Court would have to act extraordinarily quickly. Under these circumstances, the Justice Department found itself unable to move forward with its tentative plans to intervene since the Lemley ruling was still in force.[53]

Thurgood Marshall announced immediately that he would appeal the Eighth Circuit's stay order, asking Supreme Court Justice Charles Whittaker, who had jurisdiction over emergency appeals for the Eighth Circuit when the Supreme Court was in recess, to overrule it. (The Supreme Court was in recess until October 6.) Justice Whittaker, the newest member of the Supreme Court, was en route to the American Bar Association convention in Los Angeles. Contacted at a train stop in Denver, Justice Whittaker said he had the authority to rule on the request alone.[54]

The seven black children eligible to return to Central High School, of the original Nine, were at that moment in Washington, D.C. receiving another award and posing on the steps of the Supreme Court building with Thurgood Marshall. They were not sure whether they even wanted to go back to Central High School. Their parents said the children would have to make their own decisions.[55]

On Saturday, Governor Faubus issued the call for the General Assembly to meet in Little Rock on Tuesday, August 27, for one purpose: "To regulate the administration and financing of public schools and education. . . ." The governor declared, "Unless we do find some means to counteract legally what we believe to be the illegal use of armed troops or any other armed forces by the federal government, then the eventualities are what I fear and which I seek most earnestly to avoid." Faubus commented in response to questions that according to his information, the potential existed that at Central High School "there will be more violence than before." He explained that the NAACP had filed a petition with Judge Whittaker to vacate the stay of the Appeals Court, and if this were to happen, there would be no time for the legislature to act before school started.[56]

On Monday, August 25, with just one week left before the start of school, the U.S. Supreme Court announced it would convene in a rare emergency session three days later, on Thursday, August 28. Chief Justice Earl Warren was attending the ABA convention in Los Angeles, where he delivered the keynote address arguing that court delays were "corroding the very foundation of constitutional government in the United States." Other Supreme Court justices present in Los Angeles were Whittaker, William J. Brennan, and Tom Clark. William O. Douglas was vacationing on the West Coast, and Felix Frankfurter and Hugo Black were in Washington. Justice Harold Burton, vacationing in Europe, was not expected to come home. Little Rock School Board attorney Archie House was also vacationing in Europe, and he would not participate in the August 28 hearing.[57]

Tacked on to the Warren announcement of a special term was an invitation to United States Solicitor General J. Lee Rankin to join the case as *amicus curiae*. Rankin had argued the *Brown* case for the government in 1954. Warren's invitation rescued the Justice Department from its indecision about whether to request that it be involved in the case.[58]

The Little Rock School Board met Monday night and decided to postpone the opening of school until September 8, shortly after Virgil Blossom physically threw a UP reporter out of his office. The high-strung superintendent later apologized, saying, "I was pretty rough and I'm sorry for it. . . . I was under pressure." Governor Faubus met with his legislative leaders, explaining the bills he planned to introduce on Tuesday.[59]

Virgil Blossom reported in his memoir that he had talked to many members of the Arkansas legislature who were fearful for their businesses if they did not support the governor's legislative package. All the indications were that any bills the governor proposed would sail through the legislature. As one legislator remarked, "When all 75 counties voted for Faubus, they meant for the representatives to vote with him too."[60]

As the special session of the General Assembly opened, Orval Faubus strode into the House chamber through waves of applause and gave the speech of his lifetime. His central theme was that the federal courts had declared integration paramount to all other considerations—to educational standards, to the emotional well-being of students, to the maintenance of peace and order in times of crisis. Governor Faubus proposed six bills: 1) to close a school if necessary to prevent violence, or where a school had been ordered to integrate by any court and federal force was employed to enforce the order, or where it was determined that a "suitable" educational system could not be maintained because of integration; 2) to withhold state funds from any school so closed; 3) to enroll students in other schools; 4) to make it possible for a student to refuse to attend an integrated class; 5) to appropriate funds for the governor to carry out this program; and 6) to postpone the opening of "certain schools" from September 2 to September 15, 1958.[61]

Arguing that the battle for "states rights and constitutional government" was not one of his choosing but that it had been forced upon him, Faubus urged the assembled legislators not to be misled by those who would "surrender all the rights and privileges we have enjoyed to an all powerful federal government in the unwise course of action which it pursues at the present moment." When the governor finished speaking, thunderous applause lasted nearly a minute.[62]

The Arkansas legislature passed the six Faubus bills in short order, in addition to several others offered by Attorney General Bruce Bennett that were aimed at the NAACP. Four days after the session had begun, the General Assembly recessed and the legislators went home. They recessed instead of adjourning, making it legally possible for Governor Faubus to hold the adopted bills on his desk without signing them. Osro Cobb wrote years later that Faubus's failure to sign the bills immediately was "calculated to get the U.S. Supreme Court to uphold Judge Lemley's order granting a delay. . . ." Cobb quoted Faubus as saying, "I hope I never have to use them." Yet Thurgood Marshall soon brought this maneuver to the attention of the Supreme Court justices in a successful effort to harden their hearts toward the Arkansas governor.[63]

ON AUGUST 28, amid the marble columns and maroon velvet curtains of the Supreme Court, the awed Little Rock contestants acknowledged one another in hushed tones. Richard Butler arrived early, accompanied by his young assistant John Haley (on loan from the Rose Law Firm). He was soon joined by Virgil Blossom, Wayne Upton and Harold Engstrom. Dale Alford had also flown up for the occasion.[64]

Prospective spectators had started lining up outside the Supreme Court Building at 3:30 A.M., and now they scrambled to obtain one of the thirty or so seats available for uninvited guests. The remaining 150 seats were taken by senators, Supreme Court justices' wives and families, visiting dignitaries, and the like, long before the noon hour of the official opening of the Court.[65]

Promptly at noon a hush fell over the room as the nine Supreme Court justices took their seats. After the proper introductions, Chief Justice Earl Warren instructed Thurgood Marshall, as petitioner, to begin. Tall and striking in a brown-checked suit, relaxed because he had argued in this chamber fourteen times before, twelve of them successfully, Marshall spoke easily and forcefully, leaning on the lectern and shrugging his shoulders for emphasis, occasionally taking off his glasses and waving them as he gestured to make a point. From the beginning Marshall argued that the Court should not confine itself that day to a decision on his petition alone—which concerned only whether or not to vacate the Eighth Circuit's stay of its ruling—but that it should discuss the larger case "on its merits" and render a final judgment immediately. Stressing that the Little Rock School Board's request for more time would only lead to more litigation and legislative confusion, as was happening that very day in Arkansas, the NAACP's chief counsel argued that the School Board had done nothing to secure the assistance of local authorities over the past year, and that it had never indicated what it intended to do with the thirty-month delay it was seeking.[66]

As Richard Butler rose to speak, he too exuded confidence with his dignified stance, dark blue summer suit elegant and trim, and his slow southern drawl. Immediately the justices began to pepper him with questions, including ones about Marshall's unexpected suggestion that the Court should hear full argument on the case that day. In his courtly manner Butler informed the chief justice, "We have no disposition to delay the legal proceedings, but we hope that we will be given time in that event as we should to do it in an orderly fashion . . . . We would deplore being rushed into it to the extent of not having time adequately to prepare it."[67]

Richard Butler struggled to make his listeners understand that as long as popular editorialists in his community were saying that *Brown* was not the law of the land, and as long as state laws sat on the statute books that were diametrically opposed to the *Brown* decision, the people of his community were left in doubt concerning what the law actually was. And so the School Board hoped that a two and a half year delay would provide time during which "a national policy could definitely be established," and "laws could be tested so that the people would know, the people who want to obey the final word." Justice Frankfurter sat bolt upright in his chair, challenging Butler to tell him why two Supreme Court decisions (*Brown I* and *II*) were not sufficient to constitute "a national policy." Butler fumbled for words.

Chief Justice Warren jumped in, asking, "suppose every other school district in the South would do the same thing, say 'We will carry on segregation for a number of years until the law is clarified,' how would it ever be clarified?" Butler answered, "I simply say again that this School Board in Little Rock, Arkansas, was not faced with theories. It was faced with actualities which are undermining and which are going to destroy the public school system in Little Rock . . . unless they are given an opportunity to work this thing out in a climate of calm, rather than in a climate of hysteria."

Butler suggested it was difficult for many people to believe that Supreme Court decisions were the law of the land when the popular governor of their state said they were not, and until this point was resolved the people of Arkansas "have a doubt in their mind and a right to have a doubt." Chief Justice Warren came out of his chair, sputtering, "But I have never heard such an argument made in a Court of Justice before, and I have tried many a case through many a year. I never heard a lawyer say that the statement of a Governor as to what was legal or illegal should control the action of any court." It would not be easy to convince the very Court that had decided *Brown I* and *II* that they had not been clear regarding the law of the land.

Richard Butler pointed out that during the previous year the NAACP had sought no injunctions and the Justice Department had pursued no criminal actions. Furthermore, he argued, the School Board should not be expected to go out into the community and preserve the public peace. "That is not its function." Having met with Orval Faubus just days before and knowing his School Board was on the brink of yielding to defeat, Richard Butler concluded his presentation with a powerful set of questions. Shall the courts, he asked, deny a community a reasonable opportunity to reach solutions to such deep-seated problems in a period of calm and quiet rather than in an atmosphere of strife and turmoil? Shall the courts force "private citizens and officials and general assemblies" to make decisions when the air is charged with emotion? And can it logically be argued that the court's ruling can be carried out if the schools are closed? Striking the chord he had stressed all along, Butler concluded, "Patience and forbearance for a short while might save our public school system in Little Rock, which was once the pride of our community."

The justices recessed for an hour and a half, returning at five o'clock to announce they had decided to review the Court of Appeals decision reversing the order of Judge Lemley. Operating on the assumption that the Little Rock public schools would not open until September 15, they directed all parties to submit briefs to them no later than September 10. They announced plans to hear oral arguments on September 11 and their intention to defer any decision about whether or not to stay the mandate of the Appeals Court until that time. Richard Butler had carried the day.

ORVAL FAUBUS LATER claimed that in the interim between the Supreme Court sessions of August 28 and September 11, he received a confidential message from one of the justices. Delivered by "a responsible federal official of unquestioned integrity and to me well known" (possibly Brooks Hays), the message was to the effect that the prospects were good for "something to be worked out" in which the Court would relax its heretofore inflexible stand on desegregation. The message may have been designed to keep the unruly governor quiet during the interim, but if so it did not work. On September 6 Faubus suggested to the closing session of the state Democratic Party convention that the Supreme Court justices were communists. Faubus believed there was a division within the Court, and that was the reason for the decision to wait two weeks to have another hearing.[68]

The Justice Department had hoped to use the Little Rock bench rather than federal troops to forestall any potential racial unrest, by issuing injunctions against known troublemakers. Yet with Judge Lemley's retirement, Arkansas had only one federal judge left, John Miller, who faced a backlog of cases. In August the Justice Department had sent four of its attorneys to Little Rock to assist Osro Cobb in preparing injunction petitions to restrain interference with the carrying out of the court's orders. The Justice Department was trying to pave the way for the peaceful acceptance of what it thought would be the Court's "inevitable decision." Yet Attorney General Rogers also assembled a group of 137 United States marshals who were specially trained in riot control, and sent them to Little Rock.[69]

Richard Butler had left the Supreme Court justices with the clear understanding that school would not start in Little Rock until September 15. That was the date spelled out in one of Faubus's new bills, but the governor had not signed it into law, and so the formal date for school opening technically remained September 8. If, however, the high schools opened before the Court ruled, they would open segregated, and Faubus began to push for this to happen. The School Board was divided. Three of the members believed the schools should open as scheduled on the 8th, since the teachers had to be paid either way, but several board members also felt Faubus was trying to maneuver them into an open defiance of the courts. Dick Butler argued strenuously that the board did not want to prejudice its case, and that it must vote to change the date of school opening to September 15. The board at length decided to follow Butler's advice and delayed the date of school opening for the high schools only (the junior high and elementary schools opened on the 8th), but they also decided that if the Court ruled against them and Faubus ordered the schools closed, they would comply.[70]

This was the milieu in which Richard Butler struggled, under stress, in haste, and mostly alone, to write the most important brief of his legal career. Archie House was in Europe, and House's young associate John Haley was barely out of law school. Butler recalled years later that this was the hardest case he ever tried and the most strenuously he ever argued. He knew there was no room for error and little chance of success. He understood why the justices could not yield and he did not expect to win, but he hoped to secure a compromise for his School Board and his city.[71]

In the written brief he prepared for the justices' consideration Butler developed two lines of argument, stated as questions. One asked whether the courts could legally postpone the enforcement of the black children's constitutional rights in the face of "an intolerable situation and great disruption of the educational process," which by all accounts would continue to occur in the absence of a temporary delay. The other asked whether a school district had the obligation to quell violence and organized resistance to desegregation by initiating litigation and seeking injunctions.[72]

Butler's brief questioned whether the courts had the practical ability to deal with opposition such as the Little Rock School Board had encountered, but if they did, he argued, "certainly the method should not be that of placing the school board in the undeserved position of being the sole bastion of Federal authority until it destroys itself." The School Board, dependent as it was upon public support through taxation, could not be expected to expend its limited funds in "perpetual litigation and prosecutions." That board had exercised good faith with the courts in the past and would continue to do so in the future, but it should not be expected to preserve the peace. "It is not the function of a school district," Butler argued in a forthright statement of his position, "to act as a buffer in a contest between state and federal authority, and certainly not to act as the bulwark of federal authority in such a contest." If the Court did not agree with his analysis, Butler asked, and they believed that the duty for enforcing the law of the land rested on the school district, then "how can it possibly enforce the federal law and where is it to obtain funds to be used for the purpose?"

In a resounding conclusion Butler argued that if *Brown* were not sufficiently flexible to allow time for the forces of massive resistance to subside, "then it may be seriously doubted whether courts are able to effectively cope with 'state action' such as this, and perhaps the Court should so hold." In effect, Richard Butler's brief challenged the Supreme Court either to admit it did not have the power to require compliance with its mandates, or to suggest practical means for a southern school board to deal with the active opposition of the community. His analysis of the conflict between state and federal authority became the central concern of the Court.

ON SEPTEMBER 11, Richard Butler was nervous. His wife and son sat in the gallery this time, thanks to the intercession of Brooks Hays. Virgil Blossom and Archie House were there. As he had expected, he took most of the heat of the day. Thurgood Marshall spoke for twenty minutes and Lee Rankin, the solicitor general, for forty, and the justices asked each of them one question. When Butler took the floor, the justices grilled him for two hours and twelve minutes, mostly about the conflict between state and federal authority. Butler recalled years later that he wanted to say, "If we get rid of our governor and you get rid of your chief justice, this thing will be settled."[73]

Richard Butler tried to get across to the justices that what was happening in Little Rock involved more than simple defiance by the governor. The justices seemed to believe that in the absence of Orval Faubus's recalcitrance, desegregation could have proceeded with little difficulty, and that the people of Little Rock would fall into line behind more responsible leaders. Using a brief Arkansas Senator J. William Fulbright had prepared in the hope of entering the case as *amicus curiae* (the justices had denied his request), Butler began to explain the contours of "the Southern mind," which Fulbright had argued resulted from the history of having two races live over a long period of time in such close proximity. The justices would not hear of it.[74]

After attempting to develop his argument through myriad interruptions, Butler at length concluded, "We again plead for the opportunity to preserve our public education system, and that is our primary plea. In the best judgment of the School Board, it has a chance of survival so as to give effective education to the children only if some reasonable delay is given." Arguing that the NAACP and the solicitor general had failed to grasp the central problem—that the Justice Department had provided no means of enforcement and the School Board had no police powers—Butler pleaded finally for recognition that the School Board was caught in a "conflict between . . . two sovereignties," the state of Arkansas and the federal government. Until that conflict was resolved, Butler concluded, and until enforcement mechanisms were implemented that preserved educational quality, the School District should have the relief of a delay.[75]

Butler expected to fail, and he was unsurprised when the NAACP's legal team persuaded the justices that the issue was basically "whether the Court would tolerate Faubus's rebellion." In the words of one member of that team, if the Court gave comfort to Faubus in any way, "the idea of a national government would be damaged severely, perhaps fatally." At the close of oral arguments, the nine justices deliberated less than thirty minutes before deciding that the Little Rock School Board must proceed with integration, immediately.[76]

The next day, September 12, 1958, the Supreme Court announced its decision at noon, issuing only a *per curiam*, or abbreviated decision, with the promise that a fully developed ruling would follow soon. One of Orval Faubus's aides whispered the news to him just as the governor opened a committee meeting. The otherwise impassive mountaineer flushed visibly, but he continued with the business at hand and then refused to offer any comment to the press. Several hours later he signed the legislation waiting on his desk, thereby closing all the high schools in the city.[77]

RICHARD BUTLER AND Virgil Blossom flew home together that evening, reflecting on their loss. Butler later recalled that Blossom said to him, "Dick, there's a very thin line between a hero and a bum. I was almost a hero." Within a matter of months, the weary superintendent lost his job and left Little Rock, while his city descended into the chaos and turmoil of a last stand against the future.[78]

CHAPTER FOURTEEN

EMPTY SCHOOLS

Wiley Branton

I N THE EVENINGS, FINALLY, THE DRY AIR BEGAN TO COOL. THE DAY-time heat could still be blistering but the storms and the oppressive humidity had passed, and Little Rock residents once again began to visit after supper on porch swings and gliders, drinking lemonade and listening to the sounds of children playing in the gathering dusk. As the shadows lengthened, much of the conversation centered on the confusing whirl of court decisions the summer had wrought. After a year of tension and controversy Little Rock's citizens, black as well as white, were dismayed by the uncertainty facing their children and their city. They were also astonished by the new aggressiveness of the young black attorney for the NAACP, Wiley Branton.

Wiley Austin Branton lived in nearby Pine Bluff, the home of his parents and grandparents. He had grown up in unusual circumstances for a southern child of either race, surrounded by material comforts, books, and the expectation of earning a college degree. Although two of his brothers went off to college in Tennessee, Wiley had stayed home in Pine Bluff to attend Arkansas Agricultural, Mechanical, and Normal College. During his four years of college he also managed his father's cab company. In 1943, at the age of twenty, Branton was drafted into the United States Army, and by the end of World War II he was a master sergeant in an Engineer Aviation Battalion, serving on Okinawa. As he recalled many years later, fighting for freedom abroad motivated him strongly to "make home safe for democracy."[1]

Eventually resuming and completing his college studies, Branton also joined the Pine Bluff chapter of the National Association for the Advancement of Colored People. During this period he suffered a number of humiliating experiences that made him realize he wanted to be in a position to combat the discriminatory treatment black people suffered in the South, and he decided to go to law school. Branton started his legal training in a segregated classroom at the University of Arkansas Law School with individual instruction, but this form of discrimination had ceased by the time he graduated.[2]

In 1953, degree in hand, Wiley Branton and his growing family moved back to Pine Bluff, where he established a successful law practice and went to work for the NAACP. By the time the *Brown* decision was handed down in 1954, the thirty-two-year-old Branton was chairman of the NAACP's State Legal Redress Committee, and under his direction the organization filed several petitions with Arkansas school boards demanding compliance with the new Supreme Court decision. He became a close friend and avid admirer of Thurgood Marshall, whom he acknowledged as "the unquestioned master in civil rights litigation." *Aaron v. Cooper* was another in a string of landmark cases for Marshall; for Branton, it propelled him into the spotlight for the first time.[3]

Throughout late 1957 and 1958, as the case unfolded, Branton found it necessary to engage armed guards to protect his home while his family slept. He received hate mail from all over the country, some of it addressed simply to "Nigger Lawyer, Pine Bluff, Arkansas." For the rest of his life he kept on his desk a picture of a cross that unnamed cowards had burned on the Branton family's cemetery plot. But despite the many assaults on his dignity occasioned by his choosing to remain in the South throughout his life, Wiley Branton maintained a positive outlook as he followed the path of a warrior. At his death another former Pine Bluff resident said of him appreciatively ". . . the most important thing about him was the way he fought—without malice. . . . No good deed went unrecorded. Everything else he rose above."[4]

AT THE VERY MOMENT Governor Faubus announced the closing of the high schools, Margaret Jackson's attorney, Kenneth Coffelt, filed a lawsuit in the Pulaski County Courthouse challenging the governor's action. Speculation ensued immediately that this was a coordinated effort designed to give Orval Faubus political cover. If the state court threw out Act 4, the bill closing the schools, Faubus could say he had done all he could within the guidelines of state law. In the meantime, the raising of the constitutional question in a state court "thwarted a direct federal court challenge of the law."[5]

The opposition to Faubus also began to organize. That same day one of Little Rock's most revered and influential citizens, seventy-six-year-old Adolphine Fletcher Terry, Vassar College, class of 1902, telephoned Vivion Brewer, Smith College, class of 1921, and said "Are you ready to do something about Little Rock, Vivion?" Within a matter of days the two women and a young ally, Velma Powell, wife of Central High vice principal J. O. Powell, had assembled fifty-eight women in the parlor of Mrs. Terry's antebellum mansion (under the portrait of her father in his Confederate uniform), and organized the Women's Emergency Committee to Open Our Schools. The WEC soon announced its intention to act "in any emergency that might develop where a voice should be heard in the jungle of doubt, suspicion and fear which has plagued the citizens of Little Rock from the time Governor Faubus called out the National Guard to keep Negro children from attending Central High School." Faubus was chagrined by this voice raised in protest against his policies, but initially he did not expect the opposition of a few women to amount to much.[6]

As Harry Ashmore soon editorialized, "the showdown" had come in Little Rock. Governor Faubus thought the ball was now in the court of the federal government. School Board member Dr. William G. Cooper thought the next move was up to the governor. NAACP spokesmen said they were waiting for the Justice Department to act before acting themselves. According to a reporter for a national wire service, the best legal talent of the Justice Department was "divided on whether the Government has the authority to order the schools opened or to pronounce their closing a violation of the Supreme Court order."[7]

Governor Faubus felt himself to be extremely vulnerable. Recognizing the federal government's power, and having tasted it just a year before, he announced that "any effort on the part of U.S. deputy marshals to force integration of local high schools would be met by a 'cold fury' from the people." Faubus did not think the government had any legal right "to stop me from closing the Little Rock high schools," but a local stringer for the *Christian Science Monitor* reported that Faubus's intimates had indicated the governor was "prepared to go to jail if necessary" to support the mandate the people of Arkansas had given him in the recent election. Wesley Pruden reported that he, Amis Guthridge, and the governor were all in danger of being arrested, but Assistant U.S. Attorney General Malcolm Wilkey, then in Little Rock, branded these reports "nonsense."[8]

The Little Rock School Board ultimately made the next move, canceling football, band, and all other extracurricular activities associated with the high schools. To the city's legions of sports fans this was a sacrilege, especially since the Central High Tigers had dominated the state since 1951. The outcry was immediate, and Governor Faubus soon told reporters, "Blossom and his advisers did this in a war of psychology or a cold war . . ." and it was "a cruel and unnecessary blow to school children." The governor also charged the School Board with trying to turn public sentiment against him. If so, the board may have succeeded, for as an official of the Southern Regional Council soon reported, "There is a growing ground-swelling . . . to re-open the closed high

schools, even on a desegregated basis." After just one missed practice the School
Board reversed itself and reinstated football. Ironically, although the high
schools remained closed all year, a team from the darkened Little Rock Central
High went on to place second in the state championship.[9]

IT WOULD BE A very strange year. Faubus claimed that under an 1875 state
law, the vacant school buildings could be declared "surplus property" and then
leased to a private corporation for use as a "private" school complete with
equipment and teachers. School Board members worried that if they entered
into such a lease, the federal government would find them in contempt of the
court's orders to desegregate. They also worried that such a "private" school
would lose the school district's prized accreditation from the North Central
Association. Their lawyers advised them that the governor's proposed plan
would not stand up in court, and that they should seek the approval of Federal
District Judge John Miller before they entered into any such arrangement.[10]

Following the dictates of Act 4, Faubus had scheduled a referendum to let
Little Rock's citizens decide whether to keep the schools closed or reopen them
on an integrated basis. He now changed the date for that election from October 7 to September 27. Faubus denied he was responding to community pressure to reopen the schools, although 3,470 teenagers were at home and at loose
ends. The School Board found itself deluged with telephone calls from anxious
parents trying to make provisions for their children's education, as very few
children had succeeded in transferring to other schools in the county. At length
Dale Alford came up with the idea of teaching classes on television. Three of the
Little Rock television stations agreed to donate two hours a day, five days a
week, and some of Little Rock's best high school teachers started new careers in
front of the cameras.[11]

On September 17 the Little Rock Private School Corporation received a
charter from the state. Wiley Branton announced immediately his organization's intention to fight any attempt to transfer or lease public school property to this corporation. The next night Governor Faubus addressed a statewide
television audience to explain his plan for educating the children of Little
Rock.[12]

Faubus reminded his listeners that the School Board had admitted in Judge
Lemley's court it could not operate the schools well if they were integrated. He
then explained his proposal to lease the schools to the Little Rock Private School
Corporation, arguing that under the provisions of an 1875 Arkansas law and
the recently adopted Acts 4 and 5, the corporation could operate the formerly

public schools privately and segregated at state expense. Claiming his plan was lawful and even the Supreme Court had not ruled against it, Faubus crowed, "advocates of the so-called 'law of the land' can have no objection. . . ." The justices of the Supreme Court were at that moment in the process of crafting their written opinion in *Cooper v. Aaron,* and they were listening.[13]

IN THE WEEK BETWEEN the governor's televised speech and the school-closing election, the Women's Emergency Committee shifted into high gear. The WEC's progressive founding triumvirate realized very quickly they could not attract a membership if they openly espoused desegregation, and they made a crucial tactical adjustment to argue only for "open schools." Issuing the organization's first public statement, Vivion Brewer, newly elected president, informed voters that according to the rules governing the September 27 election, a majority of all registered voters (and not just a majority of those actually voting) would be necessary if the schools were to be reopened. Even worse, citizens wishing to vote for open schools would have to mark their ballots "For Integration," and the ballot was worded to suggest that such a vote would lead to complete and immediate (as opposed to partial and gradual) integration of *all* public schools, not just the high schools. The WEC statement said there was no possible way for schools to be opened on a private basis without sacrificing "all federal aid, school lunch programs, accreditation, interscholastic athletic competition and eligibility for college scholarships." Signed by Vivion Brewer, who lived outside the school district and had no children, Miss Ada May Smith, who had no children, and Mrs. Woodbridge Morris, whose children attended private schools outside Arkansas, the statement handed Orval Faubus and other WEC detractors an immediate basis for criticism.[14]

In their next public statement just three days later, the women reported they had already outgrown their downtown headquarters (ironically located on the ground floor of the seedy and disreputable Capital Hotel where women of a less exalted calling plied their trade), they had had three hundred offers of assistance from interested women, and they had named a "Steering Committee" that included several women with children in the public schools. Interestingly, while they presented themselves to the public as a "white-only" group and had no black members, they were actually engaged in a biracial effort. As a confidential report of the Arkansas Council on Human Relations made clear, "Negro women and churches raised money for the Committee; local Negro leaders used the Committee's material to rally voters. . . . This is promising for the future, though many of the group are unprepared for genuine integration."[15]

272   TURN AWAY THY SON

At this point Congressman Brooks Hays's son, Steele Hays, a young Little Rock attorney, persuaded sixty-two of his colleagues to sign a statement to be published in both local newspapers, questioning the legality of Governor Faubus's plan. This was the first instance of influential citizens, the community's traditional leadership, speaking out publicly against any of Faubus's maneuvers since the crisis began in September of 1957. This public statement both required a level of courage and reflected a measure of frustration that had remained unexpressed prior to this point. Saying simply that integration was "distasteful" but that the absence of public schools was even more unacceptable, the statement declared the attorneys' considered opinion "that existing public school facilities of this District cannot be legally operated with any public funds as segregated private schools and consequently that the real issue before the voters of this District on September 27, 1958 will be whether we shall open our schools under the Court approved plan of limited integration or close them altogether. . . ." The statement did not advocate desegregation and did not instruct voters how to vote; it simply informed them that Orval Faubus's planned lease arrangement could not withstand a court challenge.[16]

ON SEPTEMBER 23, the Little Rock School Board members petitioned Federal District Judge John E. Miller to advise them what they should do in the event of a vote to keep the schools closed in the September 27 election. Speaking for the board, Richard Butler declared its willingness to lease the public school property to the Little Rock Private School Corporation if such a course of action would not place it in contempt of court. In Washington, D.C., the *Washington Post* carried a banner headline declaring that the Little Rock School Board planned to approach Judge Miller for instructions. The same day the Supreme Court justices met to discuss their third draft of *Cooper v. Aaron*.[17]

Wiley Branton understood that his Little Rock lawsuit was rapidly becoming the test case for the implementation of *Brown,* and since the Supreme Court had ruled in his favor he was determined to force the School Board to proceed with desegregation. On September 24 he went into Judge Miller's court in Fort Smith armed with a motion challenging the board's right to participate in Governor Faubus's "private" school plan. Branton had the strong backing of the Justice Department, which entered the case as *amicus curiae.*[18]

The government's brief argued that the Faubus plan, which it identified as the School Board plan, was filled with "sham and artifice" and that it would be "an evasion of and in violation of the existing orders of this Court as confirmed by the Supreme Court." In describing the federal government's case to President

Eisenhower, Attorney General Rogers wrote, "You will notice that the courts consistently have held that a state may not use a private corporation or private person as a subterfuge for conducting public business to avoid the orders of the Court."[19]

Judge Miller faced a real dilemma. An ambitious, lifelong politician, he knew his political future rested largely in the hands of Senator John McClellan, who had just spent the summer trying to create an additional seat on the Eighth Circuit Court of Appeals for Miller. McClellan had also been speaking out at every opportunity against the Supreme Court and the *Brown* decisions, and he certainly expected Judge Miller to rule in favor of schemes to protect segregation. Miller had bailed out once before when the Little Rock school situation had become politically untenable. Now that he was the only federal judge in Arkansas, he was stuck. Predictably, he did what politicians often do in such circumstances: he waffled.[20]

After sleeping on it for a night, Judge Miller rendered an opinion. He said he lacked the authority to make a ruling since the case involved determining the constitutionality of state laws (Acts 4 and 5), and only a three-judge court could act in such a case. He also suggested that the School Board found itself in the dilemma of "not complying with an order of the court when [it] was prevented from doing so by another court of equal or concurrent jurisdiction or legislation . . . ," clearly suggesting that Arkansas laws might take precedence over federal court rulings. He dismissed the petitions of both the Little Rock School Board and the NAACP, thereby stripping the School Board of any acceptable excuse for not cooperating with Governor Faubus. Wiley Branton immediately began preparations to challenge Judge Miller's decision in the Eighth Circuit Court of Appeals.[21]

THE NIGHT BEFORE the school-closing referendum, the Women's Emergency Committee sponsored a televised panel discussion featuring Bishop Robert R. Brown of the Episcopal Church, Bishop Paul Martin of the Methodist Church, Reverend Dale Cowling, pastor of Second Baptist Church, and Reverend T. B. Hay, pastor of Pulaski Heights Presbyterian Church. Presaging a later generation's question, "What Would Jesus Do?" Bishop Brown asked his listeners, "If Christ were voting tomorrow . . . how do you think He would vote?" Bishop Martin pointed out that for most of Little Rock's youngsters "it's now or never, if they are to have an education."[22]

Dr. Dale Alford, the lone Faubus disciple on the Little Rock School Board, also took to the airwaves by paying for a spot. Obliquely attacking the Women's

Emergency Committee by suggesting the members lived in the Hall High School district and therefore had not been asked to integrate, Alford also attacked Harry Ashmore, Virgil Blossom, and the NAACP. Alford argued that the NAACP had made Little Rock's blacks the pawns of an international conspiracy, and he warned of the dangers of communism. An accomplished speaker with a deep, resonant voice (he had worked as a radio commentator in college), a handsome man with an elegant manner and impeccable social credentials, Alford was an impressive advocate for the governor's plan. He concluded his speech by saying, ". . . I am proud that I have the American privilege of voting in tomorrow's election, and I will vote for SEGREGATION."[23]

Orval Faubus and some of his key advisers watched the evening's television fare at the Governor's Mansion. After Alford finished his speech, Claude Carpenter, who had considered running against Brooks Hays in the November election until Faubus had asked him not to, commented to the governor, "He could beat Brooks Hays." Faubus agreed. The next morning, on his own initiative Carpenter called Alford and suggested he should run for Congress against Hays in November.[24]

THE DAY OF THE school-closing referendum, Harry Ashmore ran a front-page editorial and opened both barrels. Calling it "an election of doubtful legality" to choose whether or not to adopt "a private school system of doubtful legality . . . ," Ashmore contended that a "vote FOR" was an endorsement of the Little Rock School Board's plan "for gradual and limited desegregation," the only plan that had been tested in federal court and that guaranteed "local, responsible, public control of our schools." A "vote AGAINST" would be a mandate to turn the schools over to a private organization with no responsibility to the people and for an effort to maintain segregation "in the face of certain legal attack by the United States Department of Justice."[25]

In the second-largest turnout in the city's history, even though the Razorbacks were playing in Fayetteville and many educated voters were consequently out of town, Little Rock citizens voted 19,470 to 7,561 to keep their high schools closed. (The normal turnout in school elections was five to ten thousand.) Harry Ashmore understood that Little Rock people believed their governor because "he was telling them what they wanted to hear." In the face of all the evidence to the contrary, Ashmore claimed, "they accepted Governor Faubus' word that he would find a way to give them the same schools they had before, without Negro students, and by lawful means. . . ."[26]

GOVERNOR FAUBUS announced he planned to move forward "with dispatch" to open the schools. The Little Rock School Board entered into lease plan negotiations with the Little Rock Private School Corporation. Wiley Branton appealed Judge Miller's decision rejecting his petition for an injunction. Branton also said the "law was quite clear" that if the facilities were in fact leased, the institution taking them over would have to admit black students.[27]

On September 27, Wiley Branton asked the Eighth Circuit Court of Appeals to do two additional things: to enjoin the Little Rock School Board from taking any action to dispose of school property without first obtaining the court's permission; and in the event that private schools were established, to require the School Board to make provision to "secure the constitutional rights of the [Negro children] to attend Central High School and any other schools in Little Rock presently limited to white students." The second provision of this request, if granted, would have put an end to the "gradual" nature of the Blossom Plan. The very next day, a Sunday, the Eighth Circuit appointed a two-judge panel to hear the NAACP request on the following day, Monday, September 29.[28]

The extraordinary speed with which all of these maneuvers took place reflected the Eighth Circuit judges' determination to foil Faubus's plans and prevent Little Rock's schools from being reopened on a segregated basis. That speed was also a product of Thurgood Marshall's extensive contacts with constitutional lawyers throughout the country. Even though the Eighth Circuit judges were still on vacation, Marshall was able to locate two of them, who agreed to hear Branton and Marshall "on an emergency basis." Marshall met Branton in Omaha to plead for a restraining order against the School Board.[29]

Back in Little Rock, however, the School Board members had been busy. After Wiley Branton informed them on Sunday of his intention to file for an injunction on Monday morning, they met with the board members of the Little Rock Private School Corporation at 1:30 A.M. and agreed they would lease the public school property in a public meeting at 8:30 A.M. Claude Sitton of the *New York Times* wrote from Little Rock, "It was apparent that negotiations had been hurried through so that the lease could be signed before the appeals judges heard the case." The lease, representing the culmination of Governor Faubus's plan, was executed just before the hearing started in Omaha. Sitton observed that with the exception of Alford, School Board members "seemed obviously reluctant to turn over the schools for operation under the plan . . . ," but they felt they had little choice in the matter "as a result of the desegregation election's outcome and pressure from the Governor and other advocates of the plan."[30]

Claude Sitton also learned that School Board members believed the only course left to them was to lease the properties "and let the people find out for themselves that the plan could not withstand a court challenge." In concluding the lease arrangement, a School Board representative read a prepared statement which said, in part, "The Little Rock School Board is desirous of aiding any feasible plan leading to a high school education program, although it is capable of and would prefer to operate its high schools as a part of the system of public education." But since Judge Miller had refused to advise them, and Attorney General Bennett had proclaimed the lease arrangement valid under Arkansas state law, School Board members yielded to local pressures, feeling that additional delays would further impair the education of Little Rock's children, who had already been idle for three weeks.[31]

According to the *Arkansas Democrat*, "The transaction took place in the most 'open' school board meeting in history, attended by some 40 or 50 newsmen, two boards, camera crews, attorneys and Mrs. Clyde Thomason, secretary of the Central High Mothers League." The Little Rock School Board signed the lease at 9:05 A.M., and at 3:30 P.M. the Little Rock Private School Corporation announced it would open the schools segregated the next day. The six remaining black students of the Little Rock Nine said they would "await the decision of parents and attorneys as to whether they apply for admittance to the private high schools." Governor Faubus, advised that a lease arrangement had been signed for the four closed high schools, said Little Rock's high school students would be guaranteed a complete school year "unless the federal government or the NAACP interferes." The governor also expressed the hope that if further court maneuvers ensued, the children would be allowed to stay in school while the legal problems were resolved. (The Justice Department preferred to keep the schools closed so pressure would build on Governor Faubus from within the community to abandon his schemes of evasion.)[32]

For half a day the citizens of Little Rock thought they would have schools for their children on Tuesday. Yet at three o'clock, word came through from Omaha that the Eighth Circuit Court of Appeals had issued temporary restraining orders against the School Board members and 169 other school and state personnel, barring the lease of the school property. After brief deliberations, Judges Harvey J. Johnson and Joseph W. Woodrough announced the court's decision, remarking that reopening Central High as a private segregated school would not be "in harmony with the plan this Court of Appeals has previously approved." Adding that they were not ruling on either the propriety of closing the schools or on the constitutionality of Acts 4 and 5, the judges announced a more formal hearing for October 6 in St. Louis, at which point they would consider Wiley

Branton's request for a temporary injunction against the School Board. The city of Little Rock found itself in a state of complete uncertainty and confusion, not least of all because at noon the U.S. Supreme Court had handed down its formal, written decision in the case now entitled *Cooper v. Aaron.*[33]

IDEALLY THE SUPREME Court renders its judgments based on a consideration of the facts presented to it and the law as it applies to those facts. But in September of 1958 the justices allowed their decision-making process to be influenced by factors outside the generally accepted scope of their concern. As constitutional scholar Dennis Hutchinson has written of the *Cooper* decision, ". . . day-to-day reactions at the local level substantially affected the shape and tone of the Supreme Court opinion."[34]

Justice William J. Brennan drew the assignment of drafting the opinion and then circulating it among his colleagues for their comments and revisions. Successive drafts of the opinion reflected an escalating tone of concern about the unfolding situation in Arkansas. As finally signed, the decision opened saying: "As this case reaches us it involves questions of the highest importance to the maintenance of our federal system of government. It necessarily involves a claim by the Governor and Legislature of a State that there is no duty on state officials to obey federal court orders resting on this Court's considered interpretation of the United States Constitution." Ruling in favor of the NAACP and going far beyond what Branton and Marshall had asked or expected, the justices concluded, despite their expressed sympathy for the dilemma of the School Board, "the constitutional rights of children not to be discriminated against in school admission on grounds of race or color declared by this Court in the *Brown* case can neither be nullified openly and directly by state legislators or state executives or judicial officers, nor nullified indirectly by them through evasive schemes for segregation whether attempted 'ingeniously or ingenuously.'"[35]

The recent actions of Orval Faubus and the Arkansas General Assembly caused the Supreme Court to rule in haste while in the grip of strong emotions. Focusing all of their considerable wrath on the "legislators and executive officials" they believed to be at the heart of the difficulties in Little Rock, the nine justices subordinated the stated concerns of the School Board to the larger need they perceived of suppressing the current rebellion in Arkansas. The central holding of *Cooper v. Aaron* was: "The constitutional rights of respondents are not to be sacrificed or yielded to the violence and disorder which have followed upon the actions of the Governor and Legislature." While acknowledging that "the educational progress of all the students, white and colored, of that school has suffered and will continue to suffer . . . ," and "regardless of the Board's good faith," the Court concluded that "the actions of the other state agencies responsible for those conditions compel us to reject the Board's legal position."[36]

Lest anyone mistake their meaning and continue to suggest their decisions were not the law of the land, the justices added a concluding section to their opinion that made crystal clear the sources of their authority. Article VI of the United States Constitution, they reminded Orval Faubus and his ilk, made the Constitution the "supreme Law of the Land." Furthermore, *Marbury v. Madison* had established in 1803 that "it is emphatically the province and duty of the judicial department to say what the law is." In addition, since every state official is bound by oath to support the constitution, no such official can war against the constitution without violating his oath, and a governor "who asserts a power to nullify a federal court order is similarly restrained." Finally, while admitting that "the responsibility for public education is primarily the concern of the States," this responsibility must be exercised "consistently with federal constitutional requirements as they apply to state action." In short, for the benefit of all those who were currently engaged in or contemplating engaging in the practice, the justices ruled that the doctrine of interposition was dead.[37]

Toward the end of their opinion the justices inserted a passage that was clearly inspired by the new Arkansas laws and the resultant private school corporation. "State support of segregated schools," the ruling read, "through any arrangement, management, funds, or property cannot be squared with the [fourteenth] amendment's command that no State shall deny to any person within its jurisdiction the equal protection of the laws." Concluding that the Court had "unanimously reached" the *Brown* decision "only after the case had been briefed and twice argued and the issues had been given the most serious consideration . . . ," the Court now "unanimously reaffirmed" that decision and took the unprecedented step of having all nine justices sign it individually.[38]

While it thundered the primacy of federal prerogatives, *Cooper v. Aaron* nonetheless sidestepped the issues that had brought it into court and that bedeviled local school districts across the South: What did "all deliberate speed" mean? Was a delay possible under any circumstances after a school board had made a "prompt and reasonable start" toward desegregation? How were citizen school boards to control violent opposition to their programs and finance the litigation the Court of Appeals and the solicitor general had said were their responsibility? *Were* these things the responsibility of local school boards? And most important, by what means were local school officials to preserve a meaningful educational system in the face of the active resistance to integration in their communities? Driven by the imperative to buttress its own authority, which had been severely challenged by the rise of massive resistance, the Southern Manifesto, and a recent rebuke by the Association of State Chief Justices, the Court left unanswered many of the procedural questions that plagued southern school boards in ensuing years.[39]

Wiley Branton had wisely allowed Thurgood Marshall to argue *Cooper v. Aaron* before the Supreme Court, a venue in which Marshall had had spectacular successes in the past. Now armed with the legal tools and the support of the Justice Department he needed, Branton pressed his advantage aggressively. In response, segregationists in Little Rock launched a campaign against his organization that was an acknowledgement of his newfound strength. As Dr. T. J. Raney, president of the Little Rock Private School Corporation, announced to the press on September 30, "The closing of our senior high schools is now the full responsibility of the federal government and the NAACP . . . It is quite evident that they are ready to sacrifice the educational opportunities of 4,000 students to satisfy their consuming desire to mix the races in our schools, public or private." Dr. Raney considered the restraining order "unfair and unwarranted," but he acknowledged it prevented his corporation from using the public school buildings. Shortly after making this statement, Raney admitted he had authorized the placing of signs at all four of the high school buildings which read "This School Closed by Order of the Federal Goverment [*sic*]."[40]

Within a matter of days, Arkansas Attorney General Bruce Bennett launched an attack on the NAACP that he entitled a "Southern Plan for Peace," sending his proposal to senators and representatives of fourteen southern and border states. Calling the decision in *Cooper v. Aaron* "another example of judicial legislation," Bennett argued that the rights organization was "at the heart of our racial problems" and "the only way to restore our people to peace and tranquility" was to "neutralize" the NAACP. Bennett advocated a six-point program that included withdrawing the association's tax deduction privileges, inviting prosecution on barratry charges, urging increased arrests under vagrancy and "inciting riot" statutes, encouraging economic reprisals against the association's members, enacting legislation prohibiting bonus welfare payments for each illegitimate child, and urging city councils to enact ordinances requiring "certain organizations" to disclose their membership lists, as had been done in many Arkansas communities in the fall of 1957.[41]

GOVERNOR FAUBUS STUMBLED in his first attempts to find his stride after being hit by the twin blows from the Supreme Court and the Court of Appeals, but within a matter of days he found the argument that saw him through the remainder of the crisis in Little Rock. His initial reaction was that of a fighter on the ropes. "I haven't surrendered," he sputtered. "I am not ready to surrender and I don't intend to surrender." Within a week he returned to the theme he had been stressing since January, ever since he had co-opted Jim Johnson's "troops" and his central argument. Speaking in Hot Springs, Faubus said the recent rulings of the federal courts jeopardized Arkansans' freedoms of thought, choice, and belief. "If they [the courts] can make these decisions stick, they can do so in any matters and that would be judicial tyranny."[42]

Calling the race issue just a "sidelight," Faubus said the integration controversy boiled down to a question of states' rights, or "whether the state legislatures have a right to pass laws in accordance with the will of the people of their states." Acknowledging he had never claimed his stand for segregation was right, he said he was positive it was the will of the people. By this time the Arkansas governor had received a deluge of letters from all over the United States; one estimate numbered them at thirty thousand. Reflecting the tone of many of these letters, a writer for the *Chicago Tribune* concluded, "More important in the integration decision than the emotion of color mixing is this dangerously unwarranted power of Washington." Orval Faubus had now become the standard-bearer for large numbers of people throughout the country who were alarmed by the onset of what a later generation would call "the imperial judiciary."[43]

THE SCHOOLS IN Little Rock remained in chaos. The high school teachers reported to school each day and yet found no one there to teach. The students had been out of school for almost a month, and those parents who were able to do so had begun to send their children off to live with relatives in other towns or to attend private schools in other states. The Little Rock School Board had cancelled its televised classes as soon as the federal court's restraining orders arrived in Little Rock. The Vestry of Trinity Episcopal Cathedral announced that it would develop Trinity Interim Academy for the high school students of that parish, but only until the public schools could be reopened. The Baptists soon followed suit.[44]

The Little Rock Private School Corporation initiated a search for classroom space and private funding. Speaking from the conference room adjoining Governor Faubus' office, Dr. T. J. Raney made a statement to the press, saying the federal government "must somehow be made to understand that the course they have chosen is leading our nation to destruction." Amis Guthridge and the Capital Citizens' Council rushed to the defense of Dr. Raney's private school plan. "We can raise the money to educate our children," Guthridge declared in a prepared statement. "We are not beholden to the mighty tax trough. If our would-be federal masters insist on destroying our public schools, our answer is private schools—private facilities supported by private money."[45]

Wiley Branton and the Justice Department had other ideas, and they hoped to persuade the Appeals Court it should instruct Judge Miller to press on with integration. In preparation for the hearing scheduled for October 6, all sides submitted briefs for the court's consideration. The Justice Department's *amicus curiae* brief asked the three judges to instruct Judge Miller to "enter a comprehensive injunction which will in specific terms enjoin any and all persons, whether they be public officials or private individuals or organizations to prevent them from taking any action in or out of schools which would have the effect of impairing the rights of the Negroes to attend integrated schools." This was the kind of aggressive federal posture the School Board had hoped for and expected during the fall of 1957.[46]

At the last minute, instead of ruling, the Appeals Court judges announced they had decided to postpone their decision for another week, although they left their restraining orders in force. Before the October 15 hearing Wiley Branton submitted the NAACP's brief contending that at some time the Little Rock School Board "must realize that the federal Constitution and the federal courts are supreme. . . . That time is now." Richard Butler's brief for the School Board argued that the entire case involved actions by parties not named and not required to participate, in particular, the Little Rock Private School Corporation. According to Butler, "The School Board cannot be required to litigate those questions which primarily and directly involve issues with third parties not before the Court."[47]

In the St. Louis courtroom on October 15, Wiley Branton argued "Sooner or later something will have to be said to this School Board about carrying out the orders of this court. . . . The School Board is well aware of the procedure it should follow but it has decided to go along with Governor Faubus." Thurgood Marshall asked both that the court permanently enjoin the school leasing plan and direct the School Board to carry out its original integration plan, as Federal District Judge Ronald Davies had ordered it to do on September 3, 1957. Once again the judges postponed their decision, announcing they would make a final ruling "as soon as possible," and that in the meantime their temporary restraining orders would remain in force.[48]

WHILE AWAITING THE court's decision, the Little Rock Private School Corporation struggled to get under way, but the difficulties mounted at every turn.

Following the advice of their association's attorneys, the public school teachers announced they would not teach in the private schools. Faubus claimed that the School Board was refusing to release the teachers; Dr. Cooper responded that the board had not attempted in any way to advise them. State legislator Paul Van Dalsem, of neighboring Perry County, threatened that if the School Board did not release the teachers, the Arkansas legislature would abolish the Little Rock School District entirely.[49]

On October 18, Dr. Raney announced that his school had found classroom space in the old Methodist Orphanage, and that his corporation had received $61,500 in donations. Governor Faubus hinted the private school did not intend to depend on private donations, because the legislature could be expected to sanction the transfer of funds from public to private schools. Wiley Branton promptly charged that such projected transfers of funds demonstrated the private school plan to be "merely a subterfuge, in an attempt to evade previous court orders . . . ," and he promised an immediate court test. Despite the obstacles, registration proceeded in both the corporation's school (soon to be named Raney High) and the Baptist High School, to be housed in the Education Building of the Second Baptist Church in downtown Little Rock.[50]

In the meantime, State Education Commissioner Arch Ford asked Attorney General Bruce Bennett if, in light of the federal court's restraining order, he could disburse state money to the private school under the provisions of Act 5. Bennett ruled that the State Board of Education could use the funds withheld from the closed public schools, although the idled teachers continued to be paid. Bennett assured Ford this would not violate the restraining order, and Ford began to make preparations to transfer $172.66 for each student who had transferred from the Little Rock public schools into other accredited schools in the state. The new private schools were not yet accredited, and by the time they achieved accreditation in the spring, the federal courts had blocked the distribution of state funds for transfers.[51]

ON OCTOBER 21, Brooks Hays spoke to a North Little Rock men's club and called for moderation as a means of restoring national unity. "The extremists are driving the moderates off the stage . . ." Hays charged, with a complete disregard for the fury in his district over Yankee force and federal encroachment on state prerogatives. This speech handed Dale Alford all the ammunition he needed to launch a devastating attack on Hays, and within a matter of days the Little Rock ophthalmologist took the unwary congressman completely by surprise.[52]

On October 27, Alford entered the congressional race as a write-in candidate, saying Hays was "totally ineffective." In an eight-day whirlwind campaign, the mild-mannered Hays never found his stride. In the first of three televised speeches, Alford announced his intention to attack the "left-wing Supreme Court" as well as the NAACP and the disease of socialism. Hays countered feebly, pursuing a strategy he never abandoned, attacking Alford as a member of the School Board that originated "the controversial plan" for integration in Little Rock. Alford charged that Hays had never taken a forthright stand on segregation, and Hays responded he had signed the Southern Manifesto.[53]

Hays also charged that Alford had not spoken out against integration until August of 1957, which was true. Pleading for moderation, the shaken congressman argued defiance was fruitless, and a better course would be to work diligently toward bringing about a change in the Supreme Court's interpretation of the Fourteenth Amendment, or in other words gaining a reversal of *Brown*. Hays said he had been working on a constitutional amendment "that would leave no room for question . . . that the laws and regulations governing schools shall be the prerogative solely of the states and their subdivisions." Calling Alford's write-in candidacy an "undemocratic and unprecedented attempt to defraud a congressman of the support of his party," Hays said it was "a step toward the politics of the jungle." This language was uncharacteristically harsh for Congressman Hays, suggesting he was both angry and frightened. In an amazingly bold series of factual misrepresentations, Alford claimed he had never voted for the Blossom Plan, when in fact the School Board minutes reflected the plan had been adopted at his first meeting and his signature was affixed to it. On November 1 he repeated his claim, saying, "I have never voted for any integration plan and never will . . . ," even though Hays had reproduced in the newspaper the minutes of the contested board meeting.[54]

The day before the election, the Central High Mothers' League and others of like mind passed out around the city an unsigned circular featuring a photograph of Hays seated between two black men. The obvious implication was that Hays supported integration. Actually the photograph had been taken at a Baptist conference, but Hays was blindsided by the assault and unable to formulate a response. As he said several months later, "I found myself defenseless in that tragic situation. . . ." Alford's campaign manager claimed he never authorized the circular, and subsequent probes by both the FBI and a local grand jury failed to uncover sufficient information to support an indictment.[55]

On November 4 the people of Arkansas' fifth congressional district elected Dr. Dale Alford their new representative by a bare majority of one thousand votes. As *Arkansas Gazette* reporter Roy Reed assessed the situation at the time, Alford had convinced the people a moderate approach could lead only to integration. The election had sparked little interest among a people who were approaching emotional exhaustion, and toward the end of the race Hays sensed he was going to lose. As he recalled, "I saw friends walk across the street to keep from meeting me and shaking hands, old friends." Brooks Hays had failed completely to comprehend the depth of frustration and rage in his district, and he had lost touch with the concerns of his political base. Not until a year later could he see clearly enough to write, "In voting against me, I feel that many people were really voting against any assertion whatever of Federal authority in Little Rock School matters."[56]

Alford called his victory "an expression from the hearts of the people for the preservation of our American traditions and ideals, the maintenance of states' rights, and the sincere desire through legislative processes to curtail the illegal powers assumed by the United States Supreme Court." As Harry Ashmore analyzed the situation, "the voters apparently wanted a man who would shout their own frustration and defiance—and damn the consequences if he also turned out to be the most impotent figure in national politics, a freshman congressman who may not even be seated in the controlling Democratic caucus."[57]

Brooks Hays soon admitted candidly he was relieved to be out from under the pressure of representing a divided district, saying, "I feel like a great load has been lifted off my shoulders. . . ." He said years later, "I have to admit that I was tired of that effort and struggle. I felt that I wanted to step aside." Upon his return to Washington he held the largest press conference of his career. As television newsman Edward P. Morgan described it, "Almost to a man, reporters who crowded his office clambered forward to shake his hand afterwards, leaving their standard shield of cynicism behind. . . ."[58]

At this press conference, Hays told one of his signature funny stories, retiring from the limelight in the manner that had endeared him to so many constituents and colleagues. "My daddy, who is 86," Hays began, "once told me about a friend who was critically injured" when a donkey kicked him in the head. When the doctor examined the wound and told the old fellow he was going to die, the farmer pleaded to be kept alive long enough to let pneumonia set in, because "I sure do hate to have it written on my tombstone that I was killed by a jackass. . . ." Years later it pleased Hays to report that Chet Huntley and David Brinkley closed their telecast that night with the story about the old farmer, and Huntley was laughing so hard he could not say goodnight.[59]

Soon Hays launched a new initiative, explaining to an old friend, "I have at least preserved an audience outside the south that I shall try to use to save us from those who would violate the principles in which you and I believe." This idea of a "forum outside Arkansas" had become an ongoing Hays project. The *Arkansas Baptist* soon reported, "The editor of a Baptist publication has suggested that the Democratic party seriously consider Rep. Brooks Hays of Arkansas for its 1960 vice president nomination." Hays maintained that he had no political ambitions and that he planned to devote his energies to his work as president of the Southern Baptist Convention. Careful perusal of the Brooks Hays Papers, however, reveals many similar instances in which the congressman tried to plant ideas to benefit himself, without leaving telltale fingerprints.[60]

Congressman John A. Blatnik of Minnesota announced his intention to oppose Dale Alford's seating as a Democrat, and thereafter for many months he challenged Alford's legitimacy on grounds of upholding party loyalty. Arkansas Congressman Wilbur Mills rose to Alford's defense, saying he would fight Blatnik and help seat Hays's successor. In an effort to avoid a party split along sectional lines, Speaker Sam Rayburn joined the effort to defend Alford's bid for legitimacy, and even Hays ultimately assisted in helping to resolve the controversy. Hays was off now on an exciting adventure, and for the next two years he basked in his new role as the standard-bearer for the moderates.[61]

EVEN AS THE SWEET taste of victory lingered, the arch-segregationists soon had to wonder if they had overindulged in their defiant reaction to federal mandates. First the Women's Emergency Committee released a series of pamphlets, in its first public statement since the September 27 referendum, which Vivion Brewer said were designed to "inform the community of the urgency" of reopening the schools. Quoting the Governor's Advisory Committee on Education describing the public schools as "the cornerstone of our social, economic and political structure . . . ," the women charged that three of the "best high schools in the country" stood empty while "inadequate, makeshift schools" were substituted and "begging letters" were sent nationwide. Next the Arkansas Education Association, under the leadership of Brooks Hays stalwart and liberal churchman Forrest Rozzell, passed a resolution calling for the preservation of the public schools.[62]

Governor Faubus pledged to continue the fight against integration, promising never to open the high schools integrated "unless the people say so." Describing himself as neither a segregationist nor an integrationist, Faubus contended he was fighting for states' rights. He also told reporters he had received many requests to run for vice president, and it is true that before another month had passed the Gallup polling organization had listed him as number seven among rank-and-file Democrats as the choice for president in 1960. The governor became actively engaged in helping the Little Rock Private School Corporation solicit funds, speaking around the country on its behalf and signing his name to its appeals for donations.[63]

DALE ALFORD'S VICTORY had seemed to the harried Little Rock School Board members to be a clear vote of "no confidence" in their leadership. They decided to resign. Before announcing their decision, however, they invited leaders from the Chamber of Commerce to join them for dinner and revealed their intention. The incoming Chamber president, Grainger Williams, immediately convened a meeting of C of C leaders "in order to organize a slate of candidates to oppose the segregationists who were running to fill Board vacancies."[64]

Settling finally upon a strategy of asking the presidents of each of the six local banks to stand for election, Chamber leaders were stunned when two of the bankers turned them down flat and the others expressed their fears of losing east Arkansas depositors to Memphis. Several of the bank presidents even suggested that the situation was going to have to deteriorate further before Little Rock people came to their senses and decided to "accept the inevitable." At length Adolphine Terry used her influence to arrange a slate of four businessmen and one PTA mother to run against the segregationist candidates for the School Board. Mrs. Terry and the businessmen decided not to struggle to find a sixth candidate to oppose Ed I. McKinley, a former head of the state banking department who was an outspoken segregationist, because "he was a lawyer and a member of the country club, so we thought he would not cause any trouble." That decision turned out to be a serious miscalculation.[65]

ON NOVEMBER 10 the three-judge panel of the Eighth Circuit Court of Appeals finally handed down its opinion in the case Wiley Branton had filed twenty-seven days before. Whereas Branton had asked only for an injunction against the Little Rock School Board, prohibiting it from leasing its property to the private school corporation, and for the preservation of the black children's constitutional right to have equal protection under the law, the Eighth Circuit judges directed John Miller to order the School Board to "take such affirmative steps as the District Court may hereafter direct to facilitate and accomplish" integration in the Little Rock School District. The court was taking on executive responsibility, and threatening to manage the school system by proxy. The judges also outlawed the School Board's plan for leasing the high schools. In a passage that must have been particularly galling to the members of the Little Rock School Board, the Eighth Circuit judges said that under previous court orders, the School Board and the superintendent had an obligation to act on their own initiative to accomplish integration, which is what that board had attempted to do with the Blossom Plan.[66]

The judges were especially critical of the School Board for cooperating with the private school venture, saying its actions had worked to "allay most of the parental clamor and pressure" that could have been expected to help force a reopening of the public schools. They also charged that School Board members had known they were enabling the Little Rock Private School Corporation to receive state funds for segregation, and since *Cooper v. Aaron* had outlawed such "evasive schemes" the board's actions were "improper and unlawful." Finally, the judges vacated John Miller's order dismissing Branton's request for an injunction, ruling that Miller had been in error to suggest he did not have the authority to make a decision in the case. It was an unalloyed victory for Wiley Branton.[67]

One of the primary legacies of the Little Rock crisis was its crippling of the strategy of massive resistance. A part of that strategy had been to keep resistance sufficiently under the radar screen of court enforcement to avoid detection. The architects of massive resistance had hoped to be able to sustain their resolve and their recalcitrant activities long enough to convince the nation that *Brown* was unenforceable. Instead, Orval Faubus's headlong plunge into the spotlight left the federal judiciary little choice but to act in defense of its own prerogatives. In the process the courts demanded more sweeping changes than they might otherwise have been inclined to attempt.[68]

IN A SPECIAL MEETING the night of November 12, all of the members of the Little Rock School Board except Dale Alford announced their intention to resign immediately, as well as to buy up Virgil Blossom's remaining contract. As one press account described the scene, "Blossom, his forehead beaded in sweat, sat at one end of the table nervously smoking a cigarette. He and the rest of the Board members were bathed in the brightness of the newsreel floodlights." Alford objected vigorously to paying Blossom for services he would not render to the school district, asking, "On what grounds are you terminating the contract?" Brick Lile answered, "For no cause." Harold Engstrom interjected: "To the best interest of the School District." Wayne Upton added, "Through no fault of his own." The elegant New England aristocrat and former board president Willie Cooper turned to Alford and remarked, "In the first place, Dale, we hired him [Blossom]. In the second place he's worked for and with us. I feel he's our responsibility, and I feel we should deal with him fairly. It would be ungentlemanly to do otherwise." The board motion carried five-to-one, as most motions had done over the previous year. Amis Guthridge filed a lawsuit the next day challenging the board's payment to Blossom of the twenty thousand dollars outstanding on his contract, calling it a "fraud" and "collusion."[69]

Wayne Upton told a reporter the School Board resigned because they were "tired of being Governor Orval Faubus' whipping boys." The harried Upton said Faubus had identified him and the others as an "integration School Board," and the governor had "used us to win or help win three elections." As Upton explained, "All members of this Board are segregationists in feeling. But we are confronted with the problem of enforcing the law." In the days to come, the retiring School Board members received many letters thanking them for their service to the community, but Harold Engstrom often said in succeeding years, ". . . the only thing we did that pleased everybody was the day we resigned." As Harry Ashmore editorialized, those citizens who were shocked when the board resigned should not have been; after all, the community's leaders had remained silent for over a year and had offered no effective support "at any critical juncture." After years of dedicated service the repudiated School Board members retired from the field bearing scars that never healed. In the future, Little Rock found it increasingly difficult to recruit people to serve in these posts from among the community's leadership.[70]

The deadline for filing to run for the vacant School Board posts was Saturday, November 15, three days after the Blossom School Board resigned. Little Rock buzzed with activity as competing factions shaped up to vie for the leadership of the beleaguered school district. The "businessmen's slate" of candidates, headed by former Chamber of Commerce executive Everett Tucker, announced they believed in segregation and would not "voluntarily integrate the Little Rock public schools." They also said they would "never initiate any action to implement or expedite integration." They did, however, propose to preserve the integrity and stability of the public school system. Either they had not been paying close attention to the new demands of the federal courts, or they were living in a dream world. Harry Ashmore had been right when he predicted the week before that this election would undoubtedly bring "another endorsement to continued resistance to the orders of the courts," and that there was little prospect "that any alternative will be seriously debated in the campaign." While the city prepared for the third election of the fall, Dr. Raney announced the Little Rock Private School Corporation had received a total of

$225,000 in donations, and Judge Miller announced he was awaiting the mandate from the Eighth Circuit Court of Appeals instructing him how to proceed in the school case.[71]

AFTER THREE MONTHS of idleness, the five remaining black students eligible to attend Central High School (Terrence Roberts and Gloria Ray had left the city) started working with tutors and enrolled together to take correspondence courses through the University of Arkansas; the expenses were to be paid by the national office of the NAACP, which had decided it needed these children to stay in Little Rock. As one of the national officers explained in response to an inquiry, "Obviously if the Negro students currently enrolled in Central High School should leave the state for education elsewhere, there would presumably be no immediate reason why the high school could not be re-opened on an all-white basis." In light of this decision, Daisy Bates chose not to tell the five children that scholarship opportunities were available to them to attend schools elsewhere. National NAACP Executive Director Roy Wilkins spoke in Little Rock early in November and argued that blacks could not start private schools, because this was "exactly what we have been fighting against. . . . we would be betraying the nine Negro children who went through hell last year to go to Little Rock Central High School."[72]

Wilkins also described Orval Faubus as a "valuable enemy" who "fell on his face" and aroused millions to the cause of black civil rights. Wilkins told an enthusiastic and appreciative audience that Faubus had helped clarify several issues, such as destroying the utility of interposition as a strategy, highlighting the courage of the Little Rock Nine, and forcing the state legislature and the Little Rock School Board to act in such a way as to bring forth "the inclusive ruling" of the United States Supreme Court that "evasive schemes for segregation" cannot nullify orders of the court. Wilkins wished for Faubus's good health, so he could come out "on the odd-numbered days with new plans to replace those which did not work on the even-numbered days."[73]

IN MID-OCTOBER OF 1958, the *Arkansas Gazette* reported the rumor that the previous year the Faubus administration had offered Wiley Branton a deal if he would quit the integration fight. The Associated Press quoted Branton as saying, "I could have been the first Negro assistant attorney general of Arkansas if I had used my influence to get Governor Faubus off the hook through a cooling-off period. . . ." Branton immediately denied the story, saying Faubus and Bruce Bennett did not make the offers, "though certain offers have been made to me by other parties." Branton had made reference to this incident in a speech in West Virginia, and it is entirely likely the journalist who reported it misunderstood Branton's message. In fact it was probably Osro Cobb or other members of the Justice Department who offered the young NAACP lawyer a plum when they were trying to pressure him into withdrawing his clients' case in September of 1957.[74]

Whatever the truth, the fact that the story was reported in Little Rock at the very moment Branton was pushing his advantage against the School Board escalated the severe harassment he and his family had to endure. Yet he did not falter in his relentless assault on the sources of white privilege in Little Rock. Like L. C. and Daisy Bates, like the Little Rock Nine, Wiley Branton stayed the course, refusing to back down. Through their courage, their sacrifice, and especially their unyielding persistence, these black leaders and children forced their nation to take giant steps toward making real for black Americans the promise of equal protection under the law.[75]

CHAPTER FIFTEEN

THE WOMEN ORGANIZE
Vivion Brewer

V IVION BREWER DREW STRENGTH FROM THE ETERNAL STILLNESS
that embraced her at Bearskin Lake, a refuge she had chosen in her flight
from the demands of an upper-class, southern, female life. In her daily retreat
to the plantation world at Scott, where cotton fields stretched across the flat,
rich land as far as the eye could see, and where the existence side by side of privileged white gentility and mind-numbing black poverty often challenged her
certainty that the twentieth century had arrived, the fifty-seven-year-old Brewer
reviewed the circumstances and choices that had placed her at the white-hot
center of one of the most troubling episodes in her nation's history.

Born to a bank president and a society matron, young Vivion Lenon enjoyed
a traditional southern upbringing in Little Rock, although her parents had
migrated to Arkansas from Iowa. With her two siblings she reaped the rewards
of being the child of a prominent man (Warren Lenon had at one point been
mayor of Little Rock), living in a comfortable home, and relaxing at the
family's summer cottage on the edge of the Arkansas delta. Unlike her siblings,
however, the quiet, studious Vivion went east after high school, graduating with
the class of 1921 from prestigious Smith College in Northampton, Massachusetts. After college she traveled through Europe with a friend for fourteen
months, another departure from accepted southern norms, and then refused to
make her debut upon her return to Little Rock. She did, however, join the Junior
League, although she also went to work in her father's bank. Reveling in his
daughter's intelligence and undoubtedly delighted to offer her the opportunities he had not had himself, Warren Lenon sent Vivion to law school at night in
Little Rock to learn the intricacies of trust operations. When she became a vice
president of The Peoples Bank, a forerunner of Little Rock's First National
Bank, even the *New York Times* found this development sufficiently newswor-
thy to publish an announcement of her promotion.[1]

In all these ways Vivion Brewer challenged prevailing notions of acceptable behavior for a southern lady, even signing her name at the bank V. M. Lenon "so that people would think I was a man." But Brewer also "always wanted to marry and have a family . . . ," and so when handsome, dapper Joe Robinson Brewer crossed her path at the Democratic National Convention in 1928, where his uncle and boss, Arkansas Senator and Senate Majority Leader Joe T. Robinson, received the Democratic nomination for vice president on a ticket with Al Smith, Vivion fell in love. She married and followed her new husband to Washington, where she was stricken with a thyroid condition that necessitated eight years of quiet convalescence, during which she lost a baby. When Joe went overseas to serve in World War II, the slim, demure, doe-eyed Vivion returned to Arkansas to care for her aging, widowed father, and they decided to live in the summer cottage at Bearskin Lake.[2]

After the war, the Brewers settled into the lakeside home and began to notice for the first time the "feudal" conditions of the plantation life that surrounded them. Vivion refused to join the bridge clubs and church activities that defined the lives of most white women in Scott's plantation community, focusing her energies instead on winterizing the old cottage and teaching a few neighboring black children to read. Her choices rendered her an "outsider," as she had elected to be most of her life; she was not popular, but the attainment of popularity had never been one of her goals.[3]

When the Little Rock crisis broke in the fall of 1957, the sensitive Vivion's "anxiety over the 'place' of the Negro in the American way of life" heightened to the point that it "drove me to a state of illness." Convinced that Orval Faubus had engineered the situation for his own political gain, sick at heart over the damage to the city her father had helped build, and fearful of the wider, international implications of the worsening impasse, Vivion responded eagerly when in September of 1958 Adolphine Terry called and invited her to "do something" about Little Rock. The two women launched a movement that, in combination with other moderating forces, brought the Little Rock crisis to an end.[4]

Well into her seventies, Adolphine Fletcher Terry was an institution in Little Rock. Descended from two prominent Arkansas families, wife of a former United States congressman, sister of the poet laureate of Arkansas (who was also one of the Nashville "Agrarians"), Adolphine Terry had returned from Vassar in 1902 determined *not* to be a southern lady and then had spent her long life doing good things for the city and state she loved. Through fifty years of volunteering her time and her considerable means, the indefatigable Adolphine had, in addition to having four children, helped create the Little Rock Public Library, the Phyllis Wheatley (black) YWCA, the Pulaski County Juvenile Court Board, the Pulaski County Tuberculosis Association, the Little Rock branch of the American Association of University Women, the Women's City Club, the Family Service Agency, the Salvation Army, the Museum of Fine Arts, and Little Rock's Symphony Orchestra. One of her best friends recalled in the 1990s that Adolphine's devotion to Arkansas had been so strong she had described her state as "holy ground."[5]

Horrified by the actions of her governor in 1957, which she believed he had pursued purely for political gain, the outspoken Mrs. Terry at first despaired. As she recalled in her autobiography, dictated at the age of ninety-one, "For almost fifty years, our family had worked for better race relations, and so much had been quietly accomplished. I felt as if my life had been in vain; I really wanted to die." Composing herself at length, Mrs. Terry made quiet inquiries among the Central High teachers and learned of the relentless persecution of the black children. She then made a date to visit Alta Faubus, for whom she had given a party when the new governor first moved to Little Rock, imploring the governor's wife to try to sway her husband away from the course he was pursuing. Alta Faubus explained that would not be possible.[6]

In September 1958, Adolphine Terry received a letter from Velma Powell, wife of J. O. Powell, Central High School's vice principal for boys. Velma had lived with the Terrys years before while she attended school, and now she implored the older woman to act. "In the past," Powell wrote, "whenever problems have had to be faced in Little Rock, you have taken a lead in solving them. Why are you silent now?" Stung into action, Mrs. Terry invited Velma Powell and Vivion Brewer to her home to plan a crusade. Shortly after noon on September 12, the Friday the Supreme Court handed down its initial findings in *Cooper v. Aaron,* the three women met in Mrs. Terry's parlor and decided to announce a meeting for the following Tuesday, daring to hope twenty-five women would come. Mrs. Terry then put on her hat and gloves and went to see the young editor of the *Arkansas Gazette.*[7]

Sitting across the desk from Harry Ashmore in the only visit to the *Gazette* building he later recalled her ever making, the formidable, unassailable older woman announced to the man who was half her age, "Mr. Ashmore, I am disappointed in the men of Little Rock. It's clear to me that the men are not going to take the lead in turning this thing around and so the women are going to have to." Warming to her subject, Terry continued, "I'm issuing a call this afternoon. I'm going to call all the ladies down from Pulaski Heights, and from the Junior

League, and we're going to put the ladies to work on bringing this crisis to an end. And, of course, I assume that the *Gazette* is going to support me in this." As one of her many admirers recalled of her tactics, "She called in every I.O.U. that she had put out all through the years, and naturally a woman who has been this active and this intelligent and this much of a leader has many I.O.U.'s. . . . So she gathered them all in, and really held [people's] feet to the fire."[8]

ALL THROUGH THE weekend the three ladies made phone calls inviting women to attend the meeting at Mrs. Terry's home. Initially they had thought in terms of an educational effort much like that conducted by the 1930s Association of Southern Women for the Prevention of Lynching, and Mrs. Terry had been in touch with the Southern Regional Council to gather information about the earlier women's activities. At approximately the same time as Mrs. Terry sat in Harry Ashmore's office, however, Governor Faubus signed the legislation that had laid dormant on his desk for two weeks, closing the four high schools. Reading their newspapers on Saturday morning, Little Rock parents were aghast to find that schools slated to open on Monday would remain closed for another month. Three days later the young women filed down in droves from the Heights, and Mrs. Terry's two front parlors overflowed.[9]

One of the young mothers who signed in at the Terry mansion that day felt a sense of awe in the grande dame's presence, later describing the experience: "Adolphine Terry, dignified and patrician, her wispy, white hair drawn back in a bun at her neck, was dressed in a printed dress that looked like it could have, and probably did, come off the rack at Blass's, one of the town's two department stores whose building she owned." Despite her unimposing sartorial choices, however, the older woman carried the day with the young mothers. "Behind her glasses," Sara Murphy recalled, "her eyes were full of good humor and she had a whimsical smile as though she was about to share some intriguing secret with us. What came through as she spoke, along with her warmth, was a clarity about how she felt and about her intention to act. She was what I wanted to be—clear on the issues, tenacious and fearless, but with plenty of good common sense."[10]

Two issues in particular seemed clear to Terry, Brewer, and Powell. One was the need for integration. As Terry recalled years later, "Of course, few people wanted integration, but it was here and it was right." And as Vivion Brewer shared with an interviewer a decade after the crisis, "Not very many people knew that our great concern was civil rights. This came before the school situation in our minds." Velma Powell at that time was serving as secretary of the

Arkansas Council on Human Relations, the Southern Regional Council-sponsored agency developed explicitly to help implement desegregation.[11]

The other issue that the organizers saw with clarity was the need for the women, in the face of male timidity and failure, to step outside their accustomed roles as supporters of male opinion. Strong-willed women who had little patience with men (or anyone) who did not share their point of view, women of independent means who did not have to consider the economic consequences of their actions, highly intelligent women—accustomed to being heard—who felt a great disdain for those who did not see the moral issues as clearly as they did, Terry and Brewer felt tremendous irritation with the men in their community for failing to lead a crusade against the segregationists and Governor Faubus. They dismissed as inconsequential all previous efforts the School Board and the civic elite had made to resolve the crisis through legal channels and through traditional, paternalistic patterns of deference.[12]

Young Sara Murphy, who shared from the outset the older women's commitment to integration, wrote of that first meeting in Mrs. Terry's home: "The sadness of all our Southern pasts hung suspended like cobwebs in its rooms. By coming together as women, we could perhaps sweep them out of our lives and out of the life of our community." Most of the women who came to that first meeting, however, were there because of their desire to get the schools reopened, not because they were committed to integration. Even Mrs. Terry admitted years later the limits of her group's commitment to social justice. "If people had asked any of us if we were for integration," she wrote in her memoir, "we would probably have told them no, we hadn't come to that point yet. But we were for integrating the schools because there had never been enough money in Arkansas for one good school system, let alone two."[13]

Mrs. Terry addressed the group in her parlors, explaining the need for community education about improved race relations. Outlining briefly the history of the Association of Southern Women for the Prevention of Lynching, she proposed that the women develop such a group "to combat the forces destroying the peaceful progress of race relations and threatening the welfare of our city." She then nominated Vivion Brewer for the chairmanship of the group and turned the meeting over to her.[14]

As Brewer began to outline plans for contacting Negro women who shared the group's convictions, a few women slipped quietly out of the house. When she suggested inviting the celebrated black singer Marian Anderson to Little Rock for a concert, several more women vanished. Suddenly a young woman leapt from her chair in the back of the room and interrupted, saying, "This is all very fine, but what are we going to do now, *now?* My two boys must have an education and they have already lost two weeks of school. I think we have to do something now to open our schools." It was the spark that created the Women's Emergency Committee to Open Our Schools (WEC). By the next day the new organization began issuing statements to the newspapers in support of a vote for public schools.[15]

Almost as quickly, the leaders of the WEC realized they would have to distance themselves from any hint of support for integration if they were to win a wide public following. Mrs. Terry had tried to explain her thinking to Daisy Bates, asking her to stay away from the organizational meeting. Bates was offended and angered, but out of regard for Mrs. Terry, with whom she had worked in the past, she complied. The WEC then launched its first public effort, seeking votes to reopen the schools. On September 27 the citizens of Little Rock voted overwhelmingly to keep their high schools closed, but Vivion Brewer felt they had made a promising beginning since over seven thousand voters had marked their ballots "For Integration."[16]

By November, the WEC announced it had over six hundred members; by December, it claimed 850. The women had organized an operation that sent out over two thousand flyers each week, most of them composed by Vivion Brewer. Brewer also spent her time, she later remembered, "calling on men, if they'd see me. Not many would." Other women wrote daily letters commending stands in favor of public schools and answering statements opposing public schools, maintained a lending library, arranged programs and announcements on television and radio, sought voluntary financial support, staffed an office with at least two typists, called on legislators and studied legislation, and visited public hearings and School Board meetings wearing badges announcing their affiliation.[17]

Brewer thought the primary job of the WEC was to overcome the fear and numbness that had blanketed her city. As she correctly perceived, everyone was confused by the plethora of lawsuits that complicated the situation, and few had the ability or the expertise to cut through the rhetoric being spouted on all sides. But through the activities of the winter months, some citizens began to gain a measure of clarity regarding the costs of the continuing crisis. And members of the Women's Emergency Committee developed political savvy and skill.[18]

Between the school-closing referendum in September and the School Board elections on December 6, the United States Supreme Court had removed any illusion that Governor Faubus could orchestrate a private school program with public funds. Those Little Rock citizens who could cut through the fog of the segregationist outcry and of their governor's charges of federal tyranny began to perceive that some measure of integration was going to be necessary if public education were to be resumed in Little Rock. The Women's Emergency Committee worked to heighten that understanding.

Early in November an intense, tiny, and yet very commanding woman had appeared at WEC headquarters (now housed in Margaret Kolb's laundry room) and offered to take over the running of the office. A natural executive, Irene Samuel had had experience in training and management, and Vivion Brewer was delighted to turn over to her many of the burdensome bureaucratic details of running a growing organization. By the time of the School Board elections in December, Samuel had been able to organize workers by wards and precincts throughout the city and she could have them use the poll tax book to call voters (as they had done during the school-closing election, before Samuel had come on board), address and deliver cards and flyers, and set up carpools for election day. Vivion Brewer understood that because her group had begun to be identified as "integrationist," the WEC could not back the business slate openly, and most of their activities during this election remained behind the scenes.[19]

The businessmen, Everett Tucker, Billy Rector, Russell Matson, and Ted Lamb, along with WEC member Margaret Stephens, articulated their "fundamental philosophy" as segregationist. "We unequivocally feel that segregated public school education will prove better for both races than will forced integration," they announced to the press. This was not simply a campaign statement; for all except Ted Lamb, this was a clear expression of their personal views. The candidates also listed as one of the points in their platform, "Find a new Superintendent whose views on segregation are in sympathy with the Southern viewpoint." Clearly these citizens did not yet understand the legal implications of the recent court rulings, as most of the public did not. Even so, the Capital Citizens' Council branded the business slate "integrationist," and Governor Faubus concurred.[20]

In a fitting symbol of the state of the community, the election on December 6 produced a deadlock with three unyielding segregationists and three "moderates" chosen to serve on the School Board. Everett Tucker, Russell Matson, and Ted Lamb survived from the "businessmen's slate," and Robert Laster and Ben Rowland represented the opposition. Ed I. McKinley, a socially prominent attorney, had won initial endorsement as a part of the business group, but he quickly revealed himself to be an uncompromising segregationist. Some observers interpreted the outcome as a victory for moderation and a blow to

Orval Faubus, but the Capital Citizens' Council disagreed. The only thing agreed by all was that the new board would not be able to work together in harmony. None of the candidates with opposition (Ed I. McKinley had been unopposed) had won by more than 1 percent of the vote. With years of hindsight Faubus later recognized that this election "signaled the beginning of the decline in the political strength of the extreme segregationists."[21]

Harry Ashmore happily pronounced the School Board election a defeat for Orval Faubus, but he was dismayed by the businessmen's promise that they would never open the schools voluntarily. The members of the Women's Emergency Committee, which included Ashmore's wife, Barbara, were heartened by this first break in segregationist strength, and they redoubled their efforts to reach out to anyone who would listen. Eight hundred fifty WEC members included mimeographed letters in their Christmas cards proclaiming that they were "dedicated to the principle of good public education with liberty and justice for all." Vivion Brewer approached Little Rock's City Board asking it to establish a "City Commission on Civic Unity" to ease tensions between the races, and she sent a letter to the Chamber of Commerce asking for its "support and active assistance" in improving race relations in Little Rock. The City Board declined to act on Brewer's suggestion, but the Chamber of Commerce soon came to her aid.[22]

ON DECEMBER 28 the Gallup polling organization listed Orval Faubus among its ten most admired men in the world. An editorial in the *Shreveport Times* summed up his status as a martyr: ". . . no man in this particular era of American history has been subjected to organized attack embracing ridicule, belittling and general condemnation in the manner or in the volume in which such attack has been directed at the Arkansas Governor." At a Citizens' Council rally in England, Arkansas, segregationist leader Roy Harris declared that Little Rock had become "the symbol of the resistance movement in the United States today and Orval Faubus has become the leader of that movement." Others suggested that Faubus could be considered presidential timber.[23]

At the end of December the newly constituted Little Rock School Board replaced Archie House and Richard Butler as its attorneys with Herschel H. Friday Jr., from Bill Smith's law firm. Claiming they felt they needed "an entirely new deal," the School Board members suggested their new legal counsel would have to prepare them for the January 6 federal court hearing before Judge Miller. President Ed I. McKinley commented, ". . . you will be safe in assuming that the Board will strongly oppose any move toward integration."[24]

YET THE TIDE WAS beginning to turn against the segregationists in subtle ways. Arkansas Attorney General Bruce Bennett, seeking to position himself for a run for the governorship, held hearings before the Arkansas Legislative Council in December of 1958 "to determine if there are Communist influences in the Little Rock school integration crisis." He hoped to demonstrate a connection between the NAACP and the Communist Party. While claiming to be opposed to "witch hunts," Bennett said he was confident the hearings would "disclose the racial unrest in the state was the direct result of a planned, organized scheme on the part of subversive individuals and organizations . . . ," and he intended to name names.[25]

After listening from the balcony during the public hearings, Daisy Bates labeled the Red Probe a "smear," especially when witnesses suggested that she and L. C. Bates had possible communist connections. Other individuals and groups who came under suspicion were Lee and Grace Lorch, Clarence Laws, the Arkansas Council on Human Relations, the Southern Regional Council, and, of course, the National Association for the Advancement of Colored People.[26]

Key witnesses at the hearings were former Joe McCarthy aide J. B. Matthews and former communist Manning Johnson, both of whom traveled the South appearing in such communist-hunting legislative hearings and who presented much of the same testimony in each venue. ACHR Executive Director Nat Griswold reported to his board that the hearings were a flop, explaining that they "may actually have netted good rather than evil. They were long and mostly dull. Discredited witnesses gave canned and oft-published testimony. . . . In fact Mr. Bennett showed a great lack of easily available information about groups he wished to unsaddle."[27]

Bennett had similarly mixed results when he attacked the NAACP in court. Early in December Wiley Branton went into federal court in Little Rock seeking an injunction against four of Bennett's legislative bills that aimed to destroy the NAACP, and two weeks later a three-judge federal panel assumed responsibility for ruling on Branton's request. At about the same time, the Arkansas Supreme Court upheld the 1957 "Bennett Ordinance," which had required organizations, upon request, to reveal their membership lists and their contributors. The NAACP filed an appeal to the U.S. Supreme Court in March of 1959. Bennett would face a hostile bench if the Court decided to hear the case.[28]

EARLY IN DECEMBER 1958, the mandate arrived from the Eighth Circuit Court of Appeals instructing Judge Miller on how to proceed toward integrating the schools in Little Rock. It gave Judge Miller three orders: to enjoin the School Board from taking any steps toward leasing its property; to enjoin the School Board from any acts that would "impede, thwart or frustrate" integration; and to order the School Board to "take affirmative steps" toward integration. Miller set a court date for January 6, 1959, noting that he had very little room for judicial "discretion." Governor Faubus announced that if Judge Miller declared Act 4 unconstitutional, he had other plans to retain segregation. On December 30, Wiley Branton filed a pleading with Judge Miller asking explicitly for the three things the mandate required. Branton also asked Judge Miller to substitute the names of the new School Board in the case, and he noted that all of them had run on segregationist platforms.[29]

When Miller handed down his ruling, he declared there seemed to be "no alternative" to integration if the schools were to remain public. He ordered the Little Rock School Board to give him within thirty days a "specific and detailed report" of affirmative steps taken and proposed, and to "move forward" toward integration.[30]

On January 21 the Little Rock School Board asked Judge Miller for a delay of his order, requesting that it be allowed to reopen the schools segregated the following Monday. Board President Ed I. McKinley termed the request "an attempt to restore dignity to the Board." Claiming that the present plan was impossible to implement due to the "tenseness" of the situation, the School Board proposed to end the Blossom Plan and submit a new one that would be acceptable to both the court and the people of the school district. Wiley Branton immediately filed a supplement to his original brief asking that if the schools reopened, they be required to integrate.[31]

On February 3, Judge Miller denied the School Board's request. Harry Ashmore said the choice was clear: Little Rock would have to have some integration or no public schools at all. Obviously struggling with the competing demands of his office and his personal convictions, Judge Miller soon expressed his frustration before the Sebastian County Bar Association. Declaring "No judge has the right to . . . brush aside with one sweep of his hand those customs brought forth by the people over the years . . . ," Miller claimed he believed in change but declared that "changes of law should be brought about by evolution, not revolution."[32]

One piece of litigation still dangled: a fight over the constitutionality of Governor Faubus's Act 4, the law that provided for school closings. Wiley Branton was challenging it in federal district court, and the Women's Emergency Committee had decided to file a "friend of the court" brief. Weighing in on the same side as the NAACP, the WEC thereby opened itself up to further criticism as an "integrationist" group.[33]

To the delight of the WEC members, support for their open schools position had materialized through the winter from an unexpected quarter, the Chamber of Commerce. In his inaugural address in January, new Chamber president and WEC husband E. Grainger Williams had announced, to the astonishment of his audience, ". . . the time has come for us to evaluate the cost of education and the cost of the lack of it." Urging the city's business leaders to reestablish "all means of communication" so the city's problems could be discussed "without anger and hatred, without fear of reprisal . . . ," the popular Presbyterian layman, a native of Little Rock, opened the door among the community's elite to a discussion of accepting integration.[34]

Despite this promising beginning, the Chamber of Commerce board soon voted to support the Little Rock School Board in its request that Judge Miller allow them to reopen the schools segregated while they worked on developing a new plan for integration. While the Chamber leaders were undoubtedly attempting to support the School Board through a difficult transition, this action was regrettable, as it sent the wrong message to the community and to the federal courts. As Sara Murphy wrote, it was "an improvement over the silence but not a realistic solution." The Chamber board passed a resolution pledging itself to encourage a "climate of communication" in Little Rock and also to press for the conclusion of all remaining legal and legislative matters that needed resolution.[35]

LATE IN JANUARY OF 1958 the American Association of University Women released the results of a survey it had conducted among Little Rock businessmen between November and January. Based on eighty-five interviews, the women concluded that "the present prosperity is due to the expansion which took place prior to the school crisis. Since the school crisis, no new business has moved into Little Rock, which bodes ill for the future." Harry Ashmore editorialized, "It is a mark of this city's sickness that the matter of whether or not the school crisis has had an adverse effect on business has been a taboo subject, and can be frankly discussed by businessmen only under the cloak of anonymity." Disagreeing with Ashmore, Orval Faubus maintained that the school crisis had not had any adverse effect on business in Little Rock, quoting Pulitzer Prize winner Relman Morin's article on Little Rock's economic health that concluded "Little Rock never had it so good."[36]

Through the winter months, the WEC used newspaper advertisements to educate Little Rock's voters about the costs of closed schools. A visitor from Virginia encouraged them in this endeavor; the Southern Regional Council sent William M. Lightsey of the Virginia Committee for Public Schools specifically to consult with the Women's Emergency Committee. The Executive Committee of the WEC met with Lightsey, the three friendly School Board members, and several attorneys for a "gloves-off conference about opening the public schools and organizing to that end." Lightsey advised the WEC and their allies to educate the community about the economic importance of education. Within a few days, the *Arkansas Gazette* reported that Vivion Brewer and the WEC were "eager to do what the Virginia groups had done—interest businessmen in the necessity of preserving our public school system."[37]

Late in February the officials of the Chamber of Commerce conducted a poll of their entire membership asking two questions: Do you favor Little Rock's continuing with closed public high schools? Do you now favor the reopening of Little Rock's public high schools on a controlled minimum plan of integration acceptable to the federal courts? The WEC issued a statement declaring itself to be "delighted" with the poll. "We hope every man who received a questionnaire will remember not only the frightening loss of funds of our School District," the women's group declared, "but also the fact that some approximately 500,000 needed Little Rock dollars are being spent out of the state to educate displaced high school students who have been forced to break the ties of home and family in order to go to school."[38]

In March the Chamber board released a statement endorsing a "controlled minimum" integration plan. While the Chamber leaders undoubtedly were struggling not to get too far ahead of their membership, their statement proved to be the first formal step in the direction of subverting the intent of the *Brown* decision by resorting to tokenism. About the same time, the Tucker faction of the School Board released a statement arguing that Little Rock had a choice between "open[ing] the schools with controlled integration, or ... uncontrolled integration with all of its adverse effects, economic and social." The coded message was that the Little Rock School Board planned to accept as little integration as possible.[39]

Despite these limited changes, it was clear that the Women's Emergency Committee was having an effect on the growing sensibilities of thinking people in Little Rock. Adolphine Terry, Vivion Brewer, and Velma Powell were leaving their mark, and their strategy of politicizing the young women was bearing fruit. Many of the young husbands, however, were fearful of the consequences of their wives' involvement with the WEC. As member Pat House recalled,

"They were afraid for their jobs, especially local jobs. It was simply a difficult thing, because women, especially in the South, were accustomed to abiding by their husbands' wishes. Not that they were that much dominated, but this is just the culture we grew up in. And it was a tremendous break for women to insist on being active in something where their husbands were afraid. . . ." But as Pat House said later of Mrs. Terry, "So she gathered all these people, and if any of us were discouraged or if we got tired—how can you say to an 80 year old woman, you know, 'I'm tired'? Or 'I can't do this.'" Mrs. Terry cracked the whip, and the young ladies found new interests and sometimes new identities as they stepped outside traditional gender roles and expectations.[40]

IN THE WINTER OF 1959 the WEC also engaged in a more direct kind of lobbying process, attending all sessions of both houses of the Arkansas General Assembly. Eleanor Reid, legislative chair of the Arkansas branch of the American Association of University Women, had written Mrs. Terry in December pleading for the WEC to lead a lobbying effort in the legislature. "A woman's group like the Women's Emergency Committee is most formidable," she had written. "I can testify from personal experience that legislators turn pale when they see a group of polite but determined women descending on them. Perhaps it brings sudden memories of their mothers, urging them to do the right thing! Anyway, it is so, and I wish the women of Little Rock realized how much power they have, if only they appear in groups." At Mrs. Terry's direction, pretty, twenty-eight-year-old Pat House became the legislative leader in this effort. Members of the Mothers' League of Central High School also attended the meetings of the General Assembly, and the women in the two groups felt a mutual disdain for one another.[41]

From the start it was clear that the legislature intended to follow the lead of the immensely popular Governor Faubus, and the threat of abolishing public schools statewide was on everyone's mind. In his inaugural address, Faubus proposed a constitutional amendment to let local districts close their schools and disburse public money to individual students, which families could then use to purchase any form of education they chose. Faubus believed his program would permit "the continuation of segregated schools where there is no federal interference, and . . . the establishment of integrated schools where the people choose to do so." The governor's scheme promised to override the provision in the Arkansas Constitution requiring the state to provide free public schools, and he believed his plan could not be upset by the federal courts.[42]

Faubus soon commented, "Even though the federal government illegally and unconstitutionally seeks control, there is no law which says the federal government can tell a state to operate its schools." Declaring his local option proposal "foolproof," Faubus explained that by eliminating free public schools while making no mention of race or integration his plan was completely nondiscriminatory. Harry Ashmore editorialized, "Arkansas's great tragedy is that under the leadership of Orval Faubus this complex issue has been reduced to all or nothing, with the governor offering only something very close to nothing." Within a matter of days of the governor's inaugural address the General Assembly passed and referred to the voters a constitutional amendment removing the state's obligation to provide free public schools to the children of Arkansas. There were only two dissenting votes.[43]

Meanwhile, Attorney General Bruce Bennett introduced fifteen new bills aimed primarily at the NAACP, saying his legislative package was "designed to harass, to keep the enemies of America busy." The most disturbing of them prohibited paying any public funds to a member of the NAACP, which directly affected many black schoolteachers. The bill passed both houses of the legislature, although Little Rock Senator Ellis Fagan protested it strongly. In short order Governor Faubus signed it into law.[44]

Throughout the fall and winter, rumors had spread in Little Rock that segregationist groups were opposing the renewal of certain teachers' and administrators' contracts, especially at Central High School. With the teachers sitting daily in empty classrooms and with no assurances that classes would resume the following fall, teacher morale had reached an all-time low. Forrest Rozzell of the Arkansas Education Association secured a commitment from the National Education Association that the NEA would "take whatever steps were necessary to protect each and every teacher in the Little Rock system." This involved a potential commitment of half a million dollars.[45]

In February, both the WEC and the Chamber of Commerce passed resolutions urging the Little Rock School Board to renew immediately the contracts of all high school teachers in order to preserve teacher morale. The WEC wrote one of its many letters to the School Board urging it to renew the contracts of the teachers in the four closed high schools without delay. "Losing our present fine staff of teachers," the WEC letter stressed, "would be a blow to our public school system which Little Rock cannot afford. Retaining them is an obligation you owe to our children, our city and yourself. Our 1,040 members depend on you in this crisis." The WEC would soon rue the day it published a tally of its "members."[46]

The second week in February the *Arkansas Gazette* revealed that Little Rock

School District Superintendent Terrell Powell had relayed a proposition to School Board members Everett Tucker, Russell Matson, and Ted Lamb, suggesting that in return for a promise to dismiss certain administrators and teachers "the state" would return a half million dollars it had withheld from the Little Rock district under Governor Faubus' school-closing laws. The purge list included Central High School principals Jess Matthews, Elizabeth Huckaby, and J. O. Powell, and Horace Mann principal Dr. L. M. Christophe, as well as approximately one hundred teachers. Local segregation groups had compiled the list.[47]

Governor Faubus commented for the press that the three Central High principals had done "everything they could to discriminate against white students" and that if he were a member of the School Board, there were some teachers he would not rehire "under any conditions." Segregationist School Board member Ben Rowland commented that he, Laster, and McKinley agreed the three principals and "probably a few others'" should not be reemployed, because of "their views on integration and segregation."[48]

Toward the end of February, School Board President Ed I. McKinley engineered a bill in the Arkansas legislature to allow a segregationist takeover of the Little Rock School Board. Representative T. E. Tyler of Pulaski County submitted the bill, which gave the governor power to appoint three new members to the board "temporarily." Admitting he was acting at the behest of Faubus and McKinley, Tyler informed reporters that McKinley wanted the bill and had persuaded Faubus to back it. Bill Smith later explained to an Eisenhower Administration Project interviewer that Mrs. McKinley's wealth played a significant role in Faubus's decision-making processes throughout the spring of 1959. A close friend of Congressman Dale Alford and a powerful influence on the governor, Ed I. McKinley through his erratic leadership and his intemperate rhetoric dismayed many Little Rock citizens who had never thought of themselves as moderates. McKinley helped the bitter-end segregationists to overreach themselves, ultimately causing a backlash.[49]

When a group of sixteen to twenty women from the WEC confronted Tim Tyler on the steps leading to the House chamber, protesting his bill as "dictatorial" and accusing him of letting the governor control him, Tyler became addled and barked, "Lady will you please shut up?" at one persistent questioner. Pat House told him she felt the bill was uncalled for and that it threatened the city's school system. "It may break the deadlock we have on the Board," retorted Tyler. "It may even get our schools opened faster."[50]

Tim Tyler finally admitted that his bill was "a little on the dictatorship side," and when it came up for discussion in the Arkansas Senate it was tabled by a "roaring voice vote." Longtime Little Rock Senator Ellis Fagan spoke heatedly against it, saying, "This bill seeks to take away from the people the right to elect our School Board. . . . If you did this, I would resign today because we would no longer represent our people." In the House, Representative Gayle Windsor of Little Rock called the Tyler bill "a monstrous piece of legislation," and Sterling Cockrill said, "It makes as much sense for the governor to make appointments on the School Board as to appoint new senators and representatives to break a deadlock on an appropriation bill." Representative Jack Oakes of Woodruff County agreed, reminding his colleagues, "We are not fighting carpetbaggers with this. . . . These are our people, our neighbors we are fixing to harm. Let them decide their problems."[51]

The Women's Emergency Committee lobbied ferociously against the Tyler bill and felt immense gratification when it went down to defeat. The charge that "outsiders" or "intruders" were attempting to control the affairs of the Little Rock School District carried the day. Critics of the Tyler bill labeled it an effort to enable Faubus and McKinley to fire "the whole Central High staff if necessary to keep the School from reopening integrated." Yet rumors of a planned purge persisted.[52]

Orval Faubus had drawn his line in the sand and challenged the Tucker faction of the Little Rock School Board to cross over it. Segregationist School Board member Robert Laster lacked the governor's subtlety and finesse, however, and he blundered into a scenario that made it easy for Tucker, Matson, and Lamb to proclaim their independence of the Faubus forces. Toward the end of February, Laster proposed that the School Board should ignore the courts, reopen the schools segregated, and as far as the federal government was concerned, "let the devil take the hindmost." He even proposed that board members should go to jail if necessary. Then Laster came out with a second plan: "Add to the teacher contracts a clause that the contracts are automatically cancelled if the schools are desegregated. The effect would be that a school desegregated by court order would find itself without a faculty . . . and that would be the federal court's problem."[53]

Tucker and his allies issued a statement deploring Laster's tone of defiance and urging instead the approach of "controlled integration" the Chamber of Commerce membership had recently endorsed. (In a poll of its membership by mail, Chamber members had voted 819–245 in favor of a "controlled minimum" of integration.) The three concluded their statement by saying, "we, as sincere but realistic segregationists, cannot ever agree to such a foolhardy procedure when we have controlled integration available as an alternative."[54]

Tucker, Matson, and Lamb released to the press a lengthy and measured statement outlining what they claimed was "the only alternative to the state-wide abandonment of the public schools." Laying out their extraordinarily complicated situation with as much clarity as possible, they explained that Act 4 would soon come under consideration by the federal court, which had recently ruled in Virginia that a state could not operate public schools in some counties but not in others. If the court followed the Virginia decision, "and we would be naive and derelict in our duties if we did not prepare for such an eventuality," the Little Rock School Board, regardless of individual members' beliefs, would be under a court order to operate the schools on a nonsegregated basis.[55]

Additionally, since the Arkansas Constitution called for the provision of free public education to all children, the three contended that the board could not close or abandon the public schools under either federal or state law. As they explained, only the adoption of a constitutional amendment could remove the requirement that they provide free public education, a possibility that could not happen before the November 1960 elections. Therefore the ultimate choice facing Arkansas citizens, according to Tucker and his allies, was whether they wanted "non-segregated public schools or no public schools at all." It was the first challenge to Faubus's control of affairs, by a public body, since September of 1957. The governor responded by branding the three School Board members "integrationists."[56]

The Capital Citizens' Council published newspaper advertisements calling on Chamber members who were against integration to send in their names. The council promised to hold Chamber members "accountable for promoting integration," the ads said, unless they signed a statement that they did not favor it. Ed I. McKinley and Bob Laster soon announced that the Chamber poll was not representative of community sentiment.[57]

THE ARKANSAS GENERAL Assembly gaveled to a close on March 12, having passed eighty-six new laws, thirty-two of them dealing with segregation. The most ominous of these was Act 461, the Pupil Placement Act, copied from a similar law in Alabama, which enumerated sixteen criteria that local school boards could use to prevent students from transferring into a different school, none of them mentioning race. This would become the instrument that a later School Board would use to formalize a program of "tokenism." Through the last thirty-three minutes of the session, Senator Sam Levine filibustered to death a modified version of the School Board–packing bill, thereby leaving intact the leadership of the Little Rock schools.[58]

Nat Griswold reported to his superiors in Atlanta that most of the laws relating to segregation could be characterized as "delaying measures" or "harassing measures" that could easily be set aside once tested in the courts. Since most of them had to be tried at the level of the local school district, however, they would prove troublesome to invalidate. In the meantime, Griswold wrote, "the paralyzing effect of such devices upon any progress in the area of human rights may be tragic." Wiley Branton moved quickly to have the new acts of the legislature made a part of the Little Rock school integration case.[59]

ON MARCH 23, after a month of studying the issue, the Chamber of Commerce board met and decided unanimously to pass a resolution in support of compliance with court orders to desegregate. Two days later the Chamber board published its resolution as an advertisement in both local newspapers. "The decision of the Supreme Court of the United States, however much we dislike it," the resolution began, "is the declared law and is binding upon us. We think that the decision was erroneous and that it was a reversal of established law upon an unprecedented basis of psychology and sociology." Here the Chamber leaders were reflecting the majority sentiment in Little Rock, a view that had been expressed explicitly by both Arkansas senators in recent months. Nonetheless they concluded, "we must in honesty recognize that, because the Supreme Court is the court of last resort in this country, what it has said must stand until there is a correcting constitutional amendment or until the court corrects its own error. We must live and act now under the decision of that court. We should not delude ourselves about that." The Chamber board had now crossed the Rubicon, as far as Little Rock's segregationists were concerned, and the organization quickly lost 20 to 30 percent of its members. In fairly short order, however, the Chamber doubled its budget with its diminished membership, and the leadership felt that the housecleaning had been healthy for the organization.[60]

As an article in the *Louisville Courier-Journal* soon suggested, the Chamber statement represented no great "change of heart" among Little Rock people. What it did reflect was "an intelligent recognition that the deadlock in local education is bad for the community, and that some way must be found to break it." It acknowledged that the only choice open to the people of Little Rock was one between public schools with "controlled integration" and no public schools at all. While the resolution may seem mild on its face, the highly charged atmosphere in Little Rock had made rational thinking about integration close to impossible.[61]

Perhaps as a measure of its growing effectiveness, the Women's Emergency Committee began to come under organized attack in February of 1959. Whereas harassing letters and phone calls and disrupted friendships had been the price of membership to this point, in February the City Board issued a formal request that the WEC comply with the Bennett ordinance and "voluntarily" provide a list of its members and its contributors for public perusal. The women had promised anonymity to their supporters from the start, and now they perceived the difficulties inherent in their many public references to their "membership." A struggle ensued through the spring as the organization resisted the gestapo tactics of plainclothes detectives appearing at individual members' homes, at night, demanding the membership list, which was kept on index cards in a shoe-box and passed from member to member for safekeeping. The women did not comply with the city's repeated requests.[62]

At a board retreat of the Arkansas Council on Human Relations in late February, WEC member Parma Basham reported on the activities of the Women's Emergency Committee. Noting that it was the only organizational voice speaking out openly against Faubus, the attorney general, and "certain legislative acts," Basham claimed that her group now had over 1,200 members, that it regularly sent out fliers to two thousand Little Rock businessmen and to all members of the legislature, and that it was all white for strategic reasons in an attempt to show that "responsible white people also believe in public education, even more than segregation."[63]

That insight, that shift in values from maintaining segregation to preserving education, had been hard-won in Little Rock, and it came slowly and in tiny increments to most people. The Women's Emergency Committee to Open Our Schools had led the way in making the new stance respectable in Little Rock. Through an aggressive educational campaign the women nurtured the development of new insights and values among reluctant but influential businessmen and legislators who had to worry about paychecks, payrolls, and votes. Equally important, in their campaigns with the businessmen and especially in their interactions with the Arkansas legislature the "embattled ladies of Little Rock" developed a political sophistication and a commitment to political activism that would serve them well in the battles to come.

CHAPTER SIXTEEN

REBIRTH

Everett Tucker

As February nears its end and the Arkansas landscape lies covered in grey, the first promise of spring peeks out from the weather-beaten woods, fields, and flower beds. Against the somber tones of earth and sky, the brilliant mustard-yellow of the tiny crocus bloom heralds the imminent return of a more agreeable season, reminding the winter-weary that soon the deep coral of the japonica and the sunny tones of the daffodil and narcissus will burst into view at every turn. After a long, bleak winter these splashes of nature's bounty provide solace and hope, and they set the stage for the riot of color and beauty that the coming months will bring to Arkansas. In the early spring of 1959, as they looked out on lawns and landscape that were coming back to life, some in Little Rock began to hope that the school system, too, could be reborn. Yet affairs in Arkansas' capital city had to rise to a dramatic, defining climax before they could resolve themselves into a changed and more equitable pattern.

One of the new members of the Little Rock School Board typified the transformation the whole southern region faced in order to conform to the demands of the *Brown* decision. Courtly, tall, and angular, with a deep delta accent, Everett Tucker was born and raised on a cotton plantation in south Arkansas to which he was heir. His grandfather had served in the Confederate Army, and his father had studied at General Lee's college, Washington and Lee. Everett Tucker attended the Webb School, Sewanee Military Academy, and Washington and Lee before serving in the United States Army Air Corps during World War II. After a bout with tuberculosis, he moved to Little Rock and became industrial director for the Chamber of Commerce. He married one of Little Rock's most prominent young women, Frances Williams, a Vassar graduate and the granddaughter of a former United States senator from Arkansas.[1]

In the postwar years Tucker had worked closely with Richard Butler and other city leaders to develop the Little Rock Air Base and the Little Rock Industrial District, even leaving his Chamber job and forming his own private Industrial Development Company to capitalize on the promising growth in his city's economy. He had believed Little Rock was poised on the brink of a commercial takeoff before Orval Faubus called out the National Guard in September of 1957, but through the ensuing year he saw Little Rock's industrial prospects melt away to nothing as his carefully cultivated contacts told him, one by one, that they could not move their factories and their management personnel into a city that had both racial strife and no high schools.[2]

Everett Tucker had thought "it can't happen here" when the *Brown* decision was handed down in 1954. He described himself to an interviewer for the Eisenhower Administration Project as "typical of the conservative enlightened Southern viewpoint." While he had rebelled initially against doing away with the social patterns of segregation because "[t]his is what you learned at your mother's knee, and you don't learn anything bad at your mother's knee," once he got over the shock of realizing that this way of doing things was coming to an end he concluded that Virgil Blossom's approach to the new demands was "a very practical, intelligent, token approach to easing into the thing." Through many long conversations, Tucker's good friend Richard Butler had persuaded him that the *Brown* decision was in fact the law of the land and that it had to be obeyed.[3]

Toward the end of 1958 Tucker and his Chamber of Commerce colleagues had concluded they would have to take a stand against Governor Faubus if they were to have any hope of restoring the economic health of their city. As he recalled years later, he and his Chamber friends decided since there was no new industry "and since I wasn't going to have anything else to do I might as well try to get on the School Board and try to rectify the situation so that we could get back in the business of developing our economy." Forty-six years old in 1958, Tucker described himself as a "pragmatist" and a "realist" when it came to the demands of integration.[4]

Tucker's good friend Billy Rector was the rising vice president of the Little Rock Chamber of Commerce in the fall of 1958, and when the School Board resigned en masse in November, Rector persuaded Tucker that the two of them should run for the vacant positions. Rector recalled that he ran because of his embarrassment that Little Rock had become a symbol around the world of backwardness, and he knew that was not true. Rector and his board president E. Grainger Williams had badgered numerous Little Rock businessmen to stand for the School Board, but they eventually left the final selling job to Adolphine

Terry. In the December 1958 election, Billy Rector suffered defeat, largely as a result of the vigorous opposition of Governor Faubus, but Everett Tucker secured a seat on the School Board along with two other candidates from the "Businessmen's Slate," Russell Matson and Ted Lamb.[5]

Faubus had tried to argue for months that the Little Rock crisis had not had an adverse effect on the city's economy, and the vocal presence of the businessmen in the campaign was an embarrassment to him. Although he did not endorse the six candidates who supported his policies, he attacked the five-member business slate because, he said, "the people on it had worked against him in his successful bid for a third term last summer." Three men from each slate secured a seat on the reconstituted School Board, reportedly leaving Faubus "irate" over his failure to win an outright majority. This election represented the governor's first significant repudiation at the polls on a segregation issue. One *Arkansas Gazette* reporter wrote several months later that as a result of this defeat, "The magic attached to the Faubus name began to fade."[6]

ON APRIL 7, Governor Faubus, undoubtedly reacting to the new resolve of the Chamber of Commerce, the Women's Emergency Committee and the Tucker-Matson-Lamb faction of the School Board, made a statement to the press suggesting he was not opposed to "token integration" if it was necessary to resolve the·deadlock in Little Rock. Blaming the impasse on the NAACP and "other groups with other ideas," Faubus suggested if the courts upheld Acts 4 and 5 handing setbacks to the black civil rights group, African-Americans might soften their position demanding full integration and accept a modicum of compromise. Yet despite his typical shifting of blame, Faubus could not make the NAACP the point of controversy this time. Now the fight was over tokenism, and the segregationists' willingness to give an inch. Amis Guthridge, of course, immediately attacked the governor's stance, calling for the development of private schools to avoid the threatened miscegenation, and proclaiming that token integration "would never be allowed to come to pass."[7]

School Board discussion of Little Rock's teacher contracts had been scheduled for April 10, 1959. In the unsettled atmosphere of late March, with talk of a teacher purge in the air and the consideration of Acts 4 and 5 still before the courts, School Superintendent Terrell Powell burned the old contracts and sabotaged the school district's printing press to delay the decisions on contract renewal for another month. In the meantime, Tucker, Matson, and Lamb began to make visits to the closed high schools in an attempt to boost the morale of teachers who had been sitting in empty classrooms all year. The three School

Board members attempted to explain to the teachers their own understanding of the federal courts' new demands for integration, which they proposed to limit as much as possible based on extensive scholastic testing and the Pupil Placement Act

Governor Faubus and Ed I. McKinley claimed to be outraged over the three School Board members' visits with the teachers. Faubus said the three had run as segregationists "but their actions now belie their words." McKinley proclaimed "This demonstrates to what lengths the integrationists are willing to go.... I condemn the use of the words 'token' 'controlled' and/or 'limited' integration.... There can be no such thing and the integrationists know it." Tucker, Matson, and Lamb, however, predicted that the federal courts would force the opening of Central High School "on the basis of a small degree of controlled integration," and they wanted the teachers to be ready.[9]

On April 23, Powell received notification that the North Central Association might rescind the accreditation of the city's three public high schools. Within days the NCA had indeed dropped from its membership rolls the closed Little Rock schools, at the request of State Education Commissioner (and Arkansas NCA chairman) Ed McCuistion. Harry Ashmore speculated that the NCA maneuver was part of a larger design to weaken the Little Rock public schools in favor of the private system, "which the people are being led to believe will operate here next year." Teacher resignations were 50 percent higher than at the same time the previous year. The governor's assault on the public schools was taking its toll.[10]

On April 27 the Arkansas Supreme Court upheld Act 4 by a vote of four to three (with Justice Jim Johnson in the majority). Writing that they "deplored" the *Brown* decision, the justices argued "someone must guide a peaceable, safe course for its implementation ...," and concluded that Governor Faubus's decision to close the schools was a valid exercise of his police power since it was intended only as "temporary relief." The justices wrote, "That complete integration of the schools in many communities presents a social problem fraught with frightening consequences in the minds of many people is a fact that cannot be ignored or avoided." Writing for the minority, Justice Edward McFaddin also argued that the *Brown* decision had been decided in error, but he concluded that the Arkansas Constitution required a system of free public schools and that the exercise of police power was valid only in emergencies. Everyone in Arkansas officialdom seemed to agree that the *Brown* decision was wrong. For the Chamber of Commerce leaders and half of the School Board members to argue that it had to be obeyed required courage.[11]

This was the climate in which Everett Tucker, Russell Matson, and Ted Lamb walked into the regularly scheduled May meeting of the Little Rock School Board, a meeting in which the renewal of teacher contracts was the main item on the agenda. The two factions of the School Board had bickered through every meeting since their election in December, but they had managed to avoid an open confrontation. Now the lines were drawn: the hard-line segregation-ists on the board were aligned with Governor Faubus, who wanted to destroy the public schools; the other three were committed to reopening the schools with a minimum of integration in the fall. It is not difficult to imagine that the savvy and sophisticated Tucker, Matson, and Lamb went into the meeting determined to provoke the hot-headed McKinley, Laster, and Rowland into some kind of overreaction.[12]

On the morning of May 5, 1959, the Little Rock School Board assembled at the administrative offices downtown at Eighth and Scott. In the men's room before the meeting, Terrell Powell told Everett Tucker he planned to resign. He said Ed I. McKinley had asked him not to rehire forty-four teachers and admin-istrators, but he was unwilling to follow McKinley's recommendation. He said McKinley had offered to take him out to the Governor's Mansion, but since Powell had already refused a half-dozen invitations to dine with the governor because "he shut my schools down and he's withholding my money," he declined.[13]

As Powell recalled the experience years later, McKinley had told him he could recommend the forty-four be fired or he could return to his old position as principal at Hall High School. Powell added that among those the segrega-tionists had slated to be released were some of the finest in the school system, outstanding teachers who had devoted as many as thirty years to their teaching careers, and he was unwilling to recommend that they not be rehired. Powell said he had told McKinley he would just go back to Hall High School. Powell explained that he did not want to have his own firing on his personnel record, so he had decided to resign. Tucker persuaded him not to do so.[14]

Before an unusually large crowd of spectators that included members of the Women's Emergency Committee, the Mothers' League of Central High School, the American Association of University Women, the League of Women Voters, and several classroom teachers' organizations, Ed I. McKinley called the May School Board meeting to order at 9:00 A.M. The first item on the agenda was the renewal of Terrell Powell's contract. The board split three to three, allowing McKinley to rule that the motion had failed and that Powell was removed. Ted Lamb then moved that the contracts of all teachers be renewed. Again the Board split three to three, and the motion failed. Similarly, when Ben Rowland moved that contracts of all teachers in any school closed for any reason including "forced integration" be terminated automatically, the three-to-three vote killed the motion. The meeting proceeded with this kind of deadlock through the morning, until all finally agreed on something: to break for lunch at 11:00.[15]

During the break the Tucker faction and Powell conferred with their attorneys (probably including School Board attorney Herschel Friday, who was a close personal friend of Russell Matson), and devised a strategy. The attorneys advised that according to a Supreme Court case, if members announced they were leaving a meeting, then the quorum would no longer exist, and all ensuing actions would be null and void. When the meeting resumed at 1:00 P.M. Everett Tucker read a prepared statement saying his faction favored "re-employment of all personnel recommended by the school superintendent," which followed current administrative policies. Tucker then announced, "We are now withdrawing from this meeting and declaring that no quorum exists upon our withdrawal."[16]

After Tucker, Matson, and Lamb left the room, McKinley announced that the current board had never formally adopted the old administrative procedures that included the quorum rule, and he did not regard them as binding. Bob Laster then said the record should show that "when the board had begun its second session at 1 P.M. all six members were present and that the three had voluntarily left the meeting." The three remaining members proceeded to terminate the contracts of forty-four teachers, principals, and administrative personnel, twenty-six of them at Central High School. Women's Emergency Committee member Billie Wilson took the floor to ask for an explanation. Ed McKinley responded that the floor was not open for questions. Wilson slipped out into the hall and called Vivion Brewer, who was conducting the May meeting of the WEC at Mrs. Terry's home. Shaken by the call, Brewer returned to the meeting and announced, "They're firing our teachers right and left."[17]

WEC member Pat House realized that the segregationist members of the School Board had created just the kind of issue her organization needed. As she recalled years later, ". . . actually they did us a favor, by giving us a cause of righteousness." The women had been working all spring with pamphlets and meetings and educational programs, but they did not have a central issue the citizens of Little Rock could rally around, one that engaged their emotions enough to overcome the threatening bugaboo of "integration." With the firing of the teachers, according to House, "Even the segregationists could identify with a person being fired without notice and for obeying the law. This was a patently, grossly unfair thing to do." All at once, many people who had remained silent through the turmoil at Central High, through the closing of the schools, amid the growing atmosphere of fear in Little Rock, at last found a way to oppose Orval Faubus without having to declare themselves in favor of integration. In one stroke, the issue of fairness to the teachers preempted all others, and the city took its first halting steps toward recovering its equilibrium.[18]

THE NIGHT OF THE teacher purge, Everett Tucker spoke at the dedication of a new elementary school that had been named in honor of his wife's father and grandfather, both of whom were former members of the Little Rock School Board. As they entered the packed auditorium, both Tucker and Russell Matson received a standing ovation from the angry and energized school patrons. Seizing the opportunity to explain his position, Tucker told his audience Little Rock had two options: implement some plan that had received court approval, or liquidate the public schools. Noting that he and his allies had run as segregationists, and that "we have not changed our attitude one iota," he argued nonetheless that it was "an absurd distortion of logic and of facts" to suggest that any action taken pursuant to a federal court order was "voluntary."[19]

One of the purged principals was Miss Opal Middleton of Franklin School, who had taught in Little Rock for forty years. Grainger Williams had studied under her in sixth grade. Another purged principal was Frances Sue Wood of Forest Park School, twenty-nine years in the system. Wood's sister, Irene Samuel, had by this time become "the mastermind of the WEC infrastructure" and was, according to one of her lieutenants, "now ready to deploy the troops that she had been training in minor skirmishes for a major showdown with the segregationist forces." Miss Middleton and Mrs. Wood reportedly were dismissed because they had sent letters home with the children the previous fall explaining the school-closing referendum and urging their patrons to vote "for integration" so the schools would remain open. In fact, the citywide Parent-Teacher Association had prepared these letters and (according to press reports) the principals "didn't have anything to do with them."[20]

Ted Lamb called the actions of the McKinley faction "diabolical," and many people agreed. The Executive Committee of the Little Rock Council of Parent-Teacher Associations suggested that the offending School Board members should be recalled. The American Association of University Women passed a resolution concluding that the segregationists "aimed at weakening and destroying the Little Rock school system. . . ." The Executive Committee of the

Classroom Teachers Association advised all teachers against signing the contracts the School Board had offered them. Arkansas Education Association Executive Director Forrest Rozzell announced "court action will definitely be taken. . . ."[21]

Ed McKinley lamely claimed that the firings were personnel matters, discussed privately in order to spare the teachers any embarrassment. Yet McKinley confirmed that teachers' attitudes toward integration were among the criteria considered and added "several teachers in Central High School said integration didn't work because too few Negroes were admitted, that 250–300 should have been admitted." McKinley meanwhile instructed the remaining teachers to sign their contracts or risk losing their jobs.[22]

On May 6, four hundred patrons of Forest Park School, located in an affluent Heights neighborhood, filled the elementary school's auditorium and adopted two resolutions. One condemned the McKinley faction for the actions, the other commended Forest Park's principal, Frances Sue Wood. Billie Wilson presided, as PTA president, over the passage of the two resolutions and a standing ovation for Everett Tucker and Ted Lamb, and then she turned the meeting over to Tom Eisele, a young lawyer and father, a deeply thoughtful Harvard graduate who typified many of Little Rock's men in their frustration over how to oppose the Faubus machine. Eisele introduced a resolution proposing a recall of the offending board members and denouncing as "un-American and high-handed" the tactics employed by McKinley, Laster, and Rowland in "summarily dismissing teachers employed by this District, many with long tenure and distinguished careers, without any semblance of fair procedure." The patrons adopted the resolution unanimously and noisily, and the group elected Dr. Drew Agar, father of two Forest Park students, as chairman of the recall effort. The Women's Emergency Committee assumed responsibility for circulating the recall petitions.[23]

THAT SAME DAY, a young lawyer named Maurice Mitchell ran into his friend Bill Gulley in the Pyramid Building Coffee Shop, a popular gathering place for downtown businessmen and attorneys. Learning of Gulley's dismay over the teachers' treatment but not wanting to discuss such sensitive affairs in a public place, Mitchell went upstairs to his office and called Gulley on the telephone. A law partner of Brooks Hays's son Steele, Mitchell had been one of the sixty-two young lawyers to publish a statement in opposition to Faubus's private school scheme in September of 1958, and he had suffered the consequences in lost clients, as had most of the attorneys who signed. Encouraged by Gulley's vehement response and driven by his own dismay, Mitchell then arranged a meeting for the next day at Breier's restaurant, another favorite downtown haunt. At this meeting Mitchell and four other young attorneys, Ed Lester, Bob Shults, Tom Eisele, and Tom Downie (all of whom were married to Women's Emergency Committee members), as well as Gene Fretz, a young *Arkansas Gazette* feature editor, decided that the time had come for Little Rock's men to speak out in opposition to their governor's attempts to destroy the public schools. Gene Fretz came up with a name for the group: "STOP," for Stop This Outrageous Purge. That night Mitchell, Lester, and Shults compiled a list of almost two hundred community leaders and invited them to meet the next day in the community room of the city's largest downtown bank, Union National.[24]

Meanwhile, Grainger Williams called a meeting of the Chamber of Commerce Board, which voted unanimously to adopt a resolution condemning the actions of the segregationist School Board members. "The attempted dismissal of these public servants," the indignant resolution read, "without explanation, announced reason or cause, and equally important, without affording the teachers an opportunity of defense, is without precedent. This abortive abuse of power is directly contrary to long established School Board procedure . . . is without honor and human decency, and is a disgrace to this community." The Chamber Board invited the community to join it in demanding that "this attempted purge be erased."[25]

The president of the PTA Council also called her group together the same afternoon, and the women voted 41–9 to approve the Forest Park recall and censure resolutions and send them on to the local PTA units for their endorsement. Throughout this busy day, WEC members fanned out through downtown stores and suburban neighborhoods, gathering signatures. The WEC telephone chain also functioned efficiently, lining up women to attend the many PTA meetings (twenty-six in all) that were springing up all over town.[26]

That night, May 7, Ed I. McKinley spoke at the dedication of the new Hardin-Bale School, also in the Heights. He castigated his School Board opponents, at which point Everett Tucker, Billie Wilson, and seventy-three others walked out of the auditorium. One man stood at the foot of the stage and yelled at McKinley, "You are a no good bum," before departing. Although Terrell Powell was sitting on the platform, he later claimed his wife had led the walkout.[27]

Elsewhere in the Heights, PTA president Mary Hoover had called a meeting of her patrons at Forest Heights Junior High School. An estimated eight hundred people crowded into the school's gymnasium. Mrs. Hoover opened the meeting by declaring that recent events had taken a "dictatorial turn," with a blow having been struck at the "quality and competence of those who play such important roles in the lives of our children." Before turning the microphone over to Ed Lester, Hoover suggested that the injustice to the teachers "must be fought with every weapon we can muster." Lester allowed two opponents to speak, both of whom suffered heckling from the audience. Saying that all speakers were limited to two minutes, Lester eventually removed W. H. Goodman, a member of the Raney High School Board, from the microphone. After calling for a voice vote and hearing a resounding endorsement of both of the Forest Park resolutions Lester announced they had passed by a vote of eight hundred to two.[28]

ON FRIDAY, MAY 8, one hundred seventy-nine men met at Union National Bank and formally organized the Committee to Stop This Outrageous Purge. Most of the attendees were younger, second-level employees or junior executives in Little Rock's large law firms and commercial enterprises; very few of them were from the top tier of business and professional leaders in the city. Limiting their purpose explicitly to rectifying the mistreatment of the teachers and sidestepping the issue of segregation versus integration, the aroused and enthusiastic throng signed a Statement of Principles that read in part, "We characterize the action taken by these three men as a purge which was cynical and designed to create a fear that stalks the classrooms." Dr. Agar told the crowd that many people had kept quiet about the school crisis for nearly two years because they feared it would hurt their business to speak up, admitting he had been in that timid category. He continued, however, saying "But I am not any longer. . . . Something very malevolent and dangerous has occurred and it is our duty to stop it." Maurice Mitchell challenged each man present to contribute or solicit $100. Mitchell's office became the clearinghouse for the $36,000 the organization raised in the next three weeks.[29]

Vivion Brewer and Irene Samuel slipped into the meeting uninvited. The STOP men knew they needed the expertise and the womanpower of the Women's Emergency Committee, and most members of STOP were married to WEC members, but many of them feared any public association with the controversial organization. The STOP leaders were divided on integration, and fearful of its taint. Quietly, then, the women assumed direction of recruiting workers at the grassroots. They had already broken the city down into ward and precinct levels, and now they assigned secretaries from their membership to each of those units in preparation for the upcoming recall election.[30]

As the recall petition drive gained signatures and momentum, Margaret

Jackson of the Mothers' League of Central High School circulated a counter-petition demanding the recall of the tokenists, Tucker, Matson, and Lamb. Whereas the tokenists sought signatures at the War Memorial Stadium parking lot, the Mothers' League women sought theirs at the Arkansas Livestock Show Grounds. Through a hectic weekend both groups struggled to secure the requisite 6,300 names. A provision of the recall law allowed only one election per year, and it was a race to the finish.[31]

Rumors began to surface that Congressman Dale Alford and Claude Carpenter (in short, Orval Faubus) were behind the move to recall Tucker, Matson, and Lamb. Alford denied to a *Gazette* reporter on his lawn at 11:45 P.M. Saturday night that the sixty or so people gathered at his home were working on the recall project. But McKinley and his faction had hired Alford's father to serve as superintendent when they demoted Terrell Powell, so the thread connecting McKinley, Alford, Carpenter, and Faubus seemed increasingly apparent.[32]

On Saturday, May 10, Ed McKinley released a statement to the press claiming the purged teachers either were integrationists or had collaborated with integrationists but that they could be hired back "if they will state that they support 'the public policy of racially separate schools.'" McKinley claimed that the remaining teachers "do support social separation of the races and will not implant alien racial doctrines in the minds of our children." McKinley said it was the duty of the School Board to dismiss integrationists because their offensive views ran counter to "established public policy."[33]

Amis Guthridge soon surfaced in news stories and headlines, offering the tokenists additional ammunition to use against the segregationist forces. Threatening to "name names" at Monday's PTA meeting at Pulaski Heights Junior High School, and to reveal the subversive organizations to which some of the purged teachers belonged, Guthridge also promised to tell the parents and teachers "who among the communist-fronters are now in Little Rock helping Daisy Bates and the Women's Emergency Committee and the Chamber of Commerce put on their highly organized, professional campaign to race-mix our schools."[34]

On Monday, May 11, four hundred people (388 of whom were WEC members) attended a rally at Hotel Marion in a final push to obtain signatures on STOP's recall petitions. Drew Agar encouraged the workers by saying they had "touched off a fire that is unquenchable." Fanning out across the city throughout Monday, the STOP workers pushed their total of signatures collected to almost ten thousand names, filing them that day.[35]

Yet the Mothers' League also succeeded in securing sufficient signatures on their petitions. On the afternoon of May 12 Margaret Jackson filed them. Faubus aide Claude Carpenter oversaw the collection of the Mothers' League signatures; his sister, Anita Sedberry, accompanied Margaret Jackson when she filed her petitions with the Pulaski County clerk. Prosecuting Attorney Frank Holt ruled the race a tie. He allowed both sets of recall names to be included on the same ballot, and County Clerk Bob Peters set the date of the recall election for May 25. Little Rock's citizens settled in for ten days of high-powered political theatre.[36]

PHIL STRATTON, Jim Johnson's best friend and Orval Faubus's new assistant, came up with a name for the organization that formed to support the recall of Everett Tucker, Russell Matson, and Ted Lamb, the Committee to Retain Our Segregated Schools, or CROSS. Claude Carpenter served as legal counsel. Several days after the onset of the campaign, Capital Citizens' Council president Dr. Malcolm Taylor told *Arkansas Gazette* reporter Roy Reed that the CCC had not been invited to participate in the CROSS effort. In Taylor's words, "Some pretty powerful people are behind it." Two of Faubus's key aides, Claude Carpenter and Kay Matthews, invited missionary Baptist preacher Reverend M. L. Moser to chair the CROSS committee, leaving Moser with the impression that Faubus had suggested he be named chairman.[37]

Referring to the STOP forces as "integrationists or so-called moderates," Moser announced his committee's first public initiative on May 16, a rally scheduled for that night. Moser, McKinley, Laster, and Rowland addressed the crowd gathered at Hotel Marion, and they put on a show that no invited dignitary could have topped. "There's no such thing as token integration," Reverend Moser shouted, shaking his fist. "If it's legally right for ten of them to be out there, it's going to be legal for all of them to be there." Yells and applause resounded. Quoting frequently from Scripture, Moser concluded, jarringly, "The so-called moderates make me want to vomit." McKinley suggested the fired teachers could get their jobs back if they came forward and professed to believe in segregation, but "not one has shown us the courtesy of coming forward. . . ." The audience of 350 applauded enthusiastically throughout the performance and then helped themselves to a variety of racist leaflets and booklets on their way out the door. The disconnect between STOP and CROSS was apparent: the STOP forces avoided any discussion of integration and focused explicitly on fairness to the teachers; the CROSS advocates argued that integration was the only issue.[38]

Although the CROSS effort had the political acumen of Orval Faubus at its disposal, the STOP forces scored a major coup when they persuaded W. S.

Mitchell to assume their chairmanship. A Princeton graduate, an Episcopal vestryman, an attorney in his late forties, Mitchell was one of the most respected men in the city. He had been deeply troubled by the turmoil of the past two years but had hesitated to speak out because as he told Bishop Robert R. Brown, "It is foolish just to make public statements decrying the situation when there is no avenue for positive action. Such statements ruin one's usefulness in the future." Despite his earlier reluctance to speak out, Mitchell now felt revulsion over the treatment of the teachers, and since the school closing had forced him to send his son away to private school in the Northeast he was fully aware of the damage being done to the community.[39]

Initially concerned about the impact of his involvement on his law practice, Mitchell called a few clients to see if they had any serious objections. None did, and his wife supported his decision enthusiastically. For the next week Will Mitchell devoted himself full-time to leading the STOP campaign. He met for breakfast every morning with a core group of workers, which apparently included Boyd Ridgway from the Chamber of Commerce, a young banker named Finley Vinson, and former governor Sid McMath's law partner, Henry Woods. Henry Woods demonstrated his legendary political savvy by calling Irene Samuel.[40]

Woods said, "Mrs. Samuel, I'm Henry Woods. You're controversial and I'm controversial but I think you and I ought to meet because I understand from Mr. Ashmore that you are a good organizer." Over Cokes at Smith's Drugstore Woods then proceeded to explain that the thirty thousand names of voters in the poll tax book had to be put on index cards and then sorted by ward, precinct, and political persuasion. Those who could be expected to vote for STOP would be coded as "saints." Those known to be supporters of CROSS would be called "sinners." Those whose position was not known would be labeled "savables." Woods suggested that Samuel and her WEC workers distribute the cards in shoeboxes to captains at the ward, precinct, and block levels, and that block captains see to it "that they got the 'saints' out on election day, did nothing to arouse the 'sinners' to go to the polls, and worked in the meantime on the 'savables,' hoping to win them over." It was a monumental undertaking but one that Irene Samuel tackled with relish. Under her direction WEC volunteers worked ten four-hour shifts of thirty-six women each. Working day and night, they delivered the sorted cards to the block captains in time to mount a vigorous campaign that lasted just one week. Margaret Jackson soon had reason to lament: "Never have the integrationists been so successful in disguising their real purpose."[41]

In a brilliant tactical maneuver, the STOP forces planned a rally honoring all the white teachers in the city for the night of May 18 at Robinson Auditorium downtown. The same night a rally honoring black teachers was held at the Dunbar Community Center and sponsored by STEP, or Save This Educational Program. The WEC's telephone chain functioned admirably under Jane Mendel's leadership, and two thousand white Little Rock citizens packed the Joe T. Robinson Auditorium to hear Will Mitchell proclaim, "Too long, irresponsible statements have gone unchallenged in this community. What this community needs is the restoration of its self-respect." Amid almost continuous applause and shouts of approval, Mitchell explained that the segregationists had circulated bogus letters in the black community, falsely signed by Drew Agar, that invited "our colored friends" to attend the white rally, and then he concluded, "What will happen if we abandon this community to those people next Monday?" At Dunbar, five hundred African-Americans crowded into a rally for the black teachers and heard longtime political leader I. S. McClinton endorse Everett Tucker by saying, "I've known him for years. He's one of the strongest segregationists in the state of Arkansas. But he voted to preserve our schools."[42]

Reverend Moser soon complained about the financial advantage the STOP forces had over his organization. "Our funds are extremely limited," he remarked, "and when you look at the membership of STOP it reads like the Who's Who of the Wall Street Journal." Moser declared that CROSS "will work with every effort it can command but our volunteers are working people who have to make a living and cannot turn their jobs over to assistants or secretaries." Desperate, Moser hit upon a campaign tactic, the smear, that probably cost his campaign a significant number of votes. He took out an advertisement in the *Arkansas Democrat* charging that the teachers had been fired for one or more of the following reasons: "Teaching alien doctrine, incompetency [*sic*], breaking and entering, trespassing on private property, invasion of privacy, improper punishment, intimidation of students, immorality." The attorney for the Classroom Teachers' Association responded with a $3,900,000 lawsuit for libel, $100,000 for each of the white teachers fired.[43]

The teachers' attorney, Eugene Warren, countercharged that some of his clients had been fired out of favoritism, others because they had failed to give segregationist leaders' children good grades. Warren said some teachers had been "threatened by extremist leaders for such alleged heinous acts as allowing a Negro girl to take her turn to read a passage from the Bible in the schoolroom, for administering first aid to an injured Negro boy, and for keeping order in the classrooms and the halls of their schools in accordance with the directions of their principals."[44]

Beginning to grasp that the firing of the teachers was a tactical blunder that he was unable to mask with right-wing rhetoric, McKinley made his way to the governor's office and demanded that Orval Faubus expend some of his vast political capital in support of the CROSS campaign. Reluctantly, out of a "political debt" to McKinley and against his own best judgment, the governor complied.[45]

ON MAY 20, Orval Faubus told reporters he was concerned about the tension and ill-feeling in Little Rock but said, "I'm just trying to stay out of this." Two days later he went on television with an all-out attack on the STOP forces, whom he tagged "The Cadillac Brigade." With complete disregard for the orders of the federal courts, Faubus challenged STOP to draw up a plan based on volunteer white and black students and teachers. He charged that the "prominent and wealthy leaders" of Little Rock were attempting to force integration on both blacks and the "honest white people of the middle and lower classes" using "many good, honest, hard-working Negroes in the front as the shock troops."[46]

It was too little, too late. The STOP forces had attracted over seven hundred people to their first ward meetings, and they had planned "a steady round of coffee and coke parties, door to door visiting, telephone calls, and rides to the polls" for every ward in the city. They had bombarded the newspapers with advertisements, one series of which featured individual photographs and appealing descriptions of many of the fired teachers. Most important, they bought airtime for Will Mitchell to respond to Faubus's charges. Speaking on television the night after the governor's televised address, Mitchell predicted his organization was "on the eve of a great victory which will write in the skies over Little Rock, 'Decency shall prevail here.'" Chiding Faubus for his intervention, Mitchell said, "The governor asked us to submit a plan for the future of our home town. . . . I accept that offer. Governor, leave us alone. Let us return our community to a rule of reason."[47]

The *Arkansas Democrat* finally declared itself in support of the STOP effort, after months of editorial silence in the integration controversy, arguing, "The Democrat stands with the STOP support of the teachers, as we have stood many times for other individual rights. Let us not tangle this question up with the controversy over segregation." The final night of the campaign, STOP organizer Ed Lester warned that Little Rock was in danger of losing its teachers. On the other side, M. L. Moser actually suggested he would rather be "uneducated and ignorant" than have integrated schools.[48]

On May 25, twenty-five thousand of Little Rock's forty-two thousand voters went to the polls. The STOP candidates won, by very slim majorities. Everett Tucker announced to the jubilant STOP workers at Hotel Marion, "In my judgment I think this election today indicated whether Little Rock was going to go forward or stagnate." Will Mitchell proclaimed "Mission completely accomplished" and thanked publicly for the first time in the campaign the volunteers of the Women's Emergency Committee. WEC member Sara Murphy learned of the victory at midnight, at a newsstand in Times Square, New York City. When she saw the banner headline proclaiming "Faubus Loses" she stood with tears streaming down her face and exclaimed to the stand's puzzled operator, "You don't know how happy this makes me."[49]

The members of the Women's Emergency Committee had every reason to feel happy and proud. Their efforts had been central to the success of the undertaking, even though they had worked with almost no recognition. Years later Henry Woods said of them, "the WEC won that STOP election and never received the credit they should have."[50]

Crucial as the women were to the STOP victory, it was the black vote that won the election. Four thousand blacks voted almost entirely for the STOP ticket. As Vivion Brewer acknowledged, quoting an assessment by Maurice Mitchell, "Without the Negro vote, the election would have gone the other way." Henry Woods orchestrated getting out the black vote, securing one hundred vehicles and drivers for use in the black community on election day. As Maurice Mitchell recalled, Woods, whose specialty was labor law, got a lot of "big, heavy truck drivers, and they went down into what was then a black area on 9th Street . . . and they would just knock on doors and ask 'have you voted?' and they'd say 'No' and the truck drivers would say 'Well come on, because we are going to vote.'"[51]

Henry Woods assessed the STOP victory: "We got our vote out. And the other side was not that successful. If everybody had voted, we would have lost. It was a matter of identifying the people who were with us and getting them to the polls. And we did the best job on that that's ever been done in any election."[52]

The result was a devastating blow for Orval Faubus. He had put his political prestige on the line, and as one observer assessed the result, he "got it back in a bad state of disrepair." United States Attorney Osro Cobb described the STOP election as "the first real chunk out of the Governor's armor." Faubus, however, maintained for the rest of his life that the purge issue had clouded the popular understanding in Little Rock of what was actually at stake. As he said a few days after the election, "Little Rock has not voted for integration yet," describing the purge issue as "a smoke screen behind which the integrationists now move forward."[53]

Other southerners took notice of the defeat. As a writer in Jackson, Mississippi, advised his readers, "For the best interests of Mississippi a positive program in the field of race relations appears necessary. . . . Otherwise our people, like the people of Little Rock, ultimately will be confronted with the superior legal and military power of the United States government."[54]

In Little Rock itself, the recall election brought a new clarity. As one close observer wrote, "Certainly this crisis caused more Arkansans to see the real issue: legal accommodation to the desegregation decision of the court or no public schools. They also saw that hard core segregationists are willing to sacrifice the public schools." Everett Tucker reflected that he did not think the community had suddenly decided to be in favor of integration. But it *was* in favor of getting the schools open.[55]

The STOP victory did not usher in a golden era of advancement for Little Rock's black citizens. As keen an advocate as Harry Ashmore was content with very modest expectations, writing before the week was out that the legal requirements of the federal courts would soon be forthcoming, and around those orders "it should be possible to work out a sound program of limited integration that would meet the minimum demands of the law without any major alteration in a school system that will continue to provide Negro schools to serve the great majority of our colored pupils."[56]

A FEW DAYS AFTER the recall election, a newspaper in Nashville, Tennessee, ran an article about the economic climate in Little Rock that portended dreary things for the city's future. Noting that Little Rock had been experiencing an industrial boom before the school crisis, the article stressed that not a single new industry had moved to Little Rock since August of 1957. "We don't say it's all because of the school business," the article quoted Everett Tucker as saying. "There may be other factors, too. But you don't just all of a sudden run up against a blank wall like that." Reading from one of his many letters of rejection, Tucker quoted a northern industrialist who wrote, "Our contacts with Arkansas have given us an unfavorable opinion of that state in comparison with Tennessee, Mississippi or Missouri. We have no desire to be involved in the segregation problems current in that state."[57]

Playing on the ever-present theme of miscegenation, a writer in a local paper in Sumter, South Carolina, suggested that Tucker and others in Little Rock were "wiling to subject their daughters to the dangers of an integrated school in order to secure some new industrial plants. They are willing to sell the white race down the river for a few dollars that might come their way." Reducing Tucker's motivations to the crudest level, the South Carolina editorialist wrote, "If in order to keep from losing a dollar we have to let our daughters go to school with Negroes then that must be."[58]

By the summer of 1959 the threat of miscegenation had lost its power to intimidate and confuse the businessmen in Little Rock. The dollars-and-cents argument behind accepting a "controlled minimum" of desegregation seemed persuasive to men who had grown up through the Great Depression in one of the poorest states in the nation. Even though many of them abhorred the thought of making the threatening social adjustments desegregation required, they at last had begun to achieve some clarity about the high costs of resisting the federal government. For a growing number, it was a price they were not willing to pay. As political scientist Irving Spitzberg concluded concerning this phase of the Little Rock crisis, by the end of the STOP campaign, "desegregation was the bitter pill that had to be swallowed in order to restore peace and progress to the community." But at the same time, desegregation, "too much and too fast, posed a threat in the mind of the Moderate to that which he had just saved—the public schools."[59]

ORVAL FAUBUS REMAINED unmoved by the STOP victory and the alarming economic news in Little Rock, sensing in both another call to stand and fight. As he told a group of reporters, "I have never known a time when the odds were not against me. . . . I know how to fight when the odds are against me, and Harry Ashmore . . . will have a hell of a time running me out of Arkansas." As the summer unfolded, the wily governor mounted one last campaign to withstand federal intrusions into the sphere he claimed as his own, and in the end it was Ashmore, not Faubus, who folded his tent and slipped away into the mist.[60]

CHAPTER SEVENTEEN

THE NEW ELITE CONSENSUS

Gaston Williamson

By THE SUMMER OF 1959, WITH THE FULL SCHOOL YEAR LOST AND the segregationists unmasked as being willing to destroy the public schools, a consensus began to emerge among Little Rock's social and business leadership. While they found integration as distasteful as their less sophisticated neighbors, they had come to the realization that some yielding to federal demands was unavoidable. The STOP victory had given them their voice and their direction. Now they began to manage the transition and rein in the die-hard segregationists.

Gaston Williamson was emblematic of that slow tidal shift. He had been a Rhodes Scholar in his youth, earning two law degrees in his three years at Oxford University. Accustomed to success, he had quarterbacked his high school football team, earned a Phi Beta Kappa key at the University of Arkansas, served his country with distinction in World War II, practiced law on Wall Street, and joined Little Rock's finest old legal establishment, the Rose Law Firm, where he plied his trade under the tutelage of a man he admired unreservedly and considered his mentor, Archie House. The father of three school-aged children, Williamson had a particular interest in the quality of Little Rock's public schools, which had always been very high.[1]

Short and compact with an inquisitive expression and a ready smile, Williamson had come of age in the black-belt town of Monticello, Arkansas, and was the descendant of several Confederate soldiers. He had had warm, affectionate relationships with numerous black servants in his childhood, he had grown up "wrestling and hunting and fishing" with an assortment of "colored" boys, he had roomed with a native of India at Oxford, and as a consequence his racial views were more sympathetic and advanced than many of his peers' and colleagues' in Little Rock. Perhaps most important, his values had been shaped in a close-knit, loving family that stressed respectful treatment for

all races, and throughout his life he remained a devoted Presbyterian churchman. When he moved to Little Rock and married pretty Wrenetta Worthen,
daughter of a bank president and cousin of "Aunt Adolphine" Fletcher Terry,
Gaston Williamson became a prime candidate to speak out against the racial
difficulties that engulfed his adopted city.[2]

Williamson's failure to make his voice heard before the summer of 1959
reflected some fundamental realities that confronted Little Rock's businessmen
and "power structure" before the development of the STOP campaign. As Drew
Agar had confessed in May, many men had failed to become involved in the
worsening crisis because they had feared losing clients or business. But on a
deeper level, many had felt impotent to confront Eisenhower's Army or Justice
Department, and in a city that had traditionally functioned according to paternalistic and even feudalistic principles, many felt inadequate to engage the controversy in any spirited way. Additionally, in a society that valued good
manners, most of the city's leadership had hesitated to challenge other people's
racial views, even as they struggled to clarify their own. At last the STOP campaign had changed all of that, empowering men and women to step forward
and confront the abuses they saw escalating all around them.[3]

ON JUNE 1, 1959, the *Arkansas Gazette* ran on its front page two sermons that
had been delivered in Little Rock pulpits the day before, sermons that were
prophetic in their presentation of the choices and the attendant consequences
that lay before the people of Little Rock. Both ministers were committed integrationists, significantly separated from the vast majority of their listeners in
terms of their understanding of the requirements of the Christian gospel. Both
called for a radical realignment of racial patterns and practices in their city. But
where one had tolerance for the cultural resistance to change that had built up
over three generations of legalized caste, the other demanded a clean break with
the past and a forthright disavowal of the limiting older ways.

Dale Cowling was the popular pastor at Little Rock's prestigious Second
Baptist Church, Brooks Hays's church, the wealthy downtown home of the
city's mainstream Baptists. Reverend Cowling, president of the city's interracial Ministerial Alliance, told his congregation that Jesus had taken a "gradu-
alistic" approach to the evil of the slavery that prevailed in his own day.
Cowling admonished his listeners, "We must be wise enough to follow this
same course today." A thoroughly committed integrationist who had worked
for years to improve race relations in Little Rock, Cowling nonetheless concluded, "The great social aspect of this problem can only be resolved with time.

We must be willing to make changes, but we must also be willing to do so slowly and prayerfully."[4]

Several blocks away at Trinity Episcopal Cathedral, Dean Charles Higgins minced no words in condemning the "token integration" plan the city had pursued over the past two years, a plan he described as "a scheme to comply with the letter rather than the spirit of the law," an approach that had backfired, bringing a "curse" upon Little Rock. Given the depth of the commitment to segregation among all elements of the white population, it was a significant indicator of change that the debate was no longer about whether to integrate, but only how quickly to do it.[5]

Even Harry Ashmore, the great champion of compliance with *Brown*, echoed the new elite consensus. He wrote editorials throughout the summer of 1959 arguing that although integration was now the law of the land, ". . . there is much that can be done to control and limit the degree of integration in any school system." First, Ashmore suggested, segregated schools could still be maintained on a voluntary basis, since the "vast majority" of Negro citizens had no desire to participate in desegregation and as a consequence "the white schools are under no real threat of being engulfed by a tide of Negro students." Second, "the problem of integration can be handled in a way that will bring no perceptible alteration of the social patterns in this city" because the School Board had at its disposal the two Pupil Placement Acts of 1956 and 1959.[6]

Daisy Bates's old nemesis, C. H. Jones, publisher of the competing black *Southern Mediator Journal*, provided the figures that gave hope to Harry Ashmore and Everett Tucker, announcing his belief that 20 percent of blacks were segregationists, and another 35 percent were doubtful about the efficacy of integration. Jones also ventured that only 4.5 percent of the black population belonged to the NAACP. Not surprisingly, the Pupil Placement Act became the vehicle of choice the Little Rock School Board used in the summer and fall of 1959 to limit the number of blacks in the public schools. It was a way to make desegregation acceptable to the widest possible range of school patrons in the city.[7]

THREE WEEKS AFTER the successful recall of the offending "extremist" School Board members, the Pulaski County Board of Education appointed three men to assume the vacant positions, and two of them declared themselves in favor of getting the schools reopened. J. H. Cottrell and B. Frank Mackey were destined to become active partners in the tokenist coalition of Tucker, Matson, and Lamb, and they both lived in the Fifth Ward, as did the other three. H. L. Hubbard soon discovered he was ineligible to serve, and in time he was replaced by W. C. McDonald. Within a matter of days the newly constituted School Board had expunged the record of the May 5 meeting, rehired Terrell Powell as superintendent, and reinstated thirty-nine of the forty-four fired teachers.[8]

On June 18 a three-judge federal court declared Acts 4 and 5 unconstitutional. The judges disagreed with the conclusions of the Arkansas Supreme Court, finding that Faubus's closure of the high schools in 1958 had not been a valid exercise of his police powers, and that the disbursement of state funds to private schools was unacceptable and "permanently enjoined." As a consequence, they directed the Little Rock School Board and its superintendent to "take such affirmative steps as may hereafter be directed by this court" to accomplish integration in accordance with previous federal court orders. Finally, they ruled that "the defendants and their successors in office be and are permanently enjoined from engaging in any acts which will directly or indirectly impede, thwart, delay, or frustrate the execution of the approved plan for the gradual integration of the schools of Little Rock. . . ." The three federal judges could not have made a more forceful statement of their determination to enforce both *Brown* and *Cooper v. Aaron.*[9]

Everett Tucker and his new School Board lost no time in moving to comply with the federal court's orders. Within days Tucker announced his board's intention to reopen the high schools in September, using the new Pupil Placement Act copied word for word from an Alabama placement law that the U.S. Supreme Court had upheld. Harry Ashmore rushed to endorse the pupil placement concept, writing in the next few days, "We can hope Mr. Faubus will now recognize that this is the end of the line of state obstruction . . ." and that the placement law offered "protection against the wholesale integration so many fear." Arguing that the courts "have never required integration" and that "no district is required to merge its white and colored schools," Ashmore suggested that "a fair application" of the new placement law would prevent not only "any wholesale race-mixing, but the creation of social conditions in the schools which so many white parents fear." As he would do all summer, Ashmore hammered home the theme that the *Brown* decision was the "law of the land" and that the School Board's decision to reopen the high schools conformed to the "sentiment and wishes" of the community, as the STOP victory had demonstrated.[10]

Orval Faubus disagreed. A much more astute analyst of public sentiment than his old adversary Ashmore, the governor complained that the ruling on Act 4 offered no "area of compromise," and that it not only removed his authority to close the schools but it also took away "any authority the people have to vote on what they want." Intimating that he might be ready to soften his views, he also hinted that he might call a special session of the legislature. In typical fashion, Orval Faubus was keeping all his options open.[11]

Within a week, however, the governor had concluded that the federal court ruling meant the schools would be unable to open peacefully. He suggested ominously that achieving desegregation in the fall would require "federal force" and "live ammunition." Speaking at the Raney High School graduation ceremonies, Faubus compared the private school experiment to the historic encounters at Lexington and Concord, suggesting that the Raney example could be the beginning of a new educational pattern in the South if federal authorities "and the unwise and misdirected members of the Supreme Court" did not relent in their efforts "to usurp all the powers of the state and the people by which they seek to safeguard their most precious liberties and possessions." Faubus made similar claims in a speech to the Veterans of Foreign Wars. "Why go to war and make these sacrifices and see them eaten away piecemeal?" he asked. Claiming that the Supreme Court had already destroyed eight of the ten rights in the Bill of Rights, Faubus asked "Did those men—your buddies—die for this?"[12]

Faubus was under considerable pressure. He had lost a crucial battle in the STOP campaign and felt besieged by Harry Ashmore. His administrative assistant, Rolla Fitch, told a visiting representative of the Southern Regional Council, Benjamin Muse, that while he (Fitch) feared "token integration" would lead to "white and colored falling in love . . . ," he wanted to see the whole integration matter settled "for the sake of the Governor's health." He said the "strain" was telling on Faubus, that his hand was shaking visibly.[13]

Muse tried to persuade the Arkansas governor to throw in the towel in the integration struggle. "Nobody fought integration harder than Governor Almond" [of Virginia], Muse argued, "but he came to the point where there was nothing else he could do. He was just up against Federal power, and he couldn't do any more. That was last January. The same thing has happened to Arkansas now. Arkansas has come to the same point." Faubus bristled at the suggestion and countered, "We haven't come to any such point. We can keep on fighting. The whole South can keep on fighting. We can make the Supreme Court reverse its decision." He soon announced his decision to appeal the federal court's decision on Acts 4 and 5 to the U.S. Supreme Court. Noting that the Arkansas Supreme Court had upheld the two contested acts, Faubus suggested ". . . the people of this state and of this nation have a great deal more confidence in the rulings of state courts than they do in any ruling of a federal court."[14]

THE LITTLE ROCK School Board urgently needed to determine how many students planned to attend the reopened public high schools in the fall. Many private schools, including Raney High School, Baptist High School, Trinity Interim Academy, and the Anthony School, had programs in place to accommodate displaced students, and many other youngsters perhaps intended to continue their schooling in other Arkansas communities and in private schools across the nation. Large numbers of students, especially black pupils, had simply stayed out of school during the previous year, and it was not at all clear whether they would return. Preregistration at Raney High School had taken place the day before the School Board announced its decision to reopen the high schools, and preliminary figures indicated that the number of students at the public high schools would drop significantly.[15]

Lost students were one problem; segregationist resistance was another. At its monthly June meeting, the Capital Citizens' Council reviewed all the developments on the integration front in Little Rock. Members were determined to fight the imposition of "gradual" or "token" integration. The council decided to hold weekly meetings throughout the summer and to step up its educational campaign by distributing anti-integration literature on a more regular basis. According to an FBI informant who had infiltrated the meeting, one board member "said that the Council would agitate the people until September so that 'they will be ready to do anything.'" Amis Guthridge soon announced to the press that the people of Little Rock would "never" accept integration "in any form" and that the CCC planned to take "action." The forces of organized racism soon learned to their surprise, however, that something fundamental had changed in Little Rock since the STOP campaign, and that the forces of respectability had mobilized to take back control of their city.[16]

ON JULY 2, 1959, the STOP workers held their final meeting, this time inviting members of the Women's Emergency Committee to join in their deliberations and plan for the future. Dr. Jerome Levy advised the group, "We should have a planned program shooting both barrels of propaganda to the people as to what it means to have the schools closed. If we get public opinion aroused the school board will find it easy. We should emphasize the economic, ethical and moral loss of keeping these schools closed." *Arkansas Gazette* publisher Hugh Patterson told Benjamin Muse that he felt the business community was the key to the solution of Little Rock's problems. "It is dangerous for the individual business man to 'stick his neck out,'" he said, "but when they act together they are fairly safe. 'If 100 of the leading business men of the state would unite in signing the right kind of statement,' it would do wonders in Arkansas." Hugh Patterson soon got his wish.[17]

Forrest Rozzell presented the School Board with a document bearing the imprimatur of the Arkansas Education Association (although actually created by the Arkansas Council on Human Relations) that outlined for the board the policies it should follow in getting the schools reopened "with minimum desegregation." Primary among those policies was the suggestion that "as many of the people of Little Rock as possible must become personally *committed* to the successful program of the School Board. Just because they are informed does not mean that they are committed. They must be given opportunities to become *involved* in the successful operation of the schools. They must feel that success largely depends on what they do." Under the ministrations of WEC and STOP forces, a new organization began to take shape that planned to offer large numbers of people the opportunity to become "personally committed" to the successful program of the School Board. Eventually christened the Committee for the Peaceful Operation of Free Public Schools, the new organization chose Gaston Williamson as its chair.[18]

Williamson set to work, calling about 150 people and inviting them to join in a movement to assure the peaceful opening of the public schools. On July 17 an estimated one hundred people met at the Lafayette Hotel and heard Forrest Rozzell announce the formation of the new movement. Despite the recent public comments about "live ammunition" and "action" to forestall integration, Rozzell urged his listeners to refrain from impugning the motives of the extreme segregationists, suggesting the new group must assume that "their hearts are right and their intentions honest." In that spirit the new organization adopted a resolution endorsing a system of free public schools for all children, and declaring that despite the "honest differences of opinion that now divide the people," ways must be found to resolve those differences without resorting to violence. "Therefore," the resolution concluded, "we endorse the endeavor of the Little Rock School Board to restore the public schools of our city to full operation, and we call upon the leaders of the community, public and private, to support the effort to preserve free public education and maintain peace and order."[19]

The same day that Gaston Williamson's new committee was announced publicly, the City Board of Directors declared its intention to maintain order in Little Rock and announced they had instructed the Police Department "to deal firmly and quickly in the protection of life and property should the need arise." Undoubtedly Williamson and Rozzell and other city leaders had coordinated these two announcements. Williamson soon conferred with Justice Department officials, who suggested that his group "start legal action to enjoin troublemakers from acts which would impede compliance with the Federal Court orders." Following the example of the 1957 School Board, to whom the Justice Department had made the same recommendation, Williamson's committee declined to participate in a scheme that would put them so clearly at odds with their neighbors.[20]

WHILE THE MOVEMENT to support the School Board began to gather steam, that board's president, attorney, and school superintendent planned a fact-finding mission to Charlotte, North Carolina, and Norfolk, Virginia, to study two school systems where pupil placement policies had been successfully employed. Everett Tucker, Herschel Friday, and Terrell Powell flew first to Charlotte. In meetings with his counterparts in the North Carolina city, Tucker characterized the members of the Little Rock School Board as "moderates or, at least, non-abolitionists," telling the group, "We have a wealth of inexperience." Friday said the people in Little Rock essentially "wanted public schools, wanted segregation, but could not have both. The problem," he said, was "to find a way to minimize integration. They hope the pupil placement law will do it."[21]

From New York, Daisy Bates announced that Little Rock's blacks were prepared to abide by the Pupil Placement Act, if it was administered fairly. Bates was bending over backward to cooperate with the new School Board in its efforts to get the schools reopened. In practice, pupil placement laws were highly restrictive, and they ensured that desegregation would occur with only token numbers of black students enrolled in white schools.[22]

Back in Little Rock, Everett Tucker announced that he now had "greater confidence" in the placement act since his team had talked to people "who have successfully demonstrated that this problem can be handled rationally and intelligently" to the apparent satisfaction of both races. Speaking of Norfolk he said, "It's reassuring to see the way in which the School Board's plan has been accepted by citizens of both races." The plan Tucker studied in Charlotte placed only one black child in the city's schools that year.[23]

WITH LOCAL AUTHORITIES and many influential residents on its side, with the Hall High district redrawn to add about twenty-five black families to its zone, with Raney High School available as an "escape valve" for uncompromising segregationists, and with Governor Faubus's options limited, the School Board announced plans to register high school students for the 1959–60 school year. Police Chief Gene Smith asked unaffiliated people to stay away from the high schools, promising to arrest and jail any who provoked incidents or disturbed the peace. When registration started at Hall High School, Chief Smith angrily ordered several newsmen to leave the campus with the words "All you do is start trouble." CCC president Dr. Malcolm Taylor issued a statement that "the people who resent integration in our schools do not care if our race-mixing School Board registers 10,000 Negroes now as long as the city officials do not take up where the NAACP and 101st Airborne Division left off, and assume the dirty work which Eisenhower started."[24]

Daisy Bates returned from her New York trip with a high fever, but she set to work immediately recruiting black students to register at Hall and Central. As she wrote Roy Wilkins, "Tuesday morning Sybil Jordan, a tenth grade student came in and we contacted by 'phone around fifty parents and children. . . . We were fortunate in getting our top scholastic-quality pupils to register at both Hall and Central. After much persuasion and a little pressure, we were able to get two of our leading ministers to register their children." Even though Elizabeth Eckford and Thelma Mothershed had earned enough credits through correspondence courses to enter college in the fall, Bates asked them to register at Central High, in order to "give courage to other children and parents." Both did, as did Melba Patillo and Jefferson Thomas.[25]

NAACP Regional Director Clarence Laws returned to Little Rock to help with the recruitment process and to "urge parents of Negro children to see that their children were registered at the schools that we hope will be desegregated this fall." He was particularly anxious to recruit applicants for Hall High School, where "the wealthier, more intelligent whites seem anxious to prove to Little Rock in particular, and to the rest of the world in general that there can be school integration in the city without the violence, discord and shame which attended the Central High School in 1957–58."[26]

As registration proceeded quietly at the four high schools, announcements began to appear in the newspapers that various private schools had decided to close. At the end of registration, 1,462 students remained unaccounted for, but Raney High had registered 1,208, which left slightly over 250 students, mostly white, unregistered. Both systems expected more registrations in August. Fewer than sixty black students had expressed a desire to attend formerly all-white schools. Speaking of black registration in Norfolk and Charlotte, Everett Tucker commented, ". . . in both cities the 'responsible colored people' had demonstrated 'rather significantly, I think,' that they are decreasingly interested in trying to force their children in white schools. They have never had any litigation and it is also significant to note that Charlotte has acquired 14 new manufacturing plants during the last two years, as opposed to exactly none at Little Rock last year. . . ." The School Board president clearly wanted to believe he had found a painless solution to Little Rock's desegregation difficulties.[27]

Gaston Williamson made good on his promise to place his organization's support behind the efforts of the School Board. Expressing pride in "the efficient manner in which our school administrators, our public officials and enforcement officers met the challenge for a calm approach to the usual routine of registration," Williamson commended students and parents and declared, "I am satisfied that screening by the School Board and other appropriate authority will be done with dispatch and in good faith under the terms of the state's student placement law. . . ."[28]

Of course, the segregationists had not given up. On July 28, Orval Faubus proposed an outrageous scheme to the Little Rock School Board, no doubt to be provocative. He suggested that Horace Mann and Hall be integrated racially but segregated by sex, "to forestall the inevitable increase of moral problems which have always come with integrated schools." He also proposed that Central High School be left all white. As he wrote, tauntingly, "I believe that the acceptance of this plan by the school board and the integrationists of Little Rock will bring about an immediate solution to this grave problem. . . ." Furthermore, "We would have reason to hope that the gulf of distrust and hatred which has been created between the races by the arrogance of the NAACP and the 'police-state' methods of the federal government would begin to fade away."[29]

The School Board rejected the Faubus plan, announcing that it would "involve considerably more integration than the Board contemplates under the policies which it is currently pursuing." The NAACP rejected the governor's plan out of hand, saying straightforwardly it was impractical and it did not satisfy constitutional requirements. The next day, Gaston Williamson's Advisory Committee gathered for its first (and as it turned out, only) meeting, at which time Williamson said the governor's plan would not pass muster constitutionally.[30]

Declaring the preservation of the public school system to be "a vital necessity to the future of this community in any terms you care to measure it—moral, economic, social—choose your own yardstick . . . ," Williamson proclaimed that Little Rock's schools "must be opened in compliance with constitutional law—as that law has been determined by the only court competent to do so under our Federal Constitution." This was one of the few times an Arkansas leader of any stature, other than Harry Ashmore, had proclaimed publicly that the *Brown* decision was the law of the land and had to be obeyed. Gaston Williamson had the credibility, and the *gravitas,* to speak on this subject and be believed.[31]

Acknowledging that some Little Rock citizens would refuse to send their children to integrated schools, Williamson remarked, "There will be private schools in our city and public schools elsewhere to which [segregationists] may send their children without doing violence to their own conscience." But in the face of the recent high school registration, which demonstrated that the majority of school patrons preferred free public high schools even if it involved some degree of integration, Williamson demanded that the "honest convictions of these people are also entitled to respect. Their children should not be denied an education of their choice by those who prefer a private school." In conclusion Williamson announced it would be the purpose of his organization to call upon citizens in the coming weeks to take a public stand in support of the Little Rock School Board. "Only through the *open* support of a majority of our citizens can we insure the peaceful operation of free public schools in our city."[32]

TWO DAYS LATER, Everett Tucker's group announced a decision that all sides condemned. On July 31 the Little Rock School Board assigned only six black children to the two formerly white high schools. In two years, the Little Rock Nine had been shrunk by one-third. The board sent two of the original Nine, Thelma Mothershed and Melba Patillo, back to Horace Mann. Russell Matson later explained that Mothershed had a heart problem, "and was sent back because Mann is a one-story building while Central has five floors"; Patillo, "while not a troublemaker herself, seemed to attract trouble and the board thought it better to return her to Horace Mann." The School Board had made its assignments on the basis of criteria such as physical condition, emotional stability, citizenship and academic performance, none of which mentioned race.[33]

Daisy Bates contacted Wiley Branton on the children's behalf, alerting him to start making plans "to protect their interest. . . ." She was reported to be "disturbed by the attitude of the moderates [undoubtedly Harry Ashmore] who are already putting pressure upon her to accept this token integration which is being carried out under the school placement law." She requested that NAACP Regional Director Clarence Laws return to Little Rock "to assist in the coming phase of the controversy."[34]

Bitterness and resentment developed quickly in the black community, as parents absorbed the fact that fifty-five of their children had expressed a desire to attend the formerly white schools and yet only six had survived the School Board's screening process. Parents and other concerned black citizens began to hold meetings to determine "how to arouse the community to speak out in numbers against the school board's abuse of the pupil placement law." At each of these meetings, according to reports to the national NAACP office, "the overwhelming majority felt that these 'moderates' were genuine segregationists whose actions were just as unscrupulous and much more effective than those of the racists."[35]

Others in the black community believed that the announced screening was the best that could be expected under the circumstance. As Nat Griswold wrote to the Southern Regional Council, "Knowledgeable persons indicate that the Little Rock Negro leadership generally will cooperate in the School Board's proposal if they are convinced that it is made in 'good faith.' . . . It would seem to be the case that actually there is no conflict between the desires of the Negro leadership and what the white community has been forced to accept as the price of keeping the schools open." Based on his extensive contacts in the black community, Griswold was convinced that "the School Board with the least bit of private attention to the Negro leaders can be assured of their support."[36]

The Capital Citizens' Council was as distressed about the School Board's assignments as was the NAACP. Amis Guthridge sputtered to reporters, "our answer to leaders of the diabolical race-mixing plot is NEVER!" Guthridge read a statement declaring that the "race-mixing" at Little Rock was directed by "Communists in Washington and New York, aided and abetted by Main Street merchants." Guthridge continued, "The School Board is again trying to deceive local white parents. . . . If six Negroes can force their entrance unnecassarily [*sic*] into two white high schools, then 600 have the same right." Guthridge claimed that "tokenism" was just the entering wedge that eventually would allow the white schools to be overrun by blacks.[37]

Watching from afar, with keen but quiet interest, the U.S. Department of Justice assessed the potential for successful desegregation in Little Rock. Writing to Attorney General William P. Rogers on August 4, W. Wilson White of the Civil Rights Division suggested that six factors had changed in the city since 1957, boding well for the prospects of a peaceful school opening. First and most important, significant numbers of people had now accepted "the ultimate unavoidability of complying with the principle enunciated in *Brown.*" Second, as a result of recent elections and the creation of supporting citizens' organizations, the present School Board had "the benefit of a popular endorsement which the 1957 board did not clearly have." Third, the present School Board had chosen to act "with a firmness and consistency—almost aggressiveness— which was not displayed by the school board in 1957." In addition, the School

Board had defused the class issue by enlarging the Hall High district to include more black families. The presence of segregated Raney High School could be expected to relieve some of the parental pressure on the School Board, and it would probably remove some of the troublemakers from the public schools. Finally, new Police Chief Eugene Smith was "more able and aggressive" than his predecessor.[38]

On the downside, however, White's memorandum noted that Herschel Friday had replaced Archie House as School Board attorney, and Friday's firm also represented Governor Faubus. In addition, the "sincere and energetic" Woodrow Mann was no longer mayor of Little Rock, and federal Judge Ronald Davies was no longer on the scene. White questioned whether Judge John Miller would be willing "to enter any orders enjoining interference with the operation of desegregated schools." Finally, White worried that Dale Alford, who had replaced Brooks Hays as congressman for the district, "may well insert himself into any controversy involving the opening of the schools this fall." Based on this assessment, White recommended to the attorney general that the department maintain a "continuous liaison" with the School Board and prepare the paperwork to seek an injunction in case segregationist extremists disrupted the school openings. Finally he proposed that the department arrange to mobilize one hundred federal marshals for use in Little Rock if the need arose.[39]

IN LATE JULY AND early August, Governor Faubus and the School Board engaged in a chess match of feints and maneuvers. At a July 21 meeting of the Capital Citizens' Council Board, according to an FBI informant, Jim Johnson claimed that Faubus intended to have Raney High School delay its own opening for two weeks after the opening of the public schools, during which time the Raney students could "enroll at Central to 'raise hell,' then when they get kicked out of Central, they can go to Raney High as planned." Archie House passed on to Gaston Williamson the information that "Faubus was going to try to pull the same damn thing he'd done the two previous Septembers by bringing in a big bunch of his white folks and council thugs from all over the state and bringing them in to cause a riot in September when the schools would reopen. . . ."[40]

The same FBI informant also reported that Jim Johnson had told Faubus he "had legislation drawn up to be presented to a special session of the legislature to be used in the event the Federal Government tried to force integration at Little Rock." The prospect of a special session to create more anti-integration laws was a strong gambit by Faubus, which could have presented the biggest obstacle to the successful reopening of the high schools.[41]

IN THE MIDST OF this drama, influential insurance executive Herbert Thomas approached the School Board with a plan he had devised, apparently single-handedly, to resolve the controversy. He believed that if the School Board agreed to lease Raney High School and run it as a segregated school within the Little Rock public school system, free of charge to the parents who chose to enroll their children there, everybody's problems would be solved—the School Board's, the governor's, the segregationists'. Because of Thomas's prominence, and because he was chairman of the Legislative Subcommittee for Gaston Williamson's organization, the School Board gave him a respectful hearing. The members voted 5–1 to adopt his plan.[42]

On Tuesday, August 4, the board sent J. H. Cottrell out to the Capitol bearing a letter to Governor Faubus that read in part, "We are trying hard to represent every parent in Little Rock by using your own good placement laws and permitting the smallest degree of integration and still maintain our public school system." The School Board continued, "As a demonstration of our desire to cooperate with you, as a demonstration of our desire to represent all of the tax-paying parents of Little Rock, who want a school wholly segregated . . . ," they were willing to discuss with him and the Raney board a plan to lease the private school. The School Board's letter expressed the members' collective belief that no black children would apply for admission to Raney High; if they did, however, the board members believed that "with the use of the placement program, and without violating the spirit of the court orders, we could transfer the applicants to either of the other schools." If, in fact, all of these efforts failed and the courts ordered integration of Raney High, "then in keeping with our conception of a lease provision, we would immediately return it to the private Raney Board."[43]

The scheme fell apart at the moment of its creation when *Arkansas Democrat* reporter Bobbie Forster appeared at the morning School Board meeting shortly after J. H. Cottrell had left to deliver the letter. She informed her five startled listeners that Dr. T. J. Raney had just announced Raney High School's closure. Four School Board members piled in their cars and dashed to the Capitol building, where they overtook Cottrell in the press room of the governor's office. As Vivion Brewer wrote, "it was a Marx Brothers comedy. . . ."[44]

Press reports immediately quoted Dr. Raney to the effect that his board was "broke." This may have been true, because the federal court's ruling against Act 5 left the private school without public funds. Raney explained that private contributions had dried up, and that a projected fund-raising effort had failed to generate the necessary level of interest. Raney also said that Governor Faubus was not involved in the decision to close the school.[45]

Faubus still had the threat of a special session up his sleeve, but by his own admission the Little Rock School Board "outfoxed" him that day. Coming back together after retrieving their ill-fated letter, Everett Tucker's board voted unanimously to open the high schools a month early. School would start again in Little Rock, with token integration, on August 12.[46] Faubus had no time to call the legislature together. Segregationists had no options other than public protests.

LOCAL BLACK LEADERS openly opposed the use of the screening techniques the school board had employed. Daisy Bates's neighbor, Dr. Garman Freeman, charged that the heavy-handed use of the Pupil Placement Act "negates the esteem and confidence" blacks felt for the board. I. S. McClinton said there probably would have been no protests if the numbers had been slightly higher. As it was, a group of black parents hired Wiley Branton to appeal their children's assignments to Horace Mann High School. Branton and Thurgood Marshall sought a restraining order to prohibit the Little Rock School Board from using the 1959 Pupil Placement Act. If the court granted Branton's motion, all black children living in the attendance areas of Hall or Central would have had to be admitted if they applied. Within several days the School Board replied to Branton's motion, asking Judge Miller to dismiss it as premature, because the black students had not pursued the administrative remedies specified in the Pupil Placement Act.[47]

Branton doubted that the School Board had complied with federal court orders to follow its own integration plan. The NAACP attorney pointed out to the court that by denying entrance to the black children "in their appropriate school zones" the School Board deprived the African-American students of gains they had earned in previous court actions. Branton charged that the School Board was using the Pupil Placement Act to frustrate federal court orders and circumvent the court-approved Blossom Plan, which was still in effect.[48]

Everett Tucker was stunned by this attack. He thought black citizens "should be grateful that the school board is making it possible for Negro children to resume their interrupted education." Judge Miller took the case under advisement, but he commented he was "not going to bust a trace" to hear the complaint filed by the two black attorneys.[49]

As the date for school opening drew near, the School Board and Gaston Williamson's core group met every day with city officials, planning their responses to the expected demonstrations. A group of Raney High students held an uneventful rally at their old alma mater. Amid much talk of "constitutional government" and "race-mixing," one student did turn a memorable phrase for the cameras when he intoned, "We are enrolling in an integrated school under protest. We will attend an integrated school under protest. If necessary we will graduate from an integrated school under protest."[50]

Rumors began to circulate of a demonstration on the Capitol steps the morning of the school opening. Amis Guthridge issued a statement inviting "patriotic Americans" to come to the Capitol and protest against "the illegal and arrogant threat of federally dominated tyranny over a proud and peace-loving people. We heartily endorse this right to peaceably assemble to petition our governor to hold the torch of liberty high as he has done so nobly against terrific odds. . . ." Reporters began to pour into Little Rock from all over the country and beyond. Everett Tucker made a statement to about eighty of them gathered at Woodruff School, where the board planned to meet with press members twice a day for the next few days.[51]

Gaston Williamson announced that the eighteen lawyers on his Legal Subcommittee stood ready "to move for immediate court injunctions if necessary to curb agitators," evidently responding to Justice Department prodding. Williamson also announced that caravans of segregationist protesters were reportedly headed to Little Rock from the black belt areas of West Memphis and Pine Bluff. Others were soon reported from south Mississippi County and Phillips County, both in eastern Arkansas.[52]

Faubus was initially silent on his plans about attending the rally at the Capitol, although he told reporters outside his office that the NAACP "does not want this thing [racial problems in Little Rock] settled, and neither do the Communists working in the background." The night before school started the governor went on television and discouraged violence, saying that elections were the only way to fight. "I see nothing to be gained tomorrow by disorder and violence," he admonished his listeners. Emphasizing that he was not "throwing in the sponge," the governor said if token integration were effected "there are many ways in which you who are opposed can still resist. The struggle is not by any means ended. Regardless of the outcome tomorrow you must resolve to continue the struggle for freedom." Directing particular venom at the School Board and city officials, whom he called "the puppets of the federal government," Faubus said "This is your handiwork and you will be held responsible."[53]

THE MORNING OF August 12, 1959, Hall High School reopened without incident. Central High was slated to open after lunch. The only real action in the integration story shaped up in the rally on the Capitol grounds. Throughout the crowd of one thousand to fifteen hundred souls who congregated around the Capitol steps, many waved small Confederate flags, and choruses of "Dixie" went up from time to time. Signs carried by adults and children said "Arkansas Is for Faubus," "Race Mixing is Communism," "Stop the Race Mixing," "Governor Faubus Save Our Christian America," and "We Want Americanization Not Red-ucation." The Capital Citizens' Council distributed a new circular headed "The Negro's Ambition—A Mongrel American Race."[54]

At length Governor Faubus appeared to address the unruly throng. Speaking briefly, he concluded by saying, "We are fighting for democracy. We must not violate its basic precepts but must continue the struggle as free, honest and law-abiding people." After the governor had disappeared into the rotunda of the massive Capitol building, Timothy Canada, a black worker, went to the microphone and declared Orval Faubus "the best governor we ever had" and said Negroes should "stay in our place." Several whites patted him on the back and shook his hand while other whites ordered three black reporters on the edge of the crowd to leave the scene.[55]

Police Chief Gene Smith, sporting a light blue suit and a straw hat in the scorching heat, arrested three teenagers who had canisters of tear gas in their car. State police reported that two-thirds of the people at the rally were from out of town. Some were simply curious onlookers; many were teenagers. The crowd included more women than men. At length a husky, blond former Marine named Robert J. Norwood, president of the States' Rights Council, a splinter group of the Capital Citizens' Council, encouraged the crowd to march to Central High School. About two hundred participants in the rally, most of them teenage boys, joined Norwood in his ten-block march.[56]

As *Southern School News* reported the scene, "Through the streets they walked with the sound truck blaring while the crowd chanted 'Two four six eight, We don't want to integrate' or sang along with the 'Dixie' parody: 'In Arkansas, in the state of cotton, Federal courts are good and rotten, Look away, look away, look away, Dixieland.'" Carrying their signs and their flags and marching along with great camaraderie, they were entertained along the way by a bugler who played Confederate songs. Gene Smith and his police line stood three deep in the street one block east of Central High. Some of the marchers cursed the officers, calling them communists and cowards, while Smith bellowed through a portable electric megaphone, "Your behavior is a disgraceful matter . . . let's get out of the street." Coming to within an arm's length of the police line, four men at the front of the crowd, including Robert Norwood, tried to push their way through. The police grabbed them by the arms and threw them in waiting paddy wagons. The noonday temperature was 90 degrees, and the humidity was stifling.[57]

In a well-rehearsed maneuver (Smith later admitted his men had been preparing for this for a month), the police advanced in a V-formation, dividing the marchers and pushing them out of the street. Meeting some resistance, the police used their billy clubs on several men, and then a waiting fire truck pulled up and sprayed the remaining resisters into submission. One local reporter noted it was so hot, the water evaporated from the street within thirty minutes. In a matter of minutes the police made twenty-one arrests, including one woman, two teenage girls, ten teenage boys, and eight men. All were released on bail. Thirty minutes after the confrontation was over, the doors reopened to students at Central High School for the first time in fourteen months.[58]

Eighty percent of the registered students attended Hall and Central that first day. Undoubtedly some parents kept their children home from the potential disturbances, and many students were still away on vacation or at summer camp in August. Everett Tucker reported that everything was perfectly normal inside both schools. Interviewed at Daisy Bates's home, five of the black students said they were treated well, especially at Hall, although Jefferson Thomas reported that as in the past, no one had talked to him. Harry Ashmore wrote with profound relief, "And this, we believe, finally ends the shameful chapter in which public officials incited private citizens to violence and assured them they could engage in it with impunity." While he understood that Little Rock's troubles were not over, Ashmore dared to hope they "now can be resolved by orderly process, and . . . no one will again rule this city by terror, pressure, and intimidation."[59]

GASTON WILLIAMSON released a statement commending the "vast majority" of Little Rock citizens who had measured up to their responsibilities on opening day, but he also found it regrettable that "a few persons, many of them not citizens of this school district," attempted to interfere. The earnest attorney claimed that no citizen of the Little Rock School District had been denied "his legitimate right of peaceable assembly or his right of free speech." But at the same time, he argued that "no citizen can be permitted to endanger the public safety by attempting to defy the lawful and constituted police force in the execution of its clearly apparent duty."[60]

Faubus characterized the tactics of Gene Smith's police force as "Hungarian," in a reference to the Soviet-backed repression of a popular uprising in Budapest in October and November of 1956. Amis Guthridge and Wesley Pruden complained of police "brutality." L'Moore Alford, wife of the congressman, also protested the police "brutality" at Central High School. Signing her letter as chairman of the "Committee of Harassed American Patriots at Little Rock," Mrs. Alford wrote to Mayor Werner Knoop demanding that the City Board take disciplinary action against Police Chief Gene Smith and threatening that if the board did not do so, she would protest to the National Defense Committee of the Daughters of the American Revolution.[61]

The City Board responded that it felt the police acted "in a completely legal manner in maintaining order and protecting life and property." Whereas in the past the City Board had refused to participate in implementing integration, now, under the aggressive leadership of men like Gaston Williamson and Everett Tucker, the city's leaders were stepping up to the plate.[62]

The Justice Department had continued to stay out of the public eye in Little Rock that fall. Having been roundly criticized for its performances there in both 1957 and 1958, and having failed to persuade President Eisenhower to take a strong stand in favor of civil rights, the department clearly wanted to turn over to local authorities the responsibility for enforcing court orders regarding *Brown* and *Cooper v. Aaron*. Its official stance was to "leave to local authorities the maintenance of peace and order around the high schools, but . . . lend assistance if necessary." St. John Barrett of the Civil Rights Division returned to Little Rock at the request of United States Attorney Osro Cobb, and throughout the day of the school reopenings the two men and their assistants monitored the situation by radio and telephone and in turn kept Justice Department officials in Washington, D.C., informed. The department never had to intervene. Its extensive contacts with people such as Everett Tucker and Gaston Williamson had paid off.[63]

Harry Ashmore, as always, had the last word. Despite Orval Faubus's admonitions on television and at the Capitol rally that his followers should avoid street protests and rely on the electoral process, Ashmore blamed the governor for the violence at Central High, saying he was in front of the high school in spirit if not in person. Two days later he returned to one of his major themes, an idea that by this time had become a part of his canon of beliefs about the Little Rock crisis. "The keeping of the peace at Little Rock on Wednesday was initiated and sustained by local authority, as it could have been all along if nobody had interfered." Ashmore had spent the summer reinforcing his version of Little Rock crisis history. He already knew he would be leaving the city for good in October.[64]

BY THE TIME THE schools reopened, fourteen black children had filed appeals for transfers with the Little Rock School Board. Daisy Bates had met with the students twice, and five of them had decided to remain out of school "until the regular school year started September 8th, or until the school board gave them some reason for not allowing them to attend Central." Bates's thinking in recommending they stay out of school was colored by her experience in 1957, when Virgil Blossom had persuaded eight of the seventeen students who had survived his screening process to return to Horace Mann until the situation "cooled down," promising them that they could then transfer to Central High School. In the crisis environment that ensued, Blossom did not keep his promise. Two of the protesting students in 1959 had been among the eight who returned to Horace Mann in 1957.[65]

The day after school opened, Everett Tucker announced that nineteen black students had requested transfers. The *Arkansas Gazette* reported that Sybil Jordan and William Massie planned to "strike" to protest not being assigned to Central. This maneuver infuriated Wiley Branton, who was trying to get the judge's attention and did not need his plaintiffs muddying the water by getting involved in the appeal procedure. As he wrote to Daisy Bates, "I told you specifically that *none of the original plaintiffs* or *interveners* and *none of the persons* who were *willing to intervene* should send in any appeal to the school board." While he appreciated Bates's tremendous personal sacrifices for the cause, he had dealt with her strong personality for years; he tried to blend both factors in his concluding comments, saying, "We are in a difficult position because of your failure to follow legal advice. You have done and are doing an outstanding job but you are not a lawyer and the sooner you realize that, then the sooner our work can be coordinated. Please be assured of my continued interest and support in the Little Rock School fight."[66]

On August 26 the Little Rock School Board met to assign late-registering students to the various high schools. Two white women tossed tear gas canisters into the foyer of the board's administrative offices, and the intense fumes forced the board to complete its deliberations at the Chamber of Commerce offices.[67]

On September 3 the board heard the first of several black students' requests for a transfer. On September 8 it heard seven more. The appeals procedure for black students (but not whites) required the student to come before the School Board with a parent or spokesperson to be questioned by members of the board or the board's attorney. As in 1957, any black student who wanted to pursue athletics or other extracurricular activities was denied board approval to transfer. Eventually only three black students—Sybil Jordan, Sandra Johnson, and Franklin Henderson—received transfers to Central High School.[68]

Nat Griswold agonized over the use of the Pupil Placement Act. To him it was "unquestionably the highest legal hurdle yet devised to keep from compliance with the Supreme Court's decisions." He understood that "the fearsome prospect is that the best way to avoid desegregation is neither to use massive or local resistance to the courts but so to administer the schools that Negro students will be steered away from all-white schools or may unhappily voluntarily withdraw." The real problem, as Griswold understood, was that Little Rock's officials were attempting, in his terms, "legal good faith" while ignoring "moral good faith." As he reported to his superiors, Little Rock's officials "hope to restore the 'good name' of Little Rock without practicing fair play toward the Negro students."[69]

Nat Griswold's views may have been even more progressive than those of his parent organization, the Southern Regional Council. That body had declared itself in favor of integration in 1951, but its commitment to immediate and full integration lagged far behind that of the NAACP. In fact, the SRC sponsored visits around the South by Everett Tucker and Boyd Ridgway, using the two apostles from Little Rock to spread the message that other cities could avoid Little Rock's economic downturn by accepting integration. What Tucker and Ridgway sold to their eager listeners, of course, was the gospel of tokenism.[70]

As legal historian Mark Tushnet has written, ". . . in the areas where school boards used pupil placement rules to disguise racial discrimination, relatively few African-American parents were willing to subject their children both to the intrusive inquiries and testing under the pupil placement laws and the prospect of harassment if they were admitted to white schools. As a result, it would take litigators a long time to accumulate enough evidence to make a powerful showing that the boards were using the rules to evade *Brown*." Historian Mary Dudziak concurred in this assessment: "Bureaucratizing the process meant that racial integration was minimized. School boards now had a cumbersome process that by itself would delay integration. . . . To white southerners, the path was clear: bureaucratization could accomplish most of what overt resistance had not."[71]

In November 1959, Gloster Current, national director of branches, spoke at the Arkansas NAACP's annual convention. Calling the South's proliferating pupil placement laws "a deliberate attempt to keep Negroes from enrolling in white public schools," he promised an all-out attack on them. Current roared, "There were some who thought the reopening of the schools with token integration represented progress, that Negroes should accept token integration and be grateful and not complain further. We can never be satisfied with token integration." Unfortunately, the South's new elite consensus would not be easily dislodged.[72]

A BANG AND A WHIMPER

I N AUGUST OF 1959, JEFFERSON THOMAS RETURNED TO CENTRAL High School, soon to be joined by Carlotta Walls. During the week that he was the lone black student in the school he suffered escalating attacks from a group of white toughs, some of them the same segregationist tormentors who had honed their skills in 1957–58. After a week of harassment, Jeff's father, Ellis Thomas, wrote a letter to Principal Jess Matthews chronicling the mistreatment and requesting that school officials intervene. Matthews reported these incidents to the School Board and the harassment halted temporarily. On September 9, Ellis Thomas wrote again to Jess Matthews, reporting that the incidents had resumed and were escalating. "One of the boys," Mr. Thomas wrote, "tried to bump into Jeff. Jeff turned to the side and the boy kicked him. The two other boys rushed into Jeff and one of them struck Jeff in the side. Jeff caught him and held him. While he was holding him, one of the boys struck him in the abdomen." Jefferson Thomas received supportive letters from all over the country, but the day-to-day torment inside Central High School continued.[1]

LITTLE ROCK'S CITIZENS awakened the morning after Labor Day, 1959, to the horrifying news that three dynamite bombs had shattered the evening stillness between 10:30 and 11:00 the night before. The bombers had targeted Fire Chief Gann Nalley, whose car exploded, Mayor Werner Knoop, whose office building sustained extensive damage to its facade, and the administrative offices of the Little Rock School Board, blowing a sizable hole in an outside wall. Police Chief Gene Smith immediately placed all available officers on duty and started a methodical search for the perpetrators, assisted by the FBI. Smith also stationed guards at the homes of all School Board members and city officials and placed a ring of policemen around Central High School.[2]

Little Rock's leaders were irate. The Chamber of Commerce called an emergency meeting of its officers, board of directors, and past presidents, who quickly announced a $25,000 reward for helping to capture the bombers. After the meeting one Chamber official said to waiting reporters, "I'm madder than hell this morning." Another, shaking his head said, "I don't quite understand this. Things like this just don't happen in other cities." Months later Chamber vice president Billy Rector claimed that the bombings had cost the city $30 million in new industry.[3]

Gaston Williamson issued a statement saying, "The cowardly bombings last night were the inevitable consequence of defiance of duly constituted authority and deliberate invitations to violence which have been issued by persons in high places and by irresponsible spokesmen for extremist groups." Filled with righteous indignation, and blaming if not naming Orval Faubus as well as people such as Amis Guthridge and Wesley Pruden, Williamson continued: "These tactics of terror and anarchy should awaken every responsible citizen to the danger of following blindly those who advocate departure from law and order in the solution of present local problems. The persons who planted the dynamite are not more guilty than the rabble rousers who planted the idea."[4]

Governor Faubus called the violence "sickening and deplorable," but he insisted the real blame should be placed on the integration policy of the federal government. According to the *Arkansas Gazette,* Faubus charged that the "underlying cause of the violence is the federal government's policy on racial integration." As the governor suggested, "Of course, if the causes were removed there wouldn't be dynamiting in the first place." Bishop Robert R. Brown called for prayers.[5]

About midafternoon that day, Tuesday, a telephone caller at the Chamber office asked for Grainger Williams. Told that the president was not there, he left a message: "We've got some dynamite for Williams too if he doesn't keep his damned mouth shut." The Chamber president told the press that he "wasn't worried about it"; nonetheless, since he lived outside the city limits, he hired private guards and stationed them on his property.[6]

Within forty-eight hours Gene Smith's police had targeted and the city had charged three suspects in the bombings, all of whom, along with two others, were eventually convicted. One, E. A. Lauderdale, a roofing contractor who supplied the dynamite and was eventually identified as the mastermind of the operation, was a board member of the Capital Citizens' Council. CCC President Malcolm Taylor praised Lauderdale as "a hard-working Christian patriot." He added, "If Mr. Lauderdale can be selected as the scapegoat and railroaded in prison, then no American can dare voice his honest resentment to police state tactics nor hope to find refuge in the time-honored laws and constitutional

rights of this once-great land." Thoroughly discredited by the Labor Day bombings, the Capital Citizens' Council died a quiet, slow death.[7] The bombings
undermined extremism, rather than boosting it.

Later that month, the Women's Emergency Committee released its "Little
Rock Report," filled with gloomy appraisals of the city's prospects for industrial
development. Chamber of Commerce manager Boyd Ridgway had told a local
Kiwanis Club in June that he anticipated "little outside interest in Arkansas by
industry as long as the public schools are closed." According to figures the
Arkansas Industrial Development Commission compiled, Arkansas had fallen
"from first in new job creation in an eight-state area to fourth place in 1958,
with the greatest percentage decrease of any of the eight states."[8]

Based on extensive interviews, the WEC's report stressed six points: one out
of five professional people planned or wanted to move away from the city;
skilled persons had been refusing to accept jobs in Little Rock because of the
school situation; new industry had refused to move into the area; real estate
business and home building had declined by 20 percent since 1957; business
indicators for Little Rock had not kept pace with other cities in the region; and
the number of new families moving into the city had declined. The WEC sent
copies to all members of the Arkansas legislature, and the Southern Regional
Council distributed them to thousands of business and civic leaders around the
southern region, hoping to make Little Rock a cautionary tale for other cities
facing the same resistance to integration.[9]

As *New York Times* writer Gertrude Samuels described Little Rock in September of 1959, the city had become "tired of trouble." Far from favoring
integration, however, the city's whites felt "forced to comply with an unpopular law to get their schools open again. Grudgingly but surely they . . . effected
a compromise—token integration."[10] At least now, finally, the schools were
open.

Members of the Little Rock School Board expended tremendous amounts
of energy in succeeding years, screening and limiting black applicants who
wanted to transfer into the formerly all-white schools. Most of them never
bought into the moral imperative that was at the heart of the *Brown* decision.
As historian Matthew Lassiter has concluded, white elites across the South, following lessons learned from Little Rock, "did not tell the truth about the policies of pragmatic segregation that replaced massive resistance." It was a collective
case of "bad-faith tactics that merely postponed an eventual reckoning."[11]

Southern leaders such as Everett Tucker had been imbued with ancestral
fears, widespread among southern whites. They recoiled from what they

perceived to be the dangers of race-mixing, "mongrelization," and miscegenation, and they were troubled that the nation's judicial system did not take these irrational but very real fears into consideration. Speaking of the Eighth Circuit Court of Appeals, Tucker told the Eisenhower Administration Project in 1971, ". . . it's just inconceivable to me that people who have had absolutely no personal experience can be expected to resolve equitably the kind of issues that this thing has brought to them, and that they have had the sole responsibility for laying down the law of the land."[12]

FEDERAL JUDGE AXEL BECK ruled in September of 1959 that the Pupil Placement Act was constitutional "on its face," at which point Wiley Branton challenged the Little Rock School Board's application of the act before Federal District Judge John Miller, alleging that "where we have a previously-approved plan [for school integration] they can't come in now and use the pupil placement laws as a further dilution of the original plan." Little Rock School Board attorney Herschel Friday described the placement law as "the only legal device so far by which there could be an orderly transition to desegregated schools." Judge Miller affirmed the School Board's use of the placement law, but in March of 1961 the Eighth Circuit Court of Appeals ruled that the board had discriminated against Negro students in making its placement assignments and ordered the board to stop discriminating.[13]

In 1965 black parents in Little Rock filed suit in federal district court contending that their children were being relegated to black neighborhood schools. The *Clark* litigation, as this string of suits came to be known, has continued in Little Rock in various forms down to the present day. As one observer of that litigation has written, the various plans put forward by the Little Rock School Board included "student assignments based on geographic attendance zones, plans that alternated between busing students to schools in heavily white and heavily black neighborhoods depending on the grade, and plans for elementary schools that included four all-black elementary schools in order to allow for better black/white ratios in the remaining schools." The Eighth Circuit Court of Appeals approved most of these plans with some modifications.[14]

DAISY BATES SUFFERED unremitting attacks on her home throughout the duration of the Little Rock crisis, along with threats against her life and the lives of her family members. The Ku Klux Klan burned three crosses on her lawn in separate incidents. Attackers broke out the front picture windows on numerous occasions, until the Bateses covered them with steel screens. Vandals set fire to the house twice and repeatedly threw incendiary bombs at the home from automobiles. City and state law enforcement officers never apprehended the attackers, and the Bateses resorted to employing private guards. In August of 1959 the Arkansas State Police arrested three of the friends and neighbors who had been guarding the Bates home on charges of carrying concealed weapons, one of whom was Ellis Thomas. Daisy Bates appealed without success to the president of the United States for protection. After he had to close the *Arkansas State Press,* L. C. Bates secured a position with the NAACP as a regional secretary.[15]

HARRY ASHMORE LEFT the *Arkansas Gazette* in October of 1959 to join the Center for the Study of Democratic Institutions in Santa Barbara, California. He had been serving as "liaison director" at the center since September of 1957, working with Columbia University historian Allan Nevins, *American Heritage* editor Bruce Catton, and *Newsday* publisher Alicia Patterson, as well as Center consultants Eric F. Goldman, professor of history at Princeton; Clark Kerr, president of the University of California; Henry R. Luce, editor in chief and publisher of *Time, Life,* and *Fortune;* Reinhold Niebuhr, vice president of Union Theological Seminary; and others. Ashmore would continue to shape popular images of the crisis in his many books and articles in ensuing years.[16]

ALTHOUGH BROOKS HAYS and Bruce Bennett both talked about entering the governor's race in 1960, Orval Faubus eventually announced his intention of running for a fourth term and won handily, as he did when he ran for a fifth and a sixth. He finally retired in 1967, still spouting his segregationist, anticommunist and states' rights rhetoric. He later retreated from his earlier segregationist stance, though he never apologized for the positions he had taken at Central High School, maintaining to the end that he had acted to protect students and preserve the peace.[17]

IN MARCH OF 1960 a sit-in movement developed in downtown Little Rock, led by students at Philander Smith College. In response, a "secret committee" of influential businessmen entered into negotiations with black leaders and quietly desegregated many of the city's downtown business establishments.[18]

That same month, Police Chief Gene Smith committed suicide after killing his wife. The two had argued violently just hours after their son pleaded guilty to a charge of theft.[19]

PROBABLY THE MOST intriguing, if least known, of the decisions made by participants in the Little Rock crisis in ensuing years were those of the Little Rock Nine. Confirming the worst fears of the segregationists, at least four of the nine chose white partners. Minnijean Brown Trickey married the white son of a Presbyterian minister from Illinois. Melba Patillo Beals married a white man she met in college in California. Gloria Ray married a Scandinavian boy she met at Southern Illinois University. Ernest Green married a white woman he met in college in Michigan. As Green explained his choice, after the terrible treatment he had received at Central High the enthusiasm and excitement from sympathetic white college students caused him to feel that he was "being recognized as a human being." In photographs of the Nine taken at reunions over the years, the spouses have been carefully excluded.[20]

All of the Little Rock Nine earned college degrees, and most received advanced degrees. All have had productive lives. All have struggled to transcend the experiences that shaped their lives in 1957–58. Ernest Green attended college at Michigan State University, where he earned bachelor's and master's degrees in sociology. For ten years he directed the A. Philip Randolph Education Fund, until President Jimmy Carter appointed him to serve as assistant secretary of Housing and Urban Affairs in the United States Department of Labor. In 1985 he joined the financial consulting firm of Lehman Brothers, rising eventually to become a vice president and then a partner. In December of 2001, Green was charged with federal income tax evasion for channeling funds to the Democratic Party. He was sentenced in April of 2002 to three months' home detention and fined ten thousand dollars.[21]

Elizabeth Eckford and Thelma Mothershed completed their high school requirements during the "Lost Year" and went on to college in the fall of 1959. Elizabeth moved back to Little Rock in 1974, after spending a year at Knox College in Galesburg, Illinois, serving five years in the Women's Army Corps, graduating from Central State University in Wilberforce, Ohio, and working for a time in Los Angeles. Through those years she resolutely refused to talk about the Little Rock crisis. In 1977 she granted a rare interview to Brooks Hays's son Steele, admitting to him that she had found little progress in race relations in her home city. "I think I have changed rather than it has changed," she said. "I don't expect as much." Diagnosed with post-traumatic stress disorder and chronic depression, for decades she described herself as "emotionally dead" on every subject other than Little Rock, and she could not talk about the crisis without tears. She finally accepted an invitation to speak to a group of schoolchildren in Washington, D.C., in 1996, and she continues to speak to groups of young people in an effort to promote healing, theirs and hers. She has worked for the Employment Security Division of the state of Arkansas and as a probation officer for one of Little Rock's circuit judges.[22]

Thelma Mothershed received a scholarship to attend Southern Illinois University, where she earned an undergraduate degree in education and a master's degree in counseling. She taught home economics in a junior high school in Belleville, Illinois, later becoming a school vocational counselor in East St. Louis. After her retirement she worked with abused women and then moved back to Little Rock.[23]

Gloria Ray and Terrence Roberts left Little Rock when Governor Faubus closed the schools. Both of them exceptionally strong students, Gloria went on to earn an undergraduate degree from the Illinois Institute of Technology and a postgraduate degree in Stockholm, Sweden. The founder and editor of a computer journal and a prolific science writer, she has published magazines in thirty-nine countries.[24]

Terrence Roberts earned a Ph.D. in psychology from Southern Illinois University in 1976, after completing undergraduate work at California State University in sociology and earning a master's degree in social work from UCLA. He has directed a hospital's mental health department in San Francisco, served as assistant dean of the School of Social Welfare at UCLA, taught psychology at Antioch College of Los Angeles, and conducted a private practice as a clinical psychologist. He is a frequent public speaker about the impact and the meaning of the Little Rock crisis.[25]

Melba Patillo left Little Rock when the School Board failed to return her to Central High School in the fall of 1959. She completed her high school education in Santa Rosa, California, and received an undergraduate degree in journalism from San Francisco State College. She earned an M.A. in broadcasting from Columbia University, then worked as an ABC radio talk show host and a journalist for *People* magazine. She makes frequent public appearances to speak about the Little Rock crisis.[26]

Minnijean Brown finished high school at the New Lincoln School in New York City, living with the Kenneth Clark family. She went on to Southern Illinois University to pursue a degree in nursing, married, and moved to Canada with her husband to avoid the Vietnam War draft. She had six children, all of whom she home-schooled, and she engaged in protests against the Vietnam war, nuclear testing, and damage to the environment. After finishing her education, she became a popular speaker on the lecture circuit and in high school and col-

lege classrooms. Under President Bill Clinton she served as deputy assistant secretary of the Department of the Interior responsible for diversity. In 2003 she
returned to Little Rock to write her memoir and care for her aging mother.[27]

Carlotta Walls and Jefferson Thomas returned to Central High School in
the fall of 1959 and eventually graduated there. Carlotta attended Michigan
State University for two years, then earned her degree from the University of
Northern Colorado. Settling in Denver, she became a real estate broker, developing her own business, LaNier and Company.[28]

Jefferson Thomas and his parents moved away from Little Rock on the day
of his high school graduation, his father financially ruined and unable to find
work. Drafted into the Army, Jeff served in Vietnam, then graduated from California State University in Los Angeles. After owning a record shop, he served
for many years as an accountant with the Defense Department in Anaheim,
California.[29]

In 1997 President Bill Clinton opened the doors of Little Rock Central High
School to welcome the Little Rock Nine home to mark the fortieth anniversary
of their ordeal. In 1999, he awarded them the Congressional Gold Medal. In
2005, the Arkansas secretary of state commissioned sculptures of the Nine,
which now stand on the grounds of the Arkansas State Capitol building. Also
in 2005, the U.S. Postal Service issued a "Little Rock Nine" postage stamp, along
with stamps commemorating nine other civil rights milestones. Terrence
Roberts spoke for the Nine and thousands of other Americans when he stood
in the auditorium at Central High School before the commemorative stamp
that had just been unveiled. He said he hoped that one of these days, when he
puts his hand over his heart for the Pledge of Allegiance and salutes the flag for
its promise of liberty and justice for all, he will be talking about a present reality and not just "some future possibility."[30]

In the spring of 1959, at the height of the segregationists' power, Harry
Ashmore wrote a despairing article for *Saturday Review,* reaching for the heart
of the matter. He noted that whenever the great social and economic changes
of the twentieth century touched upon relationships between the white and
Negro races, white southerners turned to the past and cried "this last surviving
remnant of the old South must remain inviolate." Preventing race-mixing "is
the inner shrine, where the mildest dissent is treason, the one place where that
vaunted individuality that is so much a part of the Southern style is denied." To
Ashmore it was "the great flaw of the Southern style," even a fatal flaw, for the
effort to "counter the reality of the present with the unreality of the past will fail

in the end, and in the process destroy the unique Southern virtues that have also been preserved in the amber of history." It was a bleak and uncharacteristically pessimistic assessment, delivered from his "foxhole."[31]

Seven years later Harry Ashmore returned to Little Rock for a grand occasion, a dinner in honor of Adolphine Fletcher Terry at which he was the featured speaker. Clearly refreshed by his years away from the South, Ashmore delivered a stunning appraisal of America's racial possibilities that unmasked the crusty, hard-bitten ironist as an idealist and a romantic. Humbled and softened by Terry's noble example, the woman who had come home from Vassar College sixty years before "to unfurl the bright banner of courage and hope she has followed all her extraordinary life," he challenged his former neighbors that "having done their worst, and failed, they may now find the way clear to do their best."[32]

Ashmore claimed that Adolphine Terry had "shown us the absurdity of so much we believed to be true, and the falsity of so many of our inherited fears." The former editor suggested, "We must know by now that we will not destroy a social order by guaranteeing justice to all its citizens. We will not amalgamate disparate races by guaranteeing that both shall have access to the facilities and amenities of the community. And we do not invite chaos, but guarantee order, when we recognize that the Constitution of the United States can admit of no exceptions in spelling out the rights of man." This was a truth that was understood, he claimed, by many southerners who did not yet proclaim it, "all that silent multitude who have suffered under the false charge of treason uttered by blind and angry men."[33]

"All that silent multitude. . . ." Where were they? With the passage of the Civil Rights Act and the Voting Rights Act recently accomplished, with Martin Luther King still talking of "the Beloved Community" and with "Burn, Baby, Burn" still in the future, Harry Ashmore wanted desperately to believe that his vision of "inevitable" southern change was not just a mirage. The Terry Dinner was a shining moment in Little Rock's process of self-definition and healing, and it offered the gifted editor-turned-analyst the opportunity to function once again as the prophet he so wanted to be. But Ashmore's bracing, touching challenge to his forsaken community proved him to be as flawed in predicting the future as he was in divining the past.

The fifty years since the Little Rock crisis have failed to bring a true spirit of community to Arkansas's capital city. While the practice of legalized segregation went by the wayside and meaningful educational and career opportunities opened for individual black citizens, residential segregation and white flight have had a devastating impact on the city. White families have moved to the far western reaches of the city and into rapidly growing neighboring communities. In addition, unremitting lawsuits over desegregation have kept the Little Rock School District embroiled in costly court battles for most of the last fifty years, and as late as 2006 the price tag of all the court battles and their judgments, according to one report, stood at $786 million, while the results in terms of racial balance and improved student performance were negligible.[34]

THE LITTLE ROCK story shows in microcosm the difficulty of extending justice to a historically powerless group in the absence of a majoritarian will to do so. Although Cold War imperatives demanded that the nation pursue at least the image of equality under the law, and although urbanization and industrialization had created the conditions for African-Americans to press their interests within the body politic, the failure to persuade white citizens in Little Rock of the necessity and morality of integration doomed that effort from the outset. In the short term, economic self-interest trumped racist values in Arkansas's capital city. But in the half century that followed the heroic efforts of nine black children to secure educational equality for themselves and their people, the nation's retreat from the quest for civil rights left the time-honored American values of white supremacy without effective challenge, and Little Rock's black citizens fighting a chimerical and faceless foe. Only when the nation chooses to name that adversary, and discuss candidly the fears that continue to animate white racism, can we hope to move at last toward the goal that one of the Little Rock Nine so forthrightly named, the hope of "liberty and justice for all."

A NOTE ON MISCEGENATION

*A*RKANSAS *GAZETTE* EDITOR HARRY ASHMORE, CALLING THE SEGRE-
gationist crusade "an aberration that ran counter to the basic good
sense, and good feeling, of the majority of Arkansans of both races . . . ," always
argued that the "real" issue in Little Rock was one of law and order. Having published a study of southern Negro education in 1954, he knew that the *Brown*
decisions of 1954 and 1955 mandating an end to segregation in the nation's
public schools would have a tremendous impact on his native region. What he
did not anticipate and could never accept was the irrational nature of the
South's impassioned response, and he routinely attempted to trivialize rather
than answer seriously the arguments of the segregationists.[1]

Senator James Eastland of Mississippi, for example, speaking before the Senate barely two weeks after the first *Brown* decision in May of 1954, called for the
creation of a southern counteroffensive, predicting that the South would never
accept the "social equality" the justices were demanding. In Eastland's view, the
heart of the matter was that the *Brown* decision was "a program designed to
mongrelize the Anglo-Saxon race . . . ," and he argued that the ultimate question
was, "Shall the white man and the Negro retain their racial identities?"[2]

Although jarring to modern sensibilities, Eastland's comments reflected
assumptions that had shaped thinking in the South and beyond. First among
these was the belief that people of color were inferior mentally and culturally to
their white neighbors, and that therefore "social equality" between the races
must never be promoted. Second was the related conviction that after the demise
of slavery, physical separation of the races and even the imposition of caste status was necessary for the maintenance of racial purity. Both of these ideas were
freighted with emotional baggage; both were indicators of the sexual threat
white southerners had long assigned to the blacks in their midst. As a contemporary writer explained southern thinking, "it is in the consistent taboos of segregation . . . that the real meaning of the institution lies. . . . beneath all of the
other trappings of segregation lie fears that are primarily sexual in origin."[3]

In polite discourse, such as a speech before the United States Senate, southern leaders were not likely to spell out the psychosexual dimensions of their thinking about the South's biracial society. Although they resorted to using code words such as "social equality" and "racial purity," their concerns about maintaining white dominance by prohibiting miscegenation emerged clearly in the segregationist literature that proliferated after 1954. Almost invariably the correlative idea emerged that the assault on segregation reflected a communist strategy to weaken American institutions. Since "everyone knew" that integration would lead to intermarriage, and that intermarriage would lead to the destruction of both the white race and Euro-American civilization, segregationist thinkers could see the hand of the communist foe in what they believed was a scheme to undermine American strength.[4]

Southern writer David L. Cohn had explained "How the South Feels" in an article in the *Atlantic Monthly* in 1944. Acknowledging that "the Negro question is insoluble . . . because it is at bottom a blood or sexual question . . . ," Cohn went on to write that "Southern whites . . . will not at any foreseeable time relax the taboos which keep the races separate. . . . They fear and believe that once a small crack is made in the walls of social segregation, the walls will eventually be breached."[5]

With the handing down of the first *Brown* decision and its legal prohibition against segregation, the South's caste arrangements seemed destined to spiral into turmoil. Integration, especially of the public schools, involved the explicit acknowledgment of social equality between the races, and as always, most white southerners equated social equality with sexual access. Deprived of the prohibitions provided by caste, the white South felt itself on the brink of the eternal southern precipice, and her loyal sons sprang into action. Having learned the folly of resorting to force of arms, however, this time southern warriors fought a guerrilla operation through a legion of Citizens' Councils. Even so, the South found itself once again the target of another federal Reconstruction.[6]

Clearly in this calamity, uncontrolled white women represented as much of a threat as uncontrolled blacks, and numerous commentators have noted the "pangs of sexual insecurity" increasingly evident in southern white male discourse. Southern writer Lillian Smith had reflected on the wellsprings of this insecurity in the 1940s. Openly acknowledging the intersection of race and sex in a region that was haunted by Protestant notions of sin, Smith had written that many southern white men developed from their earliest associations and expressed throughout their lives conflicted notions of their own sexuality. Smith argued that these men, attracted by the temptations of the accessible

Negro woman and repelled by the perceived frigidity their religion had instilled in white women, projected onto black men the guilt their own behavior engendered. Further compounding the problem, as another student of the segregationist mentality wrote in 1962, "there exists strongly among many white men of the South the old, old, insecure feeling that Negro males, if given 'social equality,' might be sexually preferred by white women."[7]

Far from being empty rhetoric designed to mask social oppression or economic exploitation, the fear of black sexual aggression was deep-seated and regionwide in the 1950s South. In the absence of the social controls slavery and then segregation had provided, this fear of a black sexual threat underlay a hardening determination to keep the Negro male "in his place," a feat that southern whites believed could not be accomplished if black children and white children interacted as equals in the schools.

In the era of massive resistance to desegregation, beneath all the rhetoric about states' rights, constitutional government, and the lovely southern lady, lay the threat that people of color represented to white male control of their "bloodlines," or in other words, of white women. The intensity of this concern seemed to increase in direct proportion to the percentage of blacks in the population. As a consequence, the black belt regions of the South were where these ideas found most vigorous expression, the cult of the Southern Lady was most oppressive, and the resistance to desegregation was most fierce.

Arkansas's most vociferous segregationist leader in the fall of 1957, Jim Johnson, told a United Press reporter his followers feared integration primarily because it would lead eventually to a "mixing" of the white and Negro races. In the words of the UP reporter, "In the end, this is what it gets down to. Segregation leaders give a dozen reasons for not wanting negroes [*sic*] in white schools. They don't often mention miscegenation. But, as one prominent leader believes, 'over the long haul,' that is what it will lead to." This fear fuelled the frantic and impassioned opposition to desegregation in Little Rock. Despite the unwillingness of such commentators as Harry Ashmore to acknowledge its force, this white fear is what almost destroyed Elizabeth Eckford in the streets outside Central High.[8]

A DEVOUT METHODIST minister committed to integration in 1957, Arkansas Council on Human Relations Executive Director Nat Griswold was an intellectually honest seeker who devoted himself throughout the next decade to understanding what had happened in Little Rock. To that end he conducted a series of unusually thoughtful interviews with Orval Faubus, from which he drew

conclusions that questioned the standard interpretation of the Little Rock crisis as a product of the Arkansas governor's moral bankruptcy and opportunism.
Instead, Griswold concluded that the crisis grew out of what Professor James
Silver had recently described as official southern orthodoxy. "The all-pervading
doctrine," Silver wrote, ". . . has been white supremacy, whether achieved
through slavery or segregation, rationalized by a professed belief in states rights
and bolstered by religious fundamentalism."[9]

Griswold argued that the deepest sources of segregationist behavior in Little Rock were to be found in the "sex taboos in Arkansas racism," and that the
guilt and fears of many white males resulting from their sexual transgressions
across the color line explained the intensity of their emotional response to the
quest for black equality. As he concluded his analysis of Governor Faubus's
behavior at Central High and that of Little Rock's school officials, ". . . they
simply acted as Southerners, loyal to Southern racial orthodoxy deeply written
in the heart of the culture. All parties alike bent to the compulsion of the
people's religious attitude toward the dogmas of that faith—white superiority
and functional separation of the races into castes."[10]

Despite Supreme Court insistence and Cold War imperatives, the nation
could not expect change until that orthodoxy changed. Segregationist thinking
was "deeply written on the heart of [the] culture," and it could not be changed
by force, no matter how worthy or urgent the compelling motives. Only when
the white leadership in Little Rock found ways to accommodate itself to the new
order, in response to motivations arising from its own purposes and values, did
Arkansas's capital city begin to undergo gradual, limited change. Sadly, the story
of changing attitudes is one that remains unfinished fifty years after the crisis
at Central High.

NOTES

Abbreviations

ABC—Arthur Brann Caldwell Papers, Special Collections, University of Arkansas Libraries, Fayetteville

ACHR—Arkansas Council on Human Relations Papers, Special Collections, University of Arkansas Libraries, Fayetteville

ACOVH—Arkansas Center for Oral and Visual History, Special Collections, University of Arkansas Libraries, Fayetteville

BLP—Benjamin Laney Papers, Torreyson Library, University of Central Arkansas, Conway

BWP—Billie Wilson Papers, in the possession of the Wilson family

CCA—Citizens' Councils of America Papers, Special Collections, University of Arkansas Libraries, Fayetteville

CCP—Colbert Cartwright Papers, Special Collections, University of Arkansas Libraries, Fayetteville

CRDP—Civil Rights Documentation Project, Moorland-Spingarn Research Center, Howard University, Washington, D.C.

DBP—Daisy Bates Papers, Special Collections, University of Arkansas Libraries, Fayetteville

DDE—Dwight David Eisenhower Papers, Dwight David Eisenhower Presidential Library, Abilene, Kansas

DGB—Daisy Gatson Bates Papers, Wisconsin Historical Society, Madison

EAP—Eisenhower Administration Project, Dwight David Eisenhower Presidential Library, Abilene, Kansas

EPH—Elizabeth Paisley Huckaby Papers, Special Collections, University of Arkansas Libraries, Fayetteville

EJC—Elizabeth Jacoway Little Rock Crisis Collection, Richard C. Butler Center for Arkansas Studies, Central Arkansas Library System, Little Rock

FBI Report—"F.B.I.—Little Rock Crisis Reports," Archives and Special Collections, University of Arkansas at Little Rock

FLP—Frank Lambright Papers, in the possession of the Lambright family

FTF—Fletcher-Terry Family Papers, Archives and Special Collections, University of Arkansas at Little Rock

GCI—Gerog C. Iggers Papers, Archives and Special Collections, University of Arkansas at Little Rock

HSA—Harry Scott Ashmore Papers, Archives and Special Collections, University of Arkansas at Little Rock

HJL—Harry J. Lemley Papers, Archives and Special Collections, University of Arkansas at Little Rock

JEM—John Elvis Miller Papers, Special Collections, University of Arkansas Libraries, Fayetteville

JGW—J. Gaston Williamson Papers, included in Elizabeth Jacoway Little Rock Crisis Collection

JJJ—Justice Jim Johnson Collection, Arkansas History Commission, Little Rock

LBH—Lawrence Brooks Hays Papers, John Fitzgerald Kennedy Presidential Library, Dorchester, Massachusetts

LDC—Lola A. Dunnavant Collection, Arkansas History Commission, Little Rock

OEF—Orval E. Faubus Papers, Special Collections, University of Arkansas Libraries, Fayetteville

PON—Papers of the National Association for the Advancement of Colored People, Library of Congress, Washington, D.C.

RBR—Richard Russell Papers, Richard B. Russell Memorial Library, University of Georgia, Athens

RCB—Richard C. Butler Papers, Torreyson Library, University of Central Arkansas, Conway

RRB—Robert R. Brown Letters, Archives and Special Collections, University of Arkansas at Little Rock

RRP—Roy Reed Papers (unprocessed), Special Collections, University of Arkansas Libraries, Fayetteville

SAM—Sara Alderman Murphy Papers, Special Collections, University of Arkansas Libraries, Fayetteville

SBC—"Southern Baptist Convention Presidents," Southern Baptist Historical Library and Archives, Nashville, Tennessee

SERS—Southern Education Reporting Service Papers, John Hope and Aurelia Franklin Library, Fisk University, Nashville, Tennessee

SHC—Southern Historical Collection, Louis Round Wilson Library, University of North Carolina, Chapel Hill

SOHP—Southern Oral History Program Collection, Southern Historical Collection, Louis Round Wilson Library, University of North Carolina, Chapel Hill

SRC—Southern Regional Council Papers, Woodruff Library, Atlanta University, Atlanta, Georgia

VTB—Virgil T. Blossom Papers, Special Collections, University of Arkansas Libraries, Fayetteville

VJP—Velma and J. O. Powell Collection, Special Collections, University of Arkansas Libraries, Fayetteville

VLB—Vivion Lenon Brewer Papers, Archives and Special Collections, University of Arkansas at Little Rock

WAB—Wiley Austin Branton Papers, Moorland-Spingarn Research Center, Howard University, Washington, D.C.

WEC—Women's Emergency Committee to Open Our Schools Papers, Archives and Special Collections, University of Arkansas at Little Rock

WPR—William P. Rogers Papers, Dwight David Eisenhower Presidential Library, Abilene, Kansas

INTRODUCTION — MISCEGENATION AND THE BEAST

1. "She Saw the Soldiers and Was Glad," *New York Post,* Sept. 8, 1957, SERS; Ted Poston, "Nine Kids Who Dared . . .", *New York Post,* Oct. 24, 1957, Bates Scrapbook, DGB; Elizabeth Eckford interview with Elizabeth Jacoway, July 5, 2004, pp. 32–33, EJC.

2. Virgil T. Blossom, *It HAS Happened Here* (New York: Harper & Bros. 1959), p. 70; "Students Report Only One Incident," *Arkansas Gazette,* Sept. 26, 1957; Colbert Cartwright, "A Portrait in Ebony," sermon delivered to Pulaski Heights Christian Church, Sept. 8, 1957, microfilm, vol. 3, CCP.

3. Marcet Haldeman-Julius, "The Story of a Lynching—An Exploration of Southern Psychology," *Haldeman-Julius Monthly* (August 1927), pp. 1–32; James R. Eison, "Dead, But She Was in a Good Place, A Church," *Pulaski County Historical Review* (Summer 1982), pp. 30–42. See also Todd E. Lewis, "Mob Justice in the 'American Congo': 'Judge Lynch' in Arkansas During the Decade after World War I," *Arkansas Historical Quarterly* (Summer 1993), pp. 156–84.

4. Eckford interview with Jacoway, July 5, 2004, p. 21.

5. Walter Lister Jr., "Barred Negro Pupils Tell of Courage and Confidence," *New York Herald Tribune,* Sept. 8, 1957, SERS. Eckford interview with Jacoway, July 5, 2004, pp. 26–27; Poston, "Nine Kids Who Dared . . ."

6. Cartwright, "A Portrait In Ebony"; Poston, "Nine Kids Who Dared . . ."; Daisy Bates interview with Elizabeth Jacoway, Oct. 11, 1976, p. 12, SOHP.

7. Daisy Bates made the same claim about Faubus and "blood . . . in the streets," perhaps based on a report she received from *New York Times* reporter Benjamin Fine, who reported this phrasing in an interview recorded on June 30, 1960; "Benjamin Fine," p. 4, Box 2, Folder 4, DGB; Bates, *The Long Shadow of Little Rock,* p. 62. Governor Faubus actually did not say those words, but the fact that Mrs. Eckford thought she heard them indicated the level of her anxiety. For the full text of the Faubus speech see "First Speech," Sept. 2, 1957, Box 496, Folder 1, OEF. For the full text of Judge Davies's order see *Race Relations Law Reporter* (October 1957), pp. 937–39. Cartwright, "A Portrait In Ebony."

8. Elizabeth Eckford, "Little Rock, 1957: The First Day," *Southern Exposure* (Summer 1979), p. 38.

9. The whites answering Bates' plea were Dr. Dunbar Ogden, pastor of Central Presbyterian Church and his son David, and Will Campbell of the National Council of Churches; the blacks were Rev. Harry Bass and Rev. Z. Z. Dryver; white minister Rev. Colbert Cartwright covered the incident as a freelance journalist. For Rev. Dryver's recollections of that episode see Z. Z. Dryver interview with FBI, Sept. 4, 1957, Box 2, Folder 8, FBI Report. Bates, *The Long Shadow of Little Rock,* p. 66; Poston, "Nine Kids Who Dared: Elizabeth Ann Eckford." General Sherman Clinger interview with FBI, Sept. 6, 1957, Box 2, Folder 2, FBI Report; see also Colonel Marion Johnson interview with FBI, Sept. 6, 1957, Box 2, Folder 2, FBI Report. For Faubus's original orders to the National Guard see Harry W. Smith, "Arkansas Army and Air National Guard: A History and Record of Events, 1820–1962," mimeographed publication dated Dec. 31, 1962, p. 47, Army and Air National Guard Museum, Camp Robinson, Ark.

10. Eckford, "Little Rock, 1957: The First Day." *New York Times,* Sept. 5, 1957, p. 1.

11. Eckford, "Little Rock, 1957: The First Day."

12. Cartwright, "A Portrait In Ebony."

13. Eckford, "Little Rock, 1957: The First Day."

14. Ibid. Wilmer Counts, *A Life Is More Than a Moment: The Desegregation of Little Rock's Central High* (Bloomington: Indiana University Press, 1999).

15. Eckford interview with Jacoway, July 5, 2004, pp. 29–30. "Benjamin Fine," pp. 7–8.

16. Eckford interview with Jacoway, July 5, 2004, p. 30.

17. Eckford, "Little Rock, 1957: The First Day." Fine later recalled he also said, "Just act brave. You will be all right"; "Benjamin Fine," p. 8. Benjamin Fine to Harry Ashmore, Oct. 1, 1957, Box 6, Folder 11, HSA. Henry Woods interview with Elizabeth Jacoway, May 30, 2000, p. 16, EJC. Eckford interview with Jacoway, July 5, 2004, p. 29. Counts, *A Life Is More Than A Moment,* p. 34.

18. Benjamin Fine, "Arkansas Troops Bar Negro Pupils; Governor Defiant," *New York Times,* Sept. 5, 1957, p. 1; Eckford interview with Jacoway, July 5, 2004, p. 30. Director's Brief, "Chronology," Vol. 1, File 3, p. B-56, FBI Report; Eckford interview with Jacoway, July 5, 2004, p. 29. The author wishes to thank Jerry Thornberry for sharing with her several documents tracing Grace and Lee Lorch's activities.

19. "Benjamin Fine," p. 9. Eckford interview with Jacoway, July 5, 2004, p. 31. Elizabeth was glad Mrs. Lorch got off the bus and had even encouraged her to do so, because she felt that Lorch's presence endangered her; Ibid.

20. Virginia Gardner, "My Child Walked to School in Little Rock Arkansas," Sept. 19(?), 1957, *Herald-Dispatch,* Box 1, Folder 5, DGB.

21. Bates, *The Long Shadow of Little Rock,* p. 65. Ogden's son David, who also walked with the ministers, later committed suicide, apparently in part because of his failure to "fit in" to southern white society after this incident; Dunbar Ogden Jr., *My Father's Little Rock,* unpublished manuscript, EJC. For an uncritical assessment of Ogden's contribution and motivations see "A Southern Profile: Little Rock Climaxes Spiritual Journey," *Southern Patriot,* September 1959, Box 2, Folder 2, DGB. Counts, *A Life Is More Than a Moment,* pp. xv, 41.

22. Hazel Bryan Massery interview with Elizabeth Jacoway, July 8, 2004, pp. 17, 24, EJC; see also Bates, *The Long Shadow of Little Rock*, p. 195. Hazel Bryan Massery interview with Sara Alderman Murphy, July 27, 1992, p. 2, Box 2, Folder 10, SAM. Hazel Bryan Massery interview with Elizabeth Jacoway and Pete Daniel, Jan. 29, 1996, pp. 3–4, EJC.

23. Massery interview with Murphy, p. 1. Massery interview with Jacoway, July 8, 2004, pp. 3, 6. Massery interview with Jacoway and Daniel, pp. 3–4.

24. Massery interview with Murphy, p. 3. J. O. Powell, *Central High School Inside Out: (A Study in Disintegration),* "Addendum," (np), Box 1, File 4, VJP; Massery interview with Jacoway, July 8, 2004, pp. 19–20.

25. Massery interview with Jacoway, July 8, 2004, pp. 5, 20, 24, 26. A cursory glance of the photograph seems to suggest that Mr. Parker, toward whom Sammie Dean has turned her head, is furious in his condemnation of Elizabeth Eckford; Hazel Massery has suggested he was, in fact, furious with Sammie Dean and Hazel for injecting themselves into such a dangerous situation, and he was demanding that they withdraw from the scene; Massery telephone conversation with Jacoway, July 18, 2004. Massery interview with Jacoway, July 8, 2004, p. 20.

26. Massery interview with Jacoway and Daniel, pp. 29–30. See Elizabeth Jacoway, "Understanding the Past: The Challenge of Little Rock," in Elizabeth Jacoway and C. Fred Williams, eds., *Understanding the Little Rock Crisis: An Exercise in Remembrance and Reconciliation* (Fayetteville: University of Arkansas Press, 1998), pp. 20–21. Massery interview with Murphy, p. 12.

27. Historian Bertram Wyatt-Brown wrote, "Fear of the contamination of blood lineage was not purely a sexual fear, but was a dread of loss of race command, the nightmare of impotence, both physical and social"; Bertram Wyatt-Brown, "W. J. Cash and Southern Culture," in Walter J. Fraser Jr. and Winfred B. Moore Jr., eds., *From the Old South to the New: Essays on the Transitional South* (Westport, Conn.: Greenwood Press, 1981), p. 209. For a fuller discussion of this phenomenon, see the Afterword, "A Note on Miscegenation."

Chapter One — Defining the Debate

1. Author's interviews with Everett Tucker, Jr., Dec. 5, 1977; B. Finley Vinson, Dec. 21, 1977; Richard C. Butler, Dec. 15, 1977; A. Howard Stebbins, Dec. 16, 1977; EJC. See also Elizabeth Jacoway, "Taken By Surprise: Little Rock Business Leaders and Desegregation" in Elizabeth Jacoway and David R. Colburn, *Southern Businessmen and Desegregation* (Baton Rouge: Louisiana State University Press, 1982).

2. For a full discussion of Little Rock's response to the *Brown* decision mandating an end to public school segregation, see Virgil T. Blossom, *It HAS Happened Here* (New York: Harper & Brothers, 1959). Information about the Good Government Campaign can be found in Jacoway, "Taken By Surprise," and in the author's interviews with William Starr Mitchell, Dec. 17, 1977; Stonewall Jackson Beauchamp, Dec. 6, 1977; Everett Tucker; and Finley Vinson. For an engaging discussion of Orval Faubus's 1957 sales tax increase see Roy Reed, *Faubus: The Life and Times of an American Prodigal* (Fayetteville: University of Arkansas Press, 1997), pp. 155–58. Historian Michael J. Klarman described Little Rock as "one of the South's most racially progressive cities"; Michael J. Klarman, "How the *Brown* Decision Changed Race Relations: The Backlash Thesis," *Journal of American History* (June 1994), p. 103; for other assessments of Little Rock's moderate race relations see Numan V. Bartley, *The Rise of Massive Resistance: Race and Politics in the South During the 1950's* (Baton Rouge: Louisiana State University Press, 1969), pp. 251–52; Neil McMillen, *The Citizens' Council: Organized Resistance to the Second Reconstruction, 1954–64* (Urbana: University of Illinois Press, 1971, 1994), pp. 94–95; Dewey Grantham, *The Regional Imagination: The South and Recent American History,* chapter titled "The Little Rock School Crisis: Negro Rights and the Struggle for an Integrated America" (Nashville: Vanderbilt University Press, 1979), p. 186; Anthony Lewis, *Portrait of a Decade: The Second American Revolution* (New York: Random House, 1964); and Griffin Smith Jr., "Localism and Segregation: Racial Patterns in Little Rock, Arkansas, 1945–1954" (Master's thesis, Columbia University, 1965). An NAACP field representative called Arkansas "the bright

spot of the South . . ."; "Has Arkansas Gone Liberal," Chicago *Defender*, May 7, 1955, as quoted in McMillen, *The Citizens' Council*, p. 94. For the reactions of visitors to the city, see the office correspondence of Harry Ashmore between 1947 and 1959, HSA.

3. Harry S. Ashmore, *Unseasonable Truths: The Life of Robert Maynard Hutchins* (Boston: Little, Brown & Co., 1989), p. 348. Harry S. Ashmore, *An Epitaph for Dixie* (New York: W. W. Norton & Co., 1958); Harry Ashmore to Harold Fleming, June 14, 1957, Box 6, Folder 8, HSA.

4. Ashmore, *An Epitaph for Dixie*, pp. 1, 118, 149.

5. Harry S. Ashmore, *Hearts and Minds: The Anatomy of Racism from Roosevelt to Reagan* (New York: McGraw-Hill Book Co., 1982), pp. 14, 70. Nathania K. Sawyer, "Harry S. Ashmore: On the Way to Everywhere" (Master's thesis, University of Arkansas at Little Rock, 2001).

6. Ashmore, *Hearts and Minds*, pp. 18–19. For the biographical details of Ashmore's life see *An Epitaph for Dixie; Hearts and Minds;* and *Civil Rights and Wrongs: A Memoir of Race and Politics, 1944–1994* (New York: Pantheon Books, 1994).

7. Louis M Lyons, ed., *The Nieman Fellows Report: An Account of an Education Experiment in its Tenth Year* (Cambridge: Harvard University Press, 1948), p. 56. For a fascinating introduction to the Harvard History Department in those years see Arthur M. Schlesinger Jr., *A Life in the Twentieth Century: Innocent Beginnings, 1917–1950* (Boston: Houghton Mifflin Co., 2000); Ashmore, *Civil Rights and Wrongs*, p. 48. Ashmore told interviewer Roy Reed many years later, "the courses I took up at Harvard were really intended to explore as best I could with people up there what kind of changes to expect"; Harry Ashmore interview with Roy Reed, June 20, 1992, p. 23, RRP. Ashmore told Reed that he read *An American Dilemma* during a two-week vacation at the beach in Massachusetts; Ashmore interview with Reed, p. 23. Sawyer, "Harry S. Ashmore," p. 27.

8. Ashmore, *Hearts and Minds*, p. 114.

9. Harry S. Ashmore, *The Man in the Middle* (Columbia: University of Missouri Press, 1966), p. 24.

10. Randall Bennett Woods, *Fulbright: A Biography* (New York: Cambridge University Press, 1995), p. 147; for an enlightening discussion of the gradualist approach of southern liberals such as Ashmore, see Anthony Lake Newberry, "Without Urgency or Ardor: The South's Middle-of-the-Road Liberals and Civil Rights, 1945-1960" (Ph.D. diss., Ohio University, 1982).

11. William K. Rutherford, "*Arkansas Gazette* Editor J. N. Heiskell: Heart and Mind" (Master's thesis, University of Arkansas at Little Rock, 1987), p. 57; Harry Ashmore to Jack B. Thompson, Jan. 17, 1949, Box 1, Folder 4, HSA. Rutherford, "J. N. Heiskell," p. 56; Hugh B. Patterson interview with Roy Reed, Feb. 16, 2000, pp. 9–12, ACOVH. Margaret Smith Ross interview with William Rutherford, March 1987, as cited in Rutherford, "J. N. Heiskell," p. 76.

12. Ashmore, *Hearts and Minds*, p. 149. Rutherford, "J. N. Heiskell," p. 60.

13. Ashmore, *Hearts and Minds*, pp. 120, 121. Ashmore, *Civil Rights and Wrongs*, p. 65.

14. Jim Lester, *A Man for Arkansas: Sid McMath and the Southern Reform Tradition* (Little Rock: Rose Publishing Co., 1976), p. 98. See, for instance, his editorial in the *Arkansas Gazette*, Feb. 21, 1948, as quoted in V. O. Key, *Southern Politics in State and Nation* (New York: Alfred A. Knopf, 1949), p. 339. For an enlightening discussion of the dynamics of white supremacy see Stephen Kantrowitz, *Ben Tillman and the Reconstruction of White Supremacy* (University of North Carolina Press, 2000).

15. Ashmore, *Civil Rights and Wrongs*, p. 69.

16. Fulbright's biographer refers to the Arkansas Plan as the Fulbright-Ashmore-Hays Plan; Woods, *Fulbright*, pp. 150–51; "The Area of Compromise," *Arkansas Gazette*, Dec. 29, 1948.

17. "The Area of Compromise"; Woods, *Fulbright*, p. 152.

18. Brooks Hays, *A Southern Moderate Speaks* (Chapel Hill: University of North Carolina Press, 1959), pp. 43, 53–62.

19. Ibid., p. 115. Ashmore interview with Jacoway, p. 59.

20. "An Address by Harry Ashmore, Executive Editor of the Arkansas Gazette, Before the Southern Governors Conference at Hot Springs, Arkansas, 12 November 1951," Box 9, Folder 3, HSA.

21. Ibid.

22. James L. Walker Jr., "Speaking Unseasonable Truths: Harry Ashmore and the Idea of Gradualism in Racial Integration" (Master's thesis, University of Northern Colorado, 1991), p. 63; Ashmore, *Hearts and Minds,* p. 173. John Egerton, *Speak Now Against the Day: The Generation Before the Civil Rights Movement in the South* (New York: Alfred A. Knopf, 1994), p. 578. John Popham to Harry Ashmore, Nov. 17, 1951, Box 2, Folder 11, HSA.

23. Harry Ashmore to Charles T. Morton, Nov. 17, 1951, Box 2, Folder 11, HSA. Harold Fleming to Harry Ashmore, Nov. 14, 1951, Box 2, Folder 11, HSA; Louis Lyons to Harry Ashmore, Dec. 3, 1951, Box 2, Folder 13, HSA.

24. Louise Patterson interview with William K. Rutherford, January 1987, quoted in Rutherford, "J. N. Heiskell," pp. 82–83. Roy Reed's Remarks, Harry S. Ashmore Memorial Service, Feb. 17, 1998, Central Arkansas Library System, Little Rock, Arkansas, EJC; see also Ray Moseley interview with Roy Reed, ACOVH.

25. Roy Reed, "The Laughing Liberal," *New York Times Magazine,* Jan. 3, 1999, p. 26.

26. Harry Ashmore to Louis Lyons, April 12, 1954, Box 4, Folder 7, HSA. Roy Reed interview with Margaret Smith Ross, p. 100, ACOVH.

27. These conclusions are drawn from numerous interviews with people who do not want to be quoted. Harry S. Ashmore, *The Negro and the Schools* (Chapel Hill: University of North Carolina Press, 1954), p. xv.

28. Harry Ashmore interview with John Egerton, June 16, 1990, p. 47, SOHP.

29. Bill Emerson, Ashmore Memorial Service, Feb. 17, 1998, Little Rock, as quoted in Sawyer, "Harry Ashmore," np.

30. Ashmore's older friend and role model, Ralph McGill of the *Atlanta Constitution,* wrote, "My heart bled for you when your effort at king-making failed"; Ralph McGill to Harry Ashmore, July 28, 1952, Box 3, Folder 6, HSA; one of Fulbright's principal backers, Sam Grundfest, wrote, "Too bad Bill didn't get the nod—but I was afraid Truman wouldn't O.K. same"; Sam Grundfest to Harry Ashmore, July 30, 1952, Box 3, Folder 6, HSA; David McCullough, *Truman* (New York: Simon & Schuster, 1992), p. 864. See Ashmore's editorial endorsing Stevenson, "A Re-dedication to the Democratic Faith," *Arkansas Gazette,* Aug. 4, 1952.

31. A leading Arkansas political scientist argued in the 1970s that Arkansas Senator John McClellan's allies promoted the highway audit in an (unsuccessful) effort to forestall a McMath race against McClellan; see Richard E. Yates, "Arkansas: Independent and Unpredictable," in William C. Havard, ed., *The Changing Politics of the South* (Baton Rouge: Louisiana State University Press, 1972), pp. 256–57. Harry Ashmore explained years later, "I was in an awkward position because they turned up enough real stuff, I mean the goddamn highway department was corrupt, it's always been corrupt and Sid had played politics with the commissioners and he had some people on the damn highway commission . . . on the take and we knew it and they did expose it and document it"; Ashmore interview with Egerton, p. 8. "Henry Woods, Blunt Federal Judge, Dies," *Arkansas Democrat-Gazette,* March 15, 2002, p. 11A. Minor W. Millwee to Francis Cherry, Aug. 14, 1952, Minor W. Millwee Papers, in the possession of the Millwee family.

32. Ashmore later recalled that ". . . they looked into all the major universities in the South, . . . and nobody would touch it with a ten-foot pole."; Ashmore interview with Jacoway, p. 11. Ashmore also recalled that the project carried with it such risk that "it also turned out to be impossible to bring together the presidents of the major Southern colleges and universities as an advisory committee. . . ." Ashmore, *An Epitaph for Dixie,* p. 161; see also Ashmore interview with Egerton, p. 23. Ashmore, *Unseasonable Truths,* pp. 348–49.

33. Ashmore later recalled that sociologist Howard Odum was one of the key advisors to the project, and Ashmore made many trips to Chapel Hill, North Carolina, to confer with him; Ashmore interview with Jacoway, p.15. Nov. 17, 1976. Ashmore completed the project without taking a leave of absence; Hugh Patterson interview with John Luter, Aug. 12, 1970, p. 4, EAP. Harry Ashmore to Robert S. Allen, July 21, 1953, Box 3, Folder 15, HSA.

34. Ashmore, *Hearts and Minds,* p. 205.

35. Ashmore, *The Negro and the Schools,* p. 139.

36. Harry Ashmore to George Mitchell, April 12, 1954, Box 4, Folder 7, HSA. Jonathan Daniels was the editior of the *Raleigh News and Observer*.

37. Willie Lawson to Harry Ashmore, April 9, 1952, Box 3, Folder 2, HSA; Marvin Bird to Harry Ashmore, Feb. 15, 1954, Box 4, Folder 5, HSA. Ashmore interview with Jacoway, p. 22. The day the Supreme Court handed down the *Brown* decision, Ashmore wrote more candidly to his compatriots at the Southern Regional Council: "Well, sir, there was a time about 3 a.m. this morning when I seemed to hear old John Calhoun whispering in my ear. Sounded like he was saying: What was that stuff that hit the fan?"; "Dred Scott" Ashmore to Phil Coombs, Phil Hammer and Harold Fleming, May 17, 1954, SRC.

38. Blossom, *It HAS Happened Here*, pp. 25, 11–12. Rutherford, "J. N. Heiskell," pp. 86, 72, 79; see also Ernest Dumas interview with Jerry Dhonau, March 3, 2000, p. 44, ACOVH.

39. B. M. Lane to Harry Ashmore, May 25, 1954, Box 4, Folder 8, HSA; Reed Sarratt to Harry Ashmore, June 21, 1954, Box 4, Folder 9, HSA; Harry Ashmore to John Ivey, June 24, 1954, Box 4, Folder 9, HSA. Harry Ashmore to Tom Waring, June 4, 1954, Box 4, Folder 9, HSA.

40. Ashmore, *Hearts and Minds*, p. 215; Ashmore to Waring, June 4, 1954; Harry Ashmore to James Colvin, Jan. 14, 1959, Box 8, Folder 5, HSA.

41. *Arkansas Recorder*, May 28, 1954, p. 2; June 18, 1954, p. 6.

42. Orval Eugene Faubus, *Down From the Hills* (Little Rock: Democrat Printing and Lithographing Co., 1980), pp.14, 16.

43. Henry Woods interview with Elizabeth Jacoway, May 26 and 30, 2000, pp. 6–7, EJC. Orval Faubus interview with Elizabeth Jacoway, May 12, 1994, pp. 62-63, EJC. Henry Woods recalled later that Faubus "worked in McMath's office with me and we had lunch every day. I just thought a hell of a lot of the guy. We were very close"; Henry Woods interview with Roy Reed, Jan. 4, 1989, p. 4, RRP. Faubus, *Down From the Hills*, p.12.

44. Woods interview with Reed, Jan. 4, 1989, p. 2. McMath believed that Faubus's race had cost him his Senate election; Sidney S. McMath, *Promises Kept* (Fayetteville: University of Arkansas Press, 2003), pp. 301–02.

45. Ashmore interview with Jacoway, p. 31; Ashmore interview with Reed, p. 1; Edwin Dunaway interview with Roy Reed, Jan. 5, 1989, p. 7, RRP; Faubus, *Down From the Hills*, p. 36.

46. Wells ultimately published his conspiracy theory as *Time Bomb: The Faubus Revolt* (Little Rock: General Publishing Co., 1962). Woods interview with Reed, Jan. 4, 1989, pp. 4–6. Dunaway interview with Reed, p. 8. See also Irving Spitzberg, *Racial Politics in Little Rock, 1954–1964* (New York: Garland Publishing, 1987), p. 34. In an interview with a college student years later, Faubus described himself as having played a more active role in writing his own speech; Orval Faubus interview with David Demuth, June 22, 1977, p. 6, EJC.

47. Reed, *Faubus*, p. 124. Ashmore interview with Jacoway, p. 32; Ashmore interview with Reed, p.4. Hugh Patterson interview with John Luter, Aug. 12, 1970, p. 9, EAP.

48. Ashmore, *The Man in the Middle*, p. 22.

49. Ashmore, *Hearts and Minds*, p. 105; Harry Ashmore to Howard W. Odum, July 16, 1954, Box 4, Folder 10, HSA.

50. Harry Ashmore to E. L. Holland, Jan. 29, 1958, Box 7, Folder, 1, HSA. Ashmore, *Hearts and Minds*, p. 209; Ashmore, *Civil Rights and Wrongs*, pp. 105–6; Richard Kluger, *Simple Justice: The History of Brown v. Board of Education and Black America's Struggle for Equality* (New York: Random House, 1975), pp. 717, 739.

51. Colbert Cartwright to Harry Ashmore, Dec. 19, 1954, Box 5, Folder 2, HSA; George Mitchell to Harry Ashmore, Nov. 15, 1954, Box 5, Folder 1, HSA. Ashmore, *Hearts and Minds*, p. 347.

52. Harry Ashmore to Mrs. David Roberts III, Feb. 28, 1955, Box 5, Folder 4, HSA. John Wells interview with Elizabeth Jacoway, July 22, 1978, pp. 1–11, EJC.

53. Harry Ashmore to the Chief Justice, May 31, 1955, Box 5, Folder 7, HSA.

54. Blossom, *It HAS Happened Here*, pp. 21–22. George Douthit interview with John Luter, Dec. 31, 1970, p.4, EAP. Ashmore, *Hearts and Minds*, p. 252; Ashmore interview with Jacoway, pp. 12–13. p. 10.

55. Ashmore, *Hearts and Minds,* p. 253. Ashmore interview with Reed, p. 36.

56. Brooks Hays to Harry Ashmore, Sept. 21, 1955, Box 5, Folder 11, HSA. Ashmore, *Civil Rights and Wrongs,* pp. 116–17.

57. Ashmore, interview with Reed, p. 19. Sawyer, "Harry S. Ashmore," p. 65.

58. Hays, *A Southern Moderate Speaks,* pp. 88–92. For the Southern Manifesto see Anthony J. Badger, "The White Reaction to *Brown:* Arkansas, the Southern Manifesto, and Massive Resistance," in Elizabeth Jacoway and C. Fred Williams, *Understanding the Little Rock Crisis: An Exercise in Remembrance and Reconciliation* (Fayetteville: University of Arkansas Press, 1999), pp. 83–98; see also Brent J. Aucoin, "The Southern Manifesto and Southern Opposition to Desegregation," *Arkansas Historical Quarterly* 60 (Summer 1996), pp. 173–93.

59. Ashmore, *An Epitaph for Dixie,* p. 32, 34. Years later Ashmore described his chagrin that he could not "deliver my own delegation to my candidate"; Ashmore interview with Reed, p. 35; Orval E. Faubus interview with John Luter, Aug. 18, 1971, p. 108, EAP.

60. Sawyer, "Harry S. Ashmore," p. 68.

61. Ashmore, *An Epitaph for Dixie,* p. 24.

62. Harry Ashmore to Don Shoemaker, June 17, 1957, Box 6, Folder 8, HSA. Rutherford, "J. N. Heiskell," p. 64.

63. Ashmore, *An Epitaph for Dixie,* p. 37. "The Crisis Mr. Faubus Made," *Arkansas Gazette,* Sept. 4, 1957; "Governor Faubus Mounts the Stump," *Arkansas Gazette,* Oct. 25, 1957.

CHAPTER TWO — MASSIVE RESISTANCE

1. Roy Reed, *Faubus: The Life and Times of an American Prodigal* (Fayetteville: University of Arkansas Press, 1997), p. 170. "Faubus Showed Unexpected Strength," *Memphis Commercial Appeal,* Aug. 5, 1958, SERS. Governor Jeff Davis was elected to a third term in 1906. As Jim Johnson's campaign manager wrote to a potential donor in the spring of 1957, "The next election in Arkansas will be an 'open' race with no incumbent seeking re-election for governor. . . . Political observers are conceding now that Johnson will either be governor or name the next governor of Arkansas"; Phil Stratton to W. H. Cullen, April 22, 1957, Box 30, Folder 12, JJJ.

2. Jim Johnson interview with Elizabeth Jacoway, April 23, 2002, p. 54, EJC; Jim interview with Roy Reed, March 24, 1994, p. 5, RRP; Reed, *Faubus,* p. 192. Arthur B. Caldwell memo titled "Segregation in Public Schools in Arkansas," to Warren Olney III, July 24, 1957, Box 5, Folder 2, ABC; Orval Eugene Faubus interview with John Luter, Aug. 18, 1971, p. 6, EAP.

3. Johnson interview with Jacoway, April 23, 2002, p. 39, EJC. See also Fletcher Knebel, "The Real Little Rock Story," *Look,* Nov. 12, 1957, Box 19, Folder 193, ACHR.

4. Jim interview with Elizabeth Jacoway, May 22, 1999, p. 7, EJC. Jim interview with Elizabeth Jacoway, Aug. 6, 1999, p. 35, EJC.

5. Johnson interview with Jacoway, Aug. 6, 1999, pp. 31–35; untitled, undated handwritten reminiscence in Box 51, Folder 13, JJJ.

6. Johnson interview with Jacoway, May 22, 1999, pp. 7, 9, 10–11, and Aug. 6, 1999, p. 15. Jim Johnson interview with Elizabeth Jacoway and Pete Daniel, Jan. 27, 1996, pp. 2–3, EJC.

7. Jim Johnson to Elizabeth Jacoway, May 16, 2002, EJC. "Address of J. Strom Thurmond, Governor of South Carolina, Before Democratic Party Rally, Jackson, Mississippi, May 10, 1948," BLP.

8. "Address of J. Strom Thurmond."

9. Thurmond did not allude to the communist threat in his May 10 speech in Jackson, but it was a common theme in most of his campaign speeches after that; see Wayne Addison Clark, "An Analysis of the Relationship Between Anti-Communist and Segregationist Thought in the Deep South, 1948–1964" (Ph.D. diss., University of North Carolina, 1976), p. 36.

10. Jim Johnson to Elizabeth Jacoway, Oct. 6, 1995, EJC. Jim Johnson, "One Picture Is Worth a Thousand Words." A 1959 editorial in the *Arkansas Gazette* claimed that Johnson first came to major office as a "liberal" with labor and black support; "Justice Johnson vs. Senator McClellan,"

Arkansas Gazette, Aug. 29, 1959, p. 4A. *Arkansas Gazette* State Editor Ken Parker had considered Johnson to be the most liberal member of the Arkansas Senate; Ken Parker interview with Elizabeth Jacoway, Dec. 19, 2005, EJC.

11. Jim Johnson classroom presentation at Arkansas College, April 25, 1991, EJC. "The Supreme Court, Segregation, and the South: Speech of Hon. James O. Eastland of Mississippi in the Senate of the United States, Thursday, May 27, 1954," Series V, Item 10, CCA.

12. Johnson interview with Jacoway, Aug. 6, 1999, p. 5.

13. See for instance Benjamin Muse, *Ten Years of Prelude: The Story of Integration Since the Supreme Court's 1954 Decision* (New York: Viking Press, 1964), pp. 16–18; and Anthony Lewis, *Portrait of a Decade: The Second American Revolution* (New York: Bantam Books, 1964).

14. The most thorough and thoughtful exploration of the Citizens' Council movement is McMillen, *The Citizens' Council.*

15. Formation of the White Citizens' Council was formally announced on Sept. 9, 1955; Tom W. Davis, "Segregationists Go Same Way But in 2 Columns; May Merge," *Arkansas Gazette,* April 1, 1956.

16. Neil McMillen, "White Citizens' Council and Resistance to School Desegregation in Arkansas," *Arkansas Historical Quarterly* 30 (Summer 1971), p. 97. "Assembly to Get Petitions Asking Vote on Integration," *Arkansas Gazette,* Feb. 19, 1955. "White America Sets Forth Its Views," *Arkansas Gazette,* June 8, 1955. See Neil McMillen, "White Citizens' Council," for a thorough treatment of Citizens' Council activities in Little Rock; see also Graeme Cope, "'Honest White People of the Middle and Lower Classes'? A Profile of the Capital Citizens' Council During the Little Rock Crisis of 1957," *Arkansas Historical Quarterly* 61 (Spring 2002), pp. 37–58, for an exploration of the lower-middle-class composition of that group. Guthridge ran for Congress against Brooks Hays in 1952 and 1958, and for Arkansas attorney general in 1960.

17. United States Census, 1950. Cook, *The Segregationists,* p. 354; see handbill advertising meeting; list of meetings taken from *Arkansas Faith,* November 1955, p. 1, Box 2, Folder 22, JJJ.

18. A more complete report on the contents of this tape can be found in *Arkansas Faith,* November 1955, pp. 19–20, Box 2, Folder 22.

19. Carl T. Rowan, *Go South to Sorrow* (New York: Random House, 1957), pp. 157–58. Cook, *The Segregationists,* p. 355. Johnson interview with Jacoway, April 23, 2002, p. 56.

20. Johnson interview with Jacoway, April 22, 2002, p. 15.

21. Rowan, *Go South to Sorrow,* pp. 159, 160.

22. Reed, *Faubus,* p. 170.

23. "A 'Morally Right' Decision," *Life,* July 25, 1955, pp. 29–31. The most detailed treatment of the Hoxie incident can be found in Jerry Vervack, "The Hoxie Imbroglio," *Arkansas Historical Quarterly* 48 (Spring 1989), pp. 16–33; for a brief overview, see J. W. Peltason, *58 Lonely Men: Southern Federal Judges and School Desegregation* (New York: Harcourt, Brace & World, 1961), pp. 149–51. *Southern School News,* September 1955, p. 10.

24. "White America, Inc. Elects L. D. Poynter State Head," *Arkansas Faith* December 1955, p. 24, Box 2, Folder 20, JJJ; Vervack, "The Hoxie Imbroglio," pp. 22, 24. "Segregationists of Little Rock Speak at Hoxie," *Arkansas Gazette,* Aug. 14, 1955; Cabel Phillips, "Integration: Battle of Hoxie, Arkansas," *New York Times Magazine,* Sep. 25, 1955, pp. 68, 69. "The Hoxie Story," *Arkansas Faith,* November 1955, p. 10, Box 2, Folder 22, JJJ. John Thomas Elliff, "The United States Department of Justice and Individual Rights, 1937–1962" (Ph.D. diss., Harvard University, 1967), p. 414.

25. Elliff, "The United States Department of Justice and Individual Rights," p. 409.

26. Ibid., pp. 409–11.

27. Untitled, undated handwritten reminiscence, Box 51, Folder 12, JJJ.

28. Ibid.

29. "Hoxie Board Upheld; Judge Reeves Holds State Laws Invalid," *Arkansas Gazette,* Jan. 10, 1956, p. 1A. For a different account of Curt Copeland's portion of the program see Curt Copeland, "Some Differences Between Arkansas and Mississippi," *Arkansas Faith,* December 1955, pp. 21–23, Box 2, Folder 20, JJJ.

30. Elliff, "The United States Department of Justice and Individual Rights," p. 412; Elizabeth Carpenter, "Native of State Doing Good Job for Civil Rights," *Arkansas Gazette*, Sep. 8, 1957. Arthur Caldwell wrote, "Actually, from the beginning, every move of the school board in this case was approved in advance here in the Department, including the pleadings which were reviewed before filing"; Arthur B. Caldwell to J. W. Peltason, Jan. 18, 1962, Box 11, Folder 15, ABC. For the conclusion that Brownell did not know about Caldwell's activities in support of the Hoxie School Board, see Elliff. Many historians have commented on Eisenhower's reluctance to be involved in advancing the cause of black civil rights; see especially Mark V. Tushnet, *Making Civil Rights Law: Thurgood Marshall and the Supreme Court, 1956–1961* (New York: Oxford University Press, 1994), p. 306; Alexander M. Bickel, *The Least Dangerous Branch: The Supreme Court at the Bar of Politics* (New Haven: Yale University Press, 1962), p. 264; J. Harvie Wilkinson III, *From Brown to Bakke: The Supreme Court and School Integration, 1954–1978* (New York: Oxford University Press, 1979), p. 24; Harvard Sitkoff, *The Struggle for Black Equality: 1954–1992* (New York: Hill & Wang, 1981), pp. 23–25.

31. Caldwell to Peltason, Jan. 18, 1962, ABC. "Hoxie 'Interference' Enjoined," *Southern School News*, December 1956, pp. 8–9; Vervack, "The Hoxie Imbroglio," p. 33; Klarman, "How *Brown* Changed Race Relations," see esp. p. 110; Elliff, *"The United States Department of Justice and Individual Rights,"* pp. 442–46; James T. Patterson, *Brown v. Board of Education: A Civil Rights Milestone and Its Troubled Legacy* (New York: Oxford University Press, 2001), pp. 112, 117; Robert A. Leflar, "Law of the Land," in Don Shoemaker, ed., *With All Deliberate Speed: Segregation-Desegregation in Southern Schools* (New York: Harper & Bros. 1957), pp. 1–14.

32. Johnson interview with Jacoway, April 23, 2002, p. 9; Johnson interview with Jacoway and Daniel, p. 4; Jim Johnson classroom presentation at Arkansas College. *Arkansas Code of 1989 Annotated* (Charlottesville, Va.: Michie Co., 1987), pp. 434–35; "Race Amendment Aim in Arkansas," *Chattanooga Times*, Feb. 3, 1956, SERS.

33. Reed, *Faubus*, p. 175. Johnson interview with Jacoway, Aug. 6, 1999, p. 7.

34. Johnson interview with Jacoway, April 23, 2002, p. 21. McMillen, *The Citizens' Council*, p. 117; "Memphis Pro-Southerners Hear Johnson," *Arkansas Faith*, March 1956, p. 4, Box 2, Folder 13, ACHR. Bartley, *The Rise of Massive Resistance*, pp. 122–23; Cook, *The Segregationists*, p. 262.

35. Johnson has written that he enjoyed "the benefit of the thinking of such men as Senator James O. Eastland, Senator Strom Thurmond, Judge Tom P. Brady, Attorney General Eugene Cook, Former Governor Ben Laney, Congressman John Bell Williams, Congressman Mendell Rivers, Congressman James M. Davis, Judge Leander Perez, Senator Walter Govan, Hon. John U. Barr, Senator Harry Byrd, Sr., Senator Richard Russell, and Former Governor James F. Byrnes"; undated, untitled handwritten reminiscences, Box 51, Folder 13, JJJ. Johnson interviews with Jacoway, May 22, 1999, pp. 22–23, April 23, 2002, p. 10; Johnson interview with Jacoway and Daniel, p. 5; Jim Johnson interview with Roy Reed, March 15, 1990, pp. 20–21, RRP.

36. Johnson interview with Jacoway, April 23, 2002, p. 50. "Petitions Filed Seeking Ban On Integration," *Arkansas Gazette*, July 4, 1956.

37. The first four issues of *Arkansas Faith* (November 1955–February 1956) are located in Box 2, Folders 20–23, JJJ; the last two issues (March and April 1956) are in Box 2, Folder 13, ACHR. "Governor Bares Knuckles to Copeland, 2 Main Foes."

38. "Now It's the South's Move," *Arkansas Faith*, November 1955, p. 3, Box 2, Folder 22, JJJ.

39. "South Closes Ranks on Race Issue: Congress Bloc Seeks Reversal of Court Decision," *Arkansas Faith*, March 1956, p. 12, Box 2, Folder 12, ACHR.

40. "Snoddy and Johnson File for Governor; Both Segregationists," *Arkansas Gazette*, May 2, 1956. Reed, *Faubus*, pp. 175–76. "Rally in Battle for Segregation Set Tomorrow," *Arkansas Gazette*, April 29, 1956; Johnson interview with Jacoway, April 23, 2002, p. 14. Mark Lowery, "'Justice' Jim Johnson: The Outsider Rhetoric of Southern Resistance," unpublished student paper, EJC. "Johnson Heeds Cries of Segregationists, Says He Will Run," *Arkansas Gazette*, May 1, 1956, p. 1A. Johnson interview with Jacoway, April 23, 2002, p. 16.

41. Black leaders also confronted Faubus about his comments, contributing to the candidate's

decision to back off the race issue; Henry Woods interview with T. Harri Baker, Dec. 8, 1972, p. 19, EAP. Reed, *Faubus,* p 169.

42. Phil Stratton to Jim Johnson, Oct. 26, 1955, Box 28, Folder 25, JJJ; Reed, *Faubus,* pp. 176–77; Jim Johnson campaign letter, May 6, 1957, Box 30, Folder 12, JJJ; Phil Stratton to Jim Johnson (nd, 1955), Box 30, Folder 11, JJJ. Davis, "Segregationists Go Same Way But in 2 Columns."

43. Anthony J. Badger, "The White Reaction to *Brown:* Arkansas, the Southern Manifesto, and Massive Resistance," in Jacoway and Williams, eds., *Understanding the Little Rock Crisis,* pp. 94–95. Orval Eugene Faubus, *Down From the Hills* (Little Rock: Democrat Printing & Lithographing Co., 1980), p. 122. Klarman, "How the *Brown* Decision Changed Race Relations," p. 104; Bartley, *The Rise of Massive Resistance,* pp. 260–62; Robert Sherrill, *Gothic Politics in the Deep South: Stars of the New Confederacy* (New York: Grossman Publishers, 1968), pp. 84–85; Richard E. Yates, "Arkansas, Independent and Unpredictable," in William C. Havard, *The Changing Politics of the South* (Baton Rouge: Louisiana State University Press, 1972), pp. 264–65.

44. "Snoddy and Johnson File for Governor." Many years later, when the two aging politicians had become good friends, Faubus's political adviser Bill Smith confessed these concerns to Johnson; Johnson interview with Jacoway and Daniel, p. 10.

45. Reed, *Faubus,* p. 154; Bartley, *The Rise of Massive Resistance,* pp. 251–69.

46. "3 Candidates Cross Swords On Integration," *Arkansas Gazette,* July 5, 1956.

47. "Governor Bares Knuckles to Copeland, 2 Main Foes." The key word in this promise was "forced"; Faubus did not commit himself to prohibit voluntary desegregation.

48. "Governor Wins in 67 Counties, Johnson Seven," *Arkansas Gazette,* Aug. 1, 1956. For an interesting analysis of this election see Thomas F. Pettigrew and Ernest Q. Campbell, "Faubus and Segregation: An Analysis of Arkansas Voting," *Public Opinion Quarterly* 24 (Fall 1960), pp. 436–47. Wallace, "Orval Eugene Faubus," p. 219. Faubus, *Down From the Hills,* p. 145; Johnson to Englehardt, April 18, 1957. Johnson interview with Jacoway, April 23, 2002, p. 1.

49. "Arkansas Voters Approve 3 Segregationist Measures," *Southern School News,* December 1956. Johnson interview with Jacoway, April 23, 2002, p. 7. Johnson interview with Jacoway and Daniel, p.14.

50. Richard McCulloch's obituary claimed he was the chief architect of the four segregation bills; "Death Claims R. B. McCulloch," *Arkansas Gazette,* March 7, 1959, p. 1A. Matilda Tuohey, "61st Assembly Produces Both Progress, Reaction," *Arkansas Gazette,* March 17, 1957. Phil Stratton to W. H. Cullen, April 22, 1957, Box 30, Folder 12, JJJ. "4 Segregation Bills Are Quickly Passed," *Memphis Commercial Appeal,* Feb. 14, 1957, SERS. Matilda Tuohey, "Segregation Bills Slip Through House Without Discussion," *Arkansas Gazette,* Feb. 14, 1957, p. 1A.

51. Ray Moseley, "State Senate Balks at Segregation Bills, Sets Public Hearing," *Arkansas Gazette,* Feb. 16, 1957, p. 1A. "2 Most Controversial Bills," *Arkansas Gazette,* Feb. 17, 1957, p. 1A; Charles Allbright and Ray Moseley, "Bills on Segregation Defended as Legal, Deplored as Unjust," *Arkansas Gazette,* Feb. 19, 1957, p. 1A; "4 Segregation Bills Head List of Issues Facing Legislature," *Arkansas Gazette,* Feb. 17, 1957, p. 1A.

52. "4 Segregation Bills Head List of Issues Facing Legislature."

53. William W. Hughes and Ray Moseley, "Backers Maneuver 4 Segregation Bills Toward Vote Today," *Arkansas Gazette,* February 15, 1957, p. 1A. Reed, *Faubus,* p. 178. See also William J. Smith interview with John Luter, August 19-20, 1971, p. 66, EAP.

54. "Faubus Says Sovereignty Unweakened," *Arkansas Gazette,* Feb. 21, 1957, p. 1A; "Faubus Signs Segregation Bills Into Law," *Arkansas Gazette,* Feb. 27, 1957, p. 1A. Faubus interview with Jacoway, May 12, 1994, p. 18, EJC.

55. Johnson interview with Jacoway, April 23, 2002, pp. 1–3. Bryce B. Miller, "White America About-Faces, Lauds Faubus," *Arkansas Gazette,* March 25, 1956, p. 3A; Davis, "Segregationists Go Same Way But in 2 Columns; May Merge."

56. McMillen, "White Citizens' Council and Resistance to School Desegregation in Arkansas," pp. 95–122. See also Amis Guthridge interview with John Luter, Aug. 21, 1970, p. 11, EAP.

57. "Gay Council Throng Applauds Griffin for Speech Flaying Race Integration," *Arkansas*

Gazette, Aug. 23, 1957, p. 2A; Jerry Dhonau, "Griffin Vows to Maintain Segregation," *Arkansas Gazette,* Aug. 23, 1957, p. 1A.

CHAPTER THREE — PATERNALISTIC GENTLEMAN

1. Harry Ashmore, "A Delayed Tribute to Archie House," *Arkansas Lawyer,* October 1992. Gaston Williamson, "Remarks at Memorial Service of Archie Franklin House," July 3, 1992, in the papers of the Rose Law Firm, Little Rock, Ark.; the author wishes to thank Phillip Carroll for bringing this information to her attention.

2. Williamson "Remarks." The Rose Law Firm would later be famous for its partners in the 1970s and 1980s, including Hillary Clinton and Vince Foster.

3. Williamson "Remarks"; A.F. House interview with Roy Reed, July 28, 1990, p. 1, RRP. A. F. House interview with John Pagan, Aug. 15, 1972, p. 15, EJC.

4. Harry Ashmore, "To the Editor of the *Gazette,*" *Arkansas Gazette,* March 22, 1970.

5. Irving Spitzberg wrote, "It seems that these men recruited, from just below their ranks, candidates to run for non-political positions on the School Board. The business elite was never afraid to engage in politics, just as long as they were not the politicians"; Irving Spitzberg Jr., *Racial Politics in Little Rock, 1954–1964* (New York: Garland Publishing, 1987), pp. 31–42. Spitzberg also wrote that the approach to "civics" employed by men such as Archie House was "paternalism in the best southern tradition." The "reform" these business leaders instituted in city government in 1956 concentrated power in the hands of the civic elite in Little Rock; it also left the city with a lame-duck mayor and City Council at the time of the Little Rock crisis; see Elizabeth Jacoway, "Taken by Surprise," in Elizabeth Jacoway and David R. Colburn, eds., *Southern Businessmen and Desegregation* (Baton Rouge: Louisiana State University Press, 1982). Harold Engstrom interview with Elizabeth Jacoway, Dec. 8, 1977, pp. 8–9, EJC; Henry Rath interview with Elizabeth Jacoway, Dec. 9, 1977, p. 11, EJC.

6. House interview with Reed, p. 4. Archie House once told an interviewer that although his father had fought in the Confederate Army, the elder House had no racial prejudice, and Archie "also tried not to be prejudiced"; Archie House interview with John Luter, Aug. 17, 1971, p. 1, EAP.

7. Sidney S. McMath interview with John Luter, Dec. 30, 1970, p. 6, EAP. Forrest Rozzell interview with John Pagan, Dec. 29, 1972, p. 1, EJC. See also Harold Engstrom interview with John Luter, Dec. 29, 1970, p. 20, EAP.

8. House interview with Reed, p. 4. Harry S. Ashmore interview with Elizabeth Jacoway, Nov. 17, 1976, pp. 13–14, EJC. Gaston Williamson concurred with Ashmore, reporting that Archie House was "largely instrumental in working out that plan with Blossom...."; J. Gaston Williamson interview with Sara Alderman Murphy, Dec. 10, 1993, p. 3, Box 5, Folder 8, SAM.

9. See Virgil T. Blossom, *It HAS Happened Here* (New York: Harper & Bros. 1959), p. 7; see also Julianne Lewis Adams and Thomas A. DeBlack, *Civil Obedience: An Oral History of School Desegregation in Fayetteville, Arkansas, 1954–1965* (Fayetteville: University of Arkansas Press, 1994); see also. Virgil T. Blossom, "The Untold Story of Little Rock," *Saturday Evening Post,* May 23, May 30, and June 6, 1959.

10. Engstrom interview with Jacoway, Dec. 8, 1977, p. 26, EJC; Harold Engstrom interview with Roy Reed, Jan. 11, 1990, pp. 22–24, RRP; Engstrom claimed that Blossom had merged the three school districts to dilute the numbers of black children in any one district; Engstrom interview with Reed, Jan. 11, 1990, pp. 22–23. Blossom, *It HAS Happened Here,* p. 26; see the office correspondence in several folders in Box 1, VTB.

11. House interview with Luter, pp. 10, 4. The board adopted the statement on May 20, 1954, and it was published in the *Arkansas Gazette* on May 23; "Statement of Little Rock Board of Education: Supreme Court Decision—Segregation in Public Schools," May 23, 1954, Box 4, Folder 16, VTB. See also "Here Is the Text of Judge Miller's Opinion in the Little Rock Integration Case," *Arkansas Gazette,* Aug. 29, 1956, p. 8A.

12. Hugh B. Patterson interview with John Pagan, Dec. 27, 1972, p. 3, EJC. Irving Spitzberg

described Blossom as a member of the "liberal clique" that included Ashmore, Patterson, and Sid McMath; Spitzberg, *Racial Politics*, p. 56. House interview with Luter, p. 6. Orval E. Faubus, *Down From the Hills* (Little Rock: Democrat Printing & Lithographing Co., 1980), p. 199.

13. Blossom, *It HAS Happened Here*, p. 10. Engstrom interview with Luter, p. 39.

14. Blossom, *It HAS Happened Here*, pp. 13–18.

15. Spitzberg, *Racial Politics*, pp. 43, 55.

16. Blossom, *It HAS Happened Here*, p. 16. Harold Engstrom interview with Roy Reed, Jan. 11, 1990, p. 2, RRP.

17. William G. Cooper interview with Roy Reed, Aug. 2, 1990, p. 12, RRP.

18. Arthur B. Caldwell to Warren Olney III, July 24, 1957, Box 5, Folder 2, ABC.

19. Georg C. Iggers, "An Arkansas Professor: The NAACP and the Grass Roots," in Wilson Record and Jane Cassels Record, *Little Rock U.S.A.: Materials for Analysis* (San Francisco: Chandler Publishing Co., 1960), pp. 286–87; see also Wilma and Georg Iggers, *Zwei Seiten der Geschinchte: Lebensbericht aus unruhigen Zeiten [Two Sides of History: An Account from Unquiet Times]* (Gottingen, Germany: Vandenhoeck und Ruprecht, 2002); the author wishes to thank Dr. Scott Darwin, professor of languages at Arkansas State University, for translating the Little Rock portion of this manuscript. For enlightening background information on the filing of *Aaron v. Cooper* see Johnny E. Williams, *African American Religion and the Civil Rights Movement in Arkansas* (Jackson: University Press of Mississippi, 2003), pp. 105–7. For a full and persuasive treatment of the activities of the NAACP in Little Rock, see Brian James Daugherity, "'With All Deliberate Speed': The NAACP and the Implementation of *Brown v. Board of Education* at the Local Level, Little Rock, Arkansas" (master's thesis, University of Montana, 1997).

20. Historian Brian Daugherity has suggested that Arkansas's *amicus curiae* brief filed with the Supreme Court in the fall of 1954 influenced Blossom to proceed even more minimally and gradually than he had first intended; Daugherity, "'With All Deliberate speed,'" pp. 39–40. ADL Report, section marked "Opinions on Desegregation."

21. "Little Rock Board of Education Plan of School Integration," p. 3 (nd) Box 4, Folder 5, VTB. In later drafts of the plan, the reference to "teachable groups" was removed; see "Little Rock Board of Education Plan of School Integration," (nd, about June 1956), Box 1, Folder 1, RCB. "Here Is the Text of Judge Miller's Opinion in the Little Rock Integration Case," *Arkansas Gazette*, Aug. 29, 1956, p. 8A. Blossom, *It HAS Happened Here*, pp. 23–24. "Little Rock Board of Education Plan of School Integration," p.17, VTB.

22. Iggers, "An Arkansas Professor," p. 287; Georg C. Iggers to Tony Freyer, Sept. 17, 1980, Box 1, Folder 7, GIP; see also John A. Kirk, *Redefining the Color Line: Black Activism in Little Rock, Arkansas, 1940–1970* (Gainesville: University Press of Florida, 2002), p. 96.

23. For thorough treatments of the deliberations surrounding *Brown II*, see Mark Tushnet, *Making Civil Rights Law: Thurgood Marshall and the Supreme Court, 1956–1961* (New York: Oxford University Press, 1994), pp. 228–31; Richard Kluger, *Simple Justice: The History of Brown v. Board of Education and Black America's Struggle for Equality* (New York: Random House, 1975), pp. 729–47; Jack Greenberg, *Crusaders in the Courts: How a Dedicated Band of Lawyers Fought for the Civil Rights Revolution* (New York: Basic Books, 1994), pp. 389–90.

24. Iggers, "An Arkansas Professor," p. 287. School Board member Harold Engstrom admitted years later that the Blossom Plan aimed to "comply barely" with the federal courts; Harold Engstrom interview with Roy Reed, Jan. 11, 1990, p. 3, RRP. Daisy Bates, *The Long Shadow of Little Rock* (New York: David McKay Co., 1962), pp. 51–52.

25. "Statement of Virgil Blossom," March 14, 1956, Box 1, Folder 1, RCB. Iggers, "An Arkansas Professor," p. 288.

26. Iggers, "An Arkansas Professor," p. 289; Iggers to Freyer, Sept. 17, 1980.

27. The local leadership was divided regarding strategy; Daugherity, "'With All Deliberate Speed,'" pp. 64–67, 72–74. Iggers, "An Arkansas Professor," p. 289. For an informative account of this recruiting process see Williams, *African-American Religion and the Civil Rights Movement in Arkansas*, p. 130. See also Ozell Sutton interview with Roy Reed, June 22, 1992, p. 6, RRP.

28. *Southern School News,* February 1956, p. 11. John Aaron was the father of the child among the thirty-three children filing suit whose name came first in the alphabet; William G. Cooper was president of the School Board. The name of the plaintiff always comes first.

29. Spitzberg, *Racial Politics,* p. 48. The description of Leon Catlett comes from Tony Freyer, *The Little Rock Crisis: A Constitutional Interpretation* (Westport, Conn.: Greenwood Press, 1984), p. 52; the assessment of Frank Chowning's racial views comes from Spitzberg, *Racial Politics,* p. 48; information about the other two lawyers comes from the author's personal experience and knowledge. For a rich sampling of these memos as well as the fullest available collection of briefs and correspondence emanating from *Aaron v. Cooper,* see RCB.

30. A. F. House to Attorney Group, March 15, 1956, Box 1, Folder 1, RCB; see also A. F. House to Attorney Group, March 23, 1956, Box 1, Folder 1, RCB. A. F. House to Attorney Group, March 9, 1956, Box 1, Folder 1, RCB. A. F. House to John E. Miller, May 11, 1956, Box 1, Folder 1, RCB; A. F. House to John E. Miller, April 9, 1956, Box 1, Folder 1, RCB.

31. The federal judge for the district that included Little Rock, Tom Trimble, disqualified himself because his son was in Richard Butler's law firm; "Judge Miller is Reassigned to CHS Case," *Arkansas Gazette,* Sept. 10, 1958, p. 1A. Grif Stockley, *Blood in Their Eyes: The Elaine Race Massacre of 1919* (Fayetteville: University of Arkansas Press, 2001), pp. 40, 41, 49, 108, 109, 187, 188. Apparently troubled by that experience, Miller set the record straight about the true nature of the Elaine tragedy in an oral history interview conducted over sixty years later; see Judge John E. Miller interview with Walter Brown, Sam Sizer and Bruce Parham, March 18, 1976, pp. 13–28, JEM. "Judge Miller to Carry Out Court Ruling," Box 1, Folder 1, HJL.

32. For a copy of Virgil Blossom's testimony in this trial see "Appellees Supplemental Record," (nd), Box 1, Folder 2, RCB. Iggers, "An Arkansas Professor," p. 290; Kirk, *Redefining the Color Line,* p. 99. Iggers to Freyer, Sep. 17, 1980.

33. Branton, "Little Rock Revisited." Leon B. Catlett to John E. Miller, Aug. 21, 1956, Box 1, Folder 1, RCB; see also A. F. House to John E Miller, "Aaron, et al, v. Cooper, et al," (nd), Box 1, Folder 1, RCB. Judge Miller's decision specified that he had retained jurisdiction "for the purpose of entering such other and further orders as may be necessary to obtain the effectuation of the plan"; "Negroes Challenge School Board Use of Placement Laws; Suit Contends All in Zone Are Eligible," *Arkansas Gazette,* Aug. 9, 1959, p. 1A.

34. A. F. House to Attorney Group, Aug. 16, 1956, Box 1, Folder 1, RCB. Wiley Branton explained that the NAACP decided not to appeal because "we didn't want to run the risk of having the Court adopt that one as a model plan for the nation"; Wiley A. Branton interview with James Mosby, Jan. 16, 1969, pp. 21–22, CRDP. See also Branton, "Little Rock Revisited," pp. 256–257. For a copy of the brief the Little Rock School District filed with the Eighth Circuit Court of Appeals, see A. F. House to Attorney Group, Feb. 8, 1957, Box 1, Folder 2, RCB.

35. "Judge Dismisses Suit to Hurry Integration of Little Rock Pupils," *Arkansas Gazette,* Aug. 29, 1956, p. 1A.

36. "The Little Rock Plan Meets the First Test," *Arkansas Gazette,* Aug. 29, 1956, p. 4A. *Arkansas Gazette* publisher Hugh Patterson later stressed that the *Gazette* always supported the Blossom Plan; Patterson interview with Pagan, p. 3.

37. Virgil Blossom interview with FBI, Sep. 7, 1957, Box 2, Folder 3, FBI Report. William H. Bowen interview with Elizabeth Jacoway, May 24, 2000, pp. 14–15, EJC. William J. Smith interview with John Luter, Aug. 19–20, 1971, pp. 6–7, EAP. Confidential interview with Elizabeth Jacoway, Nov. 17, 1976.

38. Terrell E. Powell, principal of Hall High School in 1957, received numerous telephone calls from Citizens' Council members in 1957 complaining about "my lily white school, my silk stocking school, my non-integrated school. . . ."; Terrell E. Powell interview with T. Harri Baker, Nov. 20, 1972, p. 5, EAP. William J. Smith and Orval Faubus interview with Roy Reed, Dec. 18, 1989, p. 39, RRP; Numan V. Bartley, *The Rise of Massive Resistance: Race and Politics in the South During the 1950's* (Baton Rouge: Louisiana State University Press, 1969), p. 254.

39. Colbert Cartwright, "Lesson from Little Rock," *Christian Century,* Oct. 9, 1957, pp. 1193–94.

40. ACHR was the Arkansas affiliate of the Southern Regional Council. Colbert Cartwright, "Failure in Little Rock," *Progressive,* June 1958, p. 13, (np), reprint included in materials on microfilm, CCA. For a suggestive examination of Cartwright See Terry D. Goddard, "White Southern Social Justice Advocate: The Rev. Colbert S. Cartwright and the Little Rock School Crisis." *Pulaski County Historical Review,* Summer, 2003, pp. 30–42.

41. Kirk, *Redefining the Color Line,* p. 93. See also John A. Kirk, "'Massive Resistance and Minimum Compliance': The Origins of the 1957 Little Rock School Crisis and the Failure of School Desegregation in the South," in Clive Webb, ed., *Massive Resistance: Southern Opposition to the Second Reconstruction* (New York: Oxford University Press, 2005), pp. 76–98.

42. Virgil T. Blossom, "The Untold Story of Little Rock," Part Two, *Saturday Evening Post,* May 30, 1959, p. 82.

43. ADL Report, section marked "Development of Policy on School Desegregation," in Clive Webb, ed., *Massive Resistance: Southern Opposition to the Second Reconstruction* (New York: Oxford University Press, 2005). pp. 76–98.

44. Ibid., section marked "Memo on Little Rock, Arkansas," February 1958. Nat Griswold concurred in this assessment of Blossom, writing, "Like his outsized body, his ego was always showing more than most people's"; Griswold, *The Second Reconstruction in Little Rock,* Book Two, Chapter 3, p. 2. As Harry Ashmore recalled years later, "I supported Blossom and damn near strangled to do it, he was an ass. . . ."; Harry Ashmore interview with Roy Reed, June 20, 1992, RRP. ADL Report, section marked "Preparation for Desegregation."

45. George Douthit interview with John Luter, Dec. 31, 1970, pp. 6 and 24, EAP. D. H. Yarrow to Hugh Moore, Oct. 15, 1957, Box 79, SRC. ADL Report, section marked "Educational Preparation." For an extended critique of the School Board's failure, and particularly Virgil Blossom's failure, to prepare the community for desegregation, see Robert R. Brown, *Bigger Than Little Rock* (Greenwich, Conn.: Seabury Press, 1958), pp. 47–54.

46. Rath interview with Jacoway, p. 6; Wayne Upton interview with Elizabeth Jacoway, Dec. 20, 1977, pp. 2–5, EJC.

47. Upton interview with Jacoway, pp. 2, 4. Rath interview with Jacoway, p. 6. "Mary Williams Rath: Owner of Gift Shop, Industrious, Creative," *Arkansas Democrat-Gazette,* Nov. 2, 2002.

48. Upton's firm was Wright, Harrison, Lindsey, & Upton; Upton interview with Jacoway, pp. 3, 8, 19.

49. Rath interview with Jacoway, pp. 4, 11, 12. Rath's brother-in-law was Grainger Williams; his niece was Brownie Williams Ledbetter. Upton interview with Jacoway, p. 25. Rath interview with Jacoway, p. 14. For information on Little Rock voting patterns see Corinne Silverman, *The Little Rock Story,* Inter-University Case Program, No. 41 (University, Ala.: University of Alabama Press, 1959), pp. 36–38; and Henry M. Alexander, *The Little Rock Recall Election,* Eagleton Institute Case Studies in Practical Politics, Case No. 17 (New Brunswick: Rutgers University Press, 1960), p. 32.

50. William G. Cooper interview with Roy Reed, Aug. 2, 1990, p. 5, RRP; Cooper interview with John Luter, Dec. 28, 1970 pp. 1, 3, EAP. House interview with Luter, p. 6. House interview with Reed, p. 19. Cooper interview with Reed, p. 4.

51. Lile interview with Jacoway, p. 7. House interview with Reed, p. 14; Upton interview with Jacoway, pp. 23–24; Wayne Upton interview with John Luter, December 1971, p. 44, EAP. Cooper interview with Luter, p. 20. R. A. Lile interview with John Luter, Aug. 19, 1971, pp. 1, 6, EAP; Lile interview with Jacoway, pp. 1, 4, 5, 10.

52. Engstrom interview with Jacoway, p. 5. House interview with Reed, p. 14. Dale Alford interview with Pete Daniel and Elizabeth Jacoway, Jan. 26, 1996, pp. 24, 6, EJC.

53. Engstrom interview with Luter, p. 13. Upton interview with Jacoway, p. 24.

54. Engstrom interview with Jacoway, pp. 4–7.

55. Robert Ewing Brown to Governor Orval E. Faubus, April 30, 1956, Box 4, Folder 3, VTB.

56. Ibid.

57. Ibid.

58. "On the spot" was a phrase Faubus used in numerous communications, and it found its way into Virgil Blossom's thinking and his book; *It HAS Happened Here*, p. 36.

59. House to Caldwell, July 21, 1958. Arthur B. Caldwell memo, "Segregation in Public Schools, Little Rock, Arkansas," May 28, 1957, Box 5, Folder 2, ABC; Elizabeth Carpenter, "Native of State Doing Good Job for Civil Rights," *Arkansas Gazette*, Sept. 8, 1957.

60. Caldwell to Olney, July 24, 1957.

61. Carpenter, "Native of State Doing Good Job." Robert S. Allen, "Several Shun Civil Rights Positions," *Mobile Press*, Oct. 1, 1957, Box 1, Folder 17, ABC.

62. Allen, "Several Shun Civil Rights Positions." Robert A. Caro, *Master of the Senate: The Years of Lyndon Johnson* (New York: Alfred A. Knopf, 2002) makes no mention of Caldwell. Caro, *Master of the Senate*, p. 916.

63. Allen, "Several Shun Civil Rights Positions"; Robert Caro agreed that Eisenhower was furious when he found out what was in Section III; Caro, *Master of the Senate*, pp. 918–19.

64. Caldwell to Olney, July 24, 1957. Engstrom interview with Luter, p. 30.

65. A. B. Caldwell to Judge A. F. House, June 19, 1958, Box 5, Folder 7, ABC; Caldwell continued, "You will recall how close the Department came at one time to joining with the NAACP in attacking it as a plan which fell short of a sincere attempt at compliance."

66. Caldwell to House, June 19, 1958.

67. Caldwell to Olney, July 24, 1958.

68. House interview with Pagan, pp. 4, 14.

CHAPTER FOUR — BLUE-COLLAR OPPOSITION

1. Roy Reed interview with Mamie Ruth Williams, June 25, 1996, RRP.

2. Amis Guthridge interview with John Luter, Aug. 19, 1971, p. 2, EAP.

3. Guthridge interview with Luter, p. 1. "Support of Public Officials Claimed by Segregationists," *Arkansas Gazette*, March 21, 1956; Henry M. Alexander, *The Little Rock Recall Election*, Eagleton Institute Case Studies in Practical Politics, Case No. 17 (New Brunswick: Rutgers University Press, 1960), p. 4.

4. Harry S. Ashmore, *An Epitaph for Dixie* (New York: W. W. Norton & Co., 1958), pp. 103, 189. B. Cooper Jacoway interview with Elizabeth Jacoway, Nov. 5, 1975. A. F. House interview with John Luter, Aug. 17, 1971, p. 17, EAP. Harry Ashmore interview with Roy Reed, June 20, 1992, p. 36, RRP. Business leader Finley Vinson recalled years later that Guthridge had "no influence in business or public leadership in the community. . . ."; Finley Vinson interview with Elizabeth Jacoway, Dec. 21, 1977, p. 13, EJC. For the class makeup of the Capital Citizens' Council, see Graeme Cope, "'Honest White People of the Middle and Lower Classes'? A Profile of the Capital Citizens' Council During the Little Rock Crisis of 1957," *Arkansas Historical Quarterly* (Spring 2002), pp. 36–58, and Thomas F. Pettigrew and Ernest Q. Campbell, *Christians in Racial Crisis: A Study of the Little Rock Ministry* (Washington, D.C.: Public Affairs Press, 1959), pp. 41–62. For the quote, see "Virgil Blossom and Little Rock School Board: Speak Up So We Can Hear You!," *Arkansas Democrat*, July 15, 1957, p. 16. For an insightful examination of lower-middle-class white fears of the expected loss of respectability resulting from integration see Pete Daniel, *Lost Revolutions: The South in the 1950s* (Chapel Hill: University of North Carolina Press, 2000), esp. p. 270.

5. "Difficulty Predicted By White Group Head," *Arkansas Gazette*, June 2, 1955, p. 1A. "White America Sets Forth Its Views," *Arkansas Gazette*, June 8, 1955, p. 1B.

6. "White America Sets Forth Its Views." For a helpful discussion of the sect ministers' views on the biblical bases for segregation, see Pettigrew and Campbell, *Christians in Racial Crisis*, Chapter Three, "Sects and Segregation."

7. "White America Wants Change in Constitution," *Arkansas Gazette*, Aug. 3, 1955, p. 1B. "Segregationists of Little Rock Speak at Hoxie," *Arkansas Gazette*, Aug. 14, 1955, p. 9A.

8. "Outside Influences Indicated at Hoxie," *Memphis Commercial Appeal*, Aug. 23, 1955, SERS; "Hoxie Board Upheld; Judge Reeves Holds State Laws Invalid," *Arkansas Gazette*, Jan. 10, 1956, p. 10. "Segregationists of Little Rock Speak at Hoxie."

9. At that time Arkansas public schools were primarily dependent on a property tax that had to be approved by the voters every other year. William W. Hughes, "Segregationist Outlines Plans in School Fight," *Arkansas Gazette*, Oct. 16, 1955, p. 4A.

10. "White America About-Faces, Lauds Faubus," *Arkansas Gazette*, March 25, 1956, p. 3A. Neil McMillen, "White Citizens' Council and Resistance to School Desegregation in Arkansas," *Arkansas Historical Quarterly* 30 (Summer 1971), pp. 99–101. Just a year later political scientist Henry Alexander described the CCC as "the most vocal and potent group within the community"; Alexander, *The Little Rock Recall Election*, p. 4.

11. For a careful analysis of the composition of the membership, see Cope, "'Honest White People of the Middle and Lower Classes'?" Irving Spitzberg, *Racial Politics in Little Rock, 1954–1964* (New York: Garland Publishing, 1987), p. 40; Graeme Cope, "'A Thorn in the Side'? The Mothers' League of Central High School and the Little Rock Desegregation Crisis of 1957," *Arkansas Historical Quarterly* 57 (Summer 1998), p. 176. Hugh Patterson interview with John Luter, Aug. 12, 1970, p. 48, EAP.

12. Robert E. Baker, "Faubus' Bogeyman Born of 3d-Term Ambition," *Washington Post*, Sept. 8, 1957, SERS. Amis Guthridge interview with John Pagan, Dec. 28, 1973, p. 10, EJC; Guthridge interview with Luter, p. 5. Forrest Rozzell interview with John Pagan, Dec. 29, 1972, p. 11, EJC.

13. Bobbie Forster, "700 Students to Use New High School," *Arkansas Democrat*, Aug. 25, 1957, p. 14A. C. Fred Williams overstated the case when he wrote that "the Little Rock school crisis in 1957 was more about class than race"; C. Fred Williams, "Class: The Central Issue in the 1957 Little Rock School Crisis," *Arkansas Historical Quarterly* 56 (Autumn 1997), pp. 341–44. Pettigrew and Campbell, *Christians in Racial Crisis*, p. 47. Bem Price, "Integration Barriers Cracking in South," *Arkansas Gazette*, Sept. 1, 1957, p. 1A.

14. Cope, "'A Thorn in the Side'?," p. 166; Pete Daniel interview with Wesley Pruden Jr., Dec. 6, 1995, p. 16, EJC; the author is grateful to Professor Daniel for sharing this interview; Pettigrew and Campbell, *Christians in Racial Crisis*, p. 180. For a suggestive examination of Wesley Pruden see Terry D. Goddard, "Race, Religion and Politics: Rev. Wesley Pruden of Arkansas, Modern Day Jim Crow," *Pulaski County Historical Review*, Winter 2004, pp. 107–118.

15. Blossom had discussed this screening process with Federal Judge John E. Miller; John A. Kirk, *Redefining the Color Line: Black Activism in Little Rock, Arkansas, 1940–1970* (Gainesville: University Press of Florida, 2002), p. 107. Virgil T. Blossom, "The Untold Story of Little Rock," Part Two, *Saturday Evening Post*, May 30, 1959, p. 82. Eight of the seventeen eligible black children withdrew after Governor Faubus surrounded Central High School with the Arkansas National Guard; Daisy Bates later suggested that Virgil Blossom persuaded three of these children to return to Horace Mann, promising them "that when the nine went in, he would transfer them back to Central"; Daisy Bates to Roy Wilkins, Aug. 24, 1959, Microfilm Series, Part 3, Series D, Reel 2, Folder: "Desegregation Schools Arkansas Little Rock, Central High, 1959," PON.

16. Wiley A. Branton interview with James Mosby, Jan. 16, 1969, p. 21, CRDP.

17. Spitzberg, *Racial Politics*, p. 53. Sutton interview with Reed, p. 8.

18. Guthridge interview with Luter, p. 4.

19. For perceptive insights into this phenomenon, see Jeff Woods, *Black Struggle, Red Scare: Segregation and Anti-Communism in the South, 1948–1968* (Baton Rouge: Louisiana State University Press, 2003); and George Lewis, *The White South and the Red Menace: Segregationists, Anticommunism, and Massive Resistance, 1945–1965* (Gainesville: University Press of Florida, 2004). Wesley Pruden, "Can a Christian be a Segregationist?," *Arkansas Democrat*, Oct. 12, 1957, as quoted in Terry Goddard, "Disruption of Harmony in Dixie: Politics, Religion, and the Little Rock School Crisis," p. 106, unpublished manuscript, EJC. Guthridge interview with Luter, p. 26.

20. Wesley Pruden interview with John Pagan, Aug. 17, 1972, p. 1, EJC. Wesley Pruden interview with John Luter, Dec. 28, 1970, p. 6, EAP; McMillen, "White Citizens' Council," pp. 101–2.

21. "Segregation Issue Aired in Tulsa," *Arkansas Democrat,* June 23, 1957, p. 10A; Guthridge interview with Luter, p. 6; Pruden interview with Luter, p. 25.

22. *Southern School News,* August 1957. "Here Is the Text of Judge Miller's Opinion in the Little Rock Integration Case," *Arkansas Gazette,* Aug. 29, 1956, p. 8A.

23. *Southern School News,* August 1957. Bobbie Forster, "Board Asked to Provide Segregation," *Arkansas Democrat,* June 28, 1957, p. 4. *Southern School News,* September 1957. "Chancery Suit Demands High School for Whites," *Arkansas Gazette,* Aug. 20, 1957, p. 1A.

24. *Southern School News,* September 1957.

25. "Faubus Gets Demand for Segregation," *Arkansas Democrat,* July 1, 1957, p. 1; Pruden interview with Luter, p. 7. "Race Mixing in Little Rock, North Little Rock, Ft. Smith and All Arkansas Schools Can Be Stopped By the Governor," *Arkansas Democrat,* July 1, 1957, p. 10; Baker, "Faubus' Bogeyman."

26. Roy Reed, *Faubus: The Life and Times of an American Prodigal* (Fayetteville: University of Arkansas Press, 1997), pp. 186, 188. Orval Eugene Faubus, *Down From the Hills* (Little Rock: Democrat Printing & Lithographing Co., 1980), p. 185; Alta Haskins Faubus interview with Elizabeth Jacoway, April 9, 1996, p. 11.

27. "People of Arkansas vs. Race Mixing!," *Arkansas Democrat,* July 9, 1957, p. 13. Reed, *Faubus,* p. 178.

28. Reed, *Faubus,* p. 188. "Pastor Quizzes School Board on Integration," *Arkansas Gazette,* July 9, 1957, p. 2A.

29. Amis Guthridge to Little Rock School Board and Mr. Virgil T. Blossom, Superintendent, July 10, 1957, Box 4, Folder 3, VTB.

30. "Virgil Blossom and Little Rock School Board: SPEAK UP SO WE CAN HEAR YOU!," *Arkansas Democrat,* July 15, 1957, p. 16.

31. Cope, "'A Thorn in the Side'?," p. 170; David Chappell, "Diversity Within a Racial Group: White People in Little Rock, 1957–1959," *Arkansas Historical Quarterly* 54 (Winter 1995), p. 446. Blossom, *It HAS Happened Here,* p. 42.

32. James T. Karam interview with John Luter, Aug. 20, 1971, pp. 5, 28, 3, EAP; Fred B. Routh to State Board of Directors, July 22, 1955, Box 16, Folder 152, ACHR.

33. Guthridge interview with Luter, p. 12. Karam interview with Luter, pp. 1–3.

34. Reed, *Faubus,* pp. 123, 187. Nat Griswold interview with John Luter, Aug. 21, 1971, p. 44, EAP. Karam interview with Luter, p. 4.

35. Guthridge interview with Luter, pp. 1–15. Guthridge interview with Pagan, p. 10; Reed, *Faubus,* p. 90.

36. Claude Carpenter interview with Roy Reed, Aug. 1, 1990, p. 5, RRP.

37. Karam interview with Luter, pp. 21–22. Orval Faubus interview with Roy Reed, Dec. 22, 1988, #16, pp. 8, 10, RRP; as Orval Faubus said to Roy Reed, "the door of opportunity ... for blacks, needed to be opened wider and kept opened. And no one ever went to that office of governor with stronger desire to do that than me."; Ibid., p. 6. Guthridge interview with Luter, p. 18. Karam interview with Luter, pp. 3, 14.

38. Blossom, *It HAS Happened Here,* p. 36. William W. Hughes, "Minister Tells White Council Integration Is 'Devil's Work,'" *Arkansas Gazette,* July 17, 1957, p. 6A; *Southern School News,* August 1957.

39. *Southern School News,* August 1957. William T. Shelton interview with Sara Alderman Murphy, Dec. 1, 1993, p. 8, SAM. Guthridge interview with Luter, p. 17.

40. For a copy of this statement see A. F. House, "Memorandum," (nd), Box 1, Folder 2, RCB. *Southern School News,* August 1957.

41. Blossom, *It HAS Happened Here,* p. 39. "School Board to Hear Plan By Guthridge," *Arkansas Gazette,* July 25, 1957, p. 2A.

42. "School Board to Hear Plan By Guthridge." *Southern School News,* August 1957.

43. Little Rock School Board to Amis Guthridge, July 26, 1957, Box 4, Folder 3, VTB.

44. Cooper interview with Reed, Aug. 2, 1990, p. 4. Harold J. Engstrom interview with John Luter, Dec. 29, 1970, p. 12, EAP.

45. Orval Faubus interview with Roy Reed, Dec. 19, 1988, #14, p. 16, RRP. Orval Faubus interview with Roy Reed, Dec. 19, 1988, #15, p. 17, RRP; Orval Faubus interview with Sara Alderman Murphy, Aug. 19, 1992, p. 12, SAM. One teacher told Daisy Bates, speaking of Farrell Faubus, "From the day he entered he was set upon and beaten; only he fought back. He was called 'Backwoods,' 'Hill-billy,' and 'Commie.' He was treated so badly that he refused to return to Central for his junior and senior year, instead attending school in Huntsville"; draft copy of Bates manuscript, section entitled "faubus—13," Reel 1, DGB.

46. Henry Woods interview with Sara Alderman Murphy, August 30, 1992, p. 5, SAM. Roy Reed, "Orval E. Faubus: Out of Socialism Into Realism," *Arkansas Historical Quarterly,* LIV (Spring 1995), pp. 13-29. Faubus interview with Reed, #14, p. 21.

47. Spitzberg, *Racial Politics,* p. 56; Harold Engstrom interview with Roy Reed, Jan. 11, 1990, pp. 3, 4, RRP; Faubus interview with Luter, p. 33; William J. Smith interview with John Luter, Aug. 19–20, 1971, p. 7, EAP; Claude Carpenter interview with Elizabeth Jacoway, Nov. 12, 2001, EJC; Orval Faubus and William J. Smith interview with Roy Reed, Dec. 18, 1989, p. 9, RRP; Claude Carpenter interview with Roy Reed, Aug. 1, 1990, pp. 15–16, RRP. Engstrom interview with Luter, p. 41.

48. Engstrom interview with Luter, pp. 42–43, 45. Future School Board member Ted Lamb concurred in this assessment, telling Daisy Bates, "Blossom is a sheer opportunist. He wanted to go into office as Governor, saw himself . . . as the savior of the South"; "Memo re Lamb," Nov. 23, 1960, p. 8, Box 2, Folder 4, DGB.

49. Engstrom interview with Reed, Aug. 21, 1991, pp. 4–5; William G. Cooper interview with Roy Reed, Aug. 21, 1991, pp. 11–12; Henry Rath interview with Elizabeth Jacoway, Dec. 9, 1977, p. 24, EJC. Elizabeth Huckaby, *Crisis at Central High: Little Rock, 1957–58* (Baton Rouge: Louisiana State University Press, 1980), p. 20; Faubus and Smith interview with Reed, p. 7; R. A. Lile interview with John Luter, Aug. 19, 1971, p. 12, EAP; Wayne Upton interview with Elizabeth Jacoway, Dec. 20, 1977, p. 16, EJC; Engstrom interview with Luter, p. 41. Lile interview with Luter, p. 10; R. A. Lile interview with Elizabeth Jacoway, Dec. 22, 1977, p. 18, EJC; Engstrom interview with Reed, January 11, 1990, p. 4; Harry Ashmore to Elizabeth Jacoway, Nov. 25, 1976, EJC. Blossom's memoir revealed that he had been the target of gunfire; "Forthcoming Blossom Book Reveals Crisis' Only Gunfire," *Arkansas Gazette,* April 24, 1959, p. 1A.

50. Alta Faubus interview with Jacoway, April 9, 1996, p. 11. Faubus, *Down From the Hills,* pp. 185, 205; Faubus ultimately called off the Leggett electrocution after nationally acclaimed psychiatrists declared the boy insane; "Doctors' Report to Faubus Halts Leggett Death," *Arkansas Gazette,* Aug. 26, 1957, p. 1; "Leggett Lawyer May File Plea in Rape Cases to Beat Chair," *Arkansas Democrat,* Aug. 28, 1957, p. 1. Faubus interview with Reed, #15, p. 7; Blossom, *It HAS Happened Here,* p. 52; Orval Faubus to Virgil Blossom, Feb. 11, 1957, and Virgil Blossom to Orval Faubus, Feb. 12, 1957, Box 1, Folder 10, VTB; Faubus interview with Luter, pp. 3, 4. Orval Faubus interview with Roy Reed, July 24, 1992, p. 1, RRP.

51. Faubus interview with Luter, p. 6. Blossom and Faubus attended a meeting together in Kentucky where Superintendent Omer Carmichael had attributed the success of the Louisville desegregation effort largely to the absence of any politician attempting to make political capital out of the situation; see also Omer Carmichael and Weldon James, *The Louisville Story* (New York: Simon & Schuster, 1957). Engstrom interview with FBI. Engstrom interview with Luter, pp. 8–9.

52. Blossom, *It HAS Happened Here,* pp. 49–50.

53. Engstrom interview with Luter, pp. 8–9. Faubus interview with Luter, p. 5; Faubus and Smith interview with Reed, p. 10; Engstrom interview with Reed, Jan. 11, 1990, p. 6.

54. Blossom, *It HAS Happened Here,* p. 53. Griswold interview with Luter, p. 28. Faubus interview with Luter, p. 12; Faubus said in an interview with a national magazine in the summer of

1958, and also in his memoir, that Virgil Blossom was the major source of his information about the potential for violence at Central High School; "The Story of Little Rock—As Governor Faubus Tells it," *U.S. News & World Report,* June 20, 1958, pp. 101–6.

55. Wayne Upton interview with FBI, Sept. 7, 1957, Box 2, Folder 3, FBI Report; Arthur Brann Caldwell to Warren Olney, III, Aug. 30, 1957, Box 5, Folder 2, ABC; Faubus told interviewers he knew his Resolution of Interposition "had no binding effect"; Faubus interview with Luter, p. 37; Faubus interview with Jacoway, May 12, 1994, p. 16. Faubus and Smith interview with Reed, p. 19. Faubus, *Down From the Hills,* p. 223.

56. Blossom, *It HAS Happened Here,* p. 53. Faubus interview with Reed, #14, p. 21; also Faubus, *Down From the Hills,* p. 198. Faubus interview with Luter, p. 30.

57. Guthridge interview with Luter, p. 16; Cope, "'A Thorn in the Side'?," pp. 163–64, 170.

58. "Gay Council Throng Applauds Griffin for Speech Flaying Race Integration," Aug. 23, 1957, *Arkansas Gazette,* p. 2A; Jerry Dhonau, "Griffin Vows to Maintain Segregation," Aug. 23, 1957, *Arkansas Gazette,* p. 1A. Guthridge interview with Luter, p. 16. "Griffin Guest at Citizens [*sic*] Council Meet," *Arkansas Gazette,* Aug. 22, 1957, p. 1; "Faubus Not to Hear Griffin," *Arkansas Democrat,* Aug. 21, 1957, p. 1. Faubus had consulted Harry Ashmore for advice on how to handle the Griffin visit, and Ashmore, who was still advising Faubus at that point, had suggested that Faubus could avoid the event by saying he had to be out of town; Hugh B. Patterson interview with Elizabeth Jacoway, Oct. 11, 2002, p. 6, EJC.

59. "Segregation Leaders Urge Non-Violence," *Arkansas Democrat,* Aug. 28, 1957, p. 1. "Law and Order," *Arkansas Gazette,* Aug. 29, 1957, p. 4A. "Petition Adopted at 'Mothers League' Meeting Asks Faubus to Prevent Integration of School," *Arkansas Gazette,* Aug. 28, 1957, p. 1B.

60. "Segregation Leaders Urge Non-Violence."

61. "Petition Adopted at 'Mothers League' Meeting Asks Faubus to Prevent Integration of School." "Faubus Says Integration 'Pressured,'" *Arkansas Democrat,* Aug. 28, 1957, p. 1.

62. *Mrs. Clyde Thomason vs. Dr. William G. Cooper et al,* Aug. 27, 1957, Box 5, Folder 13, VTB. Faubus's position of waiting for judicial clarification was legally sound; see Alexander Bickel, "The Decade of School Desegregation: Progress and Prospects," *Colorado Law Review,* 1964, pp. 200–1.

CHAPTER FIVE — A TIME OF PANIC

1. Ralph Brodie interview with Elizabeth Jacoway, Oct. 9, 2002, EJC.

2. For details of Blossom's childhood and education see his memoir, Virgil T. Blossom, *It HAS Happened Here* (New York: Harper & Bros., 1959). Susan Blossom Streng telephone interview with Elizabeth Jacoway, July 30, 2002. The author's mother, a cousin of Clarrene Tribble, was a bridesmaid in this wedding; Daisy Tribble Jacoway interview with Elizabeth Jacoway, Aug. 25, 1975.

3. Wayne Upton interview with John Luter, Dec. 1971, p. 42, EAP.

4. Nat Griswold interview with John Luter, Aug. 21, 1971, p. 16, EAP. Harold Engstrom interview with Roy Reed, Jan. 11, 1990, p, 3, RRP; Harold Engstrom interview with John Luter, Dec. 29, 1970, p. 41, EAP.

5. See Blossom *It HAS Happened Here,* pp. 50–51; Faubus, *Down From the Hills,* p. 203; Orval Faubus interview with Roy Reed, Dec. 19, 1988, #14, p. 17, and Dec. 19, 1988, #15, p. 7, RRP. Harold Engstrom suggested that the competitive Blossom was jealous of Faubus's political success; Engstrom interview with Luter, p. 45. Blossom reported to the FBI that Faubus had told him on numerous occasions at the mansion that he wanted a delay in implementing the Blossom Plan for political reasons, always stressing that he needed political cover when Blossom asked him to make a statement that he would preserve law and order; Virgil Blossom interview with FBI, Sept. 5, 6, 7, 1957, Box 2, Folder 3, FBI Report.

6. Wayne Upton interview with FBI, Sept. 7, 1957, Box 2, Folder 3, FBI Report.

7. Wayne Upton interview with Elizabeth Jacoway, Dec. 20, 1977, p. 16, EJC.

8. Upton interview with FBI. Orval Faubus interview with John Luter, Aug. 18, 1971, pp. 9–10,

EAP; see also Faubus's description of the meeting in Orval E. Faubus, *Down From the Hills* (Little Rock: Democrat Printing & Lithographing Co., 1980), p. 201. Actually, as Blossom and Upton understood, their plan was no longer voluntary. Ever since the decision in *Aaron v. Cooper* they had been under court order to proceed with the Blossom Plan exactly as they had outlined it at that time. Blossom, *It HAS Happened Here,* pp. 53–54.

9. Faubus interview with Luter, p. 9. Faubus also reported this incident to Nat Griswold in 1967; see Nat R. Griswold, "The Second Reconstruction in Little Rock," Book One, Chapter 2, p. 15, Box 11, Folder 8, SAM. Archie House knew nothing about such a suit at the time, although later he heard repeatedly Faubus's charge that some School Board official had helped with the preparation of the petition; when told the particulars thirty years later, House replied that if Upton did such a thing he was "doing it behind my back," and he was a "damn duplicitous scoundrel"; Archie House interview with Roy Reed, p. 9, July 28, 1990, RRP. Witt Stephens, one of Faubus's closest political allies and financial backers, recalled years later having heard the story that Blossom and Upton tried to get Faubus to block their own School Board plan; W. R. Stephens interview with Elizabeth Jacoway, Dec. 21, 1977, p. 13, EJC.

10. Bill Lewis, "Attorney Named by Sovereignty Body," *Arkansas Gazette,* Aug. 31, 1957, p. 2A; "Death Claims R. B. McCulloch," *Arkansas Gazette,* March 7, 1959, p. 1A; Roy Reed, *Faubus: The Life and Times of an American Prodigal* (Fayetteville: University of Arkansas Press, 1997), p. 177; see also Numan V. Bartley, *The Rise of Massive Resistance: Race and Politics in the South During the 1950's* (Baton Rouge: Louisiana State University Press, 1969), p. 101. Bex Shaver interview with John Pagan, Aug. 22, 1972, p. 1, EJC; Reed, *Faubus,* p. 177.

11. Pagan interview with Shaver, p. 1. Faubus, *Down From the Hills,* p. 201. Orval Faubus interview with John Pagan, Aug. 16, 1962, p. 11, EJC.

12. Upton interview with FBI. Smith and Faubus interview with Reed, pp. 4-6, 12.

13. William J. Smith interview with FBI, Sept. 6, 1957, Box 2, Folder 3, FBI Report; Faubus and Smith interview with Reed, pp. 5, 7. Summary of William J. Smith interview with John Pagan, July 27, 1972, p. 1, EJC. In an interview with the FBI three weeks later, Blossom denied knowing anything about a drawer of weapons; Blossom interview with FBI, Sept. 7, 1957.

14. William J. Smith interview with John Luter, Aug. 19–20, 1971, pp. 7–10, EAP. Upton interview with FBI.

15. Smith interview with Luter, pp. 8–9. Faubus and Smith interview with Reed, p. 9. For another version of this incident see Spitzberg, *Racial Politics,* pp. 64–65. Wayne Upton denied this part of the story in his interview with the FBI, but he may have walked across the street to his home by that time; Upton interview with FBI.

16. Smith interview with Luter, pp. 9–10. Faubus and Smith interview with Reed, p. 9.

17. Smith interview with Luter, p.10.

18. Kay Matthews telephone interview with Elizabeth Jacoway, Nov. 19, 2002. Arthur Frankel interview with FBI, Sept. 7, 1957, Box 2, Folder 3, FBI Report. Jim Johnson and Amis Guthridge also refused to answer the FBI's questions; Jim Johnson interview with FBI, Sept. 8, 1957, Box 2, Folder 3, FBI Report; Amis Guthridge interview with FBI, Sept. 7, 1957, Box 2, Folder 3, FBI Report. Blossom interview with FBI, Sept. 7, 1957; Upton interview with FBI. Archie House interview with FBI, Sept. 7, 1957, Box 2, Folder 6, FBI Report.

19. Spitzberg, *Racial Politics,* p. 64. Faubus, *Down From the Hills,* p. 174. Griswold, "The Second Reconstruction in Little Rock," Book One, Chapter 2, p. 13. During this period Faubus aide Claude Carpenter frequently had breakfast with Blossom at Hotel Marion, and he recalled that Blossom was often shaking noticeably; Claude Carpenter interview with Elizabeth Jacoway, Nov. 13, 2001, EJC.

20. William F. Rector interview with FBI, Sept. 9, 1957, Box 2, Folder 10, FBI Report. Blossom interview with FBI, Sept. 7, 1957.

21. On Rector's hesitation to go so far as to file for an injunction against the School Board see William F. Rector interview with FBI, Sept. 9, 1957, Box 2, Folder 10, FBI Report. W. F. Rector, *EX PARTE, "Complaint for Declaratory Judgment,"* (nd), Box 5, Folder 13, VTB. Orval Faubus

later revealed publicly that Blossom was behind the Rector suit; "Governor Attacks Blossom's Book," *Arkansas Gazette,* June 4, 1959, p. 1B. Upton interview with FBI. Richard C. Butler interview with John Luter, Aug. 17, 1971, p. 43, EAP, italics added.

22. Engstrom interview with Reed, Jan. 11, 1990, pp. 7, 10.

23. Blossom interview with FBI, Sept. 7, 1957. Upton interview with FBI.

24. Engstrom interview with Reed, Aug. 21, 1991, p. 2; Engstrom interview with Luter, pp. 58–59.

25. The Rector suit died a quiet death, sitting on the docket of the Pulaski County Chancery Court until Sept. 5, 1979, when it was marked "dismissed for want of prosecution under Rule 10." House interview with Reed, p. 14. Harry Ashmore recalled that House knew about the negotiations with Miller but "took a dim view of it"; Harry S. Ashmore interview with Elizabeth Jacoway, Nov. 17, 1976, p. 49, EJC. School Board President William G. Cooper reported he had no recollection of being informed about a meeting with Judge Miller, as did Henry Rath and Brick Lile; William G. Cooper interview with Roy Reed, Aug. 21, 1991, p. 9, RRP; Henry Rath interview with Elizabeth Jacoway, Dec. 9, 1977, pp. 16–17, EJC; R. A. Lile interview with John Luter; Aug. 19, 1971, p. 6, EAP. *Arkansas Gazette* publisher Hugh Patterson heard otherwise; he reported years later that he had heard that Virgil Blossom had been involved in such a scheme; Hugh Patterson interview with Elizabeth Jacoway, Oct. 11, 2002, EJC.

26. Engstrom interview with Reed, Jan. 11, 1990, p. 15; Blossom interview with FBI, Sept. 5 and 7, 1957. Arkansas' Sovereignty Commission never had the poisonous effect that its sister organization had in Mississippi, at least in part because Governor Faubus never supported it with enthusiasm. Carol Griffee, ed., *Osro Cobb of Arkansas: Memoirs of Historical Significance* (Little Rock: Rose Publishing Co., 1989), p. 182.

27. Arthur B. Caldwell to Warren Olney III, Aug. 21, 1957, ABC. Faubus later reported he had called Attorney General Brownell's office three times without receiving a response; Orval Faubus interview with Elizabeth Jacoway, May 12, 1994, p. 48, EJC. Faubus, *Down From the Hills,* p. 197.

28. House interview with Reed, p. 10; A. F. House interview with John Luter, Aug. 17, 1971, p. 17, EAP. Engstrom interview with Reed, Aug. 21, 1991, p. 1. Ashmore interview with Jacoway, Nov. 17, 1976, p. 3, EJC.

29. Robert Alfred Lile interview with FBI, Sept. 5, 1957, Box 2, Folder 6, FBI Report; Harold James Engstrom interview with FBI, Sept. 5, 1957, Box 2, Folder 6, FBI Report; Upton interview with FBI. House interview with Reed, p. 5; Archie House interview with John Pagan, Aug. 22, 1972, p. 5, EJC. Arthur B. Caldwell to Warren Olney III, Aug. 30, 1957, Box 5, Folder 2, ABC.

30. Caldwell to Olney, Aug. 30, 1957. Blossom, *It HAS Happened Here,* p. 59. See also House interview with Reed, p. 5; Blossom interview with FBI, Sept. 7, 1957; "School Board Statement," June 17, 1958, VTB. Interestingly, Wayne Upton told researcher John Pagan he had no recollection of this meeting; Upton interview with Pagan, Aug. 22, 1972, p. 1, EJC. House interview with Pagan, p. 17.

31. *Mrs. Clyde Thomason v. Dr. William G. Cooper, et al.* Aug. 27, 1957, Box 5, Folder 13, VTB. For an exhaustive discussion of the 1957 Civil Rights Bill and its tortuous route to passage, see Robert A. Caro, *Master of the Senate: The Years of Lyndon Johnson* (New York: Alfred A. Knopf, 2002).

32. "John Hamilton Caldwell, 1881–1959," Box 1, Folder 7, ABC; Elizabeth Carpenter, "Native of State Doing Good Job for Civil Rights," Box 1, Folder 17, ABC; Arthur B. Caldwell to Archie House, Aug. 1, 1958, Box 5, Folder 7, ABC. Robert S. Allen, "Several Shun Civil Rights Positions," Oct. 1, 1957, *Mobile Press,* Box 1, Folder 17, ABC.

33. Allen, "Several Shun Civil Rights Positions"; Faubus, *Down From the Hills,* p. 197. Faubus agreed to keep the meeting confidential and did so until he heard the encounter had been reported in the *New York Times;* at that point he related his side of the story to the *Arkansas Democrat;* George Douthit, "U.S. Will Not Help Preserve Order If Violence Breaks Out at Central High, Faubus Says," *Arkansas Democrat,* Aug. 31, 1957, p. 1; Faubus, *Down From the Hills,* p. 197.

34. Caldwell to Olney, Aug. 30, 1957.

35. Ibid. Warren Olney III, "A Government Lawyer Looks at Little Rock," Oct. 3, 1957, p. 5, Box 5, Folder 5, ABC.

36. Faubus, *Down From the Hills,* p. 198. Caldwell to Olney, Aug. 30, 1957.

37. Faubus, *Down From the Hills,* p. 145; Faubus interview with Jacoway, May 12, 1994, p. 83; Faubus interview with Luter, p. 30.

38. Caldwell to Olney, Aug. 30, 1957.

39. Ibid.

40. Griffin Smith interview with Roy Reed, Jan. 4, 1989, p. 2, RRP; Faubus attorney William J. Smith believed that Virgil Blossom asked Griffin Smith to replace Arthur Frankel; William J. Smith interview with Luter, p. 11. Mrs. Clyde Thomason interview with FBI. Both Amis Guthridge and Wesley Pruden later reported they knew nothing about the Thomason suit. If this suit had truly been a creature of the Central High Mothers' League and the Capital Citizens' Council, Guthridge and Pruden would not only have known about it but would have served as attorney and witness. Amis Guthridge interview with John Pagan, Dec. 28, 1973, p. 10, EJC; Wesley Pruden interview with John Pagan, Aug. 17, 1972, p. 8, EJC.

41. Forrest Rozzell interview with John Pagan, Dec. 29, 1972, p. 10, EJC. Faubus interview with Luter, p. 13.

42. House interview with Pagan, p. 6.

43. *Mrs. Clyde Thomason vs. Dr. William G. Cooper, et al.* George Bentley and Ernest Valachovic, "State Court Rules Against Integration," *Arkansas Gazette,* Aug. 30, 1957, p. 1A. Griffin Smith interview with Reed, p. 5.

44. Caldwell to Olney, Aug. 30, 1957. Bentley and Valachovic, "State Court Rules Against Integration."

45. The order of testimony in this trial was irregular, perhaps because the governor was late, as a courtesy to him. The transcript of this trial has disappeared from the Pulaski County Courthouse and also its storage facility. The author has reconstructed the testimony from newspapers, Virgil Blossom's and Orval Faubus's memoirs, and Arthur Caldwell's description. Bentley and Valachovic, "State Court Rules Against Integration."

46. Faubus, *Down From the Hills,* pp. 201–2. The *Arkansas Gazette* reported that Blossom said he "anticipated no violence"; Bentley and Valachovic, "State Court Rules Against Integration."

47. Faubus interview with Luter, p. 13. Faubus, *Down From the Hills,* pp. 201–02.

48. "Background Information on Little Rock, Arkansas," Southern Regional Council Memorandum, (nd), Box 62, SRC. Fletcher Knebel, "The Real Little Rock Story," Nov. 12, 1957, *Look,* p. 32. Bentley and Valachovic, "State Court Rules Against Integration." Caldwell to Olney, Aug. 30, 1957.

49. Engstrom interview with Reed, Aug. 21, 1991, pp. 3–4.

50. Blossom interview with FBI, Sept. 6, 1957. School Board member Dale Alford reported in his memoir that through the summer of 1957, Virgil Blossom communicated repeatedly to the board his concerns about violence, and that he had discussed these concerns with Governor Faubus; Dale and L'Moore Alford, *The Case of the Sleeping People (Finally Awakened By Little Rock School Frustrations)* (Little Rock: Pioneer Press, 1959), p. 8.

51. Bentley and Valachovic, "State Court Rules Against Integration." "Temporary Restraining Order," Aug. 29, 1957, *Race Relations Law Reporter* (October 1957), p. 933. Griffin Smith interview with Reed, p. 3.

52. Caldwell to Olney, Aug. 30, 1957. Years later, Harry Ashmore reported that the night after Judge Reed handed down his decision, Archie House stopped to eat in a restaurant in Stifft Station on his way to his home in the Heights; Judge Reed was also eating in the same restaurant, and the venerable House went over to the judge's table and "just chewed his ass out," telling the judge that his decision was outrageous. As Ashmore recalled, that was the kind of thing "Archie could do"; Ashmore interview with Reed, June 20, 1992, p. 13.

53. Caldwell to Olney, Aug. 30, 1957. "Judge Arrives to Clear Jam, Finds U.S. Cases Not Ready,"

Arkansas Gazette, Aug. 27, 1957, p. 1B.

54. Herbert Brownell to President Dwight Eisenhower, Nov. 7, 1957, Box 5, Folder 4, ABC. Olney, "A Government Lawyer Looks at Little Rock," p. 7. Engstrom interview with Reed, Aug. 21, 1991, p. 8. "East Arkansas Federal Judgeship Still Wide Open," *Arkansas Gazette,* Aug. 31, 1957, p. 1A.

55. Blossom, *It HAS Happened Here,* p. 60; see also Blossom interview with FBI, Sept. 7, 1957.

56. Faubus, *Down From the Hills,* p. 202. Faubus told this interviewer that Blossom said, "Oh, I want to thank you, I want to thank you, and I want to tell you that anything I can ever do for you in the future or otherwise, you just have to call on me"; Orval Faubus interview with Elizabeth Jacoway, May 12, 1994, p. 20, EJC. Faubus, *Down From the Hills,* p. 202. Although Faubus told one interviewer that he and Blossom had been "quite close friends" for many years, Faubus told Nat Griswold in 1967 that Blossom's testimony in Judge Reed's court led to an irreparable breech in their relationship; Orval Faubus interview with Sara Alderman Murphy, Aug. 19, 1992, p. 13, SAM; Griswold, "The Second Reconstruction in Little Rock," Book One, Chapter 2, pp. 18–19.

57. Faubus, *Down From the Hills,* p. 202. Faubus wrote, ". . . it is difficult for me to believe that Blossom was a willing part of such deceit. There were those behind him, however, whom I believe were quite capable of planning and carrying out such a scheme"; Faubus, *Down From the Hills,* p. 203.

58. Sam Faubus said, "I think my son got embittered for some reason. I don't know what it was. . . . I've never been opposed to any race myself. I don't hold any race prejudice. He didn't use to think that way. There's none of the rest of his family does either"; *Pine Bluff Commercial,* Aug. 27, 1966, as quoted in Griswold, "The Second Reconstruction in Little Rock," Book 1, Chapter 2, p. 26.

INTERREGNUM — THE CHOSEN FEW

1. Untitled, undated, unsigned handwritten report (apparently written by Arkansas Council on Human Relations Executive Secretary Nat Griswold), Box 2, Folder 12, RRB. For Blossom's explanation for the screening see Transcript, Lemley Hearing, June 3, 1958, pp. 334–35, Box 5, Folder 7, VTB. "Report of Conference Between Little Rock School Superintendent and NAACP Representatives," May 29, 1957, group III, series A, container 98, in folder marked "Desegregation of Schools, Arkansas, Little Rock, Central High, 1956–1957," PON; Mrs. L. C. Bates to Mr. Robert L. Carter, Aug. 2, 1957, group III, series A, container 98, in folder marked "Desegregation of Schools, Arkansas, Little Rock, Central High, 1956–1957," PON; "Citizens Delegation Says School Board Superintendent Blossom Intimidating Students," *Arkansas State Press,* June 7, 1957.

2. Daisy Bates interview with Elizabeth Jacoway, Oct. 11, 1976, pp. 14–15, SOHP. "Citizens Delegation Says School Board Superintendent Blossom Intimidating Students." Blossom, *It HAS Happened Here,* p. 20.

3. As the principal of Horace Mann, Dr. L. M. Christophe, recalled years later, when he told Virgil Blossom that seventy-eight students had expressed an interest in attending Central High, Blossom replied, "Seventy-eight would be too many. . . ." LeRoy Matthew Christophe, *The Arkansas African American Hall of Fame* (Little Rock: National Dunbar Alumni Association of Little Rock, Arkansas, 1993), p. 104. Bates interview with Jacoway, pp. 11–12; Christopher C. Mercer Jr., interview with Elizabeth Jacoway, Aug. 11, 2003, p. 11, EJC. Audrey Edwards and Dr. Craig K. Polite, "Don't Let Them See You Cry," *Parade,* Feb. 16, 1992, p. 10. As Wiley Branton recalled, ". . . it's interesting to note that for the next six or seven years, not a one of the 33 ever had an opportunity to go to a previously all white school. And yet, they were the ones who bore the brunt and their parents who subjected themselves when the litigation first arose"; Wiley A. Branton interview with James Mosby, Jan. 16, 1969, pp. 21, 23, CRDP.

4. "Daisy Bates: Arkansas Fighter," p. 8. "Citizens Delegation Says School Board Superinten-

dent Blossom Intimidating Students." "Report of Conference Between Little Rock School Superintendent and NAACP Representatives." As Wiley Branton explained later, "We were on the verge
of going back into court to cite the Little Rock School Board for contempt because they were using
an elaborate screening process to limit the number of Negroes who would be coming to Little
Rock schools, formerly all white schools, despite their plan, when Governor Faubus started making noises which were designed to prevent any Negroes from going. So our effort then shifted from
one of being concerned about the fact that they didn't have but so many coming in, to protecting the rights of the few who were trying to go in."; Wiley A. Branton interview with Steven Lawson, Oct. 21, 1970, p. 55, EAP.

5. "Report of Conference between Little Rock School Superintendent and NAACP Representatives," May 29, 1957; Bates interview with Jacoway, p. 11. Mercer interview with Jacoway, p. 9;
Bates also enlisted volunteer "foot soldiers" such as Ozell Sutton to go door to door trying to persuade black children to attend Central High; Ozell Sutton interview with Roy Reed, June 22, 1992,
p. 6, RRP Ozell Sutton interview with Elizabeth Jacoway, June 7, 2003, EJC.

6. Her employer was Dr. Joseph Buchman; Elizabeth Eckford interview with Elizabeth
Jacoway, Aug. 14, 2003, p. 38, EJC. Eckford interview with Jacoway, Aug. 14, 2003, p. 26; Ted Poston, "Nine Kids Who Dared: Elizabeth Ann Eckford," Oct. 23, 1957, *New York Post Daily Magazine*, Bates Scrapbook, DGB.

7. Bates, *The Long Shadow of Little Rock*, p. 139; "White Pupils Curious to Know What We're
Like, Negro Says," *Baltimore Evening Sun*, Sept. 26, 1957, SERS; Adren Cooper, "After the First
Social Contact, A Pattern in Loneliness," *Nashville Tennessean*, Dec. 16, 1957, SERS.

8. Cooper, "After the First Social Contact, A Pattern in Loneliness"; Jefferson Thomas, "Negro
Boy, 15, Tells Story of His Morning in School," *New York Herald Tribune*, Sept. 24, 1957, SERS.
Bates, *The Long Shadow of Little Rock*, p. 122; Bette Orsini, "2 Negro Students Reveal Feelings,"
St. Petersburg Times, Sept. 30, 1957, SERS.

9. Ted Poston, "9 Kids Who Dared . . . Carlotta Walls," *New York Post*, Oct. 30, 1957, Bates
Scrapbook, DGB. Bates, *The Long Shadow of Little Rock*, p. 130; Cooper, "After the First Social Contact, A Pattern in Loneliness."

10. Thelma's mother worried about whether her daughter could take the stress of integrat-
ing Central High because of her congenital heart disorder, but when Thelma persisted, Mrs.
Mothershed told her, "You're a strong girl. Just show them how strong you are"; "Hosanna Claire
Mothershed: LR Nine Member's Mom Quiet, Strong", *Arkansas Democrat-Gazette*, Jan. 9, 2005, p.
4B. Bates, *The Long Shadow of Little Rock*, p. 138; Ted Poston, "Nine Kids Who Dared: Thelma
Mothershed," Oct. 26, 1957, *New York Post*, Bates Scrapbook, DGB; "Child of Integration: Thelma
Mothershed," *New York Times*, Sept. 10, 1957.

11. David Halberstam, *The Fifties* (New York: Villard Books, 1993), p. 670. Bates, *The Long
Shadow of Little Rock*, p. 138; Ted Poston, "Nine Kids Who Dared: Terrence Roberts," Oct. 31, 1957,
New York Post, Bates Scrapbook, DGB. Mrs. Huckaby was so impressed by Terrence's bearing that
she believed he must have had a "royal ancestor"; Elizabeth Huckaby interview with T. Harri Baker,
Oct. 25, 1972, p. 35, EAP.

12. Bates, *The Long Shadow of Little Rock*, p. 139; Ted Poston, "Nine Kids Who Dared: Melba
Patillo," Oct. 22, 1957, *New York Post*, Bates Scrapbook, DGB. Cooper, "After the First Social Con-
tact, A Pattern in Loneliness"; Press release, Oct. 19, 1957, group III, series A, container 98, PON;
Melba Patillo Beals, *Warriors Don't Cry: A Searing Memoir of the Battle to Integrate Little Rock's
Central High* (New York: Simon & Schuster, 1994), p. 9.

13. Bates, *The Long Shadow of Little Rock*, p. 116; Ted Poston, "Nine Kids Who Dared: Minnijean Brown," Oct. 25, 1957, *New York Post*, Bates Scrapbook, DGB; Minnijean Brown Trickey
interview with Elizabeth Jacoway, Sept. 16, 2003, p. 64, EJC.

14. For a poignant story of Green's friendship with a young Jewish boy in Little Rock, see Halberstam, *The Fifties*, p. 680. Bates, *The Long Shadow of Little Rock*, p. 145; Ernest Green interview
with Sara Alderman Murphy, Dec. 7, 1992, p. 2, Box 1, Folder 25, SAM; Ted Poston, "Nine Kids
Who Dared: Ernest Green," Oct. 24, 1957, *New York Post*, Bates Scrapbook, DGB. Ernest Green

interview with Elizabeth Jacoway, April 21, 2006, pp. 11-12, EJC.

CHAPTER SIX — THE CRISIS BREAKS
   1. Orval Faubus interview with Elizabeth Jacoway, May 12, 1994, p. 41, EJC; Orval Faubus interview with John Luter, Aug. 18, 1971, p. 127, EAP.
   2. For a sensitive, compelling treatment of Orval Faubus's childhood and life see Roy Reed, *Faubus: The Life and Times of an American Prodigal* (Fayetteville: University of Arkansas Press, 1997). The descriptions spring from the author's experience with Faubus in numerous late-in-life interviews and conversations. Nat R. Griswold, "The Second Reconstruction in Little Rock," Book Two, Chapter 3, p. 4, Box 11, Folder 8, SAM. See also Orval Eugene Faubus, *In This Faraway Land* (Conway, Ark.: River Road Press, 1971).
   3. Faubus genuinely believed himself to be "the most progressive governor in the nation"; Jack Bass and Walter De Vries interview with Faubus, June 14, 1974, p. 23, SHC. Jim Johnson interview with Roy Reed, March 13, 1990, p. 7, RRP; Jim Johnson interview with Elizabeth Jacoway, June 17, 2002, pp. 31–32, EJC. Faubus interview with Jacoway, May 12, 1994, p. 31; Orval Faubus interview with Elizabeth Jacoway, July 11, 1978, p. 38, EJC; Faubus interview with Luter, p. 111, EAP. About this same time in early 1957, Little Rock business leader Joshua Shepherd told Faubus he could win a third term; Irving Spitzberg, *Racial Politics in Little Rock, 1954–1964* (New York: Garland Publishing, 1987), p. 60. On May 24, 1957, *Arkansas Democrat* columnist Karr Shannon speculated in print that Faubus might seek a third term; Karr Shannon, "Run of the News," *Arkansas Democrat*, May 24, 1957, p. 12. A political cartoon in the *Arkansas Democrat* on June 6, 1957 portrayed Faubus considering a run for a third term; see Orval E. Faubus, *Down From the Hills* (Little Rock: Democrat Printing & Lithographing Co., 1980), p. 180. *Arkansas Democrat* reporter George Douthit reported to the Eisenhower Administration Project that Faubus was very attracted to the prospect of seeking a third term; George Douthit interview with John Luter, Dec. 31, 1970, p. 11, EAP.
   4. Nathania K. Sawyer, "Harry S. Ashmore: On the Way to Everywhere" (Master's thesis, University of Arkansas at Little Rock, 2001), p. 65; Faubus interview with Luter, pp. 107–8, EAP; Henry Woods interview with T. Harri Baker, Dec. 8, 1972, pp. 23–24, EAP. Reed, *Faubus,* pp. 80, 84; Bill Terry, "The Hobo Who Became Governor: Orval E. Faubus Remembers," *Arkansas Times,* October 1975, p. 13. Orval Faubus's wife told this interviewer that her husband originally had planned to run for the Senate after he left the Governor's Mansion, and that was why he needed to build a large house; Alta Haskins Faubus interview with Elizabeth Jacoway, April 9, 1996, p. 7, EJC; see also Alta Faubus interview with Roy Reed, June 15, 1989, p. 1, RRP. Claude Carpenter interview with Roy Reed, Aug. 1, 1990, p. 27, RRP; Claude Carpenter interview with Elizabeth Jacoway, Nov. 13, 2001, EJC. Faubus claimed he would never have run against Senator McClellan because McClellan did him the favor of remaining neutral during Faubus's 1954 contest against Francis Cherry; Faubus interview with Jacoway, May 12, 1994, p. 68; see also Adolph L. Reed, "Orval E. Faubus: (In the Perspective of the American Liberal)," student paper based on a 1966 interview with Faubus, EJC. Hugh B. Patterson interview with John Luter, Aug. 12, 1970, p. 5, EAP. Patterson thought Faubus wanted to be the head of the Arkansas Highway Commission. Faubus, *Down From the Hills,* p. 198; Faubus interview with Luter, p. 30, EAP; Faubus interview with Jacoway, May 12, 1994, p. 32.
   5. FBI interviews with J. M. Malone Sr., Arnold Sikes, W. T. Ball, Carl Elbert Adams, all on Sept. 8, 1957, Box 2, Folder 12, FBI Report.
   6. FBI interviews with Harvey G. Combs, Carl Adams, and Arnold Sikes, all on Sept. 8, 1957, Box 2, Folder 12, FBI Report. Kelly Cornett interview with FBI, Sept. 8, 1957, Box 2, Folder 12, FBI Report. Carpenter interview with Reed, p. 13; Carpenter interview with Jacoway.
   7. Carpenter interview with Reed, p. 13; Carpenter interview with Jacoway. Cornett interview with FBI.

8. Cornett interview with FBI. Combs interview with FBI. Integrationist activist Irene Samuel told an interviewer for the Eisenhower Administration Project that she had in her possession shorthand notes she had taken of a tape recording Commerce Commissioner Bill Berry claimed to have made at this meeting. Samuel claimed "It really came out of that meeting. . . . The decision to keep the blacks out of the schools"; Irene Samuel interview with John Luter, Dec. 30, 1970, p. 28, EAP. This researcher asked Irene Samuel about her shorthand notes, but Mrs. Samuel was unable to find them; Irene Samuel interview with Elizabeth Jacoway, July 10, 1996, EJC. Berry soon stepped down as commerce commissioner and became a source of anti-Faubus information for the FBI. A careful reading of the FBI's interviews with Cabinet members reveals that while the group discussed the possibility of using the National Guard, they made no decision. Virgil Blossom interview with FBI, Sept. 6, 1957, Box 2, Folder 3, FBI Report.

9. Virgil T. Blossom, *It HAS Happened Here* (New York: Harper & Brothers, 1959), p. 61. Among those who most coveted the appointment to the vacant federal judgeship were Republicans Osro Cobb, the United States attorney in Little Rock, and Richard C. Butler, one of the attorneys for the Little Rock School Board, as well as longtime Democratic Congressman Brooks Hays; "Smith Henley Is Considered for U. S. Judge," *Arkansas Gazette,* Aug. 20, 1957, p. 1B. "Judge Arrives to Clear Jam, Finds U. S. Cases Not Ready," *Arkansas Gazette,* Aug. 27, 1957, p. 1B. "Events, Information, Statements, Etc., Prior to September 3, 1957," Box 2, Folder 2, FBI Report. "State Injunction Voided," *Race Relations Law Reporter,* October 1957, p. 935.

10. "State Injunction Voided." Wiley A. Branton, "Desegregation to Resegregation," *Journal of Negro Education,* Summer 1983, p. 259.

11. Ernest Valachovic, "U.S. Judge Rejects Chancery Injunction; Integration to Start Tuesday," *Arkansas Gazette,* Aug. 31, 1957, p. 1A. "State Injunction Voided," *Race Relations Law Reporter,* October 1957, pp. 935–36; Bobbie Forster, "Court Rules Out Changes in Integration," *Arkansas Democrat,* Aug. 31, 1957, p. 1A. Branton, "Desegregation to Resegregation," p. 259.

12. Robert Alfred Lile interview with FBI, Sept. 5, 1957, Box 2, Folder 6, FBI Report. Hugh Patterson interview with John Pagan, Dec. 27, 1972, p. 1, EJC.

13. Faubus, *Down From the Hills,* p. 203. Virgil Blossom interview with FBI, Sept. 5, 1957. Orval Faubus interview with John Luter, Aug. 18, 1971, p. 9, EAP.

14. Faubus, *Down From the Hills,* p. 203; Harold Engstrom interview with John Luter, Dec. 29, 1970, p. 11, EAP. R. A. Lile interview with John Luter, Aug. 19, 1991, pp. 4–5, EAP.

15. Lile interview with Luter, pp. 4–5; see also R. A. Lile interview with Elizabeth Jacoway, Dec. 22, 1977, p. 10, EJC. Faubus, *Down From the Hills,* p. 203; Wayne Upton interview with Elizabeth Jacoway, Dec. 20, 1977, p. 14, EJC. Reed, *Faubus,* p. 6. Sam Faubus, Orval's father, told *Time* magazine that he had instructed Orval as a boy "not to hate anybody of any race. I told him people would think he was narrow-minded and would look down on him. That's one thing Orval always hated—to be looked down on"; *Time,* Sept. 23, 1957, p. 13.

16. Harold Engstrom interview with Roy Reed, Jan. 11, 1990, p. 26, RRP. Harold Engstrom interview with John Luter, Dec. 29, 1970, p.11, EAP. Upton interview with Jacoway, p. 14.

17. William G. Cooper interview with Roy Reed, Aug. 2, 1990, p. 10, RRP; Faubus, *Down From the Hills,* p.203. Faubus interview with Luter, p. 25.

18. Faubus, *Down From the Hills,* p. 203.

19. Faubus aide Claude Carpenter told interviewer Roy Reed years later that Herman Lindsey and the Arkansas State Police had conducted an extensive investigation at the governor's request; Carpenter interview with Reed, p. 13. Reed concluded based on other interviews that the investigation had been less than thorough; Reed, *Faubus,* p. 202. Faubus, *Down From the Hills,* pp. 203–4.

20. "School Board Issues Call for Cooperation and Understanding," *Arkansas Gazette,* Sept. 1, 1957, p. 1A. Even the board's strong segregationist, Dr. Dale Alford, signed this document.

21. Wayne Glenn interview with Elizabeth Jacoway, Jan. 13, 2004, p. 3, EJC. By the time of this interview, Glenn had thrown away all of his appointment calendars, and he could not pinpoint the date of his meeting with Faubus; Ibid., pp. 5–6. Glenn also recalled that he shared his con-

cerns about this visit with Henry Woods. After Faubus called out the National Guard, Glenn came to the conclusion that the governor had been planning to do so from the start; Ibid., pp. 7, 9. At some point during the summer Faubus visited with his chief financial backer, Witt Stephens, who assured the governor, "go either way you want to and we'll sell it. . . ."; Faubus interview with Jacoway, May 12, 1994, p. 57. Faubus realized that if he chose to allow desegregation, Stephens would suffer some of the consequences; he reflected nearly forty years later, "Oh boy, he would have got his eyes on me then if I'd have gone the other way and he started to sell it. They'd have boycotted him like they did the *Arkansas Gazette*"; Ibid., p. 58.

22. George Douthit, "U.S. Will Not Help Preserve Order if Violence Breaks Out at Central High, Faubus Says," *Arkansas Democrat,* Aug. 31, 1957, p. 1A. Assistant Attorney General Warren Olney reported in a speech in October 1957 that Faubus had twisted Caldwell's information suggesting the federal government was powerless to intervene into a rationale for his subsequent use of the Arkansas National Guard at Central High School; Warren Olney III, "A Government Lawyer Looks at Little Rock," Oct. 3, 1957, Box 5, Folder 5, ABC.

23. Gene Foreman, "School Board Issues Call for Cooperation and Understanding," *Arkansas Gazette,* Sept. 1, 1957, p. 1A.

24. Sidney S. McMath interview with John Luter, Dec. 30, 1970, pp. 4–5, EAP. Thirty years later, Faubus claimed "I think, as nearly as I can determine in my own conscience and in my own thoughts, I was not trying to make a decision based on political reality. . . . I felt the whole thing was detrimental to my political fortunes at the time"; Orval Faubus speech at the centennial celebration of Dwight Eisenhower's birth, June 5, 1990, Abilene, Kan., p. IV, 11, as transcribed by Roy Reed, RRP. See also Faubus interview with Luter, pp. 30, 34; Faubus interview with Jacoway, May 12, 1994, p. 32.

25. Woods interview with Baker, pp. 29–30. Patterson interview with Luter, p. 10; Harry Ashmore interview with Roy Reed, June 20, 1992, p. 12, RRP. The Sam Peck was Harry Reasoner's favorite Little Rock hostelry; Harry Reasoner, *Before the Colors Fade* (New York: Alfred A. Knopf, 1981), p. 64. Spitzberg, *Racial Politics in Little Rock,* p. 34. Ashmore interview with Reed, p. 13. See also Patterson interview with Luter, p. 10.

26. Orval Faubus and William J. Smith interview with Roy Reed, Dec. 18, 1989, p. 17, RRP. Harry Ashmore to Elizabeth Jacoway, Oct. 19, 1979, EJC. Caldwell to Olney, Sept. 3, 1957.

27. Lile interview with FBI. Lile interview with Jacoway, pp. 3–4. Lile interview with Luter, p. 18.

28. "A Time of Testing," *Arkansas Gazette,* Sept. 1, 1957, p. 1A.

29. Faubus, *Down From the Hills,* p. 205.

30. Faubus interview with Reed, Dec. 19, 1988, pp. 4, 15, RRP.

31. "Little Rock Quiet on Eve of Opening Integrated Schools," *Arkansas Gazette,* Sept. 2, 1957, p. 1A. Jim interview with Elizabeth Jacoway, April 23, 2002, pp. 49, 53–54, EJC; see also Reed, *Faubus,* pp. 192–193. Carpenter interview with Reed, p. 30.

32. Faubus interview with Luter, pp. 26, 27; Spitzberg, *Racial Politics in Little Rock,* p. 65. Smith interview with Luter, p. 13. Faubus and Smith interview with Reed, p. 16.

33. Faubus and Smith interview with Reed, pp. 4, 16, 22. Smith described Harold Engstrom and Brick Lile as being among his "closest friends"; Smith interview with Luter, p. 12. Based on these two friendships, Smith felt confident in his assessment that ". . . the School Board were all convinced they were going to have violence and plenty of it." Fletcher Knebel, "The Real Little Rock Story," *Look,* Nov. 12, 1957, p. 32.

34. Daisy Bates explained in her memoir: "I was not notified of the meeting, but the parents called me and asked me to be present"; Bates, *The Long Shadow of Little Rock,* p. 63.

35. Ernest Green interview with Sara Alderman Murphy, Dec. 7, 1992, p. 2, Box 1, Folder 25, SAM.

36. Ernest Green interview with John Pagan, Jan. 26, 1973, p. 1, Box 1, Folder 25, SAM.

37. Eckford interview with Jacoway, p. 22; Ted Poston, "Nine Kids Who Dared: Elizabeth Ann Eckford," Oct. 23, 1957, *New York Post,* Bates Scrapbook, DGB.

38. Thelma Mothershed Wair interview with Elizabeth Jacoway, Aug. 15, 2003, pp. 5–6, 19, EJC.

39. Minnijean Brown Trickey interview with Elizabeth Jacoway, Sept. 15, 2003, p. 16, EJC.

40. Blossom, *It HAS Happened Here*, p. 63.

41. Ozell Sutton recalled the reactions he received from parents who were contemplating sending their children to Central High: some were interested, but more often they were reluctant; some were not convinced that integration was the proper strategy to achieve the "equality of opportunity" that Sutton claimed was the goal of the NAACP; some feared losing their jobs; others feared mistreatment of their children, and many believed that blacks could get a better education in black schools than in discriminatory white schools; Sutton interview with Jacoway.

42. Daisy Bates to Roy Wilkins, Aug. 24, 1959, Microfilm Series, Part 3, Series D, Reel 2, Folder: "Desegregation Schools Arkansas Little Rock, Central High, 1959," PON. Dallas Poe Raney interview with FBI, Sept. 6, 1957, Box 2, Folder 4, FBI Report. Jane Hill did not withdraw until Sept. 22.

43. Faubus, *Down From the Hills*, p. 207. Faubus interview with Reed, Dec. 19, 1988, pp. 2–3. Lile interview with FBI.

44. Faubus, *Down From the Hills*, p. 207; Faubus interview with Reed, Dec. 19, 1988, p. 3.

45. J. Edgar Hoover to Herbert Brownell, Sept. 9, 1957, Box 5, Folder 2, ABC. R. A. Lile interview with FBI.

46. Hoover to Brownell, Sept. 9, 1957. Faubus interview with Jacoway, May 12, 1994, p. 37. Ten years after the fact, based on interviews with people who had by that time become Faubus's bitter enemies, Sid McMath and Harry Ashmore, journalist Robert Sherrill repeated a quote that *Time* magazine had carried in September of 1957, reporting that Faubus had said to Rockefeller, "I'm sorry, but I'm already committed. I'm going to run for a third term, and if I don't do this, Jim Johnson and Bruce Bennett . . . will tear me to shreds"; Robert Sherrill, *Gothic Politics in the Deep South: Stars of the New Confederacy* (New York: Grossman Publishers, 1968), p. 89. The original quote was in "What Orval Hath Wrought," *Time,* Sept. 23, 1957, pp. 13–14. Sherrill's account is one of the most vituperative of the scornful genre of political reporting about the civil rights South, referring to "little Orval's" "savage rubes," and describing Faubus as having "the kind of stubbornness that serves impoverished, untutored hillbillies as the extra evolutionary gene needed to pull them out of the mud and onto the sunlit shore of civilization . . . ," where Sherrill presumably thought he, himself, resided. Among Sherrill's many errors is the undocumented claim that Faubus had "pre-determined with his staff two weeks earlier" that he would mobilize the National Guard (p. 100). Sherrill apparently was referring to the August 30 and 31 Cabinet meetings where use of the National Guard was discussed, but not decided upon. Harry Ashmore endorsed Sherrill's assessment of Faubus; Harry S. Ashmore, *Hearts and Minds: The Anatomy of Racism from Roosevelt to Reagan* (New York: McGraw-Hill Book Co., 1982), p. 261. Robert Sherrill's flawed sketch of Orval Faubus became a much-quoted shorthand interpretation of Arkansas politics; see, for example Neal Pierce, *The Deep South States of America: People, Politics and Power in the Seven Deep South States* (New York: W. W. Norton & Co., 1974), p. 132. James T. Karam interview with John Luter, Aug. 20, 1971, p. 9, EAP.

47. In his memoir, Virgil Blossom quoted Faubus as saying, "Democratic friends urged me to integrate in Little Rock, dangling before me the Vice Presidency"; Blossom, *It HAS Happened Here* (1959), p. 59; see also "Vice-Presidency Offered to Him, Faubus Asserts," *Arkansas Gazette,* Dec. 18, 1958, p. 1A; see also "Faubus Says Segregationists Deserve Thanks for 'Fight,'" *Arkansas Gazette,* May 8, 1959, p. 5A. Karam interview with Luter, pp. 9, 11, 16.

48. Faubus interview with Reed, Dec. 22, 1988, #16, p. 11. Karam interview with Luter, pp. 9, 11, 16. Many people have wondered how a questionable character like Jimmy Karam managed to get so close to Orval Faubus; Bill Smith offered this explanation: "Well, you have to know Jimmy to understand him. Then you don't understand him. . . . You can't insult Jimmy. You can't run him off. . . . Jimmy purported to exercise a great influence on Governor Faubus, but I don't know of any decision the Governor ever made, to my knowledge, predicated on advice from Jimmy Karam"; Smith interview with Luter, pp. 59–60; see also Faubus interview with Luter, p. 106.

49. Blossom, *It HAS Happened Here,* pp. 65–66; Summary of Virgil Blossom interviews, in section marked "Interviews Based on the Smith Interview," Box 2, Folder 3, FBI Report.

50. Numan V. Bartley's excellent *The Rise of Massive Resistance: Race and Politics in the South During the 1950s* (Baton Rouge: Louisiana State University Press, 1969) is the most notable exception to this generalization. Faubus interview with Luter, pp. 30–31.

51. Faubus interview with Luter, pp. 30–31. In his interview with the Eisenhower Administration Project, Bill Smith also denied that Faubus had made a deal with east Arkansas legislators to stop integration in return for their support of his proposed tax increase; as Faubus's legislative liaison, Smith would have been in a position to know if such a deal had been made; Smith interview with Luter, pp. 30, 18.

52. Faubus interview with Luter, p. 33. See especially, Orval E. Faubus, "The Faubus Years: January 11, 1955 to January 10, 1967," p. 22, a pamphlet dated Jan. 21, 1991, that Faubus prepared and personally distributed, EJC.

53. Knebel, "The Real Little Rock Story," p. 33. "Faubus Calls National Guard to Keep Schools Segregated," *Arkansas Gazette,* Sept. 3, 1957, p. 1A.

54. Smith interview with Luter, pp. 12–13.

55. Faubus interview with Luter, p. 26. Faubus, *Down From the Hills,* p. 206. Faubus later wrote, "I had served with a front line infantry division in all five major campaigns on the continent of Europe in World War Two and participated in the major battles of Normandy, Mortain [*sic*] and the Battle of the Bulge and I knew something about bloodshed. This I could not permit when it was in my power to see that it did not happen"; Faubus, "The Faubus Years," p. 25.

56. In *Down From the Hills* and in a number of interviews, Faubus located this call on Sunday afternoon; Blossom in *It HAS Happened Here* located it on Monday, as did the *Arkansas Gazette* article by Ray Moseley, "Troops Take Over at Central High: Negroes Told: Wait," *Arkansas Gazette,* Sept. 3, 1957, p. 1A, and Knebel, "The Real Little Rock Story," p. 33. Faubus, *Down From the Hills,* p. 206.

57. Blossom, *It HAS Happened Here,* pp. 70–71.

58. Ashmore to Jacoway, June 14, 1979. Ashmore, *Hearts and Minds,* p. 258; see also Harry S. Ashmore interview with Elizabeth Jacoway, Nov. 17, 1976, p. 28, EJC. Patterson interview with Luter, p. 20.

59. Blossom interview with FBI, Sept. 6, 1957; Harold Engstrom interview with FBI, Sept. 6, 1957, Box 2, Folder 6, FBI Report. Wayne Upton interview with FBI, Sept. 5, 1957, Box 2, Folder 3, FBI Report. Blossom, *It HAS Happened Here,* p. 71. Knebel, "The Real Little Rock Story," p. 33. Engstrom interview with Reed, Jan. 11, 1990, p. 20. For the full text of the Faubus speech see "First Speech," Sept. 2, 1957, Box 496, Folder 1, OEF.

60. Moseley, "Troops Take Over at Central High," p. 1A.

61. Ibid.

62. Harry W. Smith, "Arkansas Army and Air National Guard: A History and Record of Events, 1820–1962," mimeographed publication dated Dec. 31, 1962, p. 47, Army and Air National Guard Museum, Camp Robinson, Ark. Perhaps protecting himself against a contempt citation, Faubus may have intended to rely on verbal cues to Adjutant General Sherman T. Clinger of the Arkansas National Guard "to maintain the relationship as it has been" between the races, which is what General Clinger told the press the next day he had done; "30 Newsmen, Cameramen Hear Faubus at Conference," *Arkansas Gazette,* Sept. 4, 1957, p. 13A.

63. Irene Samuel interview with John Luter, Dec. 30, 1970, p.11, EAP. "What Did Governor Say In His Address?" *Arkansas Gazette,* Sept. 3, 1957, p. 1A. Arthur B. Caldwell to Warren Olney III, Sept. 3, 1957, Box 5, Folder 2, ABC. "Governor Discusses Action in Calling National Guard," *Arkansas Gazette,* Sept. 4, 1957, p. 13A; Bartley, *The Rise of Massive Resistance,* p. 265.

64. "Troops Take Over at Central High," p. 2A; Edwin L. Hawkins interview with FBI, Sept. 6, 1957, Box 2, Folder 6, FBI Report. The tenth student, Jane Hill, withdrew after the initial attempt to enter Central High School on September 4. Upton interview with FBI, Sept. 5, 1957.

65. Caldwell to Olney, Sept. 3, 1957. Hawkins interview with FBI. Virgil T. Blossom inter-

view with FBI, Sept. 6, 1957, Box 2, Folder 3, FBI Report; Fred Graham interview with FBI, Sept. 6, 1957, Box 2, Folder 6, FBI Report. Student lunches on September 3 consisted of sandwiches; Transcript, Lemley Hearing, June 3, 1958, p. 105, June 4, 1958, p. 260, Box 5, Folder 7, VTB. Blossom, *It HAS Happened Here,* p. 76; Ernest Valachovic, "Judge Orders Start of Integration Today," *Arkansas Gazette,* Sept. 4, 1957, p. 1A.

66. The author is indebted to Arkansas Senator David Pryor for sharing this information, which he gained from Margaret Ross, *Arkansas Gazette* historian; David Pryor conversation with Elizabeth Jacoway, April 15, 2000, EJC. In submitting material for Ashmore's Pulitzer Prize nomination, Hugh Patterson wrote, "During the period of the integration crisis in Little Rock Mr. Ashmore personally directed the entire news operation of the paper. . . ."; Hugh B. Patterson to John Hohenberg, Dec. 26, 1957, Box 6, Folder 13, HSA. "Faubus Calls National Guard to Keep Schools Segregated," *Arkansas Gazette,* Sept. 3, 1957, p. 1A.

67. Reverend Dale Cowling videotaped interview with Mimi Dortch, (nd), EJC; the author is grateful to Mimi Dortch for sharing her interviews. Reverend Dale Cowling interview with Elizabeth Jacoway, Feb. 23, 2005, p. 5, EJC. For an interesting assessment of Faubus's motives see Thomas F. Pettigrew and Ernest Q. Campbell, "Faubus and Segregation: An Analysis of Arkansas Voting," *Public Opinion Quarterly* (Fall 1960), p. 446.

68. Jerry Dhonau, "Crowd of 400 Watches White Students Enroll," *Arkansas Gazette,* Sept. 4, 1957, p. 1A; Caldwell to Olney, Sept. 3, 1957. *Arkansas Gazette* city editor Bill Shelton reported to the FBI that he received a telephone call from the Mothers' League informing him that Governor Faubus wanted a crowd at Central High School; William T. Shelton interview with FBI, Sept. 10, 1957, Box 2, Folder 14, FBI Report. See also " 'Right To Assembly': Little Rock Segregation Leader Will Continue Anti-Mixing Fight," *The State* (Columbia, S.C.), Sept. 3, 1957, SERS. *Arkansas Gazette* reporter Jerry Dhonau wrote that the Central High Mothers' League formed the "hard core" of the crowd outside the school all that week; Jerry Dhonau, "Daily Crowds at School Scene, Mostly Curious, Usually Well-Behaved Despite Obvious Tension," *Arkansas Gazette,* Sept. 8, 1957, p. 4A. One of the mothers claimed that her organization was hoping to prevent violence, and that is why they were at Central High School; Grace Fitzhugh interview with FBI, Sept. 8, 1957, Box 2, Folder 14, FBI Report. Graeme Cope, " 'A Thorn in the Side'? The Mothers' League of Central High School and the Little Rock Desegregation Crisis of 1957," *Arkansas Historical Quarterly* 57 (Summer 1998), p. 179. Dhonau, "Crowd of 400 Watches White Students Enroll." Caldwell to Olney. Sept. 3, 1957.

69. Reed, *Faubus,* p. 213. Claude Carpenter later admitted that he, Robert Ewing Brown, and Wesley Pruden orchestrated most of these phone calls; Carpenter interview with Reed, p. 30.

70. Reed, *Faubus,* p. 223. Faubus interview with Jacoway, May 12, 1994, p. 51; Henry Hampton and Steve Fayer, *Voices of Freedom: An Oral History of the Civil Rights Movement from the 1950s through the 1980s* (New York: Bantam Books, 1990), pp. 41–42. See also "Caravans Coming to Little Rock," *Arkansas Democrat,* Aug. 11, 1959, p. 1A.

71. "Here's What Eisenhower Said About Little Rock," *Arkansas Gazette,* Sept. 4, 1957, p. 2A.

72. John Thomas Elliff, "The United States Department of Justice and Individual Rights, 1937–1962" (Ph.D. diss., Harvard University, 1967), p. 804. James C. Duram, *A Moderate Among Extremists: Dwight D. Eisenhower and the School Desegregation Crisis* (Chicago: Nelson-Hall, 1981), pp. 143–72; Robert Frederick Burk, *The Eisenhower Administration and Black Civil Rights* (Knoxville: University of Tennessee Press, 1984), pp. 174–203; Stephen E. Ambrose, *Eisenhower, the President,* Vol. 2 (New York: Simon & Schuster, 1984); Stanley I. Kutler, "Eisenhower, the Judiciary, and Desegregation: Some Reflections," in Gunter Bischof and Stephen E. Ambrose, eds., *Eisenhower: A Centenary Assessment* (Baton Rouge: Louisiana State University Press, 1995), pp. 87–100.

73. "Letters and Telegrams Say Faubus Has 'Saved the State,' " *Arkansas Gazette,* Sept. 4, 1957, p. 1B. "30 Newsmen, Cameramen Hear Faubus at Conference." "Governor Discusses Action in Calling National Guard." "Arkansas National Guard Troops Used in Emergencies and/or Disasters for the Year 1924 through November 1957," Nov. 12, 1957, Box 487, Folder 16, OEF.

74. "30 Newsmen, Cameramen Hear Faubus at Conference."

75. Valachovic, "Judge Orders Start of Integration Today." Davies thought that because of the wording of Governor Faubus's statement, which had allowed him to "dodge the issue," there would be no clear-cut violation of the judge's order "until the colored children do go over to the school and are turned back by guards. . . ."; Caldwell to Olney, Sept. 3, 1957. Carol Griffee, ed., *Osro Cobb of Arkansas: Memoirs of Historical Significance* (Little Rock: Rose Publishing Co., 1989), pp. 190–91. For the full text of Judge Davies's order see *Race Relations Law Reporter,* October 1957, pp. 937–39.

76. Faubus, *Down From the Hills,* p. 209. See also General Sherman Clinger interview with FBI, Sept. 9, 1957, Box 2, Folder 2, FBI Report. Faubus interview with Jacoway, May 12, 1994, p. 45.

77. Orval Faubus speech at the centennial celebration of Dwight Eisenhower's birth, June 5, 1990, Abilene, Kan., p. III, 31, as transcribed by Roy Reed, RRP. Faubus interview with Luter, pp. 37, 41; Orval Faubus interview with John Pagan, Aug. 16, 1972, p. 20, EJC.

78. Elliff, "The United States Department of Justice and Individual Rights, 1937–1962," p. 486.

79. "The Crisis Mr. Faubus Made," *Arkansas Gazette,* Sept. 4, 1957, p. 1A.

80. Patterson interview with Jacoway, Oct. 11, 2002. Smith interview with Luter, p. 45; Smith also told Luter he had sponsored Ashmore for membership in the Riverdale Country Club; Ibid., p. 44.

81. McMath interview with Luter, pp. 2, 3, 4. Faubus favorite George Douthit reported to the Eisenhower Administration Project that McMath had expected to run the Faubus administration; Douthit interview with Luter, pp. 21–22.

82. Forrest Rozzell interview with John Pagan, Dec. 29, 1972, EJC.

83. Jim Johnson recalled almost fifty years later that massive resistance leaders Senator James Eastland of Mississippi, Senator Richard Russell of Georgia, and others made frantic calls to Johnson when they were unable to get through to Faubus at the Governor's Mansion after Faubus called out the National Guard; Johnson claimed that at that point Faubus knew almost nothing of the strategy of massive resistance; Johnson interview with Jacoway, April 23, 2002, pp. 26–27, 41–42; Faubus also recalled that Senator Richard Russell offered his services; Faubus interview with Luter, pp. 129–31. "Governor Discusses Action in Calling National Guard." Harry Ashmore claimed in a number of venues that Faubus had no evidence; see, for example, Harry S. Ashmore, *Civil Rights and Wrongs: A Memoir of Race and Politics, 1944–1994* (New York: Pantheon Books, 1994), p. 126; see also Patterson interview with Luter, p. 16. For a clear statement that the FBI had in fact uncovered evidence, see Director's Brief, Box 1, Folder 2, p. A-32, FBI Report.

CHAPTER SEVEN — THE MINEFIELD IN THE MIDDLE

1. James T. Baker, *Brooks Hays* (Macon, Ga.: Mercer University Press, 1989), pp. 5–6, 51. "Steele Hays Dies at 87," *Arkansas Gazette,* June 7, 1959, p. 1A. B. Cooper Jacoway interview with Elizabeth Jacoway, Nov. 5, 1975, EJC; James T. Baker, "Brooks Hays," *Encyclopedia of Southern Culture* (Chapel Hill: University of North Carolina Press, 1989), p. 1320. Lawrence Brooks Hays interview with A. Ronald Tonks, May 20, 1975–Oct. 5, 1977, pp. 16, 72, 94, 104–13, SBC; Baker, *Brooks Hays,* p. 54; Brooks Hays, *A Southern Moderate Speaks* (Chapel Hill: University of North Carolina Press, 1959), pp. 13–24. D. Nathan Coulter, "A Political Martyr for Racial Progress in the South: Brooks Hays and the Electoral Consequences of the Little Rock Crisis" (honors thesis, Harvard University, March 25, 1982). Congressman Jacoway had helped Hays get accepted at the George Washington University Law School, had gotten him a job at the Treasury Department, and had welcomed this son of his old friend Steele Hays into his home on a regular basis, so regular as to make him almost "a part of the family"; Hays, *A Southern Moderate Speaks,* p. 9; Brooks Hays, *A Hotbed of Tranquility* (New York: Macmillan Co., 1968), p. 193; Steele Hays interview with Elizabeth Jacoway, March 17, 2003, p. 1, EJC.

2. Brooks Hays interview with Elizabeth Jacoway, Sept. 10, 1979, p. 11, EJC.

3. Untitled, undated biographical sketch in Box 36, LBH.

4. See Hays, *A Southern Moderate Speaks,* pp. 25–62, for a discussion of the Arkansas Plan; see

also Brooks Hays interview with John Luter, June 27–28, July 27, 1970, pp. 20, 96, EAP. Baker, *Brooks Hays,* p. 147

5. Hays interview with Jacoway, pp. 8, 56. Hays interview with Tonks, pp. 207, 212.

6. Baker, "Brooks Hays," p. 1320; Hays interview with Tonks, p. 204. Baker, *Brooks Hays,* p. 88. Hays claimed years later that he had "no interest whatever in being a judge." But he also recalled his pleasure in having Sherman Adams tell him, "Brooks you're going to be offered an appointment as a federal judge. . . ."; Hays interview with Jacoway, p. 20. Brooks Hays's son, Steele Hays, told this interviewer he knew his father would have loved to have the judicial appointment, but he doubted that such ambition motivated his father's actions in the Little Rock crisis; Steele Hays interview with Elizabeth Jacoway, March 17, 2003, p. 9, EJC. "Smith Henley Is Considered for U.S. Judge," *Arkansas Gazette,* Aug. 20, 1957, p. 1B.

7. Faubus interview with Jacoway, May 12, 1994, p. 51, EJC. Faubus interview with Jacoway, July 11, 1978, p. 37. In a late-in-life interview Faubus reflected, "Now, if the federal government had said this is our court order and we're taking the responsibility for it . . . I could have survived. But as governor, whoever was governor, if it had been Brooks Hays, if it had been Sid McMath, if it had been the strongest liberal that ever set foot in the state, if he had used the guard to put the blacks in the school at that time, would have been political suicide"; Orval E. Faubus interview with Roy Reed, Dec. 19, 1988, p. 15, RRP. William J. Smith interview with John Luter, Aug. 19–20, 1971, p. 32, EAP.

8. Brooks Hays interview with John Luter, June 27–28 and July 27, 1970, p. 21, EAP.

9. "Hays Plans Visit with Daughter, Family in Ohio," *Arkansas Gazette,* Sept. 4, 1957.

10. "Mann Attacks Story of Fear of Violence," *Arkansas Gazette,* Sept. 5, 1957, p. 1A. Political scientist Irving Spitzberg wrote of Mann's involvement: "Mann's actions were his one last attempt to salvage respectability from a rather tainted public life"; Irving Spitzberg Jr., *Racial Politics In Little Rock, 1954–1964* (New York: Garland Publishing, 1987), p. 74; Mann later told *Arkansas Democrat* reporter George Douthit he had been used, and he "didn't realize what the situation was. . . ."; George Douthit interview with John Luter, Dec. 31, 1970, p. 23, EAP. "His Honor: Woodrow Wilson Mann, Sr.," *Arkansas Democrat-Gazette,* Aug. 10, 2002, p. 4B. For a copy of the grand jury report accusing Woodrow Mann of mismanagement and corruption, see "Text of Jury's Report," *Arkansas Gazette,* Sept. 22, 1956, p. 3A. See also Corinne Silverman, *The Little Rock Story,* Inter-University Case Program, No. 41 (University: University of Alabama Press, 1959), p. 8.

11. "Governor Sees Test of Laws," *Arkansas Democrat,* Sept. 3, 1957, p. 1; Ernest Valachovic, "Judge Orders Start of Integration Today," *Arkansas Gazette,* Sept. 4, 1957, p. 2A. "Ike's Anger," *Arkansas Gazette,* Sept. 18, 1957, p. 4A. Harry Ashmore, "Faubus, the White Citizens Council and History's Admonition," *Arkansas Times,* Sept. 12, 1997, pp. 19–20. For a suggestive discussion see David Halberstam, *The Fifties* (New York: Villard Books, 1993), p. 684. John Hohenberg to Harry Ashmore, Sept. 20, 1957, Box 6, Folder 10, HSA. Ashmore's friend and mentor, Ralph McGill of the *Atlanta Constitution,* nominated him for the Pulitzer Prize.

12. John Thomas Elliff, "The United States Department of Justice and Individual Civil Rights, 1937–1962" (Ph.D. diss., Harvard University, 1962), p. 466, italics added. Herbert Brownell with John P. Burke, *Advising Ike: The Memoirs of Attorney General Herbert Brownell* (Lawrence, Kan.: University Press of Kansas, 1993), p. 206.

13. Wiley A. Branton, "Little Rock Revisited: Desegregation to Resegregation," *Journal of Negro Education* (Summer 1983), p. 262. See also Wiley Austin Branton interview with Steven Lawson, Oct. 21, 1970, pp. 56–57, EAP; and Stephanie Branton, "Unsung Hero: Wiley A. Branton," *Arkansas Times,* Sept. 26, 1997, p. 7. Wiley A. Branton, "Personal Memories of Thurgood Marshall," *Arkansas Law Review,* Vol. 40, No. 4, 1987, p. 669.

14. Branton, "Personal Memories of Thurgood Marshall," p. 669. See also "Branton Disclaims Reported Account of State Job Offer," *Arkansas Gazette,* Oct. 14, 1958, p. 5A.

15. Branton, "Personal Memories of Thurgood Marshall," p. 669.

16. Elliff, "The United States Department of Justice and Individual Civil Rights," p. 472. "Eisenhower Awaits More Local Action," *Arkansas Gazette,* Sept. 8, 1957, p. 1A. Wilson White, "The

Department of Justice and the Little Rock Case," as cited in Elliff, "The United States Department of Justice and Individual Civil Rights," p. 467. J. W. Peltason, *Fifty-Eight Lonely Men: Southern Federal Judges and School Desegregation* (New York: Harcourt, Brace & World, 1961), p. 170.

17. Elliff, "The United States Department of Justice and Individual Civil Rights," p. 469. See also Anthony Lewis, "U.S. Opens Inquiry in Arkansas Case," *New York Times*, Sept. 5, 1957, p. 1. Federal Bureau of Information document #44-341-153 (a summary of the information collected between Sept. 4, 1957, and Sept. 9, 1957), obtained by the author through the Freedom of Information Act; EJC. Historian Tony Freyer secured a copy of the complete investigation, entitled "F.B.I.—Little Rock Crisis Reports" (herein cited as FBI Report) and deposited it in Archives and Special Collections, Ottenheimer Library, University of Arkansas at Little Rock.

18. "Faubus Defends His Order for Guard to Bar Negroes," *Arkansas Gazette*, Sept. 5, 1957, p. 6A. Faubus and Bill Smith had been in telephone contact that day with Senator Richard Russell of Georgia, the legislative strategist of massive resistance, who urged the Arkansas governor to stand on the high ground of his police powers; Richard Russell to Orval Faubus, Sept. 4, 1957, Box 118, Series VI, RBR. The best brief treatment of this phenomenon is Halberstam, *The Fifties*, pp. 678–84; see also Harry Ashmore's complaint that the Little Rock episode was reduced to a morality play in Harry S. Ashmore, *Arkansas: A History* (New York: W. W. Norton & Co., 1978), pp. xix–xx.

19. Ken Parker and Matilda Tuohey, "Mayor Labels Faubus Claim Hoax; Governor Sends Appeal to Ike," *Arkansas Gazette*, Sept. 5, 1957, p. 1A; "Halt in Integration Asked; Ike Says He Will Use Law," *Arkansas Gazette*, Sept. 6, 1957, p. 1A; the full text of the telegrams exchanged between President Eisenhower and Governor Faubus can be found in DDE. In his memoir, Attorney General Herbert Brownell wrote: "By this time, Faubus was clearly in danger of a contempt citation from the judge, perhaps even arrest"; Brownell, *Advising Ike*, p. 207. "Governor to Go on TV Tonight," *Arkansas Gazette*, Sept. 8, 1957, p. 1A. "School Dispute Boosts Western Union Volume," *Arkansas Gazette*, Sept. 5, 1957, p. 1B; Jerry Dhonau, "Daily Crowds at School Scene, Mostly Curious, Usually Well-Behaved Despite Obvious Tension," *Arkansas Gazette*, Sept. 8, 1957, p. 4A. "Newport Hails Ike on Arrival For Vacation," *Arkansas Gazette*, Sept. 5, 1957, p. 7A.

20. Elizabeth Jacoway, "Taken By Surprise: Little Rock Business Leaders and Desegregation," in Elizabeth Jacoway and David R. Colburn, eds., *Southern Businessmen and Desegregation* (Baton Rouge: Louisiana State University Press, 1982), pp. 12–41. "Bad Publicity Will Keep Out Industry, C of C Man Says," *Arkansas Gazette*, Sept. 7, 1957, p. 1A. Forrest Rozzell interview with John Pagan, Dec. 29, 1972, p. 3, EJC. Ray Moseley, "Board Seeks Suspension of U.S. Order," *Arkansas Gazette*, Sept. 6, 1957, p. 1A.

21. See Virgil T. Blossom interviews with FBI, Sept. 5, 1957, Sept. 6, 1957, Sept. 7, 1957, Box 2, Folder 3; Wayne Upton interview with FBI, Sept. 5, 1957, Box 2, Folder 3; A. F. House interview with FBI, Sept. 7, 1957, Box 2, Folder 6; Henry Rath interview with FBI, Sept. 5, 1957, Box 2, Folder 6; Dr. William G. Cooper interview with FBI, Sept. 6, 1957, Box 2, Folder 6; Dr. Dale Alford interview with FBI, Sept. 6, 1957, Box 2, Folder 6; Harold James Engstrom interview with FBI, Sept. 6, 1957, Box 2, Folder 6; Robert Alfred Lile interview with FBI, Sept. 5, 1957, Box 2, Folder 6, all in FBI Report. Virgil T. Blossom interview with FBI, Sept. 6, 1957, p. 84. Woodrow W. Mann interview with FBI, Sept. 5, 1957, p. 139, Box 2, Folder 3, FBI Report; Ernest Valachovic, "Mann Says Union Imperilled, Faubus Must Be Put Down," *Arkansas Gazette*, Sept. 6, 1957, p. 1A.

22. William J. Smith interview with FBI, Sept. 6, 1957, pp. 74–81, Box 2, Folder 3, FBI Report. Director's Brief, p. A-5, Box 1, Folder 2, FBI Report.

23. "Government May Try for Injunction Against Faubus in Showdown," *Arkansas Gazette*, Sept. 7, 1957, p. 1A.

24. Hays interview with Tonks, p. 267. Kenneth Johnson, "Faubus Says Guard Will Keep Negroes Out of High School Despite Ruling by U.S. Judge," *Memphis Commercial Appeal*, Sept. 8, 1957, SERS.

25. Ray Moseley, "Judge Refuses Delay in School Integration; Federals Standing By," *Arkansas Gazette*, Sept. 8, 1957, p. 1A.

26. Moseley, "Judge Refuses Delay . . ."; Ray Moseley, "Governor's Evidence Goes Before U.S.," *Arkansas Gazette,* Sept. 7, 1957, p. 1A. Stan Opotowsky, "Showdown Due in Little Rock Court; Ruling May Set Pattern for All Dixie," *New York Post,* Sept. 8, 1957, SERS.

27. "Text of Faubus Statement," *Arkansas Gazette,* Sept. 10, 1957, p. 6A. Matilda Tuohey, "8 Aldermen Back Faubus in Mann Feud," *Arkansas Gazette,* Sept. 9, 1957, p. 1A. Kenneth Johnson, "Faubus Says Guard Will Keep Negroes Out of High School Despite Ruling by U.S. Judge," *Memphis Commercial Appeal,* Sept. 8, 1957, SERS. Ernest Valachovic, "Cross Burns in Mayor's Front Yard," *Arkansas Gazette,* Sept. 7, 1957, p. 1A.

28. For a fascinating account of the Cold War implications of the Little Rock crisis see Mary L. Dudziak, *Cold War Civil Rights: Race and the Image of American Democracy* (Princeton: Princeton University Press, 2000), pp. 114–51; see especially her treatment of the "image" of Little Rock, pp. 150–51. See also Cary Fraser, "Crossing the Color Line in Little Rock: The Eisenhower Administration and the Dilemma of Race for U.S. Foreign Policy," *Diplomatic History* 24 (Spring 2000), pp. 233–64.

29. "Eisenhower Awaits More Local Action," *Arkansas Gazette,* Sept. 8, 1957, p. 1A. "Board Asks Court to Delay Integration," *Arkansas Gazette,* Feb. 21, 1958, p. 1A. Brownell, *Advising Ike,* p. 208.

30. Harry S. Ashmore, *Hearts and Minds: The Anatomy of Racism from Roosevelt to Reagan* (New York: McGraw-Hill Book Co., 1982), p. 261. Lyle Wilson, "Ike's Team Caught Off Its Guard as Faubus Moves Create Dilemma," *Arkansas Gazette,* Sept. 7, 1957, p. 6A. "Ike's Anger," *Arkansas Gazette,* Sept. 18, 1957, p. 4A.

31. Gloria Dapper to Harry Ashmore, June 28, 1957, Box 6, Folder 8, HSA; Ashmore, *Hearts and Minds,* pp. 261–62; see especially Robert A. Caro, *Master of the Senate: The Years of Lyndon Johnson* (New York: Alfred A. Knopf, 2002). *The Nation* magazine soon quoted the *New York Times* to the effect that Faubus had knotted "the 'civil rights' albatross firmly around the neck of the entire Democratic Party"; *The Nation,* Sept. 28, 1957, p. 185. David Halberstam, *The Powers That Be* (New York: Alfred A. Knopf, 1979), p. 310; Katharine Graham, *Personal History* (New York: Random House, 1998), p. 243. Baker, *Brooks Hays,* p. 187.

32. Truman had been the Faubuses' guest at the Arkansas Governor's Mansion in 1955; Alta Haskins Faubus interview with Jacoway, April 9, 1996, p. 6. Truman described Faubus in a New York press conference, saying "He's a wonderful fellow and I know him very well"; "Truman Recalls Jackson Halted 1832 'Nullification,'" *Arkansas Gazette,* Sept. 9, 1957, p. 1A. Halberstam, *The Powers That Be,* p. 310. Hays interview with Luter, p. 57. Earl Mazo, "HST Urged to Have Talk with Faubus," *Arkansas Gazette,* Sept. 9, 1957, p. 1A. "Integration Waters Get Democratic Oil," *Christian Science Monitor,* Sept. 13, 1957, SERS.

33. Smith interview with Luter, p. 21. Brownell, *Advising Ike,* p. 208.

34. Director's Brief, p. B-8, Box 1, Folder 3, FBI Report.

35. As Hays reflected years later, "I recall how puzzled I was by the apparent change in Governor Faubus' attitude. . . . I thought it was out of character as I had interpreted his philosophy"; Hays interview with Tonks, p. 258. Hays interview with Luter, pp. 103, 114.

36. Hays, *A Southern Moderate Speaks,* p. 139. Director's Brief, p. 39, Box 1, Folder 4, FBI Report; Director's Brief, p. A-16, Box 1, Folder 2, FBI Report. Orval Faubus classroom lecture at Arkansas College, Jan. 21, 1993, pp. 27–28; Alta Haskins Faubus interview with Elizabeth Jacoway, April 10, 1996, p, 46, EJC; Henry Woods interview with Elizabeth Jacoway, May 26, 2000, p. 7, EJC; Faubus, *Down From the Hills,* p. 237. One influential expression of this point of view can be found in David Lawrence, "Federal Action in Arkansas Seen Flouting Constitution," *New York Herald-Tribune,* Sept. 11, 1957, SERS.

37. Summary of FBI investigation between Sept. 4, 1957, and Sept. 9, 1957, FBI document # 44-341-153, EJC; Carol Griffee, ed., *Osro Cobb of Arkansas: Memoirs of Historical Significance* (Little Rock: Rose Publishing Co., 1989), p. 193.

38. Ray Moseley, "U.S. Begins Move to Enjoin Faubus, 2 Guard Officers; NLR Negroes Turned Back," *Arkansas Gazette,* Sept. 10, 1957, p. 1A.

39. Griffee, *Osro Cobb of Arkansas*, p. 195. Moseley, "U.S. Begins Move to Enjoin Faubus." "Text of Petition," *Arkansas Gazette*, Sept. 11, 1957, p. 8A.

40. Walter Riddick interview with Elizabeth Jacoway, March 18, 2003, p. 22, EJC.

41. "U.S. Course Plotted to Give Governor His Day in Court," *Arkansas Gazette*, Sept. 11, 1957, 1A. Elliff. "The United States Department of Justice and Individual Civil Rights," p. 472; Ray Moseley, "Court Orders to Weigh Heavily on Negotiations Between Ike, Faubus," *Arkansas Gazette*, Sept. 12, 1957, 1A. Ray Moseley, "Troops to Stay at CHS During 10-Day Respite," *Arkansas Gazette*, Sept. 11, 1957, p. 2A.

42. Robert W. Coakley, *Operation Arkansas* (Office of the Chief of Military History Monograph No. 158M, 1967), pp. 19–25. Faubus, *Down From the Hills*, p. 233. Coakley, *Operation Arkansas*, p. 22.

43. Hays, *A Southern Moderate Speaks*, p. 140. Faubus believed the president had initiated the request for a conference; Orval Faubus interview with John Luter, Aug. 18, 1971, p. 39, EAP; see also Faubus, *Down From the Hills*, p. 240. See White House log of telephone calls, Sept. 11, 1957, DDE. Sherman Adams's assessment of Faubus's thinking reflected Brooks Hays's flawed analysis. Hays interview with Luter, p. 34. Telegram, Governor Orval E. Faubus to The Honorable Dwight D. Eisenhower, Sept. 11, 1957, DDE. Sherman Adams claimed later to have caught the disparity, writing in his memoir, "It seemed to me that a desire was quite different from an intention"; Sherman Adams, *Firsthand Report: The Story of the Eisenhower Administration* (New York: Harper & Co., 1961), p. 349. Hays, *A Southern Moderate Speaks*, p. 142.

44. Hays, *A Southern Moderate Speaks*, p. 143.

45. Liz Carpenter had recently described Caldwell as working "around-the-clock" on the situation of "defiance of the law" in Little Rock; Elizabeth Carpenter, "Native of State Doing Good Job for Civil Rights," *Arkansas Gazette*, Sept. 8, 1957, Box 1, Folder 17, ABC. Warren Olney III to Herbert Brownell, Sept. 13, 1957, "Summary of FBI report in Little Rock, Arkansas integration difficulty," Box 5, Folder 2, ABC. This "Summary" apparently was widely disseminated and has made its way into a number of manuscript collections, where historians have read it and assumed, incorrectly, that it summarized fairly the voluminous FBI Report. This "Summary," therefore, has become the basis for some of the inaccurate conclusions historians have drawn about the Little Rock crisis.

46. Director's Brief, Box 1, Folders 2 and 3, FBI Report. Olney, "Summary," p. 1. Over half of these "450 interviews" were with the owners, operators, and clerks of more than one hundred hardware stores and pawn shops that the FBI checked for an increase in the sales of guns and knives, and the questioning focused on sales, not on rumors of violence. A large subset of the remaining interviews were with black personnel and students at Central High School; these interviews focused on these people's experiences at the school, not on rumors of violence. A significant number of interviewees, who were included in the inflated 450 figure, refused to give a statement to the FBI. Director's Brief, p. A-4, Box 1, Folder 2, FBI Report.

47. Dallas Poe Raney interview with FBI, Sept. 6, 1957, Box 2, Folder 4, FBI Report. Among the most graphic descriptions of rumors and threats of violence, see the FBI interviews with Clovis Copeland, Sept. 9, 1957, Box 2, File 12; Beverly Maxine Burks, Sept. 7, 1957 and Sept. 8, 1957, Box 2, Folder 3; and William Thomas McCauley, Sept. 6, 1957, Box 2, Folder 3, all in FBI Report.

48. Olney, "Summary," pp. 2–4. See also Bill Lewis, "Faubus Again Falls Short in Revealing 'Evidence,'" *Arkansas Gazette*, Jan. 18, 1981, p. 1A.

49. Benjamin Fine, "Faubus Sees Hays as Guard Keeps Watch at School," *New York Times*, Sept. 17, 1957. Henry Woods interview with Elizabeth Jacoway, May 30, 2000, p. 16, EJC. Elizabeth Carpenter, "Did Faubus Gain or Lose in Duel With Government?," *Arkansas Gazette*, Sept. 15, 1957, 1A. "Olney Quits Department of Justice," *Arkansas Democrat*, Sept. 18, 1957, p. 1. Olney's retirement went into effect on Oct. 15, 1957; on October 3 he made a speech in California which historians often cite; Warren Olney III, "A Government Lawyer Looks at Little Rock," Oct. 3, 1957, Box 5, Folder 5, ABC. That speech also came under severe criticism within the Department of Justice for its misstatements of fact. The summary of the FBI's investigation that

the staff prepared for J. Edgar Hoover read in part, "Former Assistant Attorney General Olney in a speech on October 3, 1957, before the California Bar Association reportedly said the FBI had documentary proof that Faubus directly ordered the Arkansas National Guard out to keep Negro students out of the school. Bureau's investigation only shows that Faubus used the guard in such a way to exclude the Negroes"; Director's Brief, p. A-36, Box 1, Folder 2, FBI Report. Brownell claimed in his memoir that he had told Eisenhower of his plans to resign weeks before; Brownell, *Advising Ike,* p. 205. Faubus claimed to have heard from two Arkansas congressmen, Oren Harris and Jim Trimble, that Eisenhower threw "the greatest tantrum by an infuriated President that had ever been seen in the White House, and out went Brownell"; Faubus interview with Jacoway, May 12, 1994, p. 82. For internal evidence that the Olney report was fabricated, see Director's Brief, Vol. 1, File 2, p. A-31, Box 1, Folder 2, FBI Report.

CHAPTER EIGHT — IN SEARCH OF COMPROMISE

1. Lawrence Brooks Hays interview with A. Ronald Tonks, May 20, 1975–Oct. 5, 1977, p. 321, SBC. Brooks Hays interview with John Luter, June 27–28, July 27, 1970, p. 40, EAP.

2. "Ike, Faubus Schedule Five-Man Conference," *Arkansas Gazette,* Sept. 13, 1957, 1A; see also "News Conference with James C. Hagerty," Sept. 12, 1957, Box 6, Folder marked Integration— Little Rock—1957 (1)," DDE. Orval E. Faubus interview with John Luter, Aug. 18, 1971, pp. 66, 44, EAP. Faubus remembered Eisenhower's strong states' rights speech at the Southern Governors' Conference in Williamsburg, Virginia, just a few months before, and he thought he could appeal directly to the president as a man of goodwill; Faubus, *Down From the Hills,* pp. 249, 241; Jack Bass and Walter DeVries interview with Orval Faubus, June 14, 1974, pp. 22–25, SHC. Orval E. Faubus interview with Elizabeth Jacoway, July 11, 1978, p. 3, EJC; William J. Smith interview with John Luter, Aug. 19–20, 1971, p. 28, EAP.

3. Faubus interview with Luter, p. 50. Hugh Patterson admitted years later that he and Harry Ashmore had engaged in "behind the scenes communication with people in the White House. . . . [W]e thought the President would be well advised to be flanked with the Secretary of State and the Secretary of Defense perhaps, . . . and that in effect he just be politely read off"; Hugh B. Patterson interview with John Luter, Aug. 12, 1970, p. 27, EAP.

4. Unless otherwise noted, this description of the Newport meeting is drawn from two interviews Elizabeth Jacoway conducted with Orval Faubus, on July 11, 1978, and May 12, 1994, EJC. A full discussion of the Newport meeting can be found in Faubus, *Down From the Hills,* pp. 255–58. Dwight D. Eisenhower, *Waging Peace: The White House Years, 1956–1961* (New York: Doubleday, 1965), p. 166.

5. Eisenhower, *Waging Peace,* p. 166. Eisenhower biographer Stephen Ambrose adopted the president's interpretation of the day's events, writing that Faubus subsequently betrayed Ike's trust and broke his promise about removing the troops; Stephen E. Ambrose, *Eisenhower the President,* Vol. 2 (New York: Simon & Schuster, 1984), p. 316. Three weeks after the Newport conference, after many emotional events had transpired, Eisenhower dictated his notes about the visit with Faubus, in which he included the following: "I got definitely the understanding that he was going back to Arkansas to act within a matter of hours to revoke his orders to the Guard to prevent re-entry of the Negro children into the school"; Eisenhower Diary, Oct. 8, 1957, DDE. When Faubus was made aware of this diary entry thirty years later, he swore to his biographer, Roy Reed, that he had given the president no such assurances, saying, "I don't believe Eisenhower wrote that. . . . There was nothing like that said at all, nothing"; Orval Faubus interview with Roy Reed, June 5, 1990, p. 18, RRP. Claude Carpenter interview with Roy Reed, Aug. 1, 1990, p. 5, RRP; Griffin Smith interview with Roy Reed, Jan. 4, 1989, p. 22, RRP. Eisenhower began to realize his error within a matter of days. At a press conference he held a week after sending federal troops into Little Rock, the president responded to a question about the Newport meeting by referring to "the understanding that I thought I had . . ."; Presidential Press Conference, October 3, 1957, Box 6, Folder marked "Integration—Little Rock—1957 (2)." DDE.

6. Faubus had recently made the same point in an interview with a national news magazine; "'Two Choices: Wait for Violence or Prevent It,'" *U.S. News & World Report,* Sep. 20, 1957, pp. 62–66.

7. A close reading of the correspondence in the Brooks Hays Papers reveals that segregationists argued two things consistently: 1) what was being called the "law of the land" was really a usurpation of laws by Eisenhower, Brownell, the Supreme Court, et al., and therefore it was not binding; and 2) the northern liberal establishment was simply pandering to urban black votes; LBH. Orval Faubus had bought these arguments.

8. Hays interview with Luter, p. 77.

9. Earl Warren, *The Memoirs of Earl Warren* (Garden City, N.Y.: Doubleday & Co., 1977), p. 291.

10. Corinne Silverman, *The Little Rock Story,* Inter-University Case Program, No. 41 (University of Alabama Press, 1959), p. 13. Hays, *A Southern Moderate Speaks,* p. 149.

11. At this point Faubus realized his error in not bringing Bill Smith with him to Newport, which was a decision he and Smith had reached together; Smith interview with Luter, p. 29.

12. Faubus interview with Luter, pp. 124, 52. Hays interview with Luter, p. 68; Hays, *A Southern Moderate Speaks,* pp. 149, 150; Hays interview with Tonks, p. 263. Herbert Brownell interview with Roy Reed, June 5, 1990, p. 1, RRP.

13. Faubus, *Down From the Hills,* p. 243.

14. Hays, *A Southern Moderate Speaks,* pp. 148, 150. Hays interview with Luter, pp. 69, 62.

15. Hays interview with Tonks, p. 263. Sherman Adams, *Firsthand Report: The Story of the Eisenhower Administration* (New York: Harper, 1961), pp. 352–53.

16. Hays interview with Luter, p. 83. Hays, *A Southern Moderate Speaks,* pp. 151–52; Adams, *Firsthand Report,* p. 352.

17. Hays interview with Tonks, pp. 314, 256.

18. "Text of Ike Statement," *Arkansas Gazette,* Sept. 15, 1957, p. 2A. "Faubus Set to Pull Guard 'Gracefully,'" *Arkansas Gazette,* Sept. 15, 1957, p. 1A. Faubus, *Down From the Hills,* p. 240.

19. Faubus interview with Luter, p. 132. "Faubus' Words Lead Some to Doubt Him," *Arkansas Gazette,* Sept. 3, 1958, p. 1A. Almost fifty years later, former Faubus assistant Kay Matthews claimed credit for originating the phrase "Just because I said it doesn't make it so"; Kay Matthews conversation with Elizabeth Jacoway, March 26, 2005. "Faubus Says 'Law of Land' Statement Forced on Him," *Arkansas Gazette,* Sept. 1, 1958, p. 1A. Faubus's old foe John Wells was one of the first to interpret Faubus's comment as an admission of mendacity; see "No Silver Linings," *Arkansas Recorder,* Sept. 5, 1958, Arkansas History Commission.

20. Smith interview with Luter, p. 43. "Text of Wallace-Faubus Interview," *Arkansas Gazette,* Sept. 16, 1957, p. 2A. Carol Griffee, ed., *Osro Cobb of Arkansas: Memoirs of Historical Significance* (Little Rock: Rose Publishing Co., 1989), p. 201. Faubus, *Down From the Hills,* p. 262.

21. Hays interview with Tonks, pp. 264–65. Hays interview with Luter, p. 61. Hays, *A Southern Moderate Speaks,* p. 155.

22. Hays, *A Southern Moderate Speaks,* p. 160; Hays interview with Luter, p. 109. Phil Graham was still working frantically to resolve the situation in Little Rock; see Philip L. Graham to Sherman Adams, Sept. 17, 1957, Box 732, folder marked "Little Rock, Ark—School Integration, Gov Faubus' use of Nat'l Gd (1)," DDE.

23. Faubus interview with Luter, p. 50. Hays admitted in his Eisenhower Administration Project interview that in the week after Newport he met frequently with Blossom, School Board members, and other civic and clerical leaders; Hays interview with Luter, p. 108.

24. Benjamin Fine, "Governor Faubus Says Militia Will Stay at School Today," *New York Times,* Sept. 16, 1957; see also "President, Faubus to Talk Privately Without Advisers," *Arkansas Gazette,* Sept. 14, 1957, p. 1A. Faubus, *Down From the Hills,* p. 246; Faubus interview with Jacoway, July 11, 1978, p. 35; "New Faces in the Gazette Office," *Arkansas Gazette,* Sept. 20, 1957, p. 2A; Ray Moseley interview with Roy Reed, Nov. 4, 2000, *Arkansas Gazette* Project, ACOVH. Faubus interview with Luter, p. 79. Ashmore later took exception to this portrayal, suggesting instead, "My Press Club elbow bending was almost entirely social; we talked a good deal more about sex and football than

we did about Faubus. I had spent the previous year campaigning with Adlai Stevenson and I had come to know most of the reporters assigned to Little Rock; I regarded them as friends entitled to my hospitality"; Harry Ashmore to Elizabeth Jacoway, June 14, 1979, EJC.

25. "President, Faubus to Talk Privately Without Advisers." Faubus interview with Jacoway, July 11, 1978, p. 36. "Hillbilly, Slightly Sophisticated," *Time*, Sept. 16, 1957, p. 24. Jerry Dhonau interview with Elizabeth Jacoway, July 20, 1978, pp. 3–4, EJC; *Arkansas Gazette* staffer Jerry Dhonau recalled years later that *Time* magazine reporter Jerry Olsen "was personally pretty upset over the treatment *Time* gave to a Faubus cover piece based on his reporting. . . ."; Dhonau interview with Jacoway, July 20, 1978, p. 3. See also "What Orval Hath Wrought," *Time*, Sept. 23, 1957, p. 12. In a letter to his sister that fall, Faubus wrote: "All of this doesn't bother me, because of my knowledge of history and my tolerance of other people's viewpoints. Rather than letting such stories make me angry, they only amuse me. There's no point at all in arguing with a prejudiced person. Some people don't want to know the truth, even when you tell it to them." Orval E. Faubus to Mrs. Connie Loustalot, October 16, 1957, EJC; the author is grateful to Griffin Smith, jr., for bringing this letter to her attention.

26. Brownell interview with Reed, June 5, 1990, p. 2. Herbert Brownell with John P. Burke, *Advising Ike: The Memoirs of Attorney General Herbert Brownell* (Lawrence, Kan.: University Press of Kansas, 1993), p. 210. John Thomas Elliff, "The United States Department of Justice and Individual Civil Rights, 1937–1962" (Ph.D. diss. Harvard University, 1962), p. 474.

27. Faubus interview with Jacoway, July 11, 1978, pp. 20, 21; Faubus, *Down From the Hills*, p. 262; Ray Moseley, "Federal Judge Finds School Plan Thwarted," *Arkansas Gazette*, Sept. 21, 1957, p. 1A. Hays, *A Southern Moderate Speaks*, p. 160.

28. Smith interview with Luter, p. 30.

29. Jerry Jones, "Faubus Attorneys' Walkout Astonishes Federal Counsel," *Arkansas Gazette*, Sept. 21, 1957, p. 1A. Relman Morin, "Governor Refuses to Appear—Faubus Defies U.S., Lawyers Say Federal Court Has No Jurisdiction," *Birmingham News*, Sept. 20, 1957, SERS. Ray Moseley, "Hope of Settlement Fades as Governor Faces Day in Court," *Arkansas Gazette*, Sept. 19, 1957, p. 1A. Margaret Frick, "U.S. to Subpoena Over 200 Witnesses in Preparation for Friday's Injunction Hearing," *Arkansas Democrat*, Sept. 17, 1957, p. 1. Smith interview with Luter, pp. 30, 31, 32.

30. Faubus, *Down From the Hills*, p. 266. Senator Richard Russell had advised Faubus's attorneys to take this course of action; Ibid. Kay Matthews explained that the lawyers had taken this action to establish the basis for their appeal; Gene Foreman, "City Will Maintain Order at School, Mayor Says; Ike Bids for Acceptance," *Arkansas Gazette*, Sept. 22, 1957, p. 1A; Bill Smith had developed this legal team since he expected to be called as a witness; Faubus-Smith interview with Reed, p. 23. For a discussion of the lawyers' thinking, see Faubus, *Down From the Hills*, p. 264. Robert McCord, "Newsman Recalls a 1957 Scoop," *Arkansas Times*, Sept. 12, 1997, p. 21. Robert McCord, "Faubus Says 'Now Begins Crucifixion,'" *Arkansas Democrat*, Sept. 20, 1957, p. 1.

31. McCord, "Faubus Says 'Now Begins Crucifixion.'" Earl Mazo, "Faubus Says Brownell Aimed to Crucify Him," *New York Herald Tribune*, Sept. 23, 1957, SERS.

32. Moseley, "Federal Judge Finds School Plan Thwarted."; "statement in open court Sept. 20, 1957," *Race Relations Law Reporter*, October 1957, p. 958; many analysts have argued that this was a strategic mistake, as it encouraged violence so the segregationists could say "I told you so"; for examples of this argument see J. W. Peltason, *Fifty-Eight Lonely Men: Southern Federal Judges and School Desegregation* (New York: Harcourt, Brace & World, 1961), p. 173, and Elliff, "The United States Department of Justice and Individual Civil Rights," p. 476. Walter Lister, "U.S. Injunction Orders Gov. Faubus to Admit Negro Pupils 'Without Delay,'" *New York Herald Tribune*, Sept. 21, 1957, SERS.

33. The *Arkansas Gazette* had reported on Sept. 19, "One of the government's primary weapons in the case is believed to be the FBI Report . . ." and on September 20, "The FBI report is the key document in the case"; Ray Moseley, "Hope of Settlement Fades as Governor Faces Day in Court," *Arkansas Gazette*, Sept. 19, 1957, p. 1A, and Ray Moseley, "Faubus, U.S. Government

Head Into Crucial Collision in Federal Court Today," *Arkansas Gazette,* Sept. 20, 1957, p. 1A.

34. Bill Smith said in an interview with the Eisenhower Administration Project, "When Davies entered the order requiring the Governor to withdraw the National Guard, he took the Governor out of the picture, and the Governor complied with the order. From then on it was the federal government's show"; Smith interview with Luter, p. 81; for criticism of Faubus's decision to remove the Guard see Harry Ashmore's editorial, "Orval Faubus v. The Law of the Land," *Arkansas Gazette,* Sept. 21, 1957, p. 4A.

35. Harry Ashmore called this charge "the final defense of the demagogue," claiming that Faubus "sought to divert attention from his own role by charging that he is the victim of an evil conspiracy"; "Orval Faubus v. The Law of the Land."

36. Gene Foreman and Matilda Tuohey, "Faubus Withdraws Guard After Court Enjoins Him," *Arkansas Gazette,* Sept. 21, 1957, p. 1A. Faubus believed Daisy Bates had agreed not to enroll the black students in Central High in his absence; reporter Relman Morin got this information from Orval Faubus and had heard it from other sources as well; "Get Negroes Out, Faubus Peace Formula," *Montgomery Advertiser,* Nov. 18, 1957, SERS. Hays, *A Southern Moderate Speaks,* p. 173; for a similar claim in a *U.S. News & World Report* interview with Faubus, see "Blossom Asked Protection?," *Arkansas Democrat,* June 16, 1958, p. 1.

37. On Saturday night, several of the southern governors attended the Georgia-Texas football game in Atlanta, where they were introduced. As one historian has written, "the announcement of Faubus's name evoked an unrestrained emotional outburst from the 33,000 southerners. Officials delayed the game several minutes as wave after wave of applause poured down upon the Arkansas governor. . . . Order was finally restored, but following the game crowds thronged through the streets shouting 'Faubus, Faubus!' Dixie had a new folk hero"; Thomas R. Wagy, "Governor LeRoy Collins of Florida and the Little Rock Crisis of 1957," *Arkansas Historical Quarterly* (Summer 1979), p. 106.

38. Walter Lister Jr., "Negroes to Be Tutored, Shun Little Rock School," *New York Herald Tribune,* Sept. 9, 1957, SERS; "Little Rock Negroes Get Tutors' Aid," *New York Herald Tribune,* Sept. 22, 1957, SERS; Chris Mercer recalled that the tutoring was fairly sporadic; C. C. Mercer interview with Jacoway, Aug. 11, 2003, p. 13, EJC.

39. Hays, *A Southern Moderate Speaks,* p. 166. Woodrow Mann, "The Truth About Little Rock," *New York Herald Tribune,* Jan. 27, 1958. Gene Foreman, "City Will Maintain Order at School, Mayor Says; Ike Bids for Acceptance," *Arkansas Gazette,* Sept. 22, 1957, p. 1A.

40. Hays, *A Southern Moderate Speaks,* p. 162, 164–65; "Hays to Return; Will Study Situation and Report to Ike," *Arkansas Gazette,* Sept. 21, 1957, p. 1A. Elizabeth Carpenter, "Hays' Go-Between Role Stirs Howls From Nixon's Backers," *Arkansas Gazette,* Sept. 22, 1957, p. 1A. For McClellan's support of Faubus see "GOP Leaders Rap Faubus; State's Senators Neutral," *Arkansas Gazette,* Sept. 6, 1957, p. 12A, and "McClellan Says He Doubts Crisis Will End Peacefully," *Arkansas Gazette,* Sept. 17, 1957, p. 1A. Arkansas Senator J. William Fulbright also supported Faubus's actions; "Fulbright Shuns Judging Fellow Arkansan Faubus," *Atlanta Constitution,* Sept. 20, 1957, SERS. Brooks Hays to Sherman Adams, Sept. 26, 1957, Box 80, LBH.

41. Hays, *A Southern Moderate Speaks,* p. 165. Hays interview with Luter, pp. 87–88, 109–110. Legal historian John Thomas Elliff argued that the Justice Department refused to send marshals because it was already making preparations to use the Army; Elliff, "The United States Department of Justice and Individual Civil Rights," pp. 477–78.

42. Henry Woods interview with Elizabeth Jacoway, May 20, 2000, p. 14, EJC. Hays, *A Southern Moderate Speaks,* pp. 166–67.

43. Henry Woods and Beth Deere, "Reflections on the Little Rock School Case," 44:971 *Arkansas Law Review,* 1991, p. 10; see also Harry S. Ashmore interview with Elizabeth Jacoway, Nov. 17, 1976, pp. 27–28, EJC. Woods interview with Jacoway, May 20, 2000, p. 14. Woods interview with Baker, p. 36. Irene Samuel interview with John Luter, Dec. 30, 1970, p. 29, EAP.

44. Woods interview with Jacoway, May 20, 2000, p. 15; Woods interview with Baker, pp. 37–38. Silverman, *The Little Rock Story,* p. 15.

45. Henry Woods interview with FBI, Sept. 25, 1957, p. 172, Box 3, File 6, FBI Report. Woods interview with Baker, pp. 38–39.

46. Daisy Bates, *The Long Shadow of Little Rock* (New York: David McKay & Co., 1962). Virgil T. Blossom, *It HAS Happened Here* (New York: Harper & Bros., 1959). Harold Engstrom interview with Roy Reed, Aug. 21, 1991, pp. 4–5, RRP; William G. Cooper interview with Roy Reed, Aug. 21, 1991, p. 5, RRP; Henry Rath interview with Elizabeth Jacoway, Dec. 9, 1977, p. 24, EJC; Wayne Upton interview with John Luter, December 1971, p. 21, EAP; Osro Cobb interview with Roy Reed, Oct. 3, 1992, p. 19, RRP; Faubus-Smith interview with Reed, pp. 26, 11, RRP; Faubus interview with Jacoway, May 12, 1994, p. 5. Alta Faubus interview with Elizabeth Jacoway, April 9, 1996, p. 4, EJC; Hays interview with Tonks, p. 472; Hays interview with Luter, p. 98; Wiley A. Branton, "Desegregation to Resegregation," *Journal of Negro Education* SL (Summer 1983), p. 268; Griffee, *Osro Cobb of Arkansas*, p. 192. Faubus interview with Bass and DeVries, p. 31.

47. Walter Lippmann, "False Excuse of Gov. Faubus," *St. Louis Post-Dispatch*, Sept. 20, 1957, SERS. Faubus, *Down From the Hills*, p. 261.

CHAPTER NINE — CENTRAL HIGH SCHOOL, ACT ONE

1. The Little Rock Central High School campus covers eight square blocks. Col. A. J. Almand, "John Parks Almand," *Pulaski County Historical Review*," Summer 1989, p. 39.

2. Faustine C. Jones-Wilson and Erma Glasco Davis, *Paul Lawrence Dunbar High School of Little Rock, Arkansas: "Take From Our Lips a Song, Dunbar to Thee"* (Virginia Beach: Va. Donning Co. Publishers, 2003), pp. 31–32, 42.

3. Jones-Wilson and Davis, *Paul Lawrence Dunbar High School of Little Rock, Arkansas*, pp. 40–44. Ozell Sutton interview with Elizabeth Jacoway, June 7, 2003, EJC; Annie Abrams interview with Elizabeth Jacoway, Aug. 15, 2003, EJC. Much of the local publicity referred to Horace Mann as a "million dollar" school, but records in the Little Rock School Board offices show that its construction cost was $773,799.32; Suellen Vann, LRSB Communications Director, telephone conversation with Elizabeth Jacoway, Sept. 11, 2003.

4. Daisy Bates, *The Long Shadow of Little Rock* (New York: David McKay & Co., 1962), pp. 11–12; Daisy Bates interview with Elizabeth Jacoway, Oct. 11, 1976, pp. 1–2, SOHP. Bates's biographer makes a compelling argument that the story of Bates's mother's rape and murder by three white men was fabricated; see Grif Stockley, *Daisy Bates: Civil Rights Crusader from Arkansas* (Jackson: University Press of Mississippi, 2005). For a suggestive brief account of some of the factors in Bates's thinking and development, see John Kirk, "Daisy Bates," in Peter J. Ling and Sharon Monteith, eds., *Gender and the Civil Rights Movement* (New Brunswick, N.J.: Rutgers University Press, 1999), pp. 17–40. Grif Stockley has written persuasively that Daisy Bates was L. C. Bates's mistress for over a decade before he divorced his first wife and married her; Stockley, *Daisy Bates*, p. 24. For background on L. C. Bates's life see Irene Martin Wassell, "L. C. Bates: Editor of the *Arkansas State Press*" (master's thesis, University of Arkansas at Little Rock, 1983), pp. 4, 6.

5. Bates, *The Long Shadow of Little Rock*, pp. 26–27. Christopher C. Mercer Jr. interview with Elizabeth Jacoway, Aug. 1, 2003, p. 21, EJC. Bates, *The Long Shadow of Little Rock*, pp. 32–58. For a balanced and yet largely sympathetic appraisal of Bates's personality and character see Stockley, *Daisy Bates*. Bates interview with Jacoway, p. 27. For physical descriptions of Bates see "Daisy Bates: Arkansas Fighter," *Jet*, October 17, 1957, p. 8; Lerone Bennett Jr., "First Lady of Little Rock," *Ebony*, September 1958, p. 18; John Wyllie, "Conversations in the South," p. 3, March 3, 1959, Box 498, Folder 6, OEF. The description of the Bates's social status comes from Ozell Sutton interview with Roy Reed, June 22, 1992, p. 11, RRP; Sutton interview with Jacoway; Elizabeth Eckford interview with Elizabeth Jacoway, Aug. 14, 2003, pp. 27, 29, EJC.

6. Sutton interview with Jacoway. Ernest Green recalled forty years later that one of his black neighbors thought pushing for integration was "the wrong thing to do." Green suggested, "She feared that by challenging whites, making them take us into their schools, there would be a spiraling backlash that would make life more difficult—not better—for a people still trying to chuck

aside the remaining shackles of slavery"; Ernest Green, "Casting Off the Legacy of Slavery," *Arkansas Times,* Sept. 19, 1997, p. 24. Sutton interview with Reed, p. 11. See also Bennett, "First Lady of Little Rock," p. 18. Nat R. Griswold to Fred Routh, July 22, 1955, Box 16, Folder 152, ACHR. ACHR Board President Fred Darragh occasionally flew Bates in his private airplane to meetings and speaking engagements across the South; Fred Darragh interview with Elizabeth Jacoway, Feb. 6, 2002, pp. 14–15, EJC. David Halberstam, *The Fifties* (New York: Villard Books, 1993), p. 670; see also Harry Ashmore, *Arkansas: A History* (New York: W. W. Norton & Co., 1978), p. 155.

7. Bates, *The Long Shadow of Little Rock,* p. 15. "Memo—Racists," (nd), Box 1, Folder 6, DGB.

8. Abrams interview with Jacoway, p. 16; Bennett, "First Lady of Little Rock," p. 20.

9. For an excellent overview of the NAACP's efforts to press for desegregation in Little Rock, see John Kirk, *Redefining the Color Line: Black Activism in Little Rock, Arkansas, 1940–1970* (Gainesville: University Press of Florida, 2002), pp. 86–105. See also Brian James Daugherity, "'With All Deliberate Speed': The NAACP and the Implementation of *Brown v. Board of Education* at the Local Level, Little Rock, Arkansas" (master's thesis, University of Montana, 1997). Wiley A. Branton interview with Steven Lawson, Oct. 21, 1970, p. 55, EAP.

10. Eckford interview with Jacoway, p. 1; Minnijean Brown Trickey interview with Elizabeth Jacoway, Sept. 15, 2003 pp. 18–20. Linda S. Caillouet, "High Profile: Daisy Lee Gatson Bates," *Arkansas Democrat-Gazette,* Oct. 15, 2000.

11. Bates, *The Long Shadow of Little Rock,* p. 64; Bates interview with Jacoway, p. 13. Transcript of telephone conversation between Daisy Bates, Clarence Laws, Gloster Current, and Henry Moon, Oct. 3, 1957, Box 5, Folder 2, DGB.

12. Wassell, "L. C. Bates," pp. 38–40, 19–21; Bates, The Long Shadow of Little Rock, pp. 3–5, 34–38, 41–43, 110–11. "Little Rock: The Chronology of a Contrived Crisis," (nd), group III, series A, container 98, Folder "Desegregation of Schools, Arkansas, Little Rock, Central High, 1956–1957," PON. Bates interview with Jacoway, pp. 33–37.

13. Bates, *The Long Shadow of Little Rock,* pp. 4–5. "Memorandum to Miss Geier from Mr. Current," Aug. 29, 1957, group III, series A, container 98, PON; Bates, *The Long Shadow of Little Rock,* pp. 110–11; Wassell, "L. C. Bates," p. 52. Clarence Laws had been on the scene since early September; Daisy Bates to Gloster Current, Sept. 9, 1957, group III, series A, container 98, PON. For information about Rosa Parks's training see Diane McWhorter, *Carry Me Home: Birmingham, Alabama, The Climactic Battle of the Civil Rights Revolution* (New York: Simon & Schuster, 2001), pp. 90–93. Daisy Bates to Gloster Current, Sept. 9, 1957, group III, series A, container 98, PON; Daisy Bates to Roy Wilkins, Sept. 12, 1957, group III, series A, container 98, PON.

14. See especially Relman Morin, "Get Negroes Out, Faubus Peace Formula," *Montgomery Advertiser,* Nov. 18, 1957, SERS. For a similar claim in a *U.S. News & World Report* interview with Faubus, See "Blossom Asked Protection?," *Arkansas Democrat,* June 16, 1958, p. 1. See also Ray Moseley, "Faubus Opens Up Swinging, Hurls Challenge at Ward," *Arkansas Gazette,* March 26, 1958, p. 1A. Sutton interview with Reed, p. 20. Sutton recalled this episode as occurring on September 2, but it undoubtedly occurred on September 20.

15. Bobbie Forster, "All Adults Barred from Central High," *Arkansas Democrat,* Sept. 21, 1957, p. 1. Gene Foreman, "City Will Maintain Order at School, Mayor Says; Ike Bids for Acceptance," *Arkansas Gazette,* Sept. 22, 1957, p. 1A. Transcript, telephone conversation between Daisy Bates, Clarence Laws, and Gloster Current, Sept. 24, 1957, group III, series A, container 98, PON. Three of the black children, Terrence Roberts, Jane Hill and Carlotta Walls, did say on Sunday they planned to attend school on Monday; Robert Troutt, "Negroes to Enter Central Monday; Police on Alert," *Arkansas Democrat,* Sept. 22, 1957, p. 1.

16. Transcript, telephone conversation between Daisy Bates and Gloster Current, Sept. 23, 1957, group III, series A, container 98, PON. This was a grey area at the time, but Brooks Hays believed the Justice Department officials should have acted "imaginatively" to uphold their own courts' orders; Brooks Hays, *A Southern Moderate Speaks,* pp. 170–71. Troutt, "Negroes to Enter Central Monday; Police on Alert"; Woodrow Mann, "The Truth About Little Rock," *New York Herald Tribune,* Jan. 27, 1958. Woods interview with FBI, p. 173; transcript of Eisenhower Presiden-

tial Library conference celebrating centennial of Eisenhower's birth, June 5, 1990, RRP.

17. Bates, *The Long Shadow of Little Rock,* pp. 87, 89; Blossom claimed publicly the black children's arrival had not been prearranged; "Blossom Lays Responsibility on 'Outside,'" *Arkansas Gazette,* Sept. 24, 1957, p. 1A. "City and State Police to be There Today," *Arkansas Gazette,* Sept. 23, 1957, p. 1A.

18. Mercer interview with Jacoway, pp. 14, 17. Bates, *The Long Shadow of Little Rock,* p. 89. Chris Mercer had been associate director of the Arkansas Council on Human Relations from 1955 to 1957; he had also made the top score on the Arkansas bar exam in 1954; "Arkansas Council on Human Relations (An Interpretation)," May 30, 1955, Box 16, Folder 152, ACHR.

19. Bates, *The Long Shadow of Little Rock,* p. 86. Ernest Green interview with John Pagan, Jan. 26, 1973, p. 5, EJC. Walter Lister Jr., "Police Guard Negroes if They Go to School in Little Rock Today," *New York Herald Tribune,* Sept. 23, 1957, SERS. Daisy Bates interview with John Pagan, Aug. 23, 1972, p. 2, EJC.

20. Relman Morin and Keith Fuller, "Violence Wins a Round at Little Rock School," *Louisville Courier-Journal,* Sept. 24, 1957, SERS.

21. Wyllie, "Conversations in the South," p. 2. Roy Reed, *Faubus: The Life and Times of an American Prodigal* (Fayetteville: University of Arkansas Press, 1997), p. 226.

22. Elizabeth Huckaby, *Crisis at Central High:, Little Rock, 1957–58* (Baton Rouge: Louisiana State University Press, 1980), pp. 34–35. Melba Patillo Beals, *Warriors Don't Cry: A Searing Memoir of the Battle to Integrate Little Rock's Central High* (New York: Simon & Schuster, 1994); Huckaby, *Crisis at Central High,* pp. 35–36.

23. Robert Troutt, "Growing Violence Forces Withdrawal of 8 Negro Students at Central High," *Arkansas Democrat,* Sept. 23, 1957, p. 1. Bates, *The Long Shadow of Little Rock,* p. 91.

24. The school librarian recorded in her memoir that parents arrived all through the day; Lola Alice Dunnavant, "Inside Central High School: Little Rock, Arkansas, 1957–1958," pp. 9–11, Box 1, Folder 58, LDC; see also Transcript, Lemley Hearing, June 4, 1958, p. 19, Box 5, Folder 7, VTB. Huckaby, *Crisis at Central High,* p. 38.

25. Green interview with Pagan, p. 5. "'Nothing Much Happened,'" *Arkansas Democrat,* Sept. 23, 1957, p. 1. Beals, *Warriors Don't Cry,* p. 111. Melba did, in fact, marry a white man; Beals, *Warriors Don't Cry,* p. 311. Ted Poston, "Nine Kids Who Dared: Melba Patillo," *New York Post Daily Magazine,* Oct. 22, 1957, Bates Scrapbook, DGB; Dunnavant, "Inside Central High School," pp. 9–11.

26. Carroll E. (Gene) Prescott interview with FBI, Sept. 25, 1957, p. 159, Box 4, Folder 1, FBI Report. The mob chanted "Run, Nigger, Run!" but Alex Wilson refused to run, saying, "I fought for my country, and I'm not going to run from you"; Wilmer Counts, *A Life Is More Than a Moment,* pp. xv and 47–52. "Newsmen Victims of Mob," *Arkansas Democrat,* Sept. 23, 1957, p. 1. Jack Setters, "Gov. Faubus' Stock Climbs As Events Confirm Fears," *Nashville Banner,* Sept. 24, 1957, SERS. One example of the kind of reporting that enraged Little Rock's segregationists was the article by Bob Considine titled "Solid Citizens Absent; Mob Formed by Po' Whites, Crackpots, Loafers," *Charleston* (West Virginia) *Gazette,* Sept. 16, 1957, SERS. Wassell, "L. C. Bates," p. 57.

27. Thomas F. Pettigrew and Ernest Q. Campbell, *Christians in Racial Crisis: A Study of the Little Rock Ministry* (Washington, D.C.: Public Affairs Press, 1959), p. 45. Transcript, Bates and Current, Sept. 23, 1957; transcript, Bates, Laws, and Current, Sept. 24, 1957; Bates, *The Long Shadow of Little Rock,* pp. 89–93. Stewart Alsop, "The Little Rock Mob Was Out to 'Get' Negro Children," *Nashville Tennessean,* Sept. 26, 1957, SERS. Henry Woods interview with FBI, Sept. 25, 1957, p. 176, Box 3, File 6, FBI Report; Huckaby, *Crisis at Central High,* p. 25; Reed, *Faubus,* p. 225.

28. Ray Moseley, "Crowd Erupts After 9 Negro Pupils Enter," *Arkansas Gazette,* Sept. 24, 1957, p. 1A. Harry Ashmore interview with Elizabeth Jacoway, Nov. 17, 1976, p. 78, EJC. Claude Sitton, "U.S. Marshals Would Keep Order in Little Rock, Backed by Police," Aug. 24, 1958, *Chattanooga Times,* SERS.

29. Hays, *A Southern Moderate Speaks,* p. 172. Most visiting journalists used the *Gazette* office as their headquarters and Harry Ashmore as a primary source of information; George Douthit

interview with John Luter, Dec. 31, 1970, pp. 11, 17, EAP. Relman Morin, "Monday, Sept. 23, 1957: Dark Day in Crisis," *Arkansas Democrat,* Oct. 10, 1957, p. 8.

30. Hays, *A Southern Moderate Speaks,* p. 172; Brooks Hays interview with John Luter, June 27–28, July 27, 1970, p. 110, EAP. In his memoir Hays attempted to blur his involvement in the calling of federal troops, as he also did in the summer of 1958 when he was running for Congress; Hays, *A Southern Moderate Speaks,* pp. 172–73; "Hays Disputes Charge That He Helped Bring Troops," *Arkansas Gazette,* July 26, 1958. See Hays interview with Luter, p. 89. See also Henry Woods interview with Sara Alderman Murphy, Aug. 30, 1992, p. 1, SAM. Woodrow Wilson Mann, "The Truth About Little Rock," *New York Herald Tribune,* Jan. 28, 1958, ABC. Woods interview with FBI, p. 173. Robert Troutt, "Growing Violence Forces Withdrawal of 8 Negro Students at Central High," *Arkansas Democrat,* Sept. 24, 1957, p. 1. Blossom wrote in his memoir he was surprised by Mann's appraisal of the danger, because he thought Gene Smith had the situation under control; Blossom, *It HAS Happened Here,* p. 108; Huckaby, *Crisis at Central High,* p. 38. Woodrow Mann, "The Truth About Little Rock," *New York Herald Tribune,* Jan. 28, 1958. Gene Smith later told Harry Ashmore he had removed the Nine "to keep them from being killed"; Harry Ashmore to John Temple Graves, Feb. 28, 1958, Box 7, Folder 3, HSA.

31. Caillouet, "High Profile: Daisy Lee Gatson Bates." "Negroes Out Until Ike Acts," *Arkansas Democrat,* Sept. 23, 1957, p. 1; Woodrow Mann, "The Truth About Little Rock," *New York Herald Tribune,* Jan. 29, 1958. "Subject: Factual Information," Sept. 23, 1957, Box 2, Folder 8, RRB. Keith Fuller, "President Clears Way for Use of Troops in Little Rock," *Atlanta Constitution,* Sept. 24, 1957, SERS. Huckaby, *Crisis at Central High,* p. 39. Hays, *A Southern Moderate Speaks,* p. 171.

32. Stephen E. Ambrose, *Eisenhower: The President,* Vol. 2 (New York: Simon & Schuster, 1984), p. 410. "News Conference," Sept. 23, 1957, Box 6, Folder "Integration—Little Rock, 1957," DDE; "Statement by the President," Sept. 23, 1957, Box 20, Folder "September 1957," DDE. Robert W. Coakley, "Federal Use of Militia and the National Guard in Civil Disturbances: The Whiskey Rebellion to Little Rock," in Robin Higham, ed., *Bayonets in the Streets: The Use of Troops in Civil Disturbances* (Lawrence: University Press of Kansas, 1969), pp. 18, 29; "Obstruction of Justice in the State of Arkansas by the President of the United States of America: A Proclamation," Sept. 23, 1957, Box 6, Folder "Integration—Little Rock, 1957," DDE.

33. "Faubus Challenges Ike on Using Troops," *Arkansas Gazette,* Sept. 24, 1957, p. 1A. "Faubus Says the U.S. Cannot Use Troops," *New York Times,* Sept. 24, 1957, p. 1. Even a former president of the American Bar Association waffled when asked whether or not troop use was legal; "Lawyers Mum On Right to Federalize Guard," *Baltimore Evening Sun,* Sept. 26, 1957, SERS. "Ike Clears Way to Send Troops: Commands Cease, Desist in Legal Move," *Arkansas Gazette,* Sept. 24, 1957, p. 1A. "News Conference with James C. Hagerty," Sept. 24, 1957, Box 6, Folder "Integration—Little Rock," DDE.

34. Woodrow Mann telegram to Dwight Eisenhower, Sept. 23, 1957, Box 6, Folder "Integration—Little Rock," DDE.

35. Summary, Director's Brief, Vol. 1, File 2, p. A-17, FBI Report. This investigation eventually cost $86,700; *Southern School News,* June 1958. Louis Cassels, "Faubus Is Playing a Waiting Game; How Can Ike Pull Troops?," *Delta Democrat-Times,* Oct. 11, 1957, SERS; Director's Brief, Vol. I, File 2, p. A-17, Box 1, Folder 2, FBI Report. An excellent article that outlines the FBI investigation of Karam is Anthony Lewis, "F.B.I. Head Says Gov. Faubus Lied on Bureau's Role," *New York Times,* Sept. 28, 1957, p. 1; see also Stan Opotowsky, "FBI Probing Faubus' Pal," *New York Post,* Sept. 27, 1957, Box 1, Folder 6, DGB.

36. Nat R. Griswold interview with John Luter, Aug. 21, 1971, pp. 43–44, EAP.

37. Jack Setters, "Gov. Faubus' Stock Climbs As Events Confirm Fears," *Nashville Banner,* Sept. 24, 1957, SERS. Mann's telegram specifically noted the mayor was not releasing a copy of his telegram to the press. Woodrow W. Mann interview with FBI, Sept. 24, 1957, p. 169, Box 4, File 1, FBI Report. Woods interview with FBI, p. 171.

38. "The President's Appointments," Sept. 23, 1957, Box 16, Folder "September, 1957—Schedules," DDE; transcript, Bates, Laws, and Current, Sept. 24, 1957; also Bates, *The Long Shadow of*

Little Rock, p. 96.

39. Bates, *The Long Shadow of Little Rock,* p. 111. Transcript, Bates and Current, Sept. 23, 1957. Bates also commented that Chris Mercer had been her "backbone" through this harrowing experience; transcript of telephone conversation between Daisy Bates and Gloster Current, Sept. 25, 1957, Box 5, Folder 2, DGB. "New Violence Breaks Out in Little Rock,"*Nashville Tennessean,* Sept. 24, 1957, SERS.

40. Robert Troutt, "Central High Quiet as Negroes Fail to Show; Attendance Drops," *Arkansas Democrat,* Sept. 24, 1957, p. 1; Coakley, *Operation Arkansas,* p. 51. Rodney Worthington, "Police Arrest 45 Persons In Race Rows," *Arkansas Democrat,* Sept. 24, 1957, p. 1; Transcript, Lemley Hearing, June 4, 1958, p. 223, VTB; Richard Morehead, "Federal Troops Occupy Arkansas School Grounds," *Dallas Morning News,* Sept. 25, 1957, SERS; Sy Ramsey, "School Battleground to Move into Courts," *Arkansas Democrat,* Oct. 6, 1957, p. 8A; Morin, "Sept. 23, 1957: Dark Day in Crisis." Dunnavant, "Inside Central High School," p. 13.

41. "Rumors Rife but Violence Only Minor," *Arkansas Gazette,* Sept. 26, 1957, p. 1A. Woodrow Wilson Mann, Mayor of Little Rock Arkansas, to President Dwight D. Eisenhower, (nd), Box 15, Folder "September, 1957—Dictation," DDE. Mann attempted immediately to blur his involvement in the sending of this telegram; "Call For Troops Laid to Mayor; Mann Says He 'Can't Confirm or Deny" Asking for Aid," *Arkansas Democrat,* Sept. 25, 1957, p. 1. Coakley, *Operation Arkansas,* p. 51.

42. Henry Woods interview with Elizabeth Jacoway, May 30, 2000, p. 15, EJC. Blurring his involvement at Henry Woods's house on the afternoon of September 23, Hays wrote, "Thus, on the morning of Tuesday, September 24, my struggle to prevent federal use of troops came to an end"; Hays, *A Southern Moderate Speaks,* p. 173. "Police Could Not Handle Mob, Little Rock Editor Declares; Federal Troops Were Needed," *Boston Daily Globe,* Sept. 27, 1957, Box 9, Folder 4, HSA.

43. "Integration Views Aired by Ashmore," *Arkansas Democrat,* Oct. 7, 1957, p. 2.

44. Woodrow Mann, "The Truth About Little Rock," *New York Herald Tribune,* Jan. 29, 1958. With the exception of Dale Alford the members of the Little Rock School Board voted among themselves to request soldiers if no one else did so; Harold Engstrom interview with John Luter, Dec. 29, 1970, p. 24, EAP; Dale and L' Moore Alford, *The Case of the Sleeping People (Finally Awakened By Little Rock School Frustrations)* (Little Rock: Pioneer Press, 1959), p. 9. Their connection in the Justice Department was Maxwell Rabb, who stayed in almost constant telephone contact with Woodrow Mann the morning of September 24. Rabb later described himself as "holding the hand" of Mayor Mann; Maxwell Rabb interview with Roy Reed, June 5, 1990, p. 16, RRP. Former *Arkansas Democrat* reporter Ron Burnham claimed, almost fifty years after the fact, that it was his idea to request federal intervention and that at Mann's request he had posed as Mann on the telephone and requested federal marshalls from Maxwell Rabb; Burnham also claimed to have written Mann's account of the crisis later published in the *New York Herald Tribune*; Ron Burnham interview with Jerry McConnell, September 4, 2005, pg. 10-19, ACOVH. Ashmore later tried to downplay his involvement in requesting troops in Little Rock, writing about "the durable myth that I was responsible for the dispatch of federal troops to Little Rock"; Harry S. Ashmore, *Hearts and Minds: The Anatomy of Racism from Roosevelt to Reagan* (New York: McGraw-Hill Book Co., 1982), p. 265.

45. Herbert Brownell to Dwight D. Eisenhower, Nov. 7, 1957, Box 8, Folder "Brownell, H. (1957)."

46. Ambrose, *Eisenhower,* p. 419. Eisenhower wrote in his autobiography he had decided to use troops before the telegram arrived; Dwight D. Eisenhower, *The White House Years: Waging Peace,* 1956–1961 (New York: Doubleday, 1965), p. 170. Eisenhower instructed his subordinates, "Well, if we have to do this, and I don't see any alternative, then let's apply the best military principles to it, and see that the force that we send there is strong enough so that it will not be challenged and will not result in any clash"; Herbert Brownell interview with Ed Edwin, Jan. 31, 1968, p. 212, EAP. As the Army's report explained, ". . . in its simplest terms, the philosophy was that if the federal government acted, that action must be successful"; Coakley, *Operation Arkansas,* p. 69.

John Thomas Elliff, "The United States Department of Justice and Individual Rights, 1937–1962" (Ph.D. diss., Harvard University, 1967), p. 474. For a discussion of the preparations for using federal troops see Coakley, *Operation Arkansas,* pp. 19–25.

47. "Proclamation 3204: Obstruction of Justice in the State of Arkansas by the President of the United States of America," Sept. 23, 1957, Box 6, Folder "Integration—Little Rock, 1957 (2)," DDE; Tony Freyer, *The Little Rock Crisis: A Constitutional Interpretation* (Westport, Conn.: Greenwood Press, 1984), p. 123. Herbert Brownell interview, Henry Hampton and Steve Fayer, *Voices of Freedom: An Oral History of the Civil Rights Movement from the 1950s through the 1980s* (New York: Bantam Books, 1990), p. 47.

48. "Executive Order 10730: Providing Assistance for the Removal of an Obstruction of Justice Within the State of Arkansas," Sept. 24, 1957, Box 6, Folder "Integration—Little Rock (2)," DDE. Coakley, *Operation Arkansas,* pp. 57, 63.

49. Coakley, *Operation Arkansas,* pp. 63, 65, 75, 88; the Army contingent was integrated, but no blacks were stationed at Central High; Ibid., pp. 76–77. General Walker was a graduate of West Point, and he had served in World War II and Korea; "Walker Assigned to Duty in Europe," *Arkansas Gazette,* July 18, 1959, p. 10B.

50. "Relieved of Command," *Arkansas Gazette,* Sept. 24, 1957, p. 1A. Walter Lister Jr., "Faubus Compares Role to Lee's and Lincoln's," *New York Herald Tribune,* Oct. 6, 1957, SERS. Faubus, *Down From the Hills,* p. 249. Transcript of Eisenhower Presidential Library conference celebrating the centennial of Dwight Eisenhower's birth, RRP.

51. Brownell interview, Hampton and Fayer, *Voices of Freedom,* p. 47.

52. Ambrose, *Eisenhower,* p. 421.

53. Dunnavant, "Inside Central High School," p. 14. "Governor Calls for Calm, Order; But Voices Resentment of Occupation," *Arkansas Gazette,* Sept. 26, 1957, p. 1A. A. Howard Stebbins interview with Elizabeth Jacoway, Dec. 16 1977, EJC.

54. Sidney S. McMath interview with John Luter, Dec. 30, 1970, p. 18, EAP. William J. Smith interview with John Luter, Aug. 19–20, 1971, p. 80, EAP. Wiley A. Branton, "Little Rock Revisited: Desegregation to Resegregation," *Journal of Negro Education* (Summer 1983), p. 264.

55. President's speech, Sept. 24, 1957, Box 22, Folder "Integration—Little Rock, Ark.," DDE. Ambrose, *Eisenhower,* p. 421.

56. Dwight D. Eisenhower, "Radio and Television Address to the American People on the Situation in Little Rock," Sept. 24, 1957, *Public Papers of the Presidents of the United States: Dwight D. Eisenhower, 1957,* pp. 690–94.

57. Pettigrew and Campbell, *Christians in Racial Crisis,* pp. 24, 25; "Negroes Will Try to Enter School," *New York Times,* Sept. 22, 1957; William H. Stringer, "Impact of Troop Action Pondered As President Lashes at 'Mob Rule,'" *Christian Science Monitor,* Sept. 25, 1957, SERS. Huckaby, *Crisis at Central High,* p. 42. Jack Setters, "Gov. Faubus' Stock Climbs As Events Confirm Fears," *Nashville Banner,* Sept. 24, 1957, SERS; Blossom, *It HAS Happened Here,* p. 118.

58. "Transcript of Telephone Report of Little Rock Situation by Clarence Laws," Sept. 25, 1957, group III, series A, container 98, PON. Bates, *The Long Shadow of Little Rock,* pp. 101–2.

59. "Transcript of Telephone Report of Little Rock Situation by Clarence Laws." Bates, *The Long Shadow of Little Rock,* p. 103.

60. Bates, *The Long Shadow of Little Rock,* p. 103, 104. Beals, *Warriors Don't Cry,* p. 130. Ernest Green interview, Hampton and Fayer, *Voices of Freedom,* p. 48. Melba Patillo Beals interview, Hampton and Fayer, *Voices of Freedom,* p. 48. Three of the girls—Melba Patillo, Minnijean Brown, and Thelma Mothershed—gave a press conference that night at the Dunbar Community Center and announced that "most of the students were nice to them and those that weren't just ignored them"; "Students Report Only One Incident," *Arkansas Gazette,* Sept. 26, 1957.

61. Coakley, *Operation Arkansas,* p. 80.

CHAPTER TEN — INTO THE CAULDRON

1. Transcript of telephone conversation between Clarence Laws and Gloster Current, Sept. 26, 1957, group III, series A, container 98, PON. Press release, Sept. 19, 1957, group III, series A, container 98, PON. Press release, Sept. 26, 1957, group III, series A, container 98, PON.

2. Apparently the Pulitzer Prize–winning journalist Relman Morin crafted the phrase "The Little Rock Nine," which has been used ever since to describe the nine young warriors who integrated Central High School; Relman Morin, "In This Hurricane's Eye? Calm Settles on City," *Arkansas Democrat,* Oct. 7, 1957, p. 3.

3. Transcript of telephone conversation between Clarence Laws, Gloster Current, Henry Moon, and John Morsell, Sept. 27, 1957, group III, series A, container 98, PON; Transcript of telephone conversation between Daisy Bates, Clarence Laws, and Gloster Current, Sept. 30, 1957, Box 5, Folder 2, DGB; L.E. Hamilton to Daisy Bates, Oct. 1, 1957, Box 1, Folder 6, DGB. Transcript of telephone conversation between Clarence Laws, Gloster Current, Henry Moon, and John Morsell, Sept. 27, 1957.

4. Transcript of telephone conversation between Daisy Bates and Gloster Current, Sept. 24, 1957, Box 5, Folder 2, DGB. "Daisy Bates: Arkansas Fighter," pp. 6–9.

5. Transcript of telephone conversation between Clarence Laws and Gloster Current, Sept. 26, 1957. Daisy Bates interview with Elizabeth Jacoway, Oct. 11, 1976, pp. 26–27, SOHP.

6. Robert W. Coakley, *Operation Arkansas* (Office of the Chief of Military History Monograph No. 158M, 1967), pp. 88, 90.

7. Coakley, *Operation Arkansas,* p. 81. Virgil Blossom recorded that the school was half empty on September 25; Virgil T. Blossom, *It HAS Happened Here,* (New York: Harper & Bros. 1959), p. 123; "Attendance at Central 67%," *Arkansas Democrat,* Sept. 26, 1957, p. 1. Transcript of telephone conversation between Clarence Laws and Gloster Current, Sept. 26, 1957.

8. Brooks Hays, *A Southern Moderate Speaks* (Chapel Hill: University of North Carolina Press, 1959), p. 174; the full speech is in Brooks Hays, *This World, A Christian's Workshop* (Nashville: Broadman Press, 1958), pp. 92–100. Brooks Hays interview with John Luter, June 27–28, July 27, 1970, pp. 123, 60, EAP. Brooks Hays to Sherman Adams, Sept. 26, 1957, Box 732, Folder "Little Rock, Arkansas—Governor Faubus' Use of National Guard," DDE.

9. Richard Russell telegram to Dwight Eisenhower, Sept. 26, 1957, Box 23, Folder "Little Rock, Arkansas (2)," DDE. Leroy Collins to Dwight Eisenhower, Sept. 26, 1957, Box 26, Folder "Little Rock, Arkansas," DDE. "Ike Insists on Broad Talk at Conference," *Arkansas Gazette,* Sept. 27, 1957, p. 1A.

10. The text of Faubus's speech can be found in the *Arkansas Gazette,* Sept. 27, 1957, under the title "'Grievous Error to Federalize Guard, Use U.S. Troops,'" p. 2A. The picture of the girls with bayonets at their backs was the product of some trick photography; for a suggestive if highly speculative sociologist's treatment of this incident, see Phoebe Godfrey, "Bayonets, Brainwashing, and Bathrooms: The Discourse of Race, Gender, and Sexuality in the Desegregation of Little Rock's Central High," *Arkansas Historical Quarterly* (Spring 2003), pp. 42–67. The man who received a blow to the forehead had ill-advisedly grabbed the soldier's rifle; Robert Troutt, "Spectator Bayoneted, Another Clubbed by Tough Paratroopers," *Arkansas Democrat,* Sept. 25, 1957, p. 1. The FBI heatedly refuted Faubus's claims of holding girls incommunicado; "J. Edgar Hoover Angered by Faubus Report of FBI; School Scene Is Peaceful," *Arkansas Gazette,* Sept. 28, 1957, p. 1A.

11. "Airborne Cheers for Central High Tigers," *Arkansas Gazette,* Sept. 28, 1957, p. 1A. 222 of the National Guard soldiers were high school students; 153 of them were college students; Coakley, *Operation Arkansas,* pp. 82, 92, 120, 131.

12. Coakley, *Operation Arkansas,* pp. 123, 136.

13. Ibid., pp. 101, 99. Beals, *Warriors Don't Cry,* p. 150. Senator John McClellan telegram to President Dwight D. Eisenhower, Sept. 30, 1957, Box 732, Folder "Little Rock, Arkansas—School Integration," DDE; Dwight D. Eisenhower telegram to Senator John McClellan, Oct. 1, 1957, Box 732, Folder "Little Rock, Arkansas—School Integration," DDE. Transcript of telephone conver-

sation between Clarence Laws, Gloster Current, and Henry Moon, Sept. 30, 1957, group III, series A, container 98, PON.

14. Elizabeth Huckaby, *Crisis at Central High: Little Rock, 1957–58* (Baton Rouge: Louisiana State University Press, 1980), p. 52. Transcript of telephone conversation between Daisy Bates, Clarence Laws, and Gloster Current, Oct. 2, 1957, 11:00 A.M., group III, series A, container 98, PON. Cecil Holland, "Faubus 'Standing Pat' on Integration Terms," *Washington Evening Star,* Oct. 2, 1957, SERS.

15. Transcript of telephone conversation between Daisy Bates, Clarence Laws, and Gloster Current, Oct. 2, 1957, 11:00 A.M. Huckaby, *Crisis at Central High,* p. 52. Before too much longer Eckford concluded there was no point in reporting harassment to the school authorities; Eckford interview with Jacoway, Aug. 14, 2003, p. 20.

16. "Governors Favor Troop Topic Only," *Atlanta Journal,* Oct. 1, 1957, SERS. "Faubus Accused of Double-Cross," *New York Times,* Oct. 3, 1957, Box 6, Folder "Integration—Little Rock, 1957 (2)," DDE. Jim Scott, "Gov. Griffin Drops From Ike Parley," *Nashville Banner,* Sept. 30, 1957, p. 1, SERS. "'Suggested' Statement Causes Row," *Arkansas Democrat,* Oct. 2, 1957, p. 1. "Faubus Wrote Own Conditions," *Nashville Tennessean,* Oct. 4, 1957, SERS; Brooks Hays Memo, Nov. 13, 1960, Box 45, LBH.

17. "Brownell Departure Laid to Clash with Adams on Little Rock Crisis," *Arkansas Democrat,* Oct. 31, 1957, p. 1; Jack Cleland, "Little Rock 'Mistake' Brings Brownell's Sudden Departure; Eisenhower Still Has Problem," *Arkansas Democrat,* Oct. 24, 1957, p. 1. "Little Rock Pact Hits Stalemate," *Christian Science Monitor,* Oct. 2, 1957, SERS.

18. "Ike, Governors Set on Little Rock Plan," *Charleston* (West Virginia) *Gazette,* Oct. 2, 1957, SERS. "Faubus 'Standing Pat' On Integration Terms," *Washington Evening Star,* Oct. 2, 1957, SERS; "Texts of Statements Issued by White House and Faubus," *St. Louis Post-Dispatch,* Oct. 2, 1957, SERS.

19. "Faubus Balks," *New York Herald Tribune,* Oct. 6, 1957, SERS. "Statement By the President," Oct. 1, 1957, Box 6, Folder "Integration—Little Rock, 1957 (2)," DDE. "Little Rock Pact Hits Stalemate."

20. "News Conference with James C. Hagerty," Oct. 2, 1957, Box 6, Folder "Integration—Little Rock, 1957 (2)," DDE.

21. Homer Bigart, "Faubus Insistent on Setting Policy," *New York Times,* Oct. 3, 1957. "McKeldin Accuses Faubus of Double-Cross, 'Infamy,'" *Arkansas Gazette,* Oct. 3, 1957, p. 1A; "Faubus Accused of Double-Cross," *New York Times,* Oct. 3, 1957, Box 6, Folder "Integration—Little Rock (2)," DDE; "What Faubus Did to Halt 'Armistice,'" *Charlotte Observer,* Oct. 3, 1957, SERS; Matilda Tuohey, "Governors' Top Envoy Confers with Faubus to Try for Agreement," *Arkansas Gazette,* Oct. 3, 1957, p. 1A; George Douthit, "Faubus Stands Firm; Says He Won't 'Bayonet Own People,'" *Arkansas Democrat,* Oct. 2, 1957, p. 1; Orval Faubus interview with John Luter, Aug. 18, 1971, p. 59, EAP. Failing to buy into one of the central tenets of federalism, Faubus believed that local law enforcement was his prerogative but that federal court orders should be enforced by federal authorities; Walter Lister Jr., "Faubus Stands Pat: Says Best Way to Keep Peace Is to Bar Negroes," *New York Herald-Tribune,* Oct. 2, 1957, SERS.

22. Transcript of telephone conversation between Daisy Bates, Clarence Laws, and Gloster Current, Oct. 2, 1957, 11:00 A.M.

23. Thurgood Marshall telegram to the President, White House, Oct. 1, 1957, Box 920, Folder "School—Arkansas, Initial," DDE.

24. "Official White House Transcript of President Eisenhower's Press and Radio Conference #122," Oct. 3, 1957, p. 6, Box 6, Folder "Integration—Little Rock (2)," DDE.

25. Transcript of telephone conversation between Daisy Bates, Clarence Laws, and Gloster Current, Oct. 2, 1957. Huckaby, *Crisis at Central High,* p. 54; Beals, *Warriors Don't Cry,* p. 167. Charles N. Quinn, "2 Negro Boys Chased and Kicked in School," *New York Herald Tribune,* Oct. 3, 1957, SERS.

26. Ted Poston, "Nine Kids Who Dared," *New York Post Daily Magazine,* Oct. 31, 1957, Clipping Scrapbooks, DGB. Jess W. Matthews, "Summary of Incidents: Central High Corridors Prior

to Home Room Bell," Oct. 2, 1957, Box 1, Folder 6, DGB. Huckaby, *Crisis at Central High,* p. 55. Charles N. Quinn, "2 Negro Boys Chased and Kicked in School," *New York Herald Tribune,* Oct. 3, 1957, SERS. "Inside Central High: Two of Negroes Reported Beaten," *Birmingham News,* Oct. 2, 1957, SERS.

27. Beals, *Warriors Don't Cry,* pp. 153–54.

28. Elizabeth Huckaby, untitled report on complaints of Melba Patillo and Minnijean Brown, Oct. 2, 1957, Box 1, Folder 6, DGB. Eckford interview with Jacoway, p. 6.

29. Huckaby, *Crisis at Central High,* pp. 56–57. Coakley, *Operation Arkansas,* p. 110.

30. Beals, *Warriors Don't Cry,* p. 160.

31. Transcript of telephone conversation between Daisy Bates, Clarence Laws, and Gloster Current, Oct. 2, 1957. Transcript of telephone conversation between Daisy Bates, Clarence Laws, and Gloster Current, Oct. 2, 1957, 3:30 P.M., group III, series A, container 98, PON.

32. Transcript of telephone conversation between Daisy Bates, Clarence Laws, and Gloster Current, Oct. 2, 1957, 3:30 P.M. Wayne Upton interview with John Luter, December, 1971, p. 40, EAP; William G. Cooper interview with John Luter, Dec. 28, 1970, pp. 23–24, EAP; Blossom, *It HAS Happened Here,* p. 158; Elizabeth Huckaby interview with T. Harri Baker, Oct. 25, 1972, p. 17, EAP.

33. Coakley, *Operation Arkansas,* pp. 109, 111; Bishop Brown called a former parishioner, Walter Robinson, an assistant secretary of state; Robinson passed the Bishop's message on to Brownell, who informed the president; News conference with James C. Hagerty, Oct. 1, 1957, Box 6, Folder "Integration—Little Rock, 1957," DDE; "Ike Writes Episcopal Bishop Here," *Arkansas Democrat,* Oct. 1, 1957, p. 1.

34. Coakley, *Operation Arkansas,* pp. 111, 117.

35. Ibid., pp. 112–14.

36. Transcript of telephone conversation between Daisy Bates, Clarence Laws, and Gloster Current, Oct. 2, 1957, 3:30 P.M. Bates, *The Long Shadow of Little Rock,* p. 129. Homer Bigart, "Faubus Insistent on Setting Policy," *New York Times,* Oct. 3, 1957. Earnest Green interview with John Pagan, Jan. 26, 1973, p. 11, Box 1, Folder 25, SAM. Transcript of telephone conversation between Daisy Bates, Clarence Laws, Gloster Current, and Henry Moon, Oct. 3, 1957, Box 5, Folder 2, DGB.

37. Green interview with Pagan, pp. 9–10. Eckford interview with Jacoway, p. 21. Wair interview with Jacoway, pp. 6–7. Elizabeth Jacoway, "Not Anger but Sorrow, Minnijean Brown Trickey Remembers the Little Rock Crisis," *Arkansas Historical Quarterly* (Winter 2005), p. 13. Terrence Roberts interview with Elizabeth Jacoway, Aug. 3, 2004, p. 10, EJC. Green interview with Pagan, p. 12.

38. Elizabeth Eckford interview with Elizabeth Jacoway, July 5, 2004, pp. 7–8, EJC.

39. Tilman C. Cothran and William M. Phillips, "Negro Leadership in a Crisis Situation," pp. 76, 28, included in Anti-Defamation League materials, RRP; a shortened version of this paper was published under the same title in *Phylon* (Summer, 1961), pp. 107–118. Harold R. Isaacs, "World Affairs and U.S. Race Relations: A Note On Little Rock," *Public Opinion Quarterly* (Fall 1958), p. 366. Kenneth Clark, "Some General Observations in the Negro Community of Little Rock, Arkansas," May 1958, included in Anti-Defamation League materials, RRP.

40. Transcript of telephone conversation between Daisy Bates, Clarence Laws, Gloster Current, and Henry Moon, Oct. 3, 1957. Lerone Bennett wrote, "In Little Rock almost everyone says Central High was integrated because Daisy Bates willed it"; Bennett, "First Lady of Little Rock," p. 17. Bates interview with Jacoway, p. 19.

CHAPTER ELEVEN — A CRISIS OF LEADERSHIP

1. Justice Robert L. Brown interview with Elizabeth Jacoway, Jan. 19, 2004, p. 6, EJC. "Religion in Action: Little Rock's Clergy Leads the Way," *Time,* Oct. 14, 1957, p. 30. Robert R. Brown, *Bigger Than Little Rock* (Greenwich, Conn.: Seabury Press, 1958), pp. 28–29.

2. Brown, *Bigger Than Little Rock,* pp. 4, 37–38, 67–72. For a full elaboration of this conflict and its manifestation in Little Rock, see Thomas F. Pettigrew and Ernest Q. Campbell, *Christians in Racial Crisis: A Study of the Little Rock Ministry* (Washington, D.C.: Public Affairs Press, 1959).

Wayne Upton was a member of the Executive Council of the Diocese of Arkansas; Transcript, Lemley hearing, June 3, 1958, p. 145, Box 5, Folder 7, VTB. William P. Rock, the head of the Arkansas Industrial Development Commission and an active Episcopal churchman, was Bishop Brown's source of information about Faubus's concerns.

3. Brown, *Bigger Than Little Rock,* p. 72, 74–81. The bishop began to receive threatening phone calls at home suggesting, for example, that space was being saved for him at the morgue. His wife kept a whistle by the telephone, and when these calls came through she routinely delivered a memorable blast into the caller's ear; Brown interview with Jacoway, p. 19, 37, 42.

4. Brown, *Bigger Than Little Rock,* pp. 19, 82–84.

5. Ibid., pp. 23, 26, 108, 129.

6. B. Finley Vinson interview with Elizabeth Jacoway, Dec. 21, 1977, p. 4, EJC. Henry Gemmill and Joseph Guilfoyle, "The Quiet Force in Arkansas," *Wall Street Journal,* Oct. 8, 1957, Box 83, LBH.

7. Cecil Holland, "Gov. Faubus Considers Calling Special Session," *Washington Evening Star,* Sep. 29, 1957, SERS; Brooks Hays, *A Southern Moderate Speaks* (Chapel Hill: University of North Carolina Press, 1959), p. 177. Elizabeth Jacoway, "Taken By Surprise," in Elizabeth Jacoway and David R. Colburn, eds., *Southern Businessmen and Desegregation* (Baton Rouge: Louisiana State University Press, 1982), pp. 24–25; A. Howard Stebbins III, interview with Elizabeth Jacoway, Dec. 16, 1977, pp. 15–16, EJC; Brown, *Bigger Than Little Rock,* p. 62; Robert E. Ford, "Moderate Forces to Organize," *Arkansas Democrat,* Oct. 1, 1957, p. 1.

8. Relman Morin, "In This Hurricane's Eye? Calm Settles on City," *Arkansas Democrat,* Oct. 7, 1957, p. 3. All of the members of the new City Council elected in November lived in the Fifth Ward, the "silk-stocking district." For insight into the nature of the relationship between Hays and Lowry see Hays, *A Southern Moderate Speaks,* pp. 164–65. For an engaging brief discussion of the Good Government Campaign, see Irving Spitzberg, *Racial Politics in Little Rock, 1954–1964* (New York: Garland Publishing, 1987), pp. 31–42.

9. "Resolution," *Arkansas Democrat,* Sept. 27, 1957, p. 2. Eldridge Thompson, "Faubus Will Win, Guthridge States," *Charleston News and Courier,* Nov. 18, 1957, Box 6, Folder 12, HSA. See also Relman Morin, "Little Rock Echoes Throughout the South," *Arkansas Gazette,* Nov. 17, 1957, p. 13A.

10. "Mothers Ask School Closing; Attendance Up," *Arkansas Gazette,* Sept. 28, 1957, p. 1A. "Won't Oppose McClellan, Faubus Says," *Arkansas Gazette,* Sept. 28, 1957, p. 1A.

11. Homer Bigart, "Governor May Call Solons; Door Ajar for Compromise," *New York Times,* Sept. 29, 1957. George Douthit, "New State Laws to Deal with CHS Considered," *Arkansas Democrat,* Sept. 28, 1957, p. 1. Bill Lewis, "Ike Says Mob Encouraged By Faubus; Governor Gets Plea of Mothers League; But No Plans Yet, He Says, to Call Session," *Arkansas Gazette,* Sept. 29, 1957, p. 1A.

12. See "On the Television Front: Dixiecrat Influence Seen by McMath," *Arkansas Gazette,* Sept. 30, 1957, p. 1A. Transcript, *Face the Nation,* p. 30, Box 9, Folder 3, HSA.

13. Gemmill and Guilfoyle, "The Quiet Force in Arkansas." Bicknell Eubanks, "LR Leader Typifies Moderates," *Christian Science Monitor,* Oct. 7, 1957, SERS.

14. Gemmill and Guilfoyle, "The Quiet Force in Arkansas."

15. R. B. Mayfield, "State Solons Cautious on Session Call," *Arkansas Democrat,* Sept. 29, 1957, p. 1. Ray Moseley and Matilda Tuohey, "Faubus Undecided on Special Session; Possibility 'Strong'; Civic Leaders Say Assembly Now 'Unwise,'" *Arkansas Gazette,* Oct. 1, 1957.

16. John D. Morris, "Capitol Expects Long Troop Guard Over Little Rock," *New York Times,* Oct. 6, 1957, p. 1. Holland, "Gov. Faubus Considers Calling Special Session."

17. "Business, Civic Leaders Urge Peaceful Compliance," *Arkansas Gazette,* Oct. 3, 1957, p. 1A. As a soon-to-be president of the Chamber board described the statement, "We praised motherhood and a few other things and did absolutely nothing"; E. Grainger Williams interview with John Luter, Dec. 29, 1970, p. 4, EAP.

18. "A Statement of Objectives and Rededication to Principles," Oct. 2, 1957, Box 1, Folder 2, RCB. Robert E. Ford, "Moderate Forces to Organize," *Arkansas Democrat,* Oct. 1, 1957, p. 1. Brown, *Bigger Than Little Rock,* p. 62. The idea of meeting on Columbus Day was Rabbi Sanders's; "85 Churches to Meet For Prayer," *Arkansas Democrat,* Oct. 10, 1957, p. 1. "Religion in Action:

Little Rock's Clergy Leads the Way."

19. Among those in attendance were Dr. Marion Boggs of Second Presbyterian Church, Reverend Dunbar Ogden of Central Presbyterian Church (who was also president of the Ministerial Alliance), Dr. Aubrey Walton of First Methodist Church, Rabbi Ira Sanders of Temple B'nai Israel, Congressman Brooks Hays, and Bishop Brown. Brown, *Bigger Than Little Rock,* p. 93; Pettigrew and Campbell, *Christians in Racial Crisis,* p. 26. The planners chose Columbus Day because it lent a national note to the services, and it also "served as a gesture to the co-sponsoring Roman Catholics."; Pettigrew and Campbell, *Christians in Racial Crisis,* p. 67. The idea of meeting on Columbus Day was Rabbi Sanders's; "85 Churches To Meet For Prayer," *Arkansas Democrat,* October 10, 1957, p. 1. "Religion in Action: Little Rock's Clergy Leads the Way," *Time,* October 14, 1957, p. 30.

20. "Ministers Urge All Arkansas to Join in Prayer for Solution," *Arkansas Gazette,* Oct. 4, 1957, p. 1A; this article suggests that the idea for the day of prayer originated with Brooks Hays. *Time* magazine reported that Bishop Brown sent out one hundred invitations to this planning meeting at the cathedral, but only forty ministers responded; "Religion in Action: Little Rock's Clergy Leads the Way." Brown explained in his memoir that black ministers were not invited to the meeting because "the mere presence of Negro clergy might at this preliminary stage increase the tensions and make impossible uninhibited discussion of the proposal . . . ," and also "the desegregation problem was in fact chiefly one for the white congregations to solve"; Brown, *Bigger Than Little Rock,* p. 94. Phyllis Dillaha, "Leaders of All Religious Faiths Unite in Effort to Solve Integration Crisis; Quiet Returns to Central High Front," *Arkansas Democrat,* Oct. 4, 1957, p. 1. Transcripts of many of the ministers' statements can be found in Box 2, Folder 7, RRB. Pettigrew and Campbell, *Christians in Racial Crisis,* pp. 26–27; "85 Churches to Meet for Prayer," *Arkansas Democrat,* Oct. 10, 1957, p. 1; "City Prays for Guidance in Crisis," *Arkansas Democrat,* Oct. 12, 1957, p. 1.

21. "Nation to Join City in Prayer for Integration Solution; Governor to 'Wait and See,'" p. 1.

22. Gunnar Myrdal, *An American Dilemma* (New York: Harper & Row, 1944). Pettigrew and Campbell, *Christians in Racial Crisis,* p. 60.

23. Elizabeth Huckaby, *Crisis at Central High:, Little Rock, 1957–58* (Baton Rouge: Louisiana State University Press, 1980), pp. 51–52. Relman Morin, "Monday, Sept. 23, 1957: Dark Day in Crisis," *Arkansas Democrat,* Oct. 10, 1957, p. 8.

24. "Prayer Meet on Crisis Set," *Arkansas Democrat,* Oct. 8, 1957, p. 1. "A Call To Prayer at the Central Baptist Church," *Arkansas Democrat,* Oct. 10, 1957, p. 10.

25. Bobbie Forster, "5,000 Pray Over Crisis," *Arkansas Democrat,* Oct. 13, 1957, p. 1. "85 Churches To Meet For Prayer," p. 1. A visitor to Little Rock reported "attendance at the Negro churches was very low"; Claud D. Nelson, "Confidential: Notes on a Visit to Arkansas, October 10–13, 1957," Box 9, Folder 4, HSA. Pettigrew and Campbell, *Christians in Racial Crisis,* p. 34. An interesting participant at First United Methodist church was Jimmy Karam, who sat in the back pew; Pettigrew and Campbell, *Christians in Racial Crisis,* p. 32.

26. "Can a Christian Be a Segregationist?" *Arkansas Democrat,* Oct. 12, 1957, p. 2. Historian David Chappell, in his suggestive study of the role of religion in the civil rights movement, downplayed the influence of "obscure preachers" such as Wesley Pruden and their "fringe churches." In Little Rock, the non-mainstream ministers' prominence and visibility throughout the crisis challenge this interpretation; David L. Chappell, *A Stone of Hope: Prophetic Religion and the Death of Jim Crow* (Chapel Hill: University of North Carolina Press, 2004), esp. p. 116.

27. Pettigrew and Campbell, *Christians in Racial Crisis,* pp. 36–37.

28. Pettigrew and Campbell, *Christians in Racial Crisis,* p. 37. After a flurry of endorsements of the businessmen's wordy "Statement of Objectives and Rededication to Principles," Little Rock's civic leaders largely fell silent. Homer Bigart, "Faubus Sees Peace Only if Negroes Quit," *New York Times,* Oct. 10, 1957, p. 1. Pettigrew and Campbell, *Christians in Racial Crisis,* p. 79.

29. Karr Shannon, *Supreme Court Decision is Unconstitutional* (Little Rock: Democrat Printing & Lithographing Co., 1958); George Douthit, "Governor Criticizes Conduct of Troops in School; Looks for Long Stay by Regulars," *Arkansas Democrat,* Oct. 7, 1957, p. 1. Karr Shannon's

editorials in the *Arkansas Democrat* undermined Harry Ashmore's arguments in the *Arkansas Gazette* that the *Brown* decision was the law of the land; see, for example, Transcript, Lemley hearing, June 5, 1958, p. 475, Box 5, Folder 7, VTB.

30. Spitzberg, *Racial Politics in Little Rock*, pp. 41–42; rough draft of untitled, undated unpublished study conducted for the Anti-Defamation League, section marked "The Power Structure," RRP. Harry Ashmore interview with Elizabeth Jacoway, Nov. 17, 1976, p. 19, EJC.

31. "Christian Love Answer in Crisis, Hays Says," *Arkansas Democrat*, Oct. 9, 1957, p. 2. "Fulbright Requests FBI Report," *Arkansas Democrat*, Oct. 22, 1957, p. 2. Fulbright told his friend Edwin Dunaway he thought it was more important for the nation "that he remain in the Senate than that he involve himself in the Little Rock controversy"; Spitzberg, *Racial Politics in Little Rock*, p. 75. William K. Rutherford interview with Louise Patterson, January 1987, as quoted in William K. Rutherford, "*Arkansas Gazette* Editor J. N. Heiskell: Heart and Mind" (master's thesis, University of Arkansas at Little Rock, 1987), p. 72. Apparently eastern Arkansas bankers and depositors exerted a great deal of pressure on Little Rock bankers to maintain segregation; Henry Woods interview with T. Harri Baker, Dec. 8, 1972, p. 41, EAP.

32. Robert W. Coakley, *Operation Arkansas* (Office of the Chief of Military History Monograph No. 158M, 1967), pp. 138–39, 128, 159, 143. I. Jack Martin, "Memorandum for the Record," Oct. 15, 1957, Box 921, Folder—Central Files, General File, DDE; "Governor Criticizes Conduct of Troops in School; Looks For Long Stay by Regulars," *Arkansas Democrat*, Oct. 7, 1957, p. 1. George Douthit, "Faubus Says Crisis Hinges on Complete Withdrawal of Negroes from Central High," *Arkansas Democrat*, Oct. 9, 1957, p. 1. "Guardsmen All Taking Physicals," *Arkansas Democrat*, Oct. 8, 1957, p. 1. George Douthit, "Faubus Awaits New Contact by Governors," *Arkansas Democrat*, Oct. 13, 1957, p. 1.

33. George Douthit, "Faubus Won't Surrender 'Powers of My Office,'" *Arkansas Democrat*, Oct. 3, 1957, p. 1. "Nation to Join City in Prayer for Integration Solution; Governor to 'Wait and See,'" *Arkansas Democrat*, Oct. 6, 1957, p. 1.

34. John Thomas Elliff, "The United States Department of Justice and Individual Rights, 1937–1962" (Ph.D. diss., Harvard University, 1967), p. 486 draws this conclusion.

35. Douthit, "Faubus Says Crisis Hinges on Complete Withdrawal of Negroes from Central High." Bigart, "Faubus Sees Peace Only if Negroes Quit."

36. George Douthit, "Faubus Says He Still Plans Special Session," *Arkansas Democrat*, Oct. 14, 1957, p. 1. While neither Faubus nor committee chairman Walter Guy would reveal the names of the participants, a report of the subcommittee's conference with Faubus lists five of the six: Clyde Lowry, Warren Bray, Sam Strauss, Raymond Rebsamen, and chairman Walter Guy; "Report of Subcommittee of Conference with Governor Faubus," (nd), Box 2, Folder 5, RRB. Richard Butler later admitted that he was the sixth member, but he may have been unnamed on the formal document in an effort to preserve his anonymity since he was an attorney for the School Board; Richard C. Butler interview with Elizabeth Jacoway, Dec. 15, 1977, EJC. Four of the six members of the Guy Committee, Guy, Lowry, Rebsamen, and Strauss were identified in an Anti-Defamation League report in 1957 as being among the twelve central members of "the power elite" in Little Rock; rough draft of untitled, undated unpublished study conducted for the Anti-Defamation League, section marked "The Power Structure," RRP. Ray Moseley, "Faubus Talks Over School Situation With Businessmen; 101st Division to Cut Back Force Today," *Arkansas Gazette*, Oct. 16, 1957, p. 1A; Homer Bigart, "Troop Cut Fails to Sway Faubus," *New York Times*, Oct. 16, 1957, p. 1. One member of the committee, Sam Strauss, recalled his surprise at finding that Faubus was not "a segregationist as he had been portrayed"; Sam Strauss interview with Elizabeth Jacoway, Dec. 22, 1977, EJC.

37. "Report of Sub-committee of Conference with Governor Faubus." Walter Guy later told the press that the Little Rock School Board had refused to seek a delay or a "cooling-off period" when his committee proposed it in October because Judge Davies was still on the federal bench in Little Rock, and he "possibly doesn't understand the philosophy of the South"; "Guy Describes Arbitral Role in CHS Crisis," *Arkansas Gazette*, March 18, 1958, p. 1A. The arguments spelled out in the Guy Committee report are the very arguments that one of that committee's members,

Richard Butler, used when asking the U.S. Supreme Court for a delay, or a "cooling-off-period" the following summer.

38. George Douthit, "'We're Still Occupied' Says Faubus After Army Orders Cut in Troops, Guard at Central," *Arkansas Democrat,* Oct. 15, 1957, p. 1. The Army dismissed 8,500 National Guardsmen from active duty but left 1,800 activated along with 1,000 regular Army soldiers. There were 2,000 students at Central High School.

39. "Guard Dissent Seen in Crisis," *Arkansas Democrat,* Oct. 16, 1957, p. 1.

40. "Civic Group Calls Off Session," *Arkansas Democrat,* Oct. 17, 1957, p. 1. Homer Bigart, "Troop Cut Fails to Sway Faubus," *New York Times,* Oct. 16, 1957, p. 1.

41. George Douthit, "Backstage at the Capitol: Governor Can't Control Integration Resistance," *Arkansas Democrat,* Oct. 20, 1957, p. 9C.

42. George E. Sokolsky, "The Constitutional Crisis with Arkansas Background," *Arkansas Democrat,* Oct. 14, 1957, p. 10C.

43. Roy Reed, *Faubus: The Life and Times of an American Prodigal* (Fayetteville: University of Arkansas Press, 1987).

44. Ron Burnham, "Mayor Calls for NAACP, 'Citizens' Data," *Arkansas Democrat,* Oct. 15, 1957, p. 1.

45. Untitled speech, (nd), Box 301, Folder 13, JDJ; Johnson drove over to Ruleville, Mississippi, to secure Senator Eastland's assistance in writing his speech, and he listened as Eastland and numerous confederates, including Senator Richard Russell, conferred in drafting it by telephone; untitled, undated handwritten description of Johnson's activities beginning: "In 1955 and 1956 I traveled throughout the South speaking day and night on States Rights and Constitutional Government," Box 51, Folder 13, JJJ.

46. Johnson wrote a letter to Senator Eastland reporting on a conversation he had recently had with one of Faubus's advisers, former Arkansas Governor Homer Adkins. Johnson said he had told Adkins, "the Governor's political future depended upon the vote of the segregationists and that if he didn't call a Special Session, *I would run against him for the sole purpose of splitting that vote, thereby defeating both of us.* . . . If the speech gets results, it will be worth everything for the cause for which we are fighting. If not, I can literally crucify Faubus in the next election" (italics added); Jim Johnson to Senator James O. Eastland, Oct. 15, 1957, Box 30, Folder 13, JJJ.

47. Faubus told biographer Roy Reed that the federal government's treatment of him made him become more conservative; Orval E. Faubus interview with Roy Reed, July 24, 1992, RRP. Relman Morin, "Orval E. Faubus: Gains Spot in History," *Arkansas Democrat,* Oct. 9, 1957, p. 5. "Faubus Okays Guard Return; Requests Probe," *Arkansas Gazette,* Oct. 26, 1957, p. 1A.

48. Jim Johnson interview with Elizabeth Jacoway, June 26, 2002, pp. 239–53, EJC.

49. Alta Haskins Faubus interview with Elizabeth Jacoway, April 9, 1996, p. 7, EJC. Orval Faubus wrote to his sister on October 16, 1957: "So don't let this bother you in any way. It is one of the controversies of this age that had to come sooner or later. I didn't ask to be in the middle of it, and I didn't want it in Little Rock, but we are all to some extent children of fortune and circumstance. It fell my lot to bear this part in controversy. I believe fully that I am right, and without any malice toward anyone. I, of course, shall do my duty according to the right as God gives me to see the right." Orval E. Faubus to Mrs. Connie Loustalot, October 16, 1957, EJC; the author is grateful to Griffin Smith, jr., for bringing this letter to her attention.

50. "To All 21 Candidates!," *Arkansas Democrat,* Oct. 28, 1957, p. 2.

51. "States Rights Rally!," *Arkansas Democrat,* Oct. 29, 1957, p. 4. "Guthridge Hits GGC Candidates," *Arkansas Democrat,* Oct. 31, 1957, p. 5.

52. "City to Vote Tuesday on Board of Directors," *Arkansas Gazette,* Nov. 3, 1957, p. 1A. "GGC Group Admits Issue of Race Ruled," *Arkansas Gazette,* Nov. 6, 1957, p. 1B.

53. "Little Rock Voters Choose Directors to Run City Today," *Arkansas Gazette,* Nov. 5, 1957, p. 1B. "Strange Alliance Gave GGC Candidates Victory," *Arkansas Gazette,* Nov. 10, 1957, p. 7A. Guthridge also charged that the Army's Counter Intelligence Corps had tapped his telephone, even though wiretapping was a federal offense; Norman Spell, "Little Rock Attorney Warns

Against Negro Bloc Voting" *Charleston News and Courier,* Nov. 21, 1957, HSA.; Jim Johnson charged the same thing in his televised speech on October 15; Untitled Speech, (nd), Box 301, Folder 13, JDJ.

54. Liberal activist and author Lillian Smith spoke in Little Rock on Oct. 28, 1957, a guest of the Arkansas Council on Human Relations. Colbert Cartwright to "Dad," Oct. 30, 1957, microfilm, vol. 4, CCP.

55. Frank Lyon interview with Elizabeth Jacoway, Dec. 13, 1977, pp. 9–10, EJC.

56. Ibid.

57. Pettigrew and Campbell, *Christians in Racial Crisis,* p. 80.

CHAPTER TWELVE — TORMENTS BEHIND CLOSED DOORS

1. Minnijean Brown Trickey interview with Elizabeth Jacoway, Sept. 15, 2003, pp. 16, 18, 41, EJC. Portions of this interview were published as Elizabeth Jacoway, "Not Anger but Sorrow: Minnijean Brown Trickey Remembers the Little Rock Crisis," *Arkansas Historical Quarterly* (Spring 2005), pp. 1–26. Minnijean Brown, "What They Did to Me in Little Rock," *Look,* June 24, 1958, p. 30. Melba Patillo Beals, *Warriors Don't Cry: A Searing Memoir of the Battle to Integrate Little Rock's Central High* (New York: Simon & Schuster, 1994), p. 193.

2. Elizabeth Huckaby, *Crisis at Central High: Little Rock, 1957–58* (Baton Rouge: Louisiana State University Press, 1980), pp. 114, 124, 68, 70. J. O. Powell, *Central High School Inside Out: (A Study in Disintegration),* Chapter 7: "Disintegration Well Underway," (np), Box 1, File 4, VJP; Huckaby, *Crisis at Central High,* p. 67; "Girl Loses Bid for Warrant; White Boy Tells of Threats," *Arkansas Gazette,* Jan. 31, 1958, p. 1B; Brown, "What They Did to Me in Little Rock," p. 33. Trickey interview with Jacoway, p. 35.

3. Short for hoodlum, "hood" was the term in current usage at Little Rock Central High School. Virgil T. Blossom, *It HAS Happened Here* (New York: Harper & Bro., 1959), p. 134. Even Blossom admitted that the attacks became more serious in the late fall and winter; Blossom, *It HAS Happened Here,* p. 138.

4. Blossom, *It HAS Happened Here,* p. 160. Apparently about this time, pacifist James Lawson came to Little Rock to train the nine black students in the principles of nonviolence; Elizabeth Eckford interview with Elizabeth Jacoway, July 5, 2004, p. 23, EJC. Beals, *Warriors Don't Cry,* pp. 162–75, 188–89. Huckaby, *Crisis at Central High,* pp. 85, 129; Daisy Gatson Bates, *The Long Shadow of Little Rock* (New York: David McKay & Co., 1962), p. 125.

5. Huckaby, *Crisis at Central High,* pp. 74–75. Trickey interview with Jacoway, pp. 54–56. Jacoway, "Not Anger but Sorrow," p. 17.

6. Huckaby, *Crisis at Central High,* p. 75. Ernest Green also reported that Matthews instructed him to stop having lunch with the white girl; Ernest Green interview with Elizabeth Jacoway April 21, 2000 p. 7, EJC.

7. Transcript of conversation between Daisy Bates and Gloster Current, Nov. 13, 1957, group III, series A, container 98, PON; "White Student Suspended After Striking Negro," *Arkansas Gazette,* Nov. 15, 1957, p. 1B; Huckaby, *Crisis at Central High,* p. 79; Robert W. Coakley, *Operation Arkansas* (Office of the Chief of Military History Monograph No. 158M, 1967), p. 191; Director's Brief, "Chronology," Vol. 1, File 3, p. B-30-31, FBI Report. Powell, *Central High School Inside Out,* Chapter 7: "Disintegration Well Underway"; Daisy Bates to Roy Wilkins, Dec. 17, 1957, group III, series A, container 98, PON; Clarence Laws Statement to NAACP, Nov. 14, 1957, group III, series A, container 98, PON. Bates, *The Long Shadow of Little Rock,* p. 126. Daisy Gatson Bates interview with Elizabeth Jacoway, Oct. 11, 1976, p. 21, SOHP. Blossom, *It HAS Happened Here,* p. 160.

8. Blossom, *It HAS Happened Here,* p. 160. Transcript, Bates and Current, Nov. 13, 1957.

9. Laws Statement to NAACP, Nov. 14, 1957, PON.

10. Bates, *The Long Shadow of Little Rock,* pp. 126–27; William G. Cooper interview with John Luter, Dec. 28, 1970, p. 21, EAP.

11. Laws Statement to NAACP, Nov. 14, 1957.

12. Coakley, *Operation Arkansas,* p. 189. Tilman C. Cothran and William M. Phillips, "Negro Leadership in a Crisis Situation," p. 46, RRP. Pettigrew and Campbell, *Christians in Racial Crisis,* p. 55.

13. Bates to Wilkins, Dec. 17, 1957, PON. Matthews had initially given permission for Minnijean to sing in the Christmas program, after she had tried out and made the cut, and her mother had started making her a white dress; Matthews changed his mind in response to white criticism; Brown, "What They Did to Me in Little Rock," p. 34; "Why No News From CHS," Nov. 24, 1957, Box 2, Folder 12, RRB. Ralph Brodie interview with Elizabeth Jacoway, Jan. 20, 2004, p. 15, EJC.; Frank Plegge to Elizabeth Jacoway, Dec. 24, 2003, EJC.

14. Elizabeth Huckaby described Powell as being very "volatile" and "excitable"; Elizabeth Huckaby interview with T. Harri Baker, Oct. 25, 1972, p. 47, EAP. Powell, *Central High School Inside Out,* Chapter 3: "Military Minds at Work." Student recollections of Jess Matthews fifty years later included descriptions of "a giant of a man, with a smile and gentle ways," and "a soft-spoken gentleman"; Frank Plegge to Elizabeth Jacoway, Dec. 24, 2003, EJC. The author is grateful to Frank Plegge for soliciting these reminiscences.

15. Powell, *Central High School Inside Out,* Chapter 7: "Disintegration Well Underway." Student Council President Ralph Brodie never heard Matthews use this kind of disrespectful language; Ralph Brodie to Elizabeth Jacoway, April 29. 2006, EJC.

16. The NAACP's list of offenders included only thirty; "Incidents at Central High School Reported and Known to School Officials," (nd), Box 1, Folder 6, DGB; Powell, *Central High School Inside Out,* Chapter 7: "Disintegration Well Underway." One former student recalled that Jess Matthews "was insulated normally from handing out discipline by having a vice-principal to do the dirty work. . . ."; Plegge to Jacoway.

17. Huckaby, *Crisis at Central High,* p. 86, Blossom, *It HAS Happened Here,* pp. 139–48.

18. The *Arkansas Gazette* refused to print these advertisements. For an example of one such ad, see Blossom, *It HAS Happened Here,* pp. 143–44. Blossom, *It HAS Happened Here,* pp. 140, 145.

19. Colbert S. Cartwright, "Failure in Little Rock," *Progressive,* June 1958, microfilm—vol. 5, CCP. Brooks Hays interview with John Luter, June 27–28, July 27, 1970, p. 54, EAP.

20. Relman Morin, "Faubus Sees Little Chance of Settlement," *Richmond Times-Dispatch,* Nov. 18, 1957, SERS.

21. Bates interview with Jacoway, pp. 30–31; Ozell Sutton interview with Roy Reed, June 22, 1992, p. 11, RRP.

22. Brooks Hays, *A Southern Moderate Speaks* (Chapel Hill: University of North Carolina Press, 1959), p. 187. Roy Reed, "Hays Hopeful Southern Bloc Can Stop Bills," *Arkansas Gazette,* Nov. 15, 1957, p. 1B; Gene Foreman, "Hays Proposes 'Breather' for South on Race Problem," *Arkansas Gazette,* Nov. 21, 1957, p. 1A.

23. "Removal of 101st Troops Is Official; Faubus Says Action 'Unfair.'" *Arkansas Gazette,* Nov. 20, 1957, p. 1A.

24. Huckaby, *Crisis at Central High,* p. 71. "Removal of 101st Troops Is Official."

25. Coakley, *Operation Arkansas,* pp. 195, 192.

26. Director's Brief, "Chronology," Vol. 1, Folder 3, p. B-28, Box 1, Folder 2, FBI Report. Director's Brief, Vol. 1, File 2, pp. A-31, 32, Box 1, Folder 2, FBI Report.

27. "U.S. Officials Drop Plans to Prosecute Agitators at School," *Arkansas Gazette,* Nov. 21, 1957, p. 1A. Relman Morin, "Both Sides Remain Adamant in Central High Stalemate," *Arkansas Gazette,* Nov. 24, 1957, p. 4A; "Federal Aide Will Assist School Cases," *Arkansas Gazette,* Aug. 12, 1959, p. 1A.

28. "City Manager Post Rejected by Top Choice," *Arkansas Gazette,* Dec. 12, 1957, p. 1A. "Six Are Cleared of School Charges," *Arkansas Gazette,* Nov. 21, 1957, p. 7A. Ernest Valachovic, "Three Accused in CHS Strife Get Off Lightly," *Arkansas Gazette,* Nov. 27, 1957, p. 1A; "September 23 Rioting Trials End with Two More Guilty; Robinson Suspends Fines," *Arkansas Gazette,* Nov. 28, 1957, p. 1B.

29. Nat Griswold wrote to SRC Director Harold Fleming on Nov. 29, 1957: "We have [a] reli-

able report that the school administrators with some built-up strong support expect to get back into court asking for suspension of the plan. . . ."; Nat Griswold to Harold Fleming, Nov. 29, 1957, Box 80, SRC. Richard C. Butler interview with Elizabeth Jacoway, Dec. 15, 1977, EJC.

30. Transcript of Bates and Current, Nov. 13, 1957. Griswold to Fleming, Nov. 29, 1957, SRC. "Bennett Law Test Urged by Harper," *Arkansas Gazette,* Feb. 5, 1957, p. 1A. Daisy Bates to Roy Wilkins, Dec. 17, 1957, group III, series A, container 98, PON.

31. Beals, *Warriors Don't Cry,* p. 191.

32. "An Editorial: Is Revolution the Answer?" *Arkansas Gazette,* Dec. 13, 1957, p. 1A. Harry Ashmore, Foreword to Elizabeth Huckaby, *Crisis at Central High,* p. xiii. Hugh B. Patterson interview with John Luter, Aug. 12, 1970, p. 38, EAP.

33. Beals, *Warriors Don't Cry,* p. 204. Director's Brief, "Chronology," pp. B-35, B-40. Harry Ashmore believed that Rogers's failure to press charges against the troublemakers and his silence about events in Little Rock stemmed from a "deal" the Justice Department had cut with powerful southern senators in return for their cooperation in approving Rogers's nomination; Harry Ashmore, "The Easy Chair: The Untold Story Behind Little Rock," *Harper's Magazine,* June 1958, pp. 16–17. Historian J. W. Peltason agreed with Ashmore; see J. W. Peltason, *58 Lonely Men: Southern Federal Judges and School Desegregation* (New York: Harcourt, Brace & World, 1961), p. 52.

34. Huckaby, *Crisis at Central High,* pp. 84–87. Beals, *Warriors Don't Cry,* p. 193.

35. Beals, *Warriors Don't Cry,* pp. 208–9. Thelma Mothershed Wair interview with Elizabeth Jacoway, Aug. 15, 2003, p. 6, EJC. Gloria Ray told a college representative she had "cried so much that year that she had never been able to cry since"; Huckaby interview with Baker, p. 74, EAP. Dunbar H. Ogden, "My Father's Little Rock," unpublished manuscript, EJC.

36. Beals, *Warriors Don't Cry,* p. 215. Wair interview with Jacoway, p. 22. A former Little Rock black resident who was a friend and contemporary of the Nine wrote in her dissertation on Little Rock, "Retrospectively, I can practically smell the African American community's fear of reprisal, fear of befriending, fear of supporting, fear of being there with the Nine and their families, fear of standing up"; D. LaRouth S. Perry, "The 1957 Desegregation Crisis of Little Rock, Arkansas: A Meeting of Histories" (Ph.D. diss., Bowling Green State University, 1998), p. 10. Nat R. Griswold, "The Second Reconstruction in Little Rock," Book One, Chapter 1, p. 22, unpublished manuscript, Box 11, Folder 8, SAM. Ernest Green did not have the experience of being rejected by old friends; Ernest Green interview with Elizabeth Jacoway, April 21, 2006, p. 6, EJC.

37. Huckaby, *Crisis at Central High,* pp. 91–93.

38. Ibid., pp. 93–94. Bob Troutt, "Questioning of Students Deplored; Mothers' Official Charges Mrs. Bates in on Grilling," *Arkansas Democrat,* Dec. 12, 1957, p. 1; "Step Up in Rumors, Incidents, Complaints Noted at School," *Arkansas Gazette,* Dec. 14, 1957, p. 2A. Blossom, *It HAS Happened Here,* pp. 163–64.

39. Director's Brief, "Chronology," p. B-39. Coakley, *Operation Arkansas,* p. 209.

40. Beals, *Warriors Don't Cry,* pp. 205, 218. Wair interview with Jacoway, p. 15. Elizabeth Huckaby report on Minnijean Brown, Dec. 12, 1957, Box 1, Folder 6, DGB; see also Huckaby, *Crisis at Central High,* pp. 95–98. Minnijean Brown Trickey recalled years later that the energy required to maintain her equilibrium was staggering. "Most of the time I was wanting to hold myself together," she remembered, "because the fear I had was that I would just explode and my body would just splatter on the walls of Central and on that marble floor. . . . So my energy was not really about responding to them. . . . We didn't have the energy to respond to them; we were busy holding ourselves together intact and not just go screaming out the door"; Trickey interview with Jacoway, pp. 71–72.

41. Clarence Laws to Roy Wilkins, Dec. 18, 1957, Box 1, Folder 6, DGB. "Minnijean Brown VS the White Conspiracy of CHS," Dec. 17, 1957, Box 1, Folder 6, DGB; Beals, *Warriors Don't Cry,* pp. 218–19.

42. "Minnijean Brown VS the White Conspiracy of CHS"; Trickey interview with Jacoway, p. 74. Beals, *Warriors Don't Cry,* pp. 219–20.

43. "Minnijean Brown VS the White Conspiracy of CHS." Laws to Wilkins, Dec. 18, 1957,

DGB. Untitled report, Dec. 17, 1957, Box 1, Folder 6, DGB.

44. Brodie interview with Jacoway, p. 2. Brodie reported that in numerous subsequent conversations with former white students, very few recalled observing harassment of the Nine; Ralph Brodie to Elizabeth Jacoway, April 12, 2006, Brown, *Bigger Than Little Rock*, p. 126.

45. "U.S. Appeals Court Delays Integration in Dallas Schools," *Arkansas Gazette*, Dec. 28, 1957, p. 1A. "School Board Orders Study of Dallas Case," *Arkansas Gazette*, Jan. 1, 1958, p. 1A.

46. "Arkansas Council on Human Relations Program Report, Second Quarter, 1957–1958." Coakley, *Operation Arkansas*, p. 218.

47. Powell, *Central High School Inside Out*, Chapter 6, (np); Beals, *Warriors Don't Cry*, p. 232.

48. Gertrude Samuels, "Little Rock: More Tension Than Ever," *New York Times Sunday Magazine*, March 23, 1958, p. 23. Elizabeth Huckaby, "Re: Elizabeth Eckford," Jan. 10, 1958, Box 1, Folder 6, DGB; J. O. Powell, "Re: Darlene Holloway," Jan. 10, 1958, Box 1, Folder 6, DGB; "School Officials to Go, Segregationist Vows," *Arkansas Gazette*, Jan. 21, 1958, p. 5A. Elizabeth Huckaby, untitled report, Jan. 9, 1958, Box 1, Folder 6, DGB. Elizabeth Huckaby, "Re: Melba Patillo," Jan. 9, 1958, Box 1, Folder 6, DGB.

49. Huckaby, *Crisis at Central High*, p. 123; "Incidents at Central High School Reported and Known to School Officials," (nd), Box 1, Folder 6, DGB. Ted Poston, "The 9 Who Dared: Little Rock, Four Months After," *New York Post*, Jan. 27, 1958, Box 1, Folder 6, DGB.

50. Huckaby, *Crisis at Central High*, pp. 113–16; Powell, *Central High School Inside Out*, Chapter 5. Brown, "What They Did to Me in Little Rock," p. 36. J. O. Powell, "Re: Minnijean Brown," Jan. 16, 1958, Box 1, Folder 6, DGB. "Incidents at Central High School Reported and Known to School Officials," (nd), Box 1, Folder 6, DGB. Elizabeth Huckaby, "Re: Minnijean Brown."

51. "Board Gives View on Pupil Discipline," *Arkansas Gazette*, Jan. 19, 1958, p. 1A. Ray Moseley, "Dynamite Found at CHS; Blossom Sees Campaign to Try to Close School," *Arkansas Gazette*, Jan. 21, 1958, p. 1A. "CHS Plagued by More Bomb Scare Attempts," *Arkansas Gazette*, Jan. 24, 1958, p. 1B.

52. "Arkansas Council on Human Relations Program Report, Second Quarter, 1957–1958." Powell, *Central High School Inside Out*, Chapter 9: "Chaos and Turmoil Censored."

53. Director's Brief, "Chronology," p. B-48. Blossom, *It HAS Happened Here*, pp. 154, 171. O. W. Romine died of a heart attack the next year, at the age of fifty-four; John Romine to Elizabeth Jacoway, August 15, 2002, EJC. The Little Rock School Board recognized his sacrifices by dedicating the O. W. Romine Elementary School in May 1959. Powell, *Central High School Inside Out*, Chapter 4: "Buffoonery, Bombs and Vandals." For an exhausting description of these locker searches, see Transcript, Lemley Hearing, June 3, 1958, p. 109, Box 5, Folder 7, VTB.

54. J. O. Powell, "Re: Minnijean Brown and James Cole," Jan. 27, 1958, Box 1, Folder 6, DGB.

55. Coakley, *Operation Arkansas*, p. 235. Transcript of conversation between Clarence Laws and Gloster Current, Jan. 31, 1958, group III, series A, container 98, PON.

56. Director's Brief, "Chronology," p. B-49. "Negro Girl Kicked by White Boy, Witness Reports," *Arkansas Gazette*, Jan. 30, 1958, p. 6B. "Girl Loses Bid for Warrant; White Boy Tells of Threats," *Arkansas Gazette*, Jan. 31, 1958, p. 1B. Coakley, *Operation Arkansas*, p. 228. Powell, *Central High School Inside Out*, Chapter 7: "Disintegration Well Underway." Huckaby, *Crisis at Central High*, p. 67.

57. Trickey interview with Jacoway, p. 59.

58. "Girl Loses Bid for Warrant." Coakley, *Operation Arkansas*, p. 228; Trickey interview with Jacoway, p. 70.

59. Beals, *Warriors Don't Cry*, pp. 235–236.

60. Coakley, *Operation Arkansas*, p. 237. Stan Opotowsky, "Little Rock Today; V—The Ones Who Want to Get Along," *New York Post*, April 12, 1958, Box 1, Folder 6, DGB. Director's Brief, "Chronology," p. B-51. Brown, "What They Did to Me in Little Rock," p. 36. Huckaby, *Crisis at Central High*, p. 141. A report in Attorney General Roger's files reveals that he was aware that segregationists outside the school were directing the attacks on the black children; "Little Rock, Arkansas, School Desegregation: Fall Semester 1959," Box 54, Schools, 2, WPR. School Board

member William G. Cooper told an interviewer his board believed Amis Guthridge had taken the lead in encouraging white students to cause trouble inside Central High School; Cooper interview with Luter, p. 23.

61. Director's Brief, "Chronology," p. B-51. Huckaby, *Crisis at Central High,* pp. 145–51; "Bomb Threats, Incidents Stir Central High," *Arkansas Gazette,* Feb. 7, 1958, p. 1A. Powell, *Central High School Inside Out,* Chapter 5.

62. Huckaby, *Crisis at Central High,* p. 145. "Suspension Notice" for Minnijean Brown, Feb. 6, 1958, group III, series A, container 98, PON. Trickey interview with Jacoway, pp. 69–70.

63. Huckaby, *Crisis at Central High,* pp. 146, 148.

64. Ibid., p. 148. "The Ordeal of Minnijean Brown," Feb. 19, 1958, Box 1, Folder 6, DGB; Director's Brief, "Chronology," p. B-52. "Suspension Notice" for Minnijean Brown.

65. "Negro Girl Blames 'White Trash' Outburst for Suspension from CHS," *Arkansas Gazette,* Feb. 14, 1958, p. 2A. Trickey interview with Jacoway, p. 40.

66. "Text of School Board Statement," *Arkansas Gazette,* Feb. 21, 1958, p. 1A. School Board member Harold Engstrom later admitted his group knew the nine black children were in danger inside Central High School; Harold Engstrom interview with John Luter, Dec. 29, 1970, pp. 23–24, EAP.

67. Director's Brief, "Chronology," p. B-54. Carpenter wrote to Harry Ashmore in January 1958 that she had called the Justice Department to complain about the incidents in Little Rock and see if the department shouldn't do something about them; she reported that a functionary checked with Wilson White and then told her, ". . . White felt they could make no such statement in view of the Attorney General's attitude that Little Rock should be forgotten"; Liz (Carpenter) to Harry Ashmore, (nd), Box 1, Folder 7, HSA.

68. Current to Wilkins, Feb. 6, 1958, group III, series A, container 98, PON. Transcript of telephone conversation between Gloster Current, Clarence Laws, Christopher Mercer, and Daisy Bates, Feb. 13, 1958. Huckaby, *Crisis at Central High,* p. 162. Mrs. Huckaby inaccurately dates this meeting as February 16, but it was reported in an NAACP telephone conversation on the 13th.

69. Director's Brief, "Chronology," p. B-55. Huckaby, *Crisis at Central High,* p. 151. "Statement Prepared to be Issued to the Press in Connection with the Expulsion of Minnie Jean Brown by the Little Rock School Board," (nd), group III, series A, container 98, PON. "Halt Suspension of Minnie Jean, NAACP Urges Little Rock Board," Feb. 13, 1958, group III, series A, container 98, PON.

70. Transcript, Current, Laws, Mercer, and Bates, Feb. 13, 1958. Frederick B. Routh to Thurgood Marshall, Feb. 12, 1958, Box 81, SRC.

71. Nat R. Griswold interview with John Luter, Aug. 21, 1971, p. 82, EAP. "Report of Sub-Committee—Business and Civic Leaders Group," Feb. 17, 1958, Series III, Box 1, Folder 3, RCB.

72. Oscar Cohen to Harry S. Ashmore, Feb. 11, 1958, Box 7, Folder 2, HSA.

73. Transcript, Current, Laws, Mercer, and Bates, Feb. 13, 1958. Director's Brief, "Chronology," p. B-54-55. Powell, *Central High School Inside Out,* Chapter 7: "Disintegration Well Underway." Jess Matthews claimed in a March 1958 speech that "most" students knew nothing about the harassment of the nine; this claim strains credulity; for the full text of Matthews's speech see "Talk by Jess W. Matthews to Pre N.C.A. Conference at Pere Marquette State Park, Grafton, Ill.," March 22, 1958, Box 2, Folder 26, EPH.

74. Wair interview with Jacoway, p. 24. Beals, *Warriors Don't Cry,* p. 243. Huckaby, *Crisis at Central High,* p. 161.

75. Ashmore, foreword to Huckaby, *Crisis at Central High,* p. xiii. Bishop Brown knew about the absence of discipline inside the school, as he reported in his memoir, Robert R. Brown, *Bigger Than Little Rock* (Greenwich, Conn.: Seabury Press, 1958), p. 52.

76. Ashmore, "The Story Behind Little Rock."

77. Huckaby, *Crisis at Central High,* pp. 162, 169. "Statement of Policy, by Board of Directors of Little Rock School District," *Arkansas Democrat,* Feb. 16, 1958, p. 10A.

78. Huckaby, *Crisis at Central High*, p. 163. Blossom, *It HAS Happened Here*, p. 140; Huckaby, *Crisis at Central High*, facing p. 156. Sammie Dean Parker's father charged that Ernest was winking at his daughter; Huckaby, *Crisis at Central High*, p. 189.

79. Hazel Bryan Massery interview with Elizabeth Jacoway and Pete Daniel, Jan. 29, 1996, p. 19, EJC. Huckaby, *Crisis at Central High*, p. 165; Director's Brief, "Chronology," p. B-58.

80. Huckaby, *Crisis at Central High*, p. 163–64.

81. Director's Brief, "Chronology," p. B-57. The FBI incorrectly identified Cooper as "Harold." Huckaby, *Crisis at Central High*, p. 163; "Three CHS Pupils Suspended; Minniejean [*sic*] Brown Expelled," *Arkansas Gazette*, Feb. 18, 1958, p. 1A.

82. Blossom, *It HAS Happened Here*, p. 167. "One Down . . ." *Arkansas Gazette*, March 3, 1958, p. 4A.

83. Huckaby, *Crisis at Central High*, p. 152.

84. "New Lincoln Is Experiment in Education," *Arkansas Gazette*, Feb. 20, 1958, p. 8A; Transcript, Current, Laws, Mercer, and Bates, Feb. 13, 1958. "Negro Girl to Leave Saturday; Vows to Return," *Arkansas Gazette*, Feb. 20, 1958, p. 8A.

85. "It's Lovely, Says Minnijean As She Enters New School," *Arkansas Gazette*, Feb. 25, 1958, p. 1B.

86. "Board Asks Court to Delay Integration," *Arkansas Gazette*, Feb. 21, 1958, p. 1A. "Arkansas Council on Human Relations Program Report, Second Quarter, 1957–1958."

87. "Text of School Board Statement," *Arkansas Gazette*, Feb. 21, 1958, p. 1A.

88. "2 CHS Pupils Suspended for 2 Weeks," *Arkansas Gazette*, Feb. 22, 1958, p. 1B. "Guthridge to Ask Action Against Board," *Arkansas Gazette*, Feb. 23, 1958, p. 10A.

89. Huckaby, *Crisis at Central High*, pp. 153, 170; Director's Brief, "Chronology," p. B-53.

90. Huckaby, *Crisis at Central High*, pp. 170–71.

91. Coakley, *Operation Arkansas*, p. 249; Director's Brief, "Chronology," p. B-63, B-65; "Sammie Dean Out for Year," *Arkansas Gazette*, March 1, 1958, p. 2A. "Lawyer Denies Attack Report About Parkers," *Arkansas Gazette*, March 6, 1958, p. 3A; "Parker Girl's Father Files Suit in Court," *Arkansas Gazette*, March 8, 1957, p. 2A.

92. Jerry Hulett, "Sammie's Story: A Biography of Sammie Parker Hulett," Box 1, Folder 32, SAM; Sammie Dean Parker Hulett interview with Sara Alderman Murphy, Dec. 9, 1992, pp. 10, 12, Box 1, Folder 32, SAM; Director's Brief, "Chronology," p. B-62. Huckaby, *Crisis at Central High*, p. 170. Blossom, *It HAS Happened Here*, p. 16. Many years later, an adult Sammie Dean Parker Hulett confessed she had come to believe that she had been used by the adults in 1957–58; Hulett interview with Murphy, p. 10. When asked almost fifty years later whether he had ever called Sammie Dean Parker, Ernest Green replied: "All I remember is that Sammie Dean Parker was somebody you would avoid, you'd stay a million miles away. The last thing I'd do is call Sammie Dean. . . . It was their attempt to try to rattle us, unnerve us, kind of besmirch our character, and the reality is that they didn't know anything about us, and that here were nine families that education was really the cornerstone of family life that almost everybody, brothers and sisters—I mean, if you look at what they've done, not just the nine of us, but the rest of the family members, I mean, you were expected to achieve. . . . So Sammie Dean, I don't know where she is, bless her soul, but you know she had no idea what the drive, what the ambitions, what the vision of the future was among us. And you know, at the end of the day, that is really why we were there, because we thought Central offered a better education for the dollar than we were receiving at Horace Mann and that we wanted to experience that"; Green interview with Jacoway, pp. 16–17.

93. "Parker Girl Back in CHS, Promises to Obey Rules," *Arkansas Gazette*, March 12, 1958, p. 1A. Huckaby, *Crisis at Central High*, p. 179; Director's Brief, "Chronology," p. B-66. Coakley, *Operation Arkansas*, p. 250. Stan Opotowsky, "Little Rock Today: I—Eight Kids Who Walk Alone," *New York Post*, April 8, 1958, Box 1, Folder 6, DGB. Charles Rixse, "Girl Tells Her Story on TV; Board Bares Why Expelled," *Arkansas Gazette*, March 5, 1958, p. 1A; *Southern School News*, April 1958.

94. Beals, *Warriors Don't Cry*, pp. 246, 244, 248.

95. Roy Wilkins to the Honorable Wilber M. Brucker, March 27, 1958, group III, series A, container 98, PON. Press Release—Editorial of the Week, March 27, 1958, group III, series A, container 98, PON.

Chapter Thirteen — The Battle in the Courts

1. Richard C. Butler interview with Elizabeth Jacoway, Dec. 15, 1977, EJC.

2. Gertrude Remmel Butler interview with Elizabeth Jacoway, Nov. 16, 2001, EJC. Butler's mother-in-law, Nellie Cates Remmel, a member of the Republican National Committee, had traveled to Washington, D.C., late in the summer to lobby Herbert Brownell in behalf of Dick Butler's bid for the federal judge's seat; Richard C. Butler Jr. telephone interview with Elizabeth Jacoway, Oct. 26, 2003.

3. This description is drawn from the author's personal observations. Gertrude Butler interview with Jacoway. Richard C. Butler interview with Jacoway. B. Cooper Jacoway interview with Elizabeth Jacoway, Nov. 5, 1975, EJC.

4. Richard C. Butler Jr. telephone interview with Jacoway. Gertrude Butler interview with Jacoway. Joe House and his brother Archie practiced law in different law firms. Richard C. Butler interview with Jacoway. Gertrude Butler interview with Jacoway.

5. For helpful insights into this phenomenon see Neil McMillen, ed., *Remaking Dixie: The Impact of World War II on the American South* (Jackson: University Press of Mississippi, 1997). "Little Rock XV Club Has Semi-Centennial Meeting," *Arkansas Gazette,* Jan. 16, 1955, p. 2A; the author is indebted to Charles Witsell for providing her with this information.

6. Richard C. Butler interview with John Luter, Aug. 17 and 23, 1971, pp. 2, 15, EAP.

7. "Guy Describes Arbitral Role in CHS Crisis," *Arkansas Gazette,* March 18, 1958, p. 1A. Butler interview with Luter, p. 11.

8. For the clearest expression of this point of view see Harry Ashmore, "The Story Behind Little Rock: Was Its Meaning Lost in Reporting Its Drama?" *Nieman Reports,* April 1958, Box 9, Folder 4, HSA; an abbreviated version of this paper later appeared as Harry Ashmore, "The Easy Chair: The Untold Story Behind Little Rock," *Harper's Magazine,* June 1958, pp. 16–17. *Southern School News,* March 1958; "Text of School Petition," *Arkansas Gazette,* Feb. 21, 1958, p. 1A. The School Board decided formally to seek a delay after an executive session with the six-man Guy Committee, which had advocated this course of action since October of 1957; "Guy Describes Arbitral Role in CHS Crisis," *Arkansas Gazette,* March 18, 1958, p. 1A.

9. Daisy Bates sent her assistant, Chris Mercer, to New York to confer with Thurgood Marshall about seeking an injunction against the segregationist troublemakers inside Central High School. Nothing came of this initiative; Frederick B. Routh to Thurgood Marshall, Feb. 12, 1958, Box 81, SRC. "Text of School Petition."

10. Archie House interview with John Luter, Aug. 17, 1971, p. 26, EAP. Harold Engstrom interview with John Luter, Dec. 29, 1970, p. 41, EAP; Orval Faubus interview with John Luter, Aug. 18, 1971, p. 33, EAP; see also Roy Reed, *Faubus: The Life and Times of an American Prodigal* (Fayetteville: University of Arkansas Press, 1997), p. 152.

11. "Appealing Anew to the Courts," *Arkansas Gazette,* Feb. 22, 1958, p. 4A. Ashmore, "The Story Behind Little Rock." Harry Ashmore to "Red," Jan. 29, 1958, Box 7, Folder 1, HSA. Mary Ellen Chase to Harry Ashmore, Jan. 24, 1958, Box 7, Folder 1, HSA.

12. "NAACP Asks Court to Deny Plea by Board," *Arkansas Gazette,* Feb. 27, 1958, p. 2A; *Southern School News,* April 1958, June, 1958. "NAACP Argues for Suit Dismissal," *Arkansas Gazette,* March 6, 1958, p. 7A.

13. "Governor Faubus Makes It Official," *Arkansas Gazette,* March 6, 1958, p. 1A. Jim Johnson interview with Elizabeth Jacoway, June 26, 2002, p. 228, ACOVH; Ernest Valachovic, "Johnson Submits Anti-Integration Plan," *Arkansas Gazette,* Jan. 9, 1958, p. 6A. Jim Johnson interview with Elizabeth Jacoway, March 15, 2004, EJC. "Proposed Constitutional Amendment No. 53 (By Petition) The States Rights Amendment," Arkansas Secretary of State's Office, Elections Division, Lit-

tle Rock, Ark.

14. "Jim Johnson Has Stated the Issue," *Arkansas Gazette,* Jan. 10, 1958, p. 4A. "Negro Leaders Form State Voters Group at Boisterous Session," *Arkansas Gazette,* Feb. 16, 1958, p. 8A.

15. Jim Johnson interview with Elizabeth Jacoway, June 18, 2002, p. 80, ACOVH. "Johnson Blames Communists for Integration in Little Rock," *Arkansas Gazette,* March 21, 1958, p. 9A. For an illuminating account of this phenomenon, see Jeff Woods, *Black Struggle, Red Scare: Segregation and Anti-Communism in the South, 1948–1968* (Baton Rouge: Louisiana State University Press, 2004). As historian Michael Klarman makes clear, "Massive resisters wanted to suppress opposition because they believed that only by presenting a united front could they induce the Court and the nation to retreat from *Brown*"; Michael J. Klarman, *From Jim Crow to Civil Rights: The Supreme Court and the Struggle for Racial Equality* (New York: Oxford University Press, 2004), p. 409.

16. Ray Moseley, "Thomas Advocates 'Voluntary' Plan of Desegregation," *Arkansas Gazette,* April 8, 1958, p. 1A. "Here Is Text of Thomas Plan," April 8, 1958, SERS.

17. Ibid.

18. Ibid.

19. Kenneth Johnson, "Thomas Integration Plan Is Off to a Shaky Start," *Commercial Appeal,* April 20, 1958, SERS; "Thomas Urges Moderates to Take Stand." "Education Board Skips Thomas Plan," *Arkansas Democrat,* May 2, 1958, p. 23; "Board Has No Plans to Act on Thomas Idea Before Court Hearing," *Arkansas Gazette,* May 14, 1958. Jerry Jones, "Rejected by Board, Thomas Plan Dies," *Arkansas Gazette,* June 10, 1958. For further discussion of the failure of the Thomas Plan see Karen Anderson, "The Little Rock School Desegregation Crisis: Moderation and Social Conflict," *Journal of Southern History* (August, 2004), pp. 611–619.

20. Margaret Frick, "Lemley Named to Hear CHS Integration Case; Early Ruling Hinted," *Arkansas Democrat,* April 21, 1958, p. 2. "Lemley Is Regarded As Painstaking Jurist, *Washington Star,* June 22, 1958, Lemley Scrapbook, Box 1, Folder 1, HJL. "Lemley a Judge of Sharp Conscience to Whom South 'Almost a Religion,' " *Arkansas Gazette,* June 22, 1958, p. 1A. A. F. House interview with John Luter, Aug. 17, 1971, p. 28, EAP; "Amicus Curiae Brief of the Attorney General of Arkansas," October 1954, in Philip B. Kurland and Gerhard Casper, *Landmark Briefs and Arguments of the Supreme Court of the United States: Constitutional Law,* Vol. 49 (Arlington, Va. University Publications of America, 1975), pp. 831–57. *Southern School News,* May 1958.

21. "Clarify Plea, Lemley Tells School Board," *Arkansas Gazette,* April 29, 1958, p. 1A; "Text of Judge Lemley's Statement," *Arkansas Gazette,* April 29, 1958, p. 6A.

22. Pulitzer Prize award booklet, (nd) Box 9, Folder 4, HSA. "Ike Orders Troops Out of CHS May 29," *Arkansas Democrat,* May 8, 1958, p. 1. R. B. Mayfield, "Faubus Doubts 'Withdrawal,' " *Arkansas Democrat,* May 8, 1958, p. 1.

23. "Seniors at CHS Start Annual Rush," *Arkansas Democrat,* May 1, 1958, p. 7A. Gertrude Samuels, "Little Rock: More Tension Than Ever," *New York Times Magazine,* March 23, 1958, p. 90. Elizabeth Huckaby, *Crisis at Central High: Little Rock, 1957–58* (Baton Rouge: Louisiana State University Press, 1980), pp. 188–89. Stan Opotowsky, "Little Rock Today: How Long Can the Kids Take It?" April 1958, *New York Post,* Box 1, Folder 7, DGB.

24. Robert W. Coakley, *Operation Arkansas* (Office of the Chief of Military History Monograph No. 158M, 1967), pp. 277, 275. Daisy Gatson Bates, *The Long Shadow of Little Rock* (New York: David McKay & Co., 1962), p. 148. Unsigned memo, May 22, 1958, group III, series A, container 98, PON.

25. "Tight Lid Clamped on CHS Graduation," *Arkansas Democrat,* May 25, 1958, p. 1. Bates, *The Long Shadow of Little Rock,* p. 149. For the photograph, see *Arkansas Democrat,* May 26, 1958, p. 1A. "CHS Case Passed to June 12," *Arkansas Democrat,* May 26, 1958, p. 5; *Southern School News,* July 1958.

26. For a full and touching description of the ceremony, see Huckaby, *Crisis at Central High,* pp. 210–17. King had spoken at commencement ceremonies at Arkansas A&M that morning; *Southern School News,* June 1958; Ernest Q. Campbell and Thomas F. Pettigrew, "Little Rock:

Vignettes of Ministers Amid Crisis," Charleston (W.V.) *Gazette,* Jan. 11, 1959, SERS. Irving Spitzberg Jr., *Racial Politics in Little Rock, 1954–1964* (New York: Garland Publishing, 1987), pp. 76, 91; Reed, *Faubus,* p. 238–39. Melba Patillo Beals, *Warriors Don't Cry: A Searing Memoir of the Battle to Integrate Little Rock's Central High* (New York: Simon & Schuster, 1994), p. 304. Bates, *The Long Shadow of Little Rock,* p. 150. "Ernest Green's Story," *Jet,* June 19, 1958, Box 1, Folder 7, DGB.

27. Coakley, *Operation Arkansas,* p. 272.

28. *Southern School News,* June 1958. House interview with Luter, p. 26, EAP. J. W. Peltason, *58 Lonely Men: Southern Federal Judges and School Desegregation* (New York: Harcourt, Brace, & World, 1961), p. 184. Margaret Frick, "Board Pleads for Delay," *Arkansas Democrat,* May 25, 1958, p. 1.

29. Frick, "Board Pleads for Delay." See also Tony Freyer, *The Little Rock Crisis: A Constitutional Interpretation* (Westport, Conn.: Greenwood Press, 1984), p. 145.

30. Transcript, Lemley Hearing, June 3, 1958, p. 61, Box 5, Folder 7, VTB; "Text of School Petition," *Arkansas Gazette,* Feb. 21, 1958, p. 1A.

31. "Text of School Petition." Transcript, Lemley Hearing, June 3, 1958, pp. 3–29.

32. Transcript, Lemley Hearing, June 3, 1958, pp. 144–79.

33. Ibid., June 4, 1958, pp. 235–94.

34. John Thomas Elliff, "The United States Department of Justice and Individual Civil Rights, 1937–1962" (Ph.D. diss., Harvard University, 1962), pp. 604–5.

35. Vivion Lenon Brewer, *The Embattled Ladies of Little Rock, 1958–1963: The Struggle to Save Public Education at Central High* (Fort Bragg, Calif.: Lost Coast Press, 1999), pp. 2–3. Sara Alderman Murphy, *Breaking the Silence: Little Rock's Women's Emergency Committee to Open Our Schools, 1958–1963* (Fayetteville: University of Arkansas Press, 1997), p. 64. J. N. Heiskell wrote to Adolphine Terry thanking her for "one of the greatest events in my life. . . ."; Terry, "My Life Is My Song, Also," p. 235. Huckaby, *Crisis at Central High,* p. 220. "CHS Nine, Mrs. Bates Get Medal," *Arkansas Democrat,* June 7, 1958, p. 2. Ellis Thomas to Roy Wilkins, May 28, 1958, Box 1, Folder 7, DGB; Pauli Murray to Spingarn Award Committee, May 30, 1958, Box 1, Folder 7, DGB.

36. Margaret Frick, "NAACP Files Appeal After Integration Delay Order," *Arkansas Democrat,* June 21, 1958, p. 1. "Integration Delay Order Text," *Arkansas Democrat,* June 22, 1958, p. 2A.

37. "Integration Delay Order Text," "Integration Delay Hailed by South," *Arkansas Democrat,* June 22, 1958, p. 1; "South's Leaders Voice Praise for Lemley," *Arkansas Democrat,* June 22, 1958, p. 2A; "Delay Tickles Guthridge, Pruden, Knocks Mrs. Bates 'for a Loop,'" *Arkansas Democrat,* June 22, 1958, p. 14A. Peltason, *58 Lonely Men,* p. 184.

38. Margaret Frick, "NAACP Files Appeal After Integration Delay Order"; Ed Martin, "Branton Says Negroes May Be Back in Fall," *Arkansas Democrat,* June 22, 1958, p. 1; "CHS Stay Plea Filed by NAACP," *Arkansas Democrat,* June 25, 1958, p. 8. "Little Rock Judge's Ruling," *New York Times,* June 24, 1958, p. 21. "Little Rock Case to Court Today," *New York Times,* June 23, 1958, p. 17.

39. Richard L. Lyons, "Supreme Court Asked to Hold Session on Little Rock Case," *Washington Post,* June 27, 1958, SERS; "High Court Asked to Reverse Lemley," *Arkansas Democrat,* June 26, 1958, p. 1. For a fascinating account of the maneuvers involved in this action see Jack Greenberg, *Crusaders in the Courts: How a Dedicated Band of Lawyers Fought for the Civil Rights Revolution* (New York: Basic Books, 1994), pp. 232–36.

40. George Douthit, "Faubus' Fiery Opener Points to Heated Race," *Arkansas Democrat,* June 29, 1958, p. 1.

41. Ray Moseley, "Faubus in Northwest, Hits Gazette, McMath, Says Ashmore Real Foe," *Arkansas Gazette,* July 3, 1958, p. 1B.

42. "Faubus Sweeps to Third Term; Landslide Margin Tops 2 to 1," *Arkansas Gazette,* July 30, 1958, p. 1; *Southern School News,* September 1958. Roy Reed, "Faubus Supporters Gay, Jubilant; 'Like Mardi Gras' on Markham Street," *Arkansas Gazette,* July 30, 1958, p. 1A. "Turmoil Ahead," *Time,* Aug. 11, 1958, p. 15. "Mr Faubus Wins a Famous Victory," *Arkansas Gazette,* July 31, 1958,

p. 4A.

43. "Arkansas Council on Human Relations Narrative Report, July–September, 1958," Box 27, Folder 287, ACHR. Griffin Smith jr. telephone conversation with Elizabeth Jacoway, Aug. 28, 2002.

44. "Negroes Submit Brief Attacking Lemley Ruling," *Arkansas Gazette,* July 20, 1958, p. 15A. "Court to Hear CHS Delay Appeal Today," *Arkansas Gazette,* Aug. 4, 1958, p. 1A. *Race Relations Law Reporter,* June 1958.

45. "Court Hears Pleas of NAACP, Board in Appeal of Delay," *Arkansas Gazette,* Aug. 5, 1958, p. 1A. Bobbie Forster, "CHS Hearing in St. Louis Held Near Scene of Dred Scott Case," *Arkansas Democrat,* Aug. 10, 1958.

46. Corinne Silverman, *The Little Rock Story,* Inter-University Case Program, No. 41 (University of Alabama Press, 1959), p. 19. (Italics in the original.) "Lemley Ruling Upset; Faubus Quiet on Plan," *Arkansas Gazette,* Aug. 19, 1958, p. 1. Dennis J. Hutchinson, "Unanimity and Desegregation: Decisionmaking in the Supreme Court, 1948–1958," *Georgetown Law Journal,* Vol. 68:1, 1979, p. 75. "Text of Decision," *Arkansas Gazette,* Aug. 19, 1958, p. 1A. "Gardner's Dissent," *Arkansas Gazette,* Aug. 19, 1958, p. 3A.

47. "Legislators Ready; Board Will Appeal," *Arkansas Gazette,* Aug. 19, 1958, p. 1A. Butler interview with Luter, p. 6.

48. "Legislators Ready; Board Will Appeal."

49. Butler interview with Luter, p. 6. "Judge Lemley Reported to Be Leaving Bench," *Arkansas Gazette,* Sept. 6, 1958, p. 1A. Bobbie Forster, "Lemley's Decision to Retire Attributed to Strong Feeling That CHS Slowdown Needed," *Arkansas Democrat,* Sept. 7, 1958, p. 1. Mrs. J. A. Livingston to C. Harry Lemley, Sept. 22, 1958, Box 2, Folder 5, HJL.

50. "Governor Faubus' Statement," *Arkansas Gazette,* Aug. 20, 1958, p. 3A. "Board Tells Faubus Court Appeal Only Step Planned Now," *Arkansas Gazette,* Aug. 20, 1958, p. 1A. "Faubus and Board Have 'Friendly, Amicable' Talk; Governor, Ike in Standoff," *Arkansas Gazette,* Aug. 21, 1958, p. 1A.

51. "Use of Troops Hinted Unless Court Obeyed," *Arkansas Gazette,* Aug. 21, 1958, p. 1A.

52. "Faubus Gives Blunt Reply: He Hasn't Changed, Either." "Board Bars Negroes After Stay Granted," *Arkansas Gazette,* Aug. 22, 1958, p. 1A. Nathan R. Griswold, "The Second Reconstruction in Little Rock," Book One, Chapter Two, p. 24, unpublished manuscript, Box 11, Folder 8, SAM. "Faubus and Board have a 'Friendly, Amicable' Talk"; "Governor, Ike in Standoff." "Faubus Mulls Need to Call Legislature," *Arkansas Gazette,* Aug. 22, 1958, p. 1A.

53. "Board Bars Negroes After Stay Granted." J. W. Peltason, *58 Lonely Men,* p. 187. Elliff, "The United States Department of Justice and Individual Civil Rights, 1937–1962," p. 606. Judge Gardner explained that the Court of Appeals judges had decided when they made their ruling that they would grant a stay if asked, and all seven judges had concurred; "Time Allowed to Take Case to High Court," *Arkansas Gazette,* Aug. 22, 1958, p. 1A.

54. Claude Sitton, "Action by Faubus Expected Today," *New York Times,* Aug. 23, 1958, p. 16; "Time Allowed to Take Case to High Court." "Negroes Ask Court to Set Aside Stay and Lemley's Order," *Arkansas Gazette,* Aug. 23, 1958, p. 1A.

55. "Leaders Say Negro Students Must Decide for Themselves Whether to Ask CHS Return," *Arkansas Gazette,* Aug. 24, 1958.

56. Claude Sitton, "Faubus Summons Special Session to Block Negroes," *New York Times,* Aug. 24, 1958, p. 1; "Legislature Called to Meet Tuesday," *Arkansas Gazette,* Aug. 24, 1958, p. 1A.

57. "CHS Term Delayed; Supreme Court Called as Legislators Gather," *Arkansas Gazette,* Aug. 26, 1958, p. 1A. "Washington Whispers," *U.S. News & World Report,* Sept. 12, 1958, Lemley Scrapbook, Box 1, Folder 4, HJL. This was the only special term Earl Warren convened during his tenure as chief justice, and it was only the third such term of the century; Hutchinson, "Unanimity and Desegregation," p. 75. "Warren Says Court Delays Corrode Respect for Law," *Arkansas Gazette,* Aug. 26, 1958, p. 1B. "CHS Term Delayed; Supreme Court Called as Legislators Gather." Wiley A. Branton, "Little Rock Revisited: Desegregation to Resegregation," *Journal of Negro Education* (Summer 1983), p. 266.

58. "CHS Term Delayed; Supreme Court Called as Legislators Gather." Elliff. "The United States Department of Justice and Individual Civil Rights, 1937–1962," p. 607. "Rogers Urges Compliance with Courts," *Arkansas Gazette*, Aug. 20, 1958, p. 1A; "U.S. Discloses Alternates to Troop Use at Little Rock," *Arkansas Gazette*, Aug. 22, 1958, p. 1A; Claude Sitton, "U.S. Marshals Would Keep Order in Little Rock, Backed by Police," *Chattanooga Times*, Aug. 24, 1958, SERS. "Committee Kills $500,000 Fund For Marshals," *Arkansas Gazette*, March 21, 1959, p. 1A.

59. Claude Sitton, "Faubus to Offer His Bills Today," *New York Times*, Aug. 26, 1958, SERS; "All Schools in City Open September 8," *Arkansas Gazette*, Aug. 26, 1958, p. 1A. Claude Sitton, "Faubus in Parley with Legislators," *New York Times*, Aug. 26, 1958, SERS.

60. Virgil T. Blossom, *It HAS Happened Here* (New York: Harper & Bros. 1959), p. 182. "School Closing Bill Assembled, Faubus Briefs Legislators," *Arkansas Gazette*, Aug. 25, 1958, p. 1A.

61. Governor's speech, Aug. 26, 1958, Box 496, Folder 2, OEF.

62. Ibid. Claude Sitton, "Faubus Asks Bills to Close Schools Integrated by U.S." *New York Times*, Aug. 27, 1958, p. 1A.

63. "Six Bills to Block School Integration Offered by Faubus," *Arkansas Gazette*, Aug. 27, 1958, p. 1A; "Faubus Bills Win Approval of Committee," *Arkansas Gazette*, Aug. 27, 1958, p. 2A. Ernest Valachovic, "All Faubus Bills Sail Through; House Acts Rapidly to Outstrip Court," *Arkansas Gazette*, Aug. 28, 1958, p. 1A. Orval Eugene Faubus, *Down From the Hills* (Little Rock: Democrat Printing & Lithographing Co., 1980), p. 414. Carol Griffee, ed., *Osro Cobb of Arkansas: Memoirs of Historical Significance* (Little Rock: Rose Publishing Co., 1989), p. 261.

64. Arthur Edson, "Calm in Court Belies Fierce Undercurrent," *Arkansas Gazette*, Aug. 29, 1958, p. 1A. Patricia Wiggins, "Court Air Almost School-like with Crowds Inside and Out," *Arkansas Gazette*, Aug. 29, 1958, p. 1A. Harold Engstrom and John Haley became dispirited during their stay in Washington and went to the Lincoln Memorial for inspiration at midnight, where they were arrested; Phillip Carroll telephone interview with Elizabeth Jacoway, Oct. 24, 2002. "Drama Is High in High Court," *Washington Post and Times-Herald*, Aug. 29, 1958, p. A3. Dale and L'Moore Alford, *The Case of the Sleeping People (Finally Awakened By Little Rock School Frustrations)* (Little Rock: Pioneer Press, 1959), p. 54.

65. Wiggins, "Court Air Almost School-like"; Clayton, "Drama Is High in High Court."

66. Wiggins, "Court Air Almost School-like." Unless otherwise noted, the following description comes from the transcript of the hearing titled Transcript, *Aaron v. Cooper*, Aug. 28, 1958, Box 5, Folder 15, VTB. For a concise description of the case as it was presented before the Supreme Court, see Mark V. Tushnet, *Making Civil Rights Law: Thurgood Marshall and the Supreme Court, 1956–1961* (New York: Oxford University Press, 1994), pp. 259–63. See also Tony Freyer, *The Little Rock Crisis: A Constitutional Interpretation* (Westport, Conn.: Greenwood Press, 1984), pp. 145–51, and Bernard Schwartz, *Super Chief: Earl Warren and His Supreme Court—A Judicial Biography* (New York University Press, 1983), 289–303. Edson, "Calm in Court Belies Fierce Undercurrent."

67. "Final Ruling on CHS Set by September 15," *Arkansas Gazette*, Aug. 29, 1958, p. 1A. When Butler said, "May it please the court," he added, "I represent the people of Little Rock." Earl Warren interrupted him and said "Which people?" Warren's law clerk, Michael Heyman, recalled years later "that was sort of the end of the case"; Phyllis D. Brandon, "Former Smithsonian Head Views Little Rock History," *Arkansas Democrat-Gazette*, Jan. 23, 2005, p. 7D.

68. Faubus, *Down From the Hills*, p. 415. "Faubus Berates Supreme Court in Party Talk," *Arkansas Gazette*, Sept. 7, 1958, p. 1A.

69. "Lemley Action Stirs Capital," *Arkansas Democrat*, Sept. 7, 1958, p. 1. "Judge Lemley Reported to be Leaving Bench." "Judge Miller Is Reassigned to Little Rock Case," *Arkansas Gazette*, Sept. 10, 1958, p. 1A. "Two Extra Attorneys Working in LR Office," *Arkansas Gazette*, Aug. 29, 1958. p. 1A. Elliff, "The United States Department of Justice and Individual Civil Rights, 1937–1962," p. 608. "Rogers Tells City Officials, Board of Plan," and "Plans for Enforcement Fully Co-ordinated, Cobb Asserts," *Arkansas Gazette*, Sept. 10, 1958, p. 1A.; *Southern School News*, October 1958. Claude Sitton, "Little Rock Board Willing to Weigh U.S. Proposal," *New York Times*, Sept. 10, 1958,

SERS.

70. Claude Sitton, "Little Rock Move on School Start Is Due Tomorrow," *New York Times*, August 31, 1958, p. 1. "Three School Directors Favor Opening Sept. 8; Board Decides Monday," *Arkansas Gazette*, Aug. 30, 1958, p. 3A; Claude Sitton, "School Board on Spot in Little Rock Crisis," *New York Times*, Sept. 7, 1958, p. 6E. "Here's Advice School Board's Attorney Gave," *Arkansas Gazette*, September 2, 1958, p. 2A. "High School Terms Delayed by Board Until September 15," *Arkansas Gazette*, Sept. 2, 1958, p. 1A; Claude Sitton, "Little Rock Delay to September 15 Voted by School Board," *New York Times*, Sept. 2, 1958, p. 1.

71. Butler interview with Luter, pp. 11, 19. School Board member Harold Engstrom later admitted that the board members knew they could not win, but they were primarily interested in convincing the people of Little Rock "that we had done what they wanted us to do as effectively as it could have been done"; Harold Engstrom interview with John Luter, Dec. 29, 1970, p. 35, EAP.

72. "Brief on Merits No. 1 in the Supreme Court of the United States, August Special Term, 1958, William G. Cooper, et al, Petitioners v. John Aaron, et al, Respondents on Writ of Certiorari to the United States Court of Appeals for the Eighth Circuit," available in microform from Information Handling Services, Englewood, Colorado, 1979. Unless otherwise noted, all of the following discussion will come from this brief.

73. "Court Session Attracts Spectators from Afar," *Arkansas Gazette*, Sept. 12, 1958, p. 14A. Richard C. Butler Jr., telephone conversation with Elizabeth Jacoway, March 2, 2004. "Court Hears Pleas; Decision Seen Today," *Arkansas Gazette*, Sept. 12, 1058, p. 1A; Greenberg, *Crusaders in the Courts*, p. 240. Doug Peters, "Three Tell of Events Behind Scenes in Central Crisis," *Arkansas Democrat-Gazette*, Sept. 30, 1997, p. 1A.

74. J. William Fulbright, "Motion for Leave to File a Brief as Amicus Curiae," Aug. 27, 1958, available in microform from Information Handling Service, Englewood, Colorado, 1979. Randall Bennett Woods, *Fulbright: A Biography* (Cambridge England: Cambridge University Press, 1995), pp. 226–35. Lee Riley Powell, "Massive Resistance in Arkansas: A Tale of Race Relations and an Undemocratic Political System in the 1950s," p. 67, student research paper prepared for Professor Michael Klarman at the University of Virginia in 1992; the author is indebted to Professor Klarman for sharing this paper with her. See also Lee Riley Powell, *J. William Fulbright and America's Lost Crusade: Fulbright, the Cold War and the Vietnam War* (Little Rock: Rose Publishing Co., 1984).

75. Kurland and Casper, *Landmark Briefs and Arguments*, pp. 709–10.

76. Greenberg, *Crusaders in the Courts*, p. 240. Hutchinson, "Unanimity and Desegregation," p. 78.

77. "Text of Court Ruling," *Arkansas Gazette*, Sept. 13, 1958, p. 1A. "Faubus Hears School News with Flush, Impassive Quiet," *Arkansas Gazette*, Sept. 13, 1958, p. 7A. "Faubus Closes CHS After Court Denies Delay of Integration," *Arkansas Gazette*, Sept. 13, 1958, p. 1A.

78. Blossom, *It HAS Happened Here*, p. 185. Butler interview with Luter, p. 3.

CHAPTER FOURTEEN — EMPTY SCHOOLS

1. Judith Kilpatrick, "Wiley Austin Branton: Arkansas Native Son," paper delivered at the Arkansas Historical Convention, April 20, 2002; the author wishes to thank Professor Kilpatrick for sharing this paper with her. Judge Wiley A. Branton Jr. interview with Elizabeth Jacoway, May 24, 2004, pp. 6, 16–17, EJC. Wiley. A. Branton, "Post-War Race Relations in Pine Bluff," (nd), p. 1, a reminiscence prepared at the request of the Pine Bluff *Commercial;* the author wishes to thank Paul Greenberg for sharing this brief history with her. Paul Greenberg, "What Wiley Branton Left Us," *Arkansas Democrat-Gazette*, Aug. 31, 2003, p. 4J. Biographical Sketch in Finding Aid, WAB. Wiley A. Branton interview with Steven Lawson, Oct. 21, 1970, p. 51, EAP; see also Wiley A. Branton interview with James Mosby, Jan. 16, 1969, p. 6, CRDP.

2. Branton interview with Mosby, pp. 2–10, 13. Branton interview with Jacoway, pp. 7–10, 12–16. For a brief introduction to Branton's confederates at the University, see Judith Kilpatrick,

"Arkansas' Early African-American Lawyers: A History" (University of Arkansas School of Law, 2003), pp. 21–22. Ada Lois Sipuel (*Sipuel v. Board of Regents of Oklahoma,* 1948) was a friend and classmate of Wiley Branton and Silas Hunt; John Kirk, *Redefining the Color Line: Black Activism in Little Rock, Arkansas, 1940–1970* (Gainesville: University Press of Florida, 2002), p. 61.

3. For a full and enlightening discussion of NAACP activities in Arkansas between the *Brown* decision and the Little Rock crisis, see Brian James Daugherity, "'With All Deliberate Speed': The NAACP and the Implementation of *Brown v. Board of Education* at the Local Level, Little Rock, Arkansas" (master's thesis, University of Montana, 1997). Wiley A. Branton, "Personal Memories of Thurgood Marshall, *Arkansas Law Review,* Vol. 40, No. 4, 1987, p. 667. See also Wiley A. Branton, "Little Rock Revisited: Desegregation to Resegregation," *Journal of Negro Education* (Summer 1983), p. 264.

4. Stephanie Branton, "Unsung Hero: Wiley A. Branton," *Arkansas Times,* Sept. 26, 1997, p. 7. Greenberg, "What Wiley Branton Left Us." Orval Faubus agreed with Greenberg's assessment, commenting in an interview, ". . . in my observation of Mr. Branton he seemed to be an objective man who was doing the job for his clients without rancor or malice toward anyone else, and I had that impression of him all the way through. . . ."; Orval E. Faubus interview with Roy Reed, Dec. 19, 1988, p. 1, RRP.

5. "Coffelt Files Suit to Stop CHS Closing," *Arkansas Gazette,* Sept. 13, 1958, p. 1A. *Southern School News,* October 1958; "School Closing Test Suit Goes to High Court," *Arkansas Gazette,* Dec. 27, 1958, p. 1A. See also Claude Sitton, "Faubus Says U.S. Can't Bar Closing," *New York Times,* Sept. 14, 1958, p. 1.

6. Vivion Lenon Brewer, *The Embattled Ladies of Little Rock: The Struggle to Save Public Education at Central High, 1958–1963* (Fort Bragg, Calif.: Lost Coast Press, 1999), pp. xxii, 6–9. See also Elizabeth Jacoway, "Vivion Brewer of Arkansas: A Ladylike Assault on the 'Southern Way of Life,'" in Bruce L. Clayton and John A. Salmond, eds., *"Lives Full of Struggle and Triumph": Southern Women, Their Institutions, and Their Communities* (Gainesville: University Press of Florida, 2003), pp. 264–82. Irving Spitzberg Jr., *Racial Politics in Little Rock, 1954–1964* (New York: Garland Publishing, 1987), p. 86. Henry M. Alexander, "The Little Rock Recall Election," Eagleton Institute Case Studies in Practical Politics, Case No. 17 (New Brunswick: Rutgers University Press, 1960), p. 7. Sara Alderman Murphy, *Breaking the Silence: Little Rock's Women's Emergency Committee to Open Our Schools, 1958–1963* (Fayetteville: University of Arkansas Press, 1997), p. 79.

7. "The Next Move Is Mr. Faubus'," *Arkansas Gazette,* Sept. 13, 1958, p. 4A. Jack Setters, "Faubus Tells of Threat in Force Use," *Nashville Banner,* Sept. 15, 1958, SERS; "Faubus Awaits U.S. Move," *Nashville Tennessean,* Sept. 15, 1958, SERS. "Closing of Schools Goes Unchallenged by U.S. Authority," *Arkansas Gazette,* Sept. 14, 1958, p. 1A. Ray Moseley, "Board Asks Faubus' Will On Football," *Arkansas Gazette,* Sept. 17, 1958, p. 1A. Bob Considine, "Marshals, Judge Set for Trouble," *Boston Globe,* Sept. 13, 1958, as quoted in Orval E. Faubus, *Down From the Hills* (Little Rock: Democrat Printing & Lithographing Co., 1980), p. 430.

8. Setters, "Faubus Tells of Threat in Force Use." Sitton, "Faubus Says U.S. Can't Bar Closing"; Relman Morin, "Faubus Leaves for Rest," Charleston (S.C.) *News and Courier,* Sept. 14, 1958, SERS. Robert L. McCord, "Faubus Prepared to Go to Jail; Court Attempts to Block Private School," *Christian Science Monitor,* Oct. 2, 1958, as quoted in Faubus, *Down From the Hills,* p. 431. "Faubus, 11 Others Due For Arrest?" *Charlotte Observer,* Sept. 14, 1958, SERS. "Closing of Schools Goes Unchallenged by U.S. Authority."

9. Ray Moseley, "High School Bands, Football Cancelled, Deadlock Continues," *Arkansas Gazette,* Sept. 16, 1958, p. 1A. Jerry McConnell and Charley Thornton, "Tigers, Warriors Stick Together," *Arkansas Gazette,* Sept. 16, 1958, p. 2B; Jerry McConnell, "Tigers Suffer the Crusher; Fort Smith, 19–6, Ends State Reign Since 1951," *Arkansas Gazette,* Oct. 11, 1958, p. 1B. Ernest Valachovic, "Faubus Resets Election for September 27, Rips School Board, Clergymen," *Arkansas Gazette,* Sept. 17, 1958, p. 1A. Ray Moseley, "Board Asks Faubus' Will On Football," *Arkansas*

Gazette, Sept. 17, 1958, p. 1A; Fred Routh to Harold Fleming, Sept. 16, 1958, Box 80, SRC. Ray Moseley, "Board Okays Resumption of Football," *Arkansas Gazette,* Sept. 18, 1958, p. 1A; "Game on Again, All Tigers Report," *Arkansas Gazette,* Sept. 18, 1958, p. 2B; Griffin Smith, jr. [*sic*], interview with Roy Reed, Jan. 4, 1989, p. 25, RRP. On Thanksgiving Day, 1958, Hall High played Central High for the state championship, and 5,000 Fans turned out to cheer the teams; "Central Blunts Hall's Hopes, 7-0," *Arkansas Gazette,* Nov 28, 1958, p. 1B.

10. "4 High Schools Remain Closed; All Sides Quiet," *Arkansas Gazette,* Sept. 15, 1958, p. 1A. "Memorandum to Little Rock School Board" signed by Archie House, Richard C. Butler, and John Haley, "Subject: Validity of lease of school buildings," (nd), Box 5, Folder 1, VTB.

11. Ernest Valachovic, "Faubus Resets Election for September 27, Rips School Board, Clergymen," *Arkansas Gazette,* Sept. 17, 1958, p. 1A; Claude Sitton, "Faubus in Clash with Clergymen; He Advances School Vote," *New York Times,* Sept. 17, 1958, p. 1. Brewer, *The Embattled Ladies of Little Rock,* p. 11. "Students Having Tough Time Transferring," *Arkansas Gazette,* Sept. 16, 1958, p. 1A; Ray Moseley, "High School Bands, Football Cancelled, Deadlock Continues," *Arkansas Gazette,* Sept. 16, 1958, p. 1A. Alford, *The Case of the Sleeping People,* p. 59. "3,500 Students, 15 Teachers in Little Rock's TV 'School,'" *Arkansas Gazette,* Sept. 21, 1958, p. 3A; "Screen School Starts Today," *Arkansas Gazette,* Sept. 22, 1958, p. 1A; Ronnie Farrar, "First Day of TV Classes Seen by Most as Success," *Arkansas Gazette,* Sept. 23, 1958, p. 1A.

12. "Charter Is Granted for Private Schools," *Arkansas Gazette,* Sept. 18, 1958, p. 1A.

13. "Speech of Governor Orval E. Faubus," Sept. 18, 1958, Box 496, Folder 2, OEF; see also "Here Is Text of Speech by Governor Faubus," *Arkansas Gazette,* Sept. 19, 1958, p. 1A. Bill Lewis, "Governor Tells Plan for Private Schools," *Arkansas Gazette,* Sept. 19, 1958, p. 1A; "Segregationists Find Hope in Faubus Talk," *Nashville Banner,* Sept. 19, 1958, SERS; Kenneth Johnson, "Faubus Urges Voters to Shun Propaganda, Back School Closings," *Commercial Appeal,* Sept. 19, 1958, SERS. Dennis J. Hutchinson, "Unanimity and Desegregation: Decisionmaking in the Supreme Court, 1948–1958," *Georgetown Law Journal,* Vol. 68:1, 1979, pp. 1–96.

14. Brewer, Terry, and Powell realized early that they "could not openly involve ourselves in any inter-racial associations"; Brewer, *Embattled Ladies of Little Rock,* p. 72; Ibid., pp. 11–12. Harry Ashmore forever after referred to the "rigged" election. Some citizens eventually understood that the election did not offer voters an honest choice; see "From the People: Who Really Closed High Schools?" *Arkansas Gazette,* March 6, 1959, p. 4A. "Women Organize Campaign for Opening of High Schools," *Arkansas Gazette,* Sept. 18, 1958, p. 1A.

15. "Open-School Women 'Outgrow' Quarters," *Arkansas Gazette,* Sept. 21, 1958, p. 2A. ACHR "Narrative Report."

16. Ray Moseley, "Lawyers Question Validity of Plans to Lease Schools," *Arkansas Gazette,* Sept. 21, 1958, p. 1A; "A Statement from Lawyers," *Arkansas Gazette,* Sept. 22, 1958, p. 2A. John Kyle Day, "The Fall of a Southern Moderate: Congressman Brooks Hays and the Election of 1958," *Arkansas Historical Quarterly* (Fall 2000), p. 248. Within a week's time Nat Griswold wrote confidentially, "The unconfirmed report is that all have lost clients; that they wish to avoid being permanently in the role of crusaders for anything, especially for desegregation"; ACHR, "Narrative Report."

17. Ray Moseley, "School Board Asks U.S. Court to Rule on Lease Proposal," *Arkansas Gazette,* Sept. 24, 1958, p. 1A.

18. Hutchinson, "Unanimity and Desegregation," p. 74. Ray Moseley, "U.S. Joins Move to Halt Faubus on School Plan," *Arkansas Gazettte,* Sept. 25, 1958, p. 1A. "Judge Miller's Ruling," *Southern School News,* October 1958. "Justice Department Declares War on School Lease Plans," *Arkansas Gazette,* Sept. 26, 1958, p. 1A.

19. *Race Relations Law Reporter,* October 1958, p. 881. Attorney General to the President, Sept. 25, 1958, Box 54, Folder "School (3)," WPR.

20. "Judgeship Vacancy Key Seen; Bill Creating New Posts Could Fill Arkansas Position," *Arkansas Democrat,* June 30, 1958, p. 1; "Bill Creating New Judgeships to Be Expedited," *Arkansas Gazette,* July 1, 1958, p. 1A. "Supreme Court Gets Lashing by McClellan," *Arkansas Gazette,* Sept.

27, 1958, p. 2A; "1954 School Ruling Flayed by McClellan," *Arkansas Gazette,* Oct. 2, 1958, p. 10B; "McClellan Sees Communist Plot to Rule World," *Arkansas Gazette,* Oct. 8, 1958, p. 2A.

21. "Judge Refuses to Act on School Lease Plan," *Arkansas Gazette,* Sept. 26, 1958, p. 1A. *Race Relations Law Reporter,* October 1958, p. 886. J. W. Peltason, *58 Lonely Men: Southern Federal Judges and School Desegregation* (New York: Harcourt, Brace, & World, 1961), p. 198. John Thomas Elliff, "The United States Department of Justice and Individual Civil Rights, 1937–1962" (Ph.D. diss. Harvard University, 1962), p. 611.

22. "Faubus Avers Schools to Stay Open if Voters Favor Segregation Today." All four of the ministers involved in the telecast suffered repercussions within their churches as well as in the larger community; see especially Daisy Bates, *The Long Shadow of Little Rock* (New York: David McKay & Co., 1962), and Brewer, *The Embattled Ladies of Little Rock,* p. 26.

23. "Dissenter on School Board Calls for 'No' Vote on TV," *Arkansas Gazette,* Sept. 27, 1958, p. 2A. The full text of Alford's speech can be found in Dale and L'Moore Alford, *The Case of the Sleeping People (Finally Awakened by Little Rock School Frustrations)* (Little Rock: Pioneer Press, 1959), pp. 70–79.

24. Claude Carpenter interview with Roy Reed, Aug. 1, 1990, p. 19, RRP. Day, "The Fall of a Southern Moderate," p. 251.

25. "Mark Your Ballot FOR," *Arkansas Gazette,* Sept. 27, 1958, p. 1A.

26. *Southern School News,* October 1958; Bill Lewis, "School Integration Rejected by Vote of 19,470 to 7,561," *Arkansas Gazette,* Sept. 28, 1958, p. 1A; Ray Moseley, "School Fight Reaches Voting Stage Today; Court Action Is Anticipated After Balloting," *Arkansas Gazette,* Sept. 27, 1958, p. 1A. "Ashmore Relates Little Rock Story," *Arkansas Gazette,* Oct. 2, 1958, p. 2A.

27. "NAACP Asks Injunction Against Leasing Schools," *Arkansas Gazette,* Sept. 28, 1958, p. 1A. For extensive quotation from the lease, see "Text of Order by Appeals Court," *Arkansas Gazette,* Nov. 11, 1958, p. 8A; see also "School Board Resolution Authorizing Lease," and "Agreement of Lease; Teachers' Contract," Sept. 29, 1958, *Race Relations Law Reporter,* October 1958, pp. 887–92. Jerol Garrison, "NAACP Appeals Miller's Decision," *Arkansas Gazette,* Sept. 27, 1958, p. 1A.

28. "NAACP Asks Injunction Against Leasing Schools." "U.S. Panel Named for Private School Hearing at Omaha," *Arkansas Gazette,* Sept. 29, 1958, p. 1A.

29. Branton, "Little Rock Revisited," p. 267.

30. "Text of Order by Appeals Court." Claude Sitton, "Faubus Won't Surrender; Awaits Court's Injunction," *New York Times,* Sept. 30, 1958, SERS.

31. Sitton, "Faubus Won't Surrender."

32. Bobbie Forster, "High Court Outlaws 'Evasive Schemes' As School Lease Signed," *Arkansas Democrat,* Sept. 29, 1958, p. 1. *Southern School News,* October 1958. "5 CHS Negroes Taking Courses of UA by Mail," *Arkansas Gazette,* Nov. 28, 1958, p. 5A; "Faubus Sees Full School Year Ahead," *Arkansas Democrat,* Sept. 29, 1958, p. 1.

33. "U.S. Marshals Serve Papers," *Arkansas Gazette,* Sept. 30, 1958, p. 1A. "School Injunction Plan to Be Aired by 3-Judge Panel," *Arkansas Gazette,* Oct. 1, 1958, p. 1A. Moseley, "School Opening in Doubt; Supreme Court Rules Out Evasion; Leasing Balked." The case had been styled *Aaron v. Cooper* since 1956, when Aaron was the appellant. When Cooper appealed the case to the United States Supreme Court, the case name changed to reflect that Cooper had become the appellant.

34. Hutchinson, "Unanimity and Desegregation," p. 74. For another concise description of the Supreme Court justices' deliberations among themselves, see Bernard Schwartz, *Super Chief: Earl Warren and His Supreme Court—A Judicial Biography* (New York University Press, 1983), pp. 289–304.

35. *Cooper v. Aaron, in Race Relations Law Reporter,* October 1958, pp. 855, 861.

36. Historian C. Vann Woodward described the tone of the decision at the time as "judicial rhetoric amounting to anger"; C. Vann Woodward, "The South and the Law of the Land," *Commentary* 26 (November 1958), p. 370. *Cooper v. Aaron, Race Relations Law Reporter,* October 1958, p. 860.

37. *Cooper v. Aaron, Race Relations Law Reporter,* October 1958, p. 861.

38. Ibid., p. 862; Hutchinson, "Unanimity and Desegregation," p. 82. For a suggestive discussion of the impact of *Cooper v. Aaron* see Kermit L. Hall, "The Constitutional Lessons of the Little Rock Crisis," in Elizabeth Jacoway and C. Fred Williams, *Understanding the Little Rock Crisis: An Exercise in Remembrance and Reconciliation* (Fayetteville: University of Arkansas Press, 1998), pp. 123–40.

39. Stephen L. Wasby, Anthony A. D'Amato, and Rosemary Metrailer, *Desegregation from Brown to Alexander: An Exploration of Supreme Court Strategies* (Carbondale: Southern Illinois University Press, 1977), pp. 179–180.

40. Ray Moseley, "Faubus Plan Fails, Schools Still Closed; He Vows to Fight On," *Arkansas Gazette,* Oct. 1, 1958, p. 1A.

41. "Bennett Reveals His Plan to Smash NAACP in South," *Arkansas Gazette,* Oct. 3, 1958, p. 5B.

42. Claude Sitton, "Faubus Won't Surrender; Awaits Court's Injunction," *New York Times,* Sept. 30, 1958. "Race Issue Just 'Sidelight': Faubus Says 'Tyranny' Jeopardizing Freedom," *Arkansas Gazette,* Oct. 7, 1958, p. 1A.

43. "Race Issue Just 'Sidelight': Faubus Says 'Tyranny' Jeopardizing Freedom." "Faubus has Overwhelming Support," *Chicago Tribune,* Oct. 9, 1958, as quoted in Faubus, *Down From the Hills,* p. 456.

44. "60 Per Cent of Displaced Students Find Means to Continue Schooling," *Arkansas Gazette,* Oct. 22, 1958, p. 1A; "LRU to Admit Some Top Seniors Shy of Credits," *Arkansas Gazette,* Oct. 24, 1958, p. 12A. Alford, *The Case of the Sleeping People,* p. 83. "Episcopal Interim Academy Opens Today 'For Duration,'" *Arkansas Gazette,* September 29, 1958, p. 1A. "Baptists to Operate Little Rock School," *Arkansas Gazette,* Oct. 10, 1958;" Ouachita Trustees Approve High School at LR," *Arkansas Gazette,* Oct. 18, 1958, p. 2A.

45. Claude Sitton, "Faubus Backers Expect Setback," *New York Times,* Oct. 2, 1958. See also Ernest Valachovic, "Donations Sought to Operate Schools on Private Basis," *Arkansas Gazette,* Oct. 2, 1958, p. 1A. "Plan Gets Support of Citizens Council," *Arkansas Gazette,* Oct. 2, 1958, p. 2A.

46. "Appeals Court Acts Tomorrow on School Plan," *Arkansas Gazette,* Oct. 5, 1958, p. 1A.

47. "U.S. Court Extends School Leasing Ban to October 15 Hearing," *Arkansas Gazette,* Oct. 7, 1958, p. 1A. "NAACP Asks Court to Ban School Lease," *Arkansas Gazette,* Oct. 14, 1958, p. 1A. "Board Protests Lease Hearing As 'Summary'; Brief Says Some of Main Parties Won't Be Heard," *Arkansas Gazette,* Oct. 15, 1958, p. 1A.

48. "School Lease Ban Is Kept Temporarily," *Arkansas Gazette,* Oct. 16, 1958, p. 1A.

49. "Private School May Get Start by Next Week," *Arkansas Gazette,* Oct. 17, 1958, p. 1A. "Faubus Charges Board's Balking," *Commercial Appeal,* Oct. 16, 1958, SERS; Kenneth Johnson, "Faubus Against School Abolition; but Says Such Move Might Be Forced by U.S.," *Commercial Appeal,* Oct. 25, 1958, SERS.

50. *Southern School News,* November 1958; "Private Firm Says Senior Registration to Start Monday," *Arkansas Gazette,* Oct. 18, 1958, p. 1A. "Faubus Hints Legislature to Act on School Funds," *Arkansas Gazette,* Oct. 22, 1958, p. 1A. "Faubus Clears Up Terms for Negro," *Commercial Appeal,* Oct. 19, 1958, SERS; "NAACP Studies Plans for Suit Against School," *Arkansas Gazette,* Oct. 21, 1958, p. 1A. "Corporation School for White Seniors Expects 500 Today," *Arkansas Gazette,* Oct. 18, 1958, p. 1A; "700 White Pupils Register in Private and Baptist Schools," *Arkansas Gazette,* Oct. 21, 1958, p. 1A; "Baptist School Plans to Start Classes Monday," *Arkansas Gazette,* Oct. 24, 1958, p. 1B.

51. *Southern School News,* November 1958. "Transfer Students Are Held Eligible For State Tax Aid," *Arkansas Gazette,* Oct. 25, 1958, p. 1A; "Board Ready to Start Aid Transfer," *Arkansas Gazette,* Oct. 16, 1958, p. 1A; "Bennett's Opinion on School Funds Creates Questions," *Arkansas Gazette,* Oct. 26, 1958, p. 18A. "Raney High School Asks for State Aid," *Arkansas Gazette,* Jan. 23, 1959, p. 3B; Jerol Garrison, "School Aid Transfer Banned; U.S. Court To Weigh Acts 4, 5," *Arkansas Gazette,* March 8, 1959, p. 1A.

52. "Alford Asked to Make Try for Congress," *Arkansas Gazette,* Oct. 20, 1958, p. 2A. "Hays

in Strong Plea for Moderate Position in Integration Controversy," *Arkansas Gazette,* Oct. 22, 1958, p. 1B.

53. George Douthit interview with John Luter, Dec. 31, 1970, p. 28, EAP; "Alford in Race for Congress," *Arkansas Gazette,* Oct. 28, 1958, p. 1A. "Alford Names Faubus Aide to Direct Bid for Congress," *Arkansas Gazette,* Oct. 29, 1958, p. 1A. D. Nathan Coulter, "A Political Martyr for Racial Progress in the South: Brooks Hays and the Electoral Consequences of the Little Rock Crisis" (senior honors thesis, Harvard University, 1982), Archives and Special Collections, UALR. "Court Attack Promised by Alford," *Arkansas Gazette,* Oct. 30, 1958, p. 1A. For the full text of Alford's campaign speeches, see Alford, *The Case of the Sleeping People.* "Alford Voted to Integrate, Hays Charges," *Arkansas Gazette,* Nov. 1, 1958, p. 10A.

54. "Alford Voted to Integrate, Hays Charges." "Alford Says He Did Not Vote for Plan," *Arkansas Gazette,* Nov. 1, 1958, p. 10A. "Write-in 'Stickers' for Ballot Permissible, Opinion Says," *Arkansas Gazette,* Nov. 2, 1958, p. 15A; "Dale Alford voted FOR Little Rock School Board Plan of Integration!!!" *Arkansas Gazette,* Nov. 1, 1958, p. 10A; "Dale Alford Has *Consistently* Opposed Integration!" *Arkansas Gazette,* Nov. 2, 1958, p. 5B; "Proof! That Dale Alford ATTENDED the L. R. School Board Meeting," *Arkansas Gazette,* Nov. 4, 1958, p. 11A; "Why Mislead the People, Brooks?" *Arkansas Gazette,* Nov. 4, 1958, p. 12A.

55. Jerol Garrison, "Jury Quizzes Nine in Election Probe," *Arkansas Gazette,* June 4, 1959, p. 1A. "Alford Aide Is Subpoenaed in Vote Probe," *Arkansas Gazette,* June 3, 1959, p. 2A. Elizabeth Carpenter, "Carpenter Trades Words with Hays at Election Hearing," *Arkansas Gazette,* June 5, 1959, p. 1A. Jerol Garrison, "Jury Refuses to Return Indictments in Probe of Alford Vote Circular," *Arkansas Gazette,* June 5, 1959, p. 1A; "FBI Probing Write-In Win by Dr. Alford," *Arkansas Gazette,* Feb. 3, 1959, p. 1A.

56. Roy Reed, "Hays Leads in Close Race; Democrats Pocket Congress," *Arkansas Gazette,* Nov. 5, 1958, p. 1A. "Election Lacks Wide Interest Despite Issues," *Arkansas Gazette,* Nov. 2, 1958, p. 1A. Brooks Hays, "Victorious Defeat," *Guideposts,* December 1959, p. 7, Box 42, LBH.

57. "Hays Concedes; Pulaski Vote Gives Write-In Foe Win," *Arkansas Gazette,* Nov. 6, 1958, p. 1A. Harry S. Ashmore, "They Didn't Want a Man of Reason," *The Reporter,* Nov. 27, 1958, pp. 21–22.

58. Jerol Garrison, "Hays Says He Will Continue to Seek Solution for South," *Arkansas Gazette,* Nov. 7, 1958, p. 1A. Lawrence Brooks Hays interview with A. Ronald Tonks, May 20, 1975–-October 5, 1977, pp. 348, 71–72, SBC. "Edward P. Morgan and the News," Nov. 7, 1958, Box 81, LBH.

59. "Edward P. Morgan and the News." Hays interview with Tonks, p. 339.

60. Brooks Hays to James P. Coleman, Nov. 10, 1958, Box 81, LBH. Hays interview with Tonks, p. 262. "Hays Suggested," *Arkansas Baptist,* Dec. 11, 1958, p. 7, "Scrapbook," LBH.

61. Elizabeth Carpenter, "Hays Says Faubus Broke Promise, Damaged South," *Arkansas Gazette,* Nov. 8, 1958, p. 1A. "Mills Promises to Push Hard for Dr. Alford," *Arkansas Gazette,* Nov. 11, 1958, p. 1B. "North-South Trade Seen to Seat Alford in 86th Congress," *Arkansas Gazette,* Dec. 22, 1958, p. 1A; Brooks Hays to Sam Rayburn, March 13, 1959, Box 82, LBH.

62. "Group to Release Pamphlets Calling for Open Schools," *Arkansas Gazette,* Nov. 2, 1958.

63. "Faubus Pledges Continued Fight on Integration," *Arkansas Gazette,* Nov. 9, 1958, p. 1A. "Segregationists to Fete Faubus in New Orleans," *Arkansas Gazette,* Nov. 9, 1958, p. 9A.

64. Grainger Williams interview with Elizabeth Jacoway, Dec. 21, 1977, untranscribed, EJC. For an excellent discussion of this scheme, see Irving Spitzberg Jr., *Racial Politics in Little Rock, 1954–1964* (New York: Garland Publishing, 1987), pp. 96–97.

65. Frank Lyon interview with Elizabeth Jacoway, Dec. 13, 1977, p. 7, EJC. "Contests Loom for School Board Posts," *Arkansas Gazette,* Nov. 13, 1958, p. 3A. Brewer, *The Embattled Ladies of Little Rock,* pp. 57–60. Billy Rector played a major role in formulating a list of potential candidates, but Mrs. Terry did the actual work of persuading candidates to run; Frank Lambright interview with Elizabeth Jacoway, Dec. 14, 1977, p. 13, EJC. Everett Tucker claimed that Billy Rector put together the businessmen's slate; Everett Tucker interview with John Luter, Aug. 16, 1971, p. 40,

EAP; see also Robert L. Brown, "Tucker Built Up Little Rock Industry Yet Still Yearns for Soil of Forebears," *Arkansas Business,* June 11–24, 1984, p. 10. Henry M. Alexander, *The Little Rock Recall Election,* Eagleton Institute Case Studies in Practical Politics, Case No. 17 (New Brunswick: Rutgers University Press, 1960), p. 2; Spitzberg, *Racial Politics in Little Rock,* pp. 97–98.

66. "Court Blasts Evasion, Asks Integration Start; District Judge Told to Supply Sweeping Rule," *Arkansas Gazette,* Nov. 11, 1958, p. 1A; "Text of Order by Appeals Court," *Arkansas Gazette,* Nov. 11, 1958, p. 8A.

67. Butler, House, and Haley had warned their clients this would be the court's reaction before the Board negotiated the lease; "Memorandum to Little Rock School Board" signed by Archie House, Richard C. Butler, and John Haley, "Subject: Validity of Lease of School Buildings," (nd), Box 5, Folder 1, VTB.

68. See Numan V. Bartley, *The Rise of Massive Resistance: Race and Politics in the South During the 1950's* (Baton Rouge: Louisiana State University Press, 1969), p. 320. Harry Ashmore was the first to suggest that Faubus's actions hastened the implementation of integration; Harry S. Ashmore, *An Epitaph for Dixie* (New York: W. W. Norton & Co., 1958), p. 43. Historian Michael Klarman has argued that southern strategists had hoped to see *Brown* overturned; Michael J. Klarman, *From Jim Crow to Civil Rights: The Supreme Court and the Struggle for Racial Equality* (New York: Oxford University Press, 2004), p. 409.

69. Garrison, "5 On School Board Quit After Buying Blossom Contract." See also "Response in Suit Tells Why Blossom Contract Cancelled," *Arkansas Gazette,* Dec. 4, 1958, p. 1A. "Guthridge to File Lawsuit to Block Blossom Payments," *Arkansas Gazette,* Nov. 13, 1958, p. 1A. "Blossom Takes School Position at San Antonio," *Arkansas Gazette,* Feb. 27, 1959, p. 1A; "Blossom Moves to Reduce Salary Claim on Little Rock," *Arkansas Gazette,* April 25, 1959, p. 1A.

70. "Upton Says Faubus' Abuse Cause of Board Resigning," Knoxville, Nov. 15, 1958, EJC. Harold Engstrom interview with Roy Reed, Aug. 21, 1991, p. 2, RRP. "The Departure of the School Board," *Arkansas Gazette,* Nov. 14, 1958, p. 4A. Harold and Martha Frances Engstrom interview with Elizabeth Jacoway, summer of 2000. Robert L. Brown, "The Second Crisis of Little Rock: A Report on Desegregation Within the Little Rock Public Schools," Winthrop Rockefeller Foundation, June 1988, p. 2.

71. "Contests Loom for School Board Posts," *Arkansas Gazette,* Nov. 13, 1958, p. 3A; "Laster in the Race; Karam Doesn't List His Slate for Board," *Arkansas Gazette,* Nov. 15, 1958, p. 1A; "15 Candidates File for School Board; Karam Withdraws," *Arkansas Gazette,* Nov. 16, 1958, p. 1A; Ronnie Farrar, "15 Candidates Guarded About School Remedy," *Arkansas Gazette,* Nov. 17, 1958, p. 1A. "5 School Board Candidates State Belief in Segregation," *Arkansas Gazette,* Nov. 18, 1958, p. 1A. "Tucker Leaves C of C Post for School Board Candidacy," *Arkansas Gazette,* Nov. 23, 1958, p. 3A. "A New Court Order—And a New Board?" *Arkansas Gazette,* Nov. 11, 1958, p. 4A. "Private Students Determined to Make Most of Difficulties," *Arkansas Gazette,* Nov. 23, 1958, p. 1A; "Miller Waiting for Court Rule on Procedure," *Arkansas Gazette,* Nov. 25, 1958, p. 1A.

72. Ernest Green had graduated; Terrence Roberts had moved to Los Angeles to live with his grandmother; Gloria Ray had moved to Kansas City to live with relatives, and Minnijean Brown was living in New York City with Dr. and Mrs. Kenneth Clark; "5 CHS Negroes Taking Courses of UA by Mail," *Arkansas Gazette,* Nov. 28, 1958, p. 5A. "Memorandum from Mr. Wilkins to Mr. McClain," Nov. 21, 1958, Microfilm Part 3, Series D, Reel 2, Folder "Desegregation Schools in Arkansas, Little Rock Central High, 1958, July—December," PON. The remaining five were tutored throughout the year by Art Dennis, white chemistry professor at Philander Smith (the local black college); Daisy Bates to Roy Wilkins, Feb. 10, 1960, group III, series A, container 20, Folder "Daisy Bates, 1957–1960," PON. Morsell to Gordon, Nov. 18, 1958. Elizabeth Eckford interview with Elizabeth Jacoway, Aug. 14, 2003, p. 19, EJC. Jerry Jones, "Wilkins Says Negroes Can't Set Up Schools," *Arkansas Gazette,* Nov. 3, 1958, p. 1A.

73. Jones, "Wilkins Says Negroes Can't Set Up Schools."

74. "Branton Disclaims Reported Account of State Job Offer," *Arkansas Gazette,* Oct. 14, 1958, p. 5A. In a 1970 interview Branton recalled, ". . . the Justice Department lawyers went to great

lengths to try and get me to persuade my clients to withdraw and go back to the segregated schools and allow for a cooling-off period, before proceeding further. And I of course would not accept those suggestions"; Branton interview with Lawson, p. 57.

75. Kilpatrick, "Wiley Austin Branton," p. 6.

CHAPTER FIFTEEN — THE WOMEN ORGANIZE

1. See typescript copy of "Lenon Family History" in Series II, Box 2, Folder 7, VLB. See also Elizabeth Jacoway, "Vivion Brewer of Arkansas: A Ladylike Assault on the 'Southern Way of Life,'" in Bruce L. Clayton and John A. Salmond, eds., *"Lives Full of Struggle and Triumph": Southern Women, Their Institutions, and Their Communities* (Gainesville: University Press of Florida, 2003), pp. 264–82. Vivion Lenon Brewer, *The Embattled Ladies of Little Rock: 1958–1963, The Struggle to Save Public Education at Central High* (Fort Bragg, Calif.: Lost Coast Press, 1999), p. xv. Vivion Brewer interview with Charlotte Gadberry, May 9, 1978, p. 5, EJC. Vivion Brewer interview with Elizabeth Jacoway, Oct. 15, 1976, p. 6, SOHP. "Little Rock Bank Directors Chosen," clipping dated Jan. 10, 1928, Series II, Box 2, Folder 8, VLB. For a brief overview of Brewer's life see "Vivion Brewer Knows All About Discrimination," *Arkansas Gazette*, May 1, 1979, p. 1B. One of Vivion Brewer's closest friends attributed Vivion's fine education to her mother's influence; Louise Vinson interview with Elizabeth Jacoway, Sept. 6, 1996, p. 16, EJC.

2. Brewer interview with Gadberry, pp. 13, 20, 22. The description of Joe Brewer is from Mimi Dortch interview with Elizabeth Jacoway, Sept. 3, 1996, p. 2, EJC; Brewer, *The Embattled Ladies of Little Rock*, pp. xviii, xix.

3. Dortch interview with Jacoway; *The Embattled Ladies of Little Rock*, p. xix. Brewer interview with Gadberry, p. 16; Brewer interview with Jacoway, p. 11.

4. Brewer, *The Embattled Ladies of Little Rock*, p. xx. Vivion Brewer may have been sensitive, but she was not weak. Grainger Williams said of her, "The White Citizens' Council followed her around, tried to frighten her, but she's not frightenable"; E. Grainger Williams interview with John Luter, Dec. 29, 1970, p. 18, EAP. Brewer, *The Embattled Ladies of Little Rock*, p. xxii. For Brewer's reflections on her contribution in Little Rock see Vivion Lenon Brewer, "Little Rock—Nine Years Later," *Smith Alumnae Quarterly*, Summer 1966, pp. 210–11, Box 1, Folder 6, Vivion Lenon Brewer Papers, Sophia Smith Collection, Smith College.

5. John Gould Fletcher, Adolphine's brother, was the author of twenty-four books of poetry, essays, and history, as well as an essay included in the influential "Southern Manifesto," Twelve Southerners, *I'll Take My Stand: The South and the Agrarian Tradition* (New York: Harper & Bros., 1930). For a full and perceptive biography of Fletcher see Ben F. Johnson III, *Fierce Solitude: A Life of John Gould Fletcher* (Fayetteville: University of Arkansas Press, 1994). For a brief, illuminating biography of Adolphine Fletcher Terry, see Sara Alderman Murphy, *Breaking the Silence: Little Rock's Women's Emergency Committee to Open Our Schools, 1958–1963* (Fayetteville: University of Arkansas Press, 1997), pp. 1–25; see also Mary Fletcher Worthen, Biography of Adolphine Fletcher Terry, Aesthetic Club paper, EJC. Lorraine Gates, "Power from the Pedestal: The Women's Emergency Committee and the Little Rock School Crisis," *Arkansas Historical Quarterly*, Spring 1996, p. 31. In 1961, in recognition of her extraordinary contributions to the life of her community, the trustees of Vassar College named Adolphine Terry to the list of its one hundred most distinguished alumnae; Worthen biography of Terry.

6. Adolphine Fletcher Terry with Carolyn Auge Rose, "Life Is My Song, Also," pp. 231–32, Box 2, Folder 6, FTF. Murphy, *Breaking the Silence*, pp. 52, 54. Brewer, *The Embattled Ladies of Little Rock*, pp. 6–7. See also Betty and Bill Terry interview with Sara Alderman Murphy, Aug. 13, 1992, p. 11, Box 4, Folder 10, SAM. Alta Haskins Faubus interview with Elizabeth Jacoway, April 10, 1996, pp. 44–46, EJC. Murphy, *Breaking the Silence*, p. 54; Brewer, *The Embattled Ladies of Little Rock*, p. 6.

7. Brewer, *The Embattled Ladies of Little Rock*, p. 7. Murphy, *Breaking the Silence*, p. 68; see also Vivion Brewer interview with John Luter, Aug. 20, 1971, p. 2, EAP.

8. Harry Ashmore interview with Elizabeth Jacoway, Nov. 17, 1976, p. 82, EJC. For a description of Mrs. Terry's invulnerability, see Pat House interview with John Luter, Aug. 22, 1971, pp. 12–14, EAP. Pat House interview with Luter, p. 13.

9. For a full and insightful treatment of the history of the ASWPL see Jacqueline Dowd Hall, *Revolt Against Chivalry: Jessie Daniel Ames and the Women's Campaign Against Lynching* (New York: Columbia University Press, 1979); Fred Routh to Harold Fleming, Sept. 16, 1958, Box 80, SRC. Most accounts set the number of attendees at fifty-eight; Velma Powell claimed in a late-in-life interview that seventy women actually attended, although only fifty-eight signed the list the organizers circulated; Velma Powell interview with Sandra Hubbard, March 1997, untranscribed, EJC; the author is indebted to Sandra Hubbard for sharing this interview with her. A researcher for the Eagleton Institute, Henry M. Alexander, incorrectly listed the number of attendees as forty-eight (in a report that is filled with inaccuracies), and many students have cited his figures; Henry M. Alexander, *The Little Rock Recall Election*, Eagleton Institute Case Studies in Practical Politics, Case No. 17 (New Brunswick: Rutgers University Press, 1960). See also Brewer, *The Embattled Ladies of Little Rock*, p. 9; Murphy, *Breaking the Silence*, p. 73.

10. Murphy, *Breaking the Silence*, p. 74.

11. Terry, *Life Is My Song, Also*, p. 231. *The Embattled Ladies of Little Rock*, p. 7; see also ACHR "Quarterly Report, Dec. 30, 1958," Box 71, SRC.

12. Terry's daughter-in-law said of her, ". . . if you disagreed with her she just thought you were crazy. She was strong. . . . It didn't make any difference whether there was another side to it or not. [She was] right and the other side was wrong"; Betty and Bill Terry interview with Murphy, p. 11.

13. Murphy, *Breaking the Silence*, p. xviii. In doing research for her own book, Sara Murphy penned a note at the end of John Pagan's interview with Vivion Brewer saying, "Like Vivion, I was an integrationist from the beginning"; John Pagan interview with Vivion Brewer, Jan. 4, 1973, p. 9, Box 1, Folder 8, SAM. Brewer interview with Luter, p. 2. Terry, *Life Is My Song, Also*, p. 238.

14. Brewer, *The Embattled Ladies of Little Rock*, p. 10.

15. Ibid.

16. The Virginia Committee for Public Schools also restricted membership to whites because of the "present climate of public opinion"; Matthew D. Lassiter, "The Open-Schools Revolt: The Southern Regional Council and the Construction of the Moderate South," p. 6, Conference on the Southern Regional Council and the Civil Rights Movement, University of Florida, Oct. 23–26, 2003. Atlanta's HOPE made the same decision; Ibid., p. 16. Murphy, *Breaking the Silence*, p. 73. Brewer, *The Embattled Ladies of Little Rock*, pp. 71–72; Brewer interview with Luter, p. 26. By Christmas, Bates had relented and sent flowers to Adolphine Terry; Adolphine Terry to Daisy Bates, Dec. 28, 1958, Box 1, Folder 7, DGB. Dan Wakefield, "Siege at Little Rock: The Brave Ones," *Nation*, Oct. 11, 1958, pp. 204–6.

17. "Open-School Body Triples Members," *Arkansas Gazette*, Nov. 14, 1958, p. 2A; "Committee to Open Schools Finds Interest Spreading," *Arkansas Gazette*, Dec. 3, 1958, p. 6A. Brewer, *The Embattled Ladies of Little Rock*, p. 62; Brewer interview with Luter, p. 4. Brewer interview with Jacoway, p. 34. Brewer, *The Embattled Ladies of Little Rock*, pp. 96–97.

18. Brewer, *The Embattled Ladies of Little Rock*, pp. 41, 43.

19. Ibid., pp. 51, 23, 60. Laura A. Miller, *Fearless: Irene Gaston Samuel and the Life of a Southern Liberal* (Little Rock: Center for Arkansas Studies, 2002), pp. 17–23, 41; Murphy, *Breaking the Silence*, p. 107.

20. "The Schools Won't Run Themselves," *Arkansas Gazette*, Dec. 1, 1958, p. 10B. "Business Slate Tells Platform in Board Race," *Arkansas Gazette*, Dec. 2, 1958, p. 1B. "School Board Slate of 6 Uses Faubus' Name," *Arkansas Gazette*, Dec. 4, 1958, p. 1A. "Faubus Off Fence, Calls Business Slate Integration Group 'Meddling,'" *Arkansas Gazette*, Dec. 6, 1958, p. 1A.

21. One analyst concluded that Lamb and Tucker were elected "only because a split in the White Citizens Council had put rival segregationist tickets into the field in those two races"; Jerry Neil, "The Education of Governor Faubus," *Nation*, June 6, 1959, pp. 507–9. Jerry Jones, "Slate Split Creates Threat of Deadlock for School Board," *Arkansas Gazette*, Dec. 8, 1958, p. 1A. See also

"Three on Each Side Win in School Race," *Arkansas Gazette,* Dec. 7, 1958, p. 1A; "Protests Hinted by 3 Losers in District's Strangest Race," *Arkansas Gazette,* Dec. 7, 1958, p. 1A; "New School Directors Take Office; McKinley Elected Board President," *Arkansas Gazette,* Dec. 17, 1958, p. 1B. Corinne Silverman, *The Little Rock Story,* Inter-University Case Program, No. 41 (University of Alabama Press, 1959), p. 30. Orval E. Faubus, *Down From the Hills* (Little Rock: Democrat Printing & Lithographing Co., 1980), p. 484.

22. "Two Slates and One School Board," *Arkansas Gazette,* Dec. 9, 1958, p. 4A. Murphy, *Breaking the Silence,* p. 109. "Group Sending 'Little Rock Letter' with Yule Cards, *Arkansas Gazette,* Dec. 17, 1958. Late in life Irene Samuel claimed that a preponderance of her group's members had been Jewish (her husband's faith); while many Jewish women played integral roles in the organization, it is doubtful that they sent these Christmas cards, and the group at that point only claimed 850 members; Clive Webb, *Fight Against Fear: Southern Jews and Black Civil Rights* (Athens: University of Georgia Press, 2001), pp. 153–55. "Board Asked to Establish Commission on Civic Unity," *Arkansas Gazette,* Dec. 23, 1958, p. 1A; Brewer, *The Embattled Ladies of Little Rock,* pp. 72–75, 80. *Southern School News,* February 1959, SERS. The wife of the Chamber's new president, Grainger Williams, was on the WEC's Executive Committee.

23. "Popularity Poll Has Faubus 10th," *Arkansas Gazette,* Dec. 29, 1958, p. 2A. "High Tribute Is Paid Faubus in National Poll," *Shreveport Times,* Jan. 2, 1959, as quoted in Faubus, *Down From the Hills,* p. 487. "Faubus Boomed for Presidency," *Commercial Appeal,* Dec. 31, 1958, SERS.

24. "School Board Chooses New Law Advisers," *Arkansas Gazette,* Dec. 29, 1958, p. 1A.

25. "Mr. Bennett and His Hired Witnesses," *Arkansas Gazette,* Dec. 21, 1958, p. 4E; see also "The Ambitions of the Hon. Bruce Bennett," *Arkansas Gazette,* Jan. 18, 1959, p. 5E. Bennett eventually ran for governor in 1960. "Bennett Says Red Hearings in Arkansas Set This Month," *Arkansas Gazette,* Dec. 4, 1958, p. 3A. For background on this initiative see "Bennett Reveals His Plan to Smash NAACP in South," *Arkansas Gazette,* Oct. 3, 1958, p. 5B. Ernest Valachovic, "Legislative Probe on Reds, Unrest to Begin Monday," *Arkansas Gazette,* Dec. 9, 1958, p. 1A. See also Roy Reed, "Names, Groups Listed As Red Probe Opens," *Arkansas Gazette,* Dec. 17, 1958, p. 1A.

26. "State NAACP Head Labels Red Probe 'Smear Session,'" *Arkansas Gazette,* Dec. 17, 1958, p. 1A. Roy Reed, "Reds, Integration Linked by Ex-aide to McCarthy," *Arkansas Gazette,* Dec. 18, 1958, p. 1A.

27. Reed, "Reds, Integration Linked by Ex-aide to McCarthy"; Elizabeth Carpenter, "Some Background on a Professional Witness," *Arkansas Gazette,* Dec. 18, 1958, p. 4A; "Hearings End; Red Probers See Success," *Arkansas Gazette,* Dec. 19, 1958, p. 4A; "Statement by Roy Wilkins on Report by Special Education Committee of Arkansas Legislative Council." ACHR "Quarterly Report," December 1958, Box 27, Folder 287, ACHR. For an informative treatment of the Bennett hearings see Wilma Dykeman and James Stokeley, "McCarthyism Under the Magnolias," *Progressive,* July 1959, Box 2, Folder 1, DGB.

28. "NAACP Asks 4 Bennett Bills Be Overthrown," *Arkansas Gazette,* Dec. 5, 1958, p. 1A; "3 Federal Judges Named to Rule on 'Bennett Bills,'" *Arkansas Gazette,* Dec. 16, 1958, p. 1B. "Show Records or Pay Taxes, NAACP Told," *Arkansas Gazette,* Dec. 23, 1958, p. 1A. "Court Rejects NAACP Appeal on Ordinances," *Arkansas Gazette,* Jan. 20, 1959, p. 1B.

29. "Court Mandate Arrives; Sent to Judge Miller," *Arkansas Gazette,* Dec. 5, 1958, p. 1B. "Miller to Hear Debate Tuesday on Integration," *Arkansas Gazette,* Jan. 4, 1959, p. 1A. "Miller Sets School Hearing for January 6," *Arkansas Gazette,* Dec. 9, 1958, p. 1A. "Karam Issue Hurt Ticket, Faubus Says," *Arkansas Gazette,* Dec. 11, 1958, p. 1A. "Branton Asks Court to Order Board to Act," *Arkansas Gazette,* Dec. 31, 1958, p. 2A.

30. "Judge Tells Board to 'Move Forward' on Integration Plan," *Arkansas Gazette,* Jan. 11, 1959, p. 1A; "Text of Order," *Arkansas Gazette,* Jan. 11, 1959, p. 2A.

31. Roy Reed, "Board Asks to Open Segregated Schools While It Drafts Plan," *Arkansas Gazette,* Jan. 22, 1959, p. 1A; "Text of School Board Plea for Relief," *Arkansas Gazette,* Jan. 22, 1959, p. 2A. "Board Will Plead Tuesday to Reopen Four Schools on Segregated Basis," *Arkansas Gazette,* Feb. 1, 1959, p. 3A.

32. Jerol Garrison, "Judge Spurns Plan to Reopen Schools, Delay Integration," *Arkansas Gazette,* Feb. 4, 1959, p. 1A; "Excerpt of Text in School Decision," *Arkansas Gazette,* Feb. 4, 1959, p. 5A. "The Federal Court Has Said It Again," *Arkansas Gazette,* Feb. 14, 1959, p. 1A. "Judge Miller Flays Federal Appeal Courts," *Arkansas Gazette,* Feb. 14, 1959, p. 1A.

33. "Court Allows 'Open-School' Group to File," *Arkansas Gazette,* Feb. 3, 1959, p. 2B.

34. "Time to Evaluate School Situation, Leaders Advised," *Arkansas Gazette,* Jan. 15, 1959, p. 1A. The full text of Williams's concluding remarks can be found in Brewer, *The Embattled Ladies of Little Rock,* p. 102. Williams later recalled that after his speech Louise and Hugh Patterson came up to him with tears in their eyes and said, "We've been waiting for someone to say this for a long time"; E. Grainger Williams interview with Elizabeth Jacoway, Dec. 21, 1977, EJC; Williams interview with Luter, p. 22.

35. Murphy, *Breaking the Silence,* p. 112. "Chamber of Commerce Backs School Board, Pledges Aid."

36. "Surveyed Businessmen Tell Crisis Impact on Little Rock," *Arkansas Gazette,* Jan. 25, 1959, p. 1A. "How Is Business?," *Arkansas Gazette,* Jan. 27, 1959, p. 4A. "Faubus Challenges Crisis Cost Survey, Notes Sales Upturn," *Arkansas Gazette,* Jan. 27, 1959, p. 1B; Relman Morin, "Arkansas Strife's Economic Results Worries Citizens," *Miami Herald,* Nov. 8, 1958, as quoted in Faubus, *Down From the Hills,* p. 476.

37. Spitzberg, *Racial Politics in Little Rock,* p. 103. Brewer, *The Embattled Ladies of Little Rock,* p. 106. ACHR "Narrative Quarterly Report," January–March, 1959, Box 71, SRC; Harold C. Fleming to Vivion Brewer, Feb. 12, 1959, Box 8, Folder 6, HSA. Murphy, *Breaking the Silence,* 135. "Women's School Committee to Make Expansion Effort," *Arkansas Gazette,* Feb. 26, 1959, p. 3A.

38. "Chamber Polls Its Members on Issue Of Closed Schools," *Arkansas Gazette,* Feb. 26, 1959, p. 1A.

39. "Minimum Plan Approved by 819–245 Vote," *Arkansas Gazette,* March 3, 1959, p. 1A. "Three on School Board Reject Defiance, Urge 'Controlled Integration,'" *Arkansas Gazette,* March 1, 1959, p. 1A.

40. Pat House interview with Luter, pp. 11, 14.

41. Brewer, *The Embattled Ladies of Little Rock,* p. 99; Spitzberg, *Racial Politics in Little Rock,* p. 103. Murphy, *Breaking the Silence,* pp. 115, 119, 125. Apparently the WEC women treated the Mothers' League women with little respect. As one Mothers' League member recalled, "They were rude to us. They tried to imply that we were ignorant, uneducated white trash"; Margaret Morrison interview with Sara Alderman Murphy, June 10, 1992, Box 2, Folder 17, SAM.

42. "'59 Legislature Set to Follow Faubus' Lead," *Arkansas Gazette,* Jan. 4, 1959, p. 1A. Ernest Valachovic, "Faubus Starts Third Term, Asks More School Laws," *Arkansas Gazette,* Jan. 14, 1959, p. 1A; "62nd Assembly Starts Slowly, Plenty Ahead," *Arkansas Gazette,* Jan. 18, 1959, p. 1A. The Faubus proposal was clearly modeled after North Carolina's Pearsall Plan; see William H. Chafe, *Civilities and Civil Rights: Greensboro, North Carolina and the Black Struggle for Freedom* (New York: Oxford University Press, 1980), p. 53. "Education, Governor's Address—Arkansas," *Race Relations Law Reporter,* Spring 1959, p. 179. *Southern School News,* February 1959, SERS.

43. "Virginia School Laws Killed: Faubus Says His Plan Is Answer," *Arkansas Gazette,* Jan. 20, 1959, p. 1A; Roy Reed, "Relieving State of Duty to Provide Free Schools Big Part of Faubus Plan," *Arkansas Gazette,* Jan. 25, 1959, p. 1A. "The Faubus Amendment Defines the Choice," *Arkansas Gazette,* Jan. 27, 1959, p. 4A. Throughout the two-month legislative session Harry Ashmore repeatedly characterized the governor's measures as "wrecking" the public schools; see, for example, "A Half Million Dollars Our Schools Are Losing," *Arkansas Gazette,* Feb. 21, 1959, p. 4A. Spitzberg, *Racial Politics in Little Rock,* p. 107.

44. "Bennett Offers 15 New Bills for Preserving Segregation," *Arkansas Gazette,* Feb. 5, 1959, p. 1A; "Bennett Sees Black Republic in Red Future," *Arkansas Gazette,* Feb. 17, 1959, p. 6A. The bills eventually passed the House; "Segregation Bills Approved in House," *Arkansas Gazette,* Feb. 27, 1959, p. 1A. "Bennett Proposal Against NAACP Passes in House," *Arkansas Gazette,* Feb. 7, 1959,

p. 2A. Roy Reed, "Fagan Protests As Bill to Curb NAACP Passes," *Arkansas Gazette,* Feb. 18, 1959, p. 1B; calling it a "vicious" bill, Daisy Bates promised to challenge it in the courts; "Faubus Signs Bill Aimed at NAACP," *Arkansas Gazette,* Feb. 25, 1959, p. 1B; "House Passes, Senate Tables Board Packing," *Arkansas Gazettea* March 3, 1959, p. 1A.

45. Alexander, *The Little Rock Recall Election,* p. 10. Roy Reed, "Teachers Without Classes Teach Themselves," *Arkansas Gazette,* Jan. 9, 1959, p. 1A; "Horace Mann Teachers Use Classless Days for Studying," *Arkansas Gazette,* Jan. 22, 1959, p. 6A. T. M. Stinnett and Clara B. Kennan, *All This and Tomorrow Too: The Evolving and Continuing History of the Arkansas Education Association— A Century and Beyond* (Little Rock: Arkansas Education Association, 1969), p. 366. Despite the AEA's claims that no teachers left the system, Irving Spitzberg suggested a loss of two hundred teachers; Spitzberg, *Racial Politics in Little Rock,* p. 99. Superintendent Terrell Powell eventually admitted the high schools had lost 20 percent of their "key staff members"; "Board Takes Look at School Plight, Hopes to Cut Tax," *Arkansas Gazette,* Sept. 2, 1959, p. 1B.

46. Brewer, *The Embattled Ladies of Little Rock,* p. 112; Alexander, *The Little Rock Recall Election,* p. 10. "State Aid in Return for Teacher Purge Posed to Directors," *Arkansas Gazette,* Feb. 8, 1959, p. 1A.

47. Alexander, *The Little Rock Recall Election,* p. 10.

48. "Faubus Would Fire Trio on Purge List; Plans New Aid Bill," *Arkansas Gazette,* Feb. 10, 1959, p. 1A. "Rowland Says He's for Purge of 3, or More," *Arkansas Gazette,* Feb. 10, 1959, p. 1A.

49. "School Board Packing Has Faubus' Okay," *Arkansas Gazette,* Feb. 28, 1959, p. 2A. *Southern School News,* April 1959. William J. Smith interview with John Luter, Aug. 19–20, 1971, p. 76, EAP.

50. "House Passes, Senate Tables Board Packing," *Arkansas Gazette,* March 3, 1959, p. 1A. Tyler failed to defend his own bill on the floor of the House.

51. "House Passes, Senate Tables Board Packing"; "The Plan to Pack the School Board," *Arkansas Gazette,* Feb. 28, 1959, p. 4A; "Board Packing to Meet Fight in Legislature," *Arkansas Gazette,* March 1, 1959, p. 1A. "House Passes, Senate Tables Board Packing."

52. Samuel interview with Luter, p. 4. "Backers Seek to Resurrect School Board Packing Bill," *Arkansas Gazette,* March 4, 1959, p. 1A; "Board Packing Fight Scorches Assembly Halls; 'Brutal' Pressure May Not Reverse Faubus' First Fall," *Arkansas Gazette,* March 8, 1959, p. 1A. See also "Faubus Loses Bid on School Set-up," *New York Times,* March 15, 1959, p. 85. "Purge Motive Is Uncovered in Tyler Bill," *Arkansas Gazette,* March 5, 1959, p. 1A; Roy Reed, "Board Packing Proposal Dies in Filibuster," *Arkansas Gazette,* March 13, 1959, p. 1A.

53. *Southern School News,* March 1959. When he stood for reelection for traffic judge and was defeated in the summer of 1959, Bob Laster became quite bitter and abandoned his segregationist stance, admitting he had hoped to be governor some day; Jerol Garrison, "Laster, Bitter in Defeat, Says He's Through with Segregationists, They Can 'Go to Blazes,'" *Arkansas Gazette,* July 29, 1959, p. 1A.

54. "3 Summon School Board," *Arkansas Gazette,* Feb. 28, 1959, p. 1A; "Three on School Board Reject Defiance, Urge 'Controlled Integration,'" *Arkansas Gazette,* March 1, 1959, p. 1A. "Minimum Plan Approved By 819–245 Vote," *Arkansas Gazette,* March 3, 1959, p. 1A. Nat Griswold soon wrote to his Southern Regional Council superiors of Faubus's reaction: "We understand the poll frightened him"; ACHR "Narrative Quarterly Report," January–March 1959, Box 71, SRC. "3–3 Split of School Board Was Predicted from Outset," *Arkansas Democrat,* May 24, 1959, p. 6A; Charles Portis, "School Board Meet Lacks Quorum; 3 Members Slap Laster, Tyler Plans," *Arkansas Gazette,* March 2, 1959, p. 1A.

55. "Three on School Board Reject Defiance, Urge 'Controlled Integration.'"

56. Ibid.; Jerry Jones, "Integrationist Scheme Seen by Governor," *Arkansas Gazette,* March 4, 1959, p. 1A.

57. *Southern School News,* April 1959. "School Board Splits, 3 to 3, Over Results of Chamber of Commerce Poll," *Arkansas Gazette,* March 4, 1959, p. 3A; Jones, "Integrationist Scheme Seen By Governor."

58. "Faubus Signs 86 Acts, Including Assessment and Segregation Bills," *Arkansas Gazette,* March 26, 1959, p. 1B; *Southern School News,* April 1959. "Pupil Placement, 2 Tuition Aid Laws Still in Faubus' Segregation Arsenal," *Arkansas Gazette,* June 19, 1959, p. 1A; Bill Lewis, "Pupil Placement Laws Appear as Big Weapons for Saving Segregation," *Arkansas Gazette,* June 28, 1959, p. 1A. See also Chafe, *Civilities and Civil Rights,* p. 50. Roy Reed, "Board Packing Proposal Dies in Filibuster," *Arkansas Gazette,* March 13, 1959, p. 1A.

59. ACHR "Narrative Quarterly Report," January–March 1959. "Branton Sees Test of Latest School Laws," *Arkansas Gazette,* March 15, 1959, p. 11A.

60. Alexander, *The Little Rock Recall Election*; "To Date: This Is the Position of the Little Rock Chamber of Commerce on the Little Rock School Crisis, No More—No Less!" *Arkansas Gazette,* March 25, 1959, p. 7A; Roy Reed, "C of C Board Asks School Reopenings with Pupil Placing; Backs Private Plans, Speaks for Teachers," *Arkansas Gazette,* March 25, 1959, p. 1A. "McClellan Turns Criticism on Supreme Court Again," *Arkansas Gazette,* March 10, 1959, p. 1A.; John McClellan to Frank Lambright, Feb. 27, 1959, EJC; "High Court Blistered by Sen. Fulbright," *Arkansas Democrat,* Dec. 4, 1958, p. 1. *Southern School News,* April 1959. Williams interview with Luter, p. 6; E. Grainger Williams interview with Sara Murphy, July 29, 1992, p. 8, Box 5, Folder 6, SAM.

61. "Sign of Progress: A Modest Bow to Reason by Realists in Little Rock," *Arkansas Gazette,* April 4, 1959, p. 4A.

62. "Women's Group to Be Asked to Comply With Bennett Law," *Arkansas Gazette,* Feb. 12, 1959, p. 10B. Brewer, *The Embattled Ladies of Little Rock,* pp. 115–22; Murphy, *Breaking the Silence,* pp. 129–33. "Women Asked to Observe Bennett Law," *Arkansas Gazette,* March 28, 1959, p. 5A; "Women Reply to 2d Request From Langford," *Arkansas Gazette,* April 24, 1959, p. 1B; "Open-schools Group Gets 3d Demand," *Arkansas Gazette,* April 29, 1959, p. 9A.

63. "Summary of Arkansas Council on Human Relations Board Retreat," Feb. 20–21, 1958, Box 80, SRC.

CHAPTER SIXTEEN — REBIRTH

1. Everett Tucker Jr. interview with John Luter, Aug. 16, 1971, p. 1, EAP. Everett Tucker III interview with Elizabeth Jacoway, February 2005, EJC; see also Robert L. Brown, "Tucker Built Up Little Rock Industry yet Still Yearns for Soil of Forebears," *Arkansas Business,* June 11–24, 1984, p. 10. Everett Tucker Jr. interview with Elizabeth Jacoway, Dec. 5, 1977, p. 5, EJC.

2. Tucker Jr. interview with Jacoway, pp. 3, 29–30; see also Garry Fullerton, "New Factories Thing of the Past in Little Rock," *Nashville Tennessean,* May 31, 1959.

3. Tucker Jr. interview with Jacoway, p. 5. Tucker Jr. interview with Luter, p. 34.

4. Tucker Jr. interview with Luter, p. 7.

5. E. Grainger Williams interview with Sara Murphy, July 29, 1992, p. 5, Box 5, Folder 6, SAM. W. F. Rector interview with John Pagan, Jan. 2, 1973, p. 3, EJC. Tucker Jr. interview with Luter, p. 5. *Southern School News,* March 1958.

6. Untitled clipping from the *Philadelphia Bulletin,* Dec. 7, 1959, Everett Tucker Jr. Scrapbook, in the possession of the Tucker family. The author is indebted to Everett Tucker Jr. for sharing these materials with her. Ernest Valachovic, "Faubus' Hand Was Heavy on the Wheel," *Arkansas Gazette,* March 15, 1959, p. 1A.

7. Ernest Valachovic, "Governor Changes Tack, Hints That He's Ready for School Compromise," *Arkansas Gazette,* April 7, 1959, p. 1A. See also "Faubus Warns of Trouble if Courts Deny Tuition to Segregationist Pupils," *Arkansas Gazette,* April 8, 1959, p. 1A. Valachovic, "Governor Changes Tack, Hints That He's Ready For School Compromise." "Private School Plan Is Urged By Guthridge," *Arkansas Gazette,* April 8, 1959, 2A.

8. "Purge Motive Is Uncovered in Tyler Bill," *Arkansas Gazette,* March 5, 1959, p. 1A. Terrell Powell interview with John Pagan, Aug. 22, 1972, p. 3, EJC; see also Terrell E. Powell interview with T. Harri Baker, Nov. 20, 1972, p. 14, EAP. Henry M. Alexander, *The Little Rock Recall Election,* Eagleton Institute Case Studies in Practical Politics, Case No. 17 (New Brunswick: Rutgers University

Press, 1960), p. 11. "3 Directors Visit Schools, Tell Teachers They Foresee Integrated Classes in Fall," *Arkansas Gazette,* April 9, 1959, p. 1B.

9. "Faubus, McKinley Trade Accusations With 3 on Board," *Arkansas Gazette,* April 10, 1959, p. 1B.

10. Roy Reed, "NCA Asked to Drop Idled High Schools," *Arkansas Gazette,* April 23, 1959, p. 1A. "3 Closed Schools Dropped From NCA," *Arkansas Gazette,* April 25, 1959, p. 1A. "The NCA and the Little Rock Schools," *Arkansas Gazette,* April 25, 1959, p. 4A. "Latest Report on Teachers Indicates 176 Won't Return," *Arkansas Gazette,* April 30, 1959, p. 1A.

11. Jerry Jones, "School Closing Law Upheld in 4–3 Votes by Supreme Court," *Arkansas Gazette,* April 28, 1959, p. 1A. "McFaddin: Act 4 Prevents Free Public Schools System," *Arkansas Gazette,* April 28, 1959, p. 1A.

12. Bill Lewis, "School Directors Take 'Wait, See' Stand on Split," *Arkansas Gazette,* March 15, 1959, p. 8B. "Faubus Says He Didn't Give McKinley Data," *Arkansas Gazette,* May 22, 1959, p. 1B.

13. Alexander, *The Little Rock Recall Election,* p. 11; see also Spitzberg, *Racial Politics in Little Rock,* p. 15. Spitzberg, *Racial Politics in Little Rock,* p. 14; see also Powell interview with Baker, p. 12, EAP. Powell interview with Pagan, p. 3, EJC; Spitzberg, *Racial Politics in Little Rock,* p. 14; Powell interview with Baker, p. 31.

14. Powell interview with Pagan, p. 1; Tucker, Jr., interview with Luter, p. 8; Spitzberg, *Racial Politics in Little Rock,* p. 15.

15. "Non-Signers of Affidavit to Get Ax?" *Arkansas Democrat,* May 5, 1959, p. 1. Alexander, *The Little Rock Recall Election,* p. 11. Good brief summaries of the meeting can be found in *Southern School News,* June 1959; Vivion Brewer, *The Embattled Ladies of Little Rock: 1958–1963, The Struggle to Save Public Education at Central High* (Fort Bragg, Calif.: Lost Coast Press, 1999), p. 155; Sara Alderman Murphy, *Breaking the Silence: Little Rock's Women's Emergency Committee to Open Our Schools, 1958–1963* (Fayetteville: University of Arkansas Press, 1997), pp. 11–12.

16. Brewer, *The Embattled Ladies of Little Rock,* p. 142; Bob and Barbara Shults interview with Sara Murphy, October 9, 1992, p. 9, Box 3, Folder 17, SAM; See also ACHR "Activities Report," April-June, 1959, Box 71, SRC. Bobbie Forster, "Three School Board Members Leave Deadlocked Meeting," *Arkansas Democrat,* May 5, 1959, p. 1. Alexander, *The Little Rock Recall Election,* p. 12.

17. Bill Lewis, "Teacher Organizations Call Action Illegal; Suit Planned," *Arkansas Gazette,* May 6, 1959, p. 1A. Forster, "Three School Board Members Leave Deadlocked Meeting." Roy Reed, "Teacher Purge Begun By 3 Board Members," *Arkansas Gazette,* May 6, 1959, p. 1A. "Here's List of Teachers Under Fire," *Arkansas Gazette,* May 6, 1959, p. 1A. Alexander, *The Little Rock Recall Election,* p. 13. Brewer, *The Embattled Ladies of Little Rock,* p. 155; "Group Shows Teacher Trust," *Arkansas Gazette,* May 6, 1959, p. 2A.

18. Pat House interview with John Luter, Aug. 22, 1971, pp. 20–21, EAP.

19. "Tucker States His, Matson's, Lamb's Stand," *Arkansas Gazette,* May 6, 1959, p. 1A. For the full text of the speech see "Dedication of Williams School," May 5, 1959, Tucker Scrapbook.

20. E. Grainger Williams interview with Sara Alderman Murphy, July 29, 1992, p. 2, Box 5, Folder 6, SAM. Murphy, *Breaking the Silence,* p. 164. Irene Samuel interview with John Luter, Dec. 30, 1970, p. 20, EAP. John L. Ward, "PTA Council, Irked by 'Purge,' Pushes Recall," *Arkansas Democrat,* May 6, 1959, p. 1.

21. "Lamb Fearful More Teachers Will Drop Out," *Arkansas Gazette,* May 6, 1959, p. 2A. "School, Civic Groups Assail Purge Attempt," *Arkansas Gazette,* May 7 1959, p. 1A. Ward, "PTA Council, Irked by 'Purge,' Pushes Recall," p. 1. Alexander, *The Little Rock Recall Election,* p. 14. Bobbie Forster, "Teachers Told: Don't Recognize Dismissal Action," *Arkansas Democrat,* May 6, 1959, p. 1; "Teachers Told Not to Sign Pacts," *Arkansas Democrat,* May 8, 1959, 1. Colbert S. Cartwright, "HOPE Comes to Little Rock," *Progressive,* August 1959, pp. 7–9.

22. "Attitude Not Sole Factor in Releases," *Arkansas Democrat,* May 6, 1959, p. 1; "Trio Won't Tell Teachers Why They're on List," *Arkansas Gazette,* May 7, 1959, p. 1A. Bobbie Forster, "Sign New

Contracts or Risk Loss of Job, Head of Board Warns," *Arkansas Democrat,* May 8, 1959, p. 1.

23. Murphy, *Breaking the Silence,* p. 164. "400 Forest Park Patrons Shout Approval of Proposal to Recall Three 'Purgers,'" *Arkansas Gazette,* May 7, 1959, p. 1A. The recall law had been passed as a segregationist measure in the special session of the 1958 legislature, designed to facilitate removal of board members suspected of "integrationist tendencies"; *Dallas Times Herald,* May 7, 1959, Tucker Scrapbook. Alexander, *The Little Rock Recall Election,* p. 16. The WEC had talked about a recall "at every meeting for months," and they were ready to act when the opportunity presented itself; Alexander, *The Little Rock Recall Election,* p. 17.

24. Maurice Mitchell interview with Elizabeth Jacoway, Jan. 21, 2004, pp. 16, 2, 10 EJC. ACHR "Narrative Report," July–September, 1958, Box 27, Folder 287, ACHR. Alexander, *The Little Rock Recall Election,* p. 17; Lorraine Gates, "Power From the Pedestal: The Women's Emergency Committee and the Little Rock School Crisis," *Arkansas Historical Quarterly,* Spring 1996, p. 51. Spitzberg, *Racial Politics in Little Rock,* p. 17. Alexander, *The Little Rock Recall Election,* p. 17; Murphy, *Breaking the Silence,* pp. 165–66; Murphy's chronology is a bit off on the timing of the early meetings.

25. "C of C Condemns 'Purge,'" *Arkansas Democrat,* May 7, 1959, 1; "C of C Board, AAUW, JCs Attack Firings," *Arkansas Gazette,* May 8, 1959, p. 1A. For the full text of the Chamber statement see "Little Rock Report, C of C, May 13, 1959," Tucker Scrapbook.

26. Murphy, *Breaking the Silence,* p. 166. Alexander, *The Little Rock Recall Election,* p. 18. "Petitions Circulate to Recall Purgers As Protests Swell," *Arkansas Gazette,* May 8, 1959, p. 1A. Brewer, *The Embattled Ladies of Little Rock,* p. 157. Henry Alexander claimed that the WEC "packed" the PTA meetings, and Amis Guthridge described the gatherings as "rigged, communist-like demonstrations"; Alexander, *The Little Rock Recall Election,* p. 18.

27. Roy Reed, "75 Walk Out on McKinley at Angry School Ceremony," *Arkansas Gazette,* May 8, 1959, p. 1A. Powell interview with Pagan, p. 3.

28. Bill Lewis, "Foes of Recall Proposal Get Brushoff at Forest Heights," *Arkansas Gazette,* May 8, 1959, p. 1A. George Bentley, "Laster Protests McKinley's Talk," *Arkansas Gazette,* May 9, 1959, p. 2A. Lewis, "Foes of Recall Proposal Get Brushoff at Forest Heights."

29. Alexander, *The Little Rock Recall Election,* p. 19; Spitzberg, *Racial Politics in Little Rock,* p. 19. Roy Reed, "Leading Citizens Organize 'STOP' to Combat Purge," *Arkansas Gazette,* May 9, 1959, p. 1A. Maurice Mitchell interview with Elizabeth Jacoway, Feb. 28, 2005, p. 15. Alexander, *The Little Rock Recall Election,* p. 31.

30. Brewer, *The Embattled Ladies of Little Rock,* p. 157. Spitzberg, *Racial Politics in Little Rock,* p. 18. The WEC kept two lists of the STOP members: those who were married to WEC women and those who were not; see "STOP Members Whose Wife Does Not Belong to W.E.C." Box 7, Folder 5, WEC. Brewer, *The Embattled Ladies of Little Rock,* p. 176. Vivion Brewer interview with John Luter, Aug. 20, 1971, p. 14, EAP. Alexander, *The Little Rock Recall Election,* pp. 21, 24. For a diary of WEC activities from May 6 through May 18, 1959, see Box 7, Folder 4, WEC; for a diary which begins at May 11 and goes through May 25, see "Recall Election," Series 1, Box 1, Folder 5, VLB.

31. "Recall Vote Backers May File Tomorrow; New Petitions Show; Purge Foes Seek to Beat Counter Move," *Arkansas Gazette,* May 10, 1959, p. 1A; Murphy, *Breaking the Silence,* p. 172. Bobbie Forster, "Would Vote On All Six," *Arkansas Democrat,* May 7, 1959, p. 1; "Petitions Need About 6,000 Signers; Boundary Overlap Confuses Counting," *Arkansas Gazette,* May 9, 1959, p. 3A.

32. "School Board Leader Calls On Carpenter," *Arkansas Gazette,* May 7, 1959, p. 1B; "Alford Defends Board Leader," *Arkansas Gazette,* May 9, 1959, p. 1A. "CHS Mothers Aim at Matson, Tucker, Lamb." *Arkansas Gazette,* May 10, 1959, p. 1A. "Alford's Father Offered Top Job in City Schools," *Arkansas Gazette,* May 6, 1959, p. 5A.

33. "McKinley Says Purge Victims 'Integrationists,'" *Arkansas Gazette,* May 10, 1959, p. 1A. See also "McKinley, Laster Cite Reasons," *Arkansas Democrat,* May 10, 1959, p. 1.

34. "Citizens Council Lawyer Attacks 'Communist-like' PTA Objection to Purge," *Arkansas Gazette,* May 11, 1959, p. 1A.

35. "STOP Collects 9,575 Signatures for Recall," *Arkansas Gazette,* May 12, 1959, p. 1A; Mur-

phy, *Breaking the Silence,* p. 172. "STOP Collects 9,575 Signatures for Recall."

36. The Mothers' League secured 7,754 signatures in four days; Alexander, *The Little Rock Recall Election,* p. 22. Roy Reed, "Petitions for Recall Filed by Both Sides," *Arkansas Gazette,* May 13, 1959, p. 1A. "Carpenter Said to Have Played a Role in Filing," *Arkansas Gazette,* May 13, 1959, p. 1A; Reed, "Petitions for Recall Filed by Both Sides." John L. Ward, "Both School Board Slates Approved for Recall Vote; Signatures Ruled Sufficient," *Arkansas Democrat,* May 14, 1959, p. 1; George Bentley, "School Board Recall Election Set May 25," *Arkansas Gazette,* May 16, 1959, p. 1A.

37. Alexander, *The Little Rock Recall Election,* p. 22; "Faubus Picks Phil Stratton Office Aide," *Arkansas Gazette,* April 14, 1959, p. 1B. Spitzberg, *Racial Politics in Little Rock,* p. 21. Roy Reed, "Recall Forces Swap Blasts Over Rally to Honor Teachers; Separate Meet Tonight Slated by Negroes," *Arkansas Gazette,* May 19, 1959, p. 1A. M. L. Moser interview with John Pagan, Jan. 4, 1973, pp. 1, 3, EJC. Described by an *Arkansas Gazette* reporter as "a glib young man with a tiny go-to-hell mustache that jars oddly in a fundamentalist pulpit," Moser was a political amateur, but he had been noisy and active in the crowds around Central High School in the early days of the integration crisis; Jerry Neil, "The Education of Governor Faubus," *Nation,* June 6, 1959, pp. 507–9.

38. "Segregationists' 'CROSS' to Sponsor Meeting Tonight," *Arkansas Gazette,* May 16, 1959, p. 1A. Charles Portis, "350 Cheer Board Members As CROSS Cancels Out Swift," *Arkansas Gazette,* May 17, 1959, p. 1A.

39. "Will Mitchell to Head Drive for Recall of Purge Faction," *Arkansas Gazette,* May 18, 1959, p. 1A. Spitzberg, *Racial Politics in Little Rock,* p. 91. Jim Mitchell went to Taft School in Connecticut.

40. W. S. Mitchell interview with Jacoway, p. 32; Virginia Mitchell conversation with Elizabeth Jacoway, April 14, 2001. Spitzberg, *Racial Politics in Little Rock,* pp. 17–18. Maurice Mitchell said Henry Woods and Sid McMath knew they needed to stay out of sight because they were "too hot to handle." Mitchell felt the same way about the Women's Emergency Committee, recalling, "It was a conscious decision. We just thought in the long run it would be better if they didn't" [get mentioned publicly]; Maurice Mitchell interview with Jacoway, Jan. 21, 2004, p. 19.

41. Murphy, *Breaking the Silence,* p. 175. Sara Murphy suggested that Irene Samuel had already gotten in the habit of maintaining a low profile because her husband was Jewish, and she understood that could be a liability to the WEC; Murphy, *Breaking the Silence,* p. 94. Velma Powell interview with Sandra Hubbard, March, 1977, EJC; the author is indebted to Sandra Hubbard for her generosity in sharing this interview. Alexander, *The Little Rock Recall Election,* p. 25; Brewer, *The Embattled Ladies of Little Rock,* p. 160. "School Purge Foes to Name Leader Today," *Arkansas Gazette,* May 17, 1959, p. 1A.

42. Roy Reed, "200 at Meeting Applaud Teachers, Hear Firing Protest; Speakers Call for Removal of 3 Purgers," *Arkansas Gazette,* May 20, 1959, p. 1A; "S.T.O.P.LIGHTS—Confidential," May 21, 1959, Number 4, Box 20, Folder 201, ACHR. *The Embattled Ladies of Little Rock,* p. 173; "Holt and Laster Talk on Letters," *Arkansas Gazette,* May 22, 1959, p. 1A. "Negro Teachers Honored at Rally Attended by 500," *Arkansas Gazette,* May 20, 1959, p. 2A.

43. Bobbie Forster, "STOP Slates Teacher Appreciation Meet Tonight; CROSS Television to Feature Alford, McKinley; Will Air 'Aspects of Crisis,'" *Arkansas Democrat,* May 19, 1959, p. 1. "Pro-Purge Forces Publicize New 'Reasons' for Firing 44," *Arkansas Gazette,* May 21, 1959, p. 1A; "Teachers' Lawyer Charges Some Fired for Rejecting Demands for Good Grades; Warren Cites Threats, Says He Has Proof," *Arkansas Gazette,* May 21, 1959, p. 1A. "McKinley, Moser Named in Libel Suit," *Arkansas Gazette,* May 23, 1959, p. 6A. The suit was eventually abandoned in 1962; Brewer, *The Embattled Ladies of Little Rock,* p. 161.

44. "Teachers' Lawyer Charges Some Fired for Rejecting Demands for Good Grades; Warren Cites Threats, Says He Has Proof."

45. Ed I. McKinley eventually conceded that in the purge, "the extremists finally had over-reached themselves tactically . . ."; Jerry Neil, "The Education of Governor Faubus," *Nation,* June 6, 1959, pp. 507–9. Bill Smith reported the initial exchange between Faubus and McKinley

regarding the projected purge, claiming "Faubus told him he was making a mistake, that they ought to think about it, and that they really ought not to attempt it. But Ed was adamant. He even spoke a little harshly to Faubus, that he was entitled to have his backing and this, that and the other, in what he was doing"; William J. Smith interview with John Luter, Aug. 19–20, 1971, p. 75, EAP.

46. "Governor Says Tension Rising, It Worries Him," *Arkansas Gazette,* May 21, 1959, p. 1A. Bill Lewis, "Governor Comes Out for McKinley Slate; Labels Move Against Purge 'Smokescreen,'" *Arkansas Gazette,* May 23, 1959, p. 1A.

47. "S.T.O.P.LIGHTS—Confidential," May 21, 1959. Billie Wilson wrote this series. The ads all carried the heading "This Teacher Was Purged!" Charles Portis, "STOP Leader Sees Victory and a 'Return to Reason,'" *Arkansas Gazette,* May 24, 1959, p. 1A.

48. "Be Sure Your Vote Counts," *Arkansas Democrat,* May 24, 1959, p. 8B. "STOP Finishes Fight on Purge," *Arkansas Gazette,* May 25, 1959, p. 1A; "Issue Religious, Moser Declares," *Arkansas Gazette,* May 25, 1959, p. 1A.

49. Reed, "STOP Wins Recall Victory; Purgers Thrown Off Board." As announced five days later, the vote totals in favor of the STOP candidates were Everett Tucker, 13,317 (against removal) to 12,093 (for removal); Russell Matson, 12,971 to 12,320; Ted Lamb, 12,944 to 12,513. The votes for the CROSS candidates were Robert Laster, 13,996 (for removal) to 11,235 (against removal); Ben D. Rowland, 13,693 to 11,527; Ed I. McKinley, 13,340 to 11,860; "Recall Is Made Official; Next Move up to Board," *Arkansas Gazette,* May 30, 1959, p. 2A. Jerol Garrison, "STOP Workers Cheer: Little Rock 'Awakened,'" *Arkansas Gazette,* May 26, 1959, p. 1A. Murphy, *Breaking the Silence,* p. 181.

50. Murphy, *Breaking the Silence,* p. 182. Lorraine Gates has written, "Most participants credit the WEC with STOP's success. . . . it was the women of the WEC who did the work, and it was the WEC's ward organization that ultimately made the difference on election day"; Gates, "Power from the Pedestal," p. 51.

51. Spitzberg, *Racial Politics in Little Rock,* p. 27. L. C. Bates's newspaper, the *Arkansas State Press,* explained why Little Rock blacks voted with STOP in the recall election even though STOP made a point of avoiding the integration issue. It was because STOP wanted to preserve the public schools and keep them open, whereas under Governor Faubus's program "the Negro has no chance–not even in the courts"; *Southern School News,* July 1959. Brewer, *The Embattled Ladies of Little Rock,* p. 171. Alexander, *The Little Rock Recall Election,* p. 29; Murphy, *Breaking the Silence,* p. 183. Maurice Mitchell interview with Jacoway, Jan. 21, 2004, p. 20. This was apparently an early version of the "knock-and-drag technique" that Bill Clinton introduced into national politics. See Edwin Dunaway interview with John Kirk, Sept. 26, 1992, p. 27, for an explication of the functioning and uses of this technique in Arkansas politics; the author is grateful to Professor Tony Badger for providing her with a transcription of this interview. For an excellent breakdown on voting patterns in Little Rock throughout the two-year crisis, see Corinne Silverman, *The Little Rock Story,* Inter-University Case Program, No. 41 (University of Alabama Press, 1959), pp. 36–38; see also Samuel Lubell, *White and Black: Test of a Nation* (New York: Harper & Row, 1964), pp. 72–75.

52. Murphy, *Breaking the Silence,* p. 182.

53. Thomas O'Neil, "Faubus' Political Prestige Comes Back in Disrepair," *Arkansas Gazette,* June 4, 1959, p. 4A. Faubus had suffered his third electoral setback in six months, including the School Board elections, the Tyler bill, and the recall election; he was, however, still a formidable force to be reckoned with in Arkansas politics; Roscoe Drummond, "Uprising in Little Rock: Faubus Suffers Third Setback in Six Months," *Washington Post,* May 30, 1959, SERS; Claude Sitton, "Faubus' Position Strong Despite Latest Setback," *New York Times,* May 31, 1959, p. 6E. John Thomas Elliff, "The United States Department of Justice and Individual Rights, 1937–1962" (Ph.D. diss. Harvard University, 1967), p. 613. Claude Sitton, "Faubus Unmoved by School Defeat," *New York Times,* May 28, 1959, p. 17.

54. Oliver Emmerich, "Appomattox in Little Rock Need Not Spell Defeat Here," *Jackson State*

Times, May 29, 1959, Tucker Scrapbook.

55. "A Proposed Purge . . . ," (unsigned, but handwriting is that of Nat Griswold), (nd), Box 27, Folder 277, ACHR. Tucker interview with Pagan, p. 2.

56. "The Problem Is Still with Us," *Arkansas Gazette,* May 28, 1959, p. 4A. The Little Rock–based Winthrop Rockefeller Foundation commissioned a study of race relations in Little Rock thirty years after the crisis and found distressing evidence that the city was resegregating both residentially and educationally, and that relations between the races were worsening; Robert L. Brown, "The Second Crisis of Little Rock: A Report on Desegregation Within the Little Rock Public Schools," Winthrop Rockefeller Foundation, June 1988.

57. Fullerton, "New Factories Thing of the Past in Little Rock." See also Reed Sarratt, *The Ordeal of Desegregation: The First Decade* (New York: Harper & Row, 1966), pp. 289–90.

58. "They Lack the Courage of National's Founding Fathers," *Sumter* (S.C.) *Daily Item,* Aug. 17, 1959, p. 6, Tucker Scrapbook.

59. Spitzberg, *Racial Politics in Little Rock,* p. 124.

60. Leland DuVall, "Faubus Says Press Reports Only the 'Bad,'" *Arkansas Gazette,* May 29, 1959, p. 1B.

CHAPTER SEVENTEEN — THE NEW ELITE CONSENSUS

1. J. Gaston Williamson interview with Elizabeth Jacoway, May 25, 2000, p. 2, EJC. "James Gaston Williamson: Civil Rights Leader, Attorney, War Hero," *Arkansas Democrat-Gazette,* July 2, 2002; Williamson interview with Jacoway, p. 20.

2. Steven Brawner, . . . *And A Time to Remember The Story of John and Martha Riggs,* (privately published, 2001), pp. 9–11, 26–27; the author is grateful to Lee Riggs Cress for sharing this family history with her. Williamson interview with Jacoway, p. 2. J. Gaston Williamson, "A Concise History of Second Presbyterian Church in Little Rock, Arkansas, 1882–1988," (October 1989). Williamson interview with Jacoway, pp. 5–6; Sara Alderman Murphy, *Breaking the Silence: Little Rock's Women's Emergency Committee to Open Our Schools, 1958–1963* (Fayetteville: University of Arkansas Press, 1997), pp. 191–92.

3. Mitchell described his frustration through much of the crisis by saying, "there wasn't too much that the individual could do or that a group of citizens could do, it was out of the hands of the community. . . ."; W. S. Mitchell interview with Elizabeth Jacoway, Dec. 17, 1977, p. 13, EJC.

4. "Second Baptist Minister Asks Christian Solution," *Arkansas Gazette,* June 1, 1959, p. 1A.

5. "Token Integration Seen as Scheme," *Arkansas Gazette,* June 1, 1959, p. 1A. ACHR "Quarterly Report," April–June 1959, Box 71, SRC.

6. "Why Not Let Little Rock Try?" *Arkansas Gazette,* June 7, 1959, p. 4E.

7. Bill Roller, "Hopes Rest with the Men in the Middle," *Orbit: The Magazine of the Sunday Oklahoman,* Sept. 20, 1959, Everett Tucker Jr. Scrapbook, in the possession of the Tucker family; the author is grateful to Everett Tucker Jr. for sharing this scrapbook with her.

8. George Bentley, "County Board Picks Three to Succeed Recalled," *Arkansas Gazette,* June 12, 1959, p. 1A; Irving Spitzberg Jr., *Racial Politics in Little Rock, 1954–1964* (New York: Garland Publishing, 1987), pp. 110–11; Vivion Lenon Brewer, *The Embattled Ladies of Little Rock: 1958–1963, The Struggle to Save Public Education at Central High* (Fort Bragg, Calif.: Lost Coast Press, 1999), p. 169. "Who the New Board Members Are," *Arkansas Gazette,* June 12, 1959, p. 2A; "Board Member Who Withdrew Airs Complaint," *Arkansas Gazette,* June 17, 1959, p. 2A. "Board Takes Steps to Reopen Schools As Vacancy Filled," *Arkansas Gazette,* July 10, 1959, p. 1A. "Teacher Purge Expunged; New Board Keeps Powell; Hubbard Gives Up Post," *Arkansas Gazette,* June 16, 1959, p. 1A.

9. Jerry Jones, "School Closing, Aid Switch Scrapped by Federal Court," *Arkansas Gazette,* June 19, 1959, p. 1A. "Sanborn to Leave Appellate Court; Miller Suggested as His Successor," *Arkansas Gazette,* June 10, 1959, p. 7A. "Text of Decision on School Segregation Laws," *Arkansas Gazette,* June 19, 1959, p. 10A. Colbert Cartwright claimed that many community leaders openly welcomed

the decision; in his words, "When the federal court's ruling was announced to a Rotary Club meeting the members greeted the hoped for decision with unprecedented applause"; Colbert S. Cartwright, "HOPE Comes to Little Rock," *Progressive*, August 1959, p. 7.

10. After meeting with their lawyers and conferring privately with the Civil Rights Division of the Justice Department, Tucker announced his board's decision not to appeal the ruling, explaining that it was not a defendant in the case; John Thomas Elliff, "The United States Department of Justice and Individual Civil Rights, 1937–1962" (Ph.D. diss. Harvard University, 1962), p. 613; "Lamb Urges Quick Appeal," *Arkansas Gazette,* June 19, 1959, p. 1A; "Board Decides Against Appeal of Court Ruling," *Arkansas Gazette,* June 20, 1959, p. 1A. "Board Tells Intent to Open Schools, Use Placement Act," *Arkansas Gazette,* June 26, 1959, p. 1A. "Pupil Placement, 2 Tuition Aid Laws Still in Faubus' Segregation Arsenal," *Arkansas Gazette,* June 19, 1959, p. 1A. "The School Closing Laws Are Nullified," *Arkansas Gazette,* June 19, 1959, p. 4A. "Pupil Assignment Has Met the Test," *Arkansas Gazette,* June 21, 1959, p. 4E. "We'd Better Get This Matter Straight," *Arkansas Gazette,* June 30, 1959, p. 4A; "The Decision to Open the High Schools," *Arkansas Gazette,* June 27, 1959, p. 4A.

11. Ernest Valachovic, "Faubus Says Decision Will Not Stop Conflict; Calls for Compromise," *Arkansas Gazette,* June 19, 1959, p. 1A. George Douthit, "Faubus Sees Federal Force, Trouble if Schools Open Mixed," *Arkansas Democrat,* June 24, 1959, p. 1.

12. "Faubus Sees More Woes if High Schools Reopen," *Arkansas Gazette,* June 25, 1959, p. 1A. "Faubus Lauds 'Historic Role' Of Raney's 188 Graduates," *Arkansas Gazette,* June 27, 1959, p. 2A. The largest ovation at the graduation ceremony was for Sammie Dean Parker, the segregationist student leader who had caused so much trouble inside Central High School during the 1957–58 school year; "Governor Compares Himself to Those Resisting Russia," *Arkansas Gazette,* June 28, 1959, p. 8A.

13. Benjamin Muse, "Visit to Governor Orval Faubus, June 29, 1959," July 3, 1959, SRC.

14. Ibid. Faubus to Take Ruling on Acts to High Court," *Arkansas Gazette,* July 2, 1959, p. 1A. George Douthit, "Faubus Plans Supreme Court Appeal on 3-Judge Ruling Against School Closing Acts," *Arkansas Democrat,* July 1, 1959, p. 1.

15. Bobbie Forster, "Survey of Pupils Who Would Go to Integrated High School Being Considered by Board," *Arkansas Democrat,* June 21, 1959, p. 1. "Trinity School May Continue Another Year," *Arkansas Gazette,* June 27, 1959, p. 2A; "Baptists Plan Lasting School, or None at All," *Arkansas Gazette,* July 1, 1959, p. 1A. J. Harvey Walthall found that 7 percent of whites and 50 percent of blacks had attended no school during the 1958–59 school year; J. Harvey Walthall, "A Study of Certain Factors of School Closing in 1958 As They Affected the Seniors of the White Comprehensive High Schools in Little Rock, Arkansas" (Ph.D. diss. University of Arkansas, 1963); Spitzberg, *Racial Politics in Little Rock,* p. 100; Sara Murphy claimed that 1,000 students dropped out permanently, 40 percent of them black; Murphy, *Breaking the Silence,* p. 90. "777 Register at Raney High for Study in Ensuing Term," *Arkansas Gazette,* June 25, 1959, p. 1B; "Raney High Pre-registration Nearly Double 500 Capacity," *Arkansas Gazette,* June 26, 1959, p. 1B.

16. "Little Rock, Arkansas, School Desegregation: Fall Semester 1959," Box 54, Schools, 2, WPR. "Segregation Leader Vows All-Out Fight," *Arkansas Gazette,* July 15, 1959, p. 1A.

17. Brewer, *The Embattled Ladies of Little Rock,* pp. 170, 173. Benjamin Muse, "Visit to Little Rock, Sunday, Monday, Tuesday, June 28–30, 1959," July 6, 1959, Box 80, SRC.

18. Nat Griswold to Harold Fleming, Aug. 12, 1959, Box 80, SRC. Late in life, Williamson could not remember exactly who invited him to serve as chair, but it was two or three ladies from the WEC, and "Cousin Adolphine" called him; Williamson interview with Jacoway, p. 43.

19. Williamson interview with Jacoway, p. 45. "Citizens Organize to Seek Peaceful School Reopening; Dauley Tells Law-Enforcing Aim of Board," *Arkansas Gazette,* July 18, 1959, p. 1A. See also J. Gaston Williamson, "The Reopening of Little Rock's High Schools: Statement for Commission on Civil Rights," March 21, 1960 (typed as "1959," which was before the committee was formed, then changed in pencil to read "1960?"), JGW.

20. "Citizens Organize to Seek Peaceful School Reopening; Dauley Tells Law-Enforcing Aim

of Board." Spitzberg, *Racial Politics,* p. 112.

21. Ann Sawyer, "School Forces in Charlotte Set Initial Meeting," *Arkansas Democrat,* July 15, 1959, p. 1. Untitled clipping, *Charlotte Observer,* July 16, 1959, Tucker Scrapbook.

22. "NAACP Abides by Pupil Act; Compliance Pledge to Arkansas's Law," *Arkansas Gazette,* July 17, 1959, p. 1A. After the School Board announced its decision to reopen the high schools, the *Arkansas Gazette* reviewed the implications of the Pupil Placement Law. Stressing that it had been designed "to permit voluntary segregation without permitting discrimination," the article claimed that such laws were ". . . significant in the fight against integration" because they did not lend themselves to class-action suits and because they "set up a number of administrative hurdles that must be passed before integration suits ever reach the courts, each of them intended to further reduce the number of plaintiffs who ultimately run the administrative gamut without failing"; Bill Lewis, "Pupil Placement Laws Appear as Big Weapons for Saving Segregation," *Arkansas Gazette,* June 28, 1959, p. 1A; "Act Outlines Assignment Guideposts," *Arkansas Gazette,* June 28, 1959, p. 1A.

23. "Placement Act Wins Support," *Arkansas Gazette,* July 18, 1959, p. 1A. "School Officials Study Norfolk Plan; Tncker [*sic*] Says Little Rock Has Choice," *Arkansas Gazette,* July 17, 1959, p. 1B. "Placement Act Wins Support."

24. "Schools That May Reopen Will Register Students for Fall Term This Week," *Arkansas Gazette,* July 18, 1959, p. 1A. Bill Lewis, "Hall High's Attendance Area Changed," *Arkansas Gazette,* July 15, 1959, p. 1A; "26 School Age Negroes in Area Covered by Hall," *Arkansas Gazette,* July 16, 1959, p. 1A. Jerry Dhonau, "Pupils to Register Today at Four High Schools," *Arkansas Gazette,* July 21, 1959, p. 1A. "Newsmen Banned by Smith," *Arkansas Democrat,* July 21, 1959, p. 2A.

25. Daisy Bates to Roy Wilkins, July 29, 1959, Box 2, Folder 1, DGB. Bobbie Forster and John Ward, "2 Negro Fathers Register Daughters at CHS; First Day's Activities Peaceful," *Arkansas Democrat,* July 21, 1959, p. 1A.

26. Clarence Laws to Messrs. Wilkins and Current, July 29, 1959, Microfilm Series, Part 3, Series D, Reel 2, Folder: "Desegregation Schools Arkansas Little Rock, Central High, 1959," PON.

27. "Calm Prevails As 162 Enroll for CHS Class," *Arkansas Gazette,* July 22, 1959, p. 1A; "Hall Registers 2 Negro Pupils; 3 Sign at CHS," *Arkansas Gazette,* July 23, 1959, p. 1A; "Negro Registers at 3rd School," *Arkansas Gazette,* July 24, 1959, p. 1A; "25 Negroes Sign at CHS; Total Now 48," *Arkansas Gazette,* July 25, 1959, p. 1A; "53 More Pupils Register; Negro Signs for Central," *Arkansas Gazette,* July 28, 1959, p. 1A; "'Emergency' Schools Closed by 2 Churches," *Arkansas Gazette,* July 22, 1959, p. 1A. *Southern School News,* August 1959. "Board in Better Position to Plan School Reopening," *Arkansas Gazette,* July 26, 1959, p. 1A.

28. "School Supporter Commends Order," *Arkansas Gazette,* July 25, 1959, p. 2A.

29. "Text of Governor's Letter," *Arkansas Gazette,* July 29, 1959, p. 2A.

30. "Governor Proposes Integration of Hall, Mann High Schools; Would Keep Central Open for Whites," *Arkansas Gazette,* July 29, 1959, p. 1A. "NAACP Rejects Faubus' Plan," *Arkansas Gazette,* July 29, 1959, p. 1A. "Civic Leaders Stress Stand for Schools," *Arkansas Gazette,* July 30, 1959, p. 1A.

31. J. Gaston Williamson, "Committee for the Peaceful Operation of Free Public Schools, Statement by Chairman," July 29, 1959, JGW; the author is grateful to James G. Williamson Jr. for sharing this and other documents with her. See also "Text of Statement by Schools Committee Chairman," *Arkansas Gazette,* July 30, 1959, p. 8C.

32. Williamson, "Committee for the Peaceful Operation of Free Public Schools, Statement by Chairman," July 29, 1959. Italics added.

33. "3 Negroes Assigned to Hall, 3 to Central Under '59 State Act," *Arkansas Gazette,* Aug. 1, 1959, p. 1A. The six were Elizabeth Eckford, Jefferson Thomas, and Carlotta Walls at Central, and Effie Jones, Elsie Robinson, and Estella Thompson at Hall. Elizabeth Eckford discovered she had enough credits to graduate, so her withdrawal from Central and Carlotta Walls's absence while she completed summer school left Jefferson Thomas to start school alone; Roy Reed, "Board Sets Firm Disciplinary Policy for High Schools; Only One Negro May Re-enter Central High," *Arkansas*

Gazette, Aug. 11, 1959, p. 1A. *Southern School News,* December 1959. "Board Adopts Rules to Guide Pupil Placing," *Arkansas Gazette,* July 30, 1959, p. 14C.

34. Gloster B. Current to Roy Wilkins, July 31, 1959, Microfilm Series, Part 3, Series D, Reel 2, Folder: "Desegregation Schools Arkansas Little Rock, Central High, 1959," PON.

35. Ibid. Even Gaston Williamson felt some reluctance about the course the School Board was pursuing in restricting so severely the numbers of black children enrolled in the formerly all-white schools, but he had committed himself to encouraging support for the School Board and he kept his promise; Williamson interview with Jacoway, p. 47.

36. Nat Griswold to Harold Fleming, Aug. 12, 1959, Box 80, SRC.

37. "Segregation, Negro Camps Both Attack School Board Plan; Faubus Hostile; NAACP Hints New Litigation," *Arkansas Gazette,* Aug. 2, 1959, p. 1A. "Segregation, Negro Camps Both Attack School Board Plan; Faubus Hostile; NAACP Hints New Litigation."

38. W. Wilson White, "Memorandum for the Attorney General Re: School Situation—Little Rock, Ark.," Aug. 4, 1959, Box 54, Schools, 2, WPR.

39. White, "Memorandum for the Attorney General Re: School Situation—Little Rock, Ark."

40. Federal Bureau of Investigation Report titled "Orval E. Faubus, LR 80-385 Serial 4," p. 33, which the author obtained using Freedom of Information Act. J. Gaston Williamson interview with Sara Alderman Murphy, Dec. 10, 1993, p. 11, Box 5, Folder 8, SAM.

41. "Orval E. Faubus, LR 80-385 Serial 4," p. 33. "Legislative Workers Get Special Session Feelers," *Arkansas Gazette,* July 20, 1959, p. 1A.

42. Spitzberg, *Racial Politics in Little Rock,* p. 113.

43. For the full text of the letter see Brewer, *The Embattled Ladies of Little Rock,* pp. 194–97.

44. Brewer, *The Embattled Ladies of Little Rock,* p. 197. For an engaging description of this comedy of errors, see Roy Reed, *Faubus: The Life and Times of an American Prodigal* (Fayetteville: University of Arkansas Press, 1997), p. 256.

45. Roy Reed, "Raney High to Close; Lack of Funds Cited," *Arkansas Gazette,* Aug. 5, 1959, p. 1A. "Raney's Donors Agreed to Give, but Not Enough," *Arkansas Democrat,* Aug. 5, 1959, p. 2A. Bobbie Forster, "Raney High Won't Open; Pupils, Faculty Released," *Arkansas Democrat,* Aug. 4, 1959, p. 1A; "Faubus Says Raney 'Had No Recourse,'" *Arkansas Gazette,* Aug. 5, 1959, p. 1A.

46. Spitzberg, *Racial Politics in Little Rock,* p. 114. "High Schools Set August 12 Opening," *Arkansas Gazette,* Aug. 5, 1959, p. 1A.

47. "Negro Pupils Hire Lawyers to Appeal School Assignment," *Arkansas Gazette,* Aug. 8, 1959, p. 1A. Bobbie Forster, "Negroes Ask U.S. Court for Admission to Schools on Basis of Attendance Area," *Arkansas Democrat,* Aug. 8, 1959, p. 1. "Court Sanction Sought for Policy of School Board; Negroes' Suit Is Premature, Brief Claims," *Arkansas Gazette,* Aug. 22, 1959, p. 1A.

48. Forster, "Negroes Ask U.S. Court for Admission to Schools on Basis of Attendance Area." "Negroes Challenge School Board Use of Placement Laws; Suit Contends All in Zone Are Eligible," *Arkansas Gazette,* Aug. 9, 1959, p. 1A.

49. "Faubus Hits at Violence, Integration," *Arkansas Democrat,* Aug. 12, 1959, p. 2A. "Negroes Challenge School Board Use of Placement Laws; Suit Contends All in Zone Are Eligible." "School Opening Scene Quiet; Faubus Keeps Close Tongue," *Arkansas Gazette,* Aug. 10, 1959, p. 1A.

50. Spitzberg, *Racial Politics in Little Rock,* p. 115. Bob Troutt, "Ex-Raney Pupils Stage Rally, Ask School Opening," *Arkansas Democrat,* Aug. 10, 1959.

51. "Mass Protest Rumors Heard As Segregationists Plan Rally," *Arkansas Gazette,* Aug. 11, 1959, p. 1A.

52. Roy Reed, "Police Brace; Segregationist Rally Still On," *Arkansas Gazette,* Aug. 12, 1959, p. 1A. See also "Legal Action Promised in Interference with Opening of Little Rock's Schools," *Arkansas Democrat,* Aug. 11, 1959, p. 1A. "Caravans Coming to Little Rock," *Arkansas Democrat,* Aug. 11, 1959, p. 1A.

53. "Governor Silent on Rally Plans," *Arkansas Democrat,* Aug. 9, 1959, p. 1A. "Faubus Discourages Violence; 'Struggle Was Lost' at Polls," *Arkansas Gazette,* Aug. 12, 1959, p. 1A. "Faubus Hits at Violence, Integration." "Faubus Plea Commended by Tucker," *Arkansas Gazette,* Aug. 12,

1959, p. 9A.

54. "Police Quell March On CHS; Negroes Enter School," *Arkansas Democrat*, Aug. 12, 1959, Tucker Scrapbook.

55. George Douthit, "Faubus Calls On Crowd to Avoid Clash," *Arkansas Democrat*, Aug. 12, 1959, p. 1A. Jerry Jones, "Rally at Capitol Got Paraders in Noisy Mood," *Arkansas Gazette*, Aug. 13, 1959, p. 1A. *Southern School News*, September 1959.

56. Jones, "Rally at Capitol Got Paraders in Noisy Mood"; "Police Arrest 24 in Wake of Rally, Fight Near Central," *Arkansas Gazette*, Aug. 13, 1959, p. 1B. "Coffman Cited in Gas Probe," *Arkansas Gazette*, Sept. 15, 1959, p. 1A. Before the month was out, Norwood was arrested at a black nightclub and charged with public drunkenness. The manager had wanted to close and called police when Norwood would not leave. The segregationist protester told police he was out "trying to get votes, but I must have been in the wrong place." Saying he went to the nightclub on a tip, to get a list of NAACP contributors, Norwood claimed his arrest was a frame-up by police; "Leader of School March Arrested at Negro Club," *Arkansas Gazette*, Aug. 29, 1959, p. 1A.

57. *Southern School News*, September 1959. *Arkansas Gazette* city editor Bill Shelton wrote the Arkansas portions of *Southern School News*. One of the many articles about Gene Smith described him this way: "a sort of one-man riot squad whose exploits of reckless courage have become legendary in Arkansas. When trouble breaks, Smith is among the first at the scene and he takes charge in unmistakable fashion. . . . He is detested by diehard segregationists but never has taken sides in the racial controversy, maintaining that his only duty is to uphold law and order"; Ray Moseley, "He's One-Man Riot Squad: Tough Officer Quells Racist Mob," *Detroit Free Press*, Aug. 13, 1959, p. 9, Tucker Scrapbook. *Southern School News*, September 1959.

58. Ronnie Farrar, "Code Assists Police Work; Morale High," *Arkansas Gazette*, Aug. 13, 1959, p. 1B. Jerry Dhonau, "Soggy and Cursing Marchers Never Got Near Their Target," *Arkansas Gazette*, Aug. 13, 1959, p. 1A. *Southern School News*, September 1959. Most of the teenagers were arrested for "loitering." Despite the limited nature of the confrontation, the *London Daily Herald* wrote "Mob war raged again in Little Rock, Arkansas, today . . ."; Peter Moorhead, "Batons-and-Hoses Battle at the High School: LITTLE ROCK AGAIN!; Faubus Tells the Mob 'I Am with You,'" *London Daily Herald*, Aug. 13, 1959, Tucker Scrapbook. George Douthit, "Faubus Says Police, Guard Were Ready if Needed at Schools," *Arkansas Democrat*, Aug. 14, 1959, p. 1A.

59. "80 Pct. Attend at Hall, Central," *Arkansas Gazette*, Aug. 13, 1959, p. 1A. "Integrated High Schools Called 'Entirely Normal,' Orderly in Classrooms," *Arkansas Gazette*, Aug. 13, 1959, p. 1B. See also "Board Says School Outlook Peaceful," *Arkansas Democrat*, Aug. 13, 1959, p. 1. "'Everything Was Okay,' Say 5 Negro Students," *Arkansas Gazette*, Aug. 13, 1959, p. 14C. "The Schools Are Open—And There Is Order," *Arkansas Gazette*, Aug. 13, 1959, p. 4A.

60. "Board Says School Outlook Peaceful."

61. Ernest Valachovic, "State Forces Ready for Use 'In Case,' Faubus Announces; Ban by Court of No Concern, Governor Says," *Arkansas Gazette*, Aug. 15, 1959, p. 1A. Patrick J. Owens, "Segregationist Duo Seeks Funds, Deplores 'Brutality,'" *Arkansas Gazette*, Aug. 14, 1959, p. 3A. "Board Says School Outlook Peaceful," *Arkansas Democrat*, Aug. 13, 1959, p. 1. *Southern School News*, September 1959; "Mrs. Alford Demands Action on Police 'Brutality' Charges," *Arkansas Gazette*, Aug. 18, 1959, p. 1B. Harry Ashmore could not resist, writing the next day, "We can assume that Gene Smith, having been unmoved by the mob, will be equally stoical now in the face of Mrs. Dale Alford's threat to tell on him to the DAR"; "Whose Tea Party?" *Arkansas Gazette*, Aug. 19, 1959, p. 4A.

62. "City Board Backs Police, Asks Probe of Criticisms," *Arkansas Democrat*, Aug. 19, 1959, Tucker Scrapbook.

63. "U.S. Officials Keep Close Watch," *Arkansas Gazette*, Aug. 13, 1959, p. 2A. "Federal Aide Will Assist School Cases," *Arkansas Gazette*, Aug. 12, 1959, p. 1A; "Federal Authorities 'Watching,'" *Arkansas Democrat*, Aug. 12, 1959, p. 15A; "U.S. Officials Keep Close Watch."

64. "Those Who Were There in Spirit," *Arkansas Gazette*, Aug. 14, 1959, p. 4A. "First Things First," *Arkansas Gazette*, Aug. 16, 1959, p. 4A. "Harry Ashmore Leaves Gazette Editorial Post; To Be Consultant in New Study of Mass Media," *Arkansas Gazette*, Sept. 22, 1959, p. 1A.

65. Untitled memo, Aug. 10, 1959, Microfilm Series, Part 3, Series D, Reel 2, Folder "Desegregation Schools Arkansas Little Rock, Central High, 1959," PON; Daisy Bates to Wiley Branton, Aug. 26, 1959, Box 2, Folder 1, DGB; Reed, "Board Sets Firm Disciplinary Policy for High Schools; Only One Negro May Re-enter Central High." Daisy Bates to Roy Wilkins, Aug. 24, 1959, Microfilm Series, Part 3, Series D, Reel 2, Folder: "Desegregation Schools Arkansas Little Rock, Central High, 1959," PON; see also Daisy Bates to Wiley Branton, Aug. 26, 1959, Box 2, Folder 1, DGB.

66. "Schools to Hold Half-Day Sessions; Heat, Early Start Cited as Reasons," *Arkansas Gazette,* Aug. 14, 1959, p. 1B; "18 Negroes Plan 'Strike,'" *Arkansas Gazette,* Aug. 14, 1959, p. 2A. Wiley A. Branton to Daisy Bates, Aug. 29, 1959, Microfilm Series, Part 3, Series D, Reel 2, Folder "Desegregation Schools Arkansas Little Rock, Central High, 1959," PON. In time Branton added the new plaintiffs to his suit; "Placement Act Case Gets 14 New Plaintiffs," *Arkansas Gazette,* Sept. 20, 1959, p. 1A.

67. "Board to Assign Unassigned Pupils Tonight," *Arkansas Gazette,* Aug. 27, 1959, p. 1B. "Tear Gas Tossed at School Board; 2 Women Sought," *Arkansas Gazette,* Aug. 28, 1959, p. 1A; "Clues Scant in Hunt for Tear Gas Users," *Arkansas Gazette,* Aug. 29, 1959, p. 2A.

68. "School Board Hears First Negro Seeking Transfer from Mann," *Arkansas Gazette,* Sept. 3, 1959, p. 14C; "School Board to Hear 11 More Transfer Plans Today," *Arkansas Gazette,* Sept. 8, 1959, p. 5A; "School Board Hears Appeal of 9 Students," *Arkansas Gazette,* Sept. 9, 1959, p. 1B. "Basic Information on Little Rock," [1954–63], Box 20, Folder 196, ACHR. Spitzberg, *Racial Politics in Little Rock,* p. 115–16. "3 Negro Pupils Get Transfers," *Arkansas Gazette,* Sept. 16, 1959, p. 1A. "School Board Tells of Two Dissenters on Transfers Votes," *Arkansas Gazette,* Sept. 17, 1959, p. 2A.

69. ACHR "Quarterly Report," July–September 1959, Box 71, SRC.

70. See Morton Sosna, "World War II, Democracy and the South: The Birth of the Southern Regional Council," unpublished paper, Conference on the Southern Regional Council and the Civil Rights Movement, University of Florida, October 23–26, 2003.

71. Mark V. Tushnet, *Making Civil Rights Law: Thurgood Marshall and the Supreme Court, 1956–1961* (New York: Oxford University Press, 1994), p. 253. Mary Dudziak, *Cold War Civil Rights: Race and the Image of American Democracy* (Princeton: Princeton University Press, 2000), p. 150.

72. *Southern School News,* December 1959.

Conclusion — A Bang and a Whimper

1. Ellis Thomas to Jess Matthews, Aug. 18, 1959; Daisy Bates to Roy Wilkins, Aug. 24, 1959; Ellis Thomas to Jesse [*sic*] Matthews, Sept. 9, 1959, all in Microfilm Series, Part 3, Series D, Reel 2, Folder "Desegregation Schools Arkansas Little Rock, Central High, 1959," PON.

2. Roy Reed, "Dynamite Tossers Damage Three Little Rock Targets; School Office, City Officials' Places Bombed," *Arkansas Gazette,* Sept. 8, 1959, p. 1A; Patrick J. Owens, "Jangled Nerves and Rubble Mark Scenes of Bombings," *Arkansas Gazette,* Sept. 8, 1959, p. 1A.

3. "Bombings Bring Irate Response at Little Rock; Civic Leaders Post Reward of $25,000," *Arkansas Gazette,* Sept. 9, 1959, p. 1A. *Southern School News,* March 1960. "Chamber Head Praises Work of Police, FBI," *Arkansas Gazette,* Sept. 10, 1959, p. 16C.

4. Margaret Frick, "Explosions Bring Quick Reaction," *Arkansas Democrat,* Sept. 8, 1959, p. 1.

5. "Bombings Bring Irate Response at Little Rock; Civic Leaders Post Reward of $25,000." "Bishop Calls for Prayers, Cooperation," *Arkansas Gazette,* Sept. 8, 1959, p. 2A.

6. "Bombings Bring Irate Response at Little Rock; Civic Leaders Post Reward of $25,000." E. Grainger Williams interview with Sara Alderman Murphy, July 29, 1992, p. 7, Box 5, Folder 6, SAM.

7. Roy Reed, "Members of Citizens Council, Trucker Charged in Bombing; Hearing Today; Police Question Another Suspect," *Arkansas Gazette,* Sept. 10, 1959, p. 1A. Patrick J. Owens, "Just Who Are the Three Suspects?" *Arkansas Gazette,* Sept. 10, 1959, p. 16C. "3 More Charged in

Dynamitings, Held Under Bail," *Arkansas Gazette,* Sept. 11, 1959, p. 1A. "Sims Pleads Guilty, Draws 5-Year Maximum in Bombing," *Arkansas Gazette,* Sept. 18, 1959, p. 1A; *Southern School News,* December 1959. Reed, "Members of Citizens Council, Trucker Charged in Bombing; Hearing Today; Police Question Another Suspect." "Citizens Council President Praises Bombing Suspect," *Arkansas Gazette,* Sept. 11, 1959, p. 1A.

8. "Little Rock Report: The City, Its People, Its Business, 1957–1959," The Women's Emergency Committee to Open Our Schools, August, 1959, typescript report in BWP. In January of 1959, the American Association of University Women had released a report that also concluded that the school crisis had damaged business and industrial growth; "Effect of the Little Rock School Situation on Local Business (Survey Conducted by Social and Economic Issues Committee of the AAUW, Little Rock Branch)," Jan. 24, 1959, Box 17, Folder 5, VTB. "Ridgway Hits Shut Schools," *Arkansas Democrat,* June 9, 1959, p. 1A.

9. "Women View School Closing Impact, Say Damage Will Fade in 'New Day,'" *Arkansas Gazette,* Sept. 6, 1959, p. 1A. "Little Rock Report . . . What Has Happened Since the School Crisis?," Southern Regional Council Report No. L-11, Oct. 12, 1959, SRC. See also Matthew D. Lassiter, "The Open-Schools Revolt: The Southern Regional Council and the Construction of the Moderate South," p. 11, unpublished paper, Conference on the Southern Regional Council and the Civil Rights Movement, University of Florida, October 23–26, 2003.

10. Gertrude Samuels, "Act III Opens in Little Rock," *New York Times Magazine,* Sept. 13, 1959, pp. 30–31.

11. Everett Tucker interview with John Luter, Aug. 16, 1971, p. 27, EAP. Matthew Lassiter has written, "Few white southerners during the decade after *Brown* examined deeply what racial integration and genuine educational equality would look like in practice"; Lassiter, "A 'Fighting Moderate': Benjamin Muses's Search for the Submerged South," in Matthew D. Lassiter and Andrew B. Lewis, *The Moderates' Dilemma: Massive Resistance to School Desegregation in Virginia* (Charlottesville: University Press of Virginia, 1998), p. 201. To the contrary, Little Rock's leaders thought deeply about the implications of genuine integration and found them horrifying, concluding that it would lead to miscegenation and the destruction of educational quality. Lassiter, "The Open-Schools Revolt," p. 25.

12. Tucker interview with Luter, p. 59.

13. *Southern School News,* October 1959; "Dollarway Lawyer Sees New Hearing As Crucial to South," *Arkansas Gazette,* Sept. 20, 1959, p. 3A. *Southern School News,* October 1959. "Basic Information on Little Rock," [1954–63], Box 20, Folder 196, ACHR.

14. For information on later developments in Little Rock see especially Robert L. Brown, "The Second Crisis of Little Rock: A Report on Desegregation Within the Little Rock Public Schools" (Little Rock: Winthrop Rockefeller Foundation, 1988); Robert L. Brown, "The Third Crisis of Little Rock," *Arkansas Historical Quarterly,* Spring 2006, p. 37; Polly J. Price, "The Little Rock School Desegregation Cases in Richard Arnold's Court," unpublished paper in the possession of the author; and Gary Orfield and Susan E. Eaton, *Dismantling Desegregation: The Quiet Reversal of Brown v. Board of Education* (New York: New Press, 1996), pp. 156–61.

15. Telegram from Mrs. Daisy Bates to United States Attorney General, July 8, 1959, Microfilm Series, Part 3, Series D, Reel 2, Folder "Desegregation Schools Arkansas Little Rock, Central High, 1959," PON. Mrs. L. C. (Daisy) Bates to Honorable Dwight D. Eisenhower, Aug. 13, 1959, Microfilm Series, Part 3, Series D, Reel 2, Folder "Desegregation Schools Arkansas Little Rock, Central High, 1959," PON; Bill Lewis, "NAACP Leader Appeals to Ike for Protection," *Arkansas Gazette,* Aug. 14, 1959, p. 1A. See also "Justice Department Gets Bates' Appeal," Aug. 21, 1959, group III, series A, container 174, Folder "Reprisals, Arkansas, Govt. Actions, 1958–62," PON. Soon Ellis Thomas had even greater cause for alarm when he was fired on October 1 from his job at International Harvester, after ten years with the company; Ellis Thomas to Brooks McCormick, Oct. 6, 1959, Box 2, Folder 2, DGB. After writing to the president of the company, Thomas received a dismissive reply, and the termination stood; Brooks McCormick to Ellis Thomas, Nov. 9, 1959, and News Release, Nov. 20, 1959, both in Microfilm Series, Part 3, Series D, Reel 2, Folder "Desegre-

gation Schools Arkansas Little Rock, Central High, 1959," PON. *Southern School News,* February 1960.

16. "Harry Ashmore Leaves Gazette Editorial Post; To Be Consultant in New Study of Mass Media," *Arkansas Gazette,* Sept. 22, 1959, p. 1A.

17. "Hays Attacks State Capitol Role in Crisis; Statement Hints He Would Enter Governor's Race," *Arkansas Gazette,* Sept. 13, 1959, p. 1A; "Bennett Hints Go for Governor," *Arkansas Gazette,* Sept. 2, 1959, p. 2A; *Southern School News,* April 1960. See Roy Reed, *Faubus: The Life and Times of an American Prodigal* (Fayetteville: University of Arkansas Press, 1987), pp. 263–84.

18. *Southern School News,* April 1960; "Unofficial Committee of Downtown Businessmen," (nd), Box 20, Folder 197, ACHR; Arthur Phillips interview with Elizabeth Jacoway, Dec. 20, 1977, untranscribed, EJC; Elizabeth Jacoway, "Taken by Surprise: Little Rock Business leaders and Deseg-regation," in Elizabeth Jacoway and David R. Colburn, eds., *Southern Businessmen and Desegregation* (Baton Rouge: Louisiana State University Press, 1982), pp. 15–41. See also John A. Kirk, *Redefining the Color Line: Black Activism in Little Rock, Arkansas, 1940–1970* (Gainesville: University Press of Florida, 2002), pp. 139–62.

19. *Southern School News,* April 1960; Grif Stockley, *Daisy Bates: Civil Rights Crusader from Arkansas* (Jackson: University Press of Mississippi, 2005), p. 213.

20. Elizabeth Jacoway, "Not Anger but Sorrow: Minnijean Brown Trickey Remembers the Little Rock Crisis," *Arkansas Historical Quarterly,* Spring 2005, p. 11. Melba Patillo Beals, *White Is a State of Mind: A Memoir* (New York: G. P. Putnam's Sons, 1999), p. 259. D. LaRouth S. Perry, "The 1957 Desegregation Crisis of Little Rock, Arkansas: A Meeting of Histories" (Ph.D. diss., Bowling Green State University, 1998), pp. 302–3; Perry claimed that five of the nine married whites. Minnijean Brown Trickey interview with Elizabeth Jacoway, Sept. 15, 2003, pp. 55–56, EJC.

21. http://www.centralhigh57.org/The_Little_Rock_Nine.html. "Reunion of the Little Rock Nine," in Erma Glasco Davis and Faustine Childress Wilson, eds., *The Arkansas African American Hall of Fame,* (Little Rock: National Dunbar Association of Little Rock, Ark., 1993), p. 106.

22. Perry, "The 1957 Desegregation Crisis of Little Rock, Arkansas," pp. 368, 331; Steele Hays, "20 Years Later: Vulnerability Still Lingers," *Arkansas Democrat,* Jan. 2, 1977, p. 1A.

23. "Reunion of the Little Rock Nine"; Perry, "The 1957 Desegregation Crisis of Little Rock, Arkansas," p. 340; "Whatever Happened To . . . 'The Little Rock 9'?" *Ebony,* Feb. 19, 1972, pp. 136–38.

24. Herbert H. Denton, "'Little Rock Nine' Recall School Desegregation Battle," *Boston Globe,* May 1982; "Reunion of the Little Rock Nine"; www.centralhigh57.org/The_Little_Rock_Nine.html.

25. Perry, "The 1957 Desegregation Crisis of Little Rock, Arkansas," p. 356; "Reunion of the Little Rock Nine." Denton, "'Little Rock Nine' Recall School Desegregation Battle"; www.centralhigh57.org/The_Little_Rock_Nine.html.

26. "Chose Private School for Daughter," *Arkansas Gazette,* Sept. 27, 1977, p. 1A; Beals, *White Is a State of Mind.* "Reunion of the Little Rock Nine."

27. Jacoway interview with Trickey; "Reunion of the Little Rock Nine"; www.thelavinagency.com/college/minnijeanbrown-trickey.html.

28. "Whatever Happened To . . . 'The Little Rock 9'?"; www.colorado.edu/Carillon/volume3/stories/1-nine.

29. Denton, "'Little Rock Nine' Recall School Desegregation Battle." Perry, "The 1957 Desegregation Crisis of Little Rock, Arkansas," p. 368; "Reunion of the Little Rock Nine"; "Whatever Happened To . . . 'The Little Rock 9'?"; www.centralhigh57.org/The_Little_Rock_Nine.html.

30. *Arkansas Democrat-Gazette,* Sept. 26, 1997, p. 14A; "Little Rock 9 Recognized for Hero-ism; Each Receives Top Medal Congress Gives Civilians," *Arkansas Democrat-Gazette,* Nov. 10, 1999, p. 1A.

31. Harry S. Ashmore, "The Southern Style," *Saturday Review,* May 23, 1959, pp. 16, 46.

32. "Remarks by Harry S. Ashmore, Adolphine Terry Dinner," June 14, 1966, p. 5, Box 23, Folder 239, ACHR.

33. Ibid.

34. Thirty years after the Little Rock crisis, Little Rock attorney Robert L. Brown, the son of Bishop Robert R. Brown, prepared a report on integration and race relations for a local charitable foundation in which he documented widespread residential segregation, white flight, and social suspicion; Brown, "The Second Crisis of Little Rock: A Report on Desegregation Within the Little Rock Public Schools." See also Brown, "The Third Crisis of Little Rock"; and Orfield and Eaton, *Dismantling Desegregation,* pp. 156–61; "Lawmakers Press Schools on Integration," *Arkansas Gazette,* Feb. 17, 2005, p. 1B; and Joel Anderson, "Plain Talk: The Future of Little Rock's Public Schools," University Task Force on the Little Rock School District, University of Arkansas at Little Rock, 1987.

AFTERWORD — A NOTE ON MISCEGENATION

1. "Law and Order," *Arkansas Gazette,* Aug. 29, 1957, p. 4A; Ashmore reiterated this thesis in 1980 in the Introduction to Elizabeth Huckaby's memoir, saying, "The *Gazette* stood virtually alone at the time in its insistence that the real issue was law and order. . . ."; Elizabeth Huckaby, *Crisis at Central High: Little Rock, 1957–1958* (Baton Rouge: Louisiana State University Press, 1980), p. xv. Harry S. Ashmore, *The Negro and the Schools* (Chapel Hill: University of North Carolina Press, 1954).

2. Gunnar Myrdal had written at length about the American taboo against miscegenation, explaining that "rejection of 'social equality' is to be understood as a precaution to hinder miscegenation and particularly intermarriage." Myrdal went so far as to write *"This attitude of refusing to consider amalgamation—felt and expressed in the entire country—constitutes the center in the complex of attitudes which can be described as the 'common denominator' in the problem";* Gunnar Myrdal, *An American Dilemma* (New York: Harper & Row, 1944), vol. 1, p. 58. (Italics in the original.) "The Supreme Court, Segregation, and the South: Speech of Hon. James O. Eastland of Mississippi in the Senate of the United States, Thursday, May 27, 1954," Series V, Item 10, CCA. For a revealing insight into Eastland's thinking and motivations see Hollinger F. Barnard, ed., *Outside the Magic Circle: The Autobiography of Virginia Foster Durr* (University: University of Alabama Press, 1985), pp. 171–72.

3. For helpful explorations of "the ideology of white supremacy," see especially Neil McMillen, "White Citizens' Council and Resistance to School Desegregation in Arkansas," *Arkansas Historical Quarterly* (Summer 1971), pp. 95–122; see also Neil McMillen, *The Citizens' Council: Organized Resistance to the Second Reconstruction, 1954–1964* (Urbana: University of Illinois Press, 1971), pp. 159–204; Guion Griffis Johnson, "The Ideology of White Supremacy," in Fletcher Melvin Green, ed., *Essays in Southern History* (Chapel Hill: University of North Carolina Press, 1949), pp. 124–56; James Vander Zanden, "The Ideology of White Supremacy," *Journal of the History of Ideas,* 20 (June–September 1959), pp. 385–98; George M. Fredrickson, *The Black Image in the White Mind: The Debate on Afro-American Character and Destiny, 1817–1914* (New York: Harper & Row, 1971), p. 321; Howard Odum, *Race and Rumors of Race: The American South in the Early Forties* (Baltimore: Johns Hopkins University Press, 1943, 1997), pp. 22–31. The classic exploration of southern caste arrangements is John Dollard, *Caste and Class in a Southern Town* (New Haven: Yale University Press, 1937). For explorations of the psychosexual dimensions of southern racism, see especially Winthrop Jordan, *White Over Black: American Attitudes Toward the Negro, 1550–1812* (Chapel Hill: University of North Carolina Press, 1968); Joel Williamson, *The Crucible of Race: Black-White Relations in the American South Since Emancipation* (New York: Oxford University Press, 1984); Wilbur J. Cash, *The Mind of the South* (New York: Alfred A. Knopf, 1941); Lillian Smith, *Killers of the Dream* (New York: W. W. Norton & and Co., 1949); and Jacqueline Dowd Hall, *Revolt Against Chivalry: Jessie Daniel Ames and the Women's Campaign Against Lynching* (New York: Columbia University Press, 1979). See also Lau-

rence Shore, "The Enduring Power of Racism: A Reconsideration of Winthrop Jordan's *White Over Black*," *History and Theory*, May, 2005, pp. 195– 206. For more recent explorations of the fear of miscegenation, see especially, Charles Robinson, *Dangerous Liaisons: Sex and Love in the Segregated South* (Fayetteville: University of Arkansas Press, 2003); Renee Romano, *Race Mixing: Black-White Marriage in Postwar America* (Cambridge: Harvard University Press, 2003); Peter Wallenstein, *Tell the Court I Love My Wife: Race, Marriage, and Law—An American History* (New York: Palgrave Macmillan, 2002); and Jane Dailey, "The Theology of Massive Resistance: Sex, Segregation, and the Sacred after Brown," in Clive Webb, ed., *Massive Resistance: Southern Opposition to the Second Reconstruction* (New York: Oxford University Press, 2005), pp. 151—80. The quote is from William Peters, *The Southern Temper: A Fresh Look at the People in the Segregation Crisis—With Encouraging News of What They are Doing About It* (Garden City: Doubleday & Co., 1959), p. 191.

4. See especially Tom P. Brady, "Black Monday: Segregation or Amalgamation . . . America Has Its Choice," nd [1955], Series IX, Item 3, CCA. An earlier elaboration of this theme can be found in Theodore Bilbo, *Take Your Choice: Separation or Mongrelization* (Poplarville, Miss.: Dream House Publishing Co., 1947). As Jacqueline Hall described the thinking of southern white racists in the Jim Crow era, "Any transgression of the caste system was a step toward 'social equality'; and social equality, with its connotations of personal intimacy, could end only in interracial sex"; Hall, *Revolt Against Chivalry*, p. 145. See especially Jeff Woods, *Black Struggle, Red Scare* (Baton Rouge: Louisiana State University Press, 2003); George Lewis, *The White South and the Red Menace: Segregationists, Anticommunism, and Massive Resistance, 1945–1965* (Gainesville: University Press of Florida, 2004); and Wayne Addison Clark, "An Analysis of the Relationship Between Anti-Communism and Segregationist Thought in the Deep South, 1948–1964" (Ph.D. diss., University of North Carolina, 1976). Neil McMillen argued that to southerners, "Integration always meant miscegenation. . . ."; McMillen, *The Citizens' Council*, p. 184.

5. David L. Cohn, "How the South Feels," *Atlantic Monthly*, January–June 1944, pp. 49–50.

6. Herbert Ravenel Sass, "Mixed Schools and Mixed Blood: Where Equality Leads," *Atlantic Monthly*, November 1956, pp. 45–49. This equation of social equality with sexual access was a subtext of southern white discourse that was hidden from view and therefore difficult for outgroup members to grasp; as African-American historian George Wright has written, when he and his wife first began to eat in formerly white restaurants in the South, he always wondered, "What did they think we would do in here but eat?" The answer, of course, is that "they" thought that the social equality implicit in the shared eating space would open the door to sharing space in the bedroom; George Wright, "Growing Up Segregated," in Jacoway and Williams, *Understanding the Little Rock Crisis*, p. 47. Harry Ashmore was one of the first to refer to the civil rights era as "a sort of New Reconstruction"; see Harry S. Ashmore, *An Epitaph for Dixie* (New York: W. W. Norton & Co., 1958), p. 182. Soon Yale historian C. Vann Woodward coined the phrase "the Second Reconstruction"; C. Vann Woodward, *The Burden of Southern History* (Baton Rouge: Louisiana State University Press, 1968), pp. 89–107.

7. For instance, see Numan V. Bartley, *The New South: 1945–1980* (Baton Rouge: Louisiana State University Press, 1995), p. 202; Peters, *The Southern Temper*, pp. 33, 190–205; and James Graham Cook, *The Segregationists* (New York: Appleton-Century-Crofts, 1962), p. 354. Lillian Smith, *Killers of the Dream*, pp. 102–3.

8. United Press dispatch to Don Dillon, Oct. 12, 1957, Box 30, Folder 13, JJJ.

9. Nathan R. Griswold, "The Second Reconstruction in Little Rock," unpublished manuscript, EJC. James W. Silver, *Mississippi: The Closed Society* (New York: Harcourt, Brace & World, 1964), p. 6.

10. Griswold, "The Second Reconstruction in Little Rock," Book 1, Chapter 1, pp. 27, 31, and Book 1, Chapter 2, p. 27.

Additional Manuscript Collections Consulted

Arkansas National Guard Archives, Camp Robinson, Arkansas
Beauchamp, S. J., Papers, in possession of the family
Brewer, Vivion, Papers, Smith College, Northhampton, Massachusetts
Brewer, Vivion, Papers and Photographs, in possession of the family
Butler, Richard Colburn, Papers, in possession of the family
Cobb, Judge Osro, Papers, Archives and Special Collections, University of Arkansas at Little Rock
Crenchaw, Joseph, Papers, Archives and Special Collections, University of Arkansas at Little Rock
Harris, Oren, Papers, Special Collections, University of Arkansas, Fayetteville
Hays, L. Brooks, Papers, Special Collections, University of Arkansas, Fayetteville
Hodges, Luther, Papers, Southern Historical Collection, University of North Carolina, Chapel Hill
Huckaby, Elizabeth, Papers, Archives and Special Collections, University of Arkansas at Little Rock
Lile, R.A., Papers, in possession of the author
Little Rock Crisis Collection, Eisenhower Library, Abilene, Kansas
Little Rock School Board, Minutes, Little Rock School Board Offices
Little Rock School Board, Minutes, Archives and Special Collections, University of Arkansas at Little Rock
Little Rock School Crisis Collection, Archives and Special Collections, University of Arkansas at Little Rock
Lowry, Clyde E., Scrapbook, Good Government Campaign, in possession of the family
Lyon, Frank, Papers, in possession of the family
McMath, Sidney Sanders, Papers, Special Collections, University of Arkansas, Fayetteville

McMath, Sidney Sanders, Papers, Arkansas History Commission, Little Rock
Mills, Wilbur, Papers, Hendrix College, Conway, Arkansas
Millwee, Minor W., Papers, in possession of the family
Mitchell, William Starr, Scrapbook, in possession of the family
Shelton, Bill, Papers, Archives and Special Collections, University of Arkansas at Little Rock
Thomas, Herbert L. Papers, Special Collections, University of Arkansas, Fayetteville
Tucker, Everett Jr. Scrapbook, in possession of the family
Upton, Wayne, Papers, in possession of the family
Williams, E. Grainger, Papers, Archives and Special Collections, University of Arkansas at Little Rock
Women's Emergency Committee Papers, Arkansas History Commission, Little Rock
Woods, Judge Henry, Papers, in possession of the family

Interviews

Elizabeth Jacoway Interviews

Abrams, Annie
Alford, Dr. Dale
Ashmore, Harry (2)
Bates, Daisy Lee Gatson (2)
Bates, Lucious Christopher
Beauchamp, Stonewall Jackson, Jr.
Bowen, William H.
Branton, Wiley Austin, Jr.
Brewer, Vivion Lenon
Brodie, Ralph (2)
Brown, Robert L.
Butler, Gertrude Remmel
Butler, Richard Colburn
Butler, Richard C., Jr., conversations
Carpenter, Claude
Carroll, Phillip, conversation
Margaret Windsor Clark, conversation
Cooper, Dr. William G.
Cowling, Rev. Dale
Counts, Wilmer, conversation

Darragh, Fred
Dhonau, Jerry (2)
Dortch, Mimi
Eckford, Elizabeth (2)
Engstrom, Harold (2)
Engstrom, Martha Frances
Farella, Ann Park, conversation
Faubus, Alta Haskins (2)
Faubus, Orval Eugene (3)
Gordon, Jean Thomas
Green, Ernest
Hamlen, James G.
Hays, Brooks (2)
Hays, Steele
Hodges, Harryette Morrison
House, Archie
House, Pat
Jacoway, B. Cooper
Johnson, Justice Jim (15)
Jones, Janet Morley, conversation
Lambright, Frank
Lewis, Willard, M.
Lile, Robert Alfred
Lile, Betty (Mrs. R. A.)
Lowry, Robert D.
Lowry, Robert D., Jr., conversation
Lyon, Frank, Sr.
Massery, Hazel (5)

Matthews, Kay, conversations.
McCord, Robert
McMath, Sidney Sanders
Mercer, Christopher Columbus, Jr.
Meredith, Sgt. Jack, Arkansas National
    Guard
Metcalf, Mrs. Margeurite
Mitchell, Maurice (2)
Mitchell, Virginia Grobmyer
Mitchell, William Starr
Mitchum, Jim, Arkansas National Guard
Murphy, Sara
Ottenheimer, Gus
Parker, Ken
Patterson, Hugh B. (2)
Patton, Kay Smith, conversation
Phillips, Arthur
Phillips, Barbara
Pickens, Eran Bartley
Pickens, Fred Maxfield
Poe, Fred, conversation
Pryor, David, conversation
Rath, Henry
Reasoner, Harry
Reed, Roy, conversations
Reid, Eleanor
Remmel, Ruth Rebsamen, conversation
Riddick, Walter

Riley, Eva Park, conversation
Roberts, Terrence
Rostker, Patricia
Rozzell, Forrest

Samuel, Irene, (2)
Shelton, William T.
Sizer, Sam, conversation
Smith, Griffin, jr., conversation
Stebbins, A. Howard, (2)
Stephens, W.R.
Strauss, Sam
Streng, Susan Blossom, conversation
Sutton, Ozzell
Tate, Ernest, Arkansas National Guard
Terry, Adolphine Fletcher, conversation
Terry, Bill
Trickey, Minnijean Brown
Tucker, Everett, Jr.
Tucker, Everett, III

Upton, Wayne
Vinson, B. Finley
Vinson, Louise
Wair, Thelma Mothershed
Wann, Fred, Arkansas National Guard
Ward, John
Wells, John
Williams, E. Grainger
Williams, Richard A.
Williamson, Gaston
Woods, Judge Henry (2)

JOHN LUTER INTERVIEWS

Eisenhower Administration Project,
Columbia University Oral History Program

Alford, Dr. Dale

Becker, J. Bill

Branton, Wiley Austin (by Steven Lawson)

Brewer, Mrs. Joe

Brownell, Herbert (by Ed Edwin)

Butler, Richard. C.

Cooper. Dr. William G.

Douthit, George

Engstrom, Harold

Faubus, Orval E.

Griswold, Nat R.

Guthridge, Amis

Hays, L. Brooks

House, Archie. F.

House, Mrs. Pat

Huckaby, Elizabeth (by T. Harri Baker)

Karam, James T.

Lile, R. A.

McMath, Sidney S.

Patterson, Hugh B.

Powell, Terrell E. (by T. Harri Baker)

Pruden, Wesley

Samuel, Irene

Shelton, William T.

Smith, William J.

Tucker, Everett

Upton, Wayne

Williams, E. Grainger

Woods, Henry (by T. Harri Baker)

JOHN PAGAN INTERVIEWS

Bates, Daisy

Brewer, Vivion

Metcalf, Marguerite

Mitchell, W. S.

Moser, M. L.

Murphy, Sara

Patterson, Hugh

Powell, Terrell

Pruden, Wesley

Rector, W. F.

Rozzell, Forrest

Samuel, Irene

Faubus, Orval

Green Ernest

Guthridge, Amis

House, Archie

Huckaby, Elizabeth

Karam, Jimmy

Matthews, Jess

Shaver, Bex

Smith, William J.

Terry, Adolphine

Troutt, Robert

Tucker, Everett

Upton, Wayne

SARAH MURPHY INTERVIEWS

Bates, Daisy

Darragh, Fred

Faubus, Orval E.

Green, Ernest

Hulett, Sammie Dean Parker

Massery, Hazel Bryan

Morrison, Margaret

Shelton, William T.

Shults, Barbara and Bob

Sutton, Ozell

Terry, Betty and Bill
Williamson, Gaston
Woods, Henry

Carpenter, Claude
Cobb, Osro
Cooper, William Grant
Eisele, Tom
Engstrom, Harold
Faubus, Orval (3)
Faubus, Orval and Smith, William J.
House, Archie
Johnson, Jim (3)
Karam, Jimmy
Smith, Griffin, Jr.
Sutton, Ozell
Woods, Henry (3)

MIMI DORTCH INTERVIEWS

Brown, Earline
Cartwright, Rev. Colbert
Cowling, Rev. Dale
Forster, Bobbie
Hardie, Rev. Richard
Huckaby, Elizabeth
Jones, Rev. W. S.
Mendell, Jane
O'Connell, Msr. James
O'Donnell, Msr. Don
Powell, James
Samuel, Irene
Teagarden, Dr. Kenneth
Waylon, Dr. Ewing
Williams, E. Grainger
Workman, Rev. John
Worthen, Mary
Young, Dr. Rufus King

ROY REED INTERVIEWS

Ashmore, Harry
Brownell, Herbert

MISCELLANEOUS INTERVIEWS

Ashmore, Harry, interview with John Egerton, Southern Oral History Program, Louis Round Wilson Library, University of North Carolina, Chapel Hill
Bates, Daisy, interview with John Kirk; the author is grateful to Professor Tony Badger for sharing this interview with her

Branton, Wiley A., interview with James Mosby, Civil Rights Documentation Project, Moorland-Spingarn Research Center, Howard University, Washington, D.C.

Brewer, Vivion, interview with Jacqueline Van Voris, Vivion Lenon Brewer Papers, Smith College, Northhampton, Massachusetts

Brewer, Vivion, interview with Rebecca Yarborough, Vivion Lenon Brewer Papers, Archives and Special Collections, Univesity of Arkansas at Little Rock

Dunaway, Edwin, interview with John Kirk; the author is grateful to Professor Tony Badger for sharing this interview with her

Faubus, Orval, interview with Jack Bass and Walter DeVries, Southern Historical Collection, Louis Round Wilson Library, University of North Carolina, Chapel Hill

Faubus, Orval, interview with David Demuth, June 22, 1977, in the possession of the author.

Faubus, Orval, interview with John Kirk, 12-3-92; the author is grateful to Professor Tony Badger for sharing this interview with her

Faubus, Orval, and John Ward, interview with Brooks Hays, Special Collections, University of Arkansas Libraries, Fayetteville

Hays, Brooks, interviews with Ronald Tonks (11 parts), "Southern Baptist Convention Presidents," Southern Baptist Historical Library and Archives, Nashville, Tennessee

McMath, Sidney Sanders, interview with John Kirk; the author is grateful to Professor Tony Badger for sharing this interview with her

McMath, Sidney Sanders interview with John Egerton, Southern Oral History Program, Southern Historical Collection, Louis Round Wilson Library, University of North Carolina, Chapel Hill

Miller, Judge John, interview with Walter Brown, Sam Sizer and Bruce Parham, John Miller Papers, Special Collections, University of Arkansas Libraries, Fayetteville

Powell, Velma, interview with Sandra Hubbard, March, 1997, in the possession of the author; the author is grateful to Sandra Hubbard for sharing this interview with her

Vinson, B. Finley, interview with John Kirk; the author is grateful to Professor Tony Badger for sharing this interview with her

ACKNOWLEDGMENTS

This project has shaped half of my life, and it would be impossible for me to thank adequately all the people who have contributed to its completion and to my support during the process. I owe a tremendous debt to my husband, Tim Watson, and to my sons, Timothy and Todd Watson, who have lived with this emerging story and cheered its author almost from its inception. I could not have stayed the course without the daily encouragement of all three of my men.

An undertaking of this scope is utterly dependent on the professionalism, creativity, and patience of a host of librarians, and I owe a debt of gratitude to some of the best in the business. The staff in Special Collections at the University of Arkansas, Fayetteville, has been heroic, and I have consumed so many hours of their time that I should pay a portion of the electric bill. Andrea Cantrell, Anne Prichard, Cheri Pearce, and Michael Dabrishus have guided me through a thousand mysteries, always with wisdom and good cheer, and I am deeply in their debt. Similarly, the staff in Archives and Special Collections at the University of Arkansas at Little Rock, especially Linda Pine, Jillian Barnett, and Shay Stiles have been tremendously helpful. Since I live in a tiny village that is far removed from a university library, I depended heavily on Inter-Library Loan. Ellen Crain at Newport's Billingsley Library was unfailingly cheerful in response to this unaccustomed demand on her time, and I am very grateful for all her help. Jane Hooker and Jeff Lewellen at the Arkansas History Commission guided me expertly through their many relevant collections. Dennis Dallenbach and his staff at the Eisenhower Library made my month-long stay in Abilene a productive as well as a pleasant time, even including me in their volleyball games. At Fisk University, Beth Hows and Dr. Jessie C. Smith made my repeated visits both enjoyable and fruitful. At Smith College, Sherrill Redmon gave me valuable assistance in gleaning maximum insight from the Vivion Brewer Papers, for which I am deeply appreciative. The staffs of the Wisconsin Historical Society, the John Fitzgerald Kennedy Presidential Library, and the University of Georgia Archives responded cheerfully and patiently to my many requests for assistance when I visited them, and the staffs of the Library of Congress, the Moorland-Spingarn Research Center at Howard University, and the Southern Baptist Historical Library and

Archives in Nashville guided me through numerous requests for information by telephone. I am grateful to all of these capable professionals for their expertise, efficiency, and generosity.

I inaugurated this project in 1976 with a Fellowship for Independent Study and Research from the National Endowment for the Humanities. That year off from teaching allowed me to jump-start this undertaking with twelve months of extensive travel to all of the archives and repositories listed above, as well as to accomplish interviews with many of the principals in the crisis. A later grant from the American Philosophical Society enabled me to continue the interviewing process, as did a Faculty Research Grant from the University of Arkansas at Little Rock. I am grateful to all of these institutions for their endorsement and encouragement of my work.

Researchers have collected an extraordinary amount of oral history in Little Rock over the last fifty years, and I have been the beneficiary of the work of many talented people. First among these is Roy Reed, who with characteristic generosity made available to me his superb interviews with many of the major actors in the Little Rock crisis. An accomplished journalist who established marvelous rapport with his subjects, Roy uncovered numerous nuggets of information that could not have been recovered from any other source. Roy also gave this manuscript a careful and thoughtful reading, and his helpful insights strengthened considerably the final product. John Pagan wrote a splendid undergraduate Honors paper at William and Mary on the Little Rock crisis, and he very generously shared with me the interviews that he conducted in 1972 and 1973. Once again, these have been a rich source of information, and I am deeply grateful for the opportunity to learn from them. The Columbia University Oral History Program conducted two dozen amazingly rich interviews in Little Rock as a part of the Eisenhower Administration Project in 1970 and 1971, and Sara Murphy gathered half that many while preparing her history of the Women's Emergency Committee in the 1980s. Mimi Dortch interviewed eighteen crisis participants in the 1990s and very generously shared her findings with me. John Kirk conducted many interviews in Little Rock in the 1990s, and Professor Tony Badger kindly facilitated my obtaining copies. I am grateful to these researchers for the seriousness and care with which they approached their work, all of which has enhanced my ability to tell this story with an immediacy and richness that rarely emerges from written documents. I owe a debt of gratitude as well to the many people who have allowed me to interview them over the years, and who have thereby expanded so dramatically my understanding of what happened in our city fifty years ago. Finally, I want to thank all the family members who granted me permission to quote and/or cite this great assortment of interviews.

Several friends have done me the high honor of setting aside their own work in order to read and critique mine. My dear friend Jim Jones has read every word, sometimes more than once, and he has cheered from the sidelines since the day this project made its initial appearance on his desk at the National Endowment for the Humanities. Bob Brown, Jane Dailey, Charles Eagles, Neil McMillen, Michael O'Brien, Charlotte Plegge, David Stricklin, and Joel Williamson have read extensive portions of the manuscript, each of them offering penetrating comments and suggestions. I am humbled by their generosity.

Elisabeth Curtner, Sandra Lacy, and Elizabeth Payne have been dear and steadfast friends, lavishing upon me frequent support and encouragement. My Birthday Bunch has provided honesty, empathy, and giggles since grade school. Keep it up, ladies!

One of the lovely benefits of this long project has been the new friends I have made along the way, people whom I would otherwise have missed and been much the poorer as a result. My colleagues in the Southern Association for Women Historians have been a constant source of inspiration, intellectual stimulation, and friendship, and I have benefited tremendously from my many connections with them over the years. Annie Abrams worked with me on the committee to plan the Central High School Museum Visitors' Center, and she has become a faithful friend and guide. Filmmaker Sharon LaCruise has been a source of wisdom, insight, and encouragement; not least of all, she has shared with me many of the photographs that are included in this book. Filmmaker Sandra Hubbard came into my life through our shared work on Little Rock and introduced me to her brother-in-law, former *Atlantic Monthly* editor William Whitworth, who helped me navigate the labyrinthine maze of the New York publishing world. I will be eternally grateful to these friends and many others who have provided guidance and support over the years.

I am still amazed that my fairy tale agent, Tina Bennett, swooped down from Manhattan and tapped me with her magic wand. It has been a joy to work with her, never more so than the day she brought me my wonderful editor, Bruce Nichols, who has tightened and strengthened this manuscript with an amazingly sure touch. He has had the help of a gifted assistant, Kadzi Mutizwa, who bled red ink all over my work, but who was absolutely right about what needed to stay and what needed to go. Together they have cut thirty percent from a too-long manuscript, leaving what remains to shine with a new level of clarity. I am in awe of their ability to do this without leaving me mortally wounded.

My greatest debt, as always, is to my parents. Daisy Tribble Jacoway has inspired me every day of my life to be the best that I could be, and she has shown me with her own life how to do it. Bronson Cooper Jacoway recognized in me a kindred spirit, and I in him, and I dedicate this book to him with boundless gratitude for his life, his example, and his unfailing devotion.

INDEX

ABOUT THE AUTHOR

Elizabeth Jacoway grew up in Little Rock, just two years behind the youngest of the Little Rock Nine. After earning her Ph.D. in southern history at the University of North Carolina, she returned to Arkansas and has studied southern history and the desegregation crisis ever since. She has taught at the University of Florida and the University of Arkansas at Little Rock. She has served on the Planning Committee for the Little Rock Central High Museum and is the recipient of a grant from the National Endowment for the Humanities. The mother of two grown sons, she currently lives in the northeast Arkansas farming community of Newport.